# RUINING A NATION
## and
## Nobody Cares
## By Lee E. McNulty

Copyright © 2016 by Lee McNulty
All rights reserved. This book or any portion thereof
may not be reproduced or used in any manner whatsoever
without the express written permission of the publisher
except for the use of brief quotations in a book review.

Printed in the United States of America

First Printing, 2016

**ISBN: 978-1542457187**

All photos, pictures and home videos were taken by Lee McNulty
and are the exclusive rights of Lee McNulty.

**DISCLAIMER:** This manual is being offered for education and information purposes only. All opinions are exclusively of the author. Names have been changed.

## TABLE OF CONTENTS

Forward..................................................................................................................ix

Introduction.............................................................................................................4

Top-Heavy Administration......................................................................................5

Drop-Out Rate.........................................................................................................6

Classrooms............................................................................................................12

School Year 2007 -2008........................................................................................18

October 22, 2007 – The Day of the Block Schedule Riot.....................................28

Misappropriation of Funds....................................................................................48

Anonymous Letters...............................................................................................60

Building Evacuations..........................................................................................139

My Diary.............................................................................................................152

School Year 2000-2001.......................................................................................162

School Year 2001-2002.......................................................................................170

School Year 2002-2003.......................................................................................180

School Year 2003-2004.......................................................................................198

School Year 2004-2005.......................................................................................229

School Year 2005-2006.......................................................................................245

School Year 2006-2007.......................................................................................262

School Year 2007-2008.......................................................................................289

School Year 2008-2009.......................................................................................340

School Year 2009-2010.......................................................................................347

School Year 2010-2011.......................................................................................353

2011-2012: 1st Year of Restructuring..................................................................370

2012-2013: 2nd Year of Restructuring.................................................................410

School Year 2013-2014.......................................................................................464

**Articles**..................................................................................................................469

**My Final Thoughts**.....................................................................................475

**Resources**...................................................................................................476

## ACKNOWLEDGEMENT

I would like to acknowledge my appreciation to the "**North Jersey Media Group**" for their permission and licensing agreement to reprint and utilize the following newspaper articles and clippings.

THE RECORD, June 12, 1999
**"3 Paterson students charged with carrying guns"**
By Timothy D. May & Michael Casey / Staff Writers

THE RECORD, June 21, 2001
**"Gentle soul, violent death"**
By John Chadwick & Jennifer Hughes

THE RECORD, May 26, 2004
**"Burning through millions"**
By Kathleen Carroll / Herald News

HERALD NEWS October 24, 2004
**"Fear at end of day"**
By Tom Meagher

THE RECORD, December 8, 2004
**"Audit hits school spending"**
By Whitey Kvasager / Herald News

HERALD NEWS, August 8, 2006
**"Bearing Arms"**
Special to the Herald News

HERALD NEWS September 23, 2006
**"Schedule glitch leaves kids idle"**
By Heather Haddon 973-569-7121 or haddon#northjersey.com

HERALD NEWS September 23, 2006
**"Teachers students say knock blocks off"**
By Danielle Shapiro 973-569-7100 or Shapiro@northjersey.com

HERALD NEWS Section, February 9, 2007
**"Lack of heat means early dismissal at JFK"**
By Danielle Shapiro

HERALD NEWS, February 9, 2007
**"Paterson brawl cancels girl's showdown"**
By Sheila G. Miller

HERALD NEWS, October 11, 2007
**"School Labs Safe - For Now"**
By Danielle Shapiro

HERALD NEWS, October 23, 2007
**"Fires, alarms, chaos, rule the day at JFK"**
By Ed Beeson

HERALD NEWS, October 30, 2007
**"Dropout Factory tags city schools"**
By Nancy Zuckerbrod

HERALD NEWS, November 11, 2007
Op Ed Page; **"Schools as 'dropout factories? PUHLEEEESE!**
By Roselyn O. Rauch, Ed.D.

THE HERALD NEWS, December 9, 2007
Special to the Herald News, **"Paterson community goes to work"**
By Michael E. Glascoe

THE RECORD, February 20, 2008
**"JFK teachers say school is out of control"**
By Danielle Shapiro

THE RECORD, December 7, 2012
**"Paterson principal is under scrutiny for alleged Thanksgiving announcement"**
By Nick Clunn and Leslie Brody
http://www.northjersey.com/news/paterson-principal-is-under-scrutiny-for-alleged-thanksgiving-announcement-1.361987

THE RECORD, November 25, 2014
**"Ex-teacher says chaos was norm; officials dispute view of Paterson school"**
By Hannan Adley
http://www.northjersey.com/news/ex-teacher-says-chaos-was-norm-officials-dispute-view-of-paterson-school-1.1141171

THE RECORD, December 18, 2014
Letters: **"Turmoil inside"** Regarding "Ex-teacher says chaos was the norm"
By Lee McNulty
http://www.northjersey.com/opinion/opinion-letters-to-the-editor/the-record-letters-friday-dec-19-1.1169741?page=2

I want to thank the following:

| | |
|---|---|
| Angelo Bonora | JFK Wood Shop Teacher |
| Lou Bonora | JFK History Teacher |
| Nanci Ianzano | JFK Speech Language Specialist / Teacher |
| Dave Kott | JFK Teacher & cut officer |
| Ivan Madjar | JFK Teacher & cut officer |
| Joe Pardine | JFK Teacher & cut officer |
| Mike Recca | Retired Paterson Police Officer (Lieutenant) |
| Ken Whalen | JFK Teacher |

The Paterson Police Officers.

John F. Kennedy High School security.

Bob Bowdon of "CHOICE MEDIA."

Joe Malinconico of the "PATERSON PRESS."
North Jersey Media Group

Hannan Adely of "THE RECORD."

Tamara Lane of "CHASING NEW JERSEY."

Colleen McSpirit Editor & Social Media Expert
scpeditor@gmail.com

A very special THANK YOU to all of the JFK teachers, staff, secretaries, security guards and many others who helped me a *great* deal and wish to remain anonymous, especially those who are still working there.

*Some names have been omitted or changed followed by an * after the name, to protect the identity of some of the people referenced in this book.*

In addition, any confidential information, such as email or mailing addresses, has been deleted.

All photos, unless otherwise stated, were taken by the author.

All newspaper articles appear with permission, courtesy of each respective publication.

*It is extremely important to make it clear that my overall intentions are to shed light on the issues at hand. With that being said, please know that any profit received from the production of the book will be split equally between St. Jude's Children's Hospital and funding children's education in Paterson, NJ.*

## FORWARD

Education/school is expected to be a safe haven— a learning environment where students' education, future and safety are a priority, free from exposure to what goes on in the streets.

Unfortunately, here at John F. Kennedy High School, now the John F. Kennedy Educational Complex, it is nothing more than an indoor very bad and dangerous street corner where students can come in and hang out…indoor truancy.

As you will read, JFK HIGH SCHOOL and the entire school district are more concerned with the PERCEPTION of the school and school district than education and safety of the children left in their charge.

The administration continues to lie, cover up and be watchful of the paper trail.
The Paterson Public School District administration uses the old philosophy,
"IF IT ISN'T WRITTEN, IT DIDN'T HAPPEN!" and doesn't consider this lying.

I can't take it anymore; they are "Ruining a Nation!"

As a Metal Shop Teacher in the Paterson Public School System for almost 30 years, I have witnessed a great deal. I've seen things that should have never gone on in a school— or any place for that matter.

The worse started when Gov. Chris Christie took office.

On May 16, 2011 during the Commencement Ceremony for Seton Hall at the Izod Center, in East Rutherford, NJ, Gov. Christie encouraged students to use their education to disrupt the status quo— to create change. He put a *new spin* on the status quo and labeled himself the Disrupter. His exact words? "I am going to be the Disrupter!"

For over 23 years the State of NJ took control over the Paterson Public School District, during that time the only change I saw in the district was the major disintegration of discipline and learning at JFK High School.

It seems when it comes to failing schools, everyone wants to blame everything and everyone else except those who should be blamed. Instead of dealing with the actual situation, our public schools are just another political BS game. Politicians never deal with the actual problems in the district, because it would be too much of a hot topic for their political career.

The blame lies with politicians, superintendents and the administration of the school district. Also to blame are the students with negative attitudes, the parents who don't care, and the community who is used to blaming everyone for their problems.

Don't listen to politicians telling you about school reform or about how teachers are the problems for failing schools. Contrary to that belief, the real problem with failing schools is politics and politicians. Politicians need to get your attention and your vote. It is nothing more than a political-rally cry; lies to make the taxpayers think they care and to make the taxpayer agree with and vote for them. Politicians and politics today are providing nothing more than theater! It is not about right and wrong, nor about doing what's best for the country or for the people they represent. It is about one side or the other scaring voters into believing in what they are saying and of course, it's about money, *big* money.

The chaos began when Gov. Christine Whitman and the Commissioner of Education, took control over the Paterson Public School System. These are elected officials who are lucky if they stay in the same position for 4 years - one term. How many of them have been fired? How many have left before their term was up to go fulfill another government position or return to the corporate world after they made their contacts, especially the position of Commissioner of Education?

A recent example is the Commissioner of Education Chris Cerf, who resigned in March of 2014. He was appointed by Gov. Christie in late 2010, after the governor fired his previous commissioner. He left to join an educational software company led by his old boss and former New York School Chancellor Joel Klein.

This is exactly what I mean. It is *not* about doing the job or sticking around and staying with it until you see it completed. It is about your friends and networking for your next lucrative position.

Meanwhile, the teacher is still in the classroom doing their job for 25, 30, 35, 40 and I have even seen some with over 50 years of service. So, who are the dedicated ones to the profession of education?

Today, the same goes for the superintendent of the school districts. They're only appointed for a few years. When I was a kid, there was the same superintendent prior to me starting kindergarten, up until after I left high school. Those who serve as superintendents today are vagabonds--carpet baggers who come from other states, have no vested interest other than following the money.

**Here are some of the reasons for the so-called State Takeover:**
1. Top-Heavy Administration
2. High Drop-out Rate
3. Test Scores on State Exams
4. Misappropriation of Funds
5. Low Graduation Rate

## INTRODUCTION

*"Education is the most powerful weapon which you can use to change the world."*

Nelson Mandela

This is a true story.

As you turn the pages of this book, I hope you will become outraged and disappointed in our Public Education System. This book is written in a diary format and chronicles my almost 25 years as an educator at John F. Kennedy High School in Paterson, N.J. During this period, I witnessed despicable student behavior and unforgiveable administrative decisions.

It is our responsibility as a community and a society to say, "No more" to a bureaucratic system that allows for a blatant mismanagement of funds, out-of-control students, and a disregard for students to secure a quality education that prepares them for the future.

It is not my intention to cast a cloud on all those dedicated individuals who view teaching as a noble profession, the parents who guide their children to do their best, or the students that persevere in an atmosphere of chaos. It is rather my intention and hope that you the reader will gain insight and first-hand knowledge about the "real occurrences" in one urban public high school.

After reading this book…you decide if—

***We are Ruining a Nation!***

## TOP-HEAVY ADMINISTRATION

There were too many administrators for the size of the district and number of schools. Look at the district now? Immediately after the state took over the district of Paterson numerous administrative positions were created.

Shortly afterward, the administration opened up another building of nothing but offices at 660 14th Ave., Paterson. Now, they have this huge monstrous warehouse at 90 Delaware Ave. I can only imagine what it costs to operate monthly, let alone the cost to the taxpayers of New Jersey for renovations as well as to update it with all the latest technologies.

Meanwhile, students don't have basic textbooks and the schools do not have all the supplies necessary to operate successfully.

During the 2011–12 school year, John F. Kennedy High School's name changed to John F. Kennedy Educational Complex. What a joke. That was the only thing that changed. Other than some painting and construction inside the building, the classrooms and courses remained the same. They broke the "one" school into four academies, all housed within the original building. These academies are: Architecture Construction Trades (ACT); Science Technology Engineering & Math (STEM); School of Education & Training (SET); and Business, Technology, Marketing & Finance (BTMF), but nothing has changed! In fact, some students have to go to other academies for classes, because their academy doesn't have enough teachers to teach a required course. In hindsight, these academies had already been in place for years!

What changed was the increase of administration in the building, many who received *two* pay raises within a year.

**The Breakdown:**

There are ten more administrators from the previous 2010-11 school year. Instead of one principal running the entire building, there are now two. Plus, there are four more principals, one for each academy, making it a total of six principals in the building, with each principal having their own cabinet of administrators.

We also have two retired Paterson police officers as heads of security. Unfortunately, the taxpayers have been really screwed over and have taken a beaten in order to pay for all of this. The building is absolutely out of control. Students do not have to go to class. There is no accountability for student's attendance, cuts and lateness.

**Bottom Line:**

**What is allowed to go on inside JFK this year is the worse I have ever seen.**

## DROP-OUT RATE

If a student drops out and does not return to school, it can be months— sometimes an entire school year, before he or she is removed from the attendance roster and school enrollment list. This makes it look as if the drop-out rate is lower.

This is *especially* the case with Special Education Students (SPED). This too is another scam. For students who are classified (SPED) the district receives *more* money. Not to mention, parents of classified students, receive (a stipend) extra money too.

It appears the district is very willing to classify many students that present behavioral issues. Unfortunately, many students in my class who had academic issues or ESL (English as a Second Language) never received special education help/assistance.

There are parents who receive a stipend because their child is classified for being hyper. We have case workers going crazy because parents or guardians are constantly coming to their office insisting that their child become classified. It is all about getting extra money from the taxpayers.

Meanwhile what is going on is "Ruining a Nation." No one deserves to receive extra money to go to school, but attending class is optional.

If this school district was run like a *business* and there were problems, those problems would not be allowed to exist for 23 years. However, the state of New Jersey has been running the district for over two decades and we face the same issues from day one.

I can only come to the determination that they don't care; it is just a temporary job to fill their resume requirements for that next appointment or position.

IT IS MY HOPE AFTER YOU READ THIS BOOK AND VIEW THE DOCUMENTATION YOU WILL DECIDE FOR YOURSELF THEY ARE RUINING A NATION!

*********************

As I previously mentioned, many students with behavioral problems roam the halls. The school does not offer support for the teachers or help for the students to correct these problems. Parents did not receive suggestions or counseling for their child. The problems, which often start at home, continue at school. Many students who are disruptive are in the hallways— basically they are any and every place other than their assigned classes. The administration's solution to the problem is simple— just pass them. Give them a "D," let's get them out of here. The cycle continues.

Administration *cannot* deny knowing about these problems because it is all on the school's surveillance cameras. But in the eyes of the outside looking in, we appear as if we are a *functional* school.

Teachers are always on the carpet with administration with this nonsense and procedure. These students will pass their courses and graduate, even if they have not attended classes. WHY? Teachers are threatened by administration about tenure especially if they are a beginning teacher or given classes with students that are worse the next year. Many new teachers become frustrated and leave within a few years. They will either apply for a position in another district and some have quit being a teacher altogether. There are only 181 days in a school year. Some teachers have never ever seen a student an entire school year. Students have been either absent or out of class as much as 100*plus* days and they still pass. If they are seniors the administration goes crazy in making sure those students GRADUATE. The administration wants to show attendance numbers up.

There's a 20-day absentee policy. If a student is absent from school 21 days or more, the student has a hearing along with their parent/s or guardian to decide whether they are kicked out of school, lose credit for the year, go to an alternative program or are allowed to stay in school under a specified contract. A contract means this student cann*ot* be absent anymore, cannot cut a class or be late to school or class. I have never ever seen any of these contracts work. It is giving the student another chance, another chance, and yet a third chance. This goes on and on. Meanwhile the entire student body realizes the contract is a *joke*, an empty and meaningless threat.

The school system and its administration are just pushing students through. They are just graduating and sending students out into the real world, unprepared, uneducated, lacking in basic social skills or graces, which is so important and necessary to become productive members of society. With each year, it becomes progressively worse. Like an infection, it continues to fester and the blame is placed on teachers.

**For example,** during the school year 2005-06 and in one class, I had two female students who were repeating juniors. Meaning they were held back and put in a class called 11R. "R" after a number, means repeating.

All year, both students had poor attendance, cutting, late to both class and school. These two girls were on contracts, many contracts. Not only were they on contracts but they did the same things and acted the exact same way as the year before and (eventually) lost credit for this year too, meaning they will *now* be in 11RR next year, repeating the 11th for the second time. What do you think happened?

They got a new contract and their credit back. Only to void their contract right away and lose credit again. This went on all year. Remember, they are in 11RR. Two weeks before the end of the school year, both of these students, were now in the 12th grade and actually graduated.

I went to an administrator and asked how this could happen. She replied, "Don't worry about them. Now we got them out of here." I blew up and yelled, "What are **we** doing here? This is *not* education?"

There was a lot more said, but it was a waste of my time, effort and just made me sick. She didn't care. She felt she did her job. I asked her as I ask so many administrators, "Would you send your children or grandchildren here?" As usual, she said nothing and walked away.

- *April 6, June 19, 20, 22 & July 26 entries are a continuation to one of the above students.*

Are there exceptions? Absolutely! There are many students who do their work, have good attendance, are not a behavioral problem, study and work hard. What makes it even sadder is that these students receive the same diplomas as those students who do nothing and are just pushed through. Why are these things allowed to go on in our public school system?

When a teacher tells students to move, get to class, get out of the hallway, the bell rang let's go, you're already late, you should already be in your classes, teachers are ignored, threatened, cursed at, given the finger and many times items such as bottles, food, pencils, pens and anything they can get their hands on are thrown at them. Some students are so brazenly defiant because they know administration will *not* do a thing about their behavior and actually try to start a fight by shoving or spitting at the teacher in attempts of provoking the teacher to strike back. All the while the students continue cursing, threatening the teacher and then more students join in like a pack of hungry wolves attacking their prey.

Even security guards are not allowed to do their jobs. They are not backed up, supported, and are basically undermined by administration and told to let the student or students go, don't write it up and etc.

It is absolutely disgusting what is allowed to go on and is covered up inside the school. To add insult to injury, the *teacher* is usually ignored or accused (blamed) for starting the problem by administration in the first place. This is a tactic the administration use to embarrass and frustrate teachers so teachers will now say the heck with it, what's the use, nothing is going to be done about it. They think, *I'm the one who will be accused of starting the problem, I'm the one who will be threatened about receiving a bad evaluation by my supervisor.* That's why many teachers refuse to bother with anything anymore in fear of retaliation.

**NOTE OF INTEREST:** This district's superintendent has a clause in his contract, allowing him to receive bonuses, which makes me understand the *real* reason why the administration does not want to suspend, expel, keep track of attendance, cutting and lateness, pass and graduate everyone etc. He doesn't want a paper trail or he will lose his bonuses.

According to the superintendent all those areas improved and he received his bonus!

Gov. Christie keeps telling New Jersey voters that too much money is being wasted on public education. Didn't he say that there will be a CAP on all NJ school superintendents? Please explain how the Superintendent of Paterson, NJ not only has his contract renewed but will receive a salary of $215,000 a year, plus bonuses? **What happened to the CAP?**

I ask you, who is really failing the schools and the school district?

## LOW TEST SCORES ON STATE-WIDE EXAMS

No change: however, the district will tell you differently. The administration will come up with all sorts of ways/scams to improve and increase the numbers/statistics in passing the State-wide Proficiency Exams, whatever the heck they called it that year. The test name is always changing, but yet it's the same thing.

One way was to allow *only* those students who they thought would pass to take the test. This was done by pretesting students prior to the test. Then they would take any senior who the administration thought that would *not* pass the exam and designate them as 11R, so they would be exempt from taking the test at that time. Then by the next time the test was to be administered they hope to have these students better prepared.

In August, juniors and seniors who have yet to pass the state-wide exam are required to attend school on Saturdays for preparation for exams in September. Most of the students don't show up and yet there still is the expenses that go with opening and running the school.

Then as soon as school opens in September these same students are again assigned to take weekend classes to prepare for the state exam. Once again many of the students still don't show up. All of this is at the expense of New Jersey taxpayers.

The first year of the so-called, "restructuring," was 2011–12 (My Diary entry Jan 20, 2012).Students were still refusing to show up for Saturday Test Prep classes, so the administration went around the building and any student who was *not* wearing their uniforms were assigned Saturday detention. When and *if* these students showed up for detention on Saturday, they were instead placed in the test prep classes. This method increased the number (it is always about number and statistics) of students who showed up for test prep.

Several of my students were rounded up despite being special ed and exempt from taking the test! It is all about controlling the paper trail the administration wants to submit. The numbers maybe correct, but the students that were supposed to be there in attendance were *not.*

Also in the "Restricting Year," students were removed from four periods of their regularly scheduled classes for two double periods of English and math for three weeks prior to testing, and placed in a class that was nothing more than preparing them *on how to take the test.*

This was called "HSPA BOOT CAMP!"

---

**NOTE OF INTEREST:**

Each class is a minute or two more than 40 minutes long and using 40 minutes as a means;
- 40 minutes times 5 days = 200 minutes. 200 minutes = 3 hours and 20 minutes.
- Times (4) four classes = 800 minutes a week = 13 hours and 20 minutes a week.
- Times (3) weeks = 2400 minutes a week = 40 hours total to prepare for HSPA.

- If it snows and students lose a day of school, they need to make that day up at the end of the year.
- If the school day is approximately 6½ to 7 hours long how do students make up 40 hours?
- 40 hours divided by 6½ hours = 6.15 days. 40 hours divided by 7 hours = 5.71 days.
  And it is done *TWICE* a year!

---

Furthermore, many students already have in their regularly daily schedule classes specifically designed to prepare students to take and hopefully pass the standardized test.

My question is— how is this a standardized test when preparing students to take and pass the test isn't standard?

The district many times classifies students so they don't have to take that state test. The district will institute other testing methods in order to say these students are proficient. I am sure there are many other measures administered for preparing students throughout the years to take and pass the standardized test, as to increase the scores and school/district statistics that I *don't* know about!

---

A true story— several students asked me what time it was. I replied, it's a quarter after ten. They would reply what do you mean it's a quarter after ten?

It's unfortunate that students are spending so much time throughout their school day preparing for standardized testing and they are not able to tell time unless it is digital.

---

It is *not* about education here. It is *only* about passing the statewide proficiency standardized exam.

When students fail the statewide exam, the administration goes crazy on figuring out how they can get these students to pass and graduate. They come up with so many BS excuses and programs at the cost of the New Jersey taxpayers all because the superintendent, his administration, and other school administrators continually allow students to be any and every place else other in their classrooms. This is a CRIME!

**The district also implements other ways to help students graduate. Here are** examples of the programs developed to help students graduate:

### BUY BACK PROGRAM

I have my doubts on how this is run. If a student does not go to class all year long, has failed their classes for three and a half marking period they can sign up for Buy Back.

Think about it, students can take and regain their credit in a matter of days for a class they have hardly attended all year! This is done to increase the graduation numbers/statistics.

The administration will have this program right up to a day or two before school is out for the summer.

### TWILIGHT PROGRAM

Basically, the same type of BS program. However, students must attend classes when the regular school day ends.

I believe if a student doesn't go to school, they don't get promoted and they don't graduate.

See My Diary entry January 19, 2012. That's when one of my students was assigned to the *"TWILIGHT PROGRAM."* A copy of his form is included.

### CREDIT RECOVERY/NOVA NET

This is the BIGGEST waste of taxpayers' money. A scam is going on here. So many students have told me this is GREAT! All they do at the end of the day is go to a school computer and if they log on for at least 10 minutes they get credit for that day.

I will discuss more on this BS program later. Once again, if the administration did NOT allow students to be continually out of their classes there would be no need for this.

### SUMMER SCHOOL

It is a freaking joke. Six weeks of school is expected to make up for an entire year if a student did not go to class or has failed a class or classes for an entire year and it is FREE.

During the 2011–12, school year alone, the line for summer school registration started in the front cafeteria and extended all the way out the front entrance of the school. School security had to tell parents and student registration was closed and to come back tomorrow. The next day, the same thing occurred. The line for registration remained this long up until the registration period ended.

Why is summer school *free* in Paterson, NJ? First of all, nothing is FREE! Somebody must pay. In any other school district, parents pay for the summer course upon registration.

If a student is allowed to miss 100 plus days of school a year, have many cuts in all of their classes, fail three and four marking periods and are allowed to go to summer school and miraculously pass for the year, then why don't we just shut the public school system down completely and just have summer school for six weeks? It would save the NJ taxpayers MILLIONS, if not BILLIONS, of dollars just in a few years.

**SRA (Senior Review Assessment)**

Any student the administration thinks will *not* pass the state standardized exam will be assigned to take SRA.

In fact, on May 8, 2012, Ms. Conscientious* told me that the district wanted every student who took the "Credit Recovery" and "Buy Back" programs to graduate. The administration and the building principals want Ms. Conscientious* to set these kids up with the state (DOE) so they can be evaluated. Ms. Conscientious* told me there was *no* way she is going to do this and make herself look like a fool, because the district administration and the building principals want to lie and make it look as if everything here is better now by falsifying records.

To me, it is very obvious the administration is *only* concerned with numbers, statistics, and their own personal goals and advancements rather than with actually giving every student a QUALITY bang for the buck PUBLIC EDUCATION!

- *I sent a copy of this information via e-mail to the president of the PEA.*

## CLASSROOMS

We have had several subcontracting janitorial services that come in and clean. Anybody can empty a garbage can and sweep a floor. The rooms need more than basic cleaning. They are filthy; they are never mopped unless you ask by leaving a note. There are dead bugs, rat and mice feces, dust dirt, mold etc. all over the place. Absolutely disgusting! I am sure the principals' as well as all the superintendent's offices are *not* cleaned in the same way.

There is basically a skeleton crew in the building during the day. They have their hands full with just the maintenance necessary and needed throughout each day. In many cases if it weren't for the shop classes, many things in the building that are broken, vandalized and in need of immediate repair, fabrication or installed would never be fixed or completed.

**BELOW ARE SOME PICTURES OF CLASSROOMS**

They have been this way for years. The graffiti-filled door and large hole in wall were fixed in the summer of 2011.Everything else remains the same as of 2013.

The first seven pictures were taken on March 3, 2008, the day the state-wide exam was being administered. See my complete write up in My Diary, entry March 4, 2008.

I waited until all the students were dismissed before taking photos. These are regularly used classroom occupied by students every day. As you can see, this didn't just happen overnight. In the first two photos the cabinets are filled with dirt, mold, and mice feces.

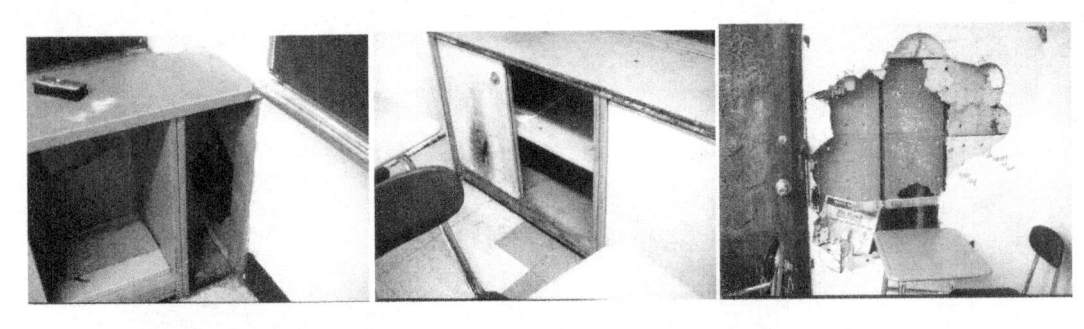

Do these pictures look like a school that is under control?

Vandalism done during school hours.    Television wires pulled right out of the wall.

The televisions are like that or worse in almost every room in the building; all done during school hours.

These are just a few small examples of vandalism that goes on here.

Once again, with evidence such as these photos, my questions remains--Why does the administration continue to allow students to roam the building all day long, every day, all year, every year?

Above is what use to be a heating radiator.    Missing fire extinguisher in foyer by auditorium.

I bet none of this was ever properly reported and documented.

## Bathrooms

Both the boys' and girls' rooms are absolutely disgusting. They are worse than any gas station bathroom or from what I remember of the Port Authority bathrooms in NYC in the 1970s. They are not just dirty, they are absolutely filthy with paper, urine, feces, Kotex, blood and every other gross thing everywhere. In many of the bathrooms the sinks, toilets, and urinals are ripped out and/or have been leaking for years. Many had to be removed permanently.

During the winter and other cold months, they are absolutely freezing because the heaters are all busted up and in some places, they had to be removed. The smell alone is horrible. You come out of them smelling like cigarettes. They are filled with graffiti. They're dangerous. Many students have been beaten up, robbed and attacked at knife point. Gambling and other illegal activity occurs regularly. It is all ignored. It just continues to go on and on, every day for years, especially during this so-called "RESTRUCTURING" period.

Some bathrooms are closed down, locked up and used as storage for office supplies. Many still functioning bathrooms are locked and students have to find a security guard to open them. This is dangerous. What if a fight or worse goes on with in the bathroom? What if a student is sick and passes out and a security guard is not around?

In 2013, one of my quiet well-behaved students was suspended because he could not find a security guard to open the bathroom. The poor kid had to go so bad and didn't know what to do, so he went (defecated) in the stairwell. This incident the school administration saw on the surveillance cameras. Everything else they don't see.

There is so much out of control chaos along with violent and uncontrollable behavior going on because students are constantly allowed to hang out all throughout the building instead of going to their classes.

What comes to mind is that this is supposed to be a place of learning and education— a school. A place where students are to have a sense of security and learn in an enriched, safe and clean environment, away from all the evils of the outside and of the city. Everything that is going on outside is going on inside. In fact, this is the place where it either starts or ends up happening all over again.

## Cafeteria-Lunch Periods

This is when the school is really at its worse. You will see anything and everything you can imagine and more, in the hallways, especially during lunch periods. The sad thing about it is that the cafeterias are on the first floor, right where the heads of security, the security office and the building's principal along with several other administrators are all located.

The noise emanating from the cafeteria is absolutely deafening and the language is absolutely disgusting. This goes on in every lunch period, every day and nothing is done about it. No one makes any effort to have any type of order, human standard or decency. It is an absolute, disgusting free for all. If anyone would act this way in any public establishment or any place outside of JFK, they would be either thrown out or arrested. This is not the way decent people act in society. This is *not* acceptable behavior in any place. Once again, the teaching of right from wrong is dead here. There have been times when I've had to go into the cafeteria and two administrators standing outside the door holding it shut have said, "You're going in there? You're braver than us."

The cafeteria itself after a lunch period is an absolute mess. It is so disgusting. It looks as if a bomb exploded, everything imaginable is all over the place. Students don't have to pick up after themselves. I have seen vice principals on several occasions clean up to get the cafeteria somewhat clean before the next lunch period. On many occasions I have seen security holding students back from entering the cafeterias because it was a disaster of a mess.

Sometimes it is so bad in the cafeteria because there was not just one food fight but several which escalated into brawls and gang fights. Then the same fight carries on into the next and all of the other lunch periods, then into the hallways, eventually the entire school itself, and sometimes on into the very next day. WHY? Because even after the police and security escorted these students out of the cafeteria to the security office, these very same students are let go and the fighting starts all over again.

**REASON:** They do not want to write anyone up. They do not want to discipline students, suspend them, or anything because then there will be a paper trail. This will hurt the perception on how things have changed. This is all a lie, and even though the administration is *not* filling out and submitting the proper forms for all of these actions, it is still a form of falsifying records and documents.

*********************

Unfortunately, many students, who are between 17 and 21 years of age, do not have a driver's license. Why? Because they can't pass the written test even when they get the driving test booklet with the answers. Some don't want to, and some don't know how to study. I blame this school system because they taught students they do not have to study or go to class— they don't have to do anything and they will still pass.

For years, I would not allow students to utilize their notes during an exam or a test.

What I did was to have each student write their notes twice. The second copy is a homework assignment. By doing it this way, I knew students read the notes twice. The next day I checked to see if they did their assignment then I sat with them to go over the notes. I asked questions and deliberately give them the wrong information to see if they are paying attention, looking for students to correct me. I did this to prep them for the quiz. After all of that, most students still failed. They don't care. After we went over the notes, I handed out the quiz. We read the eight to ten questions together out loud and then go over the answers which are *ONLY* true and false.

I marked down in my grade book for each student that we did the test together in class. If I don't do it this way, we would be on the same topic for the entire school year. The mid-term or final exam are a culmination of all the notes and quizzes. Two weeks prior to the exam students received a copy. Students signed a sheet stating they received their copy. The next day we started going over the exam in class and fill in the answers. We went over the entire exam every day right up until the day of the scheduled exam. In the meantime, students had a homework assignment. They're to make sure every question is answered (which is either multiple choice or true and false) and turn in the exam sheet to me on that day of the scheduled exam. To cover myself, I put all this information in my lesson plans and submit it to my administrator.

The mid-term and final exams are in two parts. The first part— each student must turn in their notebook having every note neatly written and in chronological order. If this is done, they automatically receive 45 to 50 percent of their exam grade, making it even easier to get a good grade for the entire exam. Their notes include the copy of their mid-term and or final exam which I gave them two weeks prior. Nothing can be missing from their notes. If there is one note missing or incomplete the student receives an "F". I make this clear to them on the very first day of class and repeat it over and over the entire school year. I especially remind students of every time we have a set of notes to complete. Plus, it is also written down in the very first set of notes they are assigned to complete. I DO NOT ACCEPT EXCUSES. Be it the scheduled mid-term or final-exam- on that day each student receives a copy of the exact exam to take the test. I cannot make it any easier if I took the test myself.

Disappointedly and disgusted, I had 60 plus percent failure rate. So many students either refuse to turn in their notebook, wouldn't do their notes, notes were missing or incomplete or didn't even have a notebook. Throughout the entire year, I have periodical notebook inspections— usually twice a month. Even at that time, if something is missing or wrong, the students are reminded to get it done or fixed. I even have days where I place all notes on a table and allow students to get caught up or make up any notes they are missing. If a student has all the notes, they receive an "A" as if it is a test grade. That was my way of encouraging students in keeping their notebook in order and handy. I kept excellent documentation on every student.

There are many students not only in my class, but in the entire school building who never show up for their final exams. They refuse to come or even make up their final exam. Now here's where your so-called teacher's evaluation comes into play. Yes, it is the end of the year. However, students did not show up and their exam was crucial in order for them to pass. Your administrator will come and ask you why this student failed. The point that aggravates me is that it's the end of the school year, the administration *all* knew which students are failing— *now* they ask the classroom teacher why this student is failing. What happened the entire school year? Why now? Is it because it's crunch time and they need to get the numbers up for passing and graduating students?

All along, parents should have received four sets of warning notices, three report cards and more than likely the teacher made several calls home. However, next year when this teacher is up for evaluations, especially if they are not tenured and are evaluated three times, what do you think is going through their mind? What do you think happens? The new teachers do not want to lose their jobs, so they are forced to lower standards even further so students *will* pass and/or graduate when they should have actually *failed*!

**NOTE OF INTEREST:** In the 2011-12 school year, the very first day of school for teachers, *both* building principals stood in front of the faculty in the auditorium and said things would be different this year. It is *ALL* about education. Any student, who does *not* want to follow the rules, would not be denied an education; they just would not go to John F. Kennedy Educational Complex. They also said, "Any student who is in the hallways, two minutes after the bell rang to be in class, will be swept up and escorted to the security office for disciplinary actions." They say this every year.

From first day of school for the students until the last day of school nothing changed except when visitors arrived. The administration then made it appear as if this was a well-run school. Once the visitors left, it was back to "normal" where chaos and insanity reigned.

There was one young man who was in the hallway all day every day, almost all year. While this young man was in the hallways, he would walk in and out of classrooms where he didn't belong. When teachers asked him to leave, they were met with a barrage of foul language including cursing and threatening remarks along with obscene hand gestures. He yelled personal and inappropriate remarks not only to the teacher but to students in the class in attempts to provoke an altercation.

This is BULLYING! Teachers are targets and allowed to be bullied. The administration encourages this by not admonishing, disciplining, or correcting this behavior. It's allowed to go on and continue because administration do NOT want any reports (paper trail) pertaining to what really happens and goes on here.

If the public knew the truth it will ruin the school, administration, and most of all, the superintendent's image/perception. Meanwhile, it is the teacher who is in the trenches and getting NO SUPPORT from the administration.

There is supposed to be a 'No Bullying Program/Campaign' throughout the country in every public school district. Now if this is not bullying, I don't know what is. *Not* once was this young man ever held responsible or disciplined for this continuous behavior.

Day after day, this went on. One of my colleagues had a 'situation' with this young man. The security guard said "What do you want me to do? I will bring him to the office and the administration will tell me to let him go." The teacher persisted. The security guard brought him into the security office, and as he said to the teacher, administration told the security guard to let him go. Once again—*how can you hold teachers responsible, if administration does nothing and allows this student, as well as hundreds of others to continue to behave and be out of their classes every day?*

Visualize the scenario— students, who are not in classes as they should be, parade the halls screaming, yelling, banging on the door, cursing, giving the finger and just basically raising hell and pitching quarters in the hallway. To make things worse there are security cameras in the exact area where all of this is going on, but the security guard does nothing! I do *not* blame the security guards. The security guard in the prior example said the same thing as the other security guard did in prior incidents. "What do you want me to do? Administration will just tell me to let them go."

This type of thing goes on and on and on all day, every day. Please, somebody tell me, who is responsible for allowing this?

However, sometime in May of 2012, I noticed a certain student was no longer around. While attending one of the districts in-services, I happened to overhear a conversation and heard his name. It seems this young man was with a younger female student. Instead of being in class they were caught in the stairwell together. The young lady was performing oral sex. **NOW** the young man was removed from the building.

This information came to my attention a while after the incident.
See June 20, 2012 & Oct. 24, 2012, in my diary for further details and information about this incident.

**There are several points I am making here:**
1. No matter what happened and who was doing what, if students were not permitted to be in the hallway and stairwells, this would have never happened.

2. If security guards who are paid with taxpayers' money were allowed to do their job and keep the hallways and stairwells (SAFE) clear of students, this would have never happened.

3. If I just found out about it how many people in this LARGE building still know nothing about it? WHY? Because the district wants it kept hushed up.

4. I would like to know how this was handled. Were the parents called in? Did the administrators fill out, submit, and file the proper and necessary paperwork and incident reports? Or as I would expect, was it hushed up and swept under the rug?

5. If what I am telling is what I know, can you imagine what goes on here that I don't know, especially when there are three more floors to this building?

**Bottom line: None of this should have ever happened. The school administration and the district superintendent should have been held liable.**

However, this is just one student in a course of any given school day. We're talking hundreds of students roaming the halls all day long, every day, doing the exact same thing; banging, kicking the classroom doors, yelling, screaming through the door to a teacher or a particular student, walking in and out of classrooms that they don't belong in and doing anything and everything to disrupt classes.

I cannot truly explain what it's really like here. It is *not* normal any place in society, let alone inside a high school. The noise is constant and unbelievably loud. All you hear is a constant roar of screaming, yelling and just the plain continuous obnoxiously loud noise in the hallways exactly like a prison documentary I watched called, "Pelican Island."

The parents, community, and taxpayers never know anything or have any idea this goes on constantly. However, according to Gov. Christie, the Commissioner of Education, and many other politicians all problems in the public school system are the fault of *teachers*.

**EXAMPLE:**
Oct. 22, 2007. The school broke out into a RIOT! This is the year the superintendent implemented block scheduling at John F. Kennedy High School.

Block Scheduling was supposed to be away to curb all of the cutting. How it works is that there are odd and even days of school, which were labeled A-days and B-days. If school started on a Monday that would be A-day and students would follow an A-day schedule; Tuesday, would be B-day, etc.

Students had their schedules cut in half between A and B-days. Whatever day students had their scheduled classes would be double periods. Meaning it is supposedly giving students more time on task and classroom. However, as I said, it was really to help with all of the cutting.

**Bottom line: It didn't work.**

First, students' schedules were all screwed up. The school did not have the program ready to begin when school started in September. This was the beginning of the problem. After a few days, the school decided to have students go back to the schedules they had from last year. Now this became a catastrophe too because some students didn't go to JFK last year. Then we had students who were new and incoming freshman starting here for the first time, and their schedules were not right. This was a mess and went on for weeks. The school was in such disarray, and the students were upset and complaining.
Below, in a chronological timeline is my documentation journal leading up to the RIOTS.

### SCHOOL YEAR 2007-2008
**Sept. 4** -Here we go, first day of school, teachers only. No students until Thursday, Sept. 6, 2007. Anyway, today, we had a meeting in the auditorium, with the principal and all of the VPs. Now here comes the interesting part. Our principal showed us a DVD that features a principal from a different school, let's call her Dr. McPhearson*

It was very good. We did not get a chance to see it all. However, the interesting part is coming. On the DVD, Dr. McPhearson*, who has impeccable education credentials, is telling a group of people that when she was a principal, a parent came in to see and speak with her. The parent explained she was mad at McPhearson* and Dr. McPhearson* asked why. The parent replied it was because she is teaching her son values that are against her teachings. For example, her son is always late to school and is getting in trouble and it is NOT fair. The parent said they teach their children to go by the natural clock. Not a clock that has to be wound up and wakes you up with an alarm; they use nature's way of waking up. Meaning, they wake up when they are ready. Soooo, Dr. McPhearson* says okay, when he wakes up send him to school.

Then the parent complained about a specific teacher who is mean to her son. He is failing him because her son is late, etc. Dr. McPhearson* says something like, okay. When he gets up and finally gets to school; when it's time to go to that class, he doesn't have to go. He can go and pick any teacher and class he wants to go to. Then the parent asked, he won't get in trouble, he won't fail? Principal Dr. McPhearson*replied, no, he will not fail. So the parents then asked if he will have to stay late, make up time and then miss his bus because he needs to leave early to catch a specific bus. The principal tells the parent that when he needs to leave, he can just leave. He can catch any bus he wants that will suit him. If he takes a bus and they don't usually stop at his stop, he can tell the bus driver to stop so he can get out.

The parent replied, "You're crazy. You can't run a school like that!"

McPhearson* sharply replied back to the parent, "You're right, so make sure your son gets here on time."

Right after that our principal stopped the DVD and turned the meeting over to VP Ms. Princess*. What does she do? Ms. Princess*, contradicts the principal saying that students are allowed to be late 15 minutes. Teachers are NOT to write cuts on students if they come to class 5 or 6 minutes late which has been the policy. She says this right after the principal just showed us a DVD about THE IMPORTANCE OF STUDENTS BEING ON TIME.

Then she said five cuts will no longer be counted as a day absent.

I had to laugh; we all said this is BS and another way to falsify records, rigging the percentages/statistics, so students will no longer lose credit. The school year hasn't even started and ALREADY, the administrators are setting it up for failure.

WHY SHOULD ANYONE BE LATE? What are we preparing students for? Then what was the purpose of the principal showing us the video?

**Sept 5** -Here we go again. The 2007–08 school year begins now! 9:18 am the fire alarm went off. We evacuated building.

**Sept 7** -NO SCHOOL, FOR THE ENTIRE DISTRICT. WHY? Because the fire marshal and the mayor closed the schools because of all the fire code violations. The superintendent and mayor are fighting and are going at it with one another.

**Sept 17** -fights all day. Two of them were right by my room. One was between a boy and a girl. Another was to the left of my classroom at approximately 12:50 pm during 6$^{th}$ -7$^{th}$ period.

**Sept 18** -it's only the 4$^{th}$ or 5$^{th}$ full day of school and the hallways are a disaster. So much for this VP Ms. Princes*, who allows students to be 15 minutes late before teachers can write a cut. If things do not change in the next day or 2, the school year will be lost. AGAIN!

**Sept 19** -12:28, fight in Cafe (AGAIN) - Security brought out a student and put him in the security office. About a minute later he walked out and had to be escorted again back by police. Both times all you hear is screaming, yelling, cursing, threats being made by this student, get your fucking hands off of me, I want to get that guy, you can't touch me, you can't do this, etc. and on and on. 1:16 p.m. student is escorted out of the building in handcuffs by police.

**Sept 20 -** 12:20 BIG FIGHT in Cafeteria AGAIN. Many students escorted out by police to the office.

**Sept 25 - period block 3&4 11:25 - A student of mine**, asked to go to the boys' room. Came back all upset set, said he will never use the bathrooms here at JFK again. He said when he went into the boys' room it was filled with kids smoking and shooting dice. One kid shoved him up against the wall and placed a knife to his throat saying we know what you look like, you better not say nothing.

I told security. Nothing was done about it.

**Sept 26 -** The band teacher was telling me yesterday he had 2 students arrested. One punk attacked one of his students trying to steal his iPod while 2 or 3 other thugs were sucker punching and kicking him.

**Since 7th period began**, kids were walking in and out of my classroom that did not belong in here. All they were doing was yelling screaming, wanting to talk to this student, giving food to that one, hanging out, swearing, cursing. I finally went out into the hallway and started yelling, why are all these students allowed in the hallway? I thought this was going to stop with block scheduling? Why are these students allowed to walk in and out of my classroom? Where is security? Where is the administration who said we were not going to allow this? Then finally Ms. Princess* came out of her office.

If I hadn't kept yelling, she would have stayed inside.

**Sept 27 - 1st period 8:15, here we go,** fire trucks, police cars, red lights flashing all around and front of the school. BOMB SCARE! We did NOT evacuate building. WHY?

**This** school year is already lost. Students are in the hallways and outside the building all day. Security is NOT allowed to do anything. Truant Officers are *not allowed* to go after and pick up students. WHY? Kids are hanging out in the hallways, bathrooms, stairwells, walking the entire building as if it is a park, screaming, cursing, running, wrestling, doing flips off the wall. I am NOT exaggerating. There are NO administrators present and so no one does a thing to stop it.

**Oct 4 -** first thing this morning. Mr. Madjar from the cut office came up to me and was livid. He said as of yesterday, (10/3/07), he has processed over 350 cuts. We have already broken the all-time record. Most of the cuts are from students cutting **BLOCKED SCHEDULED CLASSES.**

**12:46 in Café** another fight. Students were brought into security.

SPEAKING OF CAFE and a student told me I should go to the cafe during 5th & 6th periods. Sophomore Girls are giving lap dances and no one is stopping them. No one meaning, security and administration.

STILL SPEAKING OF CAFE TODAY, I went to speak to one of the vice principals. He is usually covering the cafeteria at 12. As I approached the front cafeteria door, he and a TAPs were both standing outside. They must have thought I was going to go inside and said, you're not really going in there. You should have seen it. It was a just short of a riot. It was an absolute free for all. I do NOT understand why this is allowed and NOT stopped.

**Oct 5 -** Hallways are filled with students all day long. NO CHANGE THIS YEAR? WHY? In fact, Ms. Princess*, a VP and Mr. Lance* a TAP walked right into the center hallway filled with kids and each just said, "GO TO CLASS!" All the kids just ignored them and continued doing anything and everything they want rather than go to CLASS! So did the VP & TAP, they just kept on walking as if it were just a stroll in a park. If I was at a park, that acted this way, I would be GONE and QUICK! What a joke, if students were going to listen then what are they doing in the hallways, stairwells, bathrooms, walking in and out of the building all day and every day, in the first place? I believe the administrators are allowing kids to cut so they can get over time later on with students taking NOVA NET, (for class/course recovery) the quicker fixer upper once again all BIG BUCKS at TAXPAYER'S EXPENSE.

**Oct 5 - 12:12, BIG FIGHT** again in cafeteria. 3 or 4 students were pulled out by security and police. Mr. Nickels* a VP had one kid by the neck, Mr. Pro*and Dave*a security officer each had a student and escorting them to the security office. All the while these students were being escorted, they kept trying desperately to continue fighting. I bet nothing will happen. The place is a freakin' disaster.

> Teachers still have *not* received absentee sheets in order to check daily attendance to see whose cutting, suspended, absent or late to school. However, this particular VP, Ms. Princess,*can make all sorts of flyers to place all over the school for "NOVA NET." A money making BS scam. However, for the regular and important school year there is no, "NO PAPER," for teachers to make copies.
>
> There was **NO MASTER SCHOOL ROSTER as of Oct. 5, 2007** to know where students should be during the school day??? WHY? Many students' schedules are still all screwed up.

Received a video showing the hallways are filled with 100s of students acting up, carrying on screaming and yelling. There is NO SUPERVISION. Not one VP, administrator, security guard and the place is out of control.

**Oct 7 -** Spoke with Mr. Madjar about the incident with Mr. Ken Whalen, a teacher. Approximately 2 weeks ago there was a student (female) who was acting up in his class (Special Ed) and was going to be removed by Mrs. Swift* and security. Seems this young lady, **(student built like a bull)** tackled Mr. Ken Whalen like a linebacker and threw him on his back. Consequently, Mr. Whalen has *not* been back to work because he is seriously injured, on crutches and has a great deal pain.

**NOTE OF INTEREST:** As of Nov. 2, 2007, you will see the student in the hallway all day long. I don't think she was ever suspended. Mr. Ken Whalen is still *not* back to school/work!

**UPDATE:** Because of this incident, Mr. Whalen had back problems and was in constant severe pain. After retiring he finally had no choice but to have back surgery.

**FURTHER UPDATE**: Mr. Whalen did press charges against this young lady. The school and school district would not and did not press charges. I do *not* understand this mentality. Do you really wonder why this and other incidents happen here? Students all know that the school and the district WILL NOT do anything. I would like to know why she wasn't arrested right then and there. JFK is a place of lawlessness; where laws and simple rules are on paper only, never enforced, and obviously not obeyed. Nevertheless, this young lady was found guilty and sent to a juvenile facility in Connecticut.

**Oct 9 -** Unbelievable, kids in my class in and in the hallway talking about a shootout today in school. I notified a police sergeant. He said he was aware and wanted me to speak to school security. He came to my class and spoke with that boy. Yet, it is all hushed up. If it was a suburban school and a non-state take-over school, it would be all over the news

**Oct 10** - The same, hallways filled with students acting up. There is NO SUPERVISION. Not one VP, administrator, security guard and the place is out of control.

*Unbelievable*—Mr. Madjar tells me last week Thursday, October 4, 2007, an English class with Special Ed students was being conducted in a science room chem-lab, Room 349. Seems the class was working on a project. The teacher was hanging up stuff and had a kid climbing around on chairs, desks, cabinets, all around hanging up classroom projects. However, a student who was walking along the side bench that runs adjacent to the class windows gets to the end by the back of the classroom and decides to grab a pipe (which was glass) and swing from it like Tarzan. Tube breaks. Luckily, the student did *not* get hurt. The pipe falls to the floor followed by some sort of sludge. Sludge being whatever was in that pipe. That is another problem - no one knows or knew what was in there.

Now, no matter what anybody says, it wasn't an accident like they tried to play it.

One excuse was the boy hit it with his head. However, that wasn't true, because the pipe sits *above* the fluorescent light. So, he would have hit the light, not the pipe, with his head. *Plus*, the lights are 9 feet from the floor - pretty high up. The pipe is higher. The EPA was called in; everyone from downtown was called in. No one knew what to do.

That evening, I received a phone call; a taped message from principal stating briefly that there was a problem in one of the science rooms and that there is no danger and everything is fine. He says everything is ok but had a sample testing sent out by an independent company. The results haven't comeback yet. Do not know if there were any consequences to the student. Which I would very much doubt. I wonder even if there was an incident report written and more so *filed*?

HERALD NEWS, Thursday, October 11, 2007, FRONT PAGE continues on page A4, "School Labs Safe - For Now," by Danielle Shapiro.

Still speaking with Mr. Madjar, who was very upset. He said, as of 10/1 - 10/5, **1650** cut slips have been turned in to the cut office, just for those 5 days. As of today a grand total 3100 - cuts slips have been turned in. That is JUST cut slips. The total count would be MUCH higher because many of the cut slips have multiple cuts on one slip?

REMEMBER, block scheduling was supposed to be a cure for cutting and now it is worse.

**ALL DAY LONG AGAIN**, students walking in and out of my classroom stealing safety glasses, talking to students, asking for iPods, ignoring me and refusing to leave. It is absolutely ridiculous. I went out in the hallway again yelling, why are people all over the hallway? Why are students allowed to walk in and out of my classroom, disrupting me and my students, stealing my glasses? I thought things were going to be better with BLOCK SCHEDULING? I have been here for 21 years and I have never ever seen it this bad. HEY, doesn't anybody hear me, you have to see me, you have to see what's going on you have the surveillance cameras on!

NO ONE showed up, not one administrator, or security guard, not even the new vice principal Ms. Princess* whose office is right across from my classroom. She just stayed in her office. This is actually the worse I have ever seen and it is not even half-way through October?
**FIGHT 11:20,** a boy and a girl. Boy was being escorted to Mr. Pro's* office, all the while screaming, yelling cursing and swearing. Eventually, the boy broke loose and ran away. NOTHING was done about it. They let him go.

# Ruining a Nation and Nobody Cares — Lee McNulty

Received a video on the conditions of hallway on how the students are acting up and carrying on. You will notice that there is not one administrator, security guard and the place is out of control.

Speaking with Ms. Conscientious* she told me she heard Mr. Camp* yell for security because a student (name omitted #1) had a knife. However, student (name omitted #2) dropped the knife and Ms. Conscientious* heard it. The student picked it up and ran. Security caught him, BUT! did nothing, because they didn't find it on him. Ms. Conscientious* said she saw it? This is *unfreakinbelievable*. I eventually spoke directly with Mr. Camp* and he is upset because Ms. Queenie*, an administrator in the Special-Ed department is trying to make it look as if he did *not* see the knife.

**Oct 11 - week of 10/8 - 10/11, FIGHTS** all day long and especially after school, with each dismissal period. However, I do NOT know how it is *not* in the newspapers and remains hushed up. WHY? It's only October. What is going to happen NEXT WEEK, NEXT MONTH, NO TOMORROW?

**Oct 11 -** kids in hallway all day long. The hallways are filled with at least two to three hundred *plus* students. This place is getting worse and worse DAILY. It is no wonder why teachers cannot get control of their classrooms, because the hallways, stairwells, bathrooms, basement, the entire school building is out of control. Not to mention students walking in and out of classrooms they don't belong in causing problems and disrupting class. Students come here and do as they please. With everything that is going on in New Jersey, as well as the rest of the country with bomb scares/threats, shootings, etc. why is this allowed to go on? Why are the administrators allowing this to happen and to continue day after day, all day, every day? *All* **students belong somewhere. This is NOT EDUCATION.**

As I was leaving to go home, I noticed a police officer escorting a student in handcuffs out of the building. Only to learn this student walked into a classroom *he didn't belong in* and ended up shoving the teacher (name omitted). ***Continued next entry…***

**Oct 13 -** *surprisingly* I heard about the Oct. 11 incident on WGHT Radio, this morning, on my way to work. However, on the radio they said that the boy walked into the classroom by 'mistake.' Not true. If it were a mistake, then *why* would the student shove the teacher? Why would the student be escorted out of the building in handcuffs and arrested? It is October and this is absolutely unacceptable!

**Oct 15 - 2nd period, 9:57 am, fire alarm** went off. We had to evacuate building.
Received 3 photos and some sort of video (51 seconds) of the evacuation.

Hallways filled with students. It is getting worse by the day. In fact, during 3rd period, surprisingly Vice Principal Ms. Princess* came to my classroom and moved several students who were standing in my doorway hanging out. She probably did this because she didn't want to hear me yelling in the hallway to get these kids out of here again. She and all administrators should be doing this all day every day.

**12:20,** 2 of my female students, came to my classroom asking for air freshener. Someone lit a stink bomb or something and it's stinking up the entire school. Kids are all over the place now using the smell as an excuse to roam the halls and *not* go to class. As if they need an excuse! Wonder why the cut office is processing cuts like crazy.

The administration is finally *admitting* it is unsafe and dangerous here. I received a phone call at home (a taped message) from the principal stating to all parents and teachers as of tomorrow, 10/16/07, the late and cut policy procedures will be changed. If a student is 6 minutes late to class, they WILL be marked late. If a student is 7 minutes late, student will be marked as a cut and suffer the consequences, whatever they are??

He also said all students *must* report to school 10 minutes before school starts. If a student is not in homeroom, they will need a re-admittance from Office #2 or will be marked absent. Let's see what happens. I want things to get better, *but I* have *no faith* in our public school systems and politicians.

**Oct 16 - 2nd period, 9:16 am**, fire alarms go off. Students protesting about block scheduling again. We had to evacuate the building. I do not know where the alarm was pulled. It is like a riot in here. Kids are all over the place in large mobs screaming, yelling, pushing, shoving, and going berserk. It is absolutely OUT OF FREAKIN' CONTROL! There were no security and or administrators present until much later.

Found out today 10/17/07, yesterday's alarm was pulled again in the gym by the trainer's office. **Received Video & 3 Photos.**

**2nd period, 9:43 am,** fire alarms go off. Kids still protesting about Block Scheduling. We evacuated the building again. The school is so out of control. **Received video and 3 photos.**

**Found out today 10/17/07,** that the alarm was pulled by stairwell 14-15. However, the alarms were pulled **24 times** almost simultaneously all over the building to cause even more havoc and confusion. The chief custodian went to reset the alarm after being told to turn them off. He had to go to **24 individual** fire alarm boxes because the monitor in the custodian's room showed that **24 separate** places had to be reset before he can reset the master alarm. The administration wants them turned off because the school is so out of control. Well, being that the school is so out of control, who is held responsible? If they're turning the alarms off, then why do we have them in the first place? THIS IS ILLEGAL! This is the State of NJ Running and Operating THIS School District. So that makes the Governor and Commissioner of education responsible.

**Oct 16 -** speaking with a retired Paterson Police Captain, he told me they shut off the fire alarms so the kids can pull it and nothing will happen. *And*?? I'll say it again, how is this legal? That is the superintendent and administrator's solution to the problems by allowing students *not* to be in class and have the entire school building out of freakin' control!

With all that has been going on today here, the administration is *still* allowing students to roam the building as if it is normal. Students are *not* going to class. How can that be normal, especially after yesterday's phone call by the principal, stating that no one will be allowed in the hallways? Anyone who is 7 minutes late to class will receive a cut. Well, we see what the cuts mean— ABSOLUTELY NOTHING— because, the halls are *filled* with students all day long.

In fact, at one time, VP Ms. Princess*scolded a young woman for being in the hallways. This young lady was defiant even when the vice principal told her that she would be sending her home. As expected the VP did nothing; she just turned and walked away as this young lady remained in the hallway screaming as loud as she could, "FUCK HER, FUCK, WHO THE FUCK IS SHE, SHE'S NOT MY MOTHER FUCKING MOTHER, EVEN MY MOM DON'T DARE FUCKIN TALK TO ME LIKE THAT. SO WHO THE FUCK IS SHE AND WHO THE FUCK IS SHE TO TELL ME ANYTHING. THAT MOTHER FUCKER" and on and on. Not once was she disciplined, or told to be quiet and stop with the foul language. What example did the vice principal set by walking away and allowing this young lady to continue to carry on the way she did?

**BLOOD all over the floor** from Gym room to nurse's office. In fact, the nurse called on the walkie-talkie to have a janitor clean up the blood in the nurse's room. It seems a student, wanted to leave the gym area. The teacher was instructed NOT to allow anyone to leave. The student was defiant and insistent. The teacher wouldn't allow him to leave, so the student punched the window, shattering it and slicing his hand very badly. Now, I wonder what happened. Was he suspended? Did he pay for the window? I bet nothing was even a reported.

**NOTE OF INTEREST:** OCTOBER 16, 2007 —
The place was a riot and I do not mean funny. It was seriously out of control. I heard it was the same on all 3 floors. I can understand the superintendent being concerned about teachers having their ID cards. However, he should be just as concerned about enforcing the rules by having students wear their ID cards too, especially when we have adults, children gang members, anybody, constantly walking in and out of the building all day long, that do not belong in the building, causing problems, fights, etc.

**Bottom line: The children's safety as well as everyone's safety in the building is in jeopardy when the principal has the fire alarms shut off.**

**Oct 17** - *UNBELIEVABLE,* I have today's newspaper; it contains an article about the false fire alarms and students protesting. It also states Dr. Miller said, "**EVERYTHING WAS IN CONTROL**." What a FREAKING lie! I now lost all respect for him. This place was out of control and I received video as well as the videos anyone can see on MY SPACE or You Tube.

It was a dangerous situation here and still is today. I don't know if it is true or not, supposedly Dr. Miller retired from wherever he came from. However, if that is true, I would think seeing how bad things are here, he is in a position to straighten things out, get this school to run right and to set policies. However, something must have come over him to make him lie by saying "everything was in control, "and to continually allow students to roam the entire building, cut classes all day, every day, to allow our school to be so out of control and dangerous.

Speaking with one of my students he said he read the newspaper and said it was a crock of shit. He said even outside was a disaster and so dangerous. Students were fighting in groups and gangs. Everybody was fair game. Teachers were being sucker punched, hit from behind in the head. Then he said he saw 6 *more* police cars come flying up to the front of the building spraying mace to get students and whoever else to move and disburse. Yet the principal Dr. Miller says the situation was not out of control.

**NOTE OF INTEREST**: During one of the earlier stages of the riots here at JFK, Dr. Miller's phone was either dropped or knocked out of his hand, was picked up by student/s and taken away (stolen/robbed?).

**School elevator** is not still working. Has not since last Thursday when a friend of mine, an English teacher, and several other people were stuck in it between floors, I attempted to open the doors but the safety mechanism that is used to pry the elevator door open was missing. I suggested calling the fire department. The fire department came and opened up the elevator. The fire department is here so much at JFK; they should just use the school as their fire house. It would save time and money.

The fire alarms are still shut off. The head custodian is so upset. He is afraid if something should happen, he will be held responsible, get fired and put into jail, because he knows it is against the law to shut them off. However, the principal and VP Princess* will NOT sign anything saying that they *told him to shut off the alarms*. I told him to say, "NO, let them turn it off."

**At 12:27** pm the fire department came back. The alarms **did *not* go off**, because they are **shut off**. There was a fire on the second floor, boys' bathroom, social studies wing. A combination of stuffed papers in a pail, as well as a cigarette stuffed into a smoke detector in the boys' bathroom. When the fire department came they wanted to know why the alarm wasn't working. However, the alarm was sent to the Paterson Fire Department Headquarters. Furthermore, no one was ever told to evacuate the building. This is all happening because students are allowed to walk the hallways all day long. It is getting more and more dangerous. I hope parents start suing the board of education, the superintendent, the administration, the Commissioner of Education and governors for allowing these inappropriate and unacceptable conditions to continue here at JFK High School.

**During** my lunch period, I decided to go to the West Side Café on the 3rd Floor. However, when I got to the 2nd floor, I could NOT believe my eyes. There was no security, kids were over the place, not going to class, class had already started, I took video for over 7 minutes and had enough and wanted to go get my lunch. Meanwhile, students remained in the hallways and the only administrator I remember seeing was the Head of the English Department Mr. Arthurs* just standing there. I even asked several students as they were finally walking into class what time it was on the classroom clock. I did this as a reference to show actual class time and all of the kids still in the hallways refusing to go to class. Even after I left the café, kids were still all over the place, on the 1st and 2nd floor hallways and bathrooms were overflowing with students. I did NOT bother checking the 3rd floor. Anyway, I am walking down to my room when I was met with the fire department running upstairs because of the fire in the boys' bathroom. Even as the fire department was scrambling up the stairs to get to the 2nd floor, the administrators are still allowing all of these students to be in the hallways, stairwells, and bathrooms, instead of being in their respective classes.

**Oct 18 -** first thing this morning, school didn't even start, 7:20 am the bus pulls up to the school and two girls start fighting. Then the entire place goes absolutely berserk. The entire day was shot. Nothing **but** fights all day long. I couldn't keep track, I started to, but it was one right after another, back to back.

**Speaking with** a personal aide for one of my handicap students, he said they were told by VP Ms. Princess* that all handicapped children <u>***must***</u> go to the principal's conference room for classes. The personal aide was thinking because of the problems with the elevators and asked why, since all of his students' classes are on the first floor. The VP said she didn't care; she wants him to go to the principal's conference room, because it is *"safer"* there. Safer, meaning there's acknowledgment from an administrator that the school and hallways are unsafe?

Well, why is it unsafe here? What is being done to make it safe *here*? So, because the administration continually allows the school to be out of control and is so dangerous the handicapped students are actually <u>segregated, ostracized</u> from their classes, classrooms and from being with their friends in those classes/classrooms. Is this NOT discrimination?

Remember, the principal said in the newspaper that everything is under control.

Meanwhile the administration still wants everyone to believe that everything here is Safe & Normal. Has anything I've written seem to be SAFE *or* NORMAL?

Think about this, if a teacher has a problem with their class or classes that teacher has no classroom management. Well, who is to blame when the entire school is so dangerous and out of control where handicapped students can NOT, no not allowed to go to their classes? Remember, VP Ms. Princess* is in charge of student attendance, cutting and lateness.

How many state and federal laws are being broken in just *this* entry alone?

**Each day is getting worse.** I watched a boy throw a girl down on the floor, hit her and kicked her several times. Even when a teacher told the boy to stop he looked at her and kept it up. The girl just laughed got up and then got an attitude with that teacher. I am so confused when I am here. *I have no idea anymore what is right or wrong here.*

**Oct 19 -** the principal was not in the building again today. MEETINGS? With all that is and has been going on why would he be out again? Why aren't meetings held after school? If the principal is to be at meetings, then in reality there is NO PRINCIPAL here. Then why do we need a principal? Gee I wonder if it has anything to do with what has been going on in the building as well as the e-mail I had sent including the videos that students posted on YOU TUBE/MY SPACE.

**ANOTHER FIRE** during block 2-3, on the 3rd floor boy's bathroom science wing. Fire alarms did not go off because they were turned off again. I didn't even know about it until another teacher told me. I am sure most of the other faculty as well as the students didn't either.

12:12 another fight breaks out in the caf. I watched two separate police officers escorting two separate students and both in handcuffs. One student went to the security office, the other went down the principal's wing.

I decided to take video with my camcorder during 5th period lunch. UNFREAKINBELIEVABLE. You will see a kid actually doing flips in the hallway and no one said a word.
There is so much going on. It is so dangerous and out of control.

## OCTOBER 22, 2007, THE DAY OF THE BLOCK SCHEDULE RIOT

THIS IS THE WORSE I HAVE EVER SEEN HERE AT JFK. It seems the administration is really trying to control all of this and keep it quiet. It is all spilling out of the building and into the streets. It is out of control; it is a RIOT! The entire building inside and out was filled with police. All of the surrounding streets were blocked off and directed by police. Fire department, sheriff's department, everyone, including the mayor, was here. Helicopters from all the major TV channels -12, 5, 7 and 2 - were flying all day above the school. We were outside almost the entire morning, actually the entire school day. School was a disaster. We had to be constantly evacuating the building because students were deliberately setting fires in the building and pulling false alarms. Students/gangs fighting in the building and in the streets. It's an absolute disgrace and was never in the newspaper

Break down of the day's events –

**2nd period, 9:10 am**, fire alarm went off; we had to evacuate the building. Students inside the building were going berserk. Fire was set in girls' bathroom 2nd floor by igniting paper. Once outside the building, it was the same as last time, but getting worse. A great deal of tension in the air. Have video & photos.

**2nd period, 9:54 am**, fire alarm goes off, *again*, we had to evacuate the building, *again*. Fire was set in girls' bathroom 2nd floor by igniting paper, *again*. Once we left the building, it was worse than a few minutes ago. Students are screaming and yelling, "No More BLOCK!" It was so bad inside and it worse outside. All of the news helicopters were flying over including channels 2, 4, 5 and NJ12. Received video & photos.

**Block 3/4 period, 10:46, fire** alarm went off, *again*. We had to evacuate the building, again. Fire dept. police dept. sheriff's dept., police dogs, this time the riot squad, etc. News 12 and other helicopters above. REALLY BAD AND REALLY DANGEROUS TODAY. It is so out of control right now. It is scary. I am watching my back. We came back in at 11:37 am. It is much worse than the last time we had to evacuate the building a short while ago. Unbelievable. Received a great deal of video and photos. Much to explain, it is definitely a MUST SEE VIDEO.

**11:51**, fire alarm went off, AGAIN. We had to evacuate the building, AGAIN. Fire dept., police dept., riot squad, etc. all still here and never left. It is obvious it is going to happen again. The students are going crazy. There is NO CONTROL at all. The students are running so wild. The News 2, 7, and 12 helicopters are still flying above us. Everything here is getting worse. The only change is the time.

Nobody would ever believe what is going on in and outside of this school, if you want to call it a school. I have never ever heard of any school in my entire life acting like this. Then once the students were out of the building the streets were so out of control too. Students owned the school and the block. It is time to get the STATE the hell out of here. They have ruined this school and the entire school district! I received more video.

**UNFREAKINBELIEVABLE, FIGHTS** all day long, outside during evacuations, and when we are back in the building, it is absolute chaos and pandemonium. Nothing but gang wars, Blacks against Dominicans. One Spanish kid was caught, thrown down, kicked, and beat up by a bunch of Blacks - possible broken ribs. Paramedics were brought in.

Meanwhile the students are all still in the hallways. To think this is all happening under the supervision of an administration where the administrators, right up to the superintendent— ALL OF THEM— have a minimum of a master's degree to a PhD, with all sorts of certifications. What the hell good is in having all of that crap, when you can't control your school or school district? Let's see if this makes the newspapers and TV. Anybody want to make a bet?

**The 3rd time we were out** because we had to evacuate the building, I was in the front of the building videotaping. I have a great deal of unbelievable video. Later on, DOLL*a security guard, came to see me and asked if I was videotaping. I said yes. She then said, that I am not allowed to videotape. The person from human relations said it is against the law. I turned and said that I am going to videotape all I want and they can go arrest me, not thinking or realizing that DOLL* is really catching hell from everyone because of all that is going on here. She got mad at me and said, Okay, I will go and tell them that. I replied, "It's like that? Just tell them that you told me." Later that day I saw DOLL* in the building. I apologized to her and said I was *not* upset with her and she too said she was not upset with me. She said she was just following orders then she told me to be careful, you have no idea how these people really are.

I took it as meaning that they will try to write me up or enforce some sort of disciplinary action. I believe the real reason is they want all of the evidence covered up. I also realized, more than likely nothing will happen, because if they arrest me, then the video will have to be in evidence and *now* the evidence will reveal the truth to the public. Plus, they may wonder how much more (video) there is or if I have other evidence that is damaging to all of them that will also have to be made public. Does the state run and operated school district really want that? After all, how many times did we have to evacuate the building just today and it is only OCTOBER 22! Any attorney will tell you; video is better than an eye witness and I am only documenting it.

**12:47 pm--** Hallways are so bad and dangerous. They are filled with students and they are still acting up—going wild. Why? I cannot understand why this is allowed! I bet the administration has turned off the fire alarms *again*.

**Parents** are coming into school and pulling their children out like crazy. Can you *blame* them? Good! They all should be suing the entire school district. No child/students should have to be subjected to any of this unacceptable behavior.

**1:23 pm -** I heard over a walkie-talkie someone calling for Mr. Costello* a VP. Then Mr. Costello* came into my room and used my classroom phone. Whispering, I heard him say, "Well, take them to disciplinary Mr. Lance*." Then he hung up and walked out. The administration does not discuss anything over the radios anymore. As I have said before and more so now, the administration and is working even harder in their attempts in hushing up everything here at JFK.

***THE* ENTIRE SCHOOL AND DAY WAS LOST. IT WAS AN ABSOLUTE DISASTER. STUDENTS RIOTED, TOOK OVER THE ENTIRE SCHOOL, THE SCHOOL GROUNDS AND SURROUNDING CITY BLOCKS. AND IT ALL WENT IGNORED.**

**6:58 pm** received a phone call at home this evening; a taped message, from the principal, a notification about today's situation but a real watered down version. NOT even close to what really went on. However, he did say the alarms went off *five* times!! He also said they apprehended four students due to the surveillance cameras in the building, and they will be prosecuted. They have knowledge of other students as well. Why don't they have surveillance videos of *all* the students in the hallways, stairwells, bathrooms, roaming the halls NOT going to class/cutting all day, every day. How many times did we evacuate the building this year? How many times did we evacuate the building *today*? What BS.

**MY QUESTION:** WHY, isn't the school administrators held responsible if student/s are not in their classrooms or assigned classrooms? The administrators are depriving the children of an education and encouraging students who were doing well to follow those who are doing all the wrong things getting away with it all and still passes?

THINK ABOUT IT.

What is the difference if a parent refuses to send their children to school or when the school allows the child NOT to attend their classes?

If a parent does not send their child to school, if a student does not attend school, cuts class or school, this is TRUANCY and the parent/s are held responsible?

SOOOO, why isn't the school administration as well as the board of education held responsible for allowing students to be in hallways, starting fires, disrupting other classes, smoking, fighting, rioting, robbing, mugging, vandalizing and etc.? IT IS ALL STILL TRUANCY!

If a parent refuses to send their child to school doesn't that constitute child abuse?

If so, then the school is also contributing to child abuse!

Let's see— Allowing students to roam the hallways all day long. Students do not attend class(es); Administrators just change students' grades and falsify records in order for students to pass, alter report cards, passing and graduating students who are in 10R or 11R and have lost credit yet when June comes, they are graduating, (Example: I have many.) Basically, lying about a child getting a "PROPER EDUCATION."

DOES THIS ALL NOT CONSTITUTE CHILD ABUSE?

*********************

I received this link via an ex-student of mine who stopped by to visit me and said that her professor at William Paterson College in Wayne, New Jersey, was talking about this incident/riot and showed the kids this 7 minute You Tube Video https://www.youtube.com/watch?v=ndfggce_zxs  But that was it.

**Believe it or not, there was mention the next day in the Herald News—Front page:** "Fires, alarms, chaos, rule the day at JFK," continued on page A4. But that was it.

Remember Block Scheduling was to cure students from cutting!

**By 2008 - 2009,** there was no more block scheduling!
Below are a few newspaper articles about "BLOCK SCHEDULING"

Haddon, Heather. "Schedule glitch leaves kids idle." *Herald News*, 23 September, 2006. B6. Print.

Right out of the gate, the entire program was nothing but a disaster, students and teachers didn't know what to do. This went on for months.

September 23, 2006

# Teachers, students say knock blocks off

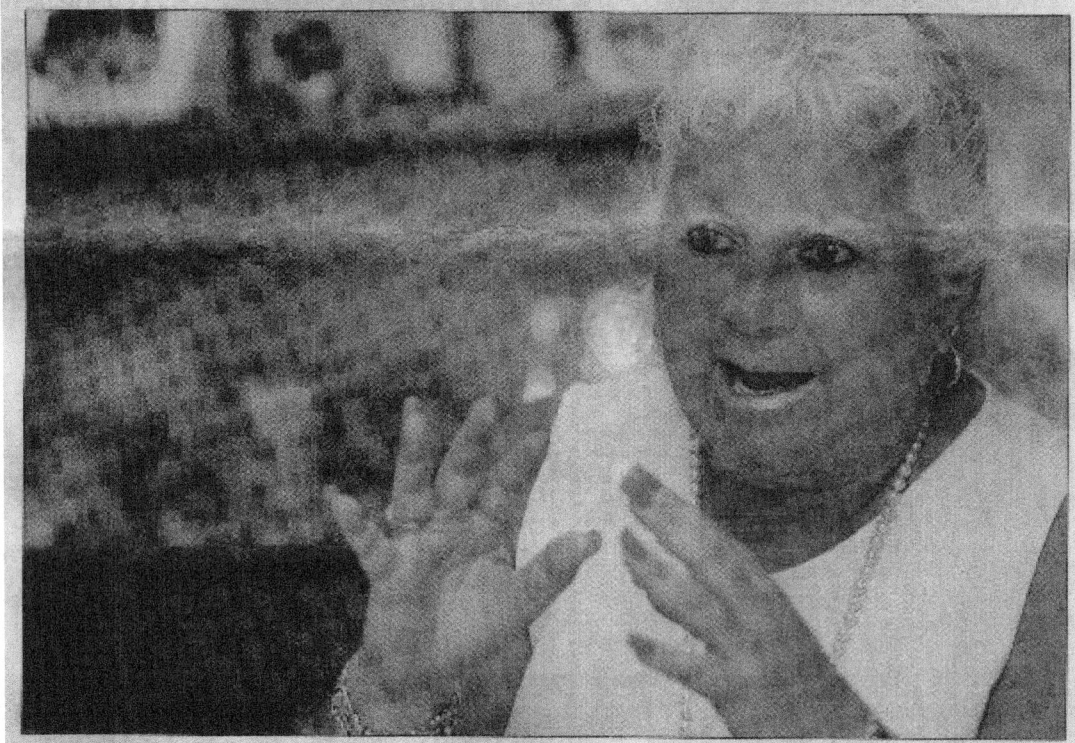

"These blocks require a teacher to be more creative, effective and efficient," says Eastside Principal Karen Johnson.

## Union to file charges on scheduling changes

By DANIELLE SHAPIRO
Herald News

PATERSON — The school district's highly touted switch to block-scheduling this year has precipitated a crescendo of opposition, fueled by allegations of no communication from administrators on the change, which will ultimately affect classroom teacher workloads.

It appears that a change in the way teachers instruct and how children learn has also spurred criticism from some students who say they prefer the status quo for classroom instruction. Other New Jersey school districts have painstakingly included community comment in assembling block-scheduling, and that is the rub, because the city school district has not, critics say.

Attorneys for the Paterson Education Association — a teachers union representing 3,800 people, 2,800 of whom are teachers — are expected to file an unfair labor practice charge soon with the Public

Please see BLOCK, A4

Shapiro, Danielle. "Teachers students say knock blocks off." *Herald News*, 23 Sept. 2006. A4. Print.

However, there was nothing ever mention about the RIOT going on inside and outside JFK on October 22, 2007 throughout the entire day!

Once again, the district just does away with another program, and more of the taxpayers' money is wasted. Why? Because students did not want to have Block Scheduling, so they rioted! Frankly, we don't need all these useless programs. All that is needed is rigorous education and *discipline*. Rules must be followed and enforced--Everyone has to work and *earn* their diplomas. Just like in the real world, you don't get something if you don't work for it.

In a school that has approximately 2500 students each year and in the last several years there were OVER 400 thousand cuts each year. What makes it worse is with the cut office students would have 100s of cuts, but nothing was done about it, so teachers didn't bother writing them anymore. Sometimes teachers would write cuts once a week. But it would be five cuts on one form. Otherwise, the total number of cuts would be higher.

So, what does the administration do now? In the 2011-2012 school year the administration decided to do away with an attendance and cut office. Why? It was to do away with the paper trail of cuts. They had to prove that the new John F. Kennedy Educational Complex is better. New and improved, and will basically just ignore cutting altogether

This way administration would have more control of statistics and the superintendent will get his contract renewed, a salary increase, and his BONUSES!

## HOMEROOM

*Oh my God*, you wouldn't believe it. What a joke.

Homeroom is supposed to be the time students get marked present in school. A place where and when students receive important information they need for the day, schedule changes, testing, etc. Instead, homeroom is a disaster.

When it comes time to saying the pledge of allegiance to the flag, students will carry on with their nonsense, talk, listen to their iPod with the head phones on, curse, yell outside the classroom, walk around, play wrestling, girls sitting on guys' laps, everything and anything else other than say the pledge of allegiance. It is absolutely disgusting. Teachers say nothing because they will be ignored or cursed at and threatened. Many students say I'm not saying the pledge of allegiance; this isn't my country. Fuck America!

When students didn't go to homeroom and didn't bother to go to the attendance office to be marked in present even if it is being marked late, they just remain in the building all day, playing or causing problems. They are in the hallways, stairwells, bathrooms, any place imaginable other than where they are supposed to be. For many students, school is merely a place to go be out of the weather, meet up with your friends and play. While there are those students all they do is look to start trouble and fights. In reality our school is nothing more and actually worse than an indoor street corner.

Hours after homeroom, you will still see so many students walking into the building *late*. They will walk in with a cup of coffee, soda, something to drink, and a donut or sandwich. They don't have a care in the world. Everything and anything is more important than being on time for school. While they are walking to wherever they are going, and for most it is *not* to homeroom or class, depending on what time they finally arrive, they are throwing the bottles, cups, wrappers, and everything else on the floor. The sad part is, administration is right there; they see this and they say nothing. If a teacher or a security guard should say something to the student or students, they are verbally attacked, threatened, and cursed at.

The reason why students act like this is because administration will do *nothing* to correct that type of behavior. So if there are no consequences, how do expect things to change? *Obviously*, if there are no consequences, things and situations *will* get worse!

Where are our politicians? Where are all the priests, community and social leaders now? Where are all these different ethnic groups now? This is no joke. People wake up. This isn't a book for a movie, this is really going on in our schools! Where are you President Obama, Gov. Christie, Commissioner of Education whoever you are today, Al Sharpton, Jessie Jackson…anybody?

**Bottom line: Our students are *not* just under educated, they are not prepared for the future and the world of work.**

Now in the school year 2011-2012, the administration, those who hold a minimum of a master's degree want discipline to be the teacher's responsibility. Think about it, if a student does not respect the teacher and has a discipline problem, how is that or any teacher to instill discipline?

I believe the administration does this purposely to frustrate teachers knowing damn well they will get fed up and eventually give up, all in attempts to keep the paper trail down on discipline and other problems.

If it is supposed to be so good and safe here, the administrators should send their children here! If they say no, then why do they allow this to go on day after day all year long? If they say yes and do not have a child or children attend this school, they're a liar.

Teachers are blamed for everything. We are NOT allowed to do our jobs. If a teacher attempts to remove a student or in many cases these students (some times as much as six or seven students will enter a classroom they don't belong in) that teacher is threatened and cursed at in the most demeaning way. They will not only threaten the teachers, they will tell the teacher that they will FUCK their daughters, kill their children and etc. You bring this to administrations attention, it falls on deaf ears. Administration will do nothing, UNTIL a teacher is attacked. Even then administration tries to blame the teacher

I'll say it over and over, when I walk into this "*School*" building, I have no idea of right and wrong anymore. It is absolutely disgusting!

## 3 Paterson students charged with carrying guns

**By TIMOTHY D. MAY and MICHAEL CASEY**
Staff Writers

### JFK incidents draw pleas for increased security

Three students at John F. Kennedy High School in Paterson were arrested this week after administrators twice discovered loaded handguns at the school, police said.

One gun — a 9mm semiautomatic — was found by school officials Monday in a student's locker, police said. And on Friday, school administrators said they discovered a .38-caliber revolver in another student's book bag.

In both cases, officials said, other students warned them that classmates had brought guns to school.

Police and school officials said there was no connection between the two incidents, and there is no evidence that the students involved — two 16-year-old sophomores and a 17-year-old freshman — had threatened or targeted anybody. Police withheld the students' names because of their age.

"The key point here is: It was the other students themselves coming forward and telling us they don't want weapons in their schools," Police Chief Lawrence Spagnola said Friday.

Kennedy Principal Richard Garibell said the district will install metal-detectors at high schools before school reopens in September.

And a city detective said Friday that Kennedy officials have asked police to scan students on Monday with hand-

See **SCHOOL** Page A-13

> teens were sent to the Passaic County Juvenile Detention Center in Haledon, their bail status was unavailable.
>
> On Monday, police arrested a 17-year-old freshman after a school administrator, acting on a tip from another student, searched the boy's locker and found the semiautomatic. The gun was outfitted with a 17-round ammunition clip loaded with 14 bullets, Spagnola said.
>
> The teen was charged with unlawful possession of a handgun, possession of a weapon for an unlawful purpose, possession of a weapon on school property, and possession of a large-capacity magazine. He remained in the Passaic County Juvenile Detention Center in Haledon on Friday; his bail status was unavailable.
>
> If convicted, the three teens each would face up to three years at the county detention center, authorities said.
>
> Garibell said the students who reported the weapons "did a very brave thing by coming forward and letting us know." He added: "We've worked with our kids so that, when they see something that doesn't belong in the school, they let us know. They understand our zero tolerance for weapons."
>
> The three suspects have been suspended from school and will have expulsion hearings, Garibell said.
>
> As news of the gun seizures got around Kennedy on Friday, teachers and parents flooded the Police Department with requests for extra security at the high school.
>
> Paterson schools Superintendent Edwin Duroy noted that four uniformed police officers work school day shifts at both Kennedy and Eastside high schools. In addition, both high schools employ about a dozen private security guards.
>
> Duroy noted that the school district had previously ordered handheld metal detectors for use at certain school functions, such as basketball games. Duroy also said extra security measures were introduced at district high schools earlier this year, such as random monthly book bag searches and unannounced patrols by gun and drug-sniffing dogs from the Passaic County Sheriff Department's K9 unit.
>
> Monday's incident was the first this year in which a Paterson student was caught with a gun in school, police said.

This is *not* the first time guns were involved at JFK. The list of similar events goes on and on. There was a young man shot several years ago, on the first day of summer school, right out front of the building with hundreds of students all waiting to come in.

The weapons that are brought into school are inconceivable. Many times, students bring machetes to school because there's going to be a fight, or they or their friends are going to be attacked. I have been given video taken by students of these crimes and turned them over to security. In the videos, you actually see a student take a machete out of his book bag, which was with him in school all day, and start swinging while students scream, "He's got a machete, look out!"

One day, a student came to me absolutely upset. He said he was behind two students going upstairs to the second floor and noticed one kid had a gun stuffed in the back of his pants. I asked if he told security. He said no, because he was afraid and didn't know what to do. I had this student go to one of the administrators, who was in her office and happened to be talking with one of the police officers. He told them the story. They start giving him a bad time. They asked him if the kid was Black, green, white, Hispanic? Then he told me that they both were yelling at him, what do you want us to do if you cannot identify them?

They should have *locked* down the building.

The only time we use metal detectors in the building is *after* something has happened. Then after a day or two, they are NOT used anymore.

What I am telling you are NOT isolated incidents. This has gone on and on ever since the State of New Jersey has taken over the District of Paterson. That is why most of this stuff is never ever on TV, newspapers and/or radio.

Obviously, some of it gets out, (leaked) to the media. However, it still continues today. Whatever happened to the District Policy RULE/LAW "ZERO TOLERANCE TO VIOLENCE?" I guess it doesn't pertain to students who threatened teachers.

There have been students who not only threatened teachers, but they actually have attacked them and gotten away with it. It is rare that a teacher presses charges. Why? Because, they fear retaliation by the student, their friends, family, and gangs. To make it worse teachers fear even the school's administration and the Superintendent of retaliation. Why? Because, the district wants everything hushed up. They want everyone to *think* that everything is going well here.

What a way to work. You have a fear of the unknown and what's going to happen today? Are you or is anybody going to get hurt, lose our job or career? A man *was* killed here. He was beaten to *death* because these students were allowed to roam the halls and walk in and out of the building.

The man's name was Mr. Hector Robles.

**June 21, 2001**

# Gentle soul, violent death
## Five teens charged in beating of homeless man

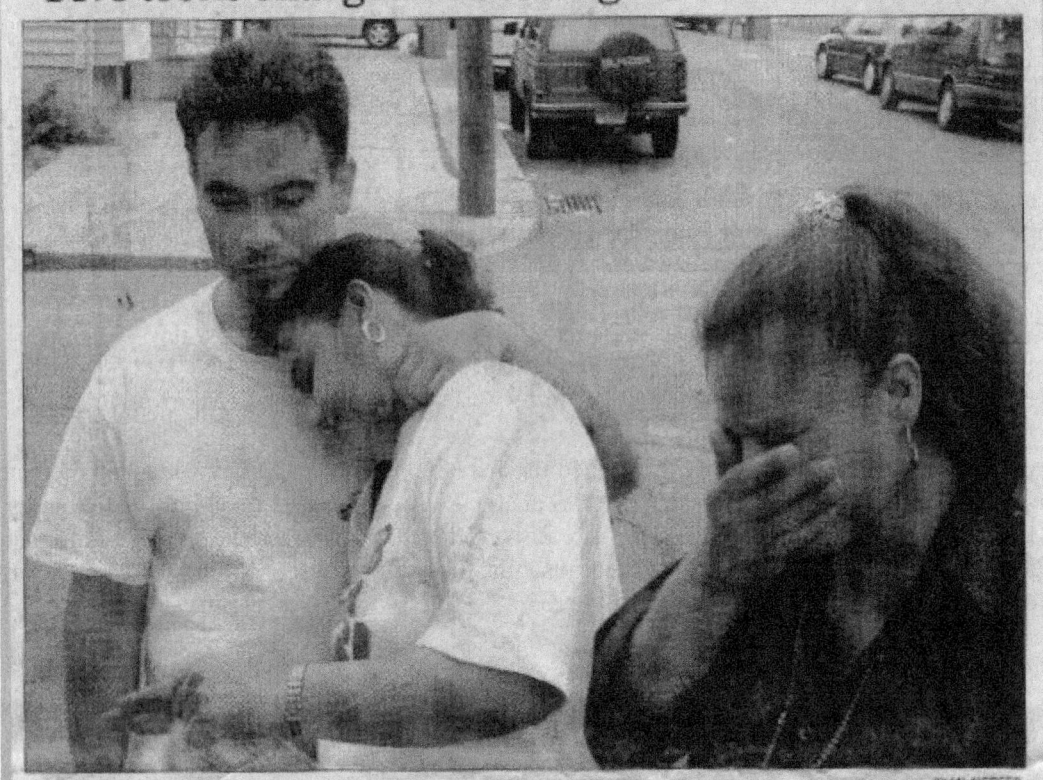

Miriam Robles, center, with husband Julio Justiniano and sister Gladys Robles on Thursday visiting the place in the Totowa section of Paterson where Hector Robles, their brother, was beaten to death Wednesday. They called his death a senseless act.

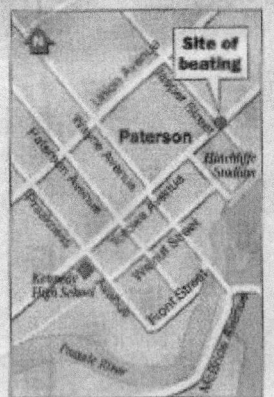

By JOHN CHADWICK and JENNIFER HUGHES
Staff Writers

Hector Robles was a homeless man who found a haven in a Paterson neighborhood. Factory workers offered him refuge in their plant. A school security guard left food outside for him. Youngsters gave him pocket change.

But on Wednesday, the slender, gentle man was killed in broad daylight by a group of rampaging teenagers, police said. The boys allegedly attacked him on the street with their hands and feet, and possibly a bottle.

By Thursday night, five teenagers had been arrested and charged with Robles' murder in what one prosecutor described as a "wilding."

Law enforcement officials said the killing was set into motion around 10:40 a.m., when about a dozen unruly students started picking fights with other teenagers outside John F. Kennedy High School. "Their adrenaline was in overdrive," Detective Lt. Craig Perrone said. "Then it got out of control."

The group left school grounds and made its way down Totowa Avenue. It was the final week of school and students were dismissed early. The brawling continued as they walked down the street.

Hector Robles in 1988.

Another student and a delivery driver were attacked, Perrone said.

The students came upon Robles, who was sitting on a tire near Jasper Street. It was one of Robles' favorite spots — close to the Electronic Transformer Corp. plant where the workers were nice to him.

See **SLAIN** Page A-10

## SLAIN
#### From Page A-1

An employee at a neighboring factory said he saw a throng of kids descend on Robles. The worker, who did not want to be named, said Robles did not fight back.

At least five teenagers are suspected of beating him to death and are in custody. Police said they expect to make more arrests.

"He was just sighted as a target," said William Purdy, Passaic County's chief assistant prosecutor. "They went after him to beat and rob him."

Three suspects, ages 15, 16, 17, were arrested hours after the attack. Two others, a 15-year-old and a 17-year-old, were arrested Thursday evening. Four are Kennedy students and one attends School 13. Their names were not released because of their age.

Rumors flew Thursday that the killing was a gang initiation rite, but authorities played that down.

"We're looking into that, but it's not necessarily jumping out that way," Purdy said. "It looks like a 'wilding' situation."

Three suspects, all friends, appeared in juvenile court Thursday morning for a detention review hearing. Superior Court Judge Nestor F. Guzman ordered them held at the county's juvenile detention center in Haledon and scheduled a probable cause hearing for Monday. No decision was initially made on whether the state will seek to try them as adults.

There was no mention of the killing at Thursday night's balloon-laden graduation ceremony for 276 Kennedy students.

But the death has left some in the city's tough-edged Totowa section in shock.

"It's really bothering me that this could happen to him, and in broad daylight," said Glen Urena, who runs an automobile dealership near where Robles was killed. "I've known him for 13 years. He was weak, and he was skinny, and he didn't give anyone any trouble."

Workers at Electronic Transformer said they were haunted by what they saw and heard Wednesday. First, the sound of breaking glass. Then Robles' anguished cries.

When they ran out, they saw Robles staggering in the street, blood pouring from a cut above his left eye. They laid him down, brought a cushion for his head, and dampened his face with water.

"I told him, 'Wake up Hector, wake up Hector, don't go to sleep,'" said June Russell.

Reinaldo Williams, one of the first on the scene, said he saw a group of kids running away down Totowa Avenue. "Somebody shouted, 'Those are the kids that did it,'" Williams said. "But I stayed and tried to help Hector."

Robles lay in the street, his eyes open and his chest thumping. He didn't say anything. He died of internal bleeding at St. Joseph's Hospital and Medical Center. He was believed to be 43.

School officials said they had received reports of a throng of students outside the school. When Kennedy Principal Richard Roberto investigated, the group had dispersed.

The killing took place about a mile from the school.

Several students said the final week of school is notorious for fights. Some said their classmates get swept into a mob mentality.

"I don't know why they would hurt Hector. He's smaller than me and I ain't nothing," Dennis Melly, a homeless man living near Union Avenue in Paterson, said Thursday of Hector Robles, who was beaten to death.

---

If you read the last paragraph of the above article, it says exactly what I have been saying for years. Sadly, this "MOB MENTALITY," still exists at John F. Kennedy High School. If a teacher should write about it on any of the social media platforms such as Facebook, they would be brought up on charges and fired! This has happened to several teachers here in Paterson, NJ. So much for "FREEDOM OF SPEECH!" Not to mention talking and telling the truth about what *really* goes on here in Paterson, NJ.

If you have seen the movie, "Lean on Me," a story about a principal at Eastside High School, in Paterson, NJ, it is absolutely worse here at John F. Kennedy High School. To think the movie is to have taken place several years *before* the State of New Jersey Takeover of the District of Paterson, NJ.

**October 24, 2004**

### PATERSON
### "When those kids come out of school, it's like, 'Forget about it.'"
ED MERCADO,
Dollar Dream Store owner

*Photos by KEVIN R. WEXLER/Herald News*

Totowa Avenue fills with John F. Kennedy High School students after school dismissal. Three years after the beating death of a homeless man by a gang of teens, neighbors say they are still afraid of the students.

# Fear at end of day
## 3 years after Robles' death, school bell still causes anxiety

By TOM MEAGHER
Herald News

Returning from the corner store Friday afternoon, 65-year-old Nurul Islam was met by a group of teenagers on the sidewalk near his Preakness Avenue home, across the street from John F. Kennedy High School. One of the boys in the crowd shoved him.

As the clustered students cheered and clapped, two other boys jostled Islam and stole the cap from his head. When Islam waved down a passing police officer, the teens ran away.

Since moving into his home in 1999, the retired writer has spent many afternoons standing in his doorway to keep watch over his front stairs and yard. Islam said he fears the brash teenagers who act so much more worldly than youths did when he was a student in his native Bangladesh. Because of the Kennedy students, he wishes he could sell his home to move away from the school.

"I cannot afford to go to another house. I have to stay here," Islam said. "I'm always afraid of that kind of

Please see **PATERSON**, A4

A Paterson police officer slowly drives up Totowa Avenue, escorting Kennedy High School students home after school.

[Newspaper clipping: "Paterson: Schools trying to put Robles' death behind them"]

As stated in the above article the district is trying to put this human being's death behind them. However, if it were at all possible the administration would rather have this incident hushed up too!

First sentence on this page- "Residents near Kennedy High School live in fear of its students." Try working in here! This poor human being, whether he was homeless or not, was beaten to death and the students who did it were from JFK.

What do you think? Do you think those students are angels in the school and classrooms? They just walked out the doors and then decide to commit crimes and acts of violence? They commit crimes right in the school every day. This place is a disaster. If it isn't, then why are there so many security and police inside and outside the building? Sadly, this man was killed, and the only reason why the story ended up in the papers is because it was done outside the school building.

August 8, 2006

# BEARING ARMS

## Schools consider getting metal detectors

Pedro Rivas, 15, a John F. Kennedy High School student, says he carried a knife to school because he felt unsafe without it. School officials are considering use of metal detectors for added security, a change that Rivas says he favors.

LESLIE BARBARO/Herald News

Special to the Herald News

Pedro Rivas is unapologetic about bringing a small knife to John F. Kennedy High School last fall. He said he simply felt unsafe without it.

But since he was caught trying to hide it from security guards in the bathroom and later arrested, he said he has had to suffice without it.

"The main reason I carry a knife is because everyone else does," he said. "I bet 11 people in my school don't carry a knife."

The 15-year-old Rivas' way of thinking is proof positive to Board of Education member Chauncey Brown that Paterson schools need metal detectors.

"We're in a post-9/11 era," he continued. "I think the safety of our students and staff is paramount. I think we should take a proactive, not a reactive approach."

Although no Paterson schools have walk-through metal detectors, hand-held wands have already been used in district high schools, said retired Paterson police Capt. James Smith, executive director of school security. Students are scanned either randomly or in targeted sweeps intended to respond to violent incidents in the community that might affect school security.

But Smith acknowledged that such meas-

"The main reason I carry a knife is because everyone else does."

PEDRO RIVAS, 15,
John F. Kennedy High School student

ures might not be enough, especially for kids like Rivas who said it was problems with kids in the neighborhood that made him bring the knife.

"Because of recent problems with gangs in the city and state, we're becoming more aware of the need to possibly upgrade to metal detectors," Smith said.

One of Brown's former colleagues on the board, Juan "Mitch" Santiago, an investigator for the Passaic County Sheriff's Department, has also been an advocate. Recalling the violent murder of a homeless man, Hector Robles, at the hands of several John F. Kennedy High School students in 2001, Santiago said the district needs to take its security to the "next level."

According to the New Jersey Department

Please see PATERSON, A8

## Paterson: Metal detectors possible

**Continued from A1**

of Education's annual report Violence, Vandalism and Substance Abuse in New Jersey's Public Schools, the total number of incidents of violence in 2004-05 was down 21 percent from 2003-04, driven primarily by a 37 percent reduction in the number of simple assaults, an 18 percent reduction in the number of fights, and a 35 percent decline in the number of threats reported. Camden City public schools and the Trenton school district accounted for a majority of the overall decline.

In Passaic County, where nearly 80,000 students are enrolled, there were 535 incidents of violence, down from 626 the year before. Still, the report cited Eastside High School as one of three in the state that is "persistently dangerous," because of incidents of violence there.

Paterson parent Elizabeth Rosado said last year her son, now 15, was threatened with a gun by two classmates at the Sports Business/Public Safety Academy in Paterson. The incident proved so disturbing that Rosado's son avoided school completely for the last several months of the year and received limited tutoring at home. Rosado, as a result, struggled to transfer him out of the district. She eventually prevailed and said he is now enrolled in a school in Wayne.

Her son, she said, seems to be responding to his new environment.

"His grades have improved 100 percent," she said. "I think he's one shot or two off of making the honor roll. He's more at ease, he's calm, he feels safe."

For Rosado, metal detectors would have made the difference in Paterson. She said that if the school had installed the devices, she would not have moved her son.

Across the nation, only 0.9 percent of public schools require students to pass through metal detectors on a regular basis, according to the National Center for Education Statistics. Schools that check students randomly account for 7.2 percent.

Smith said that he has been discussing the use of metal detectors with the superintendent, the district's leadership team, Board of Education members and even athletic directors.

Their input has been useful in determining whether the district will use metal detectors at high profile sporting events attended by crowds as large as 2,000 people. They are also deciding how to use the machines and what kind will most meet their needs – fixed or portable or a combination of the two.

Paterson school officials are not the only ones considering metal detectors. In Passaic, Schools Superintendent Robert Holster said he reserved $300,000 in this year's budget to address safety issues by installing metal detectors, electronic locks on doors and more surveillance cameras.

"The way to go is not the human factor," he said.

Schools in Atlantic City and Newark already use metal detectors. Marion Bolden, Newark schools superintendent, believes the devices, in conjunction with surveillance cameras, have made a big difference. In 1999 she said there were 751 incidents of violence or vandalism. Last year, she said, the number dropped to 331.

According to a 1999 Department of Justice report on security technologies for schools, portal metal detectors cost between $1,000 and $30,000. Those most appropriate for schools are generally between $4,000 and $5,000. However, the operating and personnel costs are apparently what make the use of metal detectors especially expensive. In one New York City public school of about 2,000 students, the report noted that nine security guards were required for about two hours every morning.

But given Paterson's tight school budget this year, Smith acknowledged that there is little money to pay for the program right now.

The district has applied for discretionary funding from the state and he said that if they are allocated enough, Paterson's high schools might begin getting metal detectors within the next school year. Aware that the wrong setup could prove troublesome, Smith wants to find the best technologically and least disruptive machines.

"If one child experiences an injury as a result of us not being able to detect it, it's worth the inconvenience," he said. "It's everywhere. Look at Newark Airport. Is it disruptive to stop a plane from blowing up?"

Rosado agreed.

"If a child has nothing on them, parents shouldn't be bothered," she said.

Even Pedro Rivas is in favor.

"I wouldn't have brought the knife, because I would've known I was safe," he said.

## FEBRUARY 20, 2008 NEWS ARTICLE HERALD

See my complete write up in "MY DIARY," entry 2/20/08

In reference to the above articles, it has changed here at JFK. NO, it has gotten worse and continues to get worse each year. During the school day the inside of the building is an absolute disaster. There is nothing but uncontrollable, unsupervised students, running the place. It is CHAOS here. Now more than ever even in 2014 the administration works even harder to cover up everything to make it look that everything has changed ever since the instituted so-called, "RESTRUCTURING" with the Academies. It is just a name; *academy*! Nothing else has changed with exception to having a great deal more administrators.

### Years later and *still* no change

As of 2014, it still continues, it's still a state run and operated school district.

As you will see sometimes incidents leak out. Or just because somewhere along the line a police report was made.

THANK GOD.

THIS IS ONLY WHAT HAS LEAKED OUT. YOU HAVE NO IDEA WHAT GOES ON HERE AND HAS BEEN SQUASHED!

**NORTHJERSEY.COM: NEWS**
"Paterson teachers' union, district joust over allegations of student violence toward Kennedy staff"
Monday March 25, 2013
By Joe Malinconico/PATERSON PRESS

PATERSON—Teachers at the city's Kennedy Educational Complex say they're feeling unsafe at the high school because of violence and threats committed by students, according to a union complaint filed with the state labor department.

Incidents outlined in the teachers' union complaint.

*Here's a list of the 19 alleged incidents outlined in the teachers' union complaint:*
**Oct. 18:** Teachers were "accidentally hit, pushed" when several fights broke out among students and non-students after dismissal on the streets around the school. Police used mace to restore order.
**Nov. 20:** A female student kicked the window in a classroom door, breaking its wire mesh glass
**Nov. 27:** Students threw "icy snowballs" at teachers in a school parking lot during a false fire alarm
**Dec. 13:** A student in a classroom tripped a substitute teacher who was seven-months pregnant
**Dec. 14:** Two students fought in a classroom
**Dec. 14:** A 14-year-old girl threatened to have a classmate shot because he reprimanded her for laughing at a student who fell in the cafeteria. The girl also struck the other student.
**Dec. 17:** A 15-year-old student struck a 14-year-old when horseplay got out of hand.
**Dec. 18:** Students vandalized a classroom.
**Dec. 19**: A 16-year-old student threatened a teacher's assistant, saying he had a gun in his book bag.
**Dec. 20:** A student said he wanted to blow up the school after an administrator told him to hurry up and go to class.
**Jan. 3:** A 15-year-old student was found in possession of a weapon on school grounds. The report lists the weapon in the "knife, blade, razor, scissors, and box cutter category.''
**Jan. 10:** A 16-year-old student pointed at other youths and said, "I am going to shoot you and you…"
**Jan. 11:** Four students vandalized the stage curtain and a video camera in the school auditorium.
**Jan. 11:** A 14-year-old student in Classroom 213 said he was going to blow up the school.
**Jan. 14:** A 15-year-old student threatened to shoot another student while exiting a fourth-period class.
**Jan. 15**: A student threatened another student.
**Jan. 23:** A student threatened to punch an art teacher in the face.
**Jan. 29:** A student in an industrial arts class broke a tool by striking it against a workbench.
**Feb. 1:** A student threw an apple into a classroom, hitting another student.

\*\*\*\*\*\*\*\*\*\*

The 79-page complaint cites 19 instances of "student violence, vandalism and threats, and assault on teachers" from Oct. 18, 2012 through Feb. 1, 2013.

The complaint comes at a time of prolonged labor negotiations between the state-governed school district and teachers who have been without a contract for nearly three years. The school board president suggested the complaint was motivated by some teachers' dissatisfaction with Amod Field, the high school principal. Union leaders deny there is any motive but safety.

"Staff feels unsafe in the building," states the complaint, which was filed with the labor department's Office of Public Employee Safety on March 1. "The District has failed to provide adequate security and enforce student discipline.

Among numerous alleged instances of violence and threats involving students, the complaint says a 14-year-old student tripped a pregnant substitute teacher during a class in December, a student threatened to punch a teacher in the face in January and students threw icy snowballs at teachers in a parking lot during a false fire alarm.

The complaint also contends that the number of violent incidents at the school has increased but provides no statistics.

James Smith, Paterson public schools' security director, questioned the legitimacy of some of the complaints, pointing out that in seven cases the incident reports were not signed by the school's principal, as required by an agreement between the union and the district.

"The absence of the principal's signature raises questions as to the credibility of the alleged acts," said Smith.

"The lack of a signature is irrelevant to the validity of the complaint," said Peter Tirri, president of the Paterson Education Association, the union that represents city teachers. Tirri asserted that in many instances, principals don't follow through and sign or file complaints submitted to them by staff members. Tirri said he was not sure whether that's what happened in the seven instances cited by Smith. "That may have happened; it happens a lot," he said.

In three other instances, Smith said the allegations did not meet criteria for the type of incidents covered by the district violence and vandalism reporting system. For example, in one case, a fight allegedly happened off school property, he said.

Smith said he thought the number of substantiated incidents cited by the union was low for a school with more than 2,000 students, 350 staff members and 315,000 square feet of space. "I don't think it constitutes excess violence," he said.

Tirri said, however, that <u>"The district tries to hide most of this stuff</u>. They try to minimize the situation. They want it to look like this is 'Little House on the Prairie' and there aren't any problems."

Christopher Irving, the school board president, said the union's safety complaint stemmed from disharmony between the Principal Amod Field, and some faculty members, rather than from any dangerous conditions at the four-school campus. Irving said some members of the school's staff — "not all, some… vehemently oppose the strong leadership" Field has brought to Kennedy.

"Kennedy is still going through transformation, and the teaching staff bears just as much responsibility for the culture of the school as does the administration," Irving said, "Each side can be blamed for it."

In recent months, there have been heightened tensions between Paterson faculty members and the district's administration because the teacher's union has gone almost three years without a new labor contract. But union representatives said their safety complaint had nothing to do with the labor contract or with disharmony with Field.

*End of Article*

THE ABOVE WAS FROM 2012–2013 SCHOOL YEAR, 22 YEARS OF STATE CONTROL

Meanwhile in 2013–2014 students are still allowed to roam the halls, stairwells, walk in and out of the building all day, every day, all year long and it is WORSE!

Today, teachers are basically targets for politicians, superintendents, administrators, parents and students. What do you want us to do, when we are not allowed to do our job and have to work under such horrendous conditions? When my colleagues and I come to work here at John F. Kennedy High School, we have no idea what is right or wrong. It is so bizarre and out of control here. Even the NEA (National Education Association, in Washington, DC) and the NJEA (New Jersey Education Association) don't do anything about it. However, they *do* automatically deduct our dues from our pay.

**MISAPPROPRIATION OF FUNDS**

In 1991, the District of Paterson, NJ was taken over by the State of New Jersey. One of the reasons was, "Misappropriation of Funds."

Next are two separate new articles on Misappropriation of Funds, 13 years of State Takeover.

### Audit hits school spending

**Report says Paterson officials misused $11 million**

By WHITNEY KVASAGER
Herald News

PATERSON – An annual audit of the district has found that school administrators spent too much money and failed to keep required paperwork on employees, students and expenditures.

It's the latest report of misman- agement in decades of problems for the school district.

The audit, obtained by the Herald News and slated for presentation at a special Board of Education meeting tonight, outlines 29 findings of financial and administrative mis- takes during the 2003-04 school year – many of them repeats from the year before.

Auditors said the district over- spent $11 million by hiring staff without positions opening up or by having a way to pay them. Of- ficials at nine schools and two ath- letic associations failed to follow proper financial procedures. Three could not produce financial records for June 2004 and one wrote $204 worth of checks payable to "cash," according to the report. The audit also said the dis- trict could not prove it had con- ducted adequate employee back- ground checks and had failed to classify special education students.

The Paterson school district was taken over by the state in 1991 be- cause of severe mismanagement

Please see **AUDIT**, A24

# Audit: $4.5 million in duplicate purchase orders found

and repeated failure to provide students with a proper education, state officials said. The school district receives almost all its money from state and federal agencies. The district's budget is nearly $300 million this year.

Board President Jonathan Hodges, Michael Azzara, the district's assistant superintendent of operations and state Department of Education spokeswoman Kathryn Forsyth would not comment regarding the audit.

Last year, an October audit showed that district officials misspent $20 million. It questioned the hiring of contractors blacklisted by the state or who have never completed construction for which the district paid, or both.

A Herald News investigation found an additional $30 million had been lost in deals with well-connected contractors.

The findings ultimately led to the removal of state-appointed Schools Superintendent Edwin Duroy. Duroy is in his last month of administrative leave, during which he was to finish a small, urban schools "special assignment" for the state.

State Commissioner of Education William Librera was not available Thursday to comment on Duroy's progress.

State-appointed interim Schools Superintendent Dennis Clancy, who took over Duroy's job in July, did not return telephone calls placed to both his office and home seeking comment.

Auditors found that Paterson district officials:

■ Wrote $4.5 million worth of duplicate purchase orders.
■ Wrote purchase orders after items had already been received or contracts already executed.
■ Failed to keep required personnel documents, including finger printing results, tuberculosis tests results and other physical exam records, Social Security card copies, federal and state W-4 forms and annual evaluation forms.
■ Failed to keep time sheets, time cards, punch cards "and other time keeping and activity monitoring tools." Auditors said the district's monthly sign-in attendance log was inadequate.
■ Failed to communicate. On Oct. 1, 2004, the district had not yet processed more than $1 million worth of services and goods received four months earlier, "due to the absence of monitoring and coordination" between two departments.
■ Failed to implement programs to protect the department's computer systems, despite auditors last year requesting that officials do so.
■ Failed to keep parental consent forms on file for four students in a five-student sample.

It is not clear from the audit how much the school district lost in financial mismanagement.

Leonora Galleros, one of the auditors at Watson Rice LLP in Rutherford, did not return a telephone call Thursday seeking comment.

Azzara, the assistant superintendent of operations, said the audit findings would be presented, along with a corrective action plan, to Board of Education members at a workshop session tonight at Eastside High School.

The session will take place at 6 p.m. in the school's library and is open to the public.

---

www.northjersey.com  Wednesday, May 26, 2004  An edition of The Record

# Burning through millions
## Records show school district ignored wasteful spending

**By KATHLEEN CARROLL**
Herald News

The Paterson school district, crunched for space and flush with state cash, has squandered millions in questionable construction deals while students crowd into century-old schoolhouses.

In striking examples of wasted tax dollars, district officials burned through at least $50 million from 1999 to 2002. Under open-ended contracts, half a dozen local construction companies were paid by the hour to renovate rented buildings or crumbling schools slated for demolition. There are few detailed records of how the work was assigned or whether projects were ever completed.

"It was a systemic and pervasive breakdown of internal controls," said Michael Azzara, the district's assistant superintendent of operations, and a former fiscal monitor for the state Department of Education. "All of the things that were put in place to prevent this, and to make sure it didn't happen, weren't followed... It took

**THE MONEY PIT**
Contractor list full of campaign contributors. A19

a lot of people to allow this to happen."

Asked why he did not discover billing irregularities, Schools Superintendent Edwin Duroy said, "I don't know what to tell you. (Internal district auditors) did have a responsibility to review documents, like we all had."

Asked specifically about renovation contracts, Duroy said he didn't know how closely they were reviewed.

The district's ballooning construction bills in early 2003 prompted the state to order a comprehensive audit and alert the state attorney general to "pervasive inefficiencies." By then, contracts that guaranteed minimum, not maximum, earnings for local contractors had already cost the district $50 million.

Federal agents and investigators from the state Attorney General's Office have seized documents and interviewed district employees, said two employees and one board member, who spoke on condition of anonymity. Investigators and spokesmen from both agencies declined to comment. Earlier this month, as part of an ongoing investigation by the state Attorney General's Office, a contractor was sentenced to five years in state prison for wage violations in Paterson and two other districts.

Please see **RECORDS**, A18

---

High school students waited eight months for their new school at the former Boris Kroll Mill on State Street. The developer took longer than expected to uphold the lease agreement.

Students of Montclair State University Pre-Collegiate Teaching Academy went on strike in March 2003 to protest conditions at their school, a rented office building on Ellison Street.

The district paid $953,000 to renovate a former dye factory on Sheridan Avenue. A five-year lease for the site, which is used as a warehouse and office facility, will cost $1.5 million.

# Records: Wasteful spending was ignored

**Continued from A1**

Under an open-government law, the Herald News obtained and reviewed hundreds of district invoices, contracts, bids, school board voting records, audits and campaign finance records.

Interviews with state and district employees helped track the spending.

The findings include:

■ The state Department of Education, which controls the district under the state takeover law through its appointee, Duroy, considered his stewardship over finances a "consuming problem" by early 2003. But the department failed to curtail or remove his authority until March 2004, six months after an October 2003 audit found the district misspent $20 million. At the time, state officials vowed they would investigate the district's facilities bills vigorously.

■ In his seven years as the state-appointed superintendent in Paterson, Duroy has leased 22 buildings throughout the city. Currently, 20 agreements cost the district $3.3 million annually. In addition, the leases require the district to pay for all repairs, renovations and taxes. None of the lease agreements include exit clauses.

■ The district has spent tens of millions of dollars renovating the rented buildings. Because of incomplete records, no precise figure is available. However, reviews of two contractors' bills show that in some years, the district paid more to renovate buildings than to rent them.

Paterson Schools Superintendent Edwin Duroy presents the district's five-year construction plan to the City Council in January 2003. An October 2003 state audit found that the district misspent $20 million.

■ Invoices show that virtually all construction work contracted by the Paterson public schools from 1999 to 2002 was paid for by "time and materials" agreements, standing deals to pay fixed hourly wages and materials fees. Even after the contracts expired, the district continued assigning work and paying the companies. Asked to calculate the total cost, Azzara estimated $50 million.

■ There are no records showing how or why private contractors were assigned certain jobs. One contractor, Paint Smart of Nutley, earned $461,465 painting School 20 and School 29. Both buildings are slated for demolition under the district's long-range facilities plan.

■ The private contractors' work assignment included routine building upgrades like installing drop ceilings and hanging doors. Meanwhile, the district employed a full-time construction and maintenance crew, which included licensed plumbers, painters and electricians. The department's current payroll of 55 workers costs $2.5 million a year.

■ In separate pitches to the local Board of Education and state officials, Duroy and district counsel Kevin Hanly have cited radically different costs for a planned 30-year lease of the downtown Fabian theater and office complex. According to a May 2002 memo, the price is $52 million, not $43 million as Duroy has stated publicly.

■ While private contractors were paid to renovate rented buildings, traditional schoolhouses in Paterson were neglected. In 2003, district officials sent 13,000 children to school buildings with outstanding safety and fire code violations, including faulty sprinkler systems and missing fire exits.

### Did anyone check the math?

According to the state's public bidding law, school districts are required to advertise projects that will cost more than $17,500 and ask companies to apply for the job with a sealed proposal, or bid. Once the agency opens the envelopes, the company with the lowest price, whose project proposal and abilities fit the assignment, is awarded the contract. The public school contracts law requires detailed project specifications, including the number of work days or the planned date of completion for bids on non-emergency work. The practice is intended to encourage competition and eliminate favoritism, ensuring that taxpayers get the most for their money.

From 1999 to 2002, the Paterson school district didn't always pay the lowest price. The district hired a handful of construction companies under elastic "time and materials" contracts, usually reserved for emergency repairs. The contracts were standing agreements to pay contractors by the hour, not by the assignment. So the companies would calculate bills based on the number of employees involved, how long they worked and the cost of their supplies.

But there's no evidence that anyone ever checked the contractors' math or declared an emergency.

One contractor has pleaded guilty to wage violations, as part of an ongoing investigation by the Division of Criminal Justice in the state Attorney General's Office. In January, Paint Smart admitted it overcharged Paterson and two other districts by $1.5 million, by overstating its employees' wages. Earlier this month, the company's vice president was sentenced to five years in prison and fined $250,000. Paint Smart is now included on New Jersey's blacklist for public contracts. It had been barred from public contracts in New York for five years for wage violations; that period has now expired.

Another Paterson contractor, Olympic Window Installers of Hawthorne, is barred in New York for willfully failing to pay prevailing wages, according to the New York State Department of Labor. The company billed the Paterson public schools about $5 million from 1999 to 2002.

The contracts for Paint Smart and Olympic, and half a dozen other contractors, did not include budget caps. Instead, the contractors signed agreements that guaranteed at least a minimum of $75,000 in work that year.

The district's facilities invoices show how well the contracts served the contractors.

For its work on just one rented building, the former Spectrachem factory on Sheridan Avenue, Paint Smart was paid $261,000. The school district uses the building for its facilities and food services offices, and as warehouse space.

Not one of Paint Smart's invoices lists the number of employees on the job, the hours worked, or the amount of materials used. For example, a bill from Sept. 18, 2000, for $38,225 reads, "Final painting of food warehouse rooms at the Sheridan Avenue warehouse."

As with all of Paint Smart's invoices, the bill was paid in full.

Other contractors were paid to do work they apparently never finished. Students at School 4 still contend with missing sinks and toilets that do not flush, even though the district paid Olympic $59,452 to repair the restrooms in October 2002.

## Overpaying vendors

The district's habit of using "time and materials" bids began in 1995, when officials hired Educational Data Services to coordinate a cooperative purchasing agreement.

EDS, of Saddle Brook, would negotiate discounted prices for time and materials contracts from private vendors. By joining the collective, the district was supposed to save money by hiring contractors at discounted rates. Currently, 350 school districts in the tri-state area, including 200 in New Jersey, have contracts with EDS, according to EDS Chairman Gilbert Wohl.

But the Paterson district didn't always take advantage of EDS's services, according to internal audits in 1998 and 2003. Internal auditors found that the district had overpaid vendors, and EDS, because of poor management and faulty paperwork. Auditors criticized the district for overpaying construction bills and for paying $38,000 to EDS for purchasing a software program that was never installed.

Although EDS provided lower "time and materials" maintenance rates for the district, there's no evidence that officials knew about or took advantage of the price breaks.

"We analyze, select a low bidder as specified, type up a report to let them know who the low bidder is and submit it," Wohl said. "Whether they use that or not, we have no idea one way or another. They decide whether they want to use it or not."

District records indicate that district facilities and business officials paid the companies without logic or question. For example, in 2002 Paint Smart was the low bidder in EDS cooperative purchasing network, based on its proposal for services paid by the square foot. But the Paterson district apparently never received notification of the deal with EDS or issued a contract with Paint Smart. That year, the company was paid $804,680 on a time and materials basis, not by the square foot.

Duroy signed a six-month contract with EDS for $43,575 in July 2002; there is no record that the Board of Education ever voted on the assignment. When asked this week if the matter came to a public vote, Duroy said he did not remember.

After district officials questioned some of the bills submitted by EDS consultant Bob Davis, the company and district ended the agreement in November 2002.

## Renovation costs exceed rent

After decades of neglect, many of the city's schools are dying. Buildings still lined with sealed asbestos depend on ancient boilers to keep students warm. Decades-old wiring hangs from low classroom ceilings. Teachers keep books and papers in strategic safe spots, because roofs and windows leak in stormy weather.

In 1960, a study of Paterson schools called for eight buildings to be replaced. None of them ever were. Now, those buildings are more than 100 years old and serve 2,700 students. Nineteen more buildings are more than 50 years old.

Compounding the problems, too many students crowd into the buildings year after year. A statewide school construction program is intended to eventually create enough classrooms for all of Paterson's students. Currently, two school buildings are under construction; two more should break ground this year.

Meantime, the district pays $3.3 million a year, or $282,000 every month, to rent 20 buildings throughout the city. Students attend class in former temples, textile mills and office buildings.

"We have limited ability to purchase buildings. We don't have the funds," said Duroy. He noted that two dozen teacher-led high school academies, all founded since 1999, have also driven the need for more, alternative space.

"Part of the attractiveness of the program was to see if we could locate sites outside of larger settings," he said.

In the past, the district has purchased new land and buildings through "lease-purchase" agreements, or short-term loan packages with some state funding assistance.

However, Abbott districts are no longer allowed to enter into long-term lease-purchase agreements, Duroy said.

A 1999 audit of the Paterson public schools by the state's independent auditor, Richard L. Fair, criticized the district's leases. He attributed the practice to "the district's inability or reluctance to obtain the funding needed to buy these buildings."

At the time, the Paterson school system rented five buildings. Fair estimated that by buying the sites, the district would have saved $320,000 annually.

The lease program has nearly quadrupled since then. In 2002-03 alone, the district signed new rental agreements on seven buildings.

Each of the district's leases is "triple net," meaning the tenant must pay rent, all taxes and maintenance for the properties. That agreement is not itself illegal, or even uncommon. Many school districts renovate rented buildings at their own expense, because they are liable for students' physical safety and must adhere to particular standards for school buildings.

But in Paterson, renovating the buildings sometimes costs more than the annual rent. In 2000-01, the district spent twice as much to renovate the Spectrachem building as to rent it. Officials paid seven companies $618,645 for renovations, and paid the landlord $303,360 in rent.

In all, the building's owner, the Spectrachem Corp. of Lodi, has received a new roof, floors, windows and doors and a fresh coat of paint – $953,130 in free upgrades, courtesy of the Paterson public schools.

Although the initial agreement allowed the district to buy the site for $1.4 million, district officials never did. Instead, Duroy signed another five-year lease in 2001 for a total cost of $1.5 million.

"We just didn't have the money to buy it," said Duroy, attributing the shortfall to the state's suspension of lease-purchase agreements.

From 1999 to 2002, the district spent $4.1 million to rent three other buildings, and paid a single contractor $1.3 million to renovate the sites. Olympic billed for basic upgrades at the Main Street Mall, a retail complex used by two high school programs; the former Don Bosco parochial school; and an Ellison Street office building. In spring 2003, the state Department of Education's Office of State-Operated School Districts began to urgently inspect the district's leasing and renovations programs, said the former director, Ben Rarick.

"My concern was piqued when my auditors began to question the appropriateness of some of the bills concerning the renovation of these (rented) and other facilities," he said in an e-mail interview.

Rarick, now a project coordinator at the University of Washington, said he ordered an internal audit of eight private companies doing business in Paterson, including Paint Smart and Olympic.

By the time the report was published internally in October 2003, auditors found $20 million in questionable time and materials contracts from 1999 to 2002. The report included a paid invoice for repairs to a Mahwah firetruck, and approved purchase orders for identical classroom clocks that cost $46.60 one month, and $365 the next.

"Following up on the complaints and the audit findings coming out of the facilities office was probably the single most consuming issue I dealt with during the spring and summer of 2003," Rarick said. "Those audits were ongoing, and as we dug deeper the problems looked progressively more serious. At a certain point, I became concerned about possible criminality and I proceeded to refer the matters to (the Division of) Criminal Justice."

### A leaky lease

Another type of lease agreement caused 150 students to attend class in the auditorium at John F. Kennedy High School until last month.

In May 2002, the district signed an agreement to lease 12,500 square feet of the former Boris Kroll textile mill from the Alpert Group, a Fort Lee developer. Unlike the district's other agreements, this lease stipulates that the developer must renovate the site. Once the construction is complete and inspectors issue a certificate of occupancy, the school system must begin to pay $26,000 per month in rent. Two high-school programs were scheduled to move into the building in September.

But the developer was at least eight months late – nearly an entire academic year. Because the lease contract didn't set a deadline for the renovations, the district was in a holding pattern, locked into the agreement no matter when it actually began.

"There was not necessarily a timeline, and that was a problem," Duroy said.

The agreement, like virtually all of the district's leases, was negotiated by the Hanly & Ryglicki law firm. A review of the law firm's bills to the Paterson school system from 1999 to 2002 shows near-daily phone calls between district lawyers and prospective landlords.

Those records include at least a dozen phone calls between Hanly and developer Joseph Alpert, as well as calls between Hanly and Alpert's attorney, Thomas Wall. The Hanly & Ryglicki firm claimed it had recused itself from the Boris Kroll lease, because it had represented Alpert in the past. The legal agreement was written by the law firm of Giblin & Giblin.

Alpert's lawyer, Wall, has offices at the same Edgewater address as the now-dissolved Hanly & Ryglicki firm. The three lawyers are former partners in the Shulman, Hanly, Ryglicki, Lindsley & Wall firm.

In the late 1990s, Alpert needed permission to develop the mill, and Hanly & Ryglicki handled its application to the city's zoning board. In 1999, Alpert obtained permission to build apartments in the mill, and received a $1 million, 1-percent, 15-year mortgage from the state Department of Community Affairs. The City of Paterson chipped in $600,000 in federal funding; then-Councilman Jose "Joey" Torres wrote the resolution authorizing the funds.

The district placed Hanly on administrative leave at full pay in March. He did not return telephone messages seeking comment.

### Revival at what price?

The formerly grand Fabian theater is a depressing eyesore, covered in plywood and padlocks. Just two blocks from City Hall and down the street from the Board of Education offices, the Fabian is a black hole in the center of downtown.

Rebuilding the school district's headquarters at a revived Fabian could boost the neighborhood's spirit. But the cost of that revival is not clear.

In public comments, Duroy has said a 30-year lease will cost $43 million. He reiterated that price on Tuesday.

But the agreement may cost $52 million, according to a memo by Hanly to the state Department of Education, which has not yet approved the deal.

When told that the memo cited $52 million, Duroy said, "this is something we're looking at very, very closely at this time."

Hanly's pitch demands a closer look. In a letter to the state, he overestimated the current cost of administrative space and underestimated the projected cost of office space in the Fabian.

Hanly wrote that the district currently spends $1.25 million annually for rented offices and parking spaces at various locations. But the real cost is $969,000.

Hanly's estimate included $280,720 in nonapplicable costs: the school district's annual $99,000 catering bill, and $181,720 to rent classroom space — not offices — at 137 Ellison St.

Then, Hanly wrote that the Fabian costs $9.55 per square foot to rent. But in a presentation to the Board of Education, Fabian developer W & C Properties estimated the rental rate at $14.91 per square foot.

The building's interior, which will be fully outfitted office space, is 100,000 square feet.

The other 82,122 square feet is a planned 199-car parking garage. To arrive at the $9.55 rate, Hanly included the parking spaces in the building's total area. The district could pay $9.55 per square foot downtown for 100,000 square feet — if it also promised to rent the parking garage at the same rate. In the developer's pitch, the parking garage would cost $3.02 per square foot.

Board members were not privy to the new numbers.

In 2002, the Board of Education approved a $43.7 million agreement, believing the district would spend $1.46 million a year for the next three decades.

If the deal is approved, the board will find it really voted to pay $1.73 million a year for the next 30 years. That's an extra $8 million that won't be spent on classroom supplies or teachers.

In late summer and early fall of 2004 New Jersey was hit by torrential rains and hurricanes. Then again, in the spring of 2005. Many areas throughout the state suffered from major flooding and water damage. New Jersey received 30 million dollars in aid.

However, around the same time the Paterson Public School District, which is still being run by the State of New Jersey, lost 50 to 60 million dollars. That's twice the amount the State of New Jersey received in Federal Aid for the floods and hurricane damage in all of New Jersey for 2004–05.

The district's superintendent was removed from his position, yet he still received his salary and is now teaching at Kean College, a state school.

Basically, it was what I call a misappropriation of funds.

**Bottom line: Our public school system is a disaster in Paterson. No one, with the exception of teachers, are held responsible.**

What is the State going to do to recoup the missing 50 plus million dollars? It is obvious that the State Controlled School District of Paterson is *not* run like a business. The NJ taxpayers are the ones constantly getting screwed. Everything that is to be ordered and purchased for the school district is to be through a State-approved bid and vending list. However, it seems everything bought for and through the district of Paterson is paid at a premium price.

See page 52 Read the very bottom paragraph of the first of three articles about paying for repairs on a Mahwah, NJ fire truck.

**Each year since 1991 John F. Kennedy High School keeps getting worse;** however, not according to the Superintendent's office and the schools administrators. The numbers, documentation, and statistics as we all know can be arranged in anyone's favor. The ONLY concerns the superintendent and administration has is students passing the state-wide exam and increasing graduation numbers. This comes to a great cost to the community and especially the taxpayers of NJ. When I say the community, I mean the future costs will be even greater, all because the administration pushed students through the school system. They did not educate nor prepare them for the real world and especially the real world of work.

It is absolutely disgusting what goes on and is allowed to go on inside our schools, while the State of New Jersey is *still* in control of the Paterson Public School District.

Before you can place any blame on the teachers and their teaching methods it is up to the administration of the building to have *control* over their building.

If the administration cannot, will not, and refuses to have control of what goes on inside the building, then how can any teacher be responsible for what goes on in their own classroom?

Chaos breeds more chaos. If you don't have control, you have anarchy and that is exactly what we have.

In 2011-12, there has been no discipline at all and is the absolute worse I have ever seen it. The building is completely out of control. Students roam the building in gangs. When confronted by security or administration, the students curse at them, ignore them and continue on with what they were doing and where they were going. All the while they should be in class! You would think now with all of this added administration this behavior would never go on. Meanwhile other students who normally never get into trouble see students act up, have poor attendance, horrible behavior even to administration, and now they too add to the discipline problems that never go properly reported and documented.

Since the so-called restructuring, there hasn't been any change warranting all of the added administration and extra people costing the New Jersey taxpayers hundreds of thousands of more dollars just from this *one* school alone. Let's not forget the salaries of the two retired Paterson police officers as heads of security. So now the taxpayers are paying *way* over a million dollars a year just for John F. Kennedy High School, compared to last year and have nothing to show for it other than a lot of money wasted.

You cannot and will not have an educational environment unless rules are followed, discipline is enforced, and standards are set, met, and increased. That does not go on here. The administration is bamboozling the parents, community, and taxpayers on what really goes on. Everything is hushed up. Teachers and support staff fear for their job and job security, if they speak up or out about what really goes on here. This includes active duty Paterson police officers who are paid by the district $28 - $33 an hour to work here on their days off. If they say or even do anything, they are removed, transferred out of the building and hopefully reassigned to another school or location. Key word is *hopefully!*

**Bottom line: What's going on inside here is *wrong*!**

I find this funny, because every public education system throughout the country has a big campaign against "bullying." It is against the law. Each school and district have policies set for "bullying!" Unfortunately, we teachers here at Paterson Public School System are not only bullied by the students, we are also bullied by the building administration, the superintendent and his staff, and now we are actually bullied by the Governor himself. If Gov. Chris Christie is so right about teachers, then how can all of this be going on in the very district he and his people are supposed to have control over?

Taxpayers, is this what we want? Politicians playing political games with teachers and the teaching profession! Playing games and making political maneuvering with the very lives of the children who attend our public school and especially a state run and operated district of Paterson, NJ. Basically, it is taxpayer's money being used, spent, mismanaged, and wasted by all of our politicians who want to play games now with our public school system for their political gains, games, and lies!

Citizens who have children that attend the Paterson Public School System, you *must* hold all of them-- each and every one of these superintendents, their administrators, principals of the entire district, the Commissioner/s of Education and the Governors all responsible for what goes on in our school building. It is UNSAFE here. Parents and guardians you have and will win a BIG LAWSUIT. Your child and children are *not* getting the proper education not only as promised, but as required by law. In fact, they are getting the opposite here. Bad behavior is allowed and actually nurtured. There is no discipline for poor, inappropriate, and criminal type behavior.

Parents work their rear ends off raising their children right, instilling values and good morals, only to have all the years of hard work to be destroyed because they send their children to our schools.

Bad behavior is not only allowed and tolerated, but our administration is actually encouraging this behavior by allowing it to continue. Students have no fear of any disciplinary action or actions taken. As I said before, *now* good students turn into bad and problem students, because they see what the other students are doing and getting away with, yet are still passing. So why should *they* be good and do their work or go to class. Won't they still get the same diploma?

To any parent or guardian, who sends their children to our school— your children are not getting a proper education. However, they *are* learning how to get over, be a criminal, and everything that a parent would NOT want their child or children exposed to.

**They learn how NOT to work and earn for what they need or desire.** However, they are taught to bully, threaten, not be responsible for anything, how to get away with it and still pass and graduate.

Our students are nothing more than cattle being pushed through the educational system.
It is not about education; it is about *money*. It is about state and federal funding. That's all the superintendents' care about-- getting that money and their *bonuses!*

In 2011-12, John F. Kennedy High School was now called the John F. Kennedy Educational Complex Educational Complex. This idea and concept of academies was talked about and supposedly in the works since 1991 when the District of Paterson was first taken over by the State of New Jersey. God only knows how much money was spent on training staff and administrators. Not to mention the cost of all the programs and ideas; the thousands of copies of papers, booklets, pamphlets, notes, statistics and all sorts of folders and handouts specially printed for every staff member. There were special training sessions with food and drink at the Brownstone Restaurant in Paterson. There were evening and after school training sessions at other establishments. The administration would have weekly evening meetings that were always catered. The money spent has to be astronomical and all of it at taxpayers' expense. Every year there was going to be a different program and new way of doing things. It is absolutely disgusting when all that was ever really needed and still is, "STRUCTURE!"

Our public school system here in Paterson is nothing more than a money pit. Somebody is making a lot of money bringing in all of these programs, which fail before they even begin. In the meantime, so many of our students in 2011–12, the first year of the so-called restructuring, did not have textbooks. It's not just the lack of textbooks, many times throughout the school year, prior to *testing*, announcements were made over PA system telling students it is *their* responsibility to bring in pencils and calculators.

However, the superintendent and administrators have everything they need - pens, pencils, erasers, calculators, computers, printers, scanners, fax machines and probably stuff they don't need. Let's not forget the superintendent also has a cell phone, bonuses, a car, a *personal driver* and God knows what other perks and all at taxpayers' expense! Meanwhile the students, who are the reason why we are all here and who the administrators are supposed to be making sure their educational needs are met, tell them that they must supply their own pencils and calculator (which have *always* been provided before) to take a mandatory state exam.

I don't understand how there can be no money for pencils and calculators, when there is money for ten more administrators, one more principal making it now two building principals and two retired Paterson police officers as heads of security. Well, that explains it.

Most parents will sacrifice and do without to make sure that their child or children have everything they need. So, why can't the superintendent and administrators do without, so our students will have what they need for their education? I thought the administration is always saying, *"children first?"*

To make things worse, I have been involved with students testing since 1987 which usually occurred twice a year. As time progressed, the number of testing days have increased.

In the last few years in the rooms that I held testing, some of the fluorescent light did not work.

Once testing was over, I would periodically go up to these rooms throughout the year and for months these lights were still not working; bulb or ballasts were not replaced. Each room is specifically assigned for a specific class and or student/s for the testing they are required to take. Even throughout the course of a school year, why are there so many classrooms that do not have all their lights working properly? Why does it take so long to fix, repair and replace whatever is necessary here?

**Bottom line: Shouldn't students' needs come first?**

It is now 2011–2012, instead of having one high school (John F. Kennedy High School) there are now four schools within the school. This was put in place supposedly to give students a choice in what they want to learn. A field they can pick. A school they can call their own.

It is ALL BS. Nothing has changed. Kids still have the same Math, English, Science, History or Social Studies, Language Arts, and Gym classes no matter what Academy, Small Learning Community they are in. Often students from all the academies have the same teachers for some of their subjects. So, how is it different?

You would think with the ACT Academy, shop classes would be the key, core classes the classes that would be most beneficial, and interdisciplinary measures to tie in all the other classes, which makes lessons easier to understand. Especially being hands on. But nooooooo, this is not the case, in fact, all the shop classes are nothing more than electives. If a student fails, the course they still graduate. What is the point of having a trade academy, when the trade classes are electives and if students don't pass these shop classes it doesn't matter?

*********************

On the very first day back to school, there was a teachers' meeting in the auditorium conducted by the two building principals. Both principals said that the following rules *will* be enforced. They both emphasized "WILL."

**1. Students were to wear uniforms, or they would be punished.**

What a freaking joke! Not one rule was ever enforced. Example: In our academy because they did not want suspensions, after school or pre-school detentions and in-school suspensions, once a student had their lunch, they were to report to the office for the rest of the lunch period. That was the discipline. Now what do you think was done when that student did not show up? That's right. *Nothing*!

**2. Two minutes after the bell to begin class, students who are not in their classes, will be swept up and disciplined.**

Unfreakinbelievable, rules are *only* enforced if there are going to be visitors. For example, when county officials visit the hall sweeps were enforced. It was nothing but smoke and mirrors, a dog and pony show.

**3. Students are not allowed to wear hats, talk on cell phones, use iPods or any electrical device or they will be confiscated. Again, not one rule was ever enforced.**

However, if students had these items on in class, administration went after the teacher. Meanwhile, students defiantly wore them as they walked into the building, in the hallways—all day in front of administrators and not one of them said or did anything. They saw nothing. They did nothing, but stood around BSing with one another, drinking their coffee.

In all of the years I have worked here, it was *only* when the state-wide exams were being administered (at that time it was the HSPT or HSPA) and for those three days *only,* the school was in control.

At least UNTIL…

**The 2011-2012 school year…**
I have never witnessed this type of out of control, chaotic, uncontrollable behavior in the hallways, and even in some classrooms, as the state-wide exams were being administered. During the entire testing time it was no different than any other day. It was out of freaking control!

The noise alone was deafening, and it was coming from all over the first floor. The entire time all we heard was screaming, yelling, cursing, at the top of their lungs, chairs and desks being shoved all over the place. It sounded as if there was a riot going on and I was on the 2nd floor. Teachers on the 2nd and 3rd floors were also complaining.

Testing starts at 8:30am and *nobody* is to be in the halls during testing. Students were just moseying into school at 10am walking up to their respective testing rooms and as usual *nothing* was done about it.

Students are in the hallways all day long, not in class. That is a security breach. Are teenagers allowed to hang out in large crowds on a street corner? Well, students are allowed to hangout all over in and out of the building here at the new John F. Kennedy Educational complex.

Every time I am in the hallway and the bell rings for students to be in class, the administration and the two heads of security guards all of a sudden disappear. I believe this is so they can say, "Well if we don't see it, this doesn't happen." Meanwhile, the hallways are filled with students fighting, yelling, cursing, screaming, wrestling, throwing food, bottles, drinks, everything and anything, other than going to class. I'll say it over and over this type of behavior would not be allowed out in public. They would be arrested.

Then to add salt to the wounds, all of these administrators (directors) received a *substantial raise* and the superintendent received BONUSES!

Meanwhile, teachers haven't had a contract in years. Students still do *not* have to go to class. Their attendance doesn't count. So many students are out 40, 50, 60, or 70 *plus* days, the same amount in cuts and with tardiness and still graduated. Some have been on roll the entire year and maybe showed up for class or school one or two weeks.

Final exams are over almost two weeks (eight) days before school is out. So, the last two weeks of school students don't even show up for class. They may show up for homeroom where attendance is taken but the rest of the day, which is a 1/2-day schedule, they don't attend any classes. Meaning they are still cutting and the superintendent, the administration and administrators are all OK with that.

My question is, why is the school year for students 181 days and the last eight days they don't have to show up? The administration will tell you, it's so students can make up their exams if they were absent. What a joke, I just said most students don't even show up to take the final exam. Many who do show up for exam day don't participate, fail and don't care. Students know that the school district will not *allow* them to fail.

Students cut school and classes all day every day. They still pass and are allowed to graduate. How can that be? Why is that allowed? Yet the politicians, governor, commissioner of education (whoever it is today), the superintendents and administrators all want to hold teachers responsible. How can teachers be responsible when students are in the hallways, stairwells, bathrooms, walking in and out of the building, in and out of classrooms they do not belong in, hanging out any and everywhere, wreaking havoc, chaos, starting fights, disrupting classes and at times having sex in the stairwells instead of being in their assigned class. Now whose fault is that? After all, it *is all on the school's surveillance cameras.*

Sadly, there were at least two Paterson police officers who were assigned to JFK this year who **did get involved** because of fighting and a threatening dangerous situation. They were banned from working in the building. Why? Because these officers had arrested students. Now the principal could NOT stop the paper trail, because these students were arrested. So, if they cannot stop the paper trail, they will stop these police officers from doing their job by not allowing them to work in the building. What kind of message do you think this relays to other students?

There are so many instances. They are *all* in "MY DIARY."

The public as well as the parents who send their children here to Paterson Public School and especially John F. Kennedy Educational complex have no idea what really goes on here because it is all hushed up. That alone is quite disturbing and a *crime*. When it comes to education in the District of Paterson, New Jersey, the New Jersey taxpayers who pay **66+ %** of their property taxes on public education are *not* getting their bang for their tax bucks. We have many security personnel in the building, both district employees and an outside contracting security agency. However, they too are not allowed to do their job.

**EXAMPLE 1:** We teachers do *not* receive a daily absentee, tardy and/or suspension list anymore. Oh, there is one and I asked for it. However, I was told by an administrator I am *not* allowed to have it because it is confidential information. Yeah, it's confidential ever since the so-called restructuring. The administration does not want to let the public or anyone else for the matter knows it is "FAILING!" They want to hide the truth on what is going on inside this school.

**EXAMPLE 2:** If a student is caught or apprehended by the school's security guards for whatever reason, once the student is brought into the security office, administration cuts them lose. They don't want them suspended because now there is a paper trail; documentation that will be part of daily and yearly statistics turned into the state.

The next section chronicles a slate of anonymous letters I have written to the governors, Commissioner of Education, NEA (National Education Association), NJEA (New Jersey Education Association) , newspapers, superintendents, about the conditions here at John F. Kennedy High School and the Paterson Public School District, looking and begging for *help*!

## ANONYMOUS LETTERS

**1994**

Below is the beginning of my documentation starting in 1994. I started writing and sending letters to the Governor and others, using a pseudo name, ZORRO. I have **omitted names** for the purpose of this book. However, verification can be used against my original documentation, notes and journals.

**Letter #1**

March 24, 1994

Dear Governor Whitman,

Please forgive me for not signing my name, but as you read on you will understand the reasons.

However, before I go any further I would like to congratulate you on your election, and on your Address to the State on Tuesday, March 15, 1994.

Governor, I work for the Paterson Public Schools in Paterson NJ. As you know the district is controlled and operated by the State of NJ. My Point is this, as you are trying to cut and save money it seems that the Paterson Public Schools Office is doing you an injustice. For an example, a VP **(Name omitted),** had instructed all students from J. F. Kennedy High School at a junior class meeting to fill out a lunch ticket. This is so the State will allocate more money to the school a program that is designed to **help** students who are economically disadvantaged.

This is embezzlement. More important this is not setting an example to our students. This school has been falsifying many school records and reports to receive more money, and to cover up the poor academic scores, the extreme acts of violence, poor attendance records, and the number of students who are suspended daily. There are students who have been absent as of this time with way over 40, 50 days. These students still receive credit because most of the days out of school are due to **suspensions.** Many students are deliberately being suspended knowing they can have the time off, and still received full credit. **(A VACATION?)**

The Principal up until the fire we had back in October, had the custodians keep all doors chained and locked. This was very scary for many students and teachers trying to evacuate the building. This was the same reason for Mr. Joe Clark being jailed.

Now if I'm not mistaken, it costs 9 to 14 thousand dollars a year for a child to attend Public School. It only cost 3 to 5 thousand dollars a year for a student to attend a private school and receive an **education?** Governor, what is done so differently in a private school compared to our public school? For example, compare the difference between J. F. Kennedy High School, Eastside High School, (Public Schools) to Don Bosco High School and Paterson Catholic High School (Private Schools). Let's not forget the schools and the students are all from the same town Paterson, NJ. Which students receive an **Education?** Which students will be prepared for the future? I don't think I have to tell you.

Our teachers have administrative responsibilities added to their regular duties, to help the State in savings. Then how does the Board of Education justify voting for themselves, either last year or the year before, to get a raise of 12.5% to 49%? Where are the savings?

When the press tried to contact the superintendent about the raise, he could not be reached for comment. Due to work related business in England? Why would someone go to another country to observe schools and ways of education, when New Jersey has many of the best schools in the country, and is also a leader in the Technology Education process?

**(Name omitted / principal at that time)**, as **(he/she)** wants to be called, is always out of the school and away to some sort of meeting or workshop.

Last week **(he/she)** was in Boston, the same week **a teacher was held up in school**, and supposedly with a fake gun. As many meetings, conferences, and workshops **(he/she)** attends, the school is not any better or safer. Why is that? Are these meetings and such for the school's benefit or for (his/hers) own resume?

The students run the school. Only **25%** of the senior class have passed the H.S.P.T. and are graduating this June. If you should visit the school unannounced you will see students sitting in front of every fire alarm box all day long. This is because, if these alarms are not guarded the students would be pulling them sometimes as often as 4 times a day. Just check with police and fire department. These students sit there sleeping, talking with other students, anything, but never do any type of school work. Some of these students are **seniors.** Let's not forget the bomb threats that are called in and the students are not evacuated. There is so much more that needs to be told, but for now this is enough. Please help our students. There is so much money spent in helping other countries children. Let's not forget our own country, our own children.

Thank you for listening.

Sincerely,
Zorro

**Letter #2**

March 29, 1994

Dear Governor Whitman,

I did not want to write to you so soon after the bundle I dropped on you last week. However, this has to be brought to your attention.

On Tuesday, March 22, 1994, there was another large fight in our school again. The fight was not the problem, the problem was, and this time there was another serious injury. A teacher was kicked until he was unconscious by a **student (name omitted)**. Now listen to this. The math teacher **(Name omitted)** is pressing charges against this **student.**

The administration, or should I say the principal **(Name omitted)** is not supportive to **(Name of teacher omitted)**. As usual, the administration is trying to cover up the incident. Many of the teachers feel the school should also press charges against this **student**, but are afraid to voice their opinion and also jeopardize their careers.

This is another case of our school setting a fine example. This is a criminal act.
Now the best part, this **student** is receiving tutoring at home which is called bedside at the taxpayers' expense. The tutor who is also a teacher receives an extra $33.00 dollars an hour while he is tutoring this **student**. This **student** performed a criminal act and should not be receiving this red carpet type of

treatment. This **student** kicked a teacher senseless and is being rewarded? The **student** is receiving this bedside treatment because, he is a choir member from the same church a particular vice principal attends.

To receive bedside tutoring there has to be a doctor's note. There is none. This is a personal favor to this particular Vice Principal, **(Name omitted)**
This student will receive credit for a full year of school as if nothing had happened. That's right, **(Name omitted)** will receive 35 credits because he will be assigned to bedside till September of '94.

**(Name omitted)** until this incident was failing most of his classes. This student should be expelled and prosecuted to the fullest extent of the law. I guess the administration figures this **student** should be protected not the teacher.

Just a note of interest, this **student** is not injured; the bedside is so this **student** does not attend classes in the school.

Just to change the subject for a second. Last year there were very many acts of violence in our school, including a shoot-out.

However, according to the local newspaper, J. F. Kennedy had only reported one act of violence in that school year.

The administration does very well in their cover-ups.

Governor our students, teachers, and school needs your help. **PLEASE** Thank-you

Respectfully,
Zorro


**Letter #3**

April 4, 1994

Dear Governor,

On Tuesday, March 29, 1994, there were a few fights. To be exact there were **5.** The best part of the story is about to be told. It seems all of the fights, involved many of the same girls. One young **lady** in particular was the instigator of all the fights.

Why was this young **woman** not sent home (suspended), instead of dealing with this type of behavior all day in a school setting?

This one particular young **lady,** who was the cause of all the trouble, was eventually beaten so bad she had lost her child. Yes, that's right. This young **lady** was pregnant.

Let's not forget Wednesday. There were **2** more fights that carried over from Tuesday's episodes.

Again, the administration does what they do best to cover up this incident.
Enclose is a copy of the Advocate. Please take notice of the amount of violence in J. F. Kennedy High School. That's right. It says only one incident in the violence category. Well, I guess according to the Advocate, every incident that I had written to you about must be a lie. On the contrary, this is the reason I

write to you. Now you can see for yourself in black and pink, how the administration covers up these incidents.

We should be setting an example to our students, and to each other, not to lie, and to stand tall when problems arise. Instead the old adage arises, **"Do as I say, not as I do."**
Governor, you have to come and see for yourself. I cannot help the feeling that these problems are not just happening in just J. F. Kennedy High School. I have to believe this is happening to all the schools in the whole district. I'm sorry but, I also have to believe this is due to the State takeover, and the orders are coming straight from the top, the Superintendent of the Paterson Public Schools. Please take notice that he had come from Boston along with his entourage. Also note the reason why he had left Boston.

I would also like to know why then would the State of New Jersey would hire him for the same position?

Enclosed are some of the incidents through-out the last two years.
1. On Tuesday, October 13, 1992, a man comes into the school with a stick 4 to 5 feet in length threatening to do serious bodily harm to some student or students. This man was finally subdued and taken directly to **(Name omitted)** office. This happened between 6th and 7th period.

2. On Wednesday, October 14, 1992, there was a large brawl on the second floor. Police had to be summoned.

3. On Thursday, October 15, 1992, a large fight breaks-out in the front cafeteria involving many young ladies ending with a guard injured. When you went to school, was their guard's in school? There were none when I went. There is a **quarter of a million dollars** spent on security in our school alone.

4. On that same day some students are sent home and suspended for bringing guns into school. *Suspended?* These students must be prosecuted! What happens to the safety of all the other students and teachers?

5. On Friday, October of 1992, a fight breaks out in the center of the school on the first floor. Involved is a student **(Name omitted)** and a VP **(Name omitted)**. The VP was violently thrown down to the floor.

6. Monday, October 26, 1992, students had started a fire on the second floor. The fire department was never summoned.

7. Wednesday, October 28, 1992, many students in hallways, by the public telephones, and congregating in hallway as if there were no school. Many teachers are trying to move the students along but students are either ignoring them or trying to start a confrontation with them. A VP **(Name omitted)** was also trying to move the students along and shouting such remarks, I'm the Vice Principal not a teacher or a guard. I assume that VP is aware of the situation with students not listening to teachers and guards.

8. Also on a Wednesday, October 28, 1992, Mrs. **(Name omitted)** who is in charge of the guards was beaten up.
9. Friday, November 29, 1992, a knife fight on the first floor between Mr. **(Name omitted)** office and the Metal Shop.
10. Tuesday, November 24, 1992, a few young men had set a young lady's hair on fire. The incident was classified as an accident. How does someone accidentally set another person's hair on fire in school?
11. December 17, 1992, the Principal was extremely upset. It seems she was sprayed in the face with MACE. Yes, this had happened in school.

12. I do not have the date. However, there was a fight on a weekend, involving a few Hispanic students and some Arab kids on Market Street in downtown Paterson NJ. On Monday, November 30, 1992, these Arab fellows had come by J. F. Kennedy High School brandishing their firearms. Later that afternoon, a few Arab fellows had shot at the same boys from the weekend's incident, by school #2.

13. You're going to love this one. On January 5, 1993, the fire alarm went off 2 or 3 times. The students and faculty were advised to disregard the fire alarm. During 5th period there was a fire in the boy's locker room. The alarm was sounded but disregarded. Many students approached me and said they did not like the situation and were afraid for their lives.

14. January 6, 1993, there was a bomb scare. No alarm was sounded. The fire department had to advise the Principal to evacuate the building. During the time outside during the evacuation from the bomb scare, many of the students were doing the following; setting leaves on fire, running in front of moving cars, and throwing dice. A sign of real control, wouldn't you think?

15. January 7, 1993, a fight broke out during 5th period in the cafeteria. A stink bomb was also ignited in the same cafeteria. This was in retaliation by the students. Students were not allowed to buy snacks. Then at 12:30 PM the fire alarm is sounded. Yes, it was a false alarm. This was also part of the retaliation.

16. Wednesday, January 20, 1993, many fights, in the girl's locker room, on the second floor, and in the main corridor on the first floor with a student **(Name omitted)**. He was beating up everyone in his path. He had hit teachers, students' boys and girls alike, guards, everyone and anyone. A teacher had to forcefully take this fellow down to the ground in order to subdue. Even at that time the student was acting like a wild man. Then threaten to come back to school with a gun.

Then later that day a student had brandished his knife in anger to a teacher. This young gentleman was not suspended. This young man was left in school as if nothing had happened. This may be verified by a teacher named Mr. **(Name omitted)**.

17. Thursday, Feb. 11, 1993, while snowing like crazy the fire alarm was again set off. Many teachers could not get out of the school due to the doors being chained and locked.

18. I do not have a date for the following incidents. However, on this particular day a fire was started in the boy's locker room, and many M80s were also ignited. There was also another incident involving someone throwing M80s at some girls in the gym room. When a VP **(Name omitted)** was asked about the situation her comments were, don't bother me about this problem. Mr. **(Name omitted)** who is in charge of the physical education department was extremely upset, because he wanted to keep the incident quiet.

19. A few freshmen girls were going to beat up this young lady. The incident was brought to the administrations' attention to prevent a situation. Nothing was done to prevent this incident, and this young lady was seriously beaten up.

Governor, I apologize for this lengthy letter, so I will end it here. I do have much more information that needs to be brought to your attention [at this time]. I will talk with you soon.   THANK YOU.
**PLEASE HELP**

Sincerely,
Zorro

**Letter #4**

April 11, 1994

Dear Governor Whitman,

It has been a relatively quiet week with the exception of a fire alarm being pulled on Friday, April 8, 1994.
Yes, that's correct. Even with a guard at each fire alarm station a false alarm had occurred.

All were evacuated from school, and the fire department, police, sheriff department, and paramedics did arrive.

The incident was reported downtown as a fire drill.
Each time there is a false alarm it costs the school $600.00. I would consider this **vandalism.**

Last year the fire alarms were pulled as much as **3** to **4** times a **day**. Let's not forget the many **bomb** scares we had, involving also the bomb squad, bomb sniffing K-9s, and the robots.

If you still have the Advocate that I had sent to you it states about **$5000.00** for that year's vandalism. I do not think they are telling the truth. Then what is considered **vandalism?** Why, is it accepted for adults to lie and cheat? Yet we preach and teach our children and students not to? Remember, the false alarm is to be reported as a fire drill? This is another lie and cover up.   **WHY?**

There is something else I would like to bring to your attention. Referring back to the Advocate, School 12 reported no incidence in the Violence department. Mrs. Whitman this is not true. A teacher was savagely and brutally attacked and beaten by a student with a baseball bat. The teacher was a Physical education instructor. This is one of many reasons why I think this is a **District wide cover up**. The **truth** is never reported, and or is always covered up.  Our districts' **parents and citizens** are being lied to and cheated. For all the reasons supposedly the State had taken over the district of Paterson's Board of Education, this new Board is committing at a larger scale the same atrocities. If this Board can lie and intimidate its administration, teachers, and all of its support staff, lie and cheat its students and citizens of Paterson, lie to the media and press, I can only imagine the lies and falsification of reports, records, and documents that are sent to you and your officers.

In J. F. Kennedy High School homeroom starts at 8:15 AM. Students are not to be permitted in the building after 8:20 AM without being accompanied by a parent. Students arrive and enter the building after 8:30 AM. Why are these rules, and so many others not enforced?

These letters I write are not written out of vindictiveness, I write them out of concern for the people of Paterson, and the most important resource our State has, its **children.**

I will now continue where I stopped with my last letter.
20. Wednesday, March 3, 1993, 3 boys were smoking dope. **(Name omitted)** and **(Name omitted)** two of the security guard picked up the boys. One boy had a beeper and had it removed by security.

When **(Name omitted)** was asked, what happened to the boys? She said they were escorted to the cut office. **(Name omitted)** was asked if the boys were taken down for a drug test. She replied with much hesitation, she didn't know.
**(Name omitted)** was asked by a teacher if she wanted him/her to write a report on the boys? **(Name omitted)** said nothing. Nothing is what was never heard of again of the incident.

21. Monday, March 8, 1993, beginning of 8th period a fight breaks out in locker room. Student **(Name omitted)** and another boy were fighting. Coach **(Name omitted)** and **(Name omitted)** stepped in to Separate them. The students end up in the Phys Ed office, and it started up again. **(Name omitted)** pushed one boy up against the wall and tried to keep the boy in check. A few choice words were spoken, then an unknown student stepped in and hit the boy **(Name omitted)** had up against the wall. **(Name omitted)** shoved this other boy out of the office. This student then struck **(Name omitted)** in the face with his fist. With this, **(Name omitted)** went after the boy swinging and throwing punches back at this student, and rightfully so.

Mr. **(Name omitted), (Name omitted), (Name omitted)** and a student **(Name omitted)** had to hold and restrain Mr. **(Name omitted)** back.

22. The week of March 11, 1993, many students are being sprayed with mace constantly. One young lady was throwing up blood after her debut with mace.

23. June 23, 1993, a bomb call was placed to the Paterson Police department. Police and Fire departments show up. No one is evacuated or told what is going on. One hour later, staff and students are informed.

24. June 24, 1993, 11:20 AM, Police and Rescue arrive. Nothing was ever said. That's right you guessed it another bomb scare, and no one was ever evacuated.

As you can see, what is a normal day at J. F. Kennedy High School, in Paterson NJ?

Governor Whitman, here are a few other problems our Public School system faces.
Parents must be held **responsible** for their children's actions, behavior, and conduct. Public Schools are not the place for parents to **dump** their children off, and have the teachers do their **parental responsibilities.**

Teachers are to instill education, not spend **60%** or more of their time with disciplinary problems. This includes babies having babies. If parents did such a good job with their own children, they wouldn't be taking care of their baby's baby. It is not the Public Schools responsibilities to teach manners, hygiene, child rearing, birth control, etc, etc. The Public School system is to help, and reinforce these areas.

I have to add to the above. Today, Tuesday, April 12, 1994, at the beginning of 7th period the fire alarm was once again set-off. This was no drill. Yes, it was another false alarm, and another bill of $600.00. Remember according to the Board Education of the Paterson Public Schools, this is not considered **vandalism.**

There are many cover-ups, and lies told by our administration. Also let's not forget that these juveniles know that nothing will happen to them, and they can and will do anything, and usually get away with it. Our Public Schools in our cities are **War Zones.** The teachers and community are losing. This disease is spreading as fast, if not faster than AIDS.

Governor, I have to communicate with you somehow and keep anonymous for obvious reasons. I do not want to just keep writing to you. I want to help you. I want to be involved in the improvement of our schools, community, and State. We cannot wait any longer.

Sincerely,
Zorro

**Letter #5**

April 19, 1994

Dear Governor,

I have a little more information for you.

On Wednesday, April 13, 1994, there was another false fire alarm sounded. As I have said to you before, the students run the school. This is after announcement was made over the schools PA system saying, that they have caught the student who has been setting the alarms off. The students in their defiance had set the alarm off once again. Rightfully so, the teachers have to guard every fire alarm during the between sessions of every class. Now a teacher is held accountable if the alarms are set off. How is a teacher to monitor student's movement, stop possible altercations, talk with and assist students, and guard a fire alarm? This is not a complaint, but if the alarm goes off, that teacher who is responsible for that particular alarm will be hung.

Remember the story I have told you about the math teacher Mr. **(Name omitted)**? He is being pressured to forget everything? He is now in a position where he may not be allowed to work his regular summer employment. He normally teaches summer school at J.F. Kennedy High School.

The student **(Name omitted)** is the young man who had inflicted serious injury to Mr. **(Name omitted)**. His stepfather is Reverend **(Name omitted)** and is the Pastor from the same church Vice Principal **(Name omitted)** attends and is also the choir director.

**(Name omitted)** is also assigned to the parents negotiating team.   Why?
He has also said to the local newspaper, "The teachers will now be forced to listen to the wishes of the parents." What is that supposed to mean?

In J. F. Kennedy High School there are 9 periods. Ninth period is supposed to be for tutorial. This was designed so if a student needs assistance, he or she has the time to get the extra help that is needed. Also if a teacher feels a student or students need help the teacher would assign the student to ninth period tutorial. If a student refuses to attend, the teacher was instructed to send in a cut on the student. Teachers are no longer allowed to send cuts on a student, for refusal to show up for their assigned tutorial. This is partially due to the students are complaining to the principal that it is unfair. **Who runs the school?**

I have written many letters to you in the last few months. I am going to send copies of these letters to our local newspapers and television stations. Possibly the TV show Crusaders. Please do not think I am threatening you, that's the furthest thing from my heart and mind. My concern is to rid the injustice, lies, threats, cover ups, and the bulling tactic the State Appointed District Board of Education inflicts on the people, parents, students, and employees, of Paterson have to contend with.

Dear Governor, I would have sent the above to you much sooner, but there is much more that must be told. I'm curious if you have seen the News Tuesday, April 19, 1994, Channel 4, with Ralph Penza? There was a teacher's hair set a fire in Eastside High School in Paterson, NJ. A spoke's person from the State Appointed District of Public Schools of Paterson, NJ. Says' it was **a childish prank**. How can someone have the nerve to be on television and say it was **a childish prank?** No, this is typical cover up. This incident is also quite a coincidence after I wrote you about a young lady last year having her hair set on fire. That was also defined as a **childish prank.** Throwing spit balls is **a childish prank.**

I would like you to be aware of the Auto Shop Teacher in J. F. Kennedy High School who also was threatened to have his hair set a fire, by a student named **(Name omitted)**. Nothing was done about that incident also. You can check with the schools Child Study Team about that incident also.

Also Tuesday, April 19, 1994, School 30 an Elementary School, the police were summoned because a student had a pistol. These are babies carrying guns. YET IT WAS ALL HUSHED UP!

I'm not sure of the date, either Monday, April 18, 1994, or Tuesday, April 19, 1994, a student **(Name omitted)** had come from behind and savagely struck a student in the face. This students name is **(Name omitted)**. **(Name omitted)** was knocked unconscious, and suffers with a broken jaw. There was no cause or provocation for **(Name omitted)** to hit **(Name omitted)**. **(Name omitted)** has a history of hitting people, and had just returned from a drug treatment center.

The parents of **(Name omitted)** are pressing charges, but our school, J. F. Kennedy High School is not. J. F. Kennedy High School is desperately trying to cover this incident up. As of today's date Friday, April 22, 1994, a State Mandate Act of Violence Form is still not filled out, for the above **childish prank**. Then again, there hasn't been many of these forms filled out in the past three years. I ask you again. Is this because our principal is not tenured? Is this also a major cover up from the State Appointed District of Public Schools of Paterson, NJ? Or is it a combination of both?

Remember, supposedly the superintendent was fired from Boston, and the State of New York. Why? I ask why, would the State of New Jersey ever consider to hire him and his entourage? Teachers have to undergo a background check. What happened here?

Getting back to the **(Name omitted)** story. I cannot give you names for obvious reasons, but check with our child study team and school Psychologists, and you will learn that the State Appointed District of Public Schools of Paterson, NJ. Do not want to take any action, and to put the disruptive children out of the Paterson District. If these students leave the district, the district will have to pay 35 thousand dollars a year for each student, and an additional 10 thousand for the student's transportation. If the student fails to take the bus in the morning, the district still has to pay transportation and program fees.
If you are under the age of 18, it is against the law for a child to have a beeper in his or her possession. It is also school policy for students not to have them. However, the students have them in plain sight, and nothing is done about it. If a teacher confiscates a beeper from a student, our administrators give it back to the students. Now the students have the beepers in their possession, and in view again, all in an act of defiance.

One last note of interest; the head of Security of J. F. Kennedy High School **(Name omitted),** and I do not know his last name, will be going to trial next week. He is being tried for illegally searching a student's locker where he had removed a firearm. The students' locker **(Name omitted)** had searched and removed the firearm from, was the same student who shot another student the next day, outside of our school. This was during our summer school session.

**THIS IS JUSTICE. HOW WE PROTECT OUR CRIMINALS!**
Thank you

Sincerely,
Zorro

**Letter #6**

April 28, 1994

Dear Governor,

On Tuesday, April 26, 1994, during third period, the fire alarm had gone off once again. Another false alarm. Now the scary part, students do not evacuate the building with any type of haste. This is due to **YEARS** of false alarms. Whenever the students, and I might add the faculty, all hear the fire alarm sound, it is now considered a hoax. This situation has now become a grave problem. With the type of students and intruders this school has to contend with on daily bases, all there has to be is A REAL BOMB THREAT, or a FIRE, and with lack of concern due to the thinking of it being another false alarm, someone will be seriously hurt if not worse. Just like, **'THE BOY WHO CRIED WOLF.'**

On Wednesday, April 27, 1994, during third period a student, by the name of **(Name omitted)**, in Mr. **(Name omitted)** class was stabbed in the **head** by an intruder who answers to the street name of Wink.

I do not know the reason for the incident, but I do know this fellow Wink, and many trespassers are always entering our building, and some sort of problem arises. The point I am trying to make here is our administration is doing their best to cover up an incident of a student being stabbed. Why, do they hide the truth? I'm sorry Governor Whitman. This is wrong. You can only imagine the information that I have not obtained, and is covered up.

Also one-day last week a student had a loaded gun in J. F. Kennedy High School. The student was removed from school quietly by the Paterson Police. This incident was also to be on the hush-hush. However, the information had leaked and was printed in a local newspaper. There were many irate administrators. Governor, there has to be **harsh** and **swift** punishment for firearms and or weapons brought into schools and within school zones.

Speaking of cover ups. A **(Name omitted)** who is a teacher at J. F. Kennedy High School, was also **threatened** with severe bodily injury by one of his students named **(Name omitted)**.

**(Name omitted),** was willing to proceed with pressing of charges against the student **(Name omitted)**, and was immediately confronted not to, or he may suffer the consequences of not be considered for summer employment.

Another cover up, another threat by, our administration.

It's a hard day when you try to work as a teacher in Paterson, New Jersey, and you have to protect yourself from intruders, students, and our own administration. We as teacher in J. F. Kennedy High School have no one to confide in or trust. This is not America as I know it to be.
I apologize for not having dates, but by giving the names, the above information can easily be investigated.

Sincerely,
Zorro

**Letter #7**

May 9, 1994

Dear Governor,

I have more information for you. Governor, I hope you will investigate all that I have written to you.

During the week of April 29, 1994, a male student walked into a classroom and proceeded to punch a female student repeatedly in the face. I do not know the reason why.

Also during the same week, a young lady (student) walked up to another young lady (student) and started to punch her repeatedly about the face. The victim during her struggle reached into her pocketbook and pulled a can of mace and sprayed her attacker. This girl then was suspended for 10 days, suspended for defending herself.

Also during this same week, a student, **(Name omitted),** a known drug dealer had sold his supplies to two students from J. F. Kennedy High School. These two students who purchased the drugs were both caught with large quantities of drugs and later removed by the Paterson Police. How does **(Name omitted)** get away unscathed? Also during this week, we had another false fire alarm.

The City of Paterson has trouble recruiting substitute teachers. The Paterson Board of Public Schools had also raised the amount of pay per day to entice recruitment of substitute teachers. In this same week an English substitute teacher was deliberately punched between his legs. The teacher did fall to the floor hurt, and embarrassed. The student gets a vacation, a 10-day suspension.

Remember students are not penalized for suspensions. Suspensions are not counted toward student's absenteeism. Students deliberately get suspended so they can have time off with-out penalty. We all wonder what's wrong with the world today. There is no **PUNISHMENT.** Yet the news media will make a big deal about an American boy in another country, who commits, and was found guilty of the crime of vandalism, and was sentenced to be caned.

Good for Singapore.
The United States should also institute **punishment to meet the crime.**

On Thursday of the same week, the fire alarm once again was set off, but were not heard in J. F. Kennedy High School. It seems the alarms were in the silent mode because of all the false alarms. However, the fire department did receive the alarm, was dispatched, and had arrived to our fair safe haven of education. It seems the alarms were silenced due to a party like atmosphere that was in our school library honoring V.P. **(Name omitted)**. I guess they did not want to be interrupted with the possibility of another false alarm.
However, you can only imagine how safe we all feel knowing that the alarms are now disconnected. It's horrible as it is and dangerous especially now, that nobody takes the fire alarms system serious anymore.

Remember the story about a student named **(Name omitted)**? Well, **(Name omitted)** was allowed back to school and class. With his return, the students who are in his classes are all upset, and extremely scared. These students, all are afraid that they may become his next prey. **(Name omitted)** also has the attitude and has been heard by students and teachers alike, saying that he has the juice, and nobody can do anything to him.

Who is to be protected here?

I truly believe the good and innocent will suffer, and always will be a victim.
This school and the laws prove this, by protecting these animals. Our administration does not hesitate to cover up all incidents, and lie, to show everyone what a good job they are doing. **NOT!**

One of these letters will eventually have news of a terrible tragedy. Before this happens, I hope you will be able to help.

Sincerely,
Zorro

**Letter #8**

September 11, 1994

Dear Governor,

I have sent you a great deal of information, and so far, nothing has been done. Now the children of Paterson, New Jerseys, 2 High Schools under the State Controlled Board of Education, are attending school from 8:15 AM to 3:05 PM, a total of 9 periods without LUNCH.

This, as you must know, is against the law.

What school district would have children attend school for 7 hours WITHOUT A LUNCH?

The law states a student can attend classes without a lunch as long there is a signed permission slip by that student's parent or guardian.
There are child labor laws, and I would imagine this issue would fall into that category. John F. Kennedy High School, if you remember has all its students fill out free lunch forms. This program is supposed to help the needy students. The school system is taking advantage of the system at the TAXPAYERS' EXPENSE.

What about the children who filled out phony lunch forms and do not even have a lunch period? As I said last year, this is embezzlement. They did remove the public phones from the school. This was not to help the students, or staff with all the violent problems the phones cause. This is so the State Controlled Board of Education of the City of Paterson, can make more money by getting another phone company.

With the new phone company, the District now receives 10 cents on each call instead of the nickel. I do not know if the price of a local phone call had changed. This will really help the children and their parents of Paterson, NJ.

Where, and what are the priorities?
The superintendent has destroyed the Paterson School System.
I hope you are aware that the teachers of Paterson, NJ are about to strike. I hope you are aware of the true reasons. Again, who suffers? The children and parents of the City of Paterson do. The next time you are eating lunch, I hope you think of the students who are NOT ALLOWED, because of the failed programs that the superintendent had implemented and is trying to cover up.

Look at the school's test scores. Check and see if the percentages are correct. As you know, numbers can be manipulated. (They are).

There are also more secretaries and staff in the Main Office downtown, than there were before the State had taken over the Paterson School District.

They were to reduce the size of personnel in that particular area. Many people had lost their jobs because of excess FAT. Now there are more people in the main office than before. The superintendent is doing a job on the City of Paterson.

I hope you will do something at least about the children not getting a lunch. When you find out about the reasons why the children do not have a lunch period, you will also see everything I said was true.

GOVERNOR, HELP OUR CHILDREN. PLEASE
Sincerely,

Zorro

**Letter #9**

October 31, 1994

Dear Governor Whitman,

Just to bring you up to date, about two weeks ago a teacher from our sister High School, Eastside, backed out of her parking spot from school and ran over and killed a homeless man. I wonder if you've heard about that.

Now, this is all because the superintendent ordered the removal of a fence that was put around the school many years ago to prevent such an incident from happening. Not only was this fence put up for that reason, it was also installed so security had more control of an enclosed area.

You see, Mrs. Whitman. Eastside High School is in an extremely rough and violent area in the city of Paterson, NJ. The fence was also helpful in keeping people from breaking in at night and during the day. It helped keep vandalism to the school and teachers' cars down to a minimum and was also helpful in the apprehension of those who try to escape from one or more of the above reasons. But, the superintendent felt it would *look better,* if the fence was taken down and removed at the hard working taxpayer's expense, naturally.

Now, because of his hastily and unthinkable choice of the removal of that fence, some poor honest and hardworking teacher has to spend the rest of her life with the thought of backing over and killing an innocent human being.

You as Governor said, "You would control spending." The children and the people of Paterson have suffered enough. The superintendent seems to implement this Paradigm program in all of the districts in which he has worked in and the program has always met with the same result, FAILURE. Now because his program has failed Teachers are losing their jobs, which is good for the States' economy. The children are now forced to have 9 straight periods of school with \out a lunch break. This is from 8:15 AM to 3:05 PM. I am sure you wouldn't want your children to go to school that long without a lunch. So why do these children have to suffer? Because they are poor? You better start investigating the house that the superintendent is building. He has deliberately made programs fail so he can be employed for 5 years at the poor people and hardworking taxpayers' expense of Paterson, NJ.

Also be advised that there is a great deal of nepotism going on in his administration. They were supposed to thin out the Central Office of unnecessary personnel. It is funny how many people from his church are employed in Central Office. Oh yes, you better have someone go over the books [really] good. It seems that there is a great deal of unaccounted expenses.

Now for the latest in Kennedy High School. Last summer the school was completely repainted. Take a look at it now. You wouldn't believe it was ever painted. The fire alarms are still going off throughout the school day, and week, falsely I might add.

It seems there was a horrific fight on the second floor Monday, October 24, 1994.

It seems there was a theft outside the school parking lot of a sound system from a student's car a week before. The amount was estimated to be well over one thousand dollars. However, because of this theft there was a very ugly beating in school. Without going into grizzly details and length, the boy who supposedly stole the equipment **(Name omitted),** was beaten by a boy **(Name omitted),** and three others so bad he is still in the hospital, with many broken bones to his face, and many other complications. Now, I would bet you there is NO incident report written and or submitted about this beating inside John F. Kennedy High School. Why? Is it not a State Mandate Directive, to have such incidents written and reported? I have said to you many times before. You have to come and see for yourself.

There are just as many students in the hallways during class time as there is in between periods.

Yes, I know I sound disgusted but so should you, for letting this go on for so long. I know many of my colleagues have written you, but it seems as if you are not doing anything about this. You have an explosive and dangerous situation here. Eventually, you will be the one who is going to take the heat for all this. Remember, the superintendent was hired by the State in which you are the Governor of. So you, and you alone are responsible for their actions, especially after many others and I have warned you of these problems and dangerous situations.

We teachers feel the superintendent is also deliberately trying to cause a strike by the teachers of Paterson, NJ. Our contract was up in June. We are all working without a contract, and in good faith. But it seems that superintendent is trying to make the teachers look bad so he can blame all his problems and failures on the teachers of Paterson, NJ.

Remember, it wasn't the teachers who implemented Paradigm program. It isn't the teachers who are forcing the children to go to school for 9 periods without a lunch. It isn't the teachers telling the students to fill out State Funded Lunch Tickets whether they need it or not. It isn't the teachers who are hiding and falsifying records. It isn't the teachers misappropriating funds. It isn't the teachers who have an address at the YMCA in Paterson, and resides someplace else. It isn't the teachers who are involved with wide spread nepotism.
Maybe I am writing to the wrong person. Maybe I should be writing to the Federal Government and the IRS, after all it is State and Federal tax money that is being misappropriated.

Disgusted,<br>Zorro

**NOTE OF INTEREST OF 2011:** The Paterson Board of Education/Superintendent's Office put up an entire new fence at Eastside High School, a few years ago. More tax dollars wasted. The fence shouldn't have been removed in the first place!

**Letter #10**

November 18, 1994

Dear Governor Whitman,

Just to keep you informed. In the last two days, November 17, and 18, there has been **four (4)** fires in J. F. Kennedy High School.

Oh yes, there was also only **one (1)** bomb scare.

One of the fires was actually started by igniting the curtains above the stage of the auditorium. All of these incidents occurred while the principal of J. F. Kennedy High School is in California.

I asked you before, why would the principal spend so much time away from **(THEIR)** school, when **(THEIR)** school is out of control?

Are these trips made to enhance his/her resume, and if she can be away from his/her school so much, then why do we need a Principal in the first place? It's only a salary of how many yens of thousand dollars a year. The State of New Jersey can afford it. If we can't, you'll just raise our taxes.

I wonder if incident reports were sent. Isn't that also the law? It would be easy to check and see how many incident reports match to how many times the police and fire department from the City of Paterson, New Jersey, were called in on scene at J. F. Kennedy High School.

Why haven't the local newspapers reported the ongoing troubles of J. F. Kennedy High School?

Why haven't the local TV Stations? Could there possible be a cover up?

The school's fire alarms are set off regularly. I have told you before the fire alarms are NOW guarded by students all day long. None of these students, who sit and guard these fire alarms, do any type of school work.

Many of these students sit at their post throughout the day just listening to their Walkman.
**(That's education?)**
Now, here's a new twist. It seems these students who sit at these fire alarm posts daily are only to be approached by three or more other students who will not only threaten them with physical harm, these animals also threaten them by administering physical harm to their families. They are not to say anything as these animals falsely activate the alarms. Now the students who are made to sit by fire alarms are not only suffering with the dilemma of him or her being physically harmed as well as their families, but also suffer the consequence of wrongly being accused of the crime, and lastly, suspension.

Why would a Public School have students in school all day long, not do any academic or remedial work, and just sit and guard a fire alarm?

I wouldn't mind it so much but the alarms are still activated continuously. By the way, I understand that the superintendent was in Israel last year. Why would he go to Israel to see how Israeli school systems operate? Is there not a school system that operates properly in the United States, let alone in our own state of New Jersey? It seems that the superintendent goes all over the world, at the expense of the taxpayers of Paterson, and the state of NEW JERSEY, with the excuse of evaluating and observing other school systems.

As I wrote to you before, your State Controlled Administration of the Public Schools of Paterson, is raping the taxpaying people of Paterson, NJ.

Before these rapists going tramping around the world at the taxpayers' Expense of Paterson, NJ, don't you think they should get control of the school's first instead of the school systems checkbook?

It was stated recently in our local newspaper that the superintendents' salary is in excess of one hundred and thirty thousand dollars. How much do you make as the Governor?

As I said to you in my last letter, the school was painted a year ago. You should see it now.

What are you waiting for Governor? Take a stand for what is **RIGHT,** not for what is politically correct.

Disgusted, Zorro

**Letter #11**

November 25, 1994

Dear Governor,

It is definite now. The school is controlled by its students. In my letter last week, I wrote about four (4), fire that where set in J. F. Kennedy High School. I also informed you that the principal was in California. When she came back she was extremely upset. She made an announcement telling all students that there will not be a pep rally for the annual Kennedy Eastside football game.

On Tuesday morning, the students walked out of the school in protest of the principal's decision with the cancellation of the pep rally for Wednesday afternoon.

Wednesday comes along, and the pep rally is not only scheduled, it becomes a reality.

Wednesday also includes the calling in of TWO BOMB SCARES that go on unannounced and the schools' premises never evacuated.
One time during one of the bomb scares, the police and fire department where actually trying to take the public phones inside the school apart. I imagine the police and fire departments are tired and fed up with the continuous false alarms and bomb scares. After all Paterson is a big city, and I don't imagine the taxpayers want the police force and fire department, spending so much of its time and resources at an educational facility on fires that are deliberately set, false alarms and bomb scares.

I find it extremely coincidental that no newspaper ever reports this. If not for anything else, the students' parents should be made aware of these problems before their sons or daughters are seriously injured or killed.

However, your State Appointed Leaders who are running the Paterson Board of Education have the nerve to tell the parents and taxpayers that everything is better and that crime, vandalism, and violence in their schools are down. These FOOLS represent YOU.

ZORRO

**Letter #12**

January 3, 1995

Dear Governor,

Before I go any further I would like to wish you and your family a Merry Christmas.

As you should be aware of there was a team of State Inspectors in Kennedy High School just before the holidays. Wrong move, you should have had them come in unannounced. There were many meetings on how we were to greet and speak to your inspection team. We were told what and what not to say, or to talk about. In fact, if we were asked a question that may be incriminating, we were told not to say anything and direct them to our administration.

The janitorial staff worked very long days preparing for their arrival. When your staff was here they had to notice the many janitors working. Wrong— we do not have that many janitors, due to cutbacks. You have to come to our schools unannounced.

Did they check school records? Did they check accident reports? Did they check vandalism reports? Did they check violent act reports, etc.? Did you especially check to see if the school records match the records in the main office?

I happened to see you on a television program the name I did not catch. I noticed you made a comment that education should be the same in Paterson as it is in Princeton. I know where that remark came from. I think that came from another teacher at Kennedy High School **(Name omitted).** So I guess you do read the letters. Before **(Name omitted)** started writing to you I have already advised you on how the teachers are treated. Mostly how dangerous it is for our students. You have to remember one thing. The students do not run the schools in Princeton, and the superintendent hasn't been put in charge by the state to run that school system yet. Or do you want Princeton to be like Paterson, N. J.?

The teachers are disciplined more than the students. I guess that explains why the students run the school.

By the way, did you receive the report on the attempted murder in Kennedy High School last week? I bet you didn't. It seems that a student named **(Name omitted)** attempted to shoot another student and the bullet did not fire. Yes, that's right, he did pull the trigger but the bullet did not fire. I also know for a fact that he and another student named **(Name omitted),** where practicing shooting the gun earlier that morning on Grand Street in Paterson, N. J. This was to prepare himself before he confronted the student he attempted to shoot.

Let's not forget the MANY fights that went on all day on Friday, December 23, 1994. There were 4 large fights before third period of December 23. I'll bet my best Christmas present that you will never receive a mandated incident report on any of these incidents.

Do you remember the information that I sent to you saying that there are NO acts of violence in Kennedy High School? Well, just what I have told you what has happened on December 23, 1994, I proved that wrong again. But that is because the incident reports are never submitted. But we know better than that.

How many have I reported to you with the dates and names? If we as teachers are told how to speak and react I can only imagine how the superintendent wants the administrators of all of the Paterson Schools to react. In essence we are all puppets of the superintendent.

I happen to find out that ASBESTOS was removed from the boiler room of John F. Kennedy High School on Tuesday, December 27, 1994. Enclosed are pictures of doors with signs on them with a WARNING TO THE ASBESTOS REMOVAL. I also know for a fact that there was a permit on the boiler room outside entrance door for the removal of ASBESTOS. It will be extremely easy to check this incident out especially when the disposal of ASBESTOS must be documented. Also somebody has to pay for the transportation of HAZARDOUS MATERIAL to its disposing area.

Now are we as student and teachers entitled for medical treatment and compensation due to ASBESTOS poisoning? A few years ago all of the ASBESTOS was supposedly removed from J. F. Kennedy High School.

I started writing letters to you 10 months ago. I know for a fact I am not the only one who writes you. Now you have to ask yourself these questions. Would you want your children to be a student or a teacher in Paterson, N. J.? Also as a taxpaying parent, would you want your school system controlled by the superintendent and his entourage?

I would have send this letter a week and a half ago but I was waiting and compiling more information for you. The company that was removing the asbestos was **(Name omitted)**.
On the white GMC truck which license plates read as X██-██L

Enclosed are pictures of a few of the many false fire alarms. If you look at the pictures closely you will notice the children's clothing and the differences in the sky and weather. This will show you that these picture are not all taken on the same day.

I will be sending you pictures of the asbestos removal, the truck, and the signs all over the school stating WARNING asbestos is being removed.

I will also send you pictures of asbestos covered pipes that are being improperly disposed of by placing them in a rented garbage dumpster.

The name and telephone number on the dumpster is clearly visible. Now, where is the asbestos being dumped? Oh, this removal of the asbestos piping was going on as school was in session. Which was the week of January 3, through the 6 of 1995.

*January 9, 1995

Last Friday, January 6, 1995, many, many fights had broken out throughout the day. One in particular was when the Principal herself witnessed a boy being savagely beaten up. Her remark was "What is going on here?" How can she make a statement like that? This has been going on daily, and goes on not reported. As in just today alone, over 8 students were suspended because of violence. Now remember they are suspended. The days of suspension are not counted toward their absence. They get a vacation for threatening or inflicting physical and mental harm.

You should check the actual suspension list because of violence, you will be shocked. Especially when you find out they go on not reported. Then they have the nerve to say that there are no acts of violence in Kennedy High School.
The teachers have no control in this school. Many are afraid for their safety and for the safety of the many good students.

Governor what are you waiting for?

HELP US

ZORRO

**Letter #13**

January 20, 1995

Dear Governor Whitman,

How are you doing? Well, I hope.

Three sets of parents aren't doing very well here in Paterson, NJ.

It seems yesterday, Thursday, January 19, 1995, approximately 8:20 am a gang of youths had savagely attacked three youths in a class room on the second floor. All three of these youths where rushed to and treated at a local hospital. One of the three attacked youths whose name is **(Name omitted)** who resides on 5th Ave. Paterson, NJ, had his skull and faced split with a pipe for which he received 15 stitches.

Another boy was stabbed in the back of the neck. I am trying to obtain his name. The third youth was beaten with a garbage can lid. I will try to obtain his name also.

One of the youths who did the attacking was **(Name omitted),** a freshman who resides on Union Ave. Paterson, NJ.

Now, I will guarantee there is no report on this incident either. In fact, I have proof. It seems a news reporter named Richard Cowen, from The Record, had heard of the incident, and cannot get any information and that includes the Paterson Police Department.

Why would that be?

Doesn't the Police Department take its orders from the Mayor? Unless the Mayor is also trying to cover all of these incidents that go on in the Paterson, School system. Why would the Mayor who is also the Assemblymen of this district be covering up these incidents why? Unless he received orders from a higher authority?
Yes, this is all a guess, but I cannot believe that the Police Department would cover up information unless instructed to.
I have heard that last week a young girl was raped in the building of Kennedy High School. It is very hard to get information on this incident. To be honest with you as I have been, I only learned of this incident today. I do not have much information on this incident and question the validity. I will investigate further.

However, two weeks ago a substitute teacher was attacked in the classroom, and is now not able to work and on compensation. It seems that the substitute teacher, **(Name omitted),** was strangled and serious damage was done to a vertebra in his neck.

Now that should be easy to check with. After all, how many substitute teachers are there whose name is **(Name omitted)**, and on compensation?

I hope you enjoyed the pictures? I will soon have others for you. One day I may send you a very special video. This is my ace in the hole.

Oh yeah, I almost forgot. Ms. **(Name omitted),** the woman in Kennedy High School who is in charge of security, was attacked again.

Let's not forget that **(Name omitted),** who is the Dean of students, was also attacked the other day.

Thanks for your help,<br>Zorro

PS
I do not expect you to stop the violence and have all the answers to every problem.
I just want to know why, are these incidents covered up?

*Enclosed, I have a report that was printed on all the (POSITIVE PROGRAMS?) The superintendent has brought to the Paterson, School System. I am sure a copy or a report of all this B S has been brought to your administration.

A note of interest, the superintendents' Paradigm program was a disaster. Just look at the HSPT test results. They are much lower.

The attendance rate of students is not true.
There are two sets of attendance, one that the school has, and the one that the school turns in to Central Office. WHY?
The same goes with suspensions.

When are you going to get wise? I have sent you names, dates, times, place, pictures, reports, etc., etc. how much proof do you need?

The children of Paterson are the ones who are suffering, while the superintendent is getting paid more than you.

Zorro

*Please note I have not included the full report sent to the superintendent. However, I do have it with my records.

**Letter #14**

January 25, 1995

Dear Governor,

Enclosed is a very interesting article. Read it before you go any further.

Did you think I was lying all this time? I'll have you know that **(Name omitted),** who is the Principal at Kennedy High School say's the article is a lie. It's funny, but there isn't a student, parent, or teacher, at Kennedy High School who think it's a lie. I have been writing to you, telling you how bad it is here.

The HSPT results were handed out yesterday. Kennedy High School's grades were terrible. Now is it the teacher's fault, as the superintendent has always said? Or, is he going to be a man and take responsibility for his FAILED PARADIGM PROGRAM, which he said is doing so well?

You have the extremely expensive flier that I sent you that was printed saying how well the PARADIGM PROGRAM is doing. The superintendent had the program dropped two years ago. Now, I have a question for you. What were the reasons for the state takeover in the first place? For all the reasons, the Board of Education of Paterson, N.J. was taken over, the superintendent and his cronies have not changed the situations but made all of them worse. Especially the HSPT results.

However, the superintendent spent more money, and given himself a 49% raise. So where is the savings? They have programs after school and on Saturday where students come to class and are prepared for the HSPT. Then upon completion they are paid for it. Yes, that's right if students do not do their assignments in class and fail, they can sign up for the same class or course and be paid for it. Where is the savings to the people of Paterson, N.J? It is obvious that the superintendent has failed here in Paterson, New Jersey also. Yet he wants his contract extended? Why, so he can take more trips at the expense of the taxpaying people of Paterson, N.J.? What is he doing to help the children?

Monday, you talked about how you have helped the state budget. However, the superintendent can tramp around the world critiquing other country's school systems. As I asked you before, there are no other schools in New Jersey worthwhile critiquing? According to you, New Jersey schools are the best in the Nation. So I ask you again, why does he, go all over the world at the taxpayers of Paterson, N.J. expense? (For example: England and Israel)

Supposedly, he has on file that he resides at the YMCA in Paterson, N.J. Does that mean his wife resides at the YMCA in Paterson, N.J. also? I don't think so. It seems she spends much time in Paterson, N.J. It seems there was a computer course offered after school, at central office, which was instructed by a professor from a local community college. At attendance in this course was his wife. She was a student, and had many conversations with teachers for which this course was offered to.

The point I am again making is, why would he say that he resides at the Paterson, YMCA? What is his wife doing taking a computer course when there are other teachers who wanted to enroll but where told that the course was filled up? His wife has nothing do with the Paterson Education system. However, she is enrolled and attends the second semester part of the computer course that was designed for the teachers of Paterson, N.J. I know for a fact that there are other teachers who wanted to take this course but could not due to the amount already enroll.

The fire alarms where falsely set on Monday and on Tuesday. There was an honors meeting and school council meeting Tuesday night, which erupted into a very heated and mudslinging debate. The worse part of it was that the arguing and fighting was done in front of the students. No, that is on professional and WRONG.

Getting back to the school council there are two of them. One the parents voted on and one that the Board appointed. I hope you can explain to me why the board would do this to the school council? I think you should speak with the parent voted school board. There is too much corruption here. The state operated and appointed Board of Education does not believe in the democratic system because they have much to hide and cover up. That is why they appointed their own school council. What else are they going to steal from the people of Paterson, who pay their salary? You wonder why people don't believe in justice and Government.

Thursday, the principal is going to have a meeting with the teachers on what can be done with the problems that plaque us here in Kennedy High School. After three years she is going to ask questions now? Is it only because of the publicity that the school and its board are getting?

Thursday's afternoon meeting was a good one. There was a list 12 miles long made up by teachers on what and how things should be done to improve the safety and education of our school.

There was a meeting Friday afternoon [about] picking choice people on how to help correct the problems here at Kennedy high School.

The principal **(Name omitted)**, still disagrees that there is a problem here, and that the newspaper article was a lie. However, she is having meetings every day addressing these problems? If there isn't a problem, then why is there so much time being taken having many hours' worth of meetings?

Well, it seems that all the lies and cover ups are coming out now finally.

No disrespect, but to no thanks to you.

Sincerely,
Zorro

**Letter #15**                                                                                                                    February 5, 1995

Dear Governor Whitman,

Enclosed is a copy of a letter I wrote and sent to Mr. Cowen.

Thank you,

ZORRO

..................................................................................................................................................................

Dear Mr. Cowen,

I have tried to call you Friday night about 8:00PM. I left a message with some fellow that ZORRO called. However, the information is this. A student named **(Name omitted)** was sent home because of a large fight. This fight involved many boys who were already on suspension from the last incident when **(Name omitted)** had his head split open.

It seems about 15 to 20 boys attacked a student named **(Name omitted)**, one of whom whose name is **(Name omitted)**. If you check the package that I sent you, **(Name omitted)**, was one of the boys who attacked **(Name omitted)** and was on suspension when this attack occurred. I told you that another fight had broken out where his brother **(Name omitted)**, or his street name Doogie, had his head bashed in with a bat. Well, this is the same incident only with more information to it.

In this incident a boy named Jerry pulled a gun on a student whose name is **(Name omitted)**. When **(Name omitted)** pulled his gun out on **(Name omitted)** another boy whose name is **(Name omitted)**, hit **(Name omitted)** causing **(Name omitted)** to drop the gun.

**(Name omitted)** picked up the gun and ran out of the building. To add to your information, **(Name omitted)** did not belong in the building. **(Name omitted)** had been kicked out of Kennedy High School for some time now. **(Name omitted)** roams these halls here at Kennedy High School almost every day.

QUESTION #1: What did **(Name omitted)** do with that gun?
QUESTION #2: What is going to happen now that **(Name omitted)** has that gun? It's scary.

Before the fight was broken up, a security guard named **(Name omitted)**, held the door open and told **(Name omitted)** to go, get out of here. When more security people arrived, that's when **(Name omitted)** changed her story by saying that **(Name omitted)** was trying to get away.

Help us Mr. Cowen. They cover up everything here.

ZORRO

**TWO NOTES OF INTEREST**:
1. Mr. Cowen was a newspaper reporter
2. In the last 2 letters, a student **(Name omitted)** eventually left John F. Kennedy High School. He ended up in jail for murder. He murdered a Paterson Fireman for piece of jewelry.

**Letter #16**

February 8, 1995
Zorro

Dear Governor Whitman,

    Enclosed is another letter I have written to Mr. Cowen.

Zorro

.................................................................................................................................................

Dear Mr. Cowen,

    Enclosed is an interesting piece of information. Look for the name **(Name omitted)**. You will notice **(Name omitted)** is listed as being on bedside as of 2/2/95.

No sir, this is not true. I spoke with **(Name omitted)** one-day last week, and he said to me that he was kicked out of Kennedy High School. Believe me, **(Name omitted)** was not and still isn't an angel, and it is for the best that he is out of Kennedy.

Now you remember the boy I wrote about **(Name omitted)**, the friend of **(Name omitted)**? I asked **(Name omitted)** where has **(Name omitted)** been? **(Name omitted)** response to me is that **(Name omitted)** was kicked out of Kennedy High School.

Now, I'll get to the point. I have said in many letters in which I have written to Governor Whitman, that there is much falsification of school records, especially enrollment here at Kennedy High School.

Now I have a question for you. Why would **(Name omitted)** be enrolled in a bedside program if he is kicked out of Kennedy?

A possible answer: So they can say we have these many students on enrollment to receive federal funds. This includes bedside. A student on bedside has a teacher sent to tutor them and that teacher is paid $33.00 an hour. The tutoring usually session starts after the regular school day. That tutor makes $33.00 an hour, above their normal salary.
I have another question. Is **(Name omitted)** on bedside?

If he isn't, is there someone receiving this tutoring compensation, and who is this person?

Any way you look at this situation, it is a lie. These types of lies and many others have been going on ever since the superintendent and his entourage have arrived in Paterson, N.J.

Thank you,

ZORRO

P S

About 9:45 today, Wednesday, February 8, 1995 there was another bomb scare that went unannounced.

I also learned today through the Paterson Police Department, that they receive 30 to 40 calls a month here at Kennedy pertaining to bomb scare.

Question:
Why aren't the people inside the school evacuated, or the staff made aware of these situations?

Will they wait till one of these calls is real and some of us are seriously hurt or killed before they take them serious?

I do not like the idea that someone can make a decision concerning my life without my knowledge, especially a place of employment.

What about the LAWS pertaining to the RIGHT TO KNOW or is that only pertaining to chemicals?

ZORRO

**Letter #17**

February 24, 1995
ZORRO

Dear Governor Whitman,
    Enclosed is a copy of a letter and contents that I sent to Mr. Cowen.

Zorro

..................................................................................................................................

    Dear Mr. Cowen,

    Enclosed are some interesting articles.

Also there are two sheets of paper, one yellow the other blue. These two pieces of information were handed out to the students on Thursday, February 23, 1995, during homeroom. They were also in all the teacher's mailbox on that same day.

Notice the date of the meeting. If the students brought these notices home, it didn't even give their parents 3 hours to make arrangements to attend.

I find this ridiculous.

You would think a matter like this; he would want the parents to be in attendance. I cannot help to think that the superintendent does not want a large turnout of concerned parents. This is another way for him

and his entourage to then say the parents just don't care, and he looks good by showing these papers and saying that he had the schools hand them out to the students in their homeroom. We all know how [students lose] things.
The people of Paterson, and especially their children, cannot afford two more years of the superintendent's lies and deteriorating tactics to the Paterson School System.

Zorro

PS
I will have another letter for you with much more information next week.

You did hear about the two teachers who were attacked in Kennedy on Wednesday, February 22, 1995, first thing in the morning?

It will be in the next letter.

**Letter #18**

March 2, 1995

Dear Governor Whitman,

Enclosed is another copy of a letter and information I sent to Mr. Cowen.
How long are you going to wait, until you get rid of this fool? He has done enough damage.

ZORRO

..................................................................................................................................

Dear Mr. Cowen,

I haven't finished my last letter but I was compelled to send you these interesting articles.

Enclosed you will find another interesting piece of information. A notice saying due to budgetary constraints, the state rules regarding transportation for students to and from school will be firmly adhered to. Please read the article about the 8.7-million-dollar surplus.
However, the superintendent, and his wife can gallivant around the world seeking alternative ways of education, at the expense of the people of Paterson, NJ.

You should also be aware that every secretary in Kennedy High School has their own computer. I am not sure about the main office has a computer. Why would a secretary need a computer when a word processor would be more than sufficient? Their forms or reports are not on the computer. Their computers are doing strictly WORD PROCESSING. But, there is no money for educational equipment, or buses for the students?
I want to remind you during the superintendent's first year here in Paterson, he gave the teachers a very bad time with the renewal of their contract, stating that there is no money. But he awards himself and his staff a twelve and one half, to a forty-nine, percent raise.

Mr. Cowen, would you like a forty-nine percent raise?

This was in the one of the local papers three years ago. I think it was in the Star Ledger. When was asked to comment about this raise he was not available, because he and his wife where in LONDON, ENGLAND, seeking alternative ways of education.

This is public knowledge. I wonder how much we are not even aware of.
Now I have a favor to ask of you. One of the articles is from a Boston newspaper; please try to locate which one of the papers printed this. Then run it in your newspaper. Thanks.

Oh yeah, I will try to finish the other letter but please be advised that yesterday there were many fights before the beginning of second period. One was basically a gang fight, and a boy was beaten till unconsciousness. Most of the students thought he was having a seizure. The truth of the matter he wasn't suffering from a seizure, and was thrashing as if he had one, because of the severity of the head injury. You can check with a teacher named Mr. **(Name omitted).** He is a Social Studies teacher.

ENJOY

ZORRO

**Note of interest:** Mr. Cowen was at that time a newspaper reporter for the Record.

**Letter #19**

February 24, 1995

Dear Governor Whitman,

Enclosed is another letter I sent to Mr. Cowen.

Zorro

...............................................................................................................................................

Dear Mr. Cowen,

Just to keep you up to date, I am sure that you are aware that a teacher was attacked here at Kennedy, on Wednesday, Feb 22, 1995, early that morning.
The name of the teacher who was attacked is **(Name omitted),** an English teacher. Another female teacher who went to the aid of the attacked teacher was also injured. The teachers here at Kennedy do not want to be out of their classrooms to monitor the students in the hallways anymore. They're afraid of not only being assaulted, but being alienated by their co-workers, and afraid of losing their career. You would think that the principal would make an announcement to the students and faculty that this type of behavior would not be permitted, and that they, the administration and the board of education, would also press charges against anyone who attacks a teacher.
I would also like to point out that the PEA, as usual, did not defend the rights of the teachers. You would think that the PEA would be upset and voice its outrage that this type of behavior could happen to its members. You would think the PEA would want to make it clear that it is not going to stand for assaults and or severe acts of violence against its members, and demand to know what the school and district are going to do to about the prevention of this type of criminal behavior ever happening again.

Believe it or not **(Name omitted)** is the PEA President, and he is never to be found or makes himself available, for comment on any of the situations that I have written about. The teachers are very displeased with his performance as the President of the PEA, especially with his non supportive roll in all of these teacher crises.

It is like a prison waiting for a riot to erupt every day here in Kennedy High School, knowing that any of us teachers can be attacked at any time and knowing there is no support by administration, and the PEA. I observed an administrator today walking past three students each on a telephone, and about six others standing around waiting for their turn. Now, this administrator looked at them, said nothing, and walked right by them as if nothing was wrong. However, a teacher would be written up if he or she did the same.

First of all, no student is allowed to use the telephones during the school day unless they have a written pass issued by a teacher or an administrator.

Take note when your article first came out. The administration cracked down hard on the lack of discipline. Now your article is like water under a bridge and the students still run this school. I can only think that this administrator did not want a confrontation with these students and may have been afraid for their own safety, so this administrator said nothing to the students on and around the telephones.

We use to have a switch in the security office that turned the telephones off in the morning and would turn them back on at the end of the day. This was so students may call home and make arrangements for their pick up and whatever. Ever since the public telephones' phones were change to another company, they will not allow the switch to be reinstalled.

I understand that the public telephones would be removed if a switch is installed because the phones would not be making enough revenue, and consequently the phones would then be removed. You are aware that most of the prank bomb scares are made here in Kennedy on these public telephones. Please be aware now not only that there is a new company supplying these public telephones phones. There are now more public phones in this building.

Question- Why was the phone company changed in the first place? Maybe, there is a little kick back involved here? What is someone to think when the phones are a problem in the first place, when they are change to another company, no cut-off switch is allowed, also the cost of a phone call is much higher? Now, the teachers and security are made to keep students from using these phones? If you want to see confrontations come in and see what a teacher or a member from security goes through every day, asking these students to hang up and go to their class. You would not believe it.

Mr. Cowen, did you ever feel unsafe when you attended school? What about your teachers, do you think they did? What is going on here? The administration here still tries to keep these incidents hushed up here. When they do come forward with any information, it is so doctored up and thought out, on how and what they are going to say.

There are many incidents when students are caught smoking marijuana in hallways and stairways and nothing is done about it.
Are you aware that there are a few students who have been quite ill and have been hospitalized? These students are threatened to be kicked out of school because of their high rate of absenteeism. Their parents are made to attend a school hearing, and then they are threatened that their son or daughter may be kicked out of school because of their poor attendance.

However, there are many students in Kennedy with 30, 40, and more days out of school because of suspensions. But suspensions are not counted as being absent. WHY? The students who have been ill and hospitalized are usually at their 20-day limit, and have written doctors' notes and proof of being in the hospital. So when a student is suspended, he/she gets a vacation. Ask any teacher how many students deliberately get suspended so they have some free time off. So why would suspension be used as a means of punishment or a deterrent?

These students who are suspended sneak back in school, roam the halls, and cause many problems throughout the day. They sneak in and out of school all day long with many other people who do not attend or belong in school looking for their prey. When and if they are caught they are usually just escorted out of the building, only to find them in the building again. The school threatens to have these people arrested but never follow through with their threats, as they so often do with all their threats. It seems the safety of the students and the faculty is of no importance. This is because they don't want the police involved and have the publicity on what a terrible job they are doing here.

Mr. Cowen, if you are doing any type of investigating? Check out the story of one of our now retired vice principals. His name is Mr. **(Name omitted),** and telephone number is **(# omitted)**. I am sure, after what happened to him, he will give you much information.

If you noticed any problem with students and their test scores, it is always made out to be the teacher's fault and how they are not doing their job properly, according to the superintendent or one of his puppets. But, if memory serves me correctly, the reason for the superintendent and his team of thieves to be here in the Paterson School System, was to change and make things better for the children. They have failed, and did more damage to the school system.

I am sure you are aware of the HSPT scores. They use the teachers as the escape goat continuously. Since the HSPT scores arrived, were made public knowledge on how terrible they were, the English and Math Department are under strict scrutiny. However, when an incident happens in any of the schools or district, why isn't the Principal's and the Board of Education held or made accountable?

It seems the superintendent is not accountable for anything that goes on in the Paterson School System.

P S
In my last letter, I said that the article about the superintendent and his band of thieves awarded themselves a twelve and a half to a forty-nine percent raise was in the Star Ledger. I may be wrong. It very well could be in the Herald News. Anyhow, it was on the front page on one of our local newspapers.

Thank you,

ZORRO
Sorry that it took so long with this letter.

**Letter #20**

March 24, 1995

Dear Governor Whitman,

Here is your copy of a letter that I sent to Mr. Cowen. Enjoy the pictures. I hope our health benefits will cover our health problems that may be related to the asbestos that is still in our school and will be removed during this summer.

Dear Mr. Cowen,
Well, this week there were supposedly some independent monitors investigating how well the state takeover has worked out. None of the teachers said much, because they are all afraid of reprisals, and losing their jobs. A few of the teachers who had talked with me were also skeptical of the monitors

because they did not know if these monitors are really rats looking for the teachers to bury. Nobody trusts anybody here. Everyone actually thinks the other person may be a spy.

Well, other than having many fights throughout the week, Friday was the worse. There were fights all day long starting at 8:30 AM. The fights were as if they were on a time schedule. One especially was when one of the security guards was jumped and beaten.
These poor security guards take a hell of a lot of abuse. They have to continuously watch their backs. These punks are always trying to set them up. Ask them yourself. Ask a specific security guard named **(Name omitted)**. **(Name omitted)** is his nick name. It's short for **(Name omitted)**, his last name.

He's one of the best security guards here at Kennedy. Ask him about the abuse he puts up with, and how many times he had to go to court because of these animals.

Mr. **(Name omitted)** is not the only security guard that has gone to court.

Remember, the first week of April we will be conducting the HSPT. We will now see again, on how well we do real soon.

*April 1, 1995

Remember Mrs. **(Name omitted),** the teacher that was attacked and assaulted here in Kennedy? Well, it seems her husband is Superintendent of Schools in Pequannock, NJ. I wonder if his influence has kept Mrs. **(Name omitted)** from ever returning to Kennedy and that she will be able to collect full disability all through the summer.

If it was anyone else here at Kennedy, we would have to fight and still loose getting our disability rights.

Enclose are pictures taken during the 94/95 school year while asbestos was being removed. At another time early in 1995, asbestos was again being removed and was not properly disposed of as these pictures will show you.

If you check the letters that I sent you where I have written to the Governor, dated on January 3, 1994, it is supposed to be 1995, you will read where I promised to send her pictures about the asbestos. They have finally arrived, and here's yours, enjoy.
A set was sent to the Governor's Office.

Zorro

*April 15, 1995

I noticed the other day in our local newspaper about how the situation of the fire alarms are under control here in Kennedy High School. There was a picture of a young lady at the desk outside in the hallways and the hallways were clear. This was a staged picture. I have been asking the governor to send someone unannounced, or under an alias, or plain clothes, and see what the school is really like, and how the halls are as if there is never a class going on. Nothing has changed here it is just covered up much better.

A disgusted Zorro

**Letter #21**

February 6, 1996

Dear Governor Christie Todd Whitman,

I am writing this letter for many reasons. One is because it has been a while since I have written. I have been holding off because of the many changes inside Kennedy High School and to see and hear what is going on. Well here it is.

Starting in September we have had a complete change of administration within. The change seemed to be long overdue and with many promises in gaining control. It didn't last long.

It seems that Mr. **(Name omitted)** the new principal has the right tools and ideas but is now getting threats and no support from central office, mainly by the superintendent.

There was a report lately in the local newspaper on how Kennedy has suspended many students and Eastside our other High School had (1) suspension for one month and none for the others. How can that be? Now I'll answer my own questions. It is because the superintendent is putting on the squeeze as always. This man is a sneak, liar and had contributed more problems within the district ever since he took over. He is also sending resumes and he definitely wants to keep all of the district problems quiet because he has not helped but hurt the children and the parents of Paterson, NJ.

The superintendent is trying his hardest to cover up the mess that **(Name omitted)** has caused with their term at Kennedy High School. In doing such, he transferred him/her to Central Office for some made up position at the taxpayer's expense. All of the administrators were sent to other schools throughout the district. It wasn't the administrators that caused the problems. It was him/her.

Now the superintendent is doing his most evil of work by making Mr. **(Name omitted)** look as if he is the idiot by making him stop gaining control of the school. I'll be a little more explicit. All measures that Mr. **(Name omitted)** implemented to gain control instill rules and regulations have been halted because of the pressure central office has put on him threatening him with lawsuits, and the removal of his position.

Another very important note of interest, including this letter, I have sent you 21 pieces of correspondence. It has been brought to my attention [that] one of my letters with many photos was intercepted by the superintendent. This was due to my error. It seems for obvious reasons, I do not go to the post office for postage, and because of that I did not put the proper amount of postage on that particular letter.

Now, I sent a copy of all letters and photographs to Mr. Richard Cowen C/O THE RECORD 1350 Route 23, Wayne, NJ 07470, Tel # 201-628-6113. This letter will be dated March 24, 1995. I will be looking for my negatives.

These pictures will be of the removal of asbestos, including the trucks with their Co. name, telephone number, and license plate numbers while school is in session. That's correct. Students and staff were in the building while this went on for quite a while. During this removal the outside uncovered or approved dumpster caught on fire and the school was filled with asbestos smoke. We all enjoyed that odor. Will our insurance coverage take care of our future medical problems because of this incident? After all, I do have the documentation, the superintendent is appointed by the state, and you are the governor now and at that time. What happened to The Right to Know Act?

There are many pieces of collected documentation in which I have not sent and I await [the] appropriate time to come forward with it.

You know this is just like the movies. You know one of those movies where you are disgusting, frustrated and all the officials cover it up with their lies, while innocent and trust worthy people suffer, and the villains just moves on upward and is made a hero.

This week as you are aware of we had police placed in J. F. Kennedy High School. This was an idea to help stop the violence acts and intruders from entering our building. I do understand there will always be people for the police and people against the police. Everyone is in titled to their opinion. Obviously I am for it and was long overdue. However, I believe this is Mr. **(Name omitted)** idea to help gain control and make this school a learning institution again.

I have a strong feeling, again this is just a feeling, and I have nothing to back up my feeling that the superintendent has put a twist to the Police patrolling the school. I understand the police are not to get involved in any situation. Even if there is a gun involved the police have to wait for a call to the police department first before they can respond to the crisis.

Now, I'll go into a little detail. Last week 3 teachers were attacked by students roaming the hall. One teacher was on the second floor, the other two were on the first floor being attacked by the same group of kids who remained roaming the hall. The police and in house security did nothing until one teacher was actually defending himself in the center of the school. Yes, the same group of students in halls causing situations and the police just watched. My question to you is--why are we paying 6 policemen to just hang out? Again the taxpaying people of Paterson get screwed again.

So that is why I think he has put the twist into the situation with the police. I have a strong gut feeling that Mr. **(Name omitted)** wanted and requested the police and probably put the pressure on the superintendent. In turn he changed the rules of engagement. This is another ploy to keep the situations as quiet as possible.
So to sum it up 6 police at $25.00 an hour, 8 hours a day, five days a week, a total cost to the taxpayer $6000.00 a week, nothing has changed and HSPT scores is still low. But he superintendent blames the teachers and everyone else. (**HE TAKES NO RESPONSIBILITY**) Just like with **(Name omitted)** he/she is transferred to a made up position in Central Office and his/her administrators are transferred to other schools, and are made to look and take the blame. Responsibility comes from the top, and that is called leadership. You watch what they try to do with Mr. **(Name omitted)**. They will make him look like a fool to cover up **(Name omitted)** inept term as principal.

Remember the superintendent is supposed to be a resident of Paterson, NJ. Why isn't he? Check his address. I would not live there unless it was my last and only choice, and your too believe that a man whose salary is in excess of $130,000.00 along with his wife would live at the Paterson YMCA on Ward Street?

I would like to know where his next position is going to be. I would have to warn these people on how he raped the children and people of Paterson, along with the state of New Jersey. This man has to be stopped. He is nothing more than a cancer, and must be cut out of the educational process.

You know it wouldn't be so bad if you actually didn't know what has been going on here, but I have been writing to you for years.

Governor, this is going to haunt your political career, because you have done nothing.

ZORRO

In between letters to the Governor, I wrote a couple of letters to the Superintendent.

**Letter "A" (A narrative version)**

April 15, 1996

Dear Superintendent,

Well, I figured it is about time that I write you. You know who I am and I understand you have intercepted one of my letters. That's good. Unfortunately, it was only one of many letters that have I sent, and not just to the Governor.

You are not above the law! You have to abide by the same rules and laws just like the rest of us. It is time to remove yourself from the position as Superintendent of Schools.

For every reason you and your entourage were sent here you have compounded the situations tenfold.

The violence in our school system is atrocious and you deny and lie that this is going on.

How do you sleep at night? How do you keep the violence, especially when teachers are beaten up, out of the newspapers? Why don't you inform the public when a teacher is beaten or threatened by a student and if they decided to press charges how they will be threatened with the possibilities of losing their job? How do you feel when your employees are being mistreated by students?

Why is everything hushed up? Who are we protecting YOU? We should have had the police in Kennedy High School a long time ago. In fact, we should have more and let them do their job. This school is out of control because you won't let the principal take control of his school.

Now you want to lay off teachers because of the budget? How do you justify this when there are double the numbers of employee's at central office since you have taken over as chief? You had to get another building on 14th Ave!

You must be very proud of your accomplishments here in Paterson. Obviously, the record of graduating students each year reflects your greatest accomplishments. By the way, how many seniors do we start out with in September, compared to the amount that graduates?

Our children that enter into the high schools are no way ready to be here. The majority cannot even add and subtract and barely read and write. Then, the high schools are held responsible for the students to pass the HSPT? If that is the case than why bother having students go to school to 8th grade? After all, when they get to high school they have to double and triple up on all their academics in order for them to possibly be prepared to pass the HSPT.

How about your big brainstorm of instituting the 9 period school day? But the students do not have to attend. Actually the only people who have to stay later in the day is the staff, because there is no actual increase of the student school day.

I await your resignation.
ZORRO

**Letter "B" (A narrative version)**

June 10, 1996

Dear Superintendent,

Congratulations on the good news of only 22 eighth grade students throughout the entire district of Paterson, passing the EWT.    You must be proud.

Well, at least you are consistent.

It is time long overdue for you to leave Paterson, NJ.


ZORRO

## CONTINUATION OF LETTERS TO THE GOVERNOR

**Letter #22**

June 5, 1996

Dear Governor Christie Todd Whitman,

It has been a while and if you haven't figured it out yet, NOTHING has changed.
Did you know in all of the eighth grade classes in all of the schools here in Paterson only **22** students passed the EWT? I further understand that there are approximately 2000 eighth graders that are to graduate this year.

Not bad after 6 years under the Bull S---- of this superintendent's control? We have gotten worse here no thanks to the state takeover and the best part I do not see it ever getting better because of the irrefutable damage that has been inflicted to our school's system by the superintendent and his pack of liars and embezzlers.

I have read a copy, briefly, and only a few were made (42) on the, "Paterson Public School District 1995 - 2000 Strategic Plan for the Systemic Improvement of Education," with Dr. Leo Klagholz and the superintendents' name on the front cover. If you have a problem identifying this literature it also has a circle in the middle of the page saying, "ALL CHILDREN CAN LEARN.

Read page 32, there are many lies on that page alone, and if all children can learn then why can only **22** eighth graders pass the EWT? Now we can leave it up to the high schools to prepare these students in four years what they should have learned in the past 8 years, plus their High School requirements.

Now what will happen when they do not pass the HSPT? Is that the high school teacher's fault?

Or, is it that the superintendent wants to lie some more and tell everybody how wonderful things are here in Paterson and cover up his mess so that it doesn't ruin his resume for his next position, and just keep passing the students on through the system?

Or, is this a master plan for you to make the public school systems look bad and make the superintendent your fall guy? Nothing would surprise me anymore. You are all a bunch of crooks. Meanwhile the children here in Paterson are not getting their proper education and the taxpayers are still paying $9,000.00 plus for each student's education yearly. I repeat, or is this a part of your master plan to make the public school systems look as if they cannot do their job?

I hope you enjoy this little bit of information. I have much more that I will use at the appropriate time.

I hope you sleep well knowing that people and **CHILDREN** of Paterson are not getting their fair share when it comes to the right of obtaining a proper education, but I guess it is more important that we protect the superintendents' reputation, and we all know what that is.

ZORRO

**Letter #23**

January 22, 1997

Dear Governor Whitman,

I decided to wait out this school year to see if there were going to be any changes.
I was correct. There was. It is worse. Actually it is horrible here.
There is no sense of order here and the students rule this building, just ask the Paterson, Police Department.
The Star Ledger gives the superintendent high marks for his work.
What work, nothing has improved, unless you give marks for lies and deceit?
Have you seen the HSPT scores yet? I have, and they are the terrible.
However, the Star Ledger states "they are a little lower than five years ago."
The scores have been in a steady decline ever since the rein of the superintendent and his entourage has taken charge six (6) years ago.

The only change is there are more bosses than Indians which was one of the reasons for a state takeover. The state takeover board is more top heavy than ever. It is approximately 150 personnel higher than before the state takeover.

The Star Ledger expresses how nice Eastside is, ever since they took down the fence that went around the building. Not to mention a drunk was killed because he fell asleep underneath a parked car in Eastside's parking lot when a teacher ran over him.

But then again what does the superintendent care? He has a personal chauffeur with a beeper and cell phone, along with his cell phone and beeper all at the people of Paterson's expense. Why?

I cannot see any reason or rationale for him or anyone in the district having a cellular phone that is paid with district funds? This is an added and unnecessary expense. These phones are nothing more than an unnecessary luxury.

Let's get our priorities straight. What do the children of Paterson, NJ, need in order to be successfully prepared for the future? It is definitely not the superintendent having a chauffeur and a cellular phone.
He is not the only one in the district with an expense paid cell phone and beeper.
Let's not forget the new vans the district bought and for what reason so their drivers can take them home, use them for their personal use, such as to drop their children off at school or go shopping?

If there were an accident, who would pay for the children's medical expense? And what if there was a lawsuit involved?

The bottom line is the people and children of Paterson keep getting screwed while these idiots live a luxurious life and hold a position with no responsibility and feed the public with lies.

# Ruining a Nation and Nobody Cares — Lee McNulty

We all know that it was supposed to be **(Name omitted)**, or **(Name omitted)** that were to be the Superintendent and for some reason or another **(Name omitted)** came into the picture. Politics has no place in the public school system.

We all have seen what politics and government has done for the people and children of Paterson, NJ.

NO CHANGE / NO RESULTS / NO IMPROVEMENT / COST MORE

Did you know that the superintendent supposedly (rumored) had sent resumes and filled out applications all throughout the country looking for employment immediately after he was assigned the position of Superintendent of Public Schools here in Paterson, NJ?
I would imagine he realized that [he'd] better keep his options open and be readily available to move again, all because of his wonderful track record of successes in Rochester and Boston.

One place in particular was Detroit.

How can a superintendent of school be loyal to the people and their children of Paterson, NJ, when he still does not live in the city of Paterson?

Yet the Star Ledger says he is doing a great job.

He is still implementing the paradigm program that has been a disaster to this district. However, to cover up this program there is no name for it and it is still forced up on the children.

You would think it would be obvious after six years of doubling up on math, reading, and writing, with no improvement of test scores, that there should be some other alternative plan for a solution.

Even the new so-called curriculums are nothing more than plagiarism. They are nothing more than taking exact information from a book or some other school's curriculum and copied. These curriculums are not meeting the needs of our students. How can they when you copy everything word for word?

Curriculums must be tailored made so they fit and are properly utilized for the effective teaching of our students of Paterson, NJ.

Again nothing but lies and deceit.
He is deliberately doing away with the Arts, Fine Arts and Music such as Music, Industrial art, Art, Chorus, and Marching Band, everything that a child should be exposed to and maybe be the difference of coming to and participating with school or not.
Why, would anyone want to go to school just to do READING, WRITING and ARITHMETIC?

I surely would not. Would you?

Ask the superintendent, how much is spent on coffee and donuts when they have conferences and meetings.

They have spent thousands for their convenience and enjoyment, all from the hard work and expense from the citizens of NJ, and people and children of Paterson, NJ.

This is a crime in itself-spending this amount of money while our students are so far behind in technological advantages and do not even have soap or paper towels in Kennedy High School. This is not including having most boys' and girls' rooms locked and the one or two that are opened in the entire building are disgusting. I would rather use the facilities in the Port Authority of NY.

Check and see that they have falsified the records on building reports.

I happen to know the person who did the inspection of the building here at John F. Kennedy only to be told to change the report because of the problems they do not want reported, such as locked doors and bathrooms.

He did it but refused to put his name in the report, because he refused to be part of a lie and become a scapegoat for the future.
He has copies of the original and addendum report.

This man is extremely honest and has much pride in himself. As long as I have known him, he has never lied and refuses to be part of a lie. He is sort of like a John Wayne type of character but is for real.

There are almost three thousand students here at Kennedy and only one boys' room and girl's room is opened for their utilization.

Some classes and classrooms are without books or even heat, and at this time of the year it is unbearable and the classrooms are like freezers where the students are nothing more than contained for 40 minutes.

This is state run education, at its best.
This is what I have been telling you about the falsification of vandalism records.
The boys' and girls' facilities are closed and locked because they have been destroyed.

Do you check the books to see where the money is going? Or is government so corrupt that it steals from their own children and their future?

All of this is going on while the test scores, discipline, and falsification of all records are being ignored.

Is this not the reason the state took over the district in the first place?

Who takes over the state when they fail and compound all the problems by 300%?

Then you have the nerve to talk about how much you saved the people of NJ. What happens when these children grow up to be responsible adults?
Most of them will either be on WELFARE, or in JAIL, only to be so-called rehabilitated again, and again at the expense of the hard working taxpayers, or they will end up dead because some police officer did their job because he/she was committing a crime and then the community starts rioting. So who saved them?

Did you know that back in October, after superintendent returned from his threatening meeting in Trenton, he in turned threatened all the principals?

He implements the plans, the programs that fail, and he wants to hold the principals responsible for following his orders.

This is just like the Vietnam War. No one is held responsible or accountable while others cannot or will not make a decisive decision. Remember, William Calley and the massacre? He followed orders and was

punished. I thought that is why we have students study history? I thought it was so we teach our children and students not to make the same mistakes again and learn from the past.
It seems the superintendent is the Teflon Don, and nothing sticks to him.

Obviously, his reputation didn't stick. Like Rochester, New York, Boston and Massachusetts where he left only to be acquired and hired by New Jersey?

What does this say about how our Government and how they care about its people and voters? It's nice way to say thanks.

On January 17, Mr. **(Name omitted)** had 3 of his computers vandalized by 5 students who refused to do their work and felt they should deliberately shut of the power to his room while he was working with two students. One computer was a newly purchased Gateway computer became jammed and locked between programs with hours of work lost which had to be reinstalled.

Then there were two other computers which he and two students were working on which that the college of NJIT had donated to Kennedy High School that also became inoperable and jammed which vital information was lost.

That does not include the hard work these two students lost on their personal floppy disks because of this deliberate act.

Only two weeks before Mr. **(Name omitted)** had all the computers reinstalled with hard drives.

They were also installed with programs to make the students work easier, only to be deliberately erases and destroyed.

Mr. **(Name omitted)** is a large and strong man however, you can see he was quite upset because he knows nothing will be done about the act of vandalism and he is afraid that this will only be done again. Mr. **(Name omitted)** has worked many long hours late into the evening after school preparing and setting up this program with NJIT. To only have his hard dedicated work destroyed, and for an administration not to back him up and do anything about it.

He said, "I wouldn't mind if I was like other teachers, but I really care, and love my work, but not to have all my work destroyed and to have nothing done about this behavior."

You can hear it in his voice that he was still quite upset and disappointed.
He just looked up at me and said, "What am I doing here?"

I replied back to him, "What about the two students you were working with?"

He said yeah, then started to smile then said thanks, but, it's still not fair for the good students who constantly get pushed a back and side because of the bad ones.
He said the same thing I have been saying all along, "We spend too much time on the disciplinary problems and not enough on the good students."

After about 3 to 4 hours of work Mr. **(Name omitted),** did finally fix and restore all the information and repaired the damage to the computers, but was still upset and disgusted.

This type of behavior goes on all of the time and is covered up and the teachers are threatened not to even discuss these problems amongst themselves or else they will be fired.

Those are the exact words that came out of the mouth of the principal of Kennedy High School.
That's only what goes on here and this is very large district.
Check on a family whose children were jumped and beaten up and had their legs broken from school #7.
The mother wanted books so she can teach her children at home.

The district obliged but when the case was thrown out of court because the students were all young juveniles they ordered this family to return the books and send her children back to school.
She is afraid for her children's safety. She reported that one of the juveniles even approached her and told her that her children are going to be hit, but the police and district are not helping her.
Our schools are supposed to be a part of the community and help parents.

Not here in Paterson, and her children will eventually become a statistic.
At Kennedy High School the students come and go to school and class as they please.

I have students who have been late to school over 40 times and nothing has been done other a notation on the tardy referral saying, "I spoke with him/her" and date it.

That's after three to four weeks after I submitted the paperwork. That's not even considering the cuts.

Some kids are in the halls all day. I mean it, all day long, walking the halls, and harassing teachers who are trying to conduct class and when these students are told to leave or disburse they end up cursing and threatening the teacher and giving them nothing but a bad time and try with all their power to provoke them into a confrontation.

The security in this building is a joke. They do nothing and actually play along with the kids and help cause problems.

I don't know if you heard about it but a couple of our security guards have been terminated because of rape charges.

A couple of school security personnel teamed up against a couple of the female students. See if you find that in any school record?

We have security in our building, but this building is not secure.

When they do approach students for an infraction, they are in turned assaulted, cussed out and or verbally abused, only for the school's administration not to back them up.

What do we expect from them? They only make $5.00 or $6.00 dollars an hour.

The police are told NOT to take part in anything here at Kennedy, unless it gets so out of control and the administration summons them.

We have six (6) cops here every day, all day, receiving premium overtime pay all at the taxpayer's expense and are not allowed to perform their job, which is to Serve and Protect.

If these students acted up outside of school environment, they would be immediately arrested. But because they are in school it's accepted?
Something is very wrong here, and with the system.

Mr. **(Name omitted)** is a teacher here at Kennedy High School and runs the early morning detention for school as part of his responsibilities. He has informed me that the students do not show up and the administration refuses to do anything about it.

When he comes across some of these students they reply I don't have to show up and what are you going to do about it? They're right. Nothing is going to be done about anything here.

There are students in the halls all day long, and you wouldn't believe school was in session or any type of class is being conducted.

This place is filled with Graffiti and to think this building was entirely repainted just two years ago. If their parents do not teach these students right from wrong, you would think that the public school system would and should be instilling these values into these students.

It seems we are only reinforcing and encouraging this type of behavior here at Kennedy High School.

I am sorry Governor, I strongly feel this is all happening because superintendent knows he has a bad track record and wants to have everything hushed and covered up for his protection.

Call him up and ask for any type of record.     They won't have any.

This is the worse I have ever seen here at Kennedy High School.

Make a surprise visit.

Sincerely,

Zorro

**Letter #24**

March 4, 1997

Dear Governor Whitman,

Well, I hope it was you who put the pressure on getting the boys' and girls' rooms opened, cleaned, and repaired.

I have never seen such chaos, scenes of extreme frantic and fast response and results, on getting them cleaned, painted, repaired, and in proper working order. There had to be many man hours of overtime spent by having all those people working over the week end getting the job done.

Who pays for this? Could it be the taxpayers again?
The taxpayer always pays, yet no one is responsible or held responsible for allowing this problem to happen after all, the entire building was only painted three years ago.

However, there is a neat little twist to this story.

Only two of each facility will be opened. Two boys and two girls' rooms. I guess it's because it is too expensive to have security guards standing guard in all of them. Yes, that's correct, we now have security guards standing guard in the boys' and girls' rooms. WHY? I am sure the taxpayers of Passaic County would also like to know why?

If students were not permitted to roam the building at will, this school would not have all this vandalism and discipline problems. That doesn't matter because administration does not turn in the violence and vandalism reports. Remember nothing goes wrong in the big city. Everything is under control as long as nobody knows. That is the superintendent's policy. It was never like that before he came here.

Yes, there has always been problems but not like it is today. These problems have escalated 100%year to year since he has been in charge. Which makes it over 600%? That's consistency and progress.

This is what I have been telling you for years. The discipline in this school and district is horrible. If you don't believe me, ask any teacher, student, janitor, security guard, secretary, social worker, the school base director and staff, and the 6 uniformed Paterson Police that stand in here every day collecting premium overtime and are not allowed to fulfill their responsibilities and duty to serve and to protect. I was told by many officers that they are not to do anything unless it is absolutely necessary. They are here because it is so bad, but it has to be basically an uncontrollable riot before they are authorized to take control or action in these situations. It's a riot here every day. The students rule and run the building. The teachers and staff are nothing more than punching bags, with no backing from administration, just their threats of losing their position if they talk.

The administration spent thousands of dollars on equipment and man hours on to print up picture IDs. All students were directed to wear them OR ELSE. Administration was proud of the list of possible alternatives that would be implemented if a student does not wear his or her ID.
Well, the administration really kept their promise. Come on down, see how well the money was spent. The students do not wear them. However, the staff does.
One of the reasons IDs were important was to easily track outsiders coming into the building.

In other words, if someone does not have an ID they do not belong in the building and would be arrested.

Well, I am sure you can figure it out now, that it isn't working. The administration is not backing the teachers up who try to enforce the rules and laws, to the students who do not wear IDs. So now we still have many, many trespassers, and all the equipment and work to make these IDs were nothing more than a waste of money and all at the expense of the taxpayers.

We have to get control of the schools before we can implement any programs to see any type of improvement in test scores, and an increase of graduating students. This place is no more than a hang out and the students can do whatever they want.

I'm letting you know this is all going to fall on your head. This is election year; I personally believe you are doing an outstanding job as Governor.
However, you are ignoring my call for help, for the people of Paterson, NJ.

When it comes to education you stink. I know this first hand, because I am on the front lines. You send your children to private school. As all you politicians do. Then you all say you know we have to improve our educational system. How are you going to do that if you allow administrators and Superintendents are not held responsible? That is why the state has taken over the District of Paterson, NJ, in the first place.

Well, I sure hope it was you who had something to do with the painting and repairs of the boys' and girls' facilities. I hope you see as I have said many times before how records are constantly being falsified. I would never send my children to this school or any school that has such behavioral, and severe disciplinary problems, such as John F. Kennedy High School, in Paterson, NJ, which is a state operated school district that appointed the superintendent.

All this school and district does is lie, falsify records, and waste money. What has it done to improve the quality of life and education for our students and their parents?

We are allowing, encouraging, and instilling improper behavior and values.

I truly believe this would never be allowed in a white school and district.

Maybe the taxpayers can spend more money later with rehabilitation when many of these students are on welfare, in jail, or both, because this state operated district which is controlled by the superintendent did not do his job and was not made accountable.

One more quick note: I am sure you are aware that the superintendent extended the school day to ten periods. This is another piece of fancy foot work. The students are not here for ten periods, just the teachers and staff. The students have an 8 period day.

You have to get off your ass and make a surprise unannounced visit and see this school in action. Then after you have been in the building for 15 minutes, let the administration know you are here. You *cannot* let anyone know that you are coming to the district. You cannot [let] the superintendent [know], [or give] any type of warning. If you can't go, send someone. But you cannot tell anyone.
I can't be lying, because I have spent too much time writing these 24 letters to you, the newspapers, and the superintendent, which is an out of pocket expense to me, not to mention my time.

The only crime I am guilty of; is persistence.

Zorro

**Letter #25**

July 8, 1998

Dear Governor Christie Todd Whitman,

It has been a long time since I have written you last.

Well you sent us another lame duck.
Or is this part of our government's plan to keep inner city kids DUMB?

Enclosed is a copy of a letter I sent to the superintendent.

You should be ashamed of yourself.     The state takeover has done NOTHING here to help us.
There are no rules and you abide NO LAWS with no one held accountable.
Yet you want to place the blame on the teachers.

Why don't you come here and work for a year without your security personnel and see if you feel safe?

Better yet, send your children here for an education.     Oh boy will they be educated real fast.

They, like you, would not believe that this behavior IS ALLOWED to go on in a SCHOOL.

Shame on you,

ZORRO

Ladies & gentlemen, just reading the above letters that I written and sent to Governor Whitman, would you send your children here?
My letters to Governor Whitman ended in 1998.There were a total of 25
I started documenting, journaling and ultimately writing this book July of 2012.
You haven't read anything yet. There are 14 more years to come.

Next, are two letters I sent to the Superintendent starting June of 1998.

**Letter #1 (A narrative version)**
June 8, 1998

Dear Superintendent,

Why is our library always closed?     In the last 5 weeks it has been open approximately 2 days.
The library is always closed for some type of meeting, party, quest, or whatever.

What about the most important reason for having a library?
Our students [seek to] gather, and compile information.
Never mind the needed practice in learning how to obtain information through the use of a library.

All other non-related activity should be conducted in a room that was built like an apartment which is located on the third floor. Or on the first floor room which was converted like a living room for banquets and meetings. Then there is the auditorium and principal's conference room.
No, we will just keep closing our school library depriving our students of access.

Why is our library not open before school?     Why is our library not open after school?

Why is there a rule for not wearing hats?
When students still wear them and give teachers and security, a horrible time when they attempt to perform their duties [and] ask students to remove them. However, administration puts the blame on the teachers, and they themselves walk the halls and do nothing and do ask, remove students that wear hats.

Why are students permitted to come in school with radios, beepers, cellular phones, toys, ski goggles, inappropriate attire (with vulgar or drug messages on them), tank tops, skirts so short it is impossible [to sit] without exposing oneself up to their trachea? Why have a dress code if it's not going to be enforced?

Why are students still on roll with 30, 40, 60, plus days of absences?
What about freshman with 20, 30 40 + days out? What happened to truancy?
What happened to having parents being held responsible?
Why are suspension days not counted towards attendance?
Why are students allowed to threaten, attack, and [beat] teachers, along with all incidents constantly covered and hushed up or to be later told that this has never happened?

Why do we have police in the building receiving overtime pay at the expense of the taxpayers when they are not allowed to perform their duties which is to serve and PROTECT?
The actions of many of these students if were carried out outside of school would be arrested. Even the very police in our building are disgusted on what is allowed to go in a place of EDUCATION.
Don't believe me, ask the police yourself.

Are we preparing our students for the next step in education to be productive members of society?
Or are we preparing them for the next institution (penal), where the process of rehabilitating and education starts all over again at the expense of the hardworking, law abiding taxpayer?
Speaking of expense; at over $9000.00 a year, which is allotted for each student towards an education and just using the number 10 (as for ten years) for easy math, equals over $90,000.00 per student.

What does the taxpayers and society have to show for this money?
Why is there a rule that NO STUDENT will be allowed to enter the building without their ID card?
Why there is a rule that the ID card must be visible at ALL times?
This is a reason why so many non-students and suspended students enter the building throughout the day, accost students and teachers, start fires, pull fire alarms, steal many items from our school, vandalize school and personal property and let's not forget graffiti.

I ask you again why, was the money wasted to purchase, make, issue ID cards, at another expense to the taxpayers if students are not made to wear them?

Why are teachers [threatening] threaten by the principal because of students who are known story fabricators and makes an accusation that he/she was sexually assaulted and says they report it to the teacher who did not report the incident, only for the principal to take the word of those students and now the problems start occurring to those teachers.
If, there was such a problem, then I ask you WHY, wasn't DYFS immediately notified?
Why wasn't your office notified?
Why wasn't an incident report filed again?
Why was the incident hushed up?
Why there are so many fires in are building in such places like the bathrooms, stairwells, and basement?
Why are not students and staff evacuated?
Why are not students and staff notified of these fires?
Why isn't the fire department called in?
Are our administrators trained in firefighting and fire prevention?
The only fire drills we have are when there is a bomb threat or a teacher calls in the fire.
There are never fire drills.
However, when the fire alarms are deliberately pulled the administration will try to cover it up by calling the fire department saying it is drill.

Why are students allowed to have 15, 20, 30 plus tardiness and only end up with a warning?

Homeroom is after first period, which is at 9:00AM and student's amber in from the streets while announcements are being made.
Let's not forget while students are supposed to be in homeroom, many of them are at the candy and soda machine and when approached by security or a teacher doing their duty and are trying to move students along only end up being yelled and cursed at, threatened, and basically being ignored, while administration walks by as if nothing is happening.

Why is eating and drinking permitted during class? I am not talking about candy and gum. I mean large sandwiches, McDonalds and Burger King, bottles of assorted drinks. If teachers say something to them they are met with a barrage of insults and threats.

The teacher is only as strong as the administration that will back them up by enforcing the rules. Why should a teacher stand in a hallway between classes, keeping students moving, off the pay phones, away from the candy and soda machines, if all the teacher is going to get is abuse, threatened and or beaten up?

Meanwhile, administration ignores these situations and when an incident does occur it is the teacher who is scolded and as usual nothing happens to the students. Other students see this and now they follow and are going to have fun, all at the teacher's expense. However, if a teacher does write an incident up NOTHING is done about it especially if the student is an athlete.
Speaking of our athletic department, WHY are students allowed to participate and play in sports or games while they are failing, on suspension, or did not attend school that day?

While students are suspended why are they permitted to roam the building?
Why are students awarded detention, while many do not attend and NOTHING is done about it?
Whatever happened to the education of following rules, regulations, and being responsible?
When a teacher is accosted why doesn't the principal call them to see how they are or how they feel?
Then when that teacher fills out a report the principal who wasn't even in the building at the time calls the teacher a liar.
Now weeks later that very same student accosts another teacher and the incident is all covered up again.

By the way the name of that student is **(Name omitted)**. His punishment for not doing anything wrong is not allowed to participate in the graduation ceremony.

Why are students allowed to roam the building all day long? Walk into classrooms they do not belong in, disrupt the class, insult and threaten the teacher, leave, only to do the same to another teacher and class?

Why are students not disciplined for fighting? Standard practice was, you fight, [you get an] automatic 10 days' suspension. Why aren't they arrested? If they fought in a mall they would be arrested?

Is school a place where anything goes?   Are the common laws not applicable here?
Why don't students carry books to class?  Why don't they take books home?
Why don't they do homework?

A good [student] who makes a mistake the administration really comes down on and is usually thrown out of school. While the enormous number of repeat offenders with horrible grade, attitudes, and attendance remain in the building. Something is extremely wrong here.

Teachers are strongly recommended to pass students for the simple reason; the administration does not want to have too many failures. So the teacher will pass them or else they may get a poor evaluation, a reprimand, not recommended for increment, not recommended for a summer school position or worse. So what choice does that teacher have? Wonder why students cannot pass the EWT and when they get to high school the HSPT.

Students are not prepared and are just pushed through the system.

However, we have to have all these meeting, in services, evaluation teams from all over researching the problem when the problem is really right here at home with the administration and parents.

We have a newly appointed teacher here at Kennedy High School. His name is Mr. **(Name omitted)**, who is extremely upset and disenchanted with what has been allowed to go on, the lack of support and discipline that he is seriously contemplating about leaving and getting out of the teaching profession.
Is there a new standard of the English Language?
It seems the only sound you hear in the hallway among all the yelling, screaming, shouting, is FUCK, FUCK YOU, and MOTHER FUCKER along with many other [choices] but inappropriate vocabulary.

It is constantly conveyed to the teachers, security, and to administrators and as usual nothing is done about it. This is NOT acceptable behavior by any standard.
So, what the hell are we teaching? It sure as hell is not values, and respect.
Speaking of teaching the only thing that is taught here is to prepare students for the HSPT.
What happened to the 9 years of education prior to high school?

Ask any student to read a ruler, just in 1/8ths. You will cry once you see the results.

However, the teacher is responsible no matter what happens in the classroom.
A teacher here at Kennedy High School is all alone. He or she has no support by the administration, who are all looking towards their next position and want to keep everything quiet so nothing interferes with getting their next position and or assignment. A teacher doesn't even get support with one and other because they all fear for their position.
EXAMPLE: MR. (OMITTED) and (OMITTED) VS (NAME OMITTED a student)

The people outside of education wonder why a teacher snaps. How can a person with morals and an education be expected to be cursed at, threatened[?] Then told by this punk that they will get their daughters, sons, and wife? Along with threats of having their house, and car vandalized.
This goes on daily and we wonder why teachers eventually get fed up and unfortunately snap, then say something back or finally smacking one of these future prison inmates.

That's what this school is, nothing more than a place where many of our students learn and have reinforced the prison mentality.
The other evening, I was watching a program on the USS Indianapolis; the ship that brought over the nuclear device during WWII and was sunk by a Japanese submarine. The point I am trying to make is that the captain was held responsible no matter what happened. It was his ship and he alone was responsible for the ship and crew and had to answer to the authorities.

Why aren't principals held responsible for what goes on and happens in the building?
It's the principal who sets the tone for the building.
If you think I am making any of this up, come on in unannounced, especially during schedule homeroom and lunch periods.

I have been writing letters to everyone asking for help for years now.
These letters were never written for teacher's benefit, other than to have a place where they are allowed to do their work and in a safe environment.

I want to make a change so we can help, prepare, guide, assist, and educate, our students and their parents in the way public schools where originally designed.

I have seen too many of students lose out because they were not properly prepared. All because teachers have to take time away from the good students to spend more and more time on discipline with the same students every day causing the same problems.
This is not a school. This is a disgusting place where students can do whatever they want, whenever they want, knowing full well nothing is going to happen to them.
A school should be a place with set standards and once these standards are met, they should be raised.
It seems all we have done is lowered standards yearly.

Most parents work and school is supposed to be a place where students are safe, receiving a proper education, knowing that they are in reliable, trustworthy, and conscientious hands of a well-disciplined environment along with a competent staff and administration.
Let's be realistic, if the educational process is so safe and reliable, then why don't the local politicians send their children here? I can't blame them. I wouldn't send my children here!

Why are students who refuse to take a final exam allowed to pass the course?
If students do not have to take a final exam, then why do we have to administer them?
There is a saying, "If we save just one kid then we have done our job." No child should ever be lost.
Every child should and must be educated. The educational process is supposed to help restore, invoke, and educate our students not just in academia but in being a good, honest hard working, on time, responsible, dependable, and positive thinking person that will be a successful part of society not only for today, but for tomorrow as well as in the future. That to me is a normal society.

The students we are sending out in the world after graduation are not even close to [meeting] most if any of the above standards.

However, you want to hold the teachers responsible for all of the student's short comings.
This lies solely with the parents, with reinforcement of a GOOD EDUCATION.
If parents have discipline, then their children will have discipline.
If a parent is unruly and undisciplined themselves, then we have to get those parents disciplined and to follow and obey the rules of a normal society.
Why aren't parents who have these behavioral problem students, not ordered by a judge to escort, follow, and stay in each class with these students?
You will see how fast the parent will obtain control of that child.

The embarrassment should be enough of a deterrent for other students not to become a future behavioral problem. Many of parents are worse than the kids. A little embarrassment many be beneficial to both in the long run.

If the parent (legal guardian) refuses to follow with the judge's ruling, then put both into the system (jail). That's where people who do not follow rules and laws end up anyway.

Then our discipline problems here at Kennedy High School should be under control.

That's only if the administration finally takes charge and follows all of the rules of discipline which they themselves have written.
Who runs this school? The administration or the lawless students!

ZORRO

**Letter #2 (Narrative version)**

September 1, 1999

Dear Superintendent,

**Did you know;**
**(Name omitted)** is always arresting someone in our school. He has said to me that he told **(Name omitted)** many times that he should be doing his job and that he better start fast, because there is no discipline here.

**1/4/99,** fire alarm was falsely pulled on the first day back to school from Christmas vacation. Mr. **(Name omitted)** was irate and let everyone know how irate he was over the PA. Then the hallways were a disaster because the students rebelled to the announcement. But nothing was done.

Whatever happened to the administrators having hallway sweeps? You would never know this was a school when you have the hallways filled all day long as if it was a mall.

**1/6/99, (Name omitted)** was attacked by a student with a knife. I have the news article.
But you choose to suspend **(Name omitted).**
Why should have **(Name omitted)** been placed in that type of situation?
What is it going to take before you people do your jobs, wait until someone is killed?

**1/7/99,** fire alarms were falsely pulled again. Seems that the students from auto-shop pulled it (Basement) because there was an announcement made over the PA by Mr. **(Name omitted)** VP for their following students to go to the principal's conference room or be suspended. I think Mr. **(Name omitted)** was out of the building? However, that should be easy enough to verify.

The same day 1/7/99, all because of the fire alarm being was falsely pulled again; Mr. **(Name omitted)** the English Department Head, was struck (by a car) by a student who would refused to stop driving out of the parking lot while students were all out during the evacuation. So the students decided to run him over. Mr. **(Name omitted)** was forced to get out of the way or be killed. Nothing was done about that.

**Same day,** 2 students were arrested for stealing a car out of the parking lot. Coincidence?
Can be verified with the police records.

Parents think that their children are safe. However, they are not aware of the truth and the sad thing about the whole mess is this district is a STATE OPERATED DISTRICT. That means the state controls ALL of the records and everything that goes on. Basically, it is dirty politics at the expense of the taxpayers, teachers' well-being and safety, and the lives of the children and their education.

In fact, wasn't there a woman teacher attacked at Eastside?

Mr. **(Name omitted)** was attacked by two female students who were involved in a fight one on one. A female student was either thrown down or knocked down the stairs when the crowd followed the fight.

**Saturday, January 31, 1999, (Name omitted a student)** wanted to come into school through the front door. The woman security guard told him that he will have to go around the building. **(Name omitted)**

kicked in the glass on the front door. A teacher insisted that the security guard call the police. The same security guard told that teacher that she told Mr. **(Name omitted)**. That same teacher repeated his/herself and said that she should have not bothered with Mr. **(Name omitted)** and that is why we have security in the building and to call the police now. She then replied that she will have to call her supervisor because she does not know what to do? Everything was repeated again and again. A little while later Mr. **(Name omitted)** comes into the building and **(Name omitted)** (head of custodian) hands Mr. **(Name omitted)** the incident report of what has happened involving **(Name omitted)**.

Now today is Tuesday, I am in the cafeteria lunch line, and who do I see, **(Name omitted) that very same student)**. Obviously NOTHING was done about it. Why, BECAUSE, he is a basketball player? So who pays for the broken door and window? Where is the vandalism report and where is the lesson for the other students to follow?

February, back to school night a fight breaks out with 3 students in center hallway. Parents and visitors cannot believe what is going on. One security guard finally made themselves available, but nothing was done. Just more arguing, cursing and screaming all at the top of their lungs. Real impressive to the parents and visitors. No one was arrested. No one was escorted out of the building. Just pushed them along as if nothing happened. One mother said out loud so everyone could hear that she fears for her daughter's life.

I HAVE THAT PARENT AND STUDENTS NAME FOR MY RECORDS.

**NOTE OF INTEREST:**
**April 6 through 8th** was HSPT and testing for all students. However, the week before and during this testing week no disciplinary actions will be taken because the administration does not want students out from testing. The students know this and they are acting up even more.
Not only do they get away with acting up, they are rewarded if they passed the test that they are supposed to take. They get to go to Liberty Science Fair, skating, and movies. Students were even paid at one time to take classes during the summer which is geared directly and specifically to take the HSPT.

Here's another joke--students can cut 5 classes then they are charged with a day of absenteeism. However, if they are suspended for 10 days those days do not count. So, it basically tells students it is ok to cut 4 classes and nothing will happen to you. I have the documentation when it comes to absenteeism, suspension, cuts, and tardiness. That is why we have students with 40, 50, 60, and even 70 plus days out and they do not count towards their attendance, because they are suspension days.
Who made up that rule?     This is not a school setting.
I have the actual records (not copies) and you will notice the administrator's signatures.

**3/12/99,** there was an incident on the 2nd floor. A chair was thrown in the classroom at the teacher and then a verbal assault, what happened afterwards I do not know. I bet there were no incident reports filed.

**3/23/99,** In-service day at Eastside High School. We were told students will not be arrested if they are found either under the influence or if with drugs or alcohol on their possessions and this is District Policy. Many teachers asked questions, but the response was, "it is not the district policy to punish kids but to help them and students will not be arrested."
Anytime someone asked a question or made an example they were told over it is district policy. One teacher stood up and said it is against the law to purchase cigarettes if you are under the age of 18. It is against the law to purchase or have alcohol if you are under the age of 21. It is also against the law to be within 1000 feet of a school with drugs. Now you're telling us if a student enters the school with it they will not be arrested?

Again, teachers were told that it is district policy not to arrest the kid. Another question was asked, does district policy override state law? Teachers were then told they are to follow district policy. A gentleman (who was part of this presentation) started talking and was irate that teachers would ask such questions. He was obnoxious and had a definite chip on his shoulder he kept telling teachers that this is a pet peeve with him and we are as employees of the district and must follow the district policy.

Then teachers were told not to fill out the Violence, Vandalism, and Substance abuse form. That is the administrator's job. Since when is that policy? As the teachers were asking more and more questions all of a sudden there was a convenient coffee break, which many teachers felt was planned in case teachers persist with their questioning. In other words, to break the momentum. You would figure that the district would want its people to ask questions and have them answered to be informed.

I learned that the next day many teachers spoke with Lt. **(Name omitted)** and explained the issue to him. He said that was BS and if he sees a kid under the influence or with possession, he will arrest him in a minute and that he is going to speak to you about this.

So is JFK a safe haven or a safe zone for students to drink, deal and take drugs?

**NOTE OF INTEREST:**
**1998-99** Eastside Fall HSPT 4% passed = 12 students
Kennedy Fall HSPT 81 students passed roughly 28%.
Administrators are contesting some of the scored because some students failed by a couple of points.

1. Is it true that Kennedy High School in Paterson, NJ, has the highest dropout rate in the country?
2. Is it true only 12 students at Eastside passed all 3 sections of the HSPT? (4%)
3. Is it true that only 81 JFK students passed all 3 parts of the HSPT? (28%)

4. Why on September 16, 1998, would all teachers receive a memo stating,
"If a student is tardy to homeroom, do not mark the student tardy (T) on the homeroom bubble sheet. Mark the student in your roll book. Complete a tardy referral as you would for students in your classes. Send the referral to the cut/tardy office. After action is taken the referral will be sent to you.
If you have any questions, please ask. Thanks for your help in this matter."
With (Name omitted) signature.
*THIS IS FALSIFYING RECORDS!*
(On page 156 there is a copy of that memo.)

5. How can a student **(Name omitted)** who was arrested because he brought a machete into school, gets incarcerated, and has those days excused? Even before this incident he already had 60 plus days absent.

6. Is foul language approved by the Paterson School District? It's not in my house. Is it in yours?

7. If we start with approximately 1000 freshman every year then why don't we have 4000 students?

8. Why do we have less than 300 students graduating?

9. I agree with you 100%.
You are absolutely right that we the staff should be energetic, motivated, ready to set the world on fire, and if we are not, we should get an attitude adjustment or leave this wonderful profession.

However, our attitude is soured when our ambitions and energies are soiled by students who are allowed to overrun the population and turn this beautiful building into nothing more than a place to strengthen their jail house mentality.

**May 13, 1999** 2nd or 3rd period a fight broke out in home economics room.
2 students came into class refused to leave and attacked a boy name **(Name omitted)**.
**(Name omitted)** was hit with a chair and taken to the hospital the other boy was suspended. No idea if charges were pressed or what happened to the other boy?
Security guard was bitten on the hand by a young lady after she called him a nigger.
She received 20 days ABC. No charges were pressed. Geesh, I wonder why?

**May 5, 1999, (Name omitted)** was arguing with Mr. **(Name omitted)** loudly in office #1 about a student who was swearing profusely at him. Mr. **(Name omitted a VP)** said, "I am not going to suspend a student for foul language. They are according to the student handbook.

**June 6, 1999, (Name omitted)** a student had a gun. He was removed from the building by police. Last week **(Name omitted)** another student had a gun. It was hushed up. I noticed on the excused list he is only marked down as suspended with a return date of June 22, 1999. I would have thought he was expelled and not coming back.

**June 16, 1999, a** security guard **(Name omitted)** was hit by a female student **(Named omitted)**. The guard pressed charges and **(Name omitted)** now wants him fired because he does not want the publicity in the paper. Could it be because he is looking for another position in another district? Or is it district policy.

**NOTE OF INTEREST:**
**(Name omitted)** is on the suspended list. He is the boy **(Name omitted)** was going to shoot.
**(Name omitted)** is on both suspension and zone. Check the excused list June 18, 1999. ZONE???
**This year 1999,** it is ironic that both Art teachers were involved with an altercation. **(Name omitted)** was involved with a fight that broke out and was hit with a chair. She was given a bad time with comp/time. However, she was finally reimbursed but not after many threats. Some teachers said that she should press charges and she replied, "I don't want to cause any waves. I only have a few years left and don't want to get into trouble now." She is scared, that's why she did not press charges.
Bottom line--the District, **(Name omitted)**, and **(Name omitted)** did nothing.
A few weeks later Ms. **(Name omitted)** took some playing cards away from a student **(Name omitted)** who then physically accosted and thrown Ms. **(Name omitted)** up against the wall. She also was given a bad time by administration for comp/time and especially because she filed charges against the boy.

Yesterday, April 15, 1999, she had her yearly evaluation done by Ms. **(Name omitted)**. It is not official yet but Ms. **(Name omitted)** was informed that it was not favorably.
She was also told that she has a discipline problem in the class.
If a teacher has a discipline problem in class is because there is a discipline problem in the school. Nevertheless, she is being punished because she is pressing charges.

**Bottom line: The administration is making it very clear that they want the incident squashed.**

Furthermore, administration is punishing Ms. **(Name omitted),** for what the administration should have done all along which was to follow the guidelines, rules and regulations written by them in the student handbook. Administration is supposed to set the tone and standard in the building so teachers can keep the tone set in the classroom.

As of April 17, Mr. **(Name omitted)** was going to have Mrs. **(Name omitted)** transferred because she wasn't sure if she was going to press charges yet.
Mr. **(Name omitted)** stopped her in the middle of the hallway and asked if she is going to press charges or not, because **(Name omitted)** wants to know now?"
Now that very same day **(Name omitted),** was going to have her transferred. However, another principal from one of the grammar schools stood up for her. (Name is withheld so there is no retaliation).
So if the law/s are broken and a teacher reports it, they are punished?
Is this district policy, or should I say is this Governor Christie Todd Whitman's' policy on handling the educational crisis in Paterson, NJ?     This will not look good on a resume!

                                                                                                   Zorro

P S

Don't you think students and their parents should be held responsible for grades, testing, attitudes, discipline, attendance, lateness, violence, and vandalism?

Or is it just politically correct to blame everything on teachers except where it actually belongs?

You should all be a shamed of yourselves for letting all of this to go on year after year.
You all act as if nothing is wrong. It is obvious you do not have a conscience.

Would you send your children here? I know the answer?

I truly hope this is a great year not for the teachers, but for the students, their parents and the community by having our school and schools the most positive and safe environment for the ability to learn and to explore the many avenues there are in this beautiful world.

If not. God help you all.

This last letter repeats many of the incidents above. I just want everyone to see that this letter went directly to the superintendent and as usual *nothing* was done about any of it.

It is 2012, and everything has become *worse* here at John F. Kennedy High School, and within the entire Paterson Public School District. However, according to the new superintendent and all of the politicians, it's the teachers' fault.

I would like the Superintendent, his administration, the Principals, the Commissioner of Education and the Governor of New Jersey EXPLAIN, how is the above allowed to go and be the teachers fault?

Next are two letters I sent to Governor Christie & the Commissioner of Education Cerf.

**Letter #1** "RESTRUCTURING"

                                                                                    February 20, 2012

Dear Governor Christopher Christie and Commissioner of Education Chris Cerf,

I know you hate teachers, think we do nothing, and everything wrong with the Public School system is our fault, [which] is the reason why I am being anonymous for the time being.

Governor and commissioner, you may not believe this, but I agree with you on so many issues about teachers, teaching and the Public School system.

To make it look as if things are better here, you will find no paper trail of poor attendance, cuts, lateness's, suspensions and violence unless it is absolutely necessary.

Prior to Christmas break, I have many students with over 35 days absent and 20 plus cuts without one means of recourse or disciplinary action taken. It is now February, I have many students with over 60 days absent and 40 of them being cuts and they still have yet to be disciplined or even removed from roll. Most of my colleagues have the same situation.

How can you hold teachers accountable if we are not allowed to do our job? With the way things are set up now, students can do whatever they want without fear of any disciplinary action, plus pass for the year as long as they passed the HSPA.

Teachers in the Special Education department were all instructed NOT TO FAIL any students. The lowest grade they are allowed to give a student is a D. Several of the teachers asked to see the directive or have some type of memo showing this demand. They were all told to do it or else.

Is this what the state run and operated school district of Paterson has come to in order to say look we have improved this school so much in one year?
Students are in the hallways all day long, screaming, yelling, cursing, running, wrestling, pushing, shoving, throwing items, eating drinking, rolling around on the floor, fighting, hanging out, banging on classroom doors, banging and kicking lockers, just disrupting the entire system. They walk in and out of the building all day long. Many of those who walk in and out don't even attend JFK. They are people from the street coming in causing fights and pulling the fire alarm in order to find the student or students they are hunting for. It is absolutely dangerous here. The police that are in the building as part of school security (while being paid over time) are told by administration they are NOT allowed to do or say anything unless they are told to by administration.
At times it is up to 20 minutes before students finally make it into their respective classrooms. Even then many students will enter a class they do not belong in. The teacher cannot get them to leave without some type of altercation because of that or those students refuses to leave. Instead the student or students will ignore, challenge, curse and threatens the teacher. Even when security comes to remove that person or persons from the classroom, they too are ignored, cursed at, and threatened. When they are finally removed, they are immediately set free only for the entire scene to happen again. This goes on every day all day long. WHY, because there is NO CONSEQUENCES for students' actions and or poor behavior. The students own the building, set the standards here and know they are free of consequences.

If there is an administrator in the hallways all they do is walk and act as if they see nothing. However, teachers and security are in the hallways attempting to move students to their classes and all the while we endure being ignored, curse at, and threatened. Our school is nothing more than in door street corner. Question--Why do we now have so manymore administrators in the building from the year before? Talk about top heavy. Why do we need so many administrators? Nothing has changed except that things have gotten worse here?

Last year we had 1 principal, 4 vice principals and three TAPs (Teacher's Aide to the Principals) specifically assigned for discipline. NOW we have 2 principals, and 24 or 25 other administrators. There are administrative roles being filled by personnel who do not even have a college degree. How can this be? To fill any type of administrative roll, one must have at least a master's degree with administrative certification?

In March, HSPA will be administered and because of that J. F. K, students now being removed from their daily scheduled assigned classes and must attend HSPA BOOT CAMP.
This started February 15, 2012. Each day, for four periods (periods 2, 3, 4 & 5), for the next three weeks, students will be missing their regularly scheduled classes to attend double classes of Math and English to prepare for the HSPA. Not to mention after school and Saturday HSPA classes at taxpayer's expense, because teachers are being paid overtime. So much for the educational process!

It is not about education here. It's about passing the HSPA and improved percentages & statistics at the cost of students forfeiting their true education. All to make the superintendents, key word is plural superintendents look good. Which brings me to another thought? Why is it when the school or schools do well the superintendents did well? On the other hand, when things go wrong and students do not perform it is the teacher's fault?

PLEASE, you must send someone undercover to see what really is going on here. It is NOT education. It is nothing more than chaos and insanity.

As an educator for almost three decades I am asking for your help. I am not looking for a fight. I want my students, I want my school, I want the people of the City and community I work for to be educated, to be gainfully employed and prepared for the future. I personally want the taxpayers of New Jersey to get the bang for their tax bucks. Right now taxpayers are not just being lied to. They are being economically raped.

After you witness what is actually going on here, you have to ask yourselves, would I send my children here? Then ask yourselves, why should anyone be forced to send their children here?

Ask the police officers who are here every day as part of our security if they would send their children here? They will all tell you NO!
Please, come and investigate what I am telling you. PLEASE!!!

I will make myself known to you once I know I am safe from administrative retaliation.

I have the documentation to back all of this up.

Sincerely,

For the time being, ZORRO

**Letter #2**     "RESTRUCTURING"

December 27, 2012

Dear Honorable Governor Chris Christie and Commissioner of Education Cerf,

I am writing to you both out of disgust and despair.

I am a teacher at John F. Kennedy High School in Paterson, NJ. As you know, Paterson is a state run and operated school district and my second attempt in getting your attention.

Ever since the state took over the district approximately 1991, our schools are out of control and Dangerous, especially here at John F. Kennedy High School.

The last school year 2011-2012 was a so-called restructuring year. It is the absolute worse I have ever seen in my almost 30 years of teaching and working at John F. Kennedy High School.
All the promises on how things are going to change and it will be a better and safer place of education, all BS.

With this so-called restructuring, there are four (4) academies, STEM, ACT, BTMF and SET. What BS! There are four (4) names but there are *not* four academies/schools. Other than the names of the academies, the only difference is each so-called academy has their own principal, two (2) to three (3) vice principals as well as other administrators for each academy.

**Bottom line: JFK is the same, with the only difference, there are more administrators. With four (4) academies, students are still attending classes with teachers from other academies just as if there were no academies at all. It is all a BIG SCAM and another big waste of taxpayer's money.**

Prior to the so-called restructuring, as for administrators here at JFK there were; one (1) principal, four (4) vice principals and three (3) teacher assistants to the principal (TAPs), as well as a department head for each department and a director of guidance. With the so-called restructuring, there has been a major increase of administrators.

It is absolutely the very worse I have ever seen. Students can do whatever they want. Not ONE school rule is enforced here. There is absolutely NO discipline. It is shear chaos here all day long.

**EXAMPLE:** In November 2012, students were assembled to the auditorium to vote for class president, etc. It was so out of control. The noise and chaos coming out of the auditorium was heard throughout the entire three floors of the building. The students would not behave. The principal who was running the elections, Mrs. **(Name omitted),** was not able to control the students. Students would not stay seated, [they] ran all around the auditorium, cursed, screamed obscenities, and threw items at the principal and the candidates. When Mrs. **(Name omitted)** was telling students to be seated, be quiet, settle down; all in attempts to obtain some sort of control, students became more wild, defiant and louder. It was basically a riot-like atmosphere. It was so bad and out of control that administrators decided to have all the students leave and go to their classes. The elections were canceled. Even the administrators could not control students. REASON: because the administration here has set the tone for the building. Students knowing this, they do and act any way they want and NOTHING will be done about it. And NOTHING was done about it. Not one student was held accountable for their behavior. When an auditorium is filled with administrators and they have no control over students, how do you think it was during the rest of the school day--not just in the building but within each classroom? Once again, there is NO record of that incident; old adage, *if it is not written down, it never happened.* How do these administrators go home every night knowing they have *not* done their jobs? They are failing not only at their jobs, but the students, the school as a whole, the district, the community as well as the State of NJ and the entire country. ABSOLUTELY DISGUSTING! Is that a requirement for becoming an administrator, not having a conscience and being conscientious of doing a good job?

That is ONLY ONE story. I can give you thousands just within the last four (4) months. I have tens of thousands since the state took over the District here in Paterson.
Better yet, speak with the security personnel and the six (6) uniformed Paterson Police Officers that are here every day. If you want lies and a cover-up, speak to the two ex-Paterson Police Officers, who are supposedly heads of security.

Bottom line--students do NOT have to go to class. I am talking 100s of them in large packs/gangs, roam the building at will, defying teachers, security and even the administration when and if administrators are present. Administration, what a joke! We now have so manymore administrators in the building and no discipline. NO, it is NOT failing teachers. It is a failing administration that will not allow teachers to do our jobs.

There is NO accountability for student behavior, attendance, lateness, cutting, disrespect, violence, vandalism, etc. etc. etc. which is rampant. There is no accountability for anything here. It is all about covering and hushing everything up here.
The last school year (2011-2012) we had at least 10 more administrators in the building. That does not include an additional principal. YES, we had two principals here at JFK, in addition to the security of the building. We also have two ex-Paterson Police Officers who are supposed to be Heads of Security. Now with all of this added administration and security in the building please explain to me why, they allow this school to be an absolute disaster, out of control, why students do NOT have to attend class and just hang out in the hallways and stairwells?

Why do we need that manymore administrators in the first place? Are favors being paid back?

Ten more administrators who are paid well over $100,000.00 a year, which equals to over a MILLION DOLLARS more each year just for John F. Kennedy High School alone. That is NOT including whatever the salaries are for the 2 retired Paterson Police Officers as heads of Security.

If we are adding taxpayer's money (which is a BIG part of the school budget), we have 6 uniformed Paterson Police officers assigned just at JFK every day at $300.00 a day.
That equals to $1,800.00 a day, times 186 days a year, which now equals $336,600.00 a year. For what? They are NOT allowed to do their jobs? They are just here to sit, stand, walk around, and eat until Mr. Dickinson* tells or gives them permission to do or say anything. If it were any place outside the school building, arrests would be made all day long. So, in reality we are teaching students and future citizens it is OK to break the law in school. Not only is all of this a waste of taxpayer's money, but what an absolute disgrace.

How can students be allowed to enter the building at any time they want? This goes on day after day, every day, all year, all last year. The school nor the district does anything to instill the responsibilities of being ON TIME! To give you an idea of how many students have been late to school just in the 2012 - 2013 school year, (four (4) months), the JFK print shop **(Name omitted)** has printed 3500 late/tardy to school slips from September to the end of November. He was asked to print up 750 more slips just a few weeks ago. You do not find this absolutely disgusting or serious? If you do not believe me, ask them. They keep accurate records with all of their printing jobs.

What is even more sickening, these same students may have already missed one (1), two (2), three (3), and even more classes due to chronic lateness, every single day. Then they will still pass each of the classes they have been missing all year. HOW, how can that be? We have students who are late every period every day, and not just a minute or two. So many are late 20 *plus* minutes every day to every class, and they too pass.

In the school year 2011–2013, there were many students that were absent 100 plus days from school, and it does not matter. They still passed and graduated. So in reality as long as a student remains on roll or left on roll, they will pass? This school year 2012–2013, in just four (4) months, so many of my colleagues and I have students with 40, and 50 plus days absent already. That's not including their cuts and lateness's.

How can students be absent so much and cut classes all year and STILL PASS?
Why is it allowed for students (gangs) to walk into any classroom that they do not belong in, refuse to leave when asked by that teacher, refuse to leave when security arrives and still start a fight/brawl?

And these incidents will all go ignored because, principal **(Name omitted),** refuses to file Violence and Vandalism reports. Teachers are threatened not to write them with fear of retaliation, of receiving a poor evaluation, being transferred, and if not a tenured teacher, FIRED! All to keep everything hushed up and made to look as if everything has improved and is better.
The abuse teachers get by students (gangs) in class and in the hallways is a crime in itself. This too goes ignored. Usually, nothing is done about it or he or she, and in many cases, *they* may be brought down to the security office and eventually let go. Once again, there is no disciplinary action, no accountability for their actions and eventually these same students to do it all over again within a few minutes.

Our poor security people, they too are NOT allowed to do their job.
Every time they apprehend a student for doing something wrong and or illegal, **(Name omitted)** tells security to let them go. Then it happens all over again. On and on and on and on all day, every day, it is out of freaking control here. My head wants to explode. This is unacceptable.
Our school is so dangerous. It is out of control. Not one rule is enforced. There is no discipline here. When I enter the building, I no longer have any idea or sense of what is right or wrong is anymore. It is that out of control, dangerous, and chaotic here. Why is this type of behavior allowed to continue?
Everything is backwards here. It is worse than any street corner at night you can imagine.
The noise alone in the building, with the students in the hallways all day long, is absolutely deafening. Even with the door closed the noise is ridiculous. With the door being closed and locked, students in defiance and causing more chaos and disruption to the class and classes going on, begin to beat, kick, and punch the door and glass. Brazenly and defiantly, student's press their faces on the glass while tapping on it to get more attention and continue with their excessive foul language and threatening remarks to the teacher/s and students, while giving the finger and screaming more and more obscenities. And there is NOT one administrator in the hallway. With all of this happening and going on and on all day every day, why is administration not making their presence known instead of hiding?

That's why students do this, because they know NOTHING will be done about it.
The noise is so loud and obscene; you would think you are in the streets during a RIOT.

There should be never be any noise of any type in an educational setting ever.
If students were made to be in their classes, there would be any students in the hallways in the first place. Which means there would be no noise in the hallways. However, this goes on day after day after day all day all year and there is no administrator around. IF, there is an administrator in the hallway while all or any of this is going on, all they will say is, "Go to class," or "Take your hat off," and keep on walking. Meanwhile, the nonsense continues and that administrator disappears into the sunset. Is this what is meant by restructuring? Why is this allowed? What are we teaching here? Why does administration allow this to continue on and on?

That is why I am contacting you Governor Christie and Commissioner of Education Cerf.
As I stated above, Paterson Public School System is Run and Operated by the State. Meaning you, the Governor of NJ and the Commissioner of Education are supposed to be in control. I do not know what information you are receiving on what is actually going on here, but believe me, what I am telling you is

the truth. If you do not believe me, do not ignore this letter PLEASE. ASK, any teacher, security personnel, and even the Paterson police officers who work here every day.

Governor, you and every politician coming [in] after [you], are blaming teachers for what is supposedly wrong with public education. We here in Paterson are NOT allowed to do our jobs.
Governor and Commissioner, this is all happening on your watch. Whether you know or do not know, with this letter, you now have no excuse or excuses.

If a parent refuses or just does not care if their child or children who are under age do not go to school, they are held responsible. This is called, "NEGLECT!" Due to neglect, DYFS, can and would be called in and the child or children can be taken away from the parent or guardian RIGHT?

Who is held responsible for deliberately allowing students not to attend their classes and roam the building all day long? Is this NOT NEGLECT?

Teachers CANNOT be held liable and or accountable if students are NOT in class. Teachers CANNOT be held responsible, liable and accountable, for a student or student's education when students are allowed to be in hallways or any and every place else within the school surroundings, instead of their respective classes and classrooms.

What makes it worse is this is deliberately breaking the law and the NJ taxpayers are paying for it now, and will continue to pay for all of this [that is] going on for years to come.

Don't you think with what I have just written and explained to you both that, DYFS should be called in on this school? This is RUINING a NATION! I have the documentation to back up and prove everything I am saying.

What are we waiting for? I sent you a letter last year.

PLEASE SIR, come here. Send someone here anonymously, undercover and without notice, to the school or district to see firsthand what really is and has been going on. If the district and especially the Principal gets wind of a visitor, they will put on the old dog and pony show. We have seen this many times when visitors are present.
I would love to contact you directly but I am afraid of retaliation. YES, I know of the whistle blowing act, however, government, politics and politicians can make and turn anything around in a way to hurt hard working, conscientious taxpaying teachers and me.

We teachers are all NOT bad. Why do you think I am writing you again sir? I want to make a difference. I want a change here at JFK and the entire school district of Paterson, NJ.

Governor, PLEASE, I beg of you, especially in the aftermath of Sandy Hook Elementary School. Sooner or later it is going to be John F. Kennedy High School, Paterson, NJ.
Do any New Jersey politicians send their children to public school/s? My question to them, and to all the administrators and superintendent/s of Paterson Public Schools, would you send your children to our school or schools?

Your honor, I do NOT understand. The Paterson Public School System (The Superintendent), is allowing our schools to fail, to be absolutely out of control and not only has his contract been renewed, he received 25 plus thousand dollars in bonuses for doing his job.

Let me understand this. He gets a bonus for doing his job. However, if he did not do his job, he still gets paid? What was the good job? Lying, falsifying paperwork on how much we have improved? How safe it is? How the dropout rate has decreased? How attendance, tardiness, cuts and the dropout rate have improved?

Well, they have to improve if there are NO records being kept! Many teachers have students whom we have yet to meet this entire 2012-2013 school year. However, these students are still on our daily, as well as the school roster. What does that tell you?

Meanwhile, we teachers who are literally in the trenches are being blamed for the failure of our school? Once again, we are NOT allowed to do our job.

As you know, we teachers here in Paterson have yet to have a contract. One of the sticking points is [that] the superintendent wants to increase the school day. I have to laugh! WHY? So students can be in the hallways longer. So they can continue threatening and bullying other students, teachers, security and whomever they want. Allowed to be in the hallways all day long, every day all year long so they can hang out, eat, drink, play, fight, wrestle, run, push people, curse, and have sex in the stairwells. YES, SEX!

I bet you did not get the memo on those incidents. Let's not forget and add to the list, gambling right in the hallways, along with anything and everything else instead of being in class. All of this is going on, and the district and school paid tens of thousands of dollars on, as the principal calls it the "STATE OF THE ART SURVEILLANCE SYSTEM." The New Jersey taxpayers got screwed again, paying for this surveillance system that isn't being used.

LENGTHEN THE SCHOOL DAY–MATH...
...if students are late to class let's say only 10 minutes. As I said, it is much longer and with many, they hardly go to class, but we will just use 10 minutes as a means.

10 Minutes  X times 9 periods = 90 Minutes.

If my math is correct, using 10 minutes as a means and if students were made to be in class on time, the school day would have increased by 90 minutes, without actually increasing the school day.

As I have been saying, so many students do not enter their classes for 20 or 30 minutes after the bell rang to be in class. If students don't go to class at all, an entire period, that's 41 minutes. Now you do the math.

Did these people really attend college?

Over the 20 plus years since the State of New Jersey has had control over the Paterson Public School District, let's not forget how many times a day, week, month, and year that we have to evacuate the building because we have false alarms. False alarms because the students want to fight! False alarms because people who do not belong in the building come in and pull the fire alarms because they are looking hunting for certain student or students to attack. Once the alarm is pulled, the building is evacuated, the gangs hunt down and attack their prey now out in the streets.

False alarms are pulled by students and outside intruders just to break up and disrupt the school day and boy does it. Once we enter back into the building, now the building environment is even worse and MORE out of control.

We have bomb scares. We have actual and deliberate fires set by students in the stairwells, Boy's and Girl's bathrooms, etc., etc. The fire department, extra added Paterson Police, Passaic County Sheriff's Office, K-9 Unit, Bomb Squad, etc., etc. have to come every time, and all at the taxpayer's continued expense.

None of it ever makes the newspaper, TV and/or radio. It is all hushed up. If it were another school or school district, and no matter how minor of an incident, it would be all over the news media. However, here in Paterson, it is all and always hushed up.

Your honor, don't you think parents and the community have the right to know what is really going on within the school and schools they send their children to? WHY, is everything always hushed up? Everything here is reactive, not proactive, and the reactive is to quickly do damage control and to hush it all up.

Bottom line-- if students are in the hallways all day long, they get bored and will do stupid stuff. If the administration did not ALLOW students to roam the hallways, 99.9% of these problems would NEVER happen. Now that makes sense.

Why is it that the only time we have absolute control over our building, meaning hallways, stairwells, and the entire perimeter of the building is when we have a Code Blue Drill? That is absolutely disgusting. In reality, with everything that goes on here at JFK, day after day all year long, we should be in a code blue for real.

This is a state run and operated school district. Especially with you, Governor Christie being at the helm, I would have expected that means tighter control, strictness and a more rigorous academic setting to our educational system here in Paterson, which is needed. Not a freaking free for all and riot like atmosphere!

Our students are not being properly educated? They are not prepared to graduate and more importantly many of our students are not prepared to enter the real world of WORK and become productive members of society!

Your honor, think about it, our young men and women today are still fighting and dying for our freedoms here in the United States.

Today they are all over the world fighting and building schools for other countries. Meanwhile, our Public School right here in Paterson, NJ, which are under State Control, is not only dangerous they are out of control and maybe the worse than any other country.

Now ask yourself, is this the very "FREEDOM" our brave service men and women have died and are still dying for?

As I write this letter, I am getting more and more nervous, anxious, and depressed knowing I will have to go back in a few days and go through all of this again for the remainder of YEAR!

I am a teacher. I am not in the military. I am not Police Officer, or Firefighter. I should not have to feel this type of anxiety, stress, disgust and despair. Unfortunately, I can't take it anymore. The stress is gonna kill me.

Gentlemen, PLEASE, I hope you will help. Or will all of us here have to endure the rest of the year without being able to do our jobs?

In a few days, 2012 will be over and 2013 will begin. Four (4) months have already gone by. Nothing has changed. Another school year will be wasted. We simply continue to push students through the Public

School System not only to be unprepared educationally, they will be unprepared socially by not being prepared for LIFE!

Come June 2013, once again we will graduate, send young men and women out into the real world unprepared, uneducated and with a high school diploma. Absolutely disgusting!

Sincerely,
ZORRO
P S

Sir, if you can make some type of sign or get the word out that I will NOT be punished, there will be no retaliation for my informative letters to you, I WILL COME FORWARD.

**1st Letter** sent to NJEA President Barbara Keshishian and Vice President Wendell Steinhauer.
A copy was also sent to the President of the NEA in Washington, DC, Dennis Van Roekel.
August 30, 2012

Dear President Barbara Keshishian and Vice President Wendell Steinhauer,

I am writing to you both out of disgust and despair.

I'm a teacher at John F. Kennedy High School in Paterson, NJ. As you are aware, it is a state run and operated school district.

Ever since the State took over the district in approximately 1991, our schools are out of control and dangerous, especially here at John F. Kennedy High School.

This past school year 2011-2012 was a so-called restructuring year. It is the absolute worse I have ever seen in my almost 30 years of teaching and working at John F. Kennedy High School. All the promises on how things are going to change and will be a better and safer place of education--all BS.
It is absolutely the very worse I have ever seen. Students can do whatever they want.
Not ONE school rule is enforced. There is absolutely *no* discipline.
Students do NOT have to go to class. I'm talking hundreds of them in large packs/ gangs, roam the building at will, defying teachers, security and even the administration.

There is NO accountability for attendance;
No accountability for lateness; No accountability for cutting.

Students can roam the building, hallways, stairwell and the entire perimeter of the outside building in gangs, and not a thing is done about it. They walk in and out of the building at will.

This past school year (2011-2012) we have at least 10 more administrators in the building. That doesn't include an additional principal. YES, we NOW have 2 principals here at JFK, **(Name omitted)** and **(Name omitted)** and we also have 2 ex-Paterson Police Officers who are supposed to be Heads of Security. Now with all of this added administration and security in the building please explain to me why they allow this school to be an absolute disaster? Why do we need that manymore administrators in the first place? Are favors being paid back?

[That is] ten (10) more administrators who are paid well over $100,000.00 a year, which equals to over a MILLION DOLLARS more each year just for John F. Kennedy High School alone. That is NOT including whatever the salaries are for the 2 ex-Paterson Police Officers as heads of security.

What for? There was no change in the building or the size of the student population. You talk about making up position and being top-heavy. This is Governor Christie's baby. He is running this district. How can you cut taxes when they are actually creating MORE administrative positions at NJ taxpayers' expense?

Boy oh boy, the New Jersey taxpayers are really getting raped here.

It is NOT a place of education.
Students can come in the building at any time they want and not be counted tardy. If they are marked tardy it doesn't matter. They will still pass. I'm not talking 2, 3, 4, or 5 or even 10 times, I am talking 50, 60, 70 and 100 lateness's. *No accountability*. They can be absent a hundred plus days from school, and it doesn't matter. They will still pass.

Whatever happened to the policy that if you are absent for 20 days you lose credit and can possibly get left back? Instead, we push them through the system. So in reality, as long as you are on roll or left on roll, you will pass?

Students can cut classes all year and *still pass*. Students can walk into any classroom that they do not belong in and start a fight. (Fight means with a student or students and teacher.) And it will all go ignored. (Ignored means just that.)

The abuse teachers get by students in class and in the hallways is a crime in itself. And that too is ignored. Either nothing is done about it or he or she, and in many cases, *they* may be brought down to the security office and eventually let go; only for these same students to do it all over again.
The poor security people they too are NOT allowed to do their job.
Every time they apprehend a student for doing something wrong, **(Name omitted)** tells security to let them go.

My head wants to explode. This is unacceptable.
Everything is backwards here.
It is worse than any street corner you can imagine.
The noise alone in the building with the students in the hallways all day long is absolutely defining. Even with the door closed the noise is ridiculous. Then with the door being closed, students beat and kick on it, hit, punch and continue tapping on the glass, curse the teacher out, give the students and teacher the finger and screaming more and more obscenities.
The students do this because they know NOTHING will be done about it.
The noise is so loud and obscene; you would think you are in a RIOT.

First of all, there should never be any noise in an educational setting ever.
If students were made to be in their classes, there wouldn't be any students in the hallways in the first place. Which means there would be no noise in the hallways. Why is this allowed?
What are we teaching here?

Why are we not going after Governor Christie and the Commissioner of Education Cerf?
As I state above, Paterson Public School System is Run and Operated by the Governor and the Commissioner of Education.

The Governor and politicians are all coming after teachers and blaming us for what is supposedly wrong with Public Education and all the while the Governor and Commissioner of education is allowing this to go on in the very school district they are supposedly in Control over???????.
THERE ARE NO EXCUSES THAT THEY DIDN'T KNOW? IT IS ON THEIR WATCH!

FOR THEM TO KNOW SO MUCH ABOUT TEACHERS AND WHAT WE DO AND DON'T DO THEN HOW CAN THEY NOT KNOW WHAT IS GOING ON IN A DISTRICT THEY ARE SUPPOSEDLY IN CONTROL OF?

If a parent refuses or just doesn't care if their child or children who are under age do not go to school, they are held responsible. DYFS, can be called in and the child or children can be taken away for neglect. RIGHT?

WELL, who is held responsible for deliberately allowing students not to attend their classes? The Superintendent/s, building administration, the Governor and Commissioner of Education must not only be held responsible, they are also liable.
Is this NOT NEGLECT?
They are not above the law.
What makes it worse they are deliberately breaking the law and at taxpayers' expense.
DON'T YOU THINK DYFS SHOULD BE CALLED ON THEM?
They are RUINING a NATION!

I have the documentation to back up and prove everything I am saying.
I have sent a great deal of documentation to the PEA and to a field rep of the NJEA, in Wayne.
What are we waiting for?

I write to them constantly. I have sent them actual on the spot reports of what is going on. I have sent them my documentation of dates, times, incident and who is involved on many incidents that have been going on here. I have asked why the NJEA has abandoned us? He has written back and assures me that the NJEA has not abandoned us.

It is not just me, it's all of us here at JFK who feel you (NJEA) have abandoned us. This place is out of control and teachers are made to be held accountable. All for a political football game in scaring and making taxpayers believe that our political people especially the Governor and Commissioner of Education are helping and making changes.

Do any of them send their children to Public School/s? My question to them, and all the administrators and superintendent of Paterson Public Schools, would you send your children to our school or schools?

I tell parents all the time that they should be suing the School District, the Superintendent, the Mayor, the Commissioner of Education and the Governor himself, for not allowing their child or children to get a proper education.

This is all LIABLE! They must be held liable.
A class action lawsuit MUST be filed.

BOTTOM LINE--WHY IS THIS ALLOWED TO GO ON?

The Paterson Public School System (The Superintendent) is allowing our schools to fail, to be absolutely out of control and the Superintendent not only has his contract renewed he received 25 plus thousand dollars in bonuses for doing a good job.
Let me understand this, he gets a bonus for doing his job.
But if he didn't do his job, he still gets paid?
Are you freaking kidding me?

What was the good job? Lying on the paperwork on how much we have improved?
How safe it is? How the dropout rate has decreased? How has attendance, tardiness, and cuts improved?
Well, they have to improve if there are NO records being kept!

In the meanwhile, we teachers who are literally in the trenches CANNOT get a contract?
One of the sticking points is they want to increase the school day.
WHY? So students can be in the hallways longer. So they can continue threatening and bully other students, teachers, security and whomever they want. Allowed to be in the hallways all day long, every day all year long so they can hang out, eat, drink, play, fight, wrestle, run, pushing people, cursing, have sex, gambling, anything and everything else instead of being in class.
YES, I said sex. That too is hushed up, BIG TIME!

Let's not forget how many times a day, week, month a year that we have to evacuate the building because we have false alarms.
False alarms because the students want to fight.
False alarms because people who do not belong in the building come in and pull the fire alarms because they are looking / hunting for certain student or students to attack.
False alarms because certain gangs want to fight.
False alarms just to break up and disrupt the school day. And boy does it. Once we enter back into the building now the building environment is even worse and MORE out of control if you can believe it.
We have bomb scares,
We have actual and deliberate fires set by students in the Boys and Girls bathrooms.
The fire department, extra added Paterson Police, Passaic County Sheriff's Office, K-9 Unit, Bomb Squad, etc., etc. has to comes every time, and all at the taxpayers continued expense.
None of it ever makes the newspaper, TV and or radio. It is all hushed up. If it were another school district and no matter how minor of an incident it would be all over the news media.
However, here in Paterson, it is all and always hushed up.

Don't parents and community have the right to know what is going on within the school and schools they send their children to?

WHY is everything hushed up?
Everything here is reactive, not proactive.
And the reactive is to quick do Damage Control and to hush it all up.
Bottom line-- students are in the hallways all day long. They get bored and do stupid stuff.
If the administration did not ALLOW students to roam the hallways, 99.9% of these problems would NEVER happen. Now that makes sense.

Ok, let's continue now with a little math.
Let's just use 10 minutes.
If students are late to class say only 10 minutes and as I said, they hardly go to class, but we'll just use 10 minutes as a means.
10 Minutes   X times 9 periods = 90 Minutes.

If my math is correct, just using 10 minutes as a means and if students were made to be in class on time, the school day would have increased by 90 minutes without actually increasing the school day.

Now students sometimes don't enter the class for 20 or 30 minutes.
If they don't go to class at all, an entire period, that's 41 minutes.

Are you kidding me? Make the school day longer so the superintendent can say, look I even extended the school day here in Paterson, look what a good boy I am so can I have another bonus. Meanwhile students are now in the hallways longer.

Once again, WHY IS THIS ALLOWED TO GO ON EVERY DAY, ALL DAY, ALL YEAR?
This is a State Run and Operated School District. Especially with Governor Christie at the helm, I would have expected that means tighter control, strictness and a more rigorous education. Not a freaking free for all and riot like atmosphere!

WHY isn't the NJEA making sure that their union members of Paterson Public School System and especially John F. Kennedy High School are working in a safe environment?

Our students are not being properly educated? They are not prepared to graduate and more importantly many of our students are not prepared to enter the real world of WORK and become productive members of society!
After all, NJEA always says, "Students Come First." Not here in Paterson.

Men and women today are still fighting and dying for our freedoms here in the United States.
Our brave service men and women are all over the world fighting, and building schools for other countries, while our Public School right here in Paterson, NJ, which are under State Control are not only dangerous they are out of control and maybe the worse than any other country.

Now ask yourself, is this the very FREEDOM are brave service men and women that have died and are still dying for?

As I have been writing this letter, I am getting more and more nervous, anxious and depressed knowing I will have to go back and go through all of this again for another YEAR!
I'm a teacher, I'm not in the Military, Policemen, and Firemen. I should not have to feel this type of stress.

PLEASE, I hope you will help.
Or will all of us here have to endure another year without being able to do our jobs.

Will 2012-2013, end up being another school year wasted of just pushing students through the Public School System not only to be unprepared educationally, they will be unprepared socially by not being prepared for LIFE!

And will we once again this year, graduate and send out thousands of young men and women into the real world unprepared, uneducated and with a high school diploma? Absolutely Disgusting!
                                          Thank you and most respectfully,
                                          Lee E McNulty

**NOTE OF INTEREST:** I never received a reply from the President & Vice President of the NJEA. However, I did receive two (2) voice mail messages from Barbara Keshishian saying she will get back to me. I never heard from her [again].

However, I did receive a reply dated October 11, 2012, from the President of the NEA.

Here is his reply and especially notice the last sentence!

**nea**
NATIONAL EDUCATION ASSOCIATION
nea.org
Great Public Schools for Every Student

1201 16th St., N.W. | Washington, DC 20036 | Phone: (202) 833-4000

Dennis Van Roekel
*President*

Lily Eskelsen
*Vice President*

Rebecca S. Pringle
*Secretary-Treasurer*

John Stocks
*Executive Director*

October 11, 2012

Lee E. McNulty
10 Summit Avenue
Butler, NJ 07405

Dear Mr. McNulty:

Thank you for your letter. Frankly, I'm alarmed by the conditions you described and have forwarded your letter to the New Jersey Education Association President and Executive Director.

The promise of a great public school for every student is one that should provide opportunity for kids to be successful throughout their lives. This isn't a privilege but a right every student in America should have. We will continue to work to ensure that all students have that opportunity, including the ones at your school.

Stay the course and remember that you have the support and encouragement of millions of teachers across the country.

Sincerely,

*Dennis Van Roekel*

Dennis Van Roekel
President

**2nd Letter** I sent to the President of the NEA & NJEA.

December 3, 2012

Dear President Dennis Van Roekel and Barbara Keshishian,

I am writing to you both out of disgust and despair.
Enclosed are e-mail messages/correspondences between Mr. **(Name omitted)** of the NJEA and the president of the PEA, all pertaining to the letter I had written to you back in the beginning of September.

I noticed that Mr. **(Name omitted)** had cc'd you, Ms. Keshishian, and others in the beginning. However, in our further correspondences I notice you were no longer in the loop.

Nevertheless, as you can tell, I am more than upset. I am truly disgusted.

EXAMPLE:
In our early e-mail, Mr. **(Name omitted)** tells me we are going to meet.
He will put together a list of dates.
Then according to the e-mail from Mr. **(Name omitted)** dated, November 16, 2012, 8:07 am, and I quote, "I am told that the PEA has arranged to visit JFK and meet with you and the other reps on Dec 4. I am glad to hear this. I also think it is best to wait until after you have had the mtg. Good Luck and let me know if you still want to meet after all."
ARE YOU FREAKING KIDDING ME?

First, I thought it was Mr. **(Name omitted),** who set up the meeting? Boy was I fooled. Secondly, why all of a sudden would he ask, if I still want to meet with him afterwards?
What is going on here? I do NOT want this swept under the rug.

Are we (we not meaning me) looking for an easy way out?
Did we (we again not meaning me) forget about protecting the rights of children's and their rights to a quality public education?
What about the NJ taxpayers?

Why is this allowed to continuously go on year after year and get progressively worse?
Because it's an urban/Abbott District, it is all right?
Because it is a state run and operated district, and we (we not meaning me) don't want to rock the boat?

Remember, Governor Christie himself said, now that you have an education use it. If you see something wrong, do something about it, be a disrupter. WELL!!!
I am so upset and disgusted right now.
I thought by contacting you both that you would be alarmed, disturbed, concerned and upset what has been and still going on and would want to do something about all of this.

Now I get the impression, NEA, NJEA & PEA want to keep quiet and sweep all of these incidents under the rug?

The President of the PEA, and some other fellow from the NJEA, (I would have to go look through my notes for his name) all know about these problems and dangerous working conditions, which have been continuously getting worse each year. I have been sending them ALL information for 7 years! This is NOT NEW!    IT IS ENOUGH!

That is why I contacted you both the NEA & NJEA Presidents.

A LAWSUIT IS NECESSARY AND DEMANDED!
How can anybody take this lightly?  I CANNOT understand and believe this!
I truly believe nobody cares. It would be different if it were your children and/or grandchildren.

In the beginning, approximately early October, Mr. **(Name omitted)** informed me of a meeting soon.

Now, it is December 3, 2012, 90 days, 1/2 of a school year later and nothing.

Everything has gotten worse. Bottom line--students are NOT BEING EDUCATED.
They are allowed NOT to attend class. OUR SCHOOL IS WORSE THAN ANY STREET CORNER.

Without going over and over the same stuff please read the e-mail messages enclosed which explains it all.

PLEASE NOTE THE FOLLOWING STATEMENT IS ABSOLUTELY RIDICULOUS:
The statement written by Mr. **(Name omitted)** in e-mail dated Friday, November 30, 2012, and I quote, "This is about process and organizing and unfortunately there are no quick and easy answers."
UNBELIEVABLE!
I say again, I have been sending information to the NJEA and the PEA for 7 years.
The state has taken over the district for over 2 decades. UNACCEPTABLE!

What nonsense. I have never ever heard of an attorney working on any case (90 plus days/3 months) without interviewing the client (ME) first and gathering evidence? Then says, let me know if you still want to meet with me? In other words, all the work he did he will now ignore?
ARE YOU KIDDING ME?     Do you think I am that stupid?

Like I said in my reply to Mr. **(Name omitted)**, "the Vietnam war was over faster."
I am sorry, but I truly believe NOBODY CARES.

Politics, politicians and education do not run like a business. That's why they are a MESS! Everything is BS and takes too long. Which is all a ploy and eventually the people forget.
Well, I am NOT going to forget, go away and/or quit.
WE (Once again, "we," not meaning me) ARE RUINING A NATION!

I don't think either of you understand. You work in a nice, clean, quiet, safe and orderly office, while my colleagues and I live and work in horrible, chaotic and dangerous places; worse than any street corner. Where we the teachers are evaluated, our jobs, lives and careers are on the line because a state run and operated district and its administration allows students to run the school. Where the teachers are blamed for failing schools and failing students.

RUN MEANS;
Students can do whatever they want without fear of retaliation.
They do not have to go to class all day every day, all year.
Where students can enter classrooms that they do not belong in and threaten (political phrase is bullying) students and teacher/s with threats and actual attacks. These incidents are ignored and or hushed up and the paperwork disappears.
And yet they are promoted to the next grade and graduate.
Meanwhile, the next year approximately 1000 brand new freshman will enter our high school and will be lucky if they have maybe a 3rd or 4th grade level of education.
Four (4) years later, approximately 300 will graduate. More than half (1/2) of them shouldn't have.
All because the administrators doctor the grades and come up with some BS program and scam to allow students to graduate who are NOT prepared, all to make the graduation numbers improve and to make it look like the district and school have improved.
Do you really believe this is acceptable? And all the street, gang, jail house mentality is not only allowed but nourished within our school building.

I ask you, shouldn't we (union members) and especially our students be zealously represented and protected so that a SAFE environment and fulfilling education is had by ALL STUDENTS?

If I do NOT hear from you, I know not only where I stand, but where the students, parents, community, the City of Paterson, the State of New Jersey as well as this entire nation all stand.

Thank you and most respectfully,

Lee E McNulty.
P S
In my last letter I stated that you were at the Brown Stone.
In fact, you mentioned it in one of your phone messages to me.
Unfortunately, and I am the blame for taking for granted on the information that was relayed to me (obviously falsely / and or mistakenly) by a PEA member.
I apologize Ms. Keshishian. I should know better to take some one word/s for it. Believe me that will never ever happen again.

Also, I do HOPE that your father is doing well. God Bless him and your family.

Once again, I thank you Ms. Keshishian.
Most respectfully,

Lee

            AS A DUES PAYING UNION MEMBER, I NEVER RECIVED A REPLY

**3rd Letter** sent to the Presidents of the NEA and NJEA.

                                                        August 8, 2013

To The Presidents of the NEA & NJEA;

Dear Mr. Dennis Van Roekel & Barbara Keshishian,

Another year has gone by and hundreds of students graduated that shouldn't and manymore promoted who never ever went to class.
I ask for your help and you both ignore me for the entire school year.
Yes, Ms. Keshishian you did call and left me 2 voice mail messages, one at work and the other at home. Those were the only time I have heard from you. However, throughout the year, I had sent you several e-mail. I received, NO REPLY or a call back from you.
Mr. Van Roekel, I sent you several e-mail throughout the 2012 - 2013 school year. However, you replied to me ONCE dated October 11, 2013.

In your letter you state:

*"Thank you for your letter. Frankly, I'm alarmed by the conditions you described and have forwarded your letter to the New Jersey Education Association President and executive Directors.*

*The promise of a great public school for every student is one that should provide opportunity for kids to be successful throughout their lives. This isn't a privilege but a right every student in America should have. We will continue to work to ensure that all students have the opportunity, including the ones at your school.*

*Stay the course and remember that you have the support and encouragement of millions of teachers across the country."*

*Sincerely,*
Your signature

(END)

Are you kidding me? You blew me off. How can millions of teachers have my support when you have not done a thing to help and support my colleagues and me other than to pass the buck to the NJEA? PLEASE explain to me what and where is the support?
Shortly after your letter Mr. Van Roekel, that is when I received the two (2) voice mail from Ms. Keshishian. Coincidence?
There is NO WAY, I am going to go through another non-productive, out of control, riot- like and violent atmosphere school year, then call it education. This is NOT EDUCATION. Students do NOT have to go to class. Why should they, when they know they will still be promoted and graduate.

Starting this year, we teachers will have to endure a MORE stringent evaluation process which is heavily based on student's performance? Are you both kidding me? As for the evaluation system especially with this new one, it is most definitely and has been always nothing more than being subjective.

**EXAMPLE:**
If a teacher's immediate supervisor who will be evaluating him or her doesn't like that person, what type of evaluation do you think they will receive?

**Here's another scenario.**
If an administrator is to doing evaluations and their supervisor doesn't like a teacher or certain teachers whom they are evaluating, what do you think will happen?
After all, who is evaluating the evaluator?

With everything that has been going on and with what I have been telling you, it's already happening here.
And it will be even worse when the new evaluation process goes into effect for 2013 - 2014 school year! Just in the last two (2) years, I was told by two (2) separate administrators who evaluated me, at two (2) separate times that they would like to give me all EXCELLENT right down the line. They both told me that they were instructed that they CANNOT! Exact words, "We CANNOT give any teacher excellent right down the line anymore!"
So what does that tell you?
Enclosed you have the following:
**1. An article from one of the local newspapers.**

The article explains that the governor at that time signed into law that DYFS is to be contacted when there are long-term and unexcused absences.

As I have been saying all along, what has been going on is NEGLECT, which administration continuously allows.

We (we meaning NJEA Wayne, NJ, PEA and myself) have proof that students are every place else besides being in their classes, and this is allowed by building administration. Including all of my documentation's and e-mail which many of them were sent to you, the Uniserv Director, two Uniserv field reps and the PEA just as it was all happening with date and timelines. My e-mail was nothing short of a blow by blow description on what was actually going as it was happening on to you both.

I received no reply from either one of you. I am ignored.
I am NOT the only one being ignored. There are over 300 teachers and other support and staff people just in JFK alone you are ignoring, not to mention the MOST important factor here. Students are in the hallways and every place else other than being in class all day every day all year long.

Am I the only person who cares? Don't you care?

**NOTE OF INTEREST**:
In the article Weinberg says that officers must be trained to notice these signs.
What signs? When attendance shows the days out what more does anyone need?
Once again I have the proof and so do you with what is in detailed in #3.

**2. End of the year and final exam schedule.** *(See page 460 for copy of exam schedule)*
Please note final exams started June 10, 2013, and ended June 14, 2013, with make ups starting on June 17 & 18, 2013. End of the year for students was June 27, 2013.

From June 17 through June 27, where were our students? Believe me or not, I did have three (3) or maybe four (4) students who did show up almost every day. That is approximately 4% of my student's enrollment. As for the rest of the building, it was worse than any street corner imaginable. Students were not in their classes. Most of them were in the hallway and stairwells until about 11:00. It was absolutely worse than I have described to you all year long. Eventually by noon most of the students left the building. Many students just never even bothered to show up for school at all. Why, because student attendance did not matter during the regular school year so why would it matter now? And it didn't! So in reality even though the end of school year was June 27, 2013, many students never showed up anymore after June 14, 2013.
Basically, for the remaining two (2) weeks there were no students going to classes.
If students are to have 180 plus days of school and are to make up days for inclement weather (Super Storm Sandy) and such, why was this allowed?

Unfortunately, there was one teacher who was in some serious hot water. All because one of his female students was caught by her mother being home instead of being in school. Mom wanted to know why she was not in school. This young lady told her mother that the teacher told her to go home. NOT TRUE! Once again the teacher was blamed. This is unacceptable. If you do not believe me, ask the PEA.
In trying to cover their tracks and protect themselves. School administration tried to hang this teacher. Unacceptable! Are you going to tell me, with all of the added administration in the building and with the state of the art surveillance system, that administration did not notice, didn't realize, did not SEE, there were no students either in the classroom/s or in the building?

Not until a parent complained, administration as usual tried to pass the buck and blame the teacher? As for the rest of the days left on the school calendar, there were still no students. NOTHING CHANGED.

This is exactly what it is like during the entire school year. Students are everywhere and anywhere other than in their classrooms. You will never ever see any supervisors or administrators clearing the hallways and stairwells making students attend their classes.

As for the few students that did show up, I asked them what happens when students do not go to class and do not turn in their texts. They replied, "What texts?" Two of the few students who showed up were seniors. It was the two seniors who told me they haven't had textbooks in years.
Can you imagine, NO TEXTBOOKS, yet the district spent how many tens (10's) of thousands of dollars for a security fence to go around the entire perimeter of the building.

Think about it, what's the point of a security fence, when students can walk in and out of the building any time they want. With such a large enrollment, we as teachers never know who is and is not a student or if a person / student actually belongs inside here. Students don't have to go to class and the inside of the building is so out of control. It just doesn't make any sense.
Then it hit me. I realized why the schedule was set up this way. Teachers were supposed to give make up final exams, etc., etc. As for me with the many students who never even showed up for their final-exams, not one student came for a makeup or for extra credit.
WHY? Because they don't have to. They know they will pass and or graduate.
That's when I realized about the end of year schedule.
These last two (2) weeks were used right up to the day of graduation for administrators to find out which seniors are not passing and what can they do to get them to pass and graduate.
One of the biggest scams is CREDIT RECOVERY. Administrator would say that students took, completed and passed CREDIT RECOVERY. It's not about school and education. It's about the numbers/percentages. All lies--smoke and mirrors.

They would also say these students took a special CREDIT RECOVERY course- but had NOTHING to do with my or other teachers' classes and courses- pass and graduate all in a couple of days. If a student cannot pass a class all year, HOW do they make up credit in a few days actually hours? Even so-called summer school is 6 weeks long.

In fact, many students that never went to CREDIT RECOVERY not only passed, they still graduated.

I was told by guidance counselors that they were told, as long as a senior passed HSPA, they WILL GRADUATE! It has nothing to do with their courses. That's the education system here in Paterson, NJ.
I have an e-mail going back and forth asking if a certain Credit Recovery course may be used to give a student credit for my class. It clearly states that they have done this in the past but should not be used next year.

For a particular student, I asked for the documentation showing the dates, and times along with the signatures on all who signed off on his satisfactory completion of the Credit Recovery. As expected, I was stalled and basically never received them. However, I am sure there still has to be some type of documentation in his records, with the guidance department chairperson and his guidance counselor.
This student was supposed to have taken and completed Credit Recovery, knowing all too well, he has never even shown up for 5 minutes.
This really irritates me, because I spoke with an administrator one (1) week prior to graduation about this student and was told he has NOT met my class/course requirements, he will fail and will not graduate. Then miraculously this student not only passed, he graduated all because of CREDIT RECOVERY?

3. Lastly, is my documentation on my class's attendance, cuts &lateness's. (Start 2006 - 2013 End)
The 2012 - 2013 is the absolute worse.
This is the first and only year I had only 5 classes. I have always had 6 classes. This is added proof of students NOT going to class as well as being in the hallways all day, every day, all year without any type of disciplinary actions taken.

This district is deliberately passing and graduating students who have not met the necessary classroom requirements all to make the district / superintendent/s look good at the expense of the taxpayers and the country. Meanwhile students were all short changed drastically out of their education and future. Not only were these students short changed, so were their parents and family, so was the town of Paterson, NJ, the county of Passaic, the State of New Jersey and this entire country. Meanwhile, taxpayers are paying--and paying for what? It is NOT education. Giving someone a diploma [doesn't] makes them prepared for their future and ready for anything.

I hope one day someone you know has to go to a doctor who received their degree in some god forsaken 3rd and 4th world country. It is NO DIFFERENT! For the most part, these children are now set up to fail their entire lives.

Even the summer school program is a joke. Why are students allowed to not attend class, fail the entire school year, then allowed to attend summer school at TAXPAYERS' EXPENSE? Students and their parent of guardian do NOT even have to pay for summer school. Let me see. Students don't have to go to class all year long, fail the entire year, are allowed to attend summer school which is only 6 weeks, and don't even have to pay to attend summer school. And this is NOT just for ONE CLASS!

If that's all that is needed, then why have a school year 180 plus days for students, when students can attend summer school for 6 weeks and pass a class / course including gym? Can you imagine failing gym? Do you know why students fail gym? It is MOSTLY because student's refuse to change and receive an F for the day. They are unprepared for the day and for the entire school year. Yet the NJ taxpayers will have to pay for students to take gym for a summer school. If a student/s fails a class for the entire year, how does a student/s then pass this class and or course by taking a six (6) week's course during summer school? Then why do students have to go to school for 180 plus days? Please, explain this to me.

Look at the money taxpayers would be saving by not paying teachers' salaries for a full school year. Bottom line--as for the student's the results would be the same!

THIS IS NOT JUST NEGLECT; IT IS A CRIME!

PLEASE Mr. Van Roekel & Ms. Keshishian, how can you ignore this?
It is so easy to prove. The NJEA of Wayne, the PEA and I all have the proof about students not going to class.

It is my understanding that the NEA and the NJEA are supposed to be concerned about teachers working conditions. If what I have been writing and sending to you both is not serious, then PLEASE, explain to me what constitutes poor working conditions?

I have forwarded many e-mails to you with the date and time line on what is going on, just as it was happening. Not only to you, but to the Uniserv Director and two Uniserv field reps. I get NO RESPONSE OR REPLY. WHY?
I have to think that you just do NOT care.

Well, how can teachers be at the top of their game / profession to ensure that each student receives a proper and an excellent quality education under the conditions I have been writing about? You are supposed to be representing us teachers and our working conditions, well what are you both waiting for?

You can interview every teacher by sending a form with questions and a comment/ remark sections for each teacher to fill out.

After all, in your letter Mr. Van Roekel, you speak about how it is the right of every student receiving an education. Well, what type of an education does a child get when they are allowed NOT to go to class and just hang out in the hallways?

How about those students who want to learn and are being distracted by the majority of students who do nothing but cause havoc in and around classrooms all day every day all year?

What about the soooo many who were good students who realized that they don't have to be good students and will still pass? What about their rights to an education?

How about those students who came to school, went to their classes, have good attendance, does not get into any serious trouble, did their assignments, took their tests, did their homework, earned their passing grade/s and receives the same diplomas as the students who did not go to class, or school, did NO work, no assignments, no homework and not only passed but graduated. Do you call that EDUCATION? Would either of you send your children here?

I have been writing to you both for a year now.
Neither one of you can say you never knew anything about it.
Sooner or later it will ALL get out.

There is NO WAY, I am going to go through this again for the 2013 - 2014 school year.
Why should I? Quoting you Mr. Van Roekel, I have the support of millions of teachers. How can that be? I don't even have your support as I am writing and reporting what is going on. How many of the million teachers you talk about even know me or who I am, and about all the information I have sent you?

For that reason alone, PLEASE explain to me what the word in your letter "support" means?
DYFS must be informed on what is or should I say is not going on.
This is a state run and operated school district. This is all the more reasons why this cannot go on any longer. OR, is this the REAL reason why I am being ignored?
I propose a possible solution. I think there should be a series of meeting with the NEA, NJEA, PEA, DYFS and myself at the NJEA office in Wayne, NJ.
Would either one of you send your children and or grandchildren here?

"WE ARE RUINING A NATION"

Do either of you have a family member in the military?
Is this what they are fighting, dying and defending our country for?

NEA and especially the NJEA should not have commercials on TV, radio and in the newspapers telling the public how much you care about New Jersey's public schools and the right of every New Jersey child to obtain an excellent education.

What about the rights of our children being able to receive a proper education in Paterson, NJ? Our Public Schools are to be exemplary institutions of EDUCATION, LEARNING and teaching vital SOCIAL SKILLS. Not a place that allows students to hang out in school hallways, stairwells and any and every place else besides being in a classroom. Not a place where students can to do whatever they want without any fear of disciplinary action, which only reinforces what many already know, which is how to hang out on a street corner.

This is NOT education. Nor is it helping our students, their parents, their community, the city, our state as well as our country by ignoring and allowing all of this to go on and on year after year. IS THIS HOW OUR TAX DOLLARS TOWARDS PUBLIC EDUCATION IS SUPPOSED TO WORK?

IF I CAN'T GET HELP **(SUPPORT)** FROM NEA & THE NJEA WHICH ARE SUPPOSED TO BE POWERFUL ORGANIZATIONS, THAT SUPPOSEDLY CARE ABOUT CHILDREN RECEIVING A PROPER PUBLIC SCHOOL EDUCATION, THEN WHERE DO I TURN TO?
AREN'T EITHER ONE OF YOU CONCERNED?
I AM SO DAMN DISGUSTED.

                                                        Most respectfully,

                                                        Lee E McNulty

P S

    IF I DON'T HEAR FROM YOU BOTH, I KNOW NOW I NEVER REALLY HAD ANY SUPPORT.
                    IT WAS JUST A WORD USED IN A LETTER.


The documents I sent along in this letter/s were;

THE DYFS ARTICLE:

FINAL EXAM SCHEDULE:

DOCUMENTATION on my classes attendance, cuts & lates (Starting 2006 - 2013 End)

Furthermore, I never heard from Ms. Keshishian, President of the NJEA.
However, I did receive a reply from President of the NEA Mr. Dennis Van Roekel.

Here's his reply:

**nea**
NATIONAL EDUCATION ASSOCIATION
Great Public Schools for Every Student

1201 16th St., N.W.   Washington, DC 20036   |   Phone: (202) 833-4000

Dennis Van Roekel
*President*

Lily Eskelsen
*Vice President*

Rebecca S. Pringle
*Secretary-Treasurer*

John Stocks
*Executive Director*

August 28, 2013

Lee McNulty
10 Summit Avenue
Butler, NJ 07405

Dear Mr. McNulty:

Thank you for your correspondence of August 8, 2013. Please know that I hear your frustration and anger, much of it due to your inability to resolve the situation directly. I share your frustration in that, as NEA President, I also cannot directly impact much of what you desire either.

While school boards, administrators, and unions can sit together to discuss and map out a way forward, no single entity can move forward alone and achieve a desirable outcome. A blueprint for improving public education must include plans to engage all stakeholders. I am willing to assist, but cannot impact to do it solo.

Sincerely,

*Dennis Van Roekel*

Dennis Van Roekel
President

**4th Letter** my reply back to the President of the NEA.

September 15, 2013

Dear President of the NEA Mr. Dennis Van Roekel,

Received your letter of response, dated August 28, 2013, thank you.
It was not what I wanted to hear but I appreciated your quick response. I have yet to hear from the NJEA. "SOLO!" Well, you now know how I've felt for years. It seems no one wants to do anything about what is SERIOUSLY WRONG.

However, in your response to last year's letter and as it is written on the NEA web page, I quote, "BECAUSE THERE IS STRENGTH IN NUMBERS."

"With 3.2 million members, the National Education Association is the **largest employee organization in the country.** And NEA's nearly half million ESP members make us the **largest organization of school support employees in the world**. This numerical strength translates into advocacy and service - for improved pay and **working conditions**, rights on the job, **improved education for the students we serve**, and great deals on products and services our members need."

I highlighted, in **BOLD,** key words to the NEA's, Mission Statement.

Even as you wrote to me last year, 3.2 million, how would that be SOLO? Once again, in your letter of last year, you told me I had the support.

I thought the point of being in an organization and Union was **"STRENGTH"** in numbers.

Mr. Van Roekel, with all due respect sir, please explain to me and every NEA member if all of what I have written to you can go on CONTINUOUSLY, then what is the point of being part of the NEA?

Before you give an answer, please read the above and NEA's Mission Statement again.

So what happens now?

I know what will happen. These problems will continue to grow and grow and all the blame will be placed up on the teachers. Have you ever heard of any politician admit to a mistake, doing anything wrong or illegal?

Can we work together? "We," meaning you, me, NEA and the NJEA.
Let's get the NEA & THE NJEA to join forces and do something about these problems.

 We CANNOT let this to continue. Politicians are using teachers for their political agenda. We CANNOT let this to go on anymore. The taxpaying citizens have no idea what really goes on in our public schools, because it kept quiet, hushed up!

By working together and joining forces, we would be even bigger and stronger. Politicians would fear us. The people/citizens would love us.

It is NOT about fear and/or love. It's about doing the right thing. Doing nothing is criminal. It is no different [than] if someone saw a person being murdered and kept quiet. It's wrong! That person MUST speak up. Keeping quiet and not fighting back is admitting to the politicians and the public that we are the problem.

You are in Washington. You have been rubbing elbows with the high and mighty. Let's set up meetings with Congress and Senate. Let me bring my information and documentation with the support and under the protection of the NEA and NJEA. The average NEA & NJEA member is afraid of losing their job and that's why they keep quiet. I too am afraid of what can happen. However, that's not the way to correct what is wrong. There is a different in being afraid and being a coward.

If that was the case, then there would have never been an American Revolution.

I am sure once it starts, other cities and states will join us. We are not just 3.2 million strong. We are teachers, educated people and problem solvers. There has to be something we can do? PLEASE let's work together and do the right thing!

WHAT IS GOING ON IS MURDER NOT ONLY TO THE TAXPAYER BUT TO THE COUNTRY.

"WE ARE RUINING A NATION!"

Thank you and most respectfully,

Lee

I have not heard back from him. On September 13, 2013, I wrote another letter but to the NEW President Wendell Steinhauer and Vice President Marie Blistan of the NJEA.

## 5th Letter

September 13, 2013
Lee E. McNulty

Dear President Wendell Steinhauer & Vice President Marie Blistan,

On August 8, 2013, I sent the enclosed letter and attached documents to the President of the NEA, Mr. Dennis Van Roekel & President of the NJEA Barbara Keshishian, certified return receipt.

I have received my return receipts from both NEA & NJEA. However, I only received a response from the NEA President Mr. Dennis Van Roekel.     Enclosed is a copy.

I am wondering Mr. Steinhauer, if you received a copy of my letter to Ms. Keshishian? If not, enclosed is a copy.

As I read through my copy of the "NJEA REPORT," vol. 57, No.1 September 2013, on front page, "A new team for a new time," 2nd paragraph, it states, "Steinhauer vowed that under his leadership, NJEA would continue to work to promote great public schools for every child in New Jersey," then continues about politics and politicians.

I hope you are very serious. In the letter I sent to Ms. Keshishian, you will read disturbing information. This is NOT the first letter I sent to Ms. Keshishian and Mr. Van Roekel.
Included are copies of all three (3) letters dating August 30, 2012, December 3, 2012, & August 8, 2013.

There is no need for me to go any further. These four (4) letters explain it all.

> I hope to hear from you soon.
>
> Thank you and most respectfully,
>
> Lee E McNulty

The NJEA(New Jersey Education Association) has a new television commercial campaign slogan— *"MAKING EVERY PUBLIC SCHOOL GREAT FOR EVERY CHILD."* Meanwhile they have done *nothing* here in Paterson, NJ.

I have never heard from or received a reply from either the new President of the NJEA, Mr. Wendell Steinhauer, or the new vice president. However, I do have my receipt and my signed certified return receipt from the NJEA. So they can't use the excuse that they didn't receive them.

They are not just ignoring me, they are ignoring our students, all of the staff and teachers at JFK who are dues paying union members and all of the problems I've described.

Persistently, I sent two more e-mails to the President of the NJEA Mr. Steinhauer. He never replied.

Three presidents, one from the NEA (National Education Association), two from the NJEA and not one of them has taken an interest. Obviously, they don't care and don't want to get involved. Then why do they call themselves president of a union?

What is the reason for teachers paying all that money into annual dues to be a part of two large organizations, if they ignore problems and allow gross negligence not only to continue, but for it all to keep escalating? So much for the NEA and the NJEA being about better Public Education, the students of New Jersey, and the rights and working conditions for their teachers!

Bottom line-- since 1994, I cannot believe with all the letters written by my colleagues and me, not one person of importance and/or of authority took an interest, made any attempt to help or even investigate. WHY?

I JUST HAD A THOUGHT: I have been writing trying to get help and to no avail. It finally came to me. It is my opinion that the NJEA & NEA do not want to *really* get involved. If they did, it would open Pandora's Box, so to speak. They would be afraid that other teachers from every district will do what I have done and then they will be over inundated with complaints and it would end up costing and losing the NEA & NJEA a great deal of *MONEY*.

This makes me wonder if the NEA & NJEA is really about public education, New Jersey children's education, as well as the working conditions of their fellow NEA & NJEA UNION MEMBERS. Or is it the same thing? *It's all about the money*!

My last letter repeated many of the incidents above. I just want everyone to know that this letter went directly to the superintendent and as usual *nothing was* done about any of it. It is 2012, and everything has become WORSE, here at John F. Kennedy High School and the entire Paterson Public School District. However, according to the superintendent and all of the politicians, it's the teachers' fault.
Over the years, I've also written e-mails to the President of the PEA (Paterson Education Association) and several officials of the NJEA, on what's been going. Many times I gave a blow by blow description

of the incidents and what was going on as they were happening in the building. The PEA president has written back. However, I have NEVER heard from the NJEA officials. I was ignored.

During the 2011–13 school years, I started writing e-mails to the building principal and all of the administrators and cc: to the PEA & the NJEA. I never received a reply from any administrator. It's obvious or it is easier for someone to say, I never received or saw your e-mail. This way, they could deny receiving it. My thought was that if I e-mailed everyone, HOW can all of them deny it? Plus, I would cc myself on all of the e-mails as well, as proof I sent them. That's why they never replied. They did not want to have a paper trail of this type of discussion going back and forth.

However, one time the principal approached me in the hallway and as usual he was accompanied with the two heads of security and said, "I received your e-mail, but why did you cc the PEA?" That was all he was concerned about.

**Bottom line: Nothing was ever done about all the problems.**

I would like the superintendent, his administration, all of the administrators, the Commissioners of Education and the governors of New Jersey EXPLAIN how is everything I described allowed to go and be the teachers fault? Since1994, I have been desperately trying to get help and not one person made an attempt to help or investigate.

With everything happening and going on in the world today, what happened to the phrase, "If you see something, say something?"

I do, I did, and I was ignored.

Typical politics, it is always nothing more than just words!

## BUILDING EVACUATIONS

As time went on I started to keep track of every fire, false alarm, bomb scare and malfunctioning fire alarm that went on at John F. Kennedy.

Many times the alarms were pulled just so students can go outside and fight. Sometimes gangs, people from the streets, who do *not* belong inside, entered the building to deliberately pull the alarms, so they can hunt down the person or persons they want to jump, attack or fight.

As I have said before, if students were not allowed to be in the hallways, 99% of the evacuations would have never happened. With exception of 1995 & 2007 when a local newspaper covered the incidents, the evacuations from John F. Kennedy High School were never mentioned in the newspaper, on TV or the radio. *Why* was this allowed to *be hushed up*? The parents, community, and taxpayers have no idea what really went on here.

All of the information has to be documented not only with the Paterson Fire Department, but with the Mayor's Office, Town Hall, Paterson Police Department, Passaic County Sheriff's Department, Passaic County Arson Squad, etc.

Who *paid* for all of these *agencies* to show up at JFK each time there was another false alarm, bomb scare or a fire that was deliberately set? You know the answer, the *taxpayers*! This is a dangerous place to work and worse for our students who come here for an education. You will be more disgusted when you learn there were many times and by order of the administration that the schools fire alarm system was deliberately turned off.

The majority of the problems started *immediately* after the State of New Jersey took over the Paterson School District in 1991. From then on, the pulling of false alarms, bomb scares, and students actually setting fires within the building went rampant. The fire alarms were going off so often throughout the day, every day teachers were made to sit and guard the fire alarms. Unfortunately, I did not actually document all the evacuations until 2001. Before I started keeping a record/diary, as previously mentioned I was writing letters to the governor, newspapers, and sometimes even the superintendents, explaining what is and has been going on, all under an alias.

Unfortunately, the information below is plenty disturbing, way too many fire alarms, and always hushed up. Remember, this is *only* documentation of the times we evacuated. This does NOT include all the FIRES we actually had inside JFK and never evacuated because the alarms never went off.

Everything below is chronicled as part of my "DIARY."

## FIRE ALARMS
### 1997

**April 3** - fire alarms went off twice. One was a bomb scare. The other was because someone pulled a false alarm. Later that day there was a fire on the 2nd floor and the alarm was never sounded.

**Apr 10** - fire alarms go off again. False alarm!

### 1999

**January 4** - fire alarms go off. False alarm!

**Jan 7** - fire alarms go off. False alarm again!

## 2000 - 2001

**Oct 4** - after 1hour after HSPT, someone pulled a false alarm.

**Oct 5** -15 - 20 minutes after the HSPT, someone pulled a false alarm. At **2:55,** another false alarm!

**Oct 23** - fire alarms go off. False alarm!

**Nov 7** - fire alarms go off. False alarm!

**January 26** - 9:45, evacuated the building. Bomb scare. K9s summoned.

**Jan 30** - another bomb-scare. We did not evacuate the building.

**Feb 5** - 6th period fire alarms go off again. Another false alarm!

**May 4** - had to evacuate the building—- bomb scare, and not only our school.

**May 23** - another bomb scare. We did *not* evacuate the building.

**May 25** - another bomb scare!

**May 30** - another bomb scare!

**May 31** - fire alarms go off. False alarm!

## 2001– 2002

**Sept 11, 2001,** we all remember the day. Since that day, we have had to evacuate the building numerous times. Bomb scares!

During the week of HSPT (High School Proficiency Testing), another bomb threat. However, we did NOT stop the testing.

**Oct 31** -7:50am, evacuated building, because of a bomb threat.

**January 9, 2002** - 6th period fire alarms go off. Evacuated building. False alarm again!
**At the end of 6th period** we had to evacuate the building *again*? Bomb threat!

**Jan 10** -7th period fire alarms go off. Evacuated building. False alarm again!

**Jan 11** - 6th period again, we had to evacuate the building.
**7th period** the fire trucks were all around the building again. We did not evacuate.

**Jan 17** – another bomb scare. We did not evacuate.

**Jan 18** - end of 6th period, we had to evacuate the building because someone pulled the fire alarms.

**June 12** - for the past week, smoke/stink bombs have been going off every day all day.

**June 20** - smoke/stink bombs still going off every day since 6/12.

## 2002 - 2003

**Sept 11** - had to evacuate the building. Don't know if it's a bomb scare or false alarm.

**Sept 30** - fire alarms go off. Evacuated the building. Fire in 3rd floor bathroom.

**Oct 7** - fire alarms goes off first thing this morning. Then at 12:50 the alarms went off again. **Same day**, 1:50 pm alarm goes off again. *Again*, the alarms go off later.

**Oct 10** - 7th period, fire alarms go off. Evacuated building. False alarm!

**Oct 15** - 8th period, fire alarms go off. Evacuated building. False alarm! Later this morning someone called in a bomb scare. We did not evacuate.

**Oct 23** - 7th period, fire alarms go off again. False alarm again!

**Oct 24** - 7th period, fire alarms go off. Evacuated building. False alarm!

**Oct 25** - smoke/stink bombs all day in hallway.

**Nov 4** - 7th period, fire alarms go off. Another false alarm!

**Nov 18** - 6th period, fire alarms go off. Evacuated the building AGAIN. Another false alarm!

**Dec 12** - fire alarm goes off. Evacuated building. Another false alarm!

**January 3, 2003** - 2nd day back from Christmas fire alarm goes off. Evacuated building. False alarm!

**Jan 7** - fire alarm goes off between 5th & 6th periods. Another false alarm!

**Jan 24** - 9:58am, fire alarms go off again. Evacuated building again. Another false fire alarm!

**Feb 21** - between 3rd & 4th periods, fire alarms go off. Evacuated building. False alarm again.

**May 9** - this is actually the first REAL fire drill we have had in years. See the reasons why?

**May 29** - 9th period alarms go off. Evacuated building. False alarm again!

**May 30** - 5th period, fire alarms go off. Evacuated building. False alarm again!

**Jun 19** - 9th period, evacuate the building because someone called the office and said there was a bomb.

## 2003– 2004

**Sept 16** - fire trucks outside school. Maybe a bomb threat again. Not sure. Did not evacuate?

**Sept 17** - fire alarm pulled. False alarm already!

**Oct 9** - 8th period, fire alarms go off. Evacuate building. Don't know the reason.

**Oct 22** - fire alarms goes off, Evacuated building again. False alarm again. Students wanted to fight.

**Oct 27** - 7th period I heard fire trucks. Someone called 911 said there was a fire. We did not evacuate.
**9th period about 2:10pm,** fire alarms go off. Evacuated building. Another false alarm!

**Oct 29** - fire alarms goes off again. Evacuated building again. False alarm again.

**Oct 30** - because of Goosey Night/day, all fire alarm boxes and posts were guarded by TEACHERS.

**Nov 3** - 9th period alarms go off. Evacuated building AGAIN. False alarms again!

**Nov 4** - 9th period the fire alarms go off again. Evacuated the building. False alarm again!

**Nov 20** - 9th period, fire alarms go off again. Another false alarm!

**Nov 25** - 3rd period, fire alarms go off. Evacuated building. False alarm!
**Later that day** fire alarms go off again. Evacuated building, another false alarm!

**Dec 9** - 6th period, alarms go off. Evacuated building again. This time there was a fire.

**Dec 23** - 7:50am, had to evacuate again. Another bomb scare!

**January 6, 2004** - 2nd day back from Christmas holiday. Bomb scare 7:10am. We evacuated the building.

**Jan 8** - another bomb scare. Instead of evacuating, everyone was told to go to the cafeterias.

**Jan 9** - 9th period, alarms go off. Evacuated building. Another false fire alarm!

**Jan 13** - 1st period, fire alarm goes off mid-term exam. Because of sensors in my classroom.
**Same day,** fire alarm went off again. Evacuated building. Another false alarm!

**Feb 25** - 5th period fire alarms go off. Evacuated building again. False alarm so students/gangs can fight.
7th period alarms go off again. Evacuated building. Don't know the reason why.

**Feb 26** - end of 8th period, the fire alarms went off. Evacuated building. False alarm AGAIN!

**Apr 28** - Fire alarms went off 5 times today.

**Apr 29** - fire alarms went off 6th period, 7th period, and 8th period. All false alarms.
9th period alarms go off. No one knows if we should evacuate or not. It was a false alarm.
9th period alarms go off *again*. No one knew what to do. *Another false alarm!*
10th period alarm goes off *again*. *Another false alarm!*

**Jun 10** - fire alarms go off twice. Don't know the reasons.

**June 11** - same as above.

**Jun 16** - 8th period someone called in a bomb scare. We did NOT evacuate the building.

**Jun 17** - fire alarms went off twice. The first time, 1:15pm and again at 1:50pm. It seems to be sensors.

**Jun 18** - about 1:30pm we evacuated the building. It was another bomb scare.
Same day fire alarm goes off again. Sensors again!

## 2004 - 2005

**Sept 9** - 8th period alarms go off. Evacuated building. Fire alarms. I do not know why?

**Oct 17** - fire alarms going off all day due to the NEW system. Then between periods 8 & 9, a false alarm.

**January 5, 2005** - 9th period approximately 1:36pm fire alarms go off; another false alarm!

**Jan 6** – 9am evacuated the building. Someone called and was very specific about a bomb going off.

**Jan 12** - fire alarms went off at 12:20pm. False alarm again! Fire alarms go off again at 12:55pm.

**Jan 28** - 2nd period, the fire alarms go off again. We don't know if we should or shouldn't evacuate.

**Feb 24** - 9th period, fire alarms go off. Did not evacuate. False alarm again!

**March 14** - 9th period fire alarms go off again. We were TOLD to evacuate. Don't know the reason.

**Mar 22** - 3rd period 9:16am false alarm! **4th period** 10:05am false alarm again!
**6th period** false alarm again! **7th period** 1:01pm *another false alarm!*

**Apr 4** - first day back from Easter vacation, 5th period, 11:14am false alarm again!

**Apr 5** - 4th period, 10:05am false alarm! Then again during 9th period, 1:40pm another false alarm!

**Apr 6** - 9th period, 1:44pm false alarm again!

**Apr 7** - 9th period, false alarm again!

**Apr 8** - 7th period fire alarms go off. False alarm again!

**Apr 15** - 7th period 12:19pm fire alarms go off. False alarm, *AGAIN!*

**Apr 20** - 3rd period 9:45am fire alarms go off. Again during 6th period 11:45am. Both were false alarms!

**Apr 21** - 7th period 12:16pm false alarm *AGAIN!*

**May 3** - 7th period 12:47pm, fire alarms go off. Another false alarm!

**May 19** - 7th period 12:37pm, another false fire alarm!

**Jun 8** - 4th period, 10am, fire alarms go off. Bomb scare, 4th period 10am evacuated building.
**9th period** 2:03pm, fire alarms go off. Sensors were triggered

**Jun 10** – 7am, fire alarm going off. I don't know why!

## 2005 - 2006

**Sept 21** - fire alarms have been going off all day.

**Oct 17** - the fire alarms have been going off all day.

**Oct 22** – 10am, fire alarms went off around.

**Oct 25** - fire alarms go off. False fire alarm again!

**Dec 21** - 5th period 10:50am, false alarm/faulty system

**January 3, 2006** - 9:56pm, fire alarms go off. Fire on the 2nd floor

**Jan 4** - 8th 1:04pm, fire alarms go off. False alarm!

**Jan 9** - 6th 11:45am, fire alarms go off. Another false alarm!

**Jan 19** - 5th period, 12:30pm fire alarms go off. False alarm!

**Jan 26** - 7th period, 12:49pm fire alarms go off. Evacuated building again. False alarm! Fire alarms go off again at 1:23pm. No one knew what to do. False alarm again!

**Jan 31** - 6:46am, fire alarms go off. / Faulty alarm this time.

**Feb 9** - 9th period, 2:20pm, fire alarms go off. Evacuated building. Real fire.

**Feb 10** - 7th 12:19pm, fire alarms go off. Evacuated the building again. False alarm!

**Feb 16** - 2nd period, 8:17am, fire alarms go off. Evacuated building. Bomb scare!

**Feb 1** - 1st period 7:41am fire alarms go off. Bomb scare again!

**Mar 15** - 5th period, 10:50am, fire alarms went off. Sensor was tripped.

**Mar 20** - 7th period 12:15pm, no alarm, fire department came, did not evacuate building. Bomb scare!

**Apr 6** - 9th period 2:17pm, fire alarms went off. There was a fire.

**Apr 25** - 9:07am, fire alarms go off. Evacuated building. False alarm!

**Apr 28** - 8th period 1:29pm, fire alarms go off. False alarm again!

**May 9** - 4th period 9:59am, fire alarms go off. Evacuated building. Fire in room 235.

**May 12** - 9th period, fire alarms go off. This time smoke smell was emanating from the elevator.

**May 22** - 6:58am, the fire alarms go off. Evacuated building. Sensors in the cafeteria.

**May 26** - 8th period 12:10pm, fire alarms go off again. Evacuated building. False alarm! 12:35, alarms go off *again*. 25 minutes later I'm bringing a *wheelchair student* down from the 3rd floor.

**Jun 1** - 7th period 12:35pm, fire alarms go off. No one knew what to do. False alarm again!

**Jun 2** - 8th period 1:13, fire alarms go off again. Evacuated building again. False alarm! 1:40pm, fire alarm goes off again. Evacuated building. *False alarm again!*

### 2006 - 2007

**Sept 13, 2006** - 8th period 1:22pm, fire alarms go off. Evacuated building. False alarm!

**Sept 18** - 10th period 3pmalarms go off. Evacuated building. A bomb scare!

**Sept 25** - 7th period 12:22pm, alarms go off. Evacuated building False alarm again!

**Oct 4** - 3rd 9:40am, fire alarms go off. Evacuated building. False alarm again!

**Oct 11** - 2nd period 8:23am, *bomb scare!* Had to evacuate building!

**Oct 17** - 5th period 10:48am, fire alarms go off. Evacuated building again. False alarm!

**Oct 25** - 9th period 1:50pm, fire alarms go off. Evacuated building again. False alarm!

**Oct 26** - 8th period1:33pm, fire alarms goes off, Evacuated building again, False alarm!

**Oct 27** - 9th period 1:43pm, fire alarms goes off. Evacuated building again, False alarm!

**Nov 1** - 6th period 11:32am, fire alarms go off again. Evacuated building again. False alarm!

**Nov 2** - 2nd period 8:40am, fire alarms go off again. Evacuated building again. Bomb scare again!

**Nov 6** - 4th period 10:19am, fire alarms go off. Evacuated building. False alarm!

**Nov 7** - 9th period 1:43pm, fire alarms go off again. Evacuated building again. False alarm! **10th period** 2:23pm, fire alarms go off again. False alarm again!

**Nov 8** - 5th period approximately 11:18am, no alarms, did not evacuate building, Bomb scare!

**Dec 14** - between 6th & 7th period, alarms did not go off. We did not evacuate. Bathroom was on fire.

**Dec 18** - 8th period 1:23pm, fire alarms go off. Evacuated building. Was told next day *Bomb scare!*

**January 16, 2007** - 3rd period 9:40pm, fire alarms go off. Evacuated building again. *Bomb scare!* **4th period** 10:20am fire alarms go off again. Evacuated building. *Another bomb scare!* **8thperiod** 1:04pm, fire alarms go off again. Evacuated building. *Another bomb scare!*

**Mar 8** - 9th period 12:57pm, fire alarms go off again. Evacuated building. False alarm!

**Mar 13** - 8th period 12:55pm, fire alarms go off. Evacuated building. False alarm again!

**Mar 19** - fire department was here. Did not evacuate building. Bomb scare!

**Mar 30** - 5th period 11:24am, fire alarms went off. Evacuated building. False alarm again!
**Between** 5th & 6th 11:39pm, fire alarms went off. Evacuated building. False alarm *again!*

**Apr 3** - 7th period fire alarms go off again. False alarm again!

**Apr4** - 4th period 10:01am, fire alarms go off. Evacuated building. False alarm!

**Apr 5** - 8th period 12:58pm, fire alarms go off. Evacuated building again.

**Apr 23** - 6th period 1:27pm, fire alarms go off. Evacuated building. Supposedly malfunction

**Apr 25** - 8th period 12:58pm, fire alarms go off again. Evacuated the building again.

**Apr 26** - 4th period 10:01am, fire alarms go off. Evacuated the building again. False alarm!

**Apr 27** - fire alarms go off Evacuated the building. Don't know what is going on.

**May 1** - 6th period 11:33am, fire alarms go off. Evacuated building. False alarm!

**May 15** - 6th period, 11:31am, fire alarms go off. Evacuated building again. False alarm.
A little later the fire alarms go off again. Evacuated the building again, *False alarm again!*

**June 19** - No classes at this time approximately 2:10. The fire alarms go off. Don't know why!

Notice the increase of evacuations? Once again another year and none of this was ever in the newspaper or on TV. It all remains to be HUSHED UP!

### 2007 - 2008

**Sept 5 - 2007** - 9:18am, alarms go off. Evacuated building. Malfunction with the sensors.

**Sept 27** - 8:15 - police and fire department arrive. We did *NOT* evacuate the building. Another bomb scare!

**Oct 15** - 2nd period 9:57am, fire alarm went off. We evacuated building.

**Oct 16** - 2nd period 9:16am, fire alarms went off. Evacuated building. False alarm!
**Again** during 2nd period 9:43, fire alarms go off. Evacuated building again. *False alarm again!*

**Oct 17** - alarms did not go off; *however*, the fire department arrived at 12:27pm. The alarms did *NOT* go off, because they were shut off. There was a fire on the second floor, boys' bathroom.

### THE DAY OF THE RIOT

**Oct 22 - 2nd** period 9:10am, fire alarms go off. Evacuated building. Fire girls' bathroom 2nd floor.
**Again 2nd** period 9:54am, fire alarms go off. Evacuated building. Fire girls' bathroom 2nd floor *AGAIN!*
**And again,** 10:46am, fire alarms go off. Evacuated building.
**And again**, 11:51am, fire alarms go off. Evacuate the building, *AGAIN!!*
Have VIDEO &digital pictures.

**Oct 23** - 7th period 2:15pm, fire alarms go off. Evacuated building. False alarm!

**Oct 24** - 12:05pm, fire alarms go off. Evacuated building. False Alarm!

**Oct 25** - 6th period 1:06pm, fire alarms go off. Evacuated building. A fire in one of the bathrooms.

**Oct 26** - 6th period 1:15pm, fire alarms go off again. Evacuated building

**Nov 2** - 6th period 12:50pm, fire alarms go off. Evacuated building again.

**Nov 13** - 7th period 1:44 pm, fire alarms go off again. Evacuated building.1:57pm fire alarms go off. Evacuated building. Came back in a few minutes later and the fire alarms go off again. *We had to evacuate the building again!*

**Nov 14** - 5th period 12:26pm, fire alarms go off. Evacuated building.
12:44pm fire alarms go off again. Evacuated the building *AGAIN!*

**Nov 26** - 6th period 1:23pm, fire alarms go off.
**7th period** 1:52pm, fire alarms go off *AGAIN!*

**Dec 17** - 7am fire alarms go off. We did not evacuate the building.

**January 17, 2008** - 2nd period 11:37am, fire alarms go off. Evacuated building. False alarm!

**Jan 30** - 3rd period 10:40am, fire alarms go off. Evacuated building. False alarm again!

**Feb 4** - 5th period 11:05 pm, fire alarms go off. Evacuated building again. False alarm again!

**Feb 8** - 4th period 11:35am, fire alarms go off. Students sprayed the sensor, making the alarm to go off.

**Feb 19** - 6th period 1:03pm, fire alarms go off again. Evacuated building again. False alarm again!

**Feb 20** - 2nd period 9:37am, fire alarms go off. Evacuated building again. There was a fire on the 2nd floor.

**Feb 28** - 3rd period 10:46am, fire alarms go off again. Evacuated building again. False alarm again!

**Apr 14** - 6th period 12:45pm, fire alarms go off. Evacuated building, AGAIN! Supposedly a malfunction??

**May 29** -7th 1:49pm, fire alarms go off. Evacuated building. A sensor was deliberately triggered.

**Jun 3** - 6th 12:54pm, fire alarms go off. Evacuated building. False alarm!

**2008 – 2009**

**Sept 29** - 6th period 11:30am, alarms go off. Evacuated building. False alarm.

**Oct 3** -7th period, 12:47pm, fire alarms go off. Evacuated building. False alarm.

**Oct 7** -7th period 12:49pm, fire alarms go off. Evacuated building.

**Oct 14** - 3rd period 9:05am fire alarms go off. Evacuated building. Supposedly it was a sensor? **Then again at**9:19am, fire alarms go off. Evacuated building again! Supposedly a sensor.

**Oct 16** - 4th period 10:37am, fire alarms go off. Evacuated building. Don't know reason why.

**Oct 20** - 1st period fire alarms go off. Evacuated building. Sensors again?

**Oct 22** - 7th period 12:30pm, fire alarms go off. Evacuated building. Sensors again?

**Nov17** - 8th period 12:59pm, fire alarms go off. Evacuated building. False alarm.

**Nov 26** - 9:01am, fire alarms go off. Evacuated building. Don't know why. Alarms went off all day long.

**Dec 12** - pulled into parking lot about 6:50am. The fire alarm was going? Don't know why.

**January 20, 2009** - 8:02am, fire alarms go off. Evacuated building. Steam pipe broke.

**Mar 12** - 3rd period 9:24am, fire alarms go off. Evacuated building. It was a sensor in my room.

**Mar 23** - 4th period 10:19am, fire alarms go off. Evacuated building. Fire in boys' room 1st floor. **5th period**10:59am, fire alarms go off again. Evacuated building again. Fire in boys' bathroom.

**Mar 24** - 4th period 9:54am fire alarms go off again. Evacuated building again. False alarm again!

**Mar 30** - 8th period1:35pm, fire alarms go off. Evacuated building. Someone lit a sensor on fire.

**Jun19** - 1:46pm, fire alarms go off. Evacuated building. However, it was a malfunction.

## 2009 – 2010

**Sept 22** - 10:55am, fire alarms go off. Evacuated building. Fire in the girl's bathroom.

**Oct14** - 3rd period 9:12am, fire alarms go off. Evacuated building. Do not know why?

**January12** - fire alarms go off, Evacuated building. It was cold and windy. False alarm!

**Apr 27** - 4th period10:22am, fire alarms go off. Evacuated building. False alarm!

**Jun 3** - 9th period, fire alarm goes off. Evacuated building. Supposedly alarm malfunctioned.

## 2010 - 2011

**Nov 12** - 4th period 10:27am, fire alarms go off. Evacuated building. False alarm!

**Jan 13, 2010** - 1:18pm, fire alarms go off. Evacuated building. Supposedly fire alarm malfunction.

**Jan 6** - 11:54am, fire alarms go off. Evacuated building, there was a fire on 2nd floor.

## FIRE ALARMS 2011 - 2012
## 1st YEAR OF RESTRUCTURING

**Oct 21, 2011** - 6th period girls' bathroom by cafeteria was set on fire. No alarm, No evacuation.

**Oct 28** - we had to evacuate the building for a fire drill.

**Dec 2** - 10:40am, fire alarms go off. Evacuated building. Students triggered sensors to go off.

**Dec 5** - 2:33pm, fire alarms go off. Evacuated building. I don't know why.

**Dec7** - 12:33pm, fire alarms go off. Evacuated the building. I don't know why.

**Dec 9** - 12:56pm, fire alarms go off. Evacuated building. I don't know why.

**January 13, 2012** - 11:58am, fire alarms go off. We finally evacuated the building. False alarm!

**Jan 20** - 9:56am, fire alarms go off again. False alarm again!

**Jan 30** - 2:30pm, fire alarms go off again. Evacuated building again. I don't know why?

**Feb 16** - 12:13pm, fire alarms go off again. Evacuated the building again. Sensor in room 11, saw dust.

**Apr 5** - 12:32pm, fire alarms go off. Evacuated building again. *FALSE ALARM, AGAIN!*

**Apr 16** - 12:46pm, fire alarms go off. Evacuated the building again. *FALSE ALARM AGAIN!*

Throughout each school year students ignite so many smoke and stink bombs within the building, not just for the smell but for the chaos it causes also. This is dangerous and a hazard for students who suffer from asthma. Nothing is ever done or attempted to try to stop this behavior. How can it NOT be on the security video?

## FIRE ALARMS 2012 – 2013
## 2nd YEAR OF RESTRUCTURING

Now the entire building perimeter is enclosed by a 10-foot fence. When we have to evacuate the building, where are the students going to go? There are over TWO THOUSAND FIVE HUNDRED students, plus teachers, secretaries, administrators, visitors, vendors and other support personnel who will now all be standing next to the building making it dangerous for the police and fire departments to get through. Absolutely ridiculous!

Nov. 15, 2012, fire in boys' bathroom. The alarms did not go off. We did not evacuate the building. See complete write up in "MY DIARY"

Unfortunately, the false alarms and bomb scares all started in 1991, when the state took over the district. At that time, I did NOT document the events because I never realized it would escalate as it did. However, because it was getting worse and worse each year, I finally started in 1997.

In fact, the next few years were so bad, the administration's solution to keep students who continuously roam the building all day, every day, all year from pulling false alarms, was to assign teachers to guard all the fire alarm boxes.
Still allowing students to roam the building all day, the students were using the school's pay phones to call in bomb threats. After a few years, the administration finally decided to remove *all* the pay phones. Several years later, Mr. Bonora, a wood shop teacher, decided to use money from his budget to purchase surveillance cameras and with the help of his students they installed them throughout the building.

Since I started documenting the false alarms, bomb scares, actual fires, etc. it took the district 13 years to finally put in cameras. Why?

Sadly, because the alarms in some years have gone off so many times, especially within a single day, sometimes in a few hours and usually false alarms, students and faculty did not take them seriously. In fact, some teachers were fired, because they thought it was just another false alarm and didn't evacuate the building. Also with so many students in the hallways all day long, once the alarm is sounded to evacuate the building, it becomes a signal for students to act up even more causing more chaos.

If a teacher does not have a class they will usually assist security, police and administrators in directing students to evacuate the building at the nearest exit. Unfortunately, they are ignored. Some students become argumentative, confrontational, curse and threaten them with shear defiance. YES, even with the police present, students act this way. It is a *big* game here. Once everyone is supposedly out of the building, you will see students who defiantly ran away from their teachers hanging out windows yelling and waving to everyone. Teachers are fired for not evacuating. I doubt if the students were even disciplined.

Once outside many students refused to stay with their teachers and class. They roam around or just leave altogether. So many times, huge gang fights broke out. If it was snowing or snow on the ground, major snowball fights erupted usually ended up with students and/or teachers pelted with snowballs and injured. There is absolutely *no control*.

There was no order for students reentering the building— just chaos. The atmosphere inside became worse than it was outside. All you saw were students gathering in large groups talking, running through the building as fast as they can, chasing and deliberately knocking anyone and everyone over. They were screaming, yelling at the top of their lungs, fighting-- basically a riot. It is so out of control. It is beyond anything that anyone would ever imagine to happen within a school. Security was in the hallway yelling for everyone to get to class, but they're wasting their breath. Students ignore them and continue to do whatever they want to do; meanwhile you will not see an administrator anywhere.

The most that may occur in attempt to control the chaos was an announcement made to inform everyone which period to go back to. Unfortunately, the noise created by the students is so loud; you cannot hear it let alone think. The only way anyone actually knew what was said during the announcement, is if an administrator tells security over the walkie-talkie. Then security yelled the information throughout the building for students to go to such and such period. Go back to your class. Go, get out of the halls. This goes on for at least 20 minutes.

It is an absolute disaster each time the alarm is sounded. The rest of the school day is absolutely lost. It is pandemonium here. The administration does NOTHING.

Not once were their instructions and added drills to teach and reinforce the importance of having a proper, safe and an orderly evacuation. It is just allowed to continue as if it is "NORMAL!"

If parents really knew what truly goes on here, they would NOT just remove their children from this school, they would have an unbelievable lawsuit against the administration, the district, the city of Paterson and the State of New Jersey.

The best way I can explain what goes on inside here- it is like Thanksgiving Day, Black Thursday, when Wal-Mart opens its doors up for shopping. It is so out of control, wild, and shear chaos, with students running all over the place, chasing and shoving one another with ill-mannered, uncivilized, disgusting behavior. It is a riot-like atmosphere, where the noise level is so deafening and grossly filled with non-stop and consistent obscene foul language filling the air long after the bell or buzzer sounds for *all* students to be in class. And this goes on all day, every day, and all year, year after year. It is absolute, "HELTER SKELTER!"

When you try to work and live in an environment like this you are in a HYPER state of *awareness*. It is nothing less than being constantly in a dangerous or combat situation, and waiting for a strike. You spend your time looking, watching and waiting as if you are constantly on guard waiting for what's going to happen next. Even when another person comes to see to speak with you, you're listening and focused on what is being said, but your eyes are all over looking, watching and being aware of your surroundings. It is always worse in the hallways. Many times unless I mentioned to the other person what they're doing, they would reply back, they didn't even realize they were doing that. Because anything, especially violence, can erupt at any time over anything and usually over nothing. When you come home from teaching you are exhausted. It is like being on constant guard duty.

The only time this school is under any type of control is when there is a "LOCK DOWN" drill. At that time, and that time ONLY (about 10 minutes), there are no students in the hallways. What's the point of having LOCK DOWN DRILL? There are always people (intruders) in the building that do NOT belong inside here.

Meanwhile for 13 *plus* years, no one was ever held responsible or accountable.

The administration decided because there were so many evacuations they never held any fire drills. They considered the evacuations as their monthly fire drill procedures for the students and staff.

What I find even more sickening and disgusting is when anyone receives a memo from any administrator and/or from the district office at the bottom of the page in large bold letters it says, **"OUR CHILDREN, OUR FUTURE."** *ARE YOU FREAKING KIDDING ME!*

Prior to the State taking over, the administration never allowed the continuous pulling of fire alarms, setting fires, setting off sensors and the consequences were severe. It is *DANGEROUS* to falsely pull a fire alarm.

In the last 3 or 4 years I taught at JFK, the superintendent/administration did NOT want to suspend students. Suspensions create a paper trail which makes the administration and all those directly involved with this continuing State Run School District look bad. If there are no suspensions and no paper trail it makes it look as if things have improved. So with the refusal to suspend or to have any type of discipline in the building, the chaos, insanity and dangerous situations not only to prevail, but continued to grow as it is all constantly ignored.

Obviously, because of the video cameras in and outside of the building, there are fewer false alarms. However, look how long it took to solve this problem. How much did it cost the district and NJ taxpayers for the fire department, fire marshals and inspectors, police department, sheriff's department, bomb squad with K9s, and riot squad having to rush here numerous times?
No parent would allow their children to act and carry on this way. If what goes on inside this school went on anywhere in public, they would be arrested.

## MY DIARY

Below is a copy of a journal, "MY DAILY DIARY," during the years I was assigned at JFK High School. Like with noting the evacuations, I started this late in my career because I use to just write letters to the governors, editors of newspapers and even to the superintendents. Once it became more and more out of control here, I began to keep an actual daily journal/diary of the day's events.

This diary/journal is to show the lack of leadership, supervision and the out of control atmosphere that goes on instead of education every day, day after day, all year and for YEARS all as the school and the entire school district of Paterson, NJ was and still is under state takeover control!

MY COMMENTS TO THE ABOVE ENTRIES:

**Remember! Teaching is the most important and noblest of professions. Teachers pass on civilization!** HOWEVER, teachers are taking the blame for everything while the administration and the schools administrators are the ones who are really at fault.

Next is a letter I had written to the Judge of Paterson Municipal Court about an evening I was jumped by a pack of students while attempting to leave John F. Kennedy High School after chaperoning a school dance.

February 15, 1995<br>Lee E McNulty<br>Address and telephone # omitted

Your Honor,

    Your Honor, because of so many cancellations and changes of court dates I compiled this letter. My witness has suffered as much as I have and maybe more in the loss of time at work. I have written this letter so in effect the dates are changed or canceled once again, my witness would not be punished for his unselfish act of getting involved by helping me during a very dangerous crisis.
    I hope you will accept this written testimony, with signatures.

Thank you,<br>Lee E McNulty

    On February 18, 1994, I, Lee E. McNulty was a chaperone for a dance at J.F. Kennedy High School, in Paterson, NJ. After the dance, I proceeded to go home. I departed the school and turned on to Preakness Ave. After only driving a few feet, many boys attacked me while I was driving my car. These kids were hitting and kicking my car as I was trying to pass. I attempted to go forth, but they jumped in front of my car and immediately surrounded me. They continued beating, kicking, throwing items and picking up objects from the garbage to hit my car. I jumped out of my car and the kids had backed off. One boy from the passenger side of my car was standing on the sidewalk had thrown a garbage can at me and it hit the trunk of my car. I picked up the garbage can and threw it back at him. This boy's name is (student name omitted #1).

Unfortunately, the garbage can hit and bounced off a snowbank, breaking the rear window of a parked car. The owner who was standing up on his balcony saw what happened and came down extremely raged. A guard from J.F. Kennedy High School witnessed the incident. He and his 2 friends had come to my assistance. This guard is named Mr. (name omitted) tried to keep the irate neighbor from attacking me. During the commotion between the neighbor and I, a boy named (student name omitted #2) had picked up a steel folding chair and proceeded to beat on my car. (The driver side.) Student #1 proceeded to kick in my grill, and also attempted to drive off with my car. That's when one of the security guard's friends stepped in, put my car back into park, and removed Student #1 from out of my car. I then decided to move my car and park it in the school parking lot. I came back to the scene and tried to reason with the neighbor, assuring him that I will take care of the damages. He was extremely violent and unreasonable, and finally made his way passed the security guard, and lunged at me. I had defended myself by wrestling him down to the street.

Student #1 wasn't finished. He then immediately started taunting the security guard. He was provoking and threatening the security guard into a fight by using the most of vulgar verbal language. Fortunately, because of my wrestling match with [the] neighbor, two police cars arrived. The security guard's attention was then averted back to my situation, and keeping well away from the taunting and agitator student #1.

Once the policemen were out of their cars and took charge of the scene, in seconds, the coward Student #1 left.
These statements I make are true.

Victim<br>Lee E McNulty

**Side note**: There has never ever been a dance after this incident at John F. Kennedy High School.

## DIARY ENTRY

**April 3, 1997** - fire alarms went off twice. First was a bomb scare. The second was because someone pulled the alarm. Later that day there was a fire in the boys' room on the 2nd floor. Security could not get in, because the door was locked. The fire alarms never went off, no one evacuated the building, and the first three fire extinguishers did work not. Smoke was billowing out of the bathroom window.

**April 10, 1997** - fire alarm goes off again. We're told it is a faulty alarm. Later they announced they caught the student who pulled the alarm and he will be prosecuted to the fullest extent of the law.

*********************

**During 7th period, I told the class a judge will be here tomorrow at 1:45 to grade their castings.**

I said to the students I would like all of you to be here. They were also instructed to clean their castings, take the magic marker, put their names on them and place them on the back table.

This was supposed to be a very easy, simple assignment and day.

However, I asked (student name omitted #1), who is lying between three desks trying to sleep to get up. He opens his eyes wide, looks up and mumbles something to me and remains lying down. I have no idea what was said, but as usual it has to be foul. I asked him again and about three more times each following with his reply of FUCK YOU. He is doing this because he wants to continue where (student name omitted #2), left off who also has a foul mouth, and I just had words with him about his behavior and language. I have young ladies in this classroom, and foul language is not allowed or tolerated. Everyone, including myself, is subjected to the penalties that accompany the use of foul language.

Student #1 kept it up, but when he called me a *MOTHER FUCKER*. Instead of stopping and behaving properly, he kept yelling this over and over again. Then he spat on me.

He got up, still carrying on and left the class as he has done all year long.

A teacher (name omitted) was trying to talk to me at the time.

At the end of the period the student comes back with three other boys, swearing, threatening, and coming at me, yelling "mother fucker, what are you going to do now mother fucker, now mother fucker, come on mother fucker, come on mother fucker, what are you going to do now mother fucker," threatening me, over and over, as two of the boys started to surround me.

This is a blatant act of intimidation by using terroristic threats. Unfortunately for them, I do not get intimidated. As they started surrounding me like a pack of wolves going in for the kill, I picked up a wooden mallet and warned them I will defend myself and told them to get the hell out of my classroom.

I approached the bigger one with the tattoos on his arm and proceeded to escort them all out of my room. They did not leave without more threats of bodily harm.

Once they were in the hallway, they started to carry on more and more; yelling more threats of bodily harm, and all the typical foul crap flowing through their filthy mouths. Such as, 'we're gonna get you, we're gonna kill you, we're going to fuck you up, we're going to get your car, we're gonna wait for you after school,' same crap over and over.

As usual there is no security or police in the center hall.

Mr. Bonora and one of the football players came by and said for me to just go inside, which I did.

About a half hour later Mr. Bonora came into my classroom to visit me and asked me if I was all right.

I said, that I was mad and damn tired of being called a mother fucker, day after day, and by the same students who come and go whenever they want, knowing nothing will be done about it. I even said that this kid is late every day, and I cannot figure out why he still has credit and is on roll. Then when someone stands up to these guys, they run crying to the administration. That's the mentality here. He can do and say anything he wants, until someone stands up to them, then they retaliate by running to administration, then getting a gang.

He asked, me if I spoke to Ms. Washington*? I said, no. However, Doll* went to Ms. Washington's* office and she advised him to go tell my supervisor, which he did.

Then Mr. Bonora and Doll* came into my room and suggested I tell my supervisor what had occurred, and to write up and fill out an incident report.

Mr. Bonora and Doll* were extremely concerned for my safety. It wasn't until they kept talking to me I finally realized that I have become desensitized to this whole environment here. It is basically an ongoing event here every day. The only people here that do not and will not put up with this nonsense and behavior are the police. I said to Mr. Bonora and Doll* I really did not know what to do.

They both suggested having the students suspended.

My supervisor comes into my classroom and I explained everything to him. He told me to lock up and leave. This was at 3:10 pm. He said he is calling the home of student #1 and tell his mother that she has to come in tomorrow (Friday, April 11). I handed him all the information on student #1.

My supervisor had security and police escort me from the building to my car for my own protection.

********************

As for those students, *nothing* was done about it.

Thinking back now, all those boys should have been arrested.

**1998**

Below, is a copy of a memo from the administration to homeroom teachers to *deliberately* falsify school records to show improvement with students being on time.

> To: Homeroom Teachers
> From: C. ▓▓▓▓▓▓▓▓
> Re: Tardies to Homeroom
> Date: September 16, 1998
>
> If a student is tardy to homeroom, *do NOT mark the student tardy (T) on the homeroom bubble sheet.*
>
> Mark the student tardy in your roll book. Complete a tardy referral as you would for students in your classes. Send the referral to the cut/tardy office. After action is taken, the referral will be returned to you.
>
> If you have any questions, please ask. Thanks for your help in this matter.

Then what is the point of taking attendance?

A LIEUTENANT in the Paterson Police Department (thankfully) is always arresting someone in our school. He told the principal that he is going to do his job and that he (principal) better start doing his because there is no discipline here.

### 1999

**January 4** - fire alarm was falsely pulled on the first day back to school from Christmas vacation. The principal was irate and let everyone know how irate he was over the PA system.

**Jan 6** - a close friend and fellow teacher Mr. Bishop*was attacked by a student with a knife.

Students can do whatever they want because they know teachers are not backed up by the administration or their own teacher's union. No matter what happens it's the teacher's fault.

**EXAMPLE:** If a teacher reminds a student to take off their hat, go to class, you don't belong in my class, get out of the hallway, get off the phones, put away the yo-yo, hat, beeper, cellular phone, Walkman, cards, dice, magazine, goggles, etc. students will only threaten, harass, degrade, scream, yell foul language and insults and at times attack that teacher. Meanwhile, the administration keeps the incident quiet or will intimidate the teacher with termination, transfers along with unfavorable comments placed in their evaluations and personnel record. Meanwhile nobody in the community knows what is actually going on inside here. Not aware of the truth, parents think their children are safe. The sad thing is this district is a state takeover, run and operated school district. Basically, it is dirty politics at the expense of the taxpayers, teachers' well-being and safety, and the lives of the children and their education.

**Jan 7** - I originally had a student arrested but later dropped the charges with an understanding from a Police Lieutenant and an apology from this student.

As usual he comes into class and I have to ask him to take off his hat. He tells me it is not a hat. I asked him to remove it any way. He persists and I then asked him to take it out of the classroom. He says no, I am not leaving. I don't care. I reply I had enough of this jackass. He then becomes indignant and obnoxious to the point where he is confronting me and wants to fight. I summon security. He does not want to be bothered and gets the attention of another security guard. All while *this student* is yelling and screaming, fuck you, I'll knock you out, I'll beat you mother fucker. I kept on walking until I got to the front desk and now *this student* is in a worse rage because I am ignoring him. He gets directly into my face. I tell him to get the hell out of my way and that is when a security guard grabs him. Finally, someone stepped in! Until then the entire time I was being threatened and stalked while everyone in the hallway just looked on. No one, not one security guard or cop came over. I let it go because an administrator made a comment that it would be in my *best* interest *not* to press charges.

**Jan 7 -** another false alarm. Students from auto-shop (basement) pulled it because there was an announcement for the following students to go to the principal's conference room or be suspended.

**Later the fire alarms went off** *again*. Mr. Logan*, the English Dept. head, was struck and pushed with car (almost run over) by a student. The student would not stop the car. Security reached in and tried to turn off the car and remove the keys. The student rolled up the window with the security persons arm still inside the car, and continued to drive through the parking that was filled with students. Mr. Logan* was forced to get out of the way or be killed. *AND, it was another false alarm*!

Same day two students were arrested for stealing a car out of the parking lot. Coincidence?

Mr. Lyons* was attacked by two female students who were already involved in a fight. One student was either thrown or knocked down the stairs, as a large crowd of students followed the fight.

**Saturday, Jan 31 -** a student wanted to come into school through the front door. The woman security guard told him that he will have to go around the building. So he kicked in the glass. I told the security guard to call the police. She said she told Mr. Carter* from the Phys. Ed department. I said it again. She says she will call her supervisor because she doesn't know what to do. The custodian supervisor tells her to call the police. A little while later the principal comes in and custodian supervisor hands him a report. Now it is Tuesday, I am in the cafeteria and who do I see, *that student*. NOTHING was done about it.

**February**—Back to school night a fight breaks out with three students in center hall. Nobody could believe what is happening. A security guard showed up but nothing was done about the incident. A mother and daughter/student were in my class and were shocked and terribly frightened. She said she fears for her daughter's safety.

**Mar 12 -** there was an incident on the 2$^{nd}$ floor. A chair was thrown in the classroom at the teacher and then verbally assaulted. What happened afterwards, I do not know. I bet there's no incident report filed.

**Mar 23 -** in-service day at Eastside high school. We were all told that students *will not be arrested* if they are found with drugs or alcohol on their possession and this is district policy. Many people got up and asked questions, but the response was it is not the district policy to punish kids but to help them and students will not be arrested. Any time someone would ask a question or make an example, we were told over and over it is district policy.

I stood up and said it is against the law to purchase cigarettes if you are under the age of 18. It is against the law to purchase or have alcohol if you are under the age of 21. Then I said it is against the law to be within 1000 feet of a school with drugs but you're telling me if you come into school the student will not be arrested? Again, I was told that it is district policy not to arrest the kid. I then asked does the district policy override state law. I was told that I am to follow district policy. Then a gentleman started talking and was irate that we would ask such questions. He was obnoxious and had a definite chip on his shoulder by telling us that this is a pet peeve with him, and as employees of the district we must follow the district policy. We were quite annoyed and started to ask more and more questions. Then we were told that we are to fill out the substance abuse form and that's it. We are not to follow up with the problem and we are not to know the outcome. We are not to fill out the Violence, Vandalism, and substance abuse form. That is the administrator's job.

To stop the momentum of teachers asking more questions the administrators decided this was a convenient time for a coffee break.

The next day I contacted the president of the PEA (Paterson Education Association) and explained what was said at the in-service. He said I may have misunderstood. I repeated myself and that we were told to follow district policy. I also asked him for a copy of the district policy. He told me to call the legal department and to fax him a copy. The next day I saw Lt. (name omitted) from the Paterson police department and explained the issue to him. He said that was bullshit. If he sees a kid, he will arrest him and that he is going to speak to [the] superintendent about this. I called the legal department and spoke with a (name omitted).I explained the situation to him and asked him if I may have a copy of the district policy. He said standard protocol is for me to speak to my principal.

Later that day I found the students with drugs and alcohol forms in my mailbox. I called him back and told him what I received and if they were the district policy. He said he did not know because the papers were not in front of him. Then he said he spoke to Ms. (name omitted),an assistant superintendent, about the situation and my phone call to him and that she wanted to talk with me. I called the assistant superintendent leaving a voice mail message and again later leaving a message with her secretary. Approximately 3:30 I received a phone call from the assistant superintendent. I find it funny that she would call me at that time, especially when we leave for the day at 3:10 and it was a Friday afternoon. Anyhow, after normal salutations, I said I understand that you wanted to talk with me. She said, no, she was told that I wanted to talk to her. Right now, I thinking someone is lying. So, I explained the situation all over again and she said what I was told is ***not district policy***.

She said she will check into it and get back to me. I said no hurry. I wasn't trying to cause any problems but felt something is wrong here and I wanted to know if district policy overrides state law. I also asked for a copy of the district's policy. She said I can get a copy from my school.
*I don't understand why no one will let me have a copy?*

**Apr 6 through 8th** is HSPT. However, all last week and during this week, administration refuses to enforce any disciplinary action because they do not want students missing the test.
The students know this, and they get away with everything.

Not only do they get away with bad behavior they are rewarded if they pass the tests that they are required to take. Some of the incentives are Liberty Science Fair, skating, and movies. *Unbelievable, some students are even paid to take classes during the summer which is geared directly to take the test (HSPT).*

Here's another joke, students who cut 5 classes are charged with a day of absenteeism. However, if they are suspended the suspension days do not count. This basically tells students it is ok to cut classes.

**Apr 26 -** during 2nd or 3rd period ***two students were having sex in stairwell 18***. I overheard a guard ask an administrator if they got suspended. The administrator replied why, ***was she pleased or was she teased?***
**In the same week**, on the 3rd floor two more students were caught having sex.

**May 5, Received the following information from our English Department**
**1998-99** Eastside Fall HSPT 4% passed 12 students.
Kennedy Fall HSPT 81 students passed roughly 28%. Administration is contesting some of the grades because some students failed by either one or a couple of points.
*And JFK has the highest drop-out rate in the country!*

**May 5** - a teacher was arguing with a VP loudly in office #1about a student who was swearing at him. The VP said I am not suspending students for foul language. According to the student handbook, students are to be punished for these infractions.

**May 13** - 2nd or 3rd period a fight broke out in home economics room. Two students came into class refused to leave and attacked a student. (Name omitted),was hit with a chair and taken to the hospital. The other boy was suspended. No idea if charges were pressed or what happened to the other boy??
Security guard was bitten on the hand by a young lady after she called him a nigger.
She received 20 days ABC. *No charges were pressed!*
ABC = **A B**etter **C**hoice which is semantics for in school suspension.
The administration did not want to say in school suspension because it sounded bad.

**May 27** - female student was attacked in stairwell, early morning, 1st or 2nd period. Boy left the building and was not found. This problem continues with intruders being in the building because the administration refuses to enforce the rule with students *NOT* wearing their IDs.

**Jun 6** - one of my students Wally* was found with a gun and was taken away by police. Incident was kept quiet. Another student Sam* had one last week. I notice on the excused list, he is only marked down as suspended and the return date is June 22, 1999. He wasn't expelled?

**NOTE OF INTEREST:** According to the excused list, one of my students, Teddy*, is both on suspension and zone? He is the boy Wally* was supposedly going to shoot. Security keeps a log on all of the incidents that go on here.

**ZONE** is another BS program where students go instead of being suspended. Unfortunately, the same students end up in ZONE over and over all year. What a waste of taxpayer's money.

**Jun16** - a security guard was hit by a female student. The security guard pressed charges and the principal wants him fired because he does not want the publicity in the paper.

**In 1999** two art teachers were involved in separate altercations. In Ms. Paul's* class a fight broke out and she was hit with a chair. I told Ms. Paul* she should press charges. She replied I don't want to cause any waves. I only have a few years left and don't want to get into trouble now.

A few weeks later Ms. Post*, the other art teacher, removed playing cards from a student and was physically accosted and thrown up against the wall. However, she said that she is pressing charges. The principal was going to have her transferred because she was going to press charges. Fortunately, the art supervisor stepped in and stood up for her stopping the transfer.

Both teachers were given a bad time by central office about workman's compensation.

Poster displayed in the center hall of J.F.K High School.

**1999-2000**

**Sept 13** - gun play with Andy Brown* threatening to shoot Zack Johnson*.

This year the administration is only allowing students who they think will pass the HSPT take the exam. This way the state operated district looks good and the newspaper prints the result more favorably. In fact, for two Saturdays in August the administration had students come in to prepare for the exam. They would have passed it anyway because these are the students that do their work and assignments.

However, the rest of the juniors and seniors were exempt from taking the exam. In fact, the administration devised alternative programs that would accommodate potentially failing students. This way those students would not have to be counted and the numbers/statistics would remain high.

Good God, testing isn't over but they are letting the rest of the students in the building. You should hear all the noise and commotion. Usually no one is allowed in the building until testing is over. But this year it is different. NO commonsense.

**Nov 1 -** I made a remark to my supervisor about having students sent home and not allowed back until they bring in their parents. He said that he has been getting a lot of heat on account of that because central office does not want to bar students from school until their parents come in. However, he said that he has no problem and will continue to do so.

Meanwhile, the district has back to school night four times a year. Most parents do not show up. I am so disgusted because in any attempt in having parents involved with the school, disciplinary situations and at times having to force parents to take part, we are met with resistance from central office.

**Nov 4 -** approximately 3:30, an administrator was telling someone from central office that a teacher had their jaw broken by a student because the student would not take off their hat. The other person from district office said, "Then why don't we just let the kids wear the hats what is the big deal. AGAIN give in because the kids won't listen. No discipline, no structure, no following of rules. It is so bad here.

**Dec ?** - Students at Eastside High School broke into the projection room and set a pile of papers on fire. The principal got on the loud speaker and evacuated the building saying this is not a drill. Police and Fire department arrive. Students were outside for approximately two hours, when a fight breaks out among the students. The district decided to send just the students home. Instead of going home the Eastside students came over to Kennedy to fight but JFK's security kept it from happening. So the students went over to Rosa Parks High School. They pulled the fire alarm, beat up and stabbed a student with a pair of scissors. A teacher went to the student's aid and the same happened to him.

There was a small newspaper article about this incident, but for the most part it was all hushed up.

**January 13, 2000 -** a security guard told a student to take his hat off. The student gave her a bad time. Security brought that student to a VP. The VP said, don't make an issue out of it. Why do we have security or rules if nothing is going to be enforced?

**Jan 13 -** I personally threw 3 kids out of school today. A student (name omitted) who was kicked out of school was walking in and tried to BS me by saying he's going to his locker. While I was checking to see if he was coming back in, at another entrance there were 4 other kids in the stairwell that did not even go to this school. In fact, they were about 20 years old or older. These bums can and are allowed to walk in and out of school all day long.

**Jan 15 - a note from a fellow teacher.** Did you see the article in the Record about the Superintendent hiring an old buddy from Hoboken? Seems the Record picked up on the nepotism and found that the chosen one has charges pending, of an assault. He was to be head of Food Service. Additionally, the superintendent failed to post the vacancy and advertise it. He just brought in one of his cronies!!!!

A secretary from **central office** told me that the district administration told all guidance counselors NOT to give out applications for Tech this year. The administration is upset that Tech gets the pick of the kids. When Tech has a problem, they ship the kids out and Kennedy or Eastside gets them but Tech keeps the money allotted to them.

**Notation:** Tech is short for Passaic County Technical School.

Students usually receive their applications before Christmas holiday. However, they did not get them until after we came back and only a few received them. I would think this has to be against the law.

I was told today that most of the seniors have exceeded 20 days out of a school. It is only January. What will they have by June? How can they graduate? Watch how the administration bends the rules.

**Feb 18 -** one of my students Ric Weaver* told me that Zach Johnson* was arrested for threatening him with a gun. Basically saying he will shoot him. I don't think there was a gun present at the time. Ric* reported it to administration. As usual, it was hushed up.

Zach Johnson* has a loooong record of assaults and threats on students. *See September 13, 1999, entry involved Johnson**

**Mar 2 -** one of our vice principals was knocked out by a student at a basketball game, all because his brother was suspended and was not allowed to play in that game.

**Apr 6 -** 12:50 a girl was arrested. There was a big fight just 30 minutes ago. She had an asthma attack and possibly some ribs busted. As usual, everything is hushed up.

**Apr 14** - a student choking. Teacher summons security. Security puts student on elevator by himself. No one knows where the student is. Then you hear over the walkie-talkie, "Please be advised no students should be left unattended when sick and placed on the elevator." The student disappeared.

**Apr 26** - Spoke with a case worker about a student. This student constantly starts fights, assaults people verbally and physically, disrespects everyone, is defiant, does not abide by any rules, or laws, is constantly suspended, fails all classes and has more than 20 days absents. The counselor said because he is Special Ed he cannot be dropped from roll, thrown out and can remain in school until age 23. Plus, the administration is afraid of some community activist who is fighting to keep this student in school. So the best thing to do is put him on bedside and just give him his diploma. This way he is out of here.

**Jun 1** - today I checked on two of my seniors. They are both horrible students. Larry Young* has 37 days absent and Joe Frasher* has 47. School policy is if you are out over 20 days you lose credit if under age of 16 and kicked out if over 16. Well, I was informed today that the principal wants them to graduate. If they have passed their courses and passed the **state exam**, let them go. They did NOT pass mine! State law mandates that every student is to attend school at least 161 days.

**Jun 1** - 3 boys from Philadelphia were arrested because they were trespassing/inside the building. Perfect reason why we need and everyone must wear ID cards?

**Jun 16** - I heard one of my students was arrested today for throwing a desk at teacher because he failed. This student failed my class too. In fact, only 28.5% of my AFTER Academy students passed. Even the six that passed I should have failed.     Boy I'm glad this year is over!

### SCHOOL YEAR 2000 – 2001

**Sept 5, 2000** - first day of school just for teachers. During our meeting in the Auditorium, the superintendent made an announcement that our drop out level has risen slightly to 13%. I don't understand. We receive 900 –1000 new freshman every year. We graduate less than 300 every year. Even at 300 that is 30% with a 70% drop out rate????

Next we had a 1½ hour presentation on gangs in our schools and what to look for. As expected, the assistant superintendent says, "Our schools are safe as can be." What does that mean, "can be?"

**Sept 18** - a parent comes to school and has been here many times before because of his son's behavior. In fact, he was here on the first day of school because of his son's behavior. Anyway, he signs in, goes to the main office, asks for a different child's schedule, (acting as if he was that child's parent), gets the info, goes to that classroom and is now looking for this student. Even with a dozen security personnel and six uniformed & armed police officers at all time in the building, the father was going to beat this kid up because of something between this kid & his son. I heard commotion and someone yelling over the walkie-talkies to have a police officer come to VP Mr. Saints* office right away. The VP was going to have the father/parent arrested. Then I hear the principal say over the walkie-talkies, "No, no, wait a minute you can't do that." Soooo, this parent/father was allowed to just go home.

**Sept ?** -a female student had a disagreement with a science teacher. The student intentionally lit the lizard cage on fire. One lizard's tail was burnt. She was suspended for 10 days. Now where is the punishment? The 10 days are not counted against her attendance. She should have been arrested and expelled.

**Oct 4** - 1hour after HSPT was completed, someone pulled the fire alarms.

**Oct 5 -** 15 - 20 minutes after HSPT was completed, someone pulled the fire alarm, only for someone to pull the alarms again at 2:55. Both times the fire department arrived.

**Oct 23 -** Fire alarms go off again. There was no fire. However, the administration is quite concerned because over the weekend a boy was stabbed & killed. So they feel the alarms may go off deliberately because this is a way to get everybody out of the building to be set up for a drive by shooting.
I heard this from two administrators. Then they said it was a malfunction. However, it is in the same alarm in the gym that keeps being pulled.

**Oct 26 -** no one was allowed to attend that boy's funeral - meaning the school would not allow anyone to attend and be excused from school. In fact, I understand that the funeral home is NOT allowing anyone to attend because they fear that there will be retaliation & more violence at the funeral home.

**Nov 2 -** a fight broke out in my room between two of my students. I kept telling them to knock it off but they kept it up. I asked a female student to get security. I didn't realize a student already went to get security. Meanwhile, the two students were really out of control. I slammed both my hands down on my desk and yelled, knock it off. In the meantime, some of my other students had intervened and separated the two. That's when Peter* swung & hit Johnny*. Johnny* then turns to me and said "what the fuck are you looking at, yeah, do you want some, get the fuck away from me." I blew up. At the same time a security guard walked into my room & heard the threatening remarks. I told security to get him out of my room and I want him arrested. Johnny* kept it up. I told security I will write up the report. I was asked to come into the security office. A policeman asked me what happened. I started to explain, that's when Johnny* ran his mouth again. I said I don't need to go through this; I want him arrested & left.

A few minutes later security and another police officer came into my room. The officer wanted to know what happened. I said I'll have it written up. He said there may be some gray area in having him arrested. I just laughed. One of my students yells out, I'm siding with the teacher (meaning me). I said, NO, you just tell the truth. I said it again to all of my 25 plus students no matter what they ask you, you are to tell the truth and the way you saw it. The only disciplinary action taken was, Johnny* was removed from my class. I would like to know; what happened to ZERO tolerance to violence in Paterson schools?

**Nov 7 -** fire alarms went off. Another false alarm.

**Dec. 2 -** students were arrested for holding up a student with a phony gun.

**January 11 -** a big fight breaks out. Shortly afterwards we hear Ms. Keys* a VP screaming over the walkie-talkies "get students out of the hallways & into the classes." She was screaming because the superintendent was either in the building or on his way over.

**Jan 11 -** another big fight breaks out and a vice principal got smacked and hard.

**Jan 12 -** a VP makes an announcement, "this is an emergency, and no one is to leave their classrooms even if the bell rings, all must wait until further notice." Shortly after an ambulance arrives all you see is police running around the building.

**Week of January 15 -** scores came back for the HSPT. From what I understand students did quite well. However, the State run board of education is taking all the accolades. Question, why is it when something is negative it is the teachers' fault? When something is positive it is the State run board of education success. Meanwhile it's the teachers who have to work continuously to prepare students towards passing the state-wide exam.

**NOTE OF INTEREST:** A great deal of money was spent having TVs installed in each classroom. **By 2014** most of them do not work because of vandalism!

**Jan 24** - a teacher was cut taking a cigarette lighter away, which was also a knife, away from a student.

**Jan 26** - first thing this morning a kid was hit by a car - hit & run (name? Gary)

Overheard a conversation in Mr. Lances* office about a male student who pulled a knife on a female student. It's all hushed up.

**9:45** - we had to evacuate the building. Bomb scare. K-9s summoned. 10:20 everyone is coming back in. The kids are all over the school, they are not going to class. Teachers and security are telling students to move on, go to class, keep it moving, but they stay right where they are refusing to go to class. Where are the administrators? Once something disrupts the schedule the day is shot. It's a mob mentality in here. It reminds me of a TV documentary on prisons with all the noise and the behavior.

**Jan 29** - every couple of weeks we are told to disregard the fire alarms because they are being worked on. This is a brand new system that never worked properly from day one. It goes off for no reasons at all.

**Jan 30** - it was obvious there was a bomb scare but we did not evacuate the building. Police & firemen were running all over the school. One of the security guards told me they were not going to evacuate anyone unless they found something. This way who ever reported the bomb scare won't think it's funny & won't try again. Pretty serious gamble!

Also, in all my years working here they have never come and checked my room for a bomb. I find that odd especially when my room has three open lines to natural gas.

**Feb 5** - 6th period fire alarms go off again. We evacuated this time. It was another false alarm. It was a cold rainy snowy damp day. What do they expect? After all these years they still allow students to roam the hallways without a pass or supervision?

**Feb 14** - the auto shop teacher, a math teacher and a VP came into my room to speak with me. It was pertaining to one of the auto shops teacher's student. It seems this student gives the auto shop teacher a horrific time every day. In fact, the VP was in the auto shop teacher's class one day and seen what went on. He asked the kid his name. Defiantly, the student said he is not allowed to speak to strangers. The VP spoke very calmly made it clear that he was a VP and again asked, what is your name? This student still being a wise ass said my mother told me not to speak with strangers. The VP suspended the student.

**Bottom line-**this kid wins and gets away with no discipline because suspension days do not count towards student's attendance. It's a vacation. Now all of the other students who observed this all know they can act like this because there will be no consequences.

The worse thing that could possibly happen is a student will be moved to a different class. Then the game of attendance starts all over. The school will NOT count that student's attendance from the class he was taken out of. And the administration says they do not understand and cannot figure out why teachers cannot get their lessons across effectively.

The VP was telling me about a student who was suspended. He has over 20 days of absences, has failed the second marking period, over 16 years of age and is a repeating freshman. He was eventually dropped from roll. The mother came in and wanted to speak with the principal but he was not in. Then she wanted to speak with the VP in charge and he wasn't in. Both were at district meetings downtown. So she spoke to him. He explained there was nothing he can do because he cannot override the VP in charge. So, the mother went to central office and speaks with the assistant superintendent. The assistant superintendent calls up and tells this VP to reinstate the child and that he deserves another chance.

We spend too much time with this nonsense and not enough time on the children that want to learn, want succeed, want to be educated.

I said to the vice principal look where my room is located I see the kids in the hallway all day, every period as if the building is nothing more than a meeting place, a mall.

Are you going to tell me the administration cannot figure out why bathrooms are set a fire, fire alarms are pulled, there's graffiti on the walls, fights breaking out throughout the building, students walking into classes they do not belong in giving that teacher a bad time. It is so f'ing sickening here. It is nothing but shear and utter chaos inside here. This is NOT A SCHOOL. This is NOT A PLACE OF EDUCATION. IT IS INSANITY, all because the administration refuses to have control of the building.

It makes me think about the people I hear crying all the time that city kids do not get as good of an education as compared to the children who live in the suburbs & especially the ones who go to private or parochial schools. All of these crybabies, bleeding hearts should have to come here to work and send their children here.

First of all, private or parochial schools have strict rules. When these rules are not obeyed the child is kicked out and ends up back here where they are allowed to become a discipline problem and do whatever they want and these same people will say you don't understand he or she has problems.

**BOTTOM LINE**-- schools are responsible for education and improving social behavior. What we are really teaching and allowing to grow inside this building is absolutely disgusting.

**Mar 26 -** speaking with the art teacher, she said a few of her students were talking about a fight that took place over the weekend and that they were going to retaliate and talked about guns. She said she spoke with one of the guidance counselors about the conversation and his reply back to her was what do you want me to do about it, babysit? The news media is going crazy with all of the school shootings in the last week. Two of them were only blocks from each other in California. We as teachers are to report any conversation and take all information on possible violence serious and what do we get? I am so discouraged. Then they will all turn around and say I can't believe this happened.

**April ? -** I was talking with Mr. Angelo Bonora and a police officer. The Mr. Bonora said to the police officer, it looks as if you're putting on a little weight. The policeman replied he had his bullet proof vest on and was glad that he wears it. He said he was a little sore because he was trying to break up a fight in the cafeteria and how the vest absorbed a lot of the punches. I asked him if the students were arrested. He said no. I asked why? He said just because that's the way they do things here.

The police are here as added security and protection in and around the building. So if and when something happens, and it does all of the time, they are already here? Or are they really here so when something happens it can be taken care of quickly alleviating any added paper trail and documentation the school and district has to hide and hush up by NOT having to call police headquarters where there will be a record.

Sadly, if an officer does their job properly which is to serve and protect they will be banned from working here. It just goes to show how much the school and school district really cares about student safety and the big push on ZERO TOLERANCE TO VIOLENCE.

**May ?** - a big fight in the cafeteria between Darlene* & some other girl Sandy*. It seems that Darlene* jumped Sandy* & beat her with a chair. They were both **only** suspended. No one was arrested. No charges pressed. I spoke with Darlene* who is my student when she returned from suspension. She said they were fighting because Sandy* and her friend jumped her and she was seeking revenge.

**May 4** - we had to evacuate the building - bomb scare & not only our school. A call was made to 4 or 5 other schools at the same time. Nothing was in the Newspapers or on the TV & Radio?

**May 8** - in the newspaper front page - Paterson Public Schools send recruiters to SPAIN, looking for teachers to teach students how to speak SPANISH. Are you kidding me, many of our students can't even speak English. There are NO qualified people in the entire state of New Jersey or the United States? This trip is one week after the teacher's contract was settled and supposedly there was no money to give teacher a raise. I never ever heard of the outcome on the Spain Trip.

Meanwhile the entire day here there was nothing but fighting going on throughout the building.

**May 9** - a senior in my 8th period class was talking about when he was a freshman and how bad it was here. He said kids were lined up in the boys' room smoking, throwing knives into the door to see how far they can stick them in.

**May 16** - fights all day long and on two of the floors at the same time. For the last few months' announcements have been made that if Mr. Lance* a TAP (Teacher Assistant to the Principal) sees you with your hat or wave cap he will take it and not return it. When the students see him or before they walk past his office they remove the head gear. However, if a teacher asks them to remove the head gear, or correct other rule infractions, it is either ignored, snotty foul mouth remarks or a defiant confrontation brought on by the student/s. Meanwhile the district wants teachers to enforce the rules. We are ignored by students and not backed up by administration. The students know this and nothing changes, and the not following of rules continues. The students do not even listen to the security guards. It is a joke here.

**NOTE OF INTEREST:** Mr. Hunter* has to watch everything he does now because he did not get a favorable evaluation. They said he does not have classroom management. Unfortunately, Mr. Hunter* had many problems last year 1999 – 2000 with his students. However, he was NOT the only one. They were disrespectful and defiant. They would constantly curse, swear and threaten him when he would ask questions pertaining to lessons in his attempts to engage them.

On account of their behavior Mr. Hunter* would eject many of them from his class and send them to me in anticipation and hoping that I will be able to help him. He did not want to deal with the administration anymore because they would turn the situation around and blame him. This poor guy had students from the AFTER Academy all day and every day. These kids were so bad that they were broken up for the 2000 - 01 year by request/demand by the entire Math and Science Departments because they had too many situations and major disciplinary problems with those students.

In the 2000 – 01 school year, Mr. Hunter* was warned/threatened that he may not be rehired or offered tenured because of the discipline problems and classroom management. I have to laugh, who warns administrators for all of the times the fire alarms are falsely pulled and fires are deliberately set in the building, the fighting and students constantly in the hallways all day, every day, all year long? Instead of no classroom management would that be *no building management*?

**May 23** - another bomb scare! Police, firemen, administrator, security are running all over the place, but they are NOT evacuating the building. Yes, this is terribly annoying for the principal, but security and student's safety must come first!

**May 24** - Special testing for three days - freshman only. All the other students come in later and go to the gym, auditorium or cafeteria. There is no school work, or anything educational going on during this time. What a freaking disaster. I had the most unfortunate pleasure of being in the cafeteria. When the students came in all they did was scream, yell, run around, play cards, roll dice, fights would break out, cursing, throwing of everything and anything they could get their hands on. It was nothing more than being present to a prison documentary. It was absolutely horrible having to be a part of this. It was OUT OF FREAKING CONTROL. No parent would allow their child to act this way in their garage, yet it is ok for them to act this way in a state run and operated school. This is not normal or proper social behavior. Meanwhile, we have to teach students about birth control, safe sex, aids, and other diseases. But we don't teach them how to act, respect others as well as themselves and property? This school is nothing more than a place to hang out, play, learn how to destroy property, be disrespectful, fight and threaten anyone [around]. All that matters are graduation numbers and passing the state-wide exam.

Once testing was finally over and it was supposed to be time for EVERY STUDENT to actually start the school day. They were all so supped up and hyper from fooling around and playing all this time that the rest of the day was a disaster/shot and even more out of control than normal; which in no means is NORMAL, by any means! Anytime there's a change of schedule or something happens it's more of a disaster here for the rest of the day.

A teacher was telling me this morning that she was assisting for the freshman testing and the students were from the After Academy, I quote, "My God they are horrible, how can you or anyone of you do it."

If parents do not have control over their own child, how can a teacher who only has them for 40 minutes a day along with approximately 30 other students in a class have control? How are we supposed to prepare these children for the real world, by not having them behave properly, and socially, instead of yelling out as loud as they can, "HEY MOTHER FUCKER, SUCK MY DICK!" etc. all day, every day, all year and year after year after year. Nothing is ever done about it.

And if it is NOT permissible, then why is it permitted to continue here?

**May 25** - another bomb scare we had to evacuate the building.

**May 29** - Mr. Ell* was so upset with Mr. Costello* a VP. He was mad because kids are not coming to class because they are *supposedly* seeing him to pay senior and trip dues. Mr. Costello* has been making announcements daily asking students to drop off their money. Every day, he says the same thing and that today is your last chance. This has been going on for weeks. The kids do NOT care. It's the same thing with permission slips and warning notices they refuse to bring them back? Students know they DO NOT have to do anything. The school and district will keep making allowances, excuses and accommodating them. There is NO regiment, no structure, no discipline and no accountability. Obviously, they're more concerned about getting the money then having students being in class!

**May 30** - another bomb scare - everyone is supposed to leave the building. One of the security guards asked a kid to leave. He replied, "NO!" At first, I thought he was just playing. She asked for him to leave again, he said no again. The security guard said are you refusing to leave. The student said, "Yes, I am refusing to leave." The security guard turned right around called the principal and said this student refuses to leave. The principal approached the student calmly and quietly said, "You have to leave." The student stood there and said, "I refuse." The principal puts his arm around the student and said, "Come on you can't fool around; you have to leave the building." The student swirled his arm around and pushed himself away from the principal and said, "No." The principal just walked away.

I watched the entire scene. If that can go on between a student and the principal of the school, now what type of clout do you think a teacher has? Remember the teacher who did not receive a favorable fitness report /evaluation because he did NOT have control of his classes?
- There seems to be a double standard here?
- That's why the teacher evaluation system is GREATLY AND DISTURBINGLY FLAWED!

**May 31** - coming back from lunch, I heard the alarms going off. I am wondering if it's a fire or a bomb scare. Turns out someone pulled the same fire alarm down in the basement again. Fire trucks arrive. There has to be a report filed with the district as well as the city. I would NOT be surprised if there isn't.
- It's 2014 and most of the fire alarms still do not work because of vandalism!

**June 5** - there was a seniors' award ceremony held in the auditorium this morning. I was told by a colleague that the principal was BOOED terribly by the students. Was BOOED even more, each time he attempted to speak. Gee, where is the so-called classroom management? Nothing was done about it.

Years ago, before the State took over the District of Paterson, if something remotely was out of order or there was a possibility of students misbehaving the principal/vice principal then would have put a screeching halt to it immediately. If anyone acted up after that, they were disciplined immediately. THIS set an example to the entire school body who is boss and it was NOT the students.

This type of behavior has progressed 100% every year ever since the State (TRENTON) took over this district. My colleague said the principal felt really bad about the incident. This alone makes me believe his hands are tied because of central offices policies & politics.

**June 6** - there was a meeting in my VPs office with one of my female students, her father and sister. The Science Department Head, a detective, a gym teacher and I were present. This is in lieu of a situation that has been brought to our attention about my student's boyfriend who has been physically abusing her. Sadly, she has been denying the allegations and has been defending him.

As expected, neither the boyfriend nor his parents showed up. My VP had security retrieve the boyfriend from class. All the dirty laundry was brought out. My VP spoke with the students that I gathered to tell him the story. Most of them did not want to come forth because they're afraid of the boyfriend. However, two students did come forward. TMO & MB. MB was present during one of the physical abuse ordeals.

My VP made it very clear that this boy will be arrested if he hears of any type of retaliation to any student or teacher. 7:15am the next day, I was in the office when MB came in telling me she was scared. She told me the boy was after her and that she had been hiding, not even 24 hours after my VP warned him he had better not retaliate. Anyhow, I told MB to stay with me and when my boss comes in, we'll see him. MB told me that she is going on a field trip today and we will do it tomorrow. In the meantime, I saw the

Science Department Head and relayed the message. She immediately turned around and went to the principal. His reply was, it's only he said, she said, I want to know the facts, hard evidence.

I said nothing after that and left disgusted. However, when administrators hear that there is going to be a fight or some type of situation after school they will summon police to surround the building and gather up the perspective kids that may be involved to prevent an incident. Isn't that he said she said as well? Or is that to protect the perception of the school?

Last night was the prom and my VP during yesterday's meeting asked if they were going to the prom. The boyfriend immediately turned to my student. The father and sister said no, and they knew nothing about it. They also said she doesn't have a dress, didn't get her hair done and with all that is going on they will not permit it. Nevertheless, I come to find out the so-called boyfriend did go to the prom but with another girl. I believe this was the plan all along with the boyfriend. However, in the office yesterday he swore to the father he never did anything like that and that he would never hurt her because he loves her.

All day I was receiving reports from concerned students on what was and is still going on. I told them to go see my boss. When they came back, they told me he said it was cut and dry and unless we have actually witnessed something, there is nothing he can do about it. I just shook my head and wondered if administration would accept that remark and situation if it were their daughter?

**June 13 -** Wednesday, a teacher's car back window was broken by student/s throwing a brick out the school window. According to administration the video camera did not see it because it does not cover that area of parking lot. So they say. It is all about covering and hushing everything up.

**June 14 -** a student of mine, who just came back from jail, is seen arguing with a female VP. The student starts yelling threats to a security guard saying he is going home to get his brass knuckles and will come back and beat his ass. I spoke with another security guard along with a *district* security guard and asked why wasn't he arrested? He just laughed and said the cops are here getting overtime and it is an easy job. If they arrest him there will be paperwork. The district doesn't want any type of paper trail showing violence. So, they don't want to get involved, because they may end up being banned from the building.

What happened to the district and State policy on "ZERO TOLERANCE TO VIOLENCE?"

**June 20 -** a BIG BRAWL started outside the school with about 20 students. It disbursed and ended up going across the street where a homeless guy (Hector Robles) was beaten to death. They caught three kids who were juveniles and JFK students. However, **Friday, June 22,** there was a teachers' meeting and the principal was very upset and said our school getting a bum's rap. We have a good school and these are isolated incidents. He was also upset about faculty members saying that there is a great deal of racial unrest in our school. The principal was mad and said that is not true and that we should all watch what we say because it has a negative impact on our school. Does he work in the same building we do? Our school is a disaster and there is a great deal of racial unrest which is usually one of the main reasons and causes for so much of the violence. All the administration does is make excuses and denies everything. They are more concerned about the school's perception. Who are we going to contact? The state is already here. Many of my colleagues and I have sent anonymous letters to newspapers and the governor on what goes on here. NOBODY CARES! Even the federal government is just as blind.

**June 21 -** 5 TEENS CHARGED OF BEATING DEATH OF HOMELESS MAN
*<u>See entire newspaper article on pages 38-40.</u>*

## SCHOOL YEAR 2001 - 2002

**Sept 11, 2001** - as we all know, the day terrorists flew into the World Trade Center buildings, the Pentagon and crashed in Pennsylvania. Since that day, we have had to evacuate the building numerous times. Bomb threats! Many of the bomb threats went on without evacuation. Understandably, because many of them were pranks, but who has the right to make that decision with other people's children lives? The calls were computer generated, sent to the State Police, to the board of education, and finally the school. Since they went to the state police, we had to evacuate the building.

However, during the week of HSPT (state exam), police and fire department were constantly in and all around the building. There were police cars and fire trucks all over the place. Obviously, we must have received another bomb threat. There must have been enough concern for the fire department having to come in and investigate, but NOT to stop the testing or evacuate the building. It seems the state exam/**TESTING** is more important than children's lives. I bet if parents knew about the decisions made here involving students' welfare and lives over testing, there would have been a major riot here and every attorney around would be lining up for a piece of the action. And I mean CLASS ACTION!

**Sept 15** -Mr. Ell*a teacher told me the secretary who does student registration was upset. She said a child came into school today & wanted to register. He said he was from Mexico but had no documentation or history of school or schools attended. No proof of his name, age, if living address is correct and if his shot records (inoculations) were up to date. *NOTHING!* However, the secretary was told she MUST admit him in our school as a student. What has happened to our immigration laws?

**Sept 24** - Mr. Ell* told me there were two students, actually brothers, who were looking for a fight. There is a police record of this. Anyhow, they were making terroristic threats screaming, Fuck the United States and on and on and in front of the principal. A fight broke out, the police had to subdue the students and they were arrested. One of them was hurt (broken nose). Now the parents want to sue. The district wants to let it blow it over. I asked Mr. Ell* why didn't the principal press charges. He said that the principal was told by central office not to. My reply was so much for zero tolerance to violence!

**Sept** - not sure of the date but there is a police, and court record on this. A student was arrested because he made threats to a teacher. The student said something to the effect that he was going to get him. He was going to blow his car up with him in it. The student was arrested and did go to court.

**Oct 26** - a bomb went off in the building stairwell above the art wing. It was a homemade firecracker with metal fragments attached to it. It was all hushed up.

**Oct 31** - 7:50am, evacuated building. Bomb threat! We were outside to 9:45. During that time many students were arrested. There was NO mention of this on TV, radio or newspapers. Now the Arabic community and the kids in school are saying the police were picking on them because they were Arabic.

**Nov 7** - fire alarms go off again. False alarm again!

**Nov 16 & 19** -the principal came on the PA system twice this week explaining why students must have and wear ID cards. He said it's to enforce school security. We don't want people in our building that don't belong here. Then he says wearing of ID cards is not being enforced other than allowing students to enter the cafeteria. I've been saying that for years! TENs of thousands of dollars wasted on the machine, man power hours and material to make ID cards for security purposes but only used to allow students to get into the cafeteria. ARE YOU FREAKING KIDDING ME!

**Nov 19 -** I was in a courtroom this evening in Wantage, NJ. One of the cases involved a young man smoking in school and on school grounds. He was fined a great deal of money. In our school you cannot enter a bathroom without leaving smelling like an ashtray. When students are caught smoking *nothing* is done about it. After all, when a student gets mugged, robbed, threatened, etc. nothing is done about it either. So why would the district do anything about smoking?

**Dec 12 -** so many big fights; actual brawls throughout the building all day long. One was when a boy knocked out a young lady in the hallway. At the beginning of 8th period a fight breaks out in my room between two students. At first I thought they were fooling around. However, Donald* damn near killed Rame*. I could not remove Donald*.I finally yelled will somebody get fuck'n security and shortly after that Donald* got off Rame*.

**Bottom line-**they both only received two days suspension.

**Dec 13 -** a student from my 8th period class was suspended for fighting a period earlier. He saw the fight in our class yesterday, how severe it was and the students only received two days suspension. So why wouldn't he get into a fight. That's the point. There is no deterrence, no discipline and no consequences. The school and district rules are ignored and meaningless. That's why there's so much fighting here. Meanwhile, the state and federal government says, "**ZERO TOLERANCE TO VIOLENCE.**" But our district is operated by the state of New Jersey and obviously like our students they too can do whatever they want.

**January 9, 2002 -** 6th period, fire alarms go off evacuated the building. False alarm again!

**Bomb threat!** At the end of 6th period we had to evacuate the building because someone slipped an explicit note in red magic marker under the principal's office door. We were outside for 70 minutes in the freezing rain. Many students didn't have anything more than a T-shirt on. I suggested we have students write a paragraph on what they want to do once they leave school so we could compare the hand writing on the note. One VP said it would take too long. When we finally came back into the building after freezing our butts off a huge fight breaks out in the center hallway. It took over 30 minutes for most students to clear and go back to their classes. The school is NOW so out of control.

**Jan 10 -** end of 7th period, we evacuated the building because of another false alarm!

**Jan 11 -** 6th period evacuated the building again! False alarm again!

**During 7th period fire trucks** were all over the building again. However, we did not evacuate the building. My guess is a bomb scare. NO ONE takes any of these alarms seriously.

**Jan 16 -** all day long students that do not belong in my class just walk in sit down and refuse to leave. I ask them politely, but it is as if I am talking to the air. They are defiant, and then when I persist for them to leave, they get indignant, curse at me, and try to provoke me into fighting them. This went on all day. I went to my supervisor at the end of the day and explained what has been going on. I also said there are and have been way too many students in the hallways and wanted to know why is this allowed? This is why we have vandalism, fights, confrontation, graffiti, fire alarms pulled, etc. As you read on OBVIOUSLY I wasted my time asking why!

**Jan 17** - police and fire departments once again summoned. Bomb scare but we did not evacuate.

**Shortly,** there was some sort of altercation. Students were brought to Mr. Lance's* office by police. In the meantime, students as usual gather by his office to hear what is going on and even get involved and instigate with the situation already in progress. It is shear lawlessness here.

One such student is a student in my 6th period class. He decides he would get out of his desk and go watch. I asked him to sit down along with others. The others went back to their seats and continued or should I say tried to continue with their test. However, this other student defiantly refuses and tells me that he doesn't have to. I get up from my desk and he continues running his foul mouth, cursing and screaming causing a bigger scene and deliberately and defiantly disrupting the class even further. Eventually I get him back to his seat. There is NO reason why any teacher should have to put up with this type of behavior.

Short time later, something else happens in the hallway, (which is an ongoing event every day, all day all year), this student again gets up and refuses to sit down, and the entire process begins again. Finally, I get up again and defiantly and challengingly he tells me to get away from him, he can do what he wants, I can't tell him what to do, and basically was warning me and taking a stance as if he was going to fight or hit me. Not intimidated, I had to set some type of an example in my class on who is boss. I walked over to him slowly and quietly. He turns and walks out of the room continuing with his cursing, threatening and carrying on and never returns. I did write it up. Guess what? NOTHING WAS DONE ABOUT IT!

**Jan 18** - 6th period we had to evacuate the building again because someone pulled the fire alarms. We were out for 10 or 15 minutes. One of my female students was jumped and beaten up by some girls for no reason. No one knows who these girls are. Soooo many kids came running into my room laughing, yelling and making fun of her. This is the second time this week someone was jumped after coming back in after an evacuation. This would have never happened if we didn't have to evacuate the building.

**Jan 20** - two students Steve* & Damian* beat up two janitors in the front cafeteria. In fact, both janitors were knocked out. They continue to stomp the janitors while they were down and out. One janitor was finally removed via the ambulance while still unconscious. There was nothing on TV, radio or in the newspapers about this attack. Obviously it was hushed up.

FOOD FOR THOUGHT-All day, every day we have 12 security guards and 6 uniformed armed police in the building. Why did this fight/assault happen? You're going to tell me the fight just happened, nothing led up to this? I do not believe that. Didn't anybody see anything for the last few days? I understand that there was some type of argument going on between the custodians and students. There's always at least two security guards in each cafeteria, as well as a VP. However, you're going to tell me, that no one saw anything and couldn't have prevented this? This just proves to me security and the police mean nothing. If a student or students want to do something they will, no matter what. Nothing is changed, or better. Do *not* blame security people or police. They're *not* to get involved until they are told to by administration!

THEN, the superintendents and the board of education keep asking for and wanting more money. Meanwhile tens of thousands of dollars they spend a month on security is wasted. This also goes for the security cameras. NOTHING has changed with the exception of more spending at the taxpayers' expense.

**Jan 25** -speaking with a colleague, he said he noticed a student giving Ms. Keys* a VP a very bad time. He was disrespectful, excessive foul language, defiant, etc., etc. He told me, he purposely looked the next day and that student was suspended for 10 days. However, if he acted that way to a teacher the administration would just brushed it off and tell the teacher they must learn to have classroom control. If the administration does not have any control inside the school building, how do they expect teachers to have control in a classroom? By administrators allowing poor and unacceptable behavior, to enter and grow in the building does anybody realizes how much harder it is for the teacher to do their job?

I noticed I was so tired today after a 4-day work week. This is because of all the chaos, distractions, out of control atmosphere with the loud, obnoxious and continuous noise that goes on all day long here. If anyone came here they would think they're in a riot, violent movie or an insane asylum. Even the school library is absolutely noisy. What happened to being quiet in a library? Then again, what happened to students going to class, not being in the hallways, stairwells, bathroom, outside the building, anyplace and every place beside being in class or where they are supposed to be doing homework, class work, being respectful, foul language being prohibited, being on time, have good attendance, passing your classes and everything else you're supposed to do in a *REAL* school?

**Feb?** - one of my students, who first reported to me on Nov. 16, already has 14 days of absences and or cuts. Furthermore, he and another student jumped a boy to take/steal his cell phone. I understand they beat that boy up pretty good. This is IN SCHOOL. That's how much control the administration has inside here when students are that brazen to not just go to class, but jump, mug and rob another student in school.

Later that day, I saw that student in the building talking with the principal, a VP and someone else. My question is why wasn't he arrested?

**Bottom line** - *zero tolerance or not*, what happened to being arrested when you mug and rob some one?

**Feb 13, 14 & 15** - I had to go outside and argue with students, because they are sitting, eating, placing their books and book bags and sodas on everyone's car. I have had my windshield broken twice, my antenna broken, my gas cap stolen always wondering if anything was ever put into my gas tank. I went to my supervisor and complained every day. He would tell me to get and tell security. Then security people would tell me to go back and see my boss and tell him to get the police.

For the past few days all I did was go around and around and around. So much nonsense. Then he finally assured me it would be taken care of. However, today Feb. 15, I went outside and it is worse than before. I went into the hallways and yelled at everyone where is security, why isn't there anyone outside watching the vehicles. Common sense when you have a group of people (students) things will happen. Come on people what is going on here?

**Bottom line**-we have security (MANY) in the building, we have cameras, we have police (uniformed) 6 every day, why isn't there anyone outside watching the vehicles. What is the point of having, cameras, security and police if this area is not going to be secure? It is so frustrating here. Nothing makes any sense here. This is NOT a school climate or setting. It is just a big indoor playground or street corner without supervision. WHAT IS THE POINT?

**Mar 8, UPDATE** –from Jan. 20 entry, Steve*came back to school today. He was ONLY suspended. You would think a 19-year-old student would be *arrested and expelled*. No, not here! Both students' names are on the suspension list. However, today they are *both* back in school

**Mar 11, UPDATE #2** on Steve*& Damian*. I asked a fellow teacher why they were back in school. He said, "Shush, this came from the district, technically, they didn't commit a crime." I assume meaning until proven in a court of law, they are innocent. Then I asked about the time when Mr. (name omitted) a teacher, was sent home and suspended until he went to court. While awaiting his court date he was not paid and for months? Furthermore, he was also found innocent. However, the teacher was punished and punitive action was taken by the district. THIS is what children are learning here. It is ok to do whatever you want in school. There are no such things as consequences. You can have poor behavior and can act any way you want, say anything and use profanity anytime you want. There are no rules here. It is OK to do what your parents would *not* allow you to do at home or in their presence. Nothing will happen to you.

It's our politicians who came up with the slogan, "Zero Tolerance to Violence," to be instituted and be implemented in our public schools. Obviously it is just words. Anything a politician says is nothing but words to get them elected or reelected. After all they do *not* send their children here. Think about everything I have been documenting and it keeps getting progressively worse, throughout the years while this school and district is Run and Operated by the State of New Jersey.

**Mar 11** – the same teacher said to me that the school received a banner saying Zero Tolerance to Violence. He also said the principal & district superintendent will not allow it to be hung in the building. Think about this, I find this sad, that a high school that was named after our president who was so ***violently assassinated,*** in which its hallways are filled with so much daily violence, is ***not*** allowed to have a banner hung up in the building against VIOLENCE.

It doesn't make any sense to me. Then again, as for everything I've documented does not make any sense to me. That's the climate here. SENSELESS!

**Mar 18 -** I just learned that Donald* the same student from Dec. 12 entry was suspended for play fighting. He was fooling around fighting with Damian* the same student from Jan. 20 entry who was involved with beating that janitor up.

It seems Donald* pushed him through a large piece of plate glass by the art room where presentations are to be displayed. It seems that Damian* was seriously injured. He had a large cut around his neck, chest, and shoulder area.

These are students who continuously act up, are disruptive, defiant and do the same things over and over and get suspended. Does administration really expect and think when they come back they have learned a lesson? Yeah right. I also heard Mr. Lance* wanted Donald* arrested. I asked why wasn't Damian* arrested and expelled from school after beating the janitor senseless?

It seems if discipline is going to be administered it depends on each day and depending how that particular or each separate administrator feels as well as who the punishment is going to be for? My colleagues and I find this sickening. I am waiting for when a smart attorney will finally hold this district culpable for what has been going on even after students have graduated.
I can honestly see when there will be a time unfortunately, when someone will get away with murder.

The defense will be that students were not only taught how to act inappropriately, but it was actually reinforced. You cannot hold this person liable. My god they were taught this behavior in school. The school and school district is at fault, not my client.

***AFTER A FEW LAWSUITS, WHO THEN WILL PAY FOR THE PATERSON PUBLIC SCHOOL DISTRICT WHEN THE MONEY IS WIPED OUT? THE TAXPAYERS WILL AGAIN AND AGAIN!***

**Mar 18 -** approximately 8:30am the principal came to my room and asked to speak with me. It was about a letter a bus company wrote stating a bus was filthy, there where alcoholic bottles left and the student kept opening and closing the emergency door.

I said another teacher and I took approximately 67 students (two buses) on a field trip and unfortunately, the students on my bus did not act very well. He continued to talk about the letter and started to scold me.

However, in his defense, I probably would have done the same thing. Once he completed his demeaning conversation telling me what supposedly went on, I then began to explain what really happened. He stated, he will have my supervisor handle it. I replied back, you are hearing one side and not asking me what happened. Then I began to talk. He was not interested. Then I said, for someone who is always saying that this is he said she said and ignores whatever a teacher says pertaining to a situation, what is this you handing me? Sounds pretty much the same thing! He knew I was right and figured he had all the info he wanted and didn't care what I had to say. I also said to the principal that no one was drinking on the bus. However, within my own investigation, I found that was not to be true. It seems a student had a bottle of rum and was sharing it with other. Then I proceeded to have all the students write their statements on paper and I collected them. I never let anyone else read them. All students were instructed to do nothing but tell the truth. Say only what they saw and exactly how they saw it. I always stressed the importance on telling the truth. I wrote up a report on two students on what they did to another smaller student. I delivered the report to my supervisor. I did *not* give him what my students wrote to me as I promised. I explained what had happened and that the principal wanted him to check into all of this. He left and said he will see the principal and find out what he wants me (my supervisor) to do?

**Mar 19** - first thing this morning the principal begins to admonish me. Never asked me once what happened? He was absolutely nasty, saying it is a disgrace and when he was at the principals meeting on the 18th he was hammered about this. I have no idea if he is telling me the truth or not. The way things run here I don't believe him or any administrator. He never once asked me to come into his office and explain. I began to get aggravated and I was about to let him have it. However, I kept quiet and just bit my tongue. It is his building and it would not be right for me to talk back especially out in the open. Even though he acted this way I was *not* going to conduct myself in the same manner. I figured I will wait and speak with him in a couple of days, *but in private, like men.*

However, what I wanted to say, after the third time he said what a disgrace, was what about the two students who beat that janitor unconscious and were allowed back in school. Then a few days later they were both suspended again. What about every time and for hours in the cold rain snow, we have to evacuate the building because of false alarms? What about all of the police and security we have and they are not allowed to anything to be proactive, wouldn't that be a disgrace? What about me having my windshield broken twice, antenna ripped off, gas cap stolen, when security should be outside is that not a disgrace? What about the ID cards that the students are supposed to have and wear at all times so security and staff knows who is and is not supposed to be in the building? What about, students are allowed to roam the building all day every day? What about HSPT days? For ½ a day the school is somewhat under control, but as soon as testing is over, the students don't even go to homeroom and just roam the building as free as canaries for the rest of the day. However, I was alone with 37 students who attend JFK high school where they learn that there are NO consequences and rules mean nothing and I am a disgrace. Usually the students do act really well on field trips. This day they did not, but they are allowed to get away with everything in school and this was a school field trip so what is the difference?

What about the time we had to evacuate the building and you asked a student to leave and that student gave you nothing but sarcastic remarks, foul language, etc., etc. and you did nothing? However, if it were a teacher, there would be comments on their evaluation about classroom management and possibly a LOW score! If a student and students can act that to the *principal*, why wouldn't they act that way with a teacher? This was not the first time either. I watched student Lyle White* tell the principal off and scream in the center hallway with no consequence. In fact, Lyle* would yell, "I run this school and no one can do anything about it," all the while the principal is standing right in front of him.

**Mar 20** - today one of my students Lyle White* came back from ANOTHER SUSPENSION. Within an hour he was being shoved into the security office because he was fighting with a girl. I have him in my 6th period class. He came in about 20 minutes into the period escorted by Mr. Lance*. I spoke with him and as usual, it is everybody's fault but his. Now it's the middle of 9th period, he is grabbed securely by security and swiftly escorted out of the school's front door. They were throwing him out trying to keep him from acting up further and causing more problems. Well it didn't work.

The entire time he was screaming obscenities, cursing and verbally threatening a security guard. He finally become so unruly, disrespectfully, defiant and to a point where you think he could not get any worse well he did. It got worse to the point where everyone had enough. He wasn't going to listen and continued with his disruptive behavior so security and police threw him back into the security office. Again, nothing was done about it. They just sent him home. He is 20 years old and is still a sophomore. However as usual, this is normal and typical behavior here at J.F. K. This goes on all day and students get away with it because the administration does not want to show it is a failing school. It isn't a failing school; it is failing administration.

The reason why all of this happened during 9th period? Well, OBVIOUSLY, it seems Lyle* didn't learn his lesson and was fighting with a girl AGAIN. Students witnessed this display of out of control, defiant behavior and realized they too can and will eventually start to act the same way.

**NOTE OF INTEREST:** How can any administrator who works here go home and feel good about themselves knowing with all that is constantly going on here they ignore, work harder in attempts to hush it up and or to get it squashed is ALL THEIR FAULT and caused by them!

**Mar 22** - I saw student Lyle White* in school. I spoke with the security guard that had to deal with him the other day. Do you know what Lyle* received for his punishment? 2-days in ZONE. Every kid that goes to zone is a constant repeat offender. Usually it's the same students, repeat offenders who get sent to Zone, over and over and when they come back NO CHANGE! This ZONE program is nothing more than an added expense to the NJ taxpayer.

**Mar 24** - there were fights all day in school including two security guards slugging it out.

**Mar 24 – 28** - Guess what? Lyle* is suspended again. Don't know why. Come late May early June the administrators will come around and will ask, "Is there anything he can do to have him pass?" Meanwhile how many days is he already out of my class and school? It doesn't matter here. It is PERCEPTION!

**April 16** - at the end of 2nd period 9am, Rodney* was attacked by a student named Perillo*. Rodney* was struck about the head and chest with a pipe. I had to finally subdue and push Rodney* into the SRA room to keep him from going after Perillo*. Shortly afterwards, Rodney* was taken out of school by ambulance. Everything was hushed up.

**Apr 18** - another one of my students was suspended again for having a knife. Why wasn't he arrested? A weapon in school, Zero Tolerance to Violence, I guess it doesn't pertain to this school. It is just words.

In fact, on **April 26,** I spoke with his mother and she said what I have been saying all along. He is going to keep on doing things and acting up until he gets suspended, because basically he isn't being punished, he gets days off that do not count against him, plus it is fun.

The mother also said to me and his case worker, that she cannot do anything to control her kids. The children threaten her all the time that they are going to call the police & DYFS (Division of Youth and

Family Services). The mother is scared. The kids come and go as they want, and the mother is afraid of getting in trouble. In fact, this boy was supposed to attend Zone today, but he refuses to go. Zone, another joke! Guess what happened? The same thing I wrote right between these brackets () NOTHING!

**Apr 26** - speaking with Mr. Ell*, I found out why the administration is doing hall sweeps. It seems that several female teachers, complained to the principal about students walking in and out of their classroom. One female teacher in particular said to the principal that she is afraid to be in the hallway. That there are too many students and they are acting up and she does not feel safe. Soooo, now the principal, is finally clamping down. Let's see how long this will last. I learned that the principal was also approached by another teacher about the same concerns and situations.

**May 3** - two kids were sitting on my car. I told them to get off. They looked at me. I repeated myself. They got off and starred me down. I warned them the next time they sat on my car, I would pull them off. One kid got smart with me and said, I'm threatening him. I turned right at him and said, there's my car, now go sit on it and let's see what happens? Go ahead both of you, you're so smart and tough go ahead and sit on it Lets see what happens wise asses?

The one kid got real smart with me and said, "Fuck you there is nothing you can do about it." I grabbed him and attempted to bring him into the principal's office. This went on for about 10 minutes and finally we entered the service entrance. However, another kid wanted to get into the act and then they both started to talk in their native Arabic tongue. Then one of them said that they are brothers.

I wouldn't let them go and there were TYPICALLY NO SECURITY, NO POLICE, NO ONE AROUND WHEN YOU NEED HELP. FIRST OF ALL, THIS SHOULDN'T EVEN BE HAPPENING. WHY ARE STUDENTS OUTSIDE THE BUILDING DURING SCHOOL TIME AND SITTING ON STAFF CARS?

Eventually, we got to Mr. Lances* office and I basically threw the other kid out. I explained to them that I am not mad at any of them but was yelling. That's when Mr. Lance* being a wise ass says to me, if I am not mad then why am I yelling. Talking to me as if I am a little kid.

My response was, because I come to you every day for weeks about the kids instead of being INSIDE the building and in their classes, they are outside the building in the parking lot, sitting on my car and other teacher's vehicles and all you do is tell me to go to Mr. Saint*. I go to Mr. Saint* and he tells me to go to security. I go to security, and they tell me that they do not have the manpower. Then I said I have had my windshield broken twice, my antenna ripped off, my gas cap stolen, and who knows if anything was poured into the gas tank. That's why I am fucking yelling.

However, before I could go any further to finish what I had to say, he gets up and went into the adjacent room to scold another kid. He did that to get away from me, because he didn't want to hear the truth.

**May 7 -** I filled out a vandalism report. I handed it to the principal's secretary to submit to the principal and a copy to the head security guard. I personally hand delivered a copy to the vice principal.

**May 8 -** the principal stops me in the middle of the hallway and starts admonishing me. I start to wonder if he is trying to set me up for an argument with him in front of others. He's upset about what I wrote. I said, I shouldn't have to go around checking on the parking lot. With all of the security guards, police, surveillance cameras, etc., etc. why is this place so out of control?

Nevertheless, the principal tells me I have to rewrite the form or he will not submit it. And that the comment about this place is out of control inside and out is ridiculous. They were not his exact words, but he was upset and was trying to place me on the defensive. I have been in contact with the president of the PEA (Paterson Education Association). I have sent him a copy of the original form submitted, by postal service and e-mail attachment along with the comments that were made by the principal. I did speak with a union rep and he advised to change it and resubmit the original to the school liaison committee, which I intend to do tomorrow, May 9th. You would think that the principal would spend more time attempting to gain control of the school and admonishing students for their behavior instead of going after teachers being concerned about how bad and unsafe the place is. He and all of the other administrators spend more time covering up and trying to keep things quiet instead of doing their jobs and having a sense of stability and control here. When I'm here, I have no idea what is right or wrong!

**May 8** - I spoke with Mr. Ell* about the above incident. He agrees and sympathizes with me and said one of the police officers made a remark to the principal saying this place is out of control. Mr. Ell* said he replied to the cop "GREAT!" But I would be quiet if I were you, because then what's the point of the police being here if this place is so out of control?

**May 13** - this one particular student roamed the hallways all during 9th period, slamming everything, beating, kicking, punching doors, lockers and windows. He was upset because someone stole his radio. First of all, students are not to bring radios in school and should not be allowed to roam the halls. He came into my room and started throwing the desks around.

I offered to sit down to talk with the kid. I asked if he wanted me to buy him a soda and would try to help him. All he kept saying is he didn't want any help. He was mad and just kept roaming the floors causing a scene. Eventually, he slammed a door and the glass broke.

> *But the school and district allows students to act this way and reinforces this type of behavior by doing nothing and ignoring it.*

Mr. White, an administrator said to Mr. Costello* a VP, "See are you happy now?" Then they went looking for the kid. The kid ran upstairs. Eventually he came back down and proceeded with the same tirade unabated. Eventually, Mr. White finally approached the student and asked him to knock it off or he will suspend him. The kid basically blew him off, ignored him and continued with his tirade and antics. The head of security did nothing but watch. Can't really blame her, if Mr. White didn't do anything with him what was she supposed to do? And this student continued to carry on and nobody did anything. My question is WHY?

This school is not just out of control it is *dysfunctional*.

**May 14** - large amounts of blood all over in the hallway by the gym. It seems another fight broke. One of my students attempted to try to stop and break it up. The next day Mr. Lance* asked him what happened? The kid explains and then Mr. Lance* says that's NOT what they had told me. Who are they? Nevertheless, what happened to ZERO TOLERANCE TO VIOLENCE?

**June 1** -the principal saw the students from yesterday that gave him and the security guard a bad time during evacuation. He had one of the TAPs, bring the student to him. The principal spoke with the kid stern but not as stern as he used to be when he was a VP. Nevertheless, I overheard the principal say to the students, hey what was your problem yesterday? When I tell you to do something you better do it and not give me any grief. Do I make myself understood? What was your reason for acting like that? You're not going to do that again, right? Then he dismisses the kid. That was the entire conversation.

There was no discipline or example set. I thought he would have said if I tell you to do something or any of my teachers, or security guards tell you to do something you better do it.

**Jun 12** - for the past week, smoke/stink bombs have been going off every day all day. However, I learned today two SENIORS were caught for lighting the smoke/stink bombs in the gymnasium and received *A Saturday detention.* There were other boys involved but they were suspended. Students told me the smell and smoke in the hallways was soooo bad. These two seniors were really not punished because the school does not graduate many students to begin with and the administration will do anything to have as many students attend the ceremony. At the very least they shouldn't have been allowed to attend their ceremony for pulling a stunt like that days before graduation. This proves how much students respect authority or have any concern about being held accountable for their behavior and actions here. The administration treated the entire incident as if it was no big deal. Now other students will do the same.

**Jun 19** - one of my female students told me that her father is friends with the principal. She told her father one day after school there were many nonstudents (Bengali) in our school on the 2$^{nd}$ floor. Her father called the principal and complained.

Why should a student have to complain to her father to the point he has to call the principal before the principal finally puts an end to the situation? What in the hell are we doing with all the police and security personnel if students and trespassers can come and go in and out of this building all day and especially after school when most of the staff has left? Isn't that the purpose of having EVERYBODY wear ID cards? Months before this even happened; the principal himself came over the school PA system and explained that ID cards were for safety issues and to keep unwanted people from being in the building. That is as far as it went. Just like all the rules and their consequences in the student teacher handbook are IGNORED! The next day students are still NOT wearing their ID cards.

**Jun 20** - the same student told her father the bathrooms are disgusting; they smell of cigarettes and there are students and security guards at the same time smoking in there. Once again, her father called the principal. The principal's response was, "There is nothing I can do about that." I told her, your father should have said back to the principal, what else goes on in school that there's nothing you can do about? Smoke/stink bombs still going off in the building and has been every day since 6/12.

**Final Exam Week-** The entire week, students were in hallway continuously. Most students are NOT even in class. Security and administrators are all in hallway and doing nothing. DO NOT blame security, they are told what they can do and when they can do it. Stands to reason if administrators and security are both standing together, and the hallways are just jammed packed with students the administration is allowing it.

Even, yesterday **June 20**, the hallways were jam filled with students. Nobody is going to class. Final exams mean NOTHING here. Students know they'll pass no matter what. There were a group of kids running through the mob as fast as they can. I yelled to stop running, knock it off. As usual I'm ignored. I was concerned for safety so I kept yelling, watch it, watch it, and coincidental, they damn near ran into and over the principal. He had to jump out of the way. Guess what, he did and said nothing.

After an entire school year is over with, I just learned from several guidance counselors there's a special class called 10R. These are the Repeating juniors that DO NOT take the state exam. This way we get better results with those who are chosen and were prepared over the summer for nothing but taking the test. It is a way to play with the numbers/percentages (keep scores up).

There was a female student who would come to my classroom often to visit and instead of spending her lunch period in the cafeteria would come and stay in my room. On a back to school night for whatever reason this young lady brought her mother in and said she wanted her mother to meet me. The mother said that her daughter talks a lot about me and hoped that she wasn't bothering me. I said no. My room is open to students who want to come in, visit, talk, look around and do anything other than being out in the hallway. From then on the mother and I became friends.

Periodically the mother would come in to check on her daughter and would stop by to visit me. Every time she would come here, she could not believe what she would see and hear. She would always ask me, where is the principal? "Why are there students always in the halls, yelling and swearing?" To be followed up with, "Does this goes on every day?" I would reply, "Yep, every day, all day and all year." She would always say each time shaking her head how much this school has changed since she was a student. She was extremely upset and didn't know what to do. I suggested writing a letter to the newspaper. She said maybe she should write a letter to the superintendent. I said no, that would be a waste of time. He already knows what's going on here.

It's almost the end of the school year and this woman decided to stop by to wish me a good vacation and gave me an envelope. In it were copies of two letters she wrote and sent to the Mayor of Paterson. I asked if I could have copies. She said no because she was afraid for her children but wanted me to read them and to let me know what she did. She hugged me, said thank you and left. I never saw her again. I do NOT know if she moved or what happened. Very sad! Really nice people!

## SCHOOL YEAR 2002 - 2003

**Sept 3** - first day of school. No students just meetings. However, superintendent makes a comment on video that the dropout rate has declined from 12 point something percent to 10 point something percent. How can that happen when we graduated approximately 270 students???

Four years ago, the class of 2002 that graduated in June, entered JFK. There were approximately 1000 new freshman. Yet we graduated approximately 270. How has that improved and how does that come out to 10%? Or is it just those who were seniors for that year compared to those who graduated? This is what the administration does; numbers, statistics are adjusted accordingly by making changes and allowances in enrollment.

**Sept 4** - first day of school for students and already the hallways are a disaster. Kids were worse than I ever seen. No security guards, no police. In fact, a couple of times the principal came out telling students to move and they ignored him. So he ignored the situation and walked away.

What chaos in the hallways? It is absolutely disgusting and it is only the first day of school with students.

> UNFREAKINBELIEVABLE! If students don't listen or respect the principal a person who is the highest of authority in the school, why would they listen or respect teachers?

All the BS the administration spoke yesterday about having more control in school with the students went out the window as soon as the students entered the building.

**Sept 8** - what a way to start a new school year. A student is so out of control and trying to mark his territory in my class by his attempts to show me and all of my students that he is boss and nothing I say or do is going to change anything. I had to write him up. He's classified as special ed because he's a behavioral problem. Do you know what we do with students who are behavioral problems? NOTHING! If they are NOT classified, then the school and district WILL have them classified.

Once a student is classified, that's IT! I have never ever heard of or seen a student that was classified because of behavioral problems, change for whatever reason and become NOT a behavioral problem.
First of all, behavioral problem is a mild term for here. Basically, they are out of freaking control!

All I hear coming out of his mouth was fuck you, I fucked your wife, I fucked your mother, I fucked your daughter, and on and on. This continues because it is allowed. The school administration and district superintendent does NOTHING to teach or to stop students like him from acting this way. If a student acts like this on the first day of school and in high school, then this type of behavior was taught, allowed and nurtured in the grammar school.

However, the administration will blame the teacher, saying that they do NOT have classroom control.

My question is, if the teacher is at fault for not having control, then why are there so many PERSONAL AIDES (at taxpayers' expense) for many of these out of control students? OR is it so the AIDE can keep a constant tab and be there to help the teacher in these situations. Even having a personal aide shadowing and going to every class with them, they still cut, walk out, act up and do whatever they want.

If it is the teachers' fault, then will somebody PLEASE explain to me how, can a student who cannot read or write, do the simplest of math end up in high school?

Any time a student who is not classified and becomes a discipline problem the administration will end up classifying them. Furthermore, many parents want their child classified because they will receive a stipend. The district also receives more money per classified student. The behavioral classified students don't have to do their class or homework, participate and come to class. Most of them have very poor attendance and continually cut classes while they remain inside the building hanging out. Even if they should do their work, they are only required to do a bare minimum.

Meanwhile they will pass, graduate and receive the same diploma as the students who do their work, come to school and do NOT cause discipline problems. How is this preparing them for the future? All the administration is doing is pushing them along and through the system.

Unfortunately, there are many students who are in need of being classified as special ed. They have birth defects, injuries, impaired vision, wheelchair bound, speech and hearing impairments as well as other medical and mental conditions. For most to all of them, they give their very best and work extremely hard in whatever they do and in any class they have.

Just as unfortunate, the behavioral problem students for the most part have no ambition or desire to do anything other than get over, getting away with whatever they can and this behavior is NEVER EVER corrected and sadly these children are never helped. It is just allowed to continue and grow. Sadly, I've seen too many of these students end up in jail and worse.

**An end to the Sept. 8, entry:** A few days later that student was removed from my class. I wrote a letter to the administration explaining safety concerns and that I was NOT going to accept responsibility for him, other students and school equipment if he is NOT removed. However, I believe the real reason why the administration removed him was because he was cutting my class almost daily and knew I wound fail him. Now all of his absences, cuts and tardiness from my class won't count anymore.

**Sept 11 -** I knew this would happen. We had to evacuate the building. I do not know if it was a bomb scare or if someone pulled the fire alarm.

The only time I saw any type of control in the school was when an assistant superintendent and some other big wig was talking to the principal.

To me it was funny. The principal looked like a duck out of water trying to move students out of the hallway. Other than that, there has to be hundreds of students every period late to class and or just out and out cutting. Gee that sure sounds like control to me. However, when it comes to HSPA/HSPT, (the state exam) nobody will be in the halls and it will be quiet as well. Then once testing is over it's an "F'ing zoo."

**Sept 26 -** gangs outside school all day, something about initiations. There have been a couple of gang related shoot outs over the weekend and a shootout after our football game.

Kids came into my classroom over hearing conversations about guns. We summoned Mr. Costello* and he said there is nothing we can do about it. Unless you give us names, we can't go and search everybody. One of my female students said she was scared.

## Standards cont.

I have to say with those five parents, I was quite pleased with their genuine concerns and active participation for the entire school year with their child or children's education and behavior. Actually it is quite refreshing. I always tell them that I get paid by the Paterson Public Schools; however, I work for the parents of Paterson, NJ. Usually a great friendship, trust and bond is formed and we worked together for a common goal, their children's education.

You CANNOT blame teachers if parents do not and refuse to get involved with their children's education. For so many students who have failed not just a marking period but the entire school year, it is the parents' fault.

Let's put this in perspective:

The failing or possible failing child receives a warning notice in the middle of each marking period a total of four a year, followed by a report card approximately four weeks later equaling seven contacts before that child has been determined failing for the year.

He replied, I know but believe me you are safe here. We are doing all that we can. There are police all over inside and outside the school. Then he said just be careful when you go home. They wouldn't be so cavalier if it were their child.

**Sept 27** - School was dead. Due to all of the publicity of the shoot outs and the gang problems, most students did not come to school. It is supposed to be worse tomorrow. Something to the effect; according to the bloods, anybody who wears red will be killed.

As for today, why didn't the administration have metal detector screening? Unbelievable, how do we know who has guns and other weapons? I think I know the answer. They do NOT want to find weapons because then they would have to REPORT it and arrests would have to be made. The administration wants to keep everything quiet as if NOTHING is wrong, happening or going on that is dangerous. After all, and unfortunately, some kids may have weapons on them only for protection.

**Sept 30** - Alarms went off again and we evacuated building. There was a fire in a 3rd floor boy's bathroom. They stuck a lit cigar behind some plastic. In fact, it was also attempted earlier in another bathroom. Sadly, nobody takes the fire alarms and evacuations seriously anymore.

**Sept 30** - a vice principal asked me to help him with the school building inspection. I said I usually do a big report on the entire school. He replies the principal doesn't want it that way. In looking at last year's report that he had, I notice it was rewritten by the principal, leaving me to think all of my hard work on that the report was never turned in.

**Bottom line: The VP ended up filling out the form using last year's form. NO CHANGE!**

Just like I said last year when I brought the principal down stairs and showed him the elevator electric with all exposed frayed wires, major cracks in the building and on another occasion I had more disturbing evidence to show him about the outside wall (cinder blocks) Separating from the concrete enough where you can see outside light plainly. His reply, "I really don't care what happens to this building."

This is why I document everything. Not to punish anyone, but to protect me. I have the original reports and saved on diskette.

**Sept 30** - today they nabbed some young boy, a freshman for
stalking a young lady who is a senior. They took care of everything in house. Again, what happened to zero tolerance to violence?

**Oct 7** - fire alarms go off first thing in the morning. However, the principal came over the PA system telling us to ignore the alarms. It
was a mistake that happened during setting. However, that afternoon approximately 12:50 the alarms went off again. Everyone was
evacuated from the building. It was a false alarm! After about 10
minutes everyone was instructed to come back inside.

---

## Standards Cont.

Unfortunately, too many students end up being room and board in a contained facility called jail. I am so freaking fed up with what goes on and the excuses that are made including the consistent lowering and lowering of standards. This is NOT progress. Meanwhile it goes on here every day while this school and district is under state control.

Approximately 1:50 pm the alarms go off again. We evacuated the building. Walking the 3rd floor with a security guard we looked at
the alarms and noticed one of them was really tampered with. The security guard had to literally take it apart to reset it. As soon as everybody came back into the building the alarms went off again. The building was in chaos. The kids were just running all over the place.

This place is out of control and it is only the beginning of October.

**Oct 8** - a VP came out of the cut office to speak to the principal. He said he suspended the boy who refused to listen to the principal for NOT taking his hat off. More than likely the student cursed him out but good as they do to teachers all day, every day all year but that's alright and allowed.

This proves this student and as well as another student don't even listen to the principal. However, the principal gets mad and an attitude with teachers because the way students act in class. If the building is out of control all day long and students are NOT in class what do you expect? Especially, if the principal allows this to continually go on day after day, all year for years.

**Oct 9** - they handed out student ID cards. My supervisor and others have been working non-stop all day making and fixing them. What I would do is take the kids' cards, tell them to see me at the end of the period, and once I received a bunch of them I put the hole in them all at one shot.

WELL, these two BIG YOUNG LADIES come in. I explained and told them to come back at the end of the period. Without missing a beat and at the top of their lungs they started screaming at me, "Fuck you, you fucking idiot, fuck this fuck that," and on and on.

I have no idea what happened or why they did this? I was shocked and surprised. They came back about an hour later, I said aren't you the two ladies with the foul mouths? I am not doing your cards. The 'fuck yous and everything starts all over again, I told them to get the hell out. When class was over, I went to see my supervisor to let me know what happened. Who do I see, the same two ladies standing by the door? Once I started to explain to my supervisor they start with their foul mouth. My supervisor tells me to bring them to Mr. Lance* and again I'm assaulted with another barrage of insults, foul language and fuck yous, you're not my father, you're not talking me anywhere. What happened to these girls? As far as I know NOTHING! Furthermore, why would my supervisor tell me to take them to see Mr. Lance*, when he already knows they have been acting up with me? Why didn't he just call security on his walkie-talkie?

**Oct 10** -12:20, 7th period, fire alarms go off. We evacuated again. It was a cold wet day False alarm again! However, signs were put up by every fire alarm box saying that the halls and alarms are under camera surveillance and anyone falsely setting off an alarm will be imprisoned.

**Oct 15** -first day of school after a long weekend, 8th period alarms go off. We evacuated the building. False alarm again! I guess students know there are no cameras and the posters mean nothing. We finally come back in and not even 5 minutes later the alarm goes off again. Another false alarm! I was also told that sometime this morning someone called in a bomb scare. We did not evacuate. However, I understand they caught the prankster, and they admitted to it. The police took him out of the building in handcuffs. Later that period, trying to make an attempt to help stop all of these false alarms, I said to the kids that the principal was going to a meeting with the Board of Ed and many big shot politicians, Mayor, Governor, etc. They are going to set a law for every minute that is wasted because of a false alarm; we will have to make it up at the end of the day but double.

Then I said anyone who is underage and who does not come back in or does not stay to make up the time will be arrested. If they are over 16, they will be arrested and kicked out of school. If that student is collecting social security because a parent is deceased, the board will make sure that the social security department is made aware of that student being kicked out and to cut off their social security. One kid jumped up and said fuck that they can't fuck with my life, they can't do that? I replied back, well those who pull false alarms are F'ing with our lives and everyone else in the community, especially, when the police and fire department are called in. The remark that was said back to me was what I expected. Unfortunately, and disgustingly that is the mentality here. *We can do whatever we want and you can't do anything about it.*

**Oct 21 -** approximately 7:10 and I hear footsteps, I turn around it is one of my students. I immediately smelled alcohol on his breathe. I mentioned it to him. He denied it. I said, no way, you have been drinking. He replies back, "I only had a sip," then walked out of the classroom fast. I reported this to Mrs. Lance*. The smell of alcohol on his breathe was unbelievably strong.

**Oct 23 -** 7$^{th}$ period, the fire alarms go off again. It's another false alarm. It is 12:41, and the hallways are a disaster. Kids are fighting, yelling screaming, cursing at the top of their lungs, running, shoving, it is like a riot. It is so out of control here. This is going on while the principal, VPs, security, and police officers are all standing in the hallways watching, as if this is acceptable behavior.

The fire alarm was deliberately pulled so groups of kids could fight. Fights began outside. Then when they came in, fighting started in and around the main hallway and cafeteria. Many innocent students were sucker punched. There was a big brawl this morning on the 2$^{nd}$ floor. The administration knows that this was all a big set up, but what are they going to do to prevent this from happening again? ***NOTHING!***

**3$^{rd}$ period**, the same student from Oct. 21, who I smelled alcohol on his breath threatens me twice. I had VP Mr. Costello* remove him from my class. As the student is walking out, he threatens me again. I said to Mr. Costello*, now you've heard him, and I want charges pressed. As far as I know not a thing was done about it. I truly believe this comes from central office to cover everything up. If someone is threatened outside of school, they would be arrested. However, civil laws do not prevail here at JFK. The administration constantly talks about raising standards, but in the meantime they allow the students to use foul language, curse, scream and threaten teachers and are allowed to gets away with it? What kind of standards are they talking about? I would like to do the same to them but I would be fired.

In fact, last week the same student was threatening me in around about way, by saying you can only tell me what to do here, out in the streets you can't. He continued saying over and over watch me, you can't do anything to me in the streets. He was confrontational, trying to provoke me and feeling me out on how I would react. I never lost my cool and talked to him in a smooth calm manner. I guess today he felt comfortable to see if he can get away with it again.

**Oct 23 -** it is soooo bad here. Kids were allowed to come to school wearing pajamas. The school was a disaster. The kids were even more out of control than ever. This school and soooo many of our students need structure. When the school is already out of control why entice them with something stupid by wearing PJs? There cannot be any type of disruptions or distractions. We cannot deviate from set guide lines or these kids will take advantage of the situation, every time. Then we cannot get what little control we did have back. The rest of the day was a freakin' disaster.

How can principals and VPs who were once teachers feel about themselves by letting this go on? What happened to; *Zero Tolerance to Violence in Schools* and from a district that is run by the state? The GOVERNOR himself says that there is zero tolerance to violence in schools. Why is it not being enforced? If a parent does not send their child to school, DYFS (District of Youth and Family Services) is called in and that child may be removed from the home, parent/s fine and possibly jailed. How can students not be made to go to class, allowed to roam the hallways and hangout throughout the building, all day every day and DYFS is not called in on the administration?

**Oct 24** - 7th period we had to evacuate the building again. Another false alarm! I believe this was a signal again for more fights. The school day was shot and complete disaster after that, especially today being a ½ day of school. There has to be a record with the fire department every time the alarm is pulled. Even if someone calls the fire department and tells them not to come, there has to be some kind of log. Then there would have to be a phone log with the telephone company.

**Oct 25** - fights all day. There was a huge fight in parking lot as I was leaving to go home. There were many police officers, detectives, security personnel, two VPs and the principal all in the parking lot. It must have been a doozy. I got the hell out of there.

Smoke/stink bombs all day in hallways.

A security guard came to me looking for one of my female students. It seems that her friend (name omitted) smacked another girl in the face with a brick. Later the security guard told me that the girl and a teacher identified her as the one who did it.

**Nov 4** - 7th period, fire alarms go off. Another false alarm! Earlier the principal and then later a VP made announcements to disregard the alarms because they're being worked on. When the alarms went off, the principal was no more than 20 feet away from me and I asked him is this for real? He just turned his back on me and I waited until the security guard yelled, *"we have to evacuate!"* This is getting real dangerous, nobody knows what to do and the principal has an attitude and refuses to respond.

**Nov 5** - 5th period, some young boy walks into my classroom screams fuck you, suck my dick cock sucker, you mother fucker. I walk outside and see Mr. White* speaking with this young man. The young man had an attitude even with him. I called over to Mr. White* and told him what that boy just did. His response was, "Yeah, I know, I heard him," and was laughing about it. TYPICALLY, and as expected, nothing was done about it. Yet, I am supposed to have control of my classroom. Meanwhile anyone can walk in, yell profanity, be caught, and that administrator just laughs it off, basically, no big deal. This is *NORMAL* and acceptable behavior? I am actually confused that I do not know what is right and wrong here. I don't know what to do or whom to turn to anymore.

A fight/brawl breaks out in the cafeteria involving one of my Bengali students' cousin. Speaking with the cousin, I asked him what happened. He said ever since the beginning of the school a bunch of Palestinian students were picking on and throwing milk cartons at him. He said everybody knew this and security did nothing about it. So, on this day the he got fed up. **I see this as racial.** But it was hushed up.

A student in my 5th period class was talking with another student. He said he was getting three days suspension and didn't know why? However, Mr. Lance* says to the boy being suspended that he smells weed. He asks him, "Were you smoking weed?" The boy says "No!" He asks, "Are you lying?" He replies "Yes!" He gave him seven more days of suspension. I do not know if a substance/violence form was ever filled out or if he went for a drug and alcohol test.

**Later**, I was speaking to a teacher Ms. Sweetness*. She was so upset because when she asked a young lady why was she was late, she starts screaming at her saying, I don't have to tell you anything, proceeded to curse her out and carried on? Ms. Sweetness* says, well you are no longer in this program. Later, Ms. Sweetness's* supervisor came down and spoke with her with the young lady present saying, you don't understand, this young lady has problems. She made Ms. Sweetness* look like a fool and now this young lady knows she can do what she wants, get in trouble, run to the supervisor, and everything will be all right and in her favor. Ms. Sweetness* is running a work program, in the health and nursing field. She tried to explain, if the young lady was working and late three times when the boss asked a question and received that snotty remark, she would be fired. How am I to do my job? The supervisor's response was we have to talk. Ms. Sweetness is so upset and says, "I can't win. I get beat up from both sides the children and then the administration. It is absolutely disgusting what goes on and is allowed to go on here!"

**Nov 15 -** a BIG food fight in cafeteria. It must have been a good one, meaning so out of control. Two VPs and the principal were summoned. It was funny, because Mr. Costello,* a VP, was the first on scene. A few seconds later he came flying out of there. I imagine he didn't want to get food on him. The screaming, yelling cursing was so loud it was as if you were in a jail house riot.

**Nov 18 -** below is a copy of what I submitted to Mr. Saint* on Tuesday, Nov. 19, 2002. I have copies of the Violence and Vandalism Form as well as the actual JFK discipline referral.

Below the incident report is a copy of a note I gave Mr. Saint* days before the November 18, incident.

INCIDENT REPORT: Nov 18, 3rd period starts off with (students name omitted) refusing to take head gear off. This is a ritual that goes on every day. As always, I asked him nicely and unfortunately repeatedly to remove his head gear only to be met with resistance. I never raised my voice little more than a whisper, attempting to keep everything quiet. The student walks over, threatens me with a remark replied he was going to slam me. I replied back that wouldn't be nice, I would rather be your friend.

He repeated it in a threatening manner again and again. I had no other choice but summon security. Security arrives, student refused to listen to the security woman. Eventually he finally took off his head gear. However, as the security woman was leaving student kept telling her fuck you, fuck you, over & over under his breath. I looked at him and he then started to say it to me. I just shook my head. About 5 minutes later I look over to I see him writing on the good table. I removed the pen from his hand. He jumps up and said, do you know who you're fucking with? I replied softly, what are you doing? The student kept threatening me by saying that he was going to fuck me up. He stood up and was directly in my face. I couldn't help it, I busted out laughing. I walked away but the student kept it up, and I asked another student calmly to get a security guard. The student walks out of the classroom. This all happened within the first 10 or 12 minutes into the period.

A few minutes before the end of the period, I receive a phone call from a security guard telling me that he has that student with him. Security said that the student was wondering around on the 2nd floor. The security guard escorted him to the security office. I explained to him what happened.

I am very surprised with this student; I have done nothing but attempt to talk with him. I asked him nicely and politely what he should and shouldn't do.

However, as I predicted this may happen and I believe this is just the beginning.
I will enclose a copy of a letter to Mr. Saint* my supervisor expressing my concerns about the student being extremely angry all of the time.

Thank you,

Mr. Lee E McNulty

I assume this incident would fall under VIOLENCE & VANDALISM.
I submitted a Discipline Referral, Violence & Vandalism Report. Sent copies to PEA.

**Below is a copy of the note I gave Mr. Saint* a few days before the above incident.**
November 14, 2002,
Mr. Saint*

Below is the name of a student who is in my 3rd period class.
I am quite concerned about him.
He is extremely angry every day.
I make many attempts in the course of each day to talk with him.
However, he just tells me to leave before he hits me.
His remarks do not bother me, but I am concerned he is going to get someone hurt if not himself.
He is NOT a discipline problem. He is NOT disrespectful.
However, he does no work. He just sits at a desk and broods.
I feel that he is a bomb that will eventually blow.
If possible, can we see if he needs and then receives counseling of some type?
I would hate to see something happen when it all could be avoided.
I hate to see a young man at such an early age to grow up extremely angry.
I feel this can manifest into something later that could be avoided.
Thank you,
Lee E McNulty

**Nov 20** - I sent the student with a security guard to Mr. Saint* with the Incident Report.
I didn't do it on the 19th because student was absent.

I gave a copy of all the paperwork to (name omitted) a PEA delegate. He will compile it with all the other paperwork that is brought to PEA's attention. He even said, the district would say that there were only 200 incidents in the entire district which is false and does not match what the PEA's records show.

**Nov. 21**- Student was in class. Obviously, nothing was done about it. *IT WAS IGNORED!*

### END OF THIS DOCUMENTATION

**Nov 18** - 6th period we had to evacuate the building AGAIN. Another false alarm!

**Nov 19** - first thing this morning a fight breaks out. No security, no administration, no police. Mr. Ell* a teacher went to Mr. Lances* office which was only 15 feet away from the fight to get the police. *NOBODY, ESPECIALLY THE ADMINISTRATION CARES.* I refuse to get involved anymore. Mr. Ell* says the same thing. This is probably what the administration wants. By frustrating us so we don't get involved and eventually become like them and don't care, which helps to keep everything all hushed up and quiet. So much for *ZERO TOLERANCE* to violence in schools!

**\*\*\* Nov 19,** (Student's name omitted) INCIDENT in my class during 5th period.

When security finally arrived the same student (name omitted) from the November 14 & 18 entry would not listen, refuse to cooperate, excessive and abusive foul language fuck you and fuck you, I want my hat you can get the cops, you can get the principal, you can get the Board of Ed., I am not leaving and I want my hat. The security woman leaves trying for over 10 minutes using her walkie-talkie and telephone she could not get in contact with an administrator or police officer. Mr. Class*a TAP (TAP = Teacher's Aide to the Principal) heard the ranting and raving of this student came over and immediately walked away saying he's sorry, but he is not getting involved because he is NOT A VP.

**REASON:** He was chewed out by the principal because he was doing the job as a VP. However, he did speak with me later that day and confirmed this as was apologizing for not coming over. I explained that I already knew, and it was all right. Mr. Class* also said it's ridiculous that I should have to go through this and all I was doing was doing my job, following orders about hats, and all of the other rules I was told to do as a teacher.

Right now, I feel as if I just shouldn't care anymore. There is no point to anything here. Nobody and especially the administration care. They are more concerned in keeping everything negative hushed up and work harder at keeping everything hushed up than running a safe an orderly school. I don't understand this. Especially this being a district that is supposed to be a state run and operated district. No street corner is like this place. I am so disgusted and feel I too will eventually just come here and let everything go. It was well into my 6th period class and no help. Eventually Doll* the security guard came over and warned the student to come out or she will have to get the police. She actually said, it will be either the easy way or if you want it will be the hard way. However, the student kept on and on. And my students and I had to put up with it. Finally, Mr. Costello* a VP came over and talked him out into the hallway. The student didn't care and kept it up. Bottom line--*NOTHING WAS DONE ABOUT IT!*

Again, if these students are allowed to talk to a vice principal like this so what is to stop them from talking and acting this way with teachers? This is a building of lawlessness. There are NO consequences for bad and unacceptable behavior. I saw this student later that afternoon. The first thing out of his mouth, I want my hat, man. I calmly explained to him, that I gave it along with the others to my supervisor. First of all let me take a break here. If the rules were enforced by administration none of this would have happened. Meanwhile, this goes on day after day; all day for me and all of the other teachers. *Why*, if we are doing what we were told by administration as being part of our jobs why is this allowed? Why aren't the very rules that are written in the teacher student handbook by administration not one of them are followed or obeyed? If the administration did their jobs, all of us teachers would *never* have to go through any of this. This whole episode is the administrations fault!

I also told this student I was very upset with him. I never disrespected him. Why would you put an act like that in my classroom? I thought we were friends. You knew I would have given your hat back later, but no, you had to act up. I also let him know that I wasn't even mad. I was more hurt that he would act that way to me; especially when he had difficulty with the police and probation officer and I covered for him. When they came in I said all good things about him. I let this student know what he did was not right and all over a stupid hat. He seemed to understand and was very quiet, but never apologized.

**Nov 21 -** the hallways were atrocious. Even one of the VPs was quite angry. Kids were all over the place. I witnessed Leo*slamming Darens* to the floor, which was followed by Darens* smashing Leo* in the back of the head. A police officer was standing next to me and I said we have a fight going on here. His reply was, "were." I looked at him as if he was retarded and pointed and said, "Those boys" The police officer walks over and talks with one of the boys and walked away. Immediately following the principal and the same VP were actually stopping students and asking "where are you going. Let's see your pass. Let's see your ID." I have never ever seen them do this. Something has to be up. One student refused to give or show his ID and said, "Who are you? I am not giving you my ID!" So, what was the result of his defiance? NOTHING!

**Dec 10** - fights breaking out all day. It's the same students. Maybe we are doing it wrong here being that everything is the opposite. The slogan should be 100% Tolerance to Violence then there wouldn't be any!

**Dec 12** - fights all day long. It was so bad students pulled the fire alarms again so they can go out to fight in the parking lot. All day police were escorting students out in handcuffs. It is so bad teachers were asking me what is going on here. One teacher said this place is an embarrassment. There are men in here working on the phones and they too can not believe what is going on with all the students in the hallway all day screaming at each other hey mother fucker, hey bitch and nothing is done about it. Why does the principal allow this she asked? This school is a place for everything wrong and disgusting to manifest. I don't understand why they allow students not to go to class? Then none of this would be happening.

**Dec 17** - Fights outside before school started. No security or police. However, they were in the building. Later the principal was with 12-14 guests in the middle of the hallway acting and carrying on as if everything is ok. It was nothing more than a dog and pony show. I noticed that there were *no students* in the hallway at that time. All a bunch of fakers and liars. It's nothing more than smoke and mirrors. Then just before 8th period begun students were fighting outside of my classroom.

Something to reflect on -if this school is NOT out of control, then why are all the supposed disciplinarians exhausted and burnt out every day and so busy all day long with discipline problems?

**Dec 18** - today there was a switch in what is considered normal. Security guards are getting everybody out of the hallways real fast. All of a sudden they do not want students in hallway. It seems a security person and a student made some sort of a proposition and money was involved. However, I do not know if it was a male security guard and a female student or vice versa. However, NOW they do not want students in the hallway. Affirmative action is involved. She said this job (affirmative action) is an all-day everyday affair. You would not believe what goes on here. There are so many cases going on and coming up. The administration wants everything all hushed up.

**Dec 19** - I have to laugh when the principal and anyone else says this school is not out of control. You should see the suspension list. It is two pages long. If that many students are suspended, then how can you say the school is not out of control? Now the district *DOES NOT* want a teacher to fail a student if they did not send out a warning notice. That is absolutely ridiculous! A student may pass ½ a marking period and in that case you do not send a warning notice home. However, if they fail the last ½ of the marking period, now you cannot fail them. This is another scam in making students *pass!* So *many* of our students should not even be in high school, they CANNOT satisfy the requirements necessary in order to be in high school. Yet they are just passed on. Then when they do attend or get to high school, they have to learn everything (13 years of schooling) in 4 years in order to pass state exam. However, here in Paterson, a state takeover, run and operated district, students are just pushed through the system. If all of this can continually go on here, then why did the State of New Jersey even bother to take over the District of Paterson and only for it to continually get worse each year?

**Example**: One of my female students graduated in June. However, she could not pass the test in order to attend Passaic County College. She was required to take all remedial courses. I do not understand how this district has not been sued by a student or their family?

**Dec 19** - Ms. Sweetness* was telling me yesterday she took the students on a field trip to qualify for CPR. However, the bus never showed up. She called the bus company and they said the district does not pay their bills, so they were not coming. She could *not* send the students home before time expected without notifying the parent/s, plus it was 6:30 in the evening and dark. Figuring many parents may not expect their child home until later she did what she thought was best. Ms. Sweetness* decided to take the students (3 trips) by her car to the location. I do NOT understand the district. The superintendent is buying all these old dilapidated buildings throughout the city but cannot pay or afford a bus for a scheduled educational field trip as promised. Leaving the teacher uninformed and embarrassed, after she had made arrangements for a person to take off from work in order to donate their time to teach, qualify and certify students for CPR? I advised her to write a grievance so it would be *documented*.

**Dec 19** - a fight breaks out again between 7th and 8th period right in front of my classroom, with one of my students and I don't know who else. As expected, NOTHING was done about it.

Rumor has it once we come back from Christmas holiday there is going to be a big student drop from roll. Why does the administration have to let things go so long? Now, many good students who got caught up with the bad students maybe on that list and dropped from roll. This is the administrations fault. They are supposed to be highly educated people making these decisions who refuse to do their jobs starting at the beginning of the school year by enforcing rules, laws and discipline. What makes it so sad to the point it is ridiculous, here at JFK we have dropout prevention people. Meanwhile the administration caused a lot of the drop out. What is so new or provocative that has not happened before that we cannot prevent? Absolutely NOTHING! THIS IS NEGLECT!

**Dec 20** - I just learned that a student/basketball player (name omitted) was suspended and arrested last week for touching a girl inappropriately. He is on the suspension list from 12/12 to 1/6. I am curious what is going to happen being he is a basketball player?

---

IMPORTANT TO THE ABOVE INFORMATION:
If anyone does not believe how badly or out of control this school is, just look at the suspension list. When you have a suspension list that is two pages filled with names what conclusion would you come up with even if it is just for being late and cuts? That alone explains what I have been saying with students being in the hallway, stairwell, bathrooms, basement, all day long, walking in and out of classes they do not belong in as well as setting fires, pulling false alarms and etc. However, according to the administration the school is NOT out of control. If many of the suspensions are for students fighting, attacking and robbing other students is that not *VIOLENCE?* I believe if the administration can keep it hushed up, then there is no record of the violence. I would love to see actual records in comparison to the suspension list. If there are no records, then why were students suspended? Would the school and districts records match mine?

---

**January 3, 2003** - second day back from Christmas vacation. Big fight breaks out in the cafeteria and we start the New Year off with the fire alarms going off at the beginning of 9th period. We evacuated the building. It was snowing, raining and miserable outside. It was another false alarm.
**Jan 7** - a gym teacher was bitten in the arm by a student while attempting to break up a fight in class.

A boy (name omitted) cut a girl on the hand with his knife. It may be an accident. According to the suspension list he is suspended from 1/8/03 to 1/22/03. He should have been arrested according to the teacher student hand book, laws of the municipality and state.
**Please note:** On the 1/9/03 suspension list there are 69 students suspended and 7 in ZONE. But the school is NOT out of control!

**Then between 5th & 6th periods** fire alarms go off *again*. It's another false alarm and a new year with the same problems and no solutions. However, students are not leaving the building properly, they are playing, fooling around and not leaving by the quickest and straightest route out. Because of the continual false alarms everybody treats it mundane, routine and casual. It is business as usual here.

**Jan 21** - we just came back from a day off for Dr. Martin Luther King. It is also midterm exam day and week. There was no HEAT. It was as cold inside as it was outside. It has been in the teens the last couple of weeks and this week it is in single digits to low teens. I spoke with the custodian supervisor and he said that there is no heat because there is NO OIL. I asked why? He said, because the jackasses from central office didn't order it. He said he told them months ago to order it, now we don't have any and everybody is yelling at me. Luckily, I have furnaces in my room for forging. It took a while, but I got the room up to comfortable. It wasn't until after 10 until there was heat for the school.

**Jan 22** - still no heat in the school. The school is horribly cold and the children are all freezing. Again, I turned on the furnace in my room. When I left my house this morning the bank sign registered the temperature outside at 8 degrees. Now, how can a district that is run & operated by the state of NJ meaning the governor's office and commissioner of education get away with this?

I attempted to videotape all that was going on in the hallway but it did not work. The kids are all hanging out long after the bell rings to start class. It is actually worse during this entire mid-term exam week. There are NO security guards, police or an administrator present. Students are fighting, running, jumping, pushing, shoving, swearing, screaming, a regular free for all. It is no wonder that the cut office is always filled with cut and late slips. The administration DOES NOT CARE! A teacher can't say a word because the students don't listen, will end up being cursed at and threatened. Then again, what's the use they don't even listen to the Principal or VPs? It's a REAL NICE PLACE!

A student told me she came here with her father on Monday while we were off for Martin Luther King Day. They went to the front door, rang the bell, security came and said that the building is closed. However, her father showed a CON Edison ID, gave some story and the security guard allowed them in. She said she showed her father all of the damages, inside and out, electrical violations especially the exposed wires in the elevator room, mold throughout the building, damaged heating systems and etc.

**Jan 23** - today is the last day of Mid-Term Exam. The hallways were out of control. One of the VPs was standing there and I just looked at him and said, why do we even have bells to tell when to go to class? The kids just don't go? He didn't even look concerned about getting them to class. It is a big free for all.

**Jan 24** - 9:58, 4$^{th}$ period, evacuated building, false alarm again! The temperature was 15 degrees. The weather was horrible. Fire department officials were in. Another expense accrued by the taxpayers for another false alarm. The principal and the fire fighters were all laughing. I don't see this being a big joke. What if the fire department had to go on a real call? The students and staff don't take the alarms serious. It's a signal and excuse for students to act up and run around the building even more.

I was told by a colleague that the school or the district was fined $10,000 because of the heat problems. It was about not having the tanks in proper working condition.

**Jan 27** - I was called into Mr. Lance's* office during 5$^{th}$ period. He asked if I could destroy and melt these. It was a pile of knives, assorted weapons and a 24" pinch bar. I showed them to a couple of my female students during 7$^{th}$ period (Lunch). As I showed them, I said, take a look what I have here. Now, if I have these that means no one was ever arrested. Meaning if students were arrested, then these items would be evidence. The two students just shook their heads and said oh my God. I then said, this is what I was given, it's not telling us what else has been confiscated that we don't know about and not reported, including guns.

During 8th period another one of my students came in and I showed him and said the same thing. I showed them to the kids as proof of what I am saying, and they can be used as a reference. I took pictures of them with the digital camera for my files. Later I realize there were 45 caliber bullets in the bag. Well if there are bullets, there was a gun or guns.

**NOTE OF INTEREST:** I also showed and said the same things to Mr. Roberts* a personal aide. He tells me a story - Wednesday of last week (Jan. 22), there was a fight with six kids, three on each side. One boy was slashed with a knife. He didn't get cut because he was wearing a heavy down jacket.

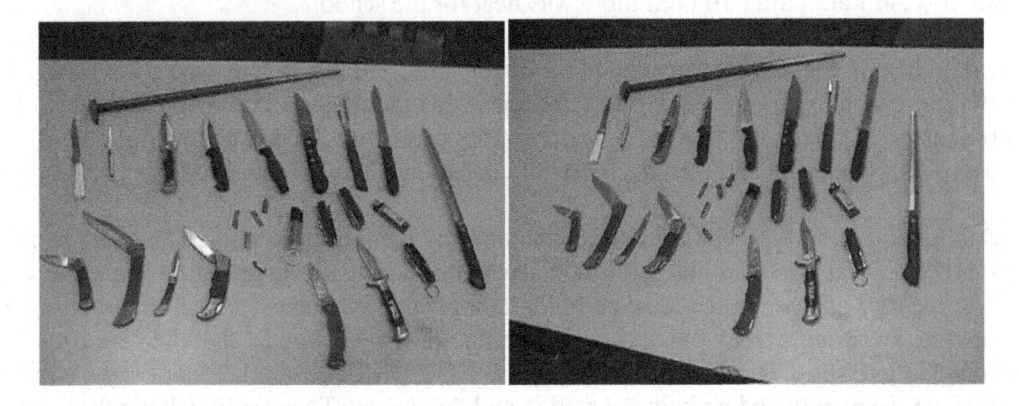

**Jan 27 -** I was talking with a secretary about all of the fighting going on. She asked me if I heard about the fighting involving (3) young ladies, students who were in so many fights all day and all of them are pregnant. I said are you kidding me. She said, NO they have been fighting with everyone all day long. I asked why in the hell are they allowed to stay here and continue to fight. Why weren't they suspended? Her exact words, "I don't know, I'm just telling what I know because I hear it over the walkie-talkies.

**Feb 20 -** speaking to a VP about a purchase order that came in from a welding company. We were both wondering why it was filled out by a secretary. The VP said it is unbelievable; Paterson does not pay its bills for 3 or 4 months. If a bill is not paid on time, it is then paid in the next 3 or 4 months making it 6 or 8 months. She says many vendors don't want to do business with Paterson Public School system. Then there is a snowball effect because teachers cannot order supplies because these companies refuse to work with us.

So who suffers? The teacher not having supplies and mostly our students by not having the supplies needed. The VP also said, it is sickening, and she can't believe how this can go on. She also said, she would rather be in the classroom then be a part of the school's operation (administration). She said this is sickening and it gets her upset.

**Feb 21 -** evacuated the building between 3rd & 4th periods. False alarm again. Kids are all over the parking lot and because it's snowing there are major snowball fights, etc. It took forever to get everyone back inside and out of hallway.

**Feb 21, 24, 28 -** I have a student Anthony* who acts up and cuts soooo much that he has to have a 35K a year personal aide shadow him all day, every day at taxpayers' expense. On the 21st Anthony* refused to come to class. In fact, he was supposed to see a counselor for his behavior. However, the personal aide tells me the counselor wasn't in her office. So, Anthony* just goes to the cafeteria. I write the cut. The next day the cut slip comes back telling me to see VP Mr. Loc*. I called Mr. Loc* on the phone and he tells me there is nothing he can do about it. I go back to the cut office they tell me there's nothing they can do about it and said it's up to Mr. Loc*. I don't know why we are told to write cuts or discipline referrals if NOTHING CAN be done about it.

Later I spoke with my supervisor. I explain the situation and how Anthony* just walks out of class. My supervisor tells me to tell the cut office to suspend the student. I call up the cut officer Mr. Pardine and explained what my supervisor said. He tells me to call up Mr. Madjar, the head cut officer. Mr. Madjar tells me to contact my supervisor again. I felt like a yo-yo. Mr. Madjar changes his mind and tells me he will contact my supervisor and confirmed what I said. The next day, I get the cut slip back saying that Anthony's* suspension is rescinded. I go to speak with my supervisor again. I was shocked, because his reply was "this is bullshit, he should have been suspended." Anthony* is a bad kid and he gets away with everything. Last year he busted a person's jaw and got away with it.

Bottom line- my supervisor comes back to me and says sorry, there is nothing he can do about it.

**Feb 28** - a fight breaks out in the cafeteria. One student is arrested because he hit a cop. Nothing would have happened if the student hit a security guard and especially a teacher.

I dropped off a bunch of cuts. The cut office was packed with students who are cutting and late. It is no wonder, when the bell rings for class to start the halls are worse than ever, nobody is in class. Obviously, whatever the punishment is, it isn't working. I know I have said this before, but why should a cut office be open the entire school day. The suspension list is almost two pages long.

What does that tell you? That the kids are NOT going to class and if they are going not on time. Many teachers say why we should spend the time to write cuts, late and discipline referrals, when nothing is done about it. I have a student that has been tardy 52 times. I turn in the referral and when I get it back there's writing by the cut officer saying 5 more. I even wrote a cut on a student's because he was marked absent. However, he was in school today and just roaming the halls.

**Mar 3** - there's a student who is supposed to be assigned to me a month or so ago for first period and has never shown up or signed in yet. However, all he does is roam the hallways and entire building all day. I summon security and it seems nothing is done about it. Now, if he has loss credit for the year, he can absolutely do whatever he wants without punishment. After all what are we going to do - FAIL HIM? He is looking to be suspended. This way he is legally allowed to be out of school. Nothing is done to change students with these bad habits? The administration should remember what it was like when they were at that age and *NOW* should know better.

Meanwhile, taxpayers are paying which will become even a bigger expense when they will have to pay even more for these children's future, because the School system deliberately allowed them to fail.

**Mar 4** - a social worker (name omitted) came to me and asked about a student. She said he complains that all he is doing is paperwork (writing). I said that is true. He is failing. He comes to class late, he doesn't do any work, he fools around, jumps, wrestles, constantly playing and doing everything but what he is supposed to do. Same with a few other students. So they're given writing assignments. The social worker says, he can't write. I replied then why is he in high school? (Mind you this week is HSPT & HSPA testing. The State Standardized Test). I replied, all of these students are being tested. If they fail, they do not graduate. However, he gets the same diploma. The counselor replied back, well that's the law. I replied, well it is wrong. The law does not allow students just to come to school to do nothing and just play. She turned away and started to talk to another teacher and walked out.

I cannot believe anyone can go to high school and not have to be up to speed or grade wise and graduate not doing any work and yet still get the same diploma as those who do their work. Now we can't figure out WHY there are so many illiterate people in this country, and they have high school diplomas??

JFK is so out of control with the cuts and late students. Today's suspension list is over a page long. Every morning the cut office is filled SRO with students and parents awaiting disciplinary action. If a student is given detention and they don't attend, they may be given another chance or add on a Saturday detention, (which teachers are paid overtime). Then if the student does not attend, they may be suspended, which is exactly what the students wants, because now they get days off that do not count toward their attendance. Where's the deterrent? Life is an ongoing process in education. School is supposed to be helping, assisting with this process. However, our school is not teaching or preparing students the most important factors of life. That is, you have to work and be on time.

When a student is called to the cut office there is such a long wait, being it is soooo busy and filled with so many students. Some students, even though they are cutting and not going to class anyway, don't want to wait. They get upset and start carrying on with their dysfunctional, unacceptable and poor behavior, making the situation worse. Screaming "I don't have to wait," "You want me, you see me now." The students can do what they want and no one can inconvenience them. Then when they are finally being processed all you hear is "you can't do that," "I don't have to do that," "you/he can't tell me to do that," "I don't have to do what they say." It goes on and on. J.F.K High School allows and ignores this behavior. Nothing is ever done to correct and improve a student's unacceptable behavior. That's why parents want a choice to use their tax dollars so they can send their children to private/parochial school where they don't allow, accept and encourage this behavior.

Kids were climbing on then jumping off my car. A teacher (name omitted) saw this and confronted the students. The students' reply "FUCK YOU." After she told me the story, I contacted the president of the PEA (Paterson Education Association).

I followed up with a violence and vandalism report and submitted it to a union rep. He told me the surveillance cameras are turned off at 2:10 p.m. I realized what is going on. This is so the administration will not have a recording, covering up student's behavior inside and outside from that time on to the end of the school day which usually includes major fighting (gang) and having a large police presence.

**Mar 12 -** I was absent but when I came back on the 13th, I learned that there is a school bus that will NO LONGER come to our school. It seems while the bus was in motion, two students (names omitted) and one of their brothers decided to destroy the bus. I understand they pulled seats out and tore them apart.

**Mar 13 -** Mr. Sharp* was telling me that Anthony* the same student from February 21, 24, & 28, cursed him out really bad and viciously. He was screaming, go fuck yourself, fuck you, get the fuck out of here mother fucker, etc. AND he was NOT suspended for his behavior either. Mr. Sharp* is quite upset and doesn't understand how Anthony* can be wondering the halls, cutting class, and NOTHING is done about it. I said last week he was finally suspended for 5 days for cutting many classes. Mr. Sharp* replied how can this be allowed when he has a personal aide who's supposed to follow him to all of his classes at taxpayers' expense? I replied because he is "SPECIAL ED" and SUPPOSEDLY cannot be kicked out of school. We both said it seems Special Ed students can do whatever they want, don't have to go to class, don't have to do school or homework, learn to read or write, don't have to take tests and still obtain the very same type diploma as the students who bust their butts, and is required to take a state exam, in order to graduate. Wonder why our taxes are always going up? Why is this allowed in a school in a district that has been taken over by the State of New Jersey and is still under state control?

**Mar 14** - one of my female students told me, two of my other students(names omitted) while sitting in classroom 238 decided to set a piece of paper on fire and throw it on the floor. As far as I know, NOTHING was done about it. To set an example, they should have been arrested for deliberately setting a fire and endangering the lives of everyone in the building. I don't understand the mentality and thinking of the administration!

**Mar 24** – talking with a secretary about the fire alarms always going off and how she does not have to leave the building. I said you know darn well the administration will tell everybody it is a fire drill. She said yes, the principal has a secretary call the fire department and tell them it is a drill. That's why it is never on TV or the news. However, it is too late. The school is supposed to notify the fire department first before having a fire drill. So, it is NOT a drill. That's why the fire department is here with all of their equipment. The administration works so hard covering everything up instead of having control of the building.

**Mar 25** - security in school is supposedly tightened because of the war and terrorist threats. Yeah right, how can that be when the hallways are packed with kids all day long? Many of my students (and I write the cuts) haven't been to class in months and are in the halls. One in particular (name omitted), I haven't seen since before Christmas. So how good is the security? How good is having IDs? This place is a joke.

**Mar 28** - one of my students was jumped and put in a hospital.

I have had enough and delivered a letter to my supervisor today relinquishing me of any responsibility with Anthony* I included all documentation and an incident referral.

**Mar 31** - Anthony* curses out his teacher Mr. Sharp* again telling him to suck his dick. He was FINALLY brought to the security office and suspended for 5 days.

**Apr 1** - fights everywhere all day. I bet there were NO reports turned in on them!

**Apr 3** - all the students who are suspended, quit and dropped from roll are inside the building hanging out everywhere with all of the other students. So much for security and students having to wear IDs.

**May 5** - at the beginning of 3rd period - a boy, throw a knife at a female student. Police chased him but did not catch him. This all happened on 1st floor in front of my room

**May 7, 8, 9** - 160 students are on the suspension list. If the school is so safe and NOT out of control, then why in May is there the same number of students suspended as there has been for the last 7 months? What are they suspended for? Most of them have to be for cuts and tardiness because they are not in class but in the halls, stairwells, bathrooms, and walking in and out of classrooms they don't belong in and etc. It is nothing but a free for all here!

**May 15** - big fight all girls in the center of the hallway outside security and front cafeteria. It started out with two girls, then another jumped in, then another and another until there were 6. In fact, there was a LARGE crowd of students gathering, watching, cheering, yelling, cursing and were all taking cheap shots at whoever they could hit. It didn't matter. It was like sharks in a feeding frenzy.

A fight breaks out and students will hit, kick and throw stuff at anyone because they enjoy hurting people. It is a sad, disgusting and dangerous place here. It took forever before the hallways were finally reasonably cleared. There are always a handful of students still trying to insight and start another commotion and situation as the administration, security and police just look on. If students feared or even respected the administration, security and the police, then why did it take so long to finally have some type of reasonable order? However, this would have never ever happened if students were in their classes instead of hanging around looking for something to do. What does administration do? They leave and continue letting students gather and congregate in the hallways all day long.

**May 16** - today the Principal came over the PA system during H/R. He had a great deal of positive things to say about, the cheerleaders, the band, the robotic people, track and all of those who participated with the Science Fair. However, these are just a few of the students and are usually the same students who participate with school, academic & any to every involvement with school.

**May 29** - 9th period evacuated the building. False alarm again! Later that period I overheard the principal talking to his secretary about staying by the phone and walkie-talkie because they have 3 to 4 minutes to call the fire department not to come because it's a false alarm/fire drill.

**May 30** - 5th period, evacuated the building again. Another false alarm! During 9th period a major fight broke out and this young girl was screaming at a female VP Ms. Ives* "fuck you, get your fucking hands off of me, who do you think you are, I'll fuck you up, you just wait and see," and on and on. A female security guard grabs her and this young lady began threatening her. Doll*, the security guard, had enough with her attitude, swearing and fighting and said, fuck it lock her ass up. Ms. Ives* didn't want that and stopped her.

Bottom line- this young lady was NOT disciplined. It was dropped as if it never happened. Other students watched and now they too will do the same. Even after the incident with this young lady the students here at J.F.K. High are *STILL* continually allowed to be in the hallways instead of being in class even more. Meanwhile, you're going to tell me that the administration wonders why the alarms are pulled, fights break out, the school has so much vandalism in, out and around the building? They know the reason, because they *are* the reason.

**Jun 13** - a pack of girls out of control carrying on, screaming, cursing, the most terrible and obscene of foul language you can imagine bellowing throughout the school. This poor security guard is trying to get them back into the cafeteria. They kept it up, ignoring him, pushing their way through as if he doesn't matter and obviously they don't care. Then again why should they? They KNOW nothing is going to happen to them. The security guard steps in front of them trying to stop them from leaving again and these girls continue. The one girl screams out at him, to get out of her fucking face, "Don't put your fucking hands on me, get the fuck out of my way, who the fuck are you? You're not my father, fuck you mother fucker, fuck you" and on and on then she gives him a shove and continues to violently curses him out more.

This is not school, this is ridiculous and disgusting! This poor man is making a little more than minimum wage and taking all of this abuse while the administration is allowing all of this behavior to continually go on all day, every day, all year, and year after year. It just keeps on getting worse here daily. The security guards can't win. It is obvious that JFK is a place for children to learn and hone their skill of bad habits. The kids can do whatever they want and get away with it without recourse. This is why you see kids instead of being in class, in the hallway, stairwells, bathrooms, at the snack machines, running, screaming, cursing in the hallways at the top of their lungs. You'll see gangs of kids walk in and out classrooms that they do not belong in. They do this to just to start a fight, upset, agitate and threaten the teacher and students, make a scene with the student, sit down and start talking with someone from that class and on many occasions to jump and beat someone. This goes on all day long, every day!

What do you expect? Security is NOT going to get beat up for minimum wage. They are NOT backed up by administration. Furthermore, many of these security guards live in the same neighborhood as the kids. They don't want to get jumped coming home from work or the store.

**Jun 19** - 4th period, hundreds of students are all over the hallway, cursing and fooling around. Few are outside the front cafeteria. VP Ms. Ives* is trying to get this young man inside the cafeteria. All this young man kept saying was fuck this shit, fuck this is shit, I don't give a shit, I don't give a fuck, I don't have to do this shit, and on and on. Nothing was done about it. God forbid if a teacher should slip because they are so frustrated in trying to do their job. What can teachers do when supervision/VPs allow this to happen in their presence? Meanwhile the teacher is held to a higher standard of having control of their classroom. I don't understand, if students don't listen to any of the administrators, and the building is so out of control, how do they expect teachers to be in control in their classrooms? The administration has set the tone and attitude for the building. What in the hell is a STANDARD, at JFK High School?

**Jun 19** - 9th period, evacuated the building. Someone called the school and said there was a bomb.

**Jun 20** - Mr. Ell* told me the principal stood fast on his decision. It seems the superintendent and assistant superintendent sent out letters to the students that took part in murdering the homeless man (Hector Robles) a few years back allowing them to walk in this year's graduation ceremony. I understand the principal was adamant this should not be allowed. Paraphrasing what I was told- the principal said, if they are allowed to walk and participate in the graduation ceremony, he will NOT attend. The superintendent and assistant superintendent rescinded the letters and those students did not participate in graduation. UNFREAKINBELIEVABLE, as if nothing happened. Is this what has become of our society just to increase the graduation rate / numbers?

**Jun 21** - I have to go to Office #2 to look through the list of names of student that are suspended and check their records for fighting, threatening to get a gun and shoot a teacher. It seems everything is so hushed up and squashed that no matter who I speak to no one wants to talk about it. They all reply they don't know what I'm talking about.

## SCHOOL YEAR 2003 – 2004
**Sept 3** - first day of school with student. Oh my God, it is an absolute free for all here already.

**Sept 9** - I spoke with a guidance counselor who was so upset. It seems back in Feb or March he attended a workshop at School 25 and the person who giving it was from central office. She said guidance counselors CANNOT call parents about school situations at work anymore because they may lose their jobs. He also said she made it very clear that she was relaying the message by order of the superintendent.

**Sept 16** - fire trucks outside of school. Possible bomb a threat again? NOT SURE. We did not evacuate?

**Sept 17** - major fights all day. Police are physically restraining students, picking them up bodily in order to get them into the security room. Students are resisting and fighting with police. Students are being arrested. Let's see if any of this makes the news or newspapers? However, students still remain in the hallway all day long. No one seems to be going to class. Not one administrator visible.

Fire alarm pulled. Here we go again. Principal was more worried if the fire department was contacted right away. He was told "no," the firemen are already here. The administration is scrambling trying to cover this up. As usual no one in the community knows about it. Later I placed 6 cuts in the cut office. The cut office drop-off bin was filled with cuts. This is NOT even the 2nd full week of school.
This place is already out of control. If we do not regain control soon, this year will be lost.

**Sept 19 -** big fight between two girls, right outside my door and Mr. Lances* office. Unbelievable, it was an extremely vicious fight. So much for ZERO TOLERANCE TO VIOLENCE! Should see the suspension list already? I am surprised they are even suspending?

**Sept 22 -** was told today our principal is up for Principal of the Year and a national award.

**Oct 1 - *BIG*** fight on 2nd floor. Hundreds of kids were gathering around watching and antagonizing the situation making it worse. It was just another excuse not to go to class. I've notice administration has slacked off and the kids are *more* wild running and pushing knocking down anyone in their way in hallway between classes. VP Ms. Ives* usually says stop it, go to class, take your hats off, just enough to be heard but keeps on walking. The students just ignore her, as if she doesn't exist and go about their business acting up and going wild. As usual they don't go to class and NOTHING is done about it. THEN during 7th period I was actually surprised because I saw the principal telling students to stop, get to class, you're in high school now, grow up, get your hats off. Sadly, the kids were ignoring him and laughing as they continued. School hasn't been open a month and it is so out of whack.

I have yet to hear anything about the vandalism on my car from 2 years ago, from either the PEA or central office.

Mr. Costello* a VP and I were talking about the kids being in the hallways all day, cutting, etc. He said there should be no students in the hallway after the bell rings. I looked at him and said, no kidding. That is why the cut office is filled with paperwork. Mr. Costello* says, "at least we have a cut office; Eastside doesn't even have a cut office." What's the point? It is not even a month into a new school year; the school is out of control and he says at least we have a cut office. I don't understand what that is supposed to mean! In reality, why should we even have to have a cut office? Every student should be in class. Our cut office is open, busy and filled with students all day long all because obviously nothing is being done about anything involving discipline, violence, control and making student attend class. Meanwhile the NJ taxpayers are paying teachers' salaries for teachers NOT to teach but to work in a cut office that means absolutely nothing. ARE YOU FREAKING KIDDING ME!

**Oct 2 -** Fights all day long in school. A big fight breaks out in the parking lot at 2:15. All you see is police, administrators and so many out of control students. It is so dangerous here.

While I was in the cut office a new teacher asked, is it true that a parent receives extra money if their child is classified? The answer was yes. Wonder why we have soooo many classified students? Also discussed was if a senior has passed all parts of the HSPA/HSPT state exams is it true that the district does NOT care how many days they are out of school or if they pass their other classes? The answer again was, "YES!" It is about numbers and percentages.

**Oct 3 -** bigger fight today. It carried out to the parking lot after school. VP Mr. Saint* was hit in the head attempting to break it up. It seems every time students have an early dismissal, half day of school, for whatever the reason, the day is a complete disaster and the school becomes even more out of control. In fact, there needs to be a great deal *more structure*. Anyhow, at the teachers meeting, the principal says we are off to a good start. Are you kidding me? How do they get the nerve to stand up in front of 300 teachers and LIE! The school is soooo out of control! You should see the suspension list already?

**NOTE OF INTEREST:** I have copies of all absentee & suspension lists since I started my documentation on what goes here at JFK high school.

Next the principal brings up that so far, we have only had *one* false fire alarm pulled. Well, if students were not cutting or late to class, mainly *not* in the hallway all day long, we wouldn't have false alarms. There should never be a false alarm. If the punishment was administered as required by state law, then maybe students would realize, and we wouldn't have ANY! Then he says it is important for teachers to keep students together while evacuating and when outside the building. What is wrong with him and administrators? Where do they work? First of all, the students *do not* listen to him. Remember, he is the same principal that was booed off the stage by seniors prior to graduation. That alarm is a signal for a free for all.

However, I do agree with him that we must take added roll call and write up all students who take off. I have been doing this for years. However, when I turn in the cut slip and discipline referral nothing is done about it. You talk about killing trees here. Is there somebody in the audience that we are not aware of watching and listening to this that he has to impress?

Then the principal asks Mr. Madjar to come up and say a few words. Mr. Madjar says Mr. Pardine, basically runs the entire show in the cut office. Many nights Mr. Pardine is in the school processing the cuts and late slips up until 11pm. However, according to the principal, the school is *not* out of control.

After we broke from the meeting in the auditorium, we went to another meeting. At this meeting a VP was talking about the all the fights, problems and the situations that are going here. I asked him, whatever happened to" ZERO TOLERANCE TO VIOLENCE" in our schools? He looked at me and then turned away. He proceeded to speak. I politely asked again. He looked at me and I looked at him waiting for an answer. He then turned his head without answering and continued with his conversation. My question is, how can they go home at night knowing that they hush up and try to keep everything quiet from parents and the public, do they actual think that they did the right thing and a good job today?

**Oct 3** - According to some of the coaches, our baseball team stinks. **REASON:** None of the kids want to attend practice. They just want to show up and play.

Once again, this shows how these children have no structure or discipline in their life and refuse to participate if it is NOT their way. This also goes for many of the other school activities.
**Bottom line -**The coach quit. He was frustrated and said, "What's the use."

I also learned (name omitted) was supposed to have a court order and restraining order NOT to be by John F. Kennedy High School, due to the murder he was involved in of Mr. Robles. However, while he is attending Eastside High School, he becomes captain of the football team and plays John F. Kennedy football team during the annual Eastside/Kennedy Football game on Thanksgiving Day. I do not understand our society or school district mentality. He killed someone in cold blood for fun, went to court, was found guilty and is *still* allowed to play school sports. I would not allow my child to play on the same team with him. This is what I mean - I have *no idea* when I am at school, the difference between right and wrong.

**Oct 9** - 8th period, fire alarms go off. Evacuated the building again. This place is so out of control. The administration still allows students to roam the building instead of going to class all day every day.

**Oct 13** - I had to write up two major safety violations for my 5th period class, in order to have two students removed. Both students were uncontrollable, abusive, foul- mouthed, disruptive, destructive and defiant. This is just a sample of what we go through every day, all day, and all year. This goes ignored unless you write it up in a way where you let administration know that you (the teacher) will NOT be held responsible and it is now in *their* hands.

### * STUDENT #1:

On 10/23 father came in. We spoke and he read the below info. We exchanged phone numbers.

**9/18** -placed out in the hallway and then was told to come in &sit in the back to write his schedule.

**9/18** - called home.

**9/29 & 9/30** - excessive foul language.

**9/29** - placed outside and had to be brought back in by order of Mrs. Ives* a V P.

**10/2** - had to be placed outside because he would not listen. Excessive foul language. Using tools and machinery improperly repeatedly. Walks away from door. Says he doesn't have to stay.

**10/6** - stealing nuts and bolts from cabinet. As I approached, he denied it. Pockets were filled with them. He said he wanted them to throw at people. He emptied his pockets and I made him sit down again. I CANNOT trust him. Is always doing something he shouldn't be doing.

**10/13** - told to sit down using equipment wrong after repeated instructions/more foul language and a barrage of insults.

**10/14** - told to sit down, using drill press improperly. Will not abide by any safety rule or regulation. When confronted puts on a big show. Cannot be allowed in this class, he is going to get hurt or cause someone else to get hurt. Extreme safety hazard. Does not talk to me without swearing and using excessive foul language. Not acceptable behavior for anyone of that age or at any age. Does *no work* at all. Only does what he wants, and it is unsafe and unacceptable.

**10/15**- defiant argumentative again. Asked to stop, he just laughs in my face and persists. I asked him to go outside and stand by the door. He was defiant and then left. I explained if you leave, I am writing a cut. He says, Mr. Saint* says I can't do that then left/walked away. This is the 2$^{nd}$time he walked away.

**10/23**- I had to go see VP Ms. Ives. He and student #2 going at it back and forth will not stop. Student #2 kept hitting student #1 on the top of the head with hand broom.

**\*November 12 dropped from class. Total: Absent (22)****Cuts (11)****Lates (11)**

### *STUDENT #2:

On 9/30 the aunt of student #2 came in and spoke with me. He complains that the test I gave him was too hard. I explained to his aunt that I gave them all the questions and answers to the test. The test was true and false with 9 questions.

**10/1** - excessive foul language, refusal of apology, and defiant.

Hitting machine with hammer, refuses to stop and had to remove hammer from him. He says I am going to get it again I had to yell at him and make him sit down. However as usual, he refused and started with the mouth and foul language, telling me he doesn't have to do what I say, so fuck you.

**10/15** - asked to sit down because he was playing with the machine after I told him not to. Then he starts yelling, swearing, throwing stuff, just will not stop and carries on.

Then he starts with his nonsense, disrespectfulness, defiance, and argumentative ways.

**10/16** - stole another students block/project

Last week he said he could not find his project. I said it is here. He starts with his foul language and that I or someone stole it. I said it is here, he then says, I will steal someone else's. I warned him if he does, I will fail him. Obviously, he stole another student's project. When he turned in his finished project, I looked at the name/initials. I then called that student over and he identified it. I called another student to verify it and she agreed and said it was NOT student #2's project.

He starts yelling, acting up, swearing, scratching, and hitting the computer with a metal rod. I ask him to stop, he kept it up. I asked him again, he tells me I don't have to. I move him away, he starts with the fuck you, get away, and get your hands off. The security guard comes in and removes him. Five minutes later, he walks out of security and starts all over again. I closed the door, and he starts to bang on it.

**10/ 21** -my supervisor spoke with him. Student came in saying you can't do that. He can't suspend me. Then it begins again, and then on and on.

**10/21** - kept on teasing kicking touching a female student after being told to stop. He refused to do his work and instead continued acting up and aggravating the female student.
**10/23** - I had to go see VP Ms. Ives. He and student #2 going at it back and forth will not stop. Student #2 kept hitting student #1 on the top of the head with hand broom.

***November 14** Dropped from class **Total: Absent (27)**      **Cuts (9)**      **Late (3)**

These were just (2) out of 100 plus students I had. Unfortunately for me, they were in the same class. Please explain to me how a teacher who has to go through all of that abuse and nonsense, endure that type of behavior is still expected to give the rest of their students the proper attention and education? Secondly, why were these students allowed to be placed in a shop setting, where every tool is a weapon? The machinery is dangerous and absolute understanding that directions must be followed is paramount. Also, let me make myself clear, not *all* students are like this. However, at JFK High School, I would say over 35% are like this or even worse. This teaches good students how to be bad, because the administration allows and encourage this behavior by ignoring it!

Please let it be known that I have and had so many good, even GREAT students. When they graduated, I was happy for them but sad because I was concerned and already started missing them. However, they could have been *better* and *greater* had I been allowed to do my job. The only way my colleagues and I can do our jobs is if and only IF the administration did their jobs.

Running around in a total panic because of all the wheeling and dealing so they can hush up or ignore problems and situations, is NOT doing their jobs.

**Oct 21** - cut office has soooo many students in there all day long/the cutting and tardiness are atrocious; the suspension list for this date is one full page. Students are hitting & threatening teachers. Nothing is being done about any of this. The administration works so hard to calm and hush up all of these problems/situation and to keep teachers from pressing press charges. What is even more disgusting is in the center hallway on the first floor, all over the walls are signs about stop the violence.

Two students, who use excessive and continuous foul language, still refuse to write their apologies. They both said, well, I will fail this marking period. I said, the apologies carry over and you will still have to do them, they will be doubled daily, and it will carry over to the next marking period. They both said, I cannot do that. I made it very clear that I will fail them. Their reply was, well we will just drop the class.

I explained to them they will NOT be able to change schedules. The first thing out of one the student's mouth was, "My guidance counselor says if I am failing or have any difficulty with any of my classes, they will change them for me." I asked why? He said, "Because I am a senior." Game, Set &Match.

The mentality here is about getting over. Doing the least amount of work possible and wanting all the rewards of an "A" student; passing and graduating. This is the mentality that is taught and instilled here by a state run and operated district on how to prepare students for a future of the real world of work and how to become a productive taxpaying member of society. Bottom line, following directions *is* a part of education. After all, when taking a written test, do you NOT have to follow explicit directions? When students are given an assignment, they have to do it over and over because they refuse to follow directions and only want to do it their way. Then because they don't get their way, they become frustrated because me/teachers will not accept anything other than the way we explained.

They say this is good enough. Why are you buggin'? What's the difference? I tell them, "The difference is it is *not* correct. I'm doing my job by preparing you for the future." Even when I have them do a simple task of copying what is on the blackboard it is not remotely close because they want to do it their way and make it shorter; do less work. Then they will argue with me saying, it *is* exactly what's on the blackboard and refuse to do it over. They just don't care because they were taught, they do *not* have to do anything and they will pass and graduate.

This is also the reason why they cannot pass the statewide exam. So, what does the district do? They remove students from their regularly assigned and scheduled classes - 4 to 5 straight periods - for several weeks prior in order to prepare them to take the exam because they CANNOT and will not follow directions. In fact, guidance counselors have to pre-grid their test booklets because the students will not and cannot follow directions and do it incorrectly.

It is not about education or anything else here. It is only about passing the State Exam

**Bottom line -** The State of New Jersey, who runs and operates the District of Paterson, NJ, has failed these students miserably. I surely hope those who read this will realize that there is a *major* lawsuit here.

**Oct 22 -** we had to evacuate the building again because someone pulled the fire alarm again. Supposedly there was to be a fight. Once again, there are too many students in hallway. I did NOT see any security or administrators. Gee, I guess that's why the fire alarm was pulled again! The administration will lie and try to cover it up by saying it's a fire drill if they notify the fire department right away. So many of us teachers refuse to say anything anymore to students as they are running around and carrying on instead of evacuating the building because they will only say something to start a confrontation.

A Special Ed student's mother came into class. She wanted to know how many students are in each class and why there are no aides. We had a discussion and she was shocked. She said, she has spoken with the newspapers and radio station and they will help. Rule of thumb-for every three students that are Special Ed, there is supposed to be an aid. She is quite concerned.

**Oct 23 -** 7th period gang fight Blacks and Arabic's gang called the PLO.

**Oct 24 -** fights continue with Blacks & Arabics. There was a beefed-up police presence around & in school. Even state police were called in. The school pulled about 100 + students out of classes for several periods due to gang war activity & had an assembly/meeting in auditorium about all of this. School is a meeting/rallying place so students can get together to attack, start fights, etc.

**Oct 27 -** first thing this morning, two female students, who come into my class every morning about 7:15, were upset. They told me that they are NOT going to take the 3:15 school #18 bus anymore. They said, Friday a bunch of kids were in the back of the bus fucking. That was their exact words. I asked questions and they said that even the bus driver would not do anything. I told them to tell their parents and contact a local newspaper. I then relayed the info to the principal. He asked me to get as much info as I can. I came back and handed him a slip with the two girls' names on it, their homeroom and verification from Friday, Oct. 24, school #18, 3:15 pm bus, noting that this was *not* the first incident.

I did express that the girls said they will *not* take this bus again. The principal took the info and said he would give it to my VP and look into it. That was the last I ever heard about it. I am not saying it was ignored or squashed, I truly don't know. As for the bus driver, I'm sure this is unusual, as well as all the other crap that goes on every day. He probably didn't do or say anything, because like I said, he sees this stuff and other worse things and figures if he does anything, he'll end up getting hurt and or fired.

**During 7th period**, I heard fire trucks. I said to a student, "I wonder where they are going? Many times they come here because someone called in a bomb threat or something and the administration doesn't even know." That's exactly what happened. In a couple of seconds, the fire trucks were here, and the fire people were in the building. The principal was right in front of my door and didn't know what was going on either. I asked a security guard and the head custodian what happened. It seems someone called 911 and said there's a fire in the basement. Nevertheless, we never evacuated the building.

**At the end of 9th period 2:10,** the fire alarms go off again. It was a cold, rainy, miserable day. We evacuated the building. *Another* false alarm. Meanwhile students still remain in the hallways all day long.

**Oct 28 -** Mr. Madjar told me they have processed about 20K cuts already. He said when he first came to the cut office, they would process over 40K cuts a year. He said some parents will come in and complain because their child was suspended for cuts, go to central office, speak to the assistant superintendent, and she would deny that such a rule is in place at and overturn the ruling.

**Oct 29 -** fights all day long and I mean big brutal fights.

**Fire alarms** were pulled *again*, between 7th and 8th period. We evacuated the building. It was pulled in the gym. Another false alarm! As we were coming back in the alarms went off again and from the same location - the GYM.

**The fire department *did* come to the school, so there is a record of it.** I was told by one of my students that Student #1, **from above entry,** told my student while they were in the cafeteria that he was going to pull the alarms. Student #1 said he will use gloves because he knows there is a substance on the alarms that can be detected on your hand. I relayed the message to VP Mr. Costello* and VP Mrs. Ives*. A few minutes later I saw Student #1 and summoned a security guard. She brought Student #1 to Mr. Lance*.

**About 15 minutes into the revised schedule for period 8, the fire alarms were pulled again.** Now the school was really out of control. Kids were going wild, screaming, yelling and running all over the place as if it was a game. We evacuated the building *AGAIN*. When we finally came back in, 8th period was over.

**During 9th period, fire alarms were pulled *again*.** Now forget it, the school was lost. It was an absolute disaster, nothing but an actual free-for-all and pandemonium.

**My concerns** are for our handicapped, wheelchair bound and special needs students with all of false alarms, bomb threats and evacuations.

Later that day, I spoke with a Mr. Costello*. He asked me what I thought. I replied, "May I answer freely?" He replied, "You always do." I said, "This is only October and the school is out of control. There are too many students in hallways, security does not ask for passes, students do not have and refuse to wear their IDs so what do you expect?" I also mentioned that we know that the gangs keep pulling the fire alarms so they can attack someone and or fight with other gangs. I asked him frankly, "What is going to happen when someone pulls a gun or guns and innocent people (teachers), children (students) are hit (shot)? He said nothing and walked away.

**Oct 30 -** Goosey Night, other than some fights in the building (again this is only what I know), the day went well. However, because of all the false alarms on Wednesday, all fire alarm boxes and posts were guarded by *teachers*. That's the administrations way of solving a problem, instead of making students attend class and keeping them out of the hallway.

**Oct 31 - found out *Student* #2 from previous entry** was arrested for pushing & shoving VP, Mr. Costello*.

**Nov 3 -** girls were fighting all day long.

**9th period,** we had to evacuate the building AGAIN. The fire alarm was pulled on the 2nd floor.

**Nov 4 -** 9th period alarms go off again. We evacuated the building. Alarm was pulled on 2nd floor.

**Now for the best.** Last week I went to office #1 and asked a secretary about a purchase order. She tells me the purchasing agent Mr. Carson* wants me to get prices from other places. This is almost 60 days later. If I didn't ask, how long would I have found out that my order was *not* processed? **Now** I am told to check with two other companies. I did and they didn't carry the material I needed. I needed STEEL and I needed it a month ago. Now, I am told to check with other companies. I was getting aggravated because I knew I'm being led on a wild goose chase, but I complied.

I finally spoke with the purchasing agent Mr. Carson*. He tells me because the company on my PO is not a state contractor, I cannot use them. He says, he thought I needed blades. How can that be when the PO says brass, aluminum, etc.? He says he now understands and tells me to contact these two companies. I did. Both places were well over $500, more than the original quote I received. Now he tells me, "We can't always go with the company that is cheaper." I said that was ridiculous. He says, "It's like that to keep people from buying stuff from friends and family." He said, "As long as the company is approved, it doesn't matter. I reply, "This is unacceptable. I have to pay $500 more for same stuff. This is not fair to the taxpayers." He replies, "If we always went with those who are cheaper, look at the money the district would save." My head almost exploded. I said, "Did you hear what you just said? What is your point? What is wrong with going someplace that is cheaper? He remained quiet. I am guessing he realized what he just said, which makes me wonder what he was really up to by sending me to all of these other vendors. I told him that I will document this and check further into it. I repeated, "This is *not* acceptable. That's what I am supposed to do. I should be getting the bang for the buck."

Then a secretary says the dumbest thing, "What do you care, it is not your money." I snapped back in anger saying, "it is my money, your money, my students' money, and all taxpayers' money." Then she said, "It's the districts!" She, like most people, just doesn't get it. Taxes are going up so schools can have a bigger budget, yet they will NOT allow teachers to purchase the same equipment, or materials for less. We have to spend the more because of the state contract. Taxpayers are getting screwed!

**Nov 13 -** I was told that our principal is in Washington, DC receiving a Principal of the Year Award.

**I also learned** today one of the reasons why our district administrator left was because she would NOT turn over *PERKINS MONEY* (a federal grant for vo-tech programs) to be spent in other areas. How it was explained to me was the superintendent would always try but she would NOT release the money to him. However, when the new superintendent came in everything here in Paterson became a different ball game. She had enough and did NOT want to get caught up with the money reallocation game and left. So in her place the superintendent hired (name omitted) who is a longtime friend of his. Bottom line, no matter what the money *IS* allocated for or where it's coming from, the district will use it for whatever they want it for. However, I am forced to pay $500 more for items needed because they are on a state contracting vendors list.

**Nov 17** - speaking to Mr. Madjar of the cut office, he said they already suspended 300 to 400 students. This is more than in April of last year. He said they are suspending 30 to 40 students a day. Students are not going to class and showing up only when they want to. He said the principal asked him what are we were doing wrong. Mr. Madjar replied that the school is out of control. The principal asked, what we can do. Mr. Madjar said he didn't know. I know, follow the rules. Many students are on probation or parole; contact the probation or parole officers. If they are collecting social security as long as they are in school, and don't show up contact social security, etc. Wrong is always wrong. Doing nothing is also wrong!

**4th period** I saw a kid savagely attack another kid in the weight room. He picked him up and slammed him to the ground and was roughing him up pretty good. The teacher finally broke it up. *No zero tolerance to violence* here. While the teacher was trying to talk to the kid who was slammed, the attacker was moving around all over the place with his hands raised, screaming and yelling in act of defiance and intimidation not only toward the student he attacked but to the teacher and everyone else around. He was just waiting to run over and strike again. The teacher tried to get him to stop but he kept it up, ignoring her as if she wasn't even there and didn't exist. NOTHING was done about it! I just sit back and watch now. I am *not* getting involved. This kid's actions showed the other students that they too can do this and get away with it. No setting of examples here!

There are about a dozen students at the far end of the building waiting for the bus. All they are doing is screaming, yelling, wrestling, throwing stuff, spitting on the floor, and carrying on, and the security guard just sits there as if this is normal. You can't blame security, because if they do anything they are told off, cursed at and threatened by the students.

I left work talking to myself repeating things that went on inside JFK knowing that it is wrong and kept saying, 'F it, what can I do? I'll just keep my mouth shut, mind my own business and forget about it. Times Square in NYC on New Year's Eve has less chaos and is in more control than JFK High School.

**Nov 18** - I was told today that Anthony*, the same student from Feb. 21, 24, 28, & March 13 & 31, 2003, went from 10R (10R = repeating sophomore) to a senior. How in the hell can a repeating sophomore jump up to a graduating senior status??? He hasn't passed any classes. He does *not* come to school; he is always absent, suspended, tardy or cutting. I would not be surprised after he graduates he and his mother sue the district because they pushed him through the system.

This is what the school and district does - just passes and gets them out. They get a diploma but are *illiterate*. What does that say about our public school system here in Paterson, that is under state takeover and control? Is this, what is meant by "no child left behind?" You mean by left behind, not left back? Once again, the taxpayers pay the price.

**ALSO,** even though this student is NOW a 12th grader, the administration still has a *teacher*/personal aide who is being paid to do NOTHING but follow/shadow him all day long. Meanwhile Anthony* still does what he wants and cuts class. The personal aide told me that Anthony* and his mother had to attend a school hearing. They had to sign a contract for him to follow or ELSE! He is NOT to be absent, cut class, be late get into trouble or anything else. However, as soon as the hearing was over, he cuts class.

**A colleague told me**, a student pinned another student down, pulled a blade or a piece of sheet metal and put it to the kid's neck. Is that not violence? How can the newspapers not know about this? There has to be a police report *if it were REPORTED*! The parents and community have NO IDEA what really goes on here because it is hushed up! If he didn't tell me, I wouldn't have known. This is another thing I will say over and over. What I am writing is *only* what I know or have learned. Can you imagine how much that goes on here that I DO NOT KNOW?

**Another fight,** one kid picked up the other kid and pushed him through the plate glass window of a show case. These things happen *because* nothing is done about it and the kids are in the hallways all day long. Common sense, where kids hang out, problems will arise. There may be a record in order to get the kid to the doctors. But *nothing* will go on file with the district and will not be part of the total violence and vandalism report for the year to the state and governor. The district does *not* need money. It needs to get control of the school and get the student heads on right for learning. Seriously, I bet there is more control at the local Juvenile Detention Center than here at JFK High School!

**Nov 19 -** 4th period, I went to the 2nd floor to check on the bulletin boards for Mr. Ell*. Oh my god. You should have seen all the students in the hallway. There had to be 200 to 300 throughout the entire hallways both sides. You could hardly move and get around. No administration, security or police. A teacher was by the elevator yelling to get to class, but no one listens. It was actually quite dangerous.

**Nov 20 -** 9th period, the fire alarms go off again. Another false alarm! With the number of students in the hallway all day what in the hell do we expect to happen? It is just a routine. Not for me, it is disgusting!

Mr. Ell* was telling me that parents get $250 a month for having a Special Ed student. He told me one of his student's mother had him quit his job because the little bit of money he made; his income put them over the limit for her to receive the money. Do we see something wrong here? Where is the incentive to work? Where is the reason to become a responsible taxpaying citizen?

A new VP attempted to stop a young man to check his ID. She politely asked for it. He said, "NO, why do I have to show you?" First of all, the students are to be wearing their IDs around their neck.

The student kept walking away and ignoring the VP all the while she is calling him. Once again, *nothing* was done about it. Me? I would have had security bring him to my office and then called his parents to come in. If they refused to come, I would have sent him home until they do. I would have used him to set an example to the rest of the students to knock it off! Let that student, the other students, and some of these parents know who runs the school and who the boss is.

Especially being a new VP, she should have made it clear that there's a NEW SHERIFF IN TOWN! But nooooooooooooo, she just ignored it.

## What happened to "Standards"?

It's time parents are MADE to be responsible for their children. That means for their wellbeing, who they hang out with, where they go and with who, what time they go to bed, did they do their homework, how are their grades, are they doing well in school, their behavior, discipline, etc. School is not a place to just drop children off and expect us to raise them. The parent is supposed to be the MOST responsible and the major influence for their children's success. Children see, watch and learn from them be it good or bad. It is that simple, it is a difficult job, but it's the responsibility of being a parent. Yes, a teacher can influence and wants to influence all of their students. However, that is if that child is paying attention, participating, not being a behavioral problem or counterproductive to the teacher, the other students and most of all wants to be influenced. Unfortunately

As I drove home today, I realized frustration and stress, that's all that there at JFK for my colleagues and I. It is so depressing knowing all that goes on here continuously is allowed, while the administration knowing full well it is wrong. It has to be illegal. After all it is neglect!

**All day long** it's stop, get away, you don't belong in here, go to class, take your hat off, put the phone away, you're not supposed to be talking on the phone, be quiet, sit down, leave him/her alone, stop pushing, stop running, stop or knock it off with the foul language, don't do that, put that down, put that away, give me that, you're going to break that, don't write on the desk, don't write in the textbooks, don't throw that, no you can't go to your guidance counselor, no you can't go to the bathroom you just got here, there's no eating or drinking in here, quit yelling, be quiet, stop talking, get out of the doorway, get back in class, sit down, do your work, where's your work and on and on and on.

The foul language is unbelievable. When you try to correct them, you get why that's a bad word or that's not a bad word. The constant loud noise in the building of students being out of control screaming along with the constant repeating of the same thing all day long and every day to the same students is absolutely exhausting and stressful. It's the same thing over and over and over again, because the students know nothing is going to be done about it.

It is all a stalling tactic instead of going to class and doing their work. They do this to wear you down, stress you out, to make you give up and to go along with all of the lunacy, to make it easier for them. They don't want to work. There is *no* work ethic. I could not believe how many students who are 16, 17, 18, 19 & 20 years old who attend JFK that DO NOT have a job. They don't believe that they have to work, and everything should be *given* to them. Once again, this is not all students. However, it is very large percentage of them, making JFK a disaster. And the biggest contributor to these problems is the administration by allowing it, ignoring it, and refusing to do anything about it.

Think about it. Teachers are to report if a child seems to be abused. How about the teacher reporting if the administration, school, and or the district is committing abuse/neglect?

**Nov 21** - back to school night. I had a pretty good turnout. I had 10 parents. I feel the reason for me having so many was because I called each student's house to inform and remind parents of back to school night. I have over 130 students and only 10 parents show up. That's less than 8%. Soooo let's hear it, for no child left behind. UNBELEIVABLE! Let's put all of the responsibility on the teacher. It is NOT just the teacher's responsibility, it is *also* the parents to see that their child is doing their work, going to school, having difficulties and what can they do to help their child or children. But nooooooo! The teacher and the school is like a restaurant. We are here to offer sustenance (education), but we *cannot* make them eat (absorb). It is up to the parents to be parents. Teachers give out the work like the restaurant gives out the food. We can't make you eat it or learn it. It is up to the student and his or her parent/s. How can a teacher be responsible for a student and or students when they have 20 or more in a class for 40 minutes a day? After all some parents have 2, 3 or even more children at home, yet they complain how hard it is for them to watch their own children!! Is there something wrong here? However, it is OK to blame teachers, who in reality are strangers and nobody to the students.

**Nov 24** - the school was a disaster. I cannot believe how many times VP Ms. Ives* asked the same students ALL day long to remove their hats, stop running, stop that, get to class, but the students ignored her, went about their merry way and did anything and everything they wanted to do.

**ALSO,** there was graffiti all over the front doors. You would think the janitors would have removed it. It was done last night. Was caught on video but the student had his hood on and they cannot identify who it was. Think about it that IS on video, but not what goes on all day every day here?

**AND** speaking with a couple of Special Ed teachers, they told me that PARENTS WANT their kids to be classified because they get 600 to 900 extra a month. I said I don't know if it is that much then started to explain a conversation and situation with another colleague and one of his student's mother having him quit his job, because she lost $250 a month.

**Nov 25 -** 3rd period, alarm goes off again. Evacuate building. False alarm again! Kids will NOT move. They're not staying with their teachers, running in hallways, will not leave the building, argue and become defiant with those who attempt to direct quick access out. Then when they do finally leave, they don't go back far enough, lean, and sit on teaches cars. Refuse to get off cars when asked. Just defiant! Then when we got back into the building, it had to be a good 15 - 20 minutes until the hallways were halfway cleared. It is shear chaos. No control. This is pep rally day and just the beginning.

**During** 5th period lunch, fighting, I'm watching security and police pull students out of the cafeteria. **COINCIDENTALLY,** in the November issue 2003 of the JFK school newspaper, "THE TORCH," on the front-page students complaining about another year of students pulling false fire alarms. It also shows a teacher having to sit in front of the fire alarm box to protect it from being falsely pulled. (I have a copy.)

**ALSO** fights all day long in the building, herds of students roaming hallways. Students walking in and out of my classroom who do not belong giving me a bad time especially when I ask them to leave.

**NEXT** during 8th period, a student was knocking, then kicking and tapping on my classroom door. First of all he should have been in class and not out in the hallways. He continued doing this for well over 10 minutes. I attempted to ignore him. When I went to the door, defiantly he wouldn't move. I had enough with this nonsense and defiance, I yelled— basically screamed at the top of my lungs to Mr. Costello* a VP, security and the police who were all standing by the security office, why is this guy in the hallway? Why is he not in class? Why is he in the hallway and nobody asks him for a pass? Why is he allowed to be standing by my door knocking, kicking, tapping, and can continue to keep making noises for over 10 minutes to deliberately distract my class? Where does he belong? And I continued yelling. They all just looked at me. The student got an attitude, went on his merry way cursing me out as if I did something wrong and was still in the hallways. Meanwhile nothing was done about it and I can guarantee this kid just went someplace else to do the same thing to another teacher's class.

Just last week, Nov 21, Mr. White* had Anthony*suspended for cursing at him? As I said before, these kids can deliberately, defiantly and maliciously cause a distraction from a class, deliberately curse and use foul language at teachers (ME) and nothing is done about it. **WHY?**

**NOTE OF INTEREST: -** I can honestly say that I have personally been all over the world. I have never seen behavior tolerated like this where defiance of authority, rules and regulations are ignored, with the deliberate and casual attitude of waste of government money day after day, year after year, while the district of Paterson, is supposed to be run and operated by the State of NJ.

**Nov 25 – IMPORTANT -** speaking with a guidance counselor he said parents/guardians will go right down to the Board of Education speak to Mr. (name omitted) and Dr. (name omitted) and complain that they want their child classified. He says it is sickening because some of these parents are not even here in this country more than a month and they complain that they are NOT getting enough money, they are not getting housing fast enough through section 8, they want their child out of certain classes, they want their child in special classes, they want their children classified so they can get an extra stipend from the government, they just come in and demand everything and have done nothing for the community let alone the country. Once again, the taxpayers get screwed.

**Nov 25** - Ms. Sweetness* had a quest speaker from Citone Institute a business school giving a presentation. The fire alarms went off. We had to evacuate the building. Ms. Sweetness*said she was so embarrassed because the guest speaker was shocked to see all that was going on. She said the guest speaker was so upset on how the students were acting and behaving. Ms. Sweetness* told me she was trying to make up all of these excuses, because she was afraid once the guest speaker went back to her office and turned in her report they would never take a child/student from JFK into their program. I said she shouldn't have made excuses. It is about time people knew what goes on here.

**Dec 1**, fights all day long. The fights are more prevalent today in the cafeteria. Nothing is ever done to change or make a change to any problem/s. Kids are in the hallways screaming, I mean actually screaming at the tops of their lungs, as if they are outside. They do this in defiance and to be disruptive. When asked to stop by a VP or principal, who speak with them "nicely" as if they are afraid of retaliation, the students actually scream and curse at them so viciously and violently. Telling them off, go F yourself, who da F are you, get the F out of my face, you can't tell me what to say and do Mother F'er, you're not my mother, get da F away from me, and on and on and they get away with it!

JFK is a school in a school district that has been taken over and is under control by the State of New Jersey because it was a failing school and school district. Are you freaking kidding me? The state says this behavior is acceptable and tolerated? Is this *not* turning our failing school district into a failing society? In fact, I was surprised one kid was going on and on cursing to one of the *nicest* administrators in the building without missing a beat, just cursing him out. Calmly, Mr. Perdue* said to the kid, I am going to suspended you for 5 days. Big deal the days do *not* count towards attendance. It's a holiday a vacation. Many students say I want to get suspended. I need/want some time off. So, what's the point? Yet we hear, "No child left behind." Don't any of these so-called leaders in DC actually know what goes on?

**Dec 3** - a parent called me at home this evening. She says she cannot believe what goes at JFK and all of you teachers allow it to go on? I replied, "All of us teachers, we have nothing to do with this. The administration allows it all to go on here every day all day long. What do you expect? Why aren't you complaining to the principal and superintendent? Go to the newspapers and tell them what you see. Don't blame the teachers. If we fight it or make a big stink, we will lose our jobs." She thought for a moment and said I was right and was going to speak with someone from central office. The superintendents and administration are responsible for failing schools. We as teachers just go along with it and are also wrong, but what the hell can we do? This is one of the reasons why I write everything down.

Earlier, speaking with my VP about my back door explaining how it is not finished being installed, only held on by 2 screws and is not sealed letting the heat out and all of the winter elements in. Anyone from the outside can pry the door off, break into the room, and the entire school building.

The work was "completed" in the middle of October. I have several conversations about the sloppy and incomplete work with the workers, maintenance, some guy in charge of facilities, head custodian, and to date NOTHING. This also includes the reinstalling of the two large exhaust fans. My supervisor said, I don't know what to tell you, all the construction people have left. He said look around the building, they did not finish the job and all the blocks that are still missing. Even my room is still incomplete and sooner or later will be broken into. I do NOT know the reasons but the district refused to pay them anymore money. I find this funny because this is with the money Governor McGreevy is always talking about being spent to fix up school and revitalization. What a waste of taxpayers' money AGAIN. NO ONE is held accountable or knows how to run a job. Other than me, it seems nobody even cares!

**Dec 4** - talking with Mr. Ell*, he said Mr. Fonda* a VP now understands what he has been talking about all this time and why he gets so upset. He could not believe that all of this has been going on and is allowed to continue to go on. He too is appalled. So, because students are allowed to have bad and dysfunctional behavior, hang out anywhere and everywhere instead of going to class, then yes, this is a failing school, but blame the administration not the teachers.

**Dec 5** - fights all day long. A big fight in cafeteria and as one boy was being escorted to the security office he yells out, I hate white people. Now, I would love to see what would happen if it was the other way around?

I have not heard anything about the letter I had written to Governor McGreevy along with copies sent to Frelinghuysen and Corzine. However, I did hear from Corzine's aide and was instructed to contact Debra Cortu in reference to my letter. I had called several times but have not received a reply back.

**Dec 8** - I went to the weight room today and no one was there. So I went inside boys' locker room. The gym teacher said nobody is taking gym because there is no heat. WELL, so much for the money being placed on renovating our schools? No heat in the gym. It was FREEZING!

**Nothing but fights/fighting all day long.** Unbelievable fights, more like brawls and gang fights. (Gang fights meaning just a large bunch of students). The biggest one I had ever seen, was between 7 and 8th period. The entire center hall was filled with kids. It was a riot. It was so scary, dangerous and out of control. Even the police could not get in. The students would not allow them to break it up. Eventually, the police had to run in, shove, plow and knock people out of the way to get to the problem. The students still would not move. It was so out of control. You couldn't hear yourself think. The hallway was FILLED, wall to wall, packed with at least half the school population and more coming. A thousand *plus* students all screaming, cursing, yelling, taking cheap shots just to get involved, starting more problems and adding to the confusion and chaos. ABSOLUTELY DISGUSTING AND DANGEROUS!

Finally, the police got to those who were fighting but it was already ready starting again with others. I am waiting for the next fight to erupt. The students are all in a frenzy looking to start up again. These problems are constant, and they just continue to feed off from these situations on and on all day long. MEANWHILE NOTHING WILL BE DONE ABOUT IT AND IT WILL BE HUSHED UP.

A simple little rule no one is to wear hats and headphones in the hallways. Even that is not enforced. During the time between classes administrators are supposed to be in the hallway. Today one VP, was telling kids - the same kids - over and over to remove their hats and head gear. Now mind you it is December, and don't you think they should know by now? As for me, I just gave up. I cannot go on and on saying the same things over and over, be ignored and not backed up by administration. This is what I mean about students wearing you down. Meanwhile the administrators make me laugh, because they're tired of telling kids to stop, take the hat or head gear off, don't run, stop yelling, stop swearing, don't run, stop wrestling, and over and over. Then when the bell rings and their presence is MOST needed, they disappear and hide before the lunacy and chaos REALLY begins. Now teachers are stuck with all of this chaos in our classrooms because students who show up are all wound up from being in the hallway.

This one student had an actual full face ski mask on. A policeman told him to remove it. The kid ignored him. The cop tapped him on the shoulder just to get this kids attention. The kid swung around and said to the cop, "get the hell off of me" and kept walking. The cop went over to him then all of a sudden just stopped. I guess he decided to let it go. Even the cops cannot do anything, because the administration tells them they are only here to be a presence. Do not get involved. Now what did this kid learn and any student who witnessed this? I can do whatever I want and even the POLICE can't do anything to me! Bottom line: Nothing was done about the student wearing the full-face mask.

**Dec 9** - speaking with one of my female students; it seems yesterday, Dec 8, she was robbed in school of her cell phone. She gave it up because the girl had a knife. Now as far as we both know; no charges were pressed. The girl was suspended. My student asked for paperwork/report pertaining to her being robbed. She said the administration didn't know if they are going to give it to her and don't know if they are going to press charges. What does that have to do in giving her a copy of the report? The next question is what is there to think about, a student was robbed? The robber had a knife. This was *IN SCHOOL!* Why is the school district so against pressing charges? I believe (think) that the administration did NOT want to give her the report in attempts from keeping her and family from pressing charges. My student also said that it seems this girl who robbed her also had drugs on her. She also said this is the 2$^{nd}$ time she was robbed in school. The first time happened last year in the cafeteria. Think about it in the cafeteria, a place loaded with students (witnesses), security and supposedly an administrator but the students are not afraid to rob someone for their phone. WHY, because they know the administration will hush it all up and they will only get suspended. Suspended a vacation where the days out do NOT count against their attendance. As if attendance truly accounts for anything here anyway. UNFREAKINBELIEVABLE!

*Who in their right mind would send their children here if they really knew what goes on inside here?*

**Dec 9** - 6$^{th}$ period, we had to evacuate the building again. This time there was *a REAL fire in a bathroom on the 3$^{rd}$ floor.* The fire department had to come and is now investigating. They were concerned if the fire went passed the insulation. We were outside for about 15 minutes. It was a miserable freezing cold wet day, with snow all over. Kids are sitting and lying all over cars and refuse to get off when asked. Students getting hit with snowballs. One of my girls got hit in the face and had a big welt. That's why she was late to class; she just came back from the nurse's office.     Then when we came in, as usual it is so out of control. Kids all over the place, not going to class, then eventually a big fight breaks out again in the center hall. Just like yesterday, students would not move and now all the kids, hundreds of them are all on the 1$^{st}$ floor. It is getting worse day by day. To think, none of this makes the newspapers. I cannot believe students don't tell their parents. It is 12:23 and you should see all the kids *STILL* in the hallways.

I'm watching the administrators and they are all upset. I have to laugh. They are upset? As usual it is reactive, but still *NOT* doing anything to stop it. Students are just going *WILD!* There has to be a record of this because there was an actual fire and the fire company had to come.

**All day,** I have students walking in and out of my class who don't belong here. Eventually, I went out in the hallway because there were 23 girls in my doorway who refuse to leave. I yell to Mr. White, "Why are people in the hallway, why are they allowed to walk in and out of my classroom, why are you guys allowing this?" Mr. White, with his wise remarks replies, "well just shut the door." Typical solution! Students are in the hallway, defiantly cutting classes, and these two administrators just ignored them, and I should shut the door as if I am the one who is wrong. Continuing his wise ass remarks he yells, "You're getting just like the guy next door!" Meaning I am complaining. Is wanting; the school to be in control, righting wrong and wanting students who do not belong in my classroom removed, is that complaining? With remarks like that, do we really wonder why this place is the way it is? I snapped back saying, "The way things are going around here, my students and I might as well sit down and do nothing, the day is shot. Meanwhile you two stand around, ignoring the situation, won't get involved so you can continue BSing with each other."

**Dec 9** - 7th period a security guard was asking a student (name omitted) who is in the hallway to stop and come here. Student replied, NO! She asked again. Again, he said, "No, I am not stopping; I don't have to, you can't tell me what to do." He continued eating a sandwich and kept on walking. At the same time a VP, Ms. Ives* was having the same type of problem with a student. It all went ignored. With that type of attitude, behavior and absolute lack of respect by students and the lack of enforcement of rules by administration, how can there be control of this school and students receiving a proper education?

**As** we were evacuating the building I was told one of our teachers Mrs. (name omitted), was deliberately shoved and injured by a student (name omitted). He was suspended for 10 days? I'm going to check to see if he remains suspended for 10 days. Assault on a teacher and nobody gets arrested?

At 2:15 I was in the nurse's office and found out what happened because the teacher who was attacked was there. Also found out this is a typical routine and a daily ongoing event with this student. PLUS, he didn't even belong in her class. It seems he asked her for some sort of an item, and she said no. Needless to say he attacked her. He threw her down, pounced on and pummeled her. Other students had to take this student off the teacher. This is more than being shoved!

At the end of 8th period another big massive fight broke out in center hallway. It is getting to be a set routine now. It is so out of control. The students do not stop and just carry on even more no matter what anybody says. It is just short of an out of control riot. It is 1:23 and you should see the hallway, wall to wall kids. The bell rang long ago to be in class. *SO MUCH FOR ZERO TOLERANCE TO VIOLENCE!* The administrators are just walking by and doing nothing?? I do not understand any of this!

**Dec 11** - I learned today that the student who murdered Mr. Robles several years ago, is NOT allowed to attend school (JFK) and was placed on bedside. Bedside is when a teacher leaves school at the end of the day, goes to a student's home who is too sick to attend school, gives instruction for a few hours each day and is paid overtime. Now these and especially this student gets complete credit for a full year of school? He receives the same DIPLOMA as a student who attends school all year for 6 plus hours a day. *So much for ZERO TOLERANCE TO VIOLENCE!*

I went to speak to a friend of mine in the attendance office. I started to ask questions and she said, do not ask me any questions because I can't answer them. Then she said, I asked the same questions you're going to ask, and I got no answer either. However, the next "student drop and loss of credit list" coming out is unbelievable with all the names on it.

> I saw a security guard with an ice pack over his eye as he was walking back to the security office.

The loss of credit students will still have to attend school. However, being that they have lost credit, they will act up even worse and do not do anything other than because more problems, disrupt the school and other classes, roam the hallways even more, will not go to their scheduled classes, but will walk in and out of classes they do not belong in. *A real solution!*

She also said on a weekly basis there are student hearings. There are so many and no one in the district presses charges on these kids for the crimes that they commit in school. She told me she asked the principal's secretary how this can go on. If students do not come to school and finally show up, they get suspended. Then when they are here, they do nothing, fail every class, in constant trouble, cutting, late to school and classes if/when they go, get an attendance hearing, brought to court, then placed on *bedside* and *GRADUATES!*

**Dec 16** - the school is freezing. There is ***NO HEAT AGAIN!*** So much for all of this renovation, our heating systems still doesn't work, and billions of dollars are being spent on fixing up our school/s. However, our windows and screens are broken, doors are filled with graffiti, and books are literally thrown out of the windows daily. During 5th period right outside my back door, I saw 20-30 books literally being thrown out the windows. This goes on and on. No one sees anything. When I report it to the administrators, I get, "Well, what do you want us to do? We will get the janitors to pick it up."

**ALSO,** with all the money being spent on renovations, they got rid of the janitorial staff in the district and hired these useless subcontracting people. There isn't a mop or a broom in the building. The janitors don't even clean my room. I used to have four brooms. They were stolen. This is funny, no one comes into my room to clean, but someone came into take my brooms! I go to the supply room and have NOT seen a broom in stock there for **YEARS.**

**Dec 17 -** big fight between periods 7 and 8. A real dragged out knock down fight with two girls. I saw cops all day long dragging kids into the security office either by force or in hand cuffs. I have been in the main office quite a bit today. So, were the police officers making copies of their reports? SOOO, remember the date, **December 17,** there has to be a police record of it. If NOT, something is wrong!

**Dec 18** - fights all day long. Many are so big they were more like brawls or mini riots. One large fight involved two brothers. In fact, yesterday, I read both brothers were on the "***LOST OF CREDIT LIST***" and have lost credit for the year. This means they will be a freshman *again* for the 3rd straight year.

One such fight I happen to see involved one of my students, who ended up in handcuffs and pretty well beaten up. It seems it is a gang thing which escalated again after school at the bridge by Wayne Ave. and McBride Ave. The name of the gangs are 5th Ave and Crazy Eighths, the gang my student and his brother are both in. Unfortunately, he and his brother are both repeating freshman and will be again according to the paperwork I received.

Mr. Ell*, Ms. Sweetness* and I were talking about the so-called academies, and how it is really a joke. All students no matter what "ACADEMY," they are in, have the exact same required classes and everything else. It is still the exact same thing and all they do is teach for the state exam and add the word "ACADEMY." One teacher said, this is another scam so the district can get (steal) more money. In fact, these academies are all supposed to be created and worked by the bottom up. Meaning the teachers are to have possession of them and have less administrators and supervisors. However, it is the complete opposite. There have been more positions available for administrators and supervisors. One of the *biggest reasons* why the state took over the district was because it was too ***TOP HEAVY*** with administrators. Now it is worse and continues to grow having more chiefs than Indians!

One of my female students, smacked the crap out of a student (student #1, from entry October 13, 2003). I did not see it but I heard it loud and clear. What a shot she gave him. It was so loud I heard it over all of the other commotion noise and ruckus going on in the hallways. This male student has been bothering her for a long time and saying some pretty nasty, disgusting and filthy things to her. In fact, earlier this morning during 2nd period, Mr. Lance* asked me to come into the office. He asked me if I heard the male student say anything to the female student about fucking her or the whole block fucking her. I said I don't really know, because he just doesn't stop with that word and when I hear the sound of his voice, I try to block him and all of the other noise in the building out. I did say that many things have been said and that male student is a pig with a filthy and nasty mouth.

Speaking with a VP, I was saying how the school is out of control. He was trying to play it down and said, why get upset? Just close your door. I said why, should I have to close my door when these students should *NOT* be in my classroom or hallway. Think about it, **close the door** is an *unacceptable* answer as well as a solution and still holds teachers accountable. The administration insists on setting policy to let all of this *chaos* go as if there is NO problem/s. Then the VP says, "You will never get the students out of the hallway." I couldn't believe it. It made no sense. I replied, "Unacceptable answer! You're telling me there is NO solution?" I also said, when the school is administering the state exams, no one is in the hallway and everything starts on time. SO, if you say we can never get the students out of the hallway then explain to me *how for 6 days a year during state-wide testing there are NO students in the hallway and the school is in control?* He just looked at me and walked away.

**Dec 18 & 19** - I noticed there has NOT been a suspension list? I asked the secretary (on the 19th); about it and she said the principal does NOT want them on the counter anymore. My guess is when visitors, guests, parents or guardians come in, they CANNOT see, read or take one home, which could cause a problem for him and the school. Once again, trying to cover things up! I replied, but why haven't I been getting them in my mailbox? She replied, Oh I don't know anything about that.

**Dec 19** - one of my female students was talking to an administrator. He told her we receive one thousand new students each year. But we only graduate exactly 4 years later about 300 students or less. Out of that 300 not many of them are from the original one thousand. Some left, dropped out, are continuously being left back year after year as 9R, 10R, 11R and then eventually drop, while some just transfer in and out. My head wanted to explode!

**Dec 19 -Another Bomb scare!** Evacuated the building AGAIN. It was another cold, damp miserable day. We eventually went to Don Bosco High School for shelter. This was after about an hour standing out in the snow and freezing cold. Due to the continuous and constant daily routine of evacuations most of the students did *not* bring their jackets figuring they will be back in the building shortly. With the weather outside being so bad these poor kids froze. I was freezing and I had all my winter clothing on including a hat and boots. I felt bad for the kids. There were two phone calls. The first call the person was being very quiet and no sound, followed by a second call with a deep manly voice being very explicit. A secretary from office #1 received the calls. She has caller ID and they found out that the calls were made at a phone booth in Montclair, NJ on Montclair Ave. Once we were allowed to come back to JFK, the majority of students did *not* come back. Those students who did come back most of them didn't go to class. They just roamed the building playing. When asked to move and get to class, students just ignored security, teachers, administrators and continued hanging out and around inside the building. The rest of the day was shot. We basically had no school.

**Dec 23** - I pull into the school parking lot approximately 7:50am, and I see teachers and students standing outside. It seems the school had to be evacuated AGAIN, because of another bomb scare.

**January 6, 2004** - 7:10 Bomb threat, 2nd day back from Christmas holiday. We had to evacuate the building. A vice principal was the only administrator in the building. She asked me to help her check the 3rd floor and to get people out of the building. She also asked another male teacher and me to check in certain places for possible items in specific areas. Obviously, whoever called was quite specific. I felt bad for her, because she was worried that the principal would be upset for evacuating the building. He was not around and she had to make a judgment call. I said she did the right thing. Students and faculty safety is paramount. I also relayed to her, I know how the boss is. She rolled her eyes and said, you don't know, really don't know, you never can do anything right. I just reassured her that she *did* the right thing.

**Jan 6** - was in the cut office when a young man received suspension for cutting classes. One class in particular he was out the entire marking period. As this same young man was walking away, he stopped, turned around offered his hand, apologized to Mr. Madjar for his behavior and foul language. However, as soon as he got out the door, he was yelling fuck this, fuck that, fuck this place, ripped up the paper, yells in the hallway as if he is in the street, swearing up a storm, and a carrying on. All he gets is "Shh Shh be quiet, don't do that." Mr. Madjar said if I see him in the building, I am going to have him arrested. Mr. Class* a TAP came into the office and wanted to know the status on this young man. Mr. Madjar said, he suspended him for 10 days. Mr. Class* replies, "explanation not necessary."

Mr. Madjar and I were talking about schools outside of this district do not have a cut office that works as hard or as long in processing cuts and lateness like JFK. He laughed saying, we process 300 to 400 cuts a day. Mr. Madjar said, if we processed cuts and gave suspension for each cut, there would be no one in school, the place would be empty. But the principal does NOT think the school is out of control.

**3rd period**, because he was not working, I asked a student if he would move please. As usual while he was talking it was nothing but non-stop continuous barrage of foul language. Unfortunately, he cannot talk unless it's foul language. His remark was Fuck it. I knew if I didn't move him, he would NOT know what to do and would have difficulties with Thursday's test. I just moved another student first for the same reason to avoid a situation. Anyhow, as expected and typically he began to give me a ration of belligerent, disgusting barrage of unacceptable foul language, saying I can't tell him what to do. I am NOT his father and just went off putting on an act, further disrupting the class and making a scene. I said to him calmly to knock it off or I will call home and I'll call while everyone is watching and listening. I find calling home right then and there in front of class usually cools and calms a student right down. WRONG! He replied defiantly and screaming, he didn't care. That he was NOT afraid. I am NOT his mother and father. You can't tell me what to do. I replied calmly, I am his mother and father while he is in my class, which seemed to aggravate him even more. He was looking for a confrontation and I wasn't going to oblige him. Then he went off like I never have seen before. He was copying from a new student and his terrible attitude and behavior. Meanwhile he continues, saying until I buy him clothes and feed him chicken, I am NOT his father and I cannot tell him what to do. This is NOT like him and was more surprising than anything. I asked him to move to a different desk, but he kept up with his disrespectful and defiant act.

I went over to him and asked him calmly to go sit outside the classroom. He starts screaming and cursing, putting on more of an act in front of the other students telling me he does not have to and he didn't have to stay in class if he didn't want to, does not have to listen to me or do what I say with every other word is Fuck or mother fucker. He gave me no choice but to call home. I am NOT having any student talk to me like that especially in front of my other students and wanted to set an example to the entire class that I'm NOT going to tolerate this. Even when I was out in hallway talking on the phone, he comes out screaming, cursing and yelling at the top of his lungs. Don't call my father he is driving a bus and starts swearing up a storm at me. When I told him that I am speaking with his mother, he starts screaming, I have had it up to here, I do not have to do what he says, I want out of this F'n class, I don't care, I have had it with this bald white cracker. I said, as he was yelling all of this, you're making it worse and showing your mother exactly how you are conducting yourself with me in class. During my phone call with MOM, he apologized. He agreed this should have never happened. After class I asked to speak with him, and we had a long conversation about today's situation. The conversation was in the fashion that I am accustomed to with him. In our conversation, I said, you know out of all of this, it is unfair because I will bet you 100 dollars to a box of donuts that your mother is upset. No parent wants to hear anything negative about their child. And that she will probably remain aggravated all the while she is at work. This was not right. He admitted he was wrong, and I said, well it's done, let's move on and use today as a guide on what not to do.
That evening Mom called me, and we had a great conversation about her son and other things of interest.

**Bottom line - This is not an isolated incident.** This happens all the time, all day, every day, all year, year after year with the only change is it keeps getting worse every year. All because the administration allows students to talk and behave this way without fear of punishment.

**Jan 8 -** we had another bomb scare. However, instead of evacuating the building and making everyone stand out in this horrible cold weather, they sent everyone to the cafeterias. Meanwhile the administrators check all floors for people and anything odd or suspicious. They asked another teacher and me to help. This is a daily routine now. They say the caller has a grown-up voice. This is scary, because no one knows when it is going to be real! I do NOT know if police or the fire departments were called. I tend to think not because, why would administrators be looking around for anything or anyone suspicious?

**Jan 9 -** another false fire alarm during 9th period. However, in attempts to have students leave the building in orderly fashion always ends up as a nightmare. Students will deliberately and defiantly refuse, then start a confrontation with every and anyone who attempts to get them to evacuate the building via the nearest exit. Students will deliberately and antagonistically try to get by you. If and when you touch them and try to turn them around, they will start a confrontation screaming and yelling at you that you cannot F'n touch me. In the meantime, we are looking at safety issues and the students are deliberately making a joke out of this and provoking trouble. They will actually come in groups of three or more to distract you and see who can get through. However, I hear supposedly they caught who pulled the alarm on the 2nd floor.

**Jan 13 -** fire alarm went off during 1st period during midterm exam. The new alarm system/sensors that were installed in my classroom were triggered because we were making castings. Why would an engineer design, installed heat and smoke detecting sensors directly overhead three foundry ovens? The ovens are so loud we didn't even hear the alarm. Doesn't anybody inspect or go over the plans for final approval?

**Alarms** went off again. We evacuated the building. Fights were breaking out all over outside the school as evacuation was being conducted. Also, when the students were coming back into the building it was horrible, nothing but chaos. Students were to go back to their last class, but instead they roamed the halls and fights were breaking out in the cafeteria. Then students decided to start a riot by throwing chairs, food, drinks and everything they can to destroy everything, just like I have seen on the prison documentaries. Students in my 8th period class were talking about it. They said it was real, scary and didn't know what to do or where to go. I always tell my students no matter what, or where you are, NEVER EVER disrespect a teacher or anyone in the school. However, if you are in trouble, scared, don't know what to do or go, politely excuse yourself and come directly to my classroom. I'll take care of everything.

**Jan 13 -** 5th period, fight in cafe. It must be a big one or maybe two. Cops are dragging boys and girls out and into security office. While being dragged to the security office students are still trying to fight, screaming, cursing, threatening and carrying on. One girl was screaming at the top of her lungs threatening the cops "I'm going to get my father." Unbelievably disgusting here! But it is NOT out of control?

**Jan 16 -** one of the SRA teachers said to me that the school is a disaster. She said even students tell her that the school is this way because the principal is afraid of us. She said she just shakes her head

**Jan 23 -** fights all day long. School is NOT getting better. This is a scary place. This is a State Takeover, Run and Operated School District, how can this even be happening?

**Jan 27** - big fight on 2nd floor, security screaming over walkie-talkies needing help, security needing help, needing help. Other security and police flew up there.

**Read School Report Card** from the Internet - The information is from North Jersey.com
http://www.northjersey.com/page.php?qstr=eXJpcnk3ZjcxN2Y3dnFlZUVFeXkyJmZnYmVsN2Y3dnFlZUVFeXk2NDc5NTUx

They have John F. Kennedy High School with only 12% of students being suspended. Eastside has less. This is funny, because Passaic County Voc Tech had 20%. Where do you think their students go when they cannot conform to their rules and regulations? Eastside & Kennedy. Yet Tech has a higher percentage of suspension??? This is what I have been saying about hushing and covering everything up, no paper trail so the numbers and statistics will be falsely adjusted. Remember, this is a state run and operated school district. This is NJ GOVERNMENT lying to its taxpayers and citizens.

**There was an incident** in cafeteria during 7th period; a policeman was attempting to escort a student to the security office. For about 2 - 3 minutes the student was yelling and screaming as loud as he could, "Fuck you, no fuck you, get your mother fucking hands off me, fuck you, no, no fuck you, get your hands off me, you white mother fucker, you fucking mother fucking bastard," and on and on.
Even one of the administrators came running out of her office which was on the other side of the hallway with her door closed to see what all of the noise and commotion was about.

This was all going on as a parent and her young child were leaving the building. They kept looking back as they were walking really slow. I knew they were not just afraid/scared, but shocked, to see what was going on. It was absolutely disgusting. And this is all the time all day long, all year long, year after year. The lack of education is due to the lack of having *control* of our school!

**Jan 30** - FIGHTS all day long every place in the building, I saw one kid going out in handcuffs. There was one on the 2nd floor and another on the 1st floor. The one on the 1st floor were two girls. One girl was kicking and a screaming fuck you, get you mother fucking hands off me, you can't touch me, fuck you, I am going to fuck you all up, and on and on and as loud as she can be as a large crowd of students (100s) were following. They kept following no matter what the VPs, security, and even the police said to keep moving, leave, get out of here, as the police were trying to escort this young lady to an office. This was during my lunch 7th period. I was standing in my doorway watching all of this with the auto shop teacher. Even after the police got her inside the office and shut the door, students gathered around and would not leave. All the while you can hear that young lady screaming and carrying on yelling FUCK YOU, you are all mother fuckers, get your fucking hands off of me, leave me the fuck alone, you can't do this, fuck you, fuck you, non-stop screaming at the police, security, teachers, a couple of VPs and the principal who were all in the office with her. So much for ZERO TOLERANCE to VIOLENCE! What do you expect to happen when the administration still allows students to be in the hallways constantly all day long instead of class? Even the police do NOT allow people to hang out on a street corner.

**Feb 2** - fights, fights and more fights all day long. School was so out of control and dangerous. One fight was 4th period in the boy's locker room. The students were going berserk. To me, it was a riot. It is jail house mentality here. The next one was at the beginning of 5th period in the school foyer. Unbelievable, there is NO control here. The students are so wild and crazy, because they are allowed to act this way. After all, most of these fights and situations would be avoided if students were in their respective classes instead of hanging out *IN* school.

**7th period** there were so many kids in hallway you thought you were in a riot. They were screaming Fuck Kennedy, Fuck Kennedy, Fuck the teachers, Fuck the principal and on and on.

It is so hard to describe because you cannot imagine this to go on inside a high school. Furthermore, a school that is under state control. Administrators had security trying to get the students to move on and out of the foyer, so the public and any possible visitors didn't see this. The students did move, but stayed together in large groups, gang, yelling and screaming as they went to gather someplace else in the building. This place is absolutely disgusting. It is NOT about education here. No one would be allowed to carry on or act this way any place else, so why is it allowed here? Meanwhile not one student was apprehended or disciplined for this behavior and basically conducting a riot like atmosphere here.
This is a normal routine here. Long after the bell rang to begin class there were still 100s of students on the 1st floor by the stairwell next to the soda machines carrying on as loud as they could.

**Feb 3** - it seemed every student was in the hallway all day. The cut office is open from 7:30 am to after 3pm and as I said before even when school is done for the day, one of the cut officers stays after school sometimes to 7 pm processing the backlog of paperwork pertaining to cuts and tardiness. When students are called to the office, they give these people such bad time with their poor attitudes, back talk and behavior and nothing is done about it. The students talk to you as if they were talking to a bum, fuck this fuck you, I don't give a fuck, fuck, fuck, fuck and on and on. The administration allows this type of behavior to continue. Gee we are really teaching young people how to act when they finally get a job. Then if the kid is lucky, they get what they want - suspension.

In fact, they ask for suspension instead of detention. This way they don't have to go to school, can stay up late, sleep late, and their suspension days don't count towards poor attendance. Then to add insult to injury what do you think they end up doing? They come to school anyway to hang out during lunch periods. With detention, they are in school longer and it is boring. It's boring because they refuse to do anything other than put their heads down on the desks and sleep the entire day. This place is a disaster, we have students who dropped out, are on suspension, are supposedly absent and where are they? They are in the hallways hanging out, playing and disrupting other classes. So much for having students wearing ID cards for security purposes!

**Feb 4** - the beginning of 4th period I smell smoke. It turned out to be firecrackers that went off by the entrance to the auditorium. The smell is strong. There is absolutely NO supervision in this building. Interesting, there is no one other than me investigating the smell. Nobody else hears, sees or SMELLS anything? How dangerous is this!

**Then** during 9th period there was about 30 students all gathering around the soda machine and the 1st floor stairwell. They're wrestling running, jumping, screaming, yelling, cursing, and throwing anything they can get their hands on even laying on the floor as if it is the beach or a park. I walked by but it doesn't matter because they know I am not going to do anything. Even if I did they are NOT going to listen anyway. In the meantime, the rental security sits at the end of hallways and watches everything.

**Feb 9** - at the end of 8th period a big fight broke out in the center hall. There was 100s of students - no exaggeration - gathering. There were 3 or 4 kids fighting. What happened or why I do not know? I usually do not get involved but I saw VP Mrs. Ives* alone in the middle trying to break it up and all of these kids surrounding her. I made my way and jumped in. I finally separated students and grabbed one kid off another. Eventually, the police and security arrived.

After the fight was finally broken up 100s of students swarmed the center hall trying to cause another situation. It is unbelievable. It is nothing more than a free for all here. The students do not listen because they know nothing will be done other than being yelled at to move. They know this so they persist to hang around and provoke more problems. They kept hanging on and banging on the walls, doors, soda machine, jumping up trying to knock the lights, ceiling tiles and exit signs down. Eventually after 10 or 15 minutes they started to disburse. However, about 1:45 another incident starts somewhere in the other direction of the school. I have no idea what it was or about, but security and police were all running. However, the hallways are still filled with students roaming and looking to start more trouble. It is shear CHAOS here. They refuse to keep students out of the hall. VP Ms., Ives* said to Doll* the security guards, BOY was I ever so glad to see you. Because she was surrounded and thought she was going to get FUCKED UP.

This place is disgusting. You think the administration would learn having students in the hallway will eventually cause problems. But NOOOOOOO, it goes on day after day with no change. I still say the superintendent, every assistant superintendent and every administrator MUST have their children attend school here. Then let's see how fast things would be DIFFERENT! The students remained in the hallway throwing items and books at us and the cops trying to provoke another situation. That's the mentality here. They want to cause problems and trouble. Then when they get caught they start screaming, cursing, threatening, kicking, punching trying to get away while telling the police to get off them, you can't do this, I'm suing you and on and on all with the F or MF word constantly being used. It is JAIL HOUSE MENTALITY HERE, NOT A PLACE OF EDUCATION.

**Feb 10** - 7th period another big cafeteria fight. I am in the cafeteria ordering a sandwich and a fight breaks out in the stairwell. Police and security rush in followed by every student in the building.

**Feb 11** - prior to HR cops and security rush up to the social studies wing. Obviously, another FIGHT! It's because students can hang out in the hallways and stairwells and don't attend homeroom?

**Feb 12** - several incidents throughout the day. However, as it has been lately, there are no security, no police, no administrators, no one of authority is around and the kids actually start a riot between 7th and 8th period. The place is out of control.

As far as I'm concern it was a riot, simply students were so out of control it was dangerous. I would yell to knock it off and naturally they would not listen. They were running, yelling, screaming, throwing anything they could get their hands on, banging on doors and windows, cursing, pushing and shoving one and other, and finally a fight breaks out going towards the boy's gym. The entire building of students runs to converge to the area. A few of us teachers, and several of the TAPs (Teacher Assistant to the Principal), were trying to get the kids to stop, go the other way, and all we get is fuck you, you can't tell us what to do, and kept pushing their way through and was working each other up more and more into a frenzy. THIS riot and out of control behavior has been going on every day for the last few weeks and at the same time. You would think the administration would have it figured out that they better have security and police in that area AT THAT TIME, EVERY DAY. There were skirmishes going on everywhere.

**9th period** another fight breaks out in the foyer by police and security. They just don't care. In fact, it is a kid who's suspended every week. Just this morning I even said to him as I shook his hand good morning, stay out of trouble, we will have a long weekend coming up. He replies, I am NOT going to get into anymore trouble. Few hours later the police are escorting him to security office, he is yelling, he has been trying to fight me for days, get your fucking hands off of me. You can't do this. You can't touch me and on and on. Meanwhile his actions are fueling more chaos in the building as the student's roam around like sharks in a feeding frenzy to start more chaos.

I don't understand any of this. When will administrators STOP allowing students from being in the hallways, stairwells and every other place other than their respective classrooms? It is disgusting. In my entire life and I have been all over the world, I have never ever seen or been any place where this type of behavior is allowed and unsupervised. Where lawlessness and blatant disrespect for any type of authority, property, and other people, where it is so uncontrollable daily you can almost set your watch to it happening the next day and it is NOT ILLEGAL. And this going on in a *state takeover run and operated school district.* The state of NJ is supposed to be in control. Does it sound like this place is in *control?*

**Feb 20** - I was speaking with the print shop and social studies teacher. The print shop teacher said the same thing I have been saying all along, "this place is so out of control!" The students just come and go as they please. The policies here *do not work.* He said he has printed over 40K **cuts slips** *since September*. However, the powers to be came up with a plan for all students who cut and are late to school and class. There will now be Saturday detention and those who work detention will get paid overtime.

**Bottom line:** *NJ TAXPAYERS GET SCREWED AGAIN!* Where do you think the money comes from to pay this added, unnecessary overtime? None of this would be necessary if the administration instilled discipline, have students follow the rules and ***disciplined*** for their infractions.

**6th period** a big fight broke out. There were 100s of kids in the hallway. There were so many students jam packed in the hallway I couldn't even open my door to exit my classroom. I called the office and said we better get security and police here it is very dangerous and out of control. The students were screaming, yelling, cursing, pushing, shoving and instigating to start more trouble /problems. It seems a teacher had subdued a student and the student was trying to fight the teacher. The teacher had control, however not without exerting a great deal of strength and effort, as well as self-restraint, keeping this student in control. The student was screaming and trying to get away. It was just plain chaos and lawlessness. Finally, Mr. Lance* opened the door to his office and the teacher threw him in. Mr. Lance* yelled at the kids to get moving but immediately went back into the office while NOTHING is being done to stop the insanity, chaos, riot like atmosphere in the hallway outside her door. It was absolutely terrible. **There were NO SECURITY AND OR POLICE around.** The police are only here to do something when it happens. NOT TO ENFORCE OR KEEP THINGS FROM HAPPENING.

**Feb 23** - Today, I received notice of students who lost credit for the year and there was Anthony's* name on it. The student from February 21, 24, 28, March 13, & 31, May 9, 2003, & Nov 18 & 21, 2003, and who went from 10r = repeating sophomore to becoming a senior in months was on it. AND he still has a personal aide following him to his classes all day, every day, all year. So much for that contract he signed. I bet he will still graduate!

**I received a phone call** from the Commissioner of Education Morris County. He apologized for not getting back to me sooner. He was following up on a letter I wrote to Governor McGreevy on November 4 in reference to the purchasing agent and how I had to pay $500 more for supplies because of state contracts. He said he is new and has a great deal to get caught up with. I assured him I am just interested in getting the most bang for my buck (my yearly budget) as a teacher and taxpayer and I have no interest in getting anyone in trouble. I thanked him for getting back to me.

*That was back in 2004, today is August 5, 2015, I have never ever heard back from him or anyone else!*

**Feb 24** - rather quiet day as far as I can tell until 9th period. I was reading a textbooks while standing in my doorway, when a student (name omitted #1) who was in my 8th period last year, threw his hat down at VP Ms. Ives* and made a bee-line to another student (name omitted #2) to start a fight over stealing his T-shirt. Obviously, he had no regards or hesitation with the VP standing right there along with me and several other teachers all in the general area. That's the mentality here. Students are NOT worried and do not care about getting in trouble, because they WON'T! I got in between the two students and broke it up. Luckily no punches were thrown. Ms. Ives* attempted to speak with (student #1), but he changed his mind and went running after (student #2) again. I caught him with one arm while I was reading my textbooks and held onto him as the police were coming. As soon as the police came over, he started with the typical nonsense we see every day here, screaming, yelling, threatening everyone, swearing, cursing, and causing a fuss as if this is normal behavior and language. Once again, this is all an act, a show they put on in front of other students as if they are tough guys. Other students watch and then they end up doing the same thing. That's the education and lessons that are taught and learned here.

This is my point. The teacher is the lowest thing on the food chain in our school. Students do NOT have to listen and or obey the teacher. The first thing out of a student's mouth when a teacher attempts to keep order or enforce any type of rules is, "YOU CAN'T DO THAT, YOU'RE NOT MY MOTHER, YOU CAN'T TELL ME WHAT TO DO and on and on and on. (This is NOT all students) Everything is entirely backwards here. Unfortunately, so many teachers just give up because the administration does nothing, and I mean absolutely nothing to enforce good behavior or enforce any type of rules and discipline. Anyhow, (student #1), is a repeating freshman and on his way to being a repeating freshman again. He showed the other students you can even act stupid with the cops in here. However, this cop was NOT going to take any of his crap. He laced into him and placed him strongly into the security office. However, other than that, that's about all that happened!

**Feb 25 -** 5th period fire alarm went off. **REASON** - So 5th Avenue and Circle Ave. gangs could fight. When we were to come back inside forget about it, shear chaos. Kids were everywhere refusing to move and would not go to class. In fact, one student comes into my classroom, takes a piece of wood from a student and starts to walk out of my classroom with it. I told him to put it down. He waves me off and proceeds to continue to walk out.

I finally yelled at the top of my lungs to put it down and went after him before he went out of my classroom. He continued to walk out. As I got close to him and still yelling at him to put it down and get back in here. He finally turns around and throws it down on the desk. I turned him around and told him to get out of here. He turns around and starts off with the mouth, swearing cursing and threatening me. He turns around and walks away while continuing to give me a barrage of insults. All the while a vice principal was there and did nothing. "Typical!" Wonder why we have these problems.
Meanwhile, all the students in the building are walking and running all over the place screaming, cursing, pushing and shoving whoever is in their way yelling "Fuck you!" at the top of their lungs. However, not one person, or an administrator comes in to intervene or see what is wrong.

Getting back to the fool trying to take a stick— how am I supposed to know what he was going to do with it? Especially, with all the CHAOS going on from all the students still in the hallway coming in from being evacuated from the building. Then for stopping him, I had to put up with that behavior, while a vice principal just ignores it?

It is so bad that most teachers just don't care. No matter what we do, it doesn't matter. So many just stay quiet, collect checks, add their time, and get out. New teachers do not last and eventually leave.
In fact, for many of the students who act up and cut, the teacher welcomes them for not being in class. Sometimes teachers wait awhile before they send any paperwork in, all in hopes that students get suspended and then the teacher doesn't have to worry for a couple of days. Real nice. That's how it is here at JFK *every freaking day!*

**7th period,** the fire alarms go off again. We evacuated the building. I am NOT sure if it is a false alarm, real fire or something else. However, when we all came back into the building, the rest of the day was shot, and the building was so out of control. Students would NOT go to class. A security guard was yelling let's keeping moving on and on as if she was just saying it for the hell of it.

**Feb 26** - immediately after the end of 8th period bell rang, the fire alarms went off. We had to evacuate the building. Another false alarm! I received the info from two of the board security officers. In fact, a VP asked a security guard if someone pulled it. He told him it was pulled. When we came back in, the rest of the school day was lost. A shocker, there were VPs in the hallways screaming for students to move and get to class. As usual the students just ignored them. Students just went about their merry way, not going to class, kept walking around and around the building screaming, yelling, cursing and playing around. Nothing changes here. Just another end of day filled with CHAOS.

**Feb 27** - Mr. Ell* was telling me that several police officers are no longer allowed to work here. Reason, there was an incident (A BIG FIGHT) and they had to get into the mix of it. They were accused of being too rough. Let me understand this - is there etiquette for breaking up a BIG FIGHT in school now? Why have the police here if you're NOT going to let them do their job? This is exactly why students do what they do here, because they can get away with it and the State Takeover, Run and Operated District allows it. If this behavior is NOT allowed in public, then why is it allowed in a PUBLIC SCHOOL?

**Mar 1** - today I went to speak with one of my student's social worker. I started to explain to her that he is not doing well and the papers that I am to fill out at the end of the class he is not given them to me. I am telling her to keep her apprised on what is happening. I told her that I keep everything documented. She starts to tell me a little about his situation and that he can't fail. I replied, if he doesn't do any work, he will fail. Then she said he doesn't have to do what the other kids do. He can do a lower level of it. And that I am to be sitting with him making sure he understands. I said, I have 20 students in my class (most to all are Special Ed to begin with) (I don't know how else I can make it any simpler for all of them) and I CANNOT sit with one student.(The words inside the brackets are my thoughts; they are NOT part of the conversation between us)

I told her that I make sure he understands, but if he chooses NOT do to his work, then he caused the problem/s. Then maybe you should get him an aid? Her face dropped. All of a sudden she got an attitude. She said there are criteria that has to be met and I should read his IAP. I said, if you just want him to pass, then why you don't just put him in a room where he can sit and do nothing and pass him. He is NOT doing anything in my class, what do you want me to do? She repeats, we should go over his IAP. I said, I am available at 4th & 7th period. She said ok as long as she would not be testing. Unfortunately, I do not know her name, anyway, she came back to my room during 4th and was as cold as ice. I thanked her for coming in. She showed me his IAP. Unfortunately, he is at 2nd & 3rd grade level of math and reading. NOW, what in the hell is he doing in high school? The system is just pushing this poor kid and soooo many other students through the system and will receive the very same high school diploma as a student who does their work, homework and passes their classes. What is the point of going to high school and study, when other students don't have to even attend, become classified and get the same diploma?

*Now*, we wonder why so many people who have high school diplomas and are illiterate. What is the point of school? Then again what goes on inside here is NOT a school. In our earlier conversation, she advised me to call home. I said, I have 168 students. I send out warning notices. I send out a letter prior to warning notices. He gets a report cards. I fill out a daily report when he decides to give it to me. Usually he does not when he didn't do any work or has acted up. What more can I do? If mom wants to speak with me she can call me. I repeated, it is her son. I have 168 other students. She said, the mother was upset because she didn't get a warning notice. I said, I do not know why. I do not give them to the students. I send them out via the postal service.

**Bottom line**- it seems everyone wants to hang the teacher for the short comings of the student and parents. No one else is wrong, just the teacher. As I always say, I am like a waiter at a restaurant. I can serve you your food, but I CANNOT make you eat it.

**Mar 10 -** Wednesday they arrested some kid who was trespassing and ended up having drug paraphernalia. It seems he didn't have an ID and that's what triggered security he was a trespasser. On Thursday, a TAP was checking every student as they came up to the 2nd floor for IDs. It is about time. It's funny, because one of my students left and moved to Clifton. He said Clifton HS is bigger, has more kids, and stricter. He just started there and forgot his ID card and received two hours of detention. He said, if anyone argues, doesn't even have to fight, they're both immediately suspended. WHY CAN'T THIS BE ENFORCED HERE? NOT ONE RULE IS ENFORCED HERE AT JFK.

**Mar 12 -** 6th period, big fight on 2nd floor. Two girls jumped another girl. Believe it or not the girl who was jumped F'ed up the two girls that jumped her really BAD. There was blood all over the place.

**During** 7th period, kids were sitting in stairwells. NOBODY should be in a stairwell. How do we know if they are trespassers, waiting to jump someone or if they are planning to do something? I mentioned it to a VP and she said, the entire Special Ed student population are going wild. It seems that 7 of the Special Ed teachers today called in sick. So the kids are running around the building as free as birds. She basically admitted the administration is not and will NOT do anything about it. Now which behavior is worse, the students for NOT being in class OR the administration not only admitting that students are in the hallways going wild and NOT doing anything about it? Students/children will do whatever they can get away with. It is up to GROWN UPS - the administration - to correct poor, bad, inappropriate and dysfunctional behavior. How else are these children supposed to learn? After all they are in a SCHOOL!

**I noticed** they don't call the suspension list/sheet, the suspension list anymore. It is NOW called "THE EXCUSED LIST!" Now the excused list, which is the suspension list, is inside the absentee list and has more names on it. Another observation, this list does not have those students on it who were suspended for cuts, late to school and/or class. More fun and playing games here with numbers and statistics instead of doing their jobs by making sure every student is IN CLASS!

**Mar 22 -** a student (name omitted) was suspended, for bringing in a BB gun. It seemed he and another boy were fooling around with it and acted as if it was a real gun. The teacher (name omitted) was frightened. I do NOT know if they were arrested. Nevertheless, (student #1) got 10 days suspension. Suspended? So much for Zero Tolerance to violence and for bringing a weapon into school! With this type of behavior by the administration and what this state run and operated district is NOT doing, it is time to send in the US MARINES. I am sure they will protect us. It is obvious our own state officials are NOT!

**Mar 24 -** speaking with a colleague, we were talking how the cut office has processed over 40k cuts already and how the hallways are constantly and continually filled with students all day long. He said he spoke with an administrator (never gave the name) on how they should conduct hall sweeps and clear out the hallways. The administrator said, what would we do with them? Again, they would rather do nothing. If an administrator can say that, it makes me believe they are following orders from the superintendent. This is NOT acceptable. That type of attitude and excuses did not work in Munich, Germany with the Nazi war crimes. And by leaving students to roam our hallways, stairwells and any and every place else other than being in their respective classrooms is a CRIME against humanity, society and civilization.

**Later** speaking with another teacher about (name omitted) and other students, we both agree it is a shame that we have students who have done nothing but constantly act up, disrupt and NOW have *finally* lost credit for the year and will still remain in class. What do you think is going to happen in class the rest of the year? These students have nothing to lose and will take away every positive learning experience from the other students for their amusement. Any responsible adult knows when children are acting up and will not stop, you have to separate them. Not here, the administration wants them to remain in class!

**Apr 1** - the cut office is open more hours processing cuts, lateness and absences, then the school itself is.

**Apr 8** - the same student from **3/22** who brought the BB gun into school is back from suspension. He and another one of my students were wrestling in the center hall of the building right outside my classroom. As they were wrestling, I noticed the student who just came back from suspension had a knife and it was OPENED. I yelled what in the hell are you doing? Don't you learn? I asked for the knife. He brought it up to me. I knew they were just playing, so I said, you found it and are giving it to me right? They both said yes. Only to find out later that the knife didn't belong to either of them!

**Apr 19** - I sent one of my female students from my 2nd period class, to retrieve her journal. She came back saying that security and police wouldn't let her upstairs because there was too much going on right now. I said what are you talking about? She said she didn't know. You can't make this stuff up.

**Later** one of my students started a fight in the cafeteria. He was suspended.

**Apr 20** - a guidance counselor came to see me and asked if I would sharpen his lawn mower blade. He said we have no idea with everything that goes on inside here that is hushed up including the weapons and guns that are confiscated. He said he had enough and is getting out of here (retiring) before he gets killed. We are both so F'n disgusted with all of this and the waste of money.

**NOTE OF INTEREST:** -This year so many students lost their credit and all of a sudden, a wand was passed, and they got it back. Only to lose it again and then given another chance and another chance and another chance.

**Bottom line:** Anyone can get a high school diploma at JFK. Any student who does not get a diploma, then there is something wrong with them.

**Apr 27** - 2:27, I am leaving. There are buses parked alongside the back of the school. Several boys opened the back emergency door of a bus and were either pushing in or pulling out a student from the bus. A VP Mr. Saint*yells to knock it off. The students ignored him. In fact, Mr. Kott was walking back into the building just covered his eyes and shook his head. Meaning administration sees nothing and does nothing and so it continues. I can only imagine what goes on daily inside those buses.

**Apr 28** - I was home today. One of the secretaries called me and I could hear the fire alarms going off. I learned they went off **5 TIMES**.

**Apr 29** - the fire alarms went off several times during 6th & 7th period. Supposedly it was a malfunction with this new alarm system. They went off again during 8th. Reason, I don't know. Meanwhile, no one knew if we were to evacuate the building or not. Some people were exiting the building while others were standing around. As for the students, they could care less - it's another excuse to act up even more.

**9th period alarm goes off again.** Talk about chaos - students running through the halls, screaming, yelling horsing around as if the circus came to town. Some people are evacuating, some are standing around not knowing what to do and some stayed in their classrooms and closed the doors. Some security personnel say leave the building others say stay. It is so very dangerous here and I just do NOT understand how this continues day after day, all day all year. Once again, another false alarm!

**GUESS WHAT? 10th period alarm goes off again,** same situations as above. However, a young man was talking to a VP Ms. Ives* and a TAP Mr. Lance*, saying he knows who did it. The entire building was out of freaking control. If people acted this way anyplace else the Paterson Police who are inside this building would have everyone arrested with NO PROBLEM!

**May 10 -** I asked students, many who are seniors, in all of my classes the following questions.
1. How many seconds are there in a minute? They did not know the answer.
2. How many minutes in an hour? Thankfully, some did know this answer.
3. If a car is going 60 MPH, how far will you travel in one minute?
Not one student in any of my classes including seniors could answer this. However, some students passed the state exam. This proves my point. All that is taught here is to prepare for and to pass the state exam.

I was telling Mr. Ell* about the questions I asked my students in the above entry. He comes back with something better. He said, let's see how many students who passed the state exam after being prepped and prepared all year just to take the exams can actually take and pass the tests for GED. He said, I bet it would be a disaster. Reason the GED is harder, and it is all reading for all sections of education. Then he says, so much for education and the state exams. I replied to him, well if you want to have another benchmark for students, how come so many 17, 18, 19, 20 & 21-year-old students do NOT have their driver's license. Reason, they CANNOT pass the written part of the test!

**May 11 -** 8th period it is unbelievable here. Absolutely unruly, disorderly chaos in the center hallway. Students are gathering, screaming, yelling, cursing, pushing, shoving each other, wrestling and carrying on. Security is yelling for everyone to move, get going, get to class and are being ignored. Two VPs Ms. Ives* and Mr. Fonda* are actually screaming as to be heard over the noise, yelling everybody is to move, go to class, get out of the hallways. The students ignore them. Meanwhile the crowd of students is getting bigger and bigger and louder and louder. In the meantime, the police are standing watching because they cannot get involved unless something happens first and then even when it does they have to wait until they are told to get involved by an administrator. This place is so out of control! What is the F'ing point?

I just learned today Anthony* the student from Feb. 21, 24, 28, Mar. 13, 31, Nov. 18, 2003 & Feb. 23, 2004, entries lost credit again for the year. However, and unfortunately, last week he and several other boys were seriously injured in a car accident. Here's the kicker. I was told today, during 9th period from his shadow/personal aide that he WILL graduate. REASON: The principal wants him OUT!

**Bottom line -** This is what I have been saying all along. You do NOT have to go to class, you can be constantly suspended, you can cut class, be late to school and to all of your classes, do not have to work, pass any tests, do homework, can inflict serious bodily harm on others, curse out, threaten teachers and staff, and still graduate.

**May 20 -** Dave* the security guard was telling me security today is real tight. There was a big fight yesterday after school. It involved gambling with a Bengali kid and a Spanish kid. Well, the Spanish kid won and the Bengali kid got mad and got his friends. Well they beat the Spanish kid up and bashed his head in with a bat. Then supposedly turned into a big brawl but lop sided. Like 10 to 1 Bengali against the Spanish. So there are cops literally patrolling on foot today outside. As always, it was still hushed up.

**May 28 -** I am to receive a new student today. Actually, I had him earlier in the year. He was no problem and did everything as asked. However, he had terrible attendance. He left to go to Clifton HS in February. Now he is back. I understand he had too many days out at Clifton. I was told by the guidance supervisor that he is back and can NOT miss anymore days. Now May 28, 2004, what does he do? He cuts my class.

This is what I am saying. They can jump from school to school and still pass and nothing is done other than a loss of taxpayers' dollars. Attendance means absolutely NOTHING here at JFK. The reason he left here to go to Clifton was because of his poor attendance. He more than likely got into trouble and had poor attendance there too, so he came back to JFK. NOW the real question is HOW MANY DAYS WAS HE OUT ALTOGETHER FOR THE ENTIRE SCHOOL YEAR?

**Jun 2** - 4th period I was going to the weight room. Who do I see walking out? One of my seniors who is supposed to be suspended. He's suspended from school BUT allowed to come to school to make up time for gym because he is a senior and is supposed to graduate? Unfreakinbelievable! He learned his lesson!

**Jun 7** - Security in school was very tight again. It was obvious there were going to be visitors and important. The administrators are all dressed up, security is doing their job and keeping the kids from routinely acting up. Then a large Mercedes bus pulls up. It says, "Rutgers New Faculty Traveling Seminar." Also written was, President of Rutgers University, Richard McCormick (Garden State 101). The theme was "Students are NOT ready for college. They are NOT properly prepared and that is why there is a large college drop out." NO "F'ing" KIDDING!

**Jun 9** - I learned that superintendent is leaving at the end of June. However, he will be paid for the remaining 6 months on his contract. WHY? It is documented that the business administrator of West Milford lost her job, her certification and will never be an administrator for a school district again, because 2 million were missing and unaccounted for. However, the superintendent goes away on scathed, with pay and still has his credentials. The commissioner of education states, "the superintendent did nothing criminal." Then who is responsible for the 60 MILLION DOLLARS?

**Jun 10** - fire alarms goes off/twice. Don't know if it's because of this new faulty system or a false alarm?

**June 11** - same as yesterday, However, a security guard said a sensor in the cafeteria was setting off the alarm and that the sensors are too sensitive and or not set up properly.

**UNBELEIVABLE,** there was NO moment of silence for President Reagan.

**ALSO,** I learned that 40 seniors did not pass one or more parts of the HSPA state exam.
I also learned that 202 students took SRA instead of the HSPA state exam.
Now we graduate less than 300 students. So, using 300 students as a mean, and 202 took SRA that leaves 98 students to take the state exam. Leaving only 68 students that passed. Now how do they manipulate these numbers statistically? This is NOT including if any failed their yearly work, lost credit for their absenteeism and how many failed SRA! As of now there is no exact count of students graduating. The administration still has plenty of time to FIX everything.

**Next week, June 21 - 23**. How much do you want to bet practically NO STUDENTS will show up for classes as required let alone show up for school, other than seniors practicing for graduation? For others they will come to school just to hang out, meet up with their friends, play and or cause problems.
Please let me be perfectly clear, there ARE some kids/students who like school, their teachers and stay involved. Unfortunately, it is a very small group. Nevertheless, the 21st to the 23rd will be lost days. So much for having scheduled days/mandatory for students to be in school!

**Jun 16** - today schedule for final exams were periods 3 & 8. During 8th period someone called in a bomb scare. However, I just learned about it from the gym teachers. Administration ignored it and once again, we DID NOT evacuate the building. The majority of us didn't even know about it.

**Once** exams were over a bunch of fire crackers went off. I thought there were gun shots. Then the hallway stunk. What does a VP say to one of the cops? "This is just typical HS stuff."

**From 1:30 on** the alarms kept going off. So they left the strobe lights flashing but silenced the alarm.

**Jun 17** - the art teacher Ms. Post* was conducting final exams. One student refused to take the exam. Instead he persisted in disrupting the class. Would not stop so she called a VP Ms. Ives*. Ms. Ives* said he has to stay because there is no place to put him. Are you kidding me?

**AGAIN,** the fire alarms went off twice. The first time was at 1:15 and again and 1:50. It seems to be something with the sensors in the cafeteria, from the heat exhaust from a refrigerator.

**June 18** - 1:30, we evacuated the building. It was a bomb scare. Exams are over so the administration decided it's now OK to evacuate the building knowing darn well most of the students will leave and not come back into the building.

**Later** the fire alarm goes off again, refrigerator sensor again. This is supposed to be a new alarm system.

**June 25** - last day of school a guidance counselor comes to me and says (name omitted), who is a student in my 1st period class, lost credit and is now getting it back. What grade do you want to give him? I replied without missing a beat, **"F."** "Doesn't come to school, if he does, he's late and late enough to be a cut. Does no work, loses credit BUT because he is Special Ed, he can get credit back? Now you're teaching him that he can do nothing for a few more years and get the same diploma as anyone who does their work to receive a diploma?" You should have seen her face.
So typical here, the last day of school and the administration are still going crazy scrambling and trying to get teachers to change students' grades who failed. Where were all of these people who are NOW so concerned about students' grades all year long?
END

THANK GOD I AM SO EXHAUSTED

**Aug 3** - a secretary was telling me that Eastside High School is on block scheduling. The new superintendent is upset because JFK is not. However, here is the kicker, the administration is saying because Eastside is on block schedule this will improve students' attendance. NOT TRUE! With block schedule, students have a 20-day attendance policy which is from Sept to Dec, then *another* 20 from Jan to June. Making it 40 days, doubling the days allowed a year for students to be absent. Are you kidding me? Already this is a scam playing with numbers, statistics and basically *LYING!*

**Aug 27** - I just woke up because I had a bad dream. I was dreaming students were soldering the classroom door lock. I realized this is because I will be starting another year next week anticipating what will be happening and again. I also think about the fools in administration and politicians who came up with the BS, *"NO CHILD LEFT BEHIND!"* This is just another way to push the blame onto the teacher. It is the parents who need to be held responsible especially when a child comes to school *repeatedly* tired and sleeps in class because they didn't go to bed until 2, 3 or 4 o'clock in the morning. The students themselves tell me. Here are some of the reasons they said why they were tired, they were at a party, watching videos, playing video games, talking on the phone, they were with their boy or girl friend, etc. Not one said anything about doing homework or making up work for other classes. Are teachers now to be held responsible for putting students to bed, getting them up and on time to school too?

## SCHOOL YEAR 2004 - 2005

**September 9, 2004** - 8th period, fire alarms went off, we evacuated the building. I don't know the reason.

**Sept 13** - I did attendance and notice there are many students already suspended and in ABC. (ABC is the same thing as ISS meaning, A Better Choice instead of In School Suspension). They changed it because it sounds better. Maybe we should forget about political correctness and get back to BASICS!
Already cutting is rampant. Kids are hanging out in the hallways, stairwells, bathrooms, loooong after the bell has sounded to be in class. These are just the first few days and the school is already lost.
HERE WE GO AGAIN! AND WHOSE FAULT IS THIS?

**Sept 14** - cut office is having mass suspensions already due to out of control cutting. Some kids are cutting ½ to all of their classes every day and they're still in the building. So much for supervision and discipline!

### INDUSTRIAL ARTS / TECHNOLOGY EDUCATION:
The Grand Poohbah of the powers- that-be decided to change INDUSTRIAL ARTS to TECH/ED. Once again semantics with words, it's STILL the same thing.
Most schools and colleges have been doing away with shops and such. Administration today emphasizes more on paperwork, testing aspect of school, as if everyone is going to be an executive / white collar worker. First of all, not everyone is a good or confident test taker. They may do well in class and turn in their assignments however when it comes to taking a test, they choke!

Even though you can turn on TV any time of the day and flick through the channels and see some sort of home improvement program such as Martha Stewart, cooking, art, painting, motorcycles and cars being made, built and manufactured, MONSTER GARAGE and etc. our public school systems are doing away with these classes. TV and movies are usually WAY ahead of the times and know what people like are interested in and seem to see the future. If they didn't, they wouldn't be in business long. They wouldn't have sponsors. NOT everyone wants to wear a shirt and a tie. How many people are capable of making repairs or even knowing enough about making an informed decision so if they have to hire someone they won't get fooled and ripped off?

Bottom line, knowledge is POWER. However, knowing stuff is only good if you are going to be a contestant on "JEOPARDY!" The importance with learning ANYTHING is being able to *"APPLY IT."* Shops of all types, as well as ye old fashion Home Economics does that. They are so essential in applying every class/course every student/s takes. Think about it, reading, measuring, math, science, history, language arts, people skills, critical think, following of directions and on and on. But NOOOOOOOOOOOO the powers to be are really more concerned in passing the STATE EXAM. I'll say it again, if our school JFK is doing so much better and the numbers/statistics have risen with students taking and passing the state exam, (as the administration is constantly saying) then why are there 17, 18, 19, 20 & 21-year old students that can NOT pass the written part of the driver's license exam?

REASON: Because so many (not all) of our students unfortunately cannot read. They were NOT taught to take the test without taking a practice after practice tests with similar questions for 5 to 6 weeks before the test is administered.

**Sept 30** - fights all day long. Many students did not come to class on time because the hallways were a mass of confusion and chaos. Some sections were actually blocked off by students swarming around trying to watch other students start and instigate more problems even with security and police present. One fight was with two of my female students. The cut office is so over inundated with cuts and lateness. Students are making deals. Instead of detention they want suspensions because suspension days do not count towards attendance. Can you imagine the administration allows students to make *DEALS* for their punishment? What student would NOT want to be suspended if the suspension days do not count? Furthermore, so many of the habitual cutters are juniors and seniors? YES, the same juniors and seniors who are removed from their regularly scheduled classes and courses in order to be prepped to take and hopefully pass the HSPA, state proficiency exam. They will choose suspension, days that do NOT count towards their attendance and then be out for the test prep. What a freaking place. The NJ taxpayers are getting *raped*, by the very state that is supposed to be running and operating this school.

**Oct 1** - like yesterday, fights again all day long. In fact, we had to evacuate the building because the fire alarm was pulled so kids could go outside to fight. Students were telling me all about the fighting going on outside during the evacuation. The building is out of control. It's not even a month into the school year. Students do NOT respect and ignore the principal and VPs. I could never even imagine this could be possible and happening. Being here is like a bad movie where you are upset on what is going on and NOBODY does anything about it other than to ignore it. What makes it more disgusting and sickening; this is *for real* and from a state run and operated school district.

**Oct 5** - prior to 5th period a fight breaks out in the hallway by my classroom. Two female VPs tried to break it up. The two boys were really going at it. They were rolling on the floor, punching, kicking, and cursing at each other. I ended up having to get involved and broke it up.

**Oct 12** - students were telling me that I CANNOT write cuts on them if they are not in my class. In other words, if I should have them 3rd period and I see them in the hallway 6th period without a pass just roaming around, they say, I have no right to write cuts. They said that they do not have to listen to me or do what we (teachers) say after they leave our class. We have no authority. I explained to them, they are wrong. We are always a voice of authority I am a teacher and you are the students. Any student doing something they shouldn't be doing or is where they should be a teacher has the authority to tell you to stop, knock it off, get to class, report it and write it up. Teachers can write a cut on any student if they are NOT in class.

I also explained just because the administration isn't doing their job and allowing students not to go to class, it doesn't mean teachers aren't going to do their job. This is our place of employment; we are not just responsible for your education we are equally and more importantly just as responsible for students' safety. First of all, no student should be in the halls at any time without a pass. Teachers are told if we see something wrong, we're to report it. (A lot of good that does.) Unfortunately, as I have been saying all along, when students act up, are roaming the hallways, stairwells, hanging out in the bathrooms, walking in and out of the building all day, every day, all year and for years and administration sees them, ignores them and does nothing about it what are students to think? Now students have the concept that it's ok and nothing will be done about it, so the teachers should be minding their own business too. There are only a few of us who do this. Most teachers are too disgusted and feel it's a waste of time. I always say, no matter what, I will do my job, even though I am also disgusted.

**Oct 14** - kids roaming halls now robbing and stealing cell phones from students. This happened to one of my students. He said one boy came up to him and said, hey, can I see your phone while another came over and held him, so the other boy could run away with it. This is happening *inside* the school building.

**During 3rd period** this kid, not assigned to my class but has been coming for weeks, again walks in. I attempted to speak with Special Ed administrator Ms. Ace* students only to have her blow me off and tell me to see a TAP. She tried to turn it around as if I am making him come to my class. I attempted to explain, he is walking into my class, he's cutting class, what do you want me to do? Then said he is better off in my class than roaming the halls. At least I know where he is and I can keep an eye on him. I am asking you for help. I don't want to see the kid getting into trouble. Either I could not get it through her thick head or she didn't want to be bothered. She was bent on making it my fault. I kept telling her, he's walking into my class; do you want me to throw him back out into to the hallway? Then she asks why isn't he in class? I snapped at her saying, I don't know, go talk to his assigned teacher. She was annoyed as if I was bothering her. Obviously, she didn't care, couldn't be bothered and just wanted to get on the elevator. She knew I was disgusted and said, well drop me a note. I said yeah, yeah, thanks a lot, what a waste of time talking to you and walked away. She really showed an interest in her job and the welfare of this student.

**SOMETHING THAT COULD & SHOULD HAVE BEEN AVOIDED**
Oct 15 - BIG FIGHT 4th period in cafeteria. This involved the same student I was attempting to help and tried talking to Ms. Ace* about. Now he is suspended. Needless to say, he didn't belong in 4th period cafeteria either. I tried to keep him from getting into trouble, but nobody would listen or help me or HIM!

**Here we go**, kids in hallways LONG after H/R has started. Students will not go to homeroom, will not move when told by security and administrators. The students are so defiant and just don't care. They get away with it. I do NOT understand any of this. This seems to be the pattern on a daily basis and getting worse. I said to a VP, the students can do whatever they want because they can get away with it. She replied, it is because they are classified, Special Ed, and the way their IAPs are written up. She said she never knew this either and is just learning about it because she is now in charge of the Special Ed department. Then she said, if we do anything we can be sued. I said to her, if they walk out of school there is a different set of rules and laws for them? She said that there is. I told her, NO WAY, I do NOT believe that. She said she has a friend who works in another district & all she does is go to court, because parents sue the school and district. Then she said, we are lucky, our parents don't.

What I am writing now was NOT part of our discussion. It is what I am thinking. Sue, sue for what? Not allowing children to be in the hallways, stairwells, bathrooms, walk in and out of the building all day instead of going to classes? Sue for giving students homework and expecting it to be done and correct? Sue for wanting and expecting students to pass their classes! Sue by not allowing students to carry or have weapons, fight, rob and mug other students in school? Are you freaking kidding me? I do not believe her. This is a school not a place to "F" around, play, roam, run, fight, hang out, and etc. all day every day. So according to this VP, Special Ed, classified students are legally allowed to destroy the educational process because the politicians say it is against the law to do anything about this behavior?

We wonder why parents want the right to choose where to send their children for an education and wanting their tax dollars to pay for it? I'll say it again; this school is the biggest waste of taxpayer's money. That's why Catholic schools do so much more for their students with A LOT LESS MONEY?

**REASON -** It's about "EDUCATION!"

Oct 17 - the fire alarms have been going off all day due to this NEW faulty system. The alarms go off over NOTHING. However, this afternoon between periods 8 & 9 the fire alarms were falsely pulled. It was pulled out by the trailers. Fire department and added police arrived.

Oct 20 – a history teacher came to see me. She was soooo upset and in tears. She said she needed someone to talk to. She was so upset because of all the violence going on in the school. She sees weapons being taken away and nothing being done about it. She said she feels helpless and doesn't know what to do. I told her to do nothing. It will be you who will suffer. They want all of this hushed up. She said that's not right. I said I know, but what will you gain by losing your job. That is why other teachers keep quiet. She left more upset.

**Bottom line-** we all see what is going on and IT IS ILLEGAL. Yet we keep quiet, (me too) because we are afraid of the consequences and we will be the ones who are punished.

**Oct 21 -** 7th period, big fight again in cafeteria. A boy is beating and punching this girl's face in.

**Later** during our ½ day**,** In-service, once again we were all talking about all of the violence here. So, once again I said to my supervisor, whatever happened to ZERO TOLERANCE to Violence. He just looked at me and never answered. Same as last year!

**HOWEVER,** here are some topics brought up by other teachers because of me asking the question again. Falls Academy, a student who was involved with the Robles murder, was allowed to play football and basketball while he was awaiting trial. What kind of message is this sending? However, if a student cuts, fails a class or is suspended, he or she cannot play sports. BUT if a student is up for murder, that is accepted and can become captain of the football team? **What is wrong with the Board of Education?**

In my opinion, the Robles murder was deliberate. In fact, there were three incidents inside the building that day and one outside prior to murdering Mr. Robles. Furthermore, it was reported one of the school's administrators heard one kid say, "Let's kill some Puerto Ricans!"

**Oct 22 -** FIGHTS all day and everywhere. One in particular was a girl fighting a security guard, making a big scene, screaming threatening swearing all because she was asked for her ID card in order to let her into the cafeteria. The cops had to literally carry her into the security office. A big chaos in sued after that.

ALL students are to have their IDs on. That's why they were given lanyards. As usual the school doesn't follow through with the very rules they wrote in the student handbook. However, administrators were quite happy and proud that the school made $8,000 last year because students didn't have or lost their IDs. I don't understand the logic AND what was done with that $8,000?Isn't there a law and school policy about "ZERO TOLERANCE TO VIOLENCE?" After all there are posters all over the building about it?

**SPEAKING** with teachers before we sign out to go home, I said, in here, (meaning the building) I do not know what right and wrong is anymore. Everything is backwards, nothing is normal here, I am confused and have no idea on how to react or what to do with everything that is going on inside here. Once I leave this I know. But in here, I have no clue. All the teachers were shaking their heads and agreeing.

**Oct 28 -** One of my female students who is in my 8th period class was telling me during 6th period, students started a fire in the girls' bathroom on the 1st floor by the cafeteria and in the boys' bathroom on the 3rd floor by a VPs office. Both were started at the same time and by the same method by piling up toilet paper to set the fire. I never knew or heard anything about this, and I am sure either did most if not all of my colleagues. Obviously, administration is hushing it up. Someone had to notice to put the fires out. So much for security and the NEW fire alarm system!

**Oct 29 -** Friday, last day of school for the month and before Halloween. Security is actually quite tight. All week-long security was checking students for eggs and what not. Of all days, today they were lax with the checking. However, as expected the alarms were sounded and we had to evacuate the building, (bomb scare). Then once we evacuated the building everything changed. The school was out of freakin' control. Students were just coming and going everywhere. Security tried to keep students moving. It's a joke here!

**NOTE OF INTEREST:** I recommended to all teachers and staff to keep a record of what they know and see. When the time comes, we will turn it all in to the authorities. Let the administration know they are being watched and we are documenting everything. Hopefully, they will do their jobs and sooner or later all of this insanity, chaos, and BS will stop. Then we can do our job which is to educate. It is important because what they are doing (or should I say *not* doing), is allowing this type of behavior and attitude to breed. It is wrong and immoral to our students, their parents, the community, the state of NJ and society.

**Nov 8 -** I have yet to receive my orders. Not only I have not received them, but I have NOT received any copies of my purchase order. I went to speak with an administrator. She said the purchasing agent went away for three weeks. Not acceptable! This is BS! I do NOT believe this entire school district CANNOT order *anything* because he is away? What would happen if he died?

I said if this place was an actual business it would be shut down. I said to the VP, I guess I'll have to contact the governor and my senator again to see why orders are not processed? She decided to call the purchasing agent, and spoke with a "Kim," who handed her off to his voice mail. Furthermore, I have called him so many times. He does NOT return calls. This too is unacceptable. Like I said, if this was a real business this DISTRICT would be shut down in two weeks. No business could ever run with this type of behavior, work ethics and practices. The VP said I should contact my district supervisor and she should be helping me and any of us in her department with this situation. Basically, she was blowing me off and pushing it onto someone else here. Typical administration BS, this happens all the time. I burst out laughing and said she has never helped or supported any of us in the department other than knocking, bullying, talking down to and or belittling us.

**Bottom line - I had everything completed and submitted in May. I had to do it all over in September and again two days later.** *Now* **it is NOVEMBER and still nothing. UNFREAKINBELIEVABLE!**

**Nov 9 -** In-service day. It was about PC #s. (Position/Personnel Control Numbers). We were told when a person leaves, retires or whatever, the principal is supposed to send the PC # to the Central Office for eligibility. *However*, what they do is instead of sending it in they keep the number and that is why there are NOT enough Special Ed counselors in the district. This was told by the person giving the In-service. You could see it on her face and hear it in her voice how upset and disgusted she was about this situation. She was genuinely concerned for all of the students we are supposed to be servicing and educating.

**Nov 10 -** 12:12 & 12:15, there were two separate incidents FIGHTS. Security is trying to get students moving and out of the hallways. A security guard is screaming clear the halls, what don't you understand, but the students' as usual knowing nothing will be done about anything are gathering and trying to instigate more problems. As each second goes by, more and more students seem to be gathering around. Basically, it is a waste of time to say anything, if the administration is NOT going to do anything.

**Nov 16 - BIG FIGHT** in cafeteria again! Mr. Fonda,* a VP, was the administrator on duty at that time. He is talking about the incident to me and another teacher. I asked her what happened to "ZERO TOLERANCE TO VIOLENCE?" He said that's at the administrator's discretion. I just shook my head. Then he said if they are Special Ed, you cannot suspend them more than ten days a year on the same infraction. I said, "I don't believe that. Show me where it says that."

UNFUCKINBELIEVABLE, you think these kids don't know this and this is why our school is failing, out of control as well as what goes on in the classrooms?? He also said we cannot have them arrested. We can't do anything. The State will not relinquish control of our schools. I said, I do NOT believe this. Sounds more like something the district came up with. Breaking the law is breaking the law. Being in school does NOT give amnesty.
If they act like this outside of school in a mall or someplace else, they would be arrested. He snapped back without missing a beat, "Oh shit yeah, in a minute!"
**See October 15 entry.** The same VP. What happened to being sued? It's an entirely different excuse.

**Nov 18 - 6th period 11:45** BIG FIGHT - Two girls being dragged out by security. The cops are all shaking their heads in disgust. They cannot do anything unless asked to. They have to sit and watch. What's the point of taxpayers having to pay for them to be here? It is obvious that the students are NOT intimidated and do not care if the police are here. They will still do whatever they want and get away with it. Meanwhile, both these girls (if you want to call them that) are screaming, swearing, cursing, and threatening at the top of their lungs.

**Nov 22 -** FIGHTS all day long all over the building boys and girls. Absolute chaos and going berserk.

**Nov 23 -** Just like yesterday, the same thing. It is so out of control here and no one is doing anything to help stop this insanity. It is the same disgusting, chaotic out of control nonsense and most of the problems are supposedly from the Special Ed students. The administration says there is nothing they can do about it. I have seen some of these students causing problems and they are NOT all Special Ed.

**LATER,** speaking with (name omitted) a case worker, I asked her some questions about our Special Ed students. In many classes, including mine, the law states there should be a certain number of aides based on the square footage of the room and how many Special Ed students are in the class. She said yes, but there are no aides. I replied, being that this is State Takeover Run and Operated School District that this still can go on for over 15 years. She just laughed and said, isn't that something. She was upset and extremely disgusted with this as well.

I asked her about those Special Ed students that are disruptive what kind of help do they get. She said counseling. I replied what kind of counseling because it is the same students who are always acting up and still do the same things? She replied they are NOT getting the proper counseling; it is basically just on the paperwork we have to turn in. I received the same answer for those students who are academically classified. They put them in a resources class but once again, there are not enough aides. I then asked her, what is the purpose of the Special Ed program if things are not being followed out properly by a state operated district as well as with those who cause nothing but problems in school every day all day long? She just smiled, shrugged her shoulders and said, "What can I say."

Obviously, JFK is NOT a place that teaches and or enforces proper behavior. In fact, it encourages it. It is jail house mentality, and it is spreading like wildfire. What is the purpose of the school district being taken over by the State of New Jersey if everything is the same and actually it is WORSE?

**TODAY** I received a bill from AGL Welding for mig-welding wire I never received. However, a B. Brown, office manager did, whoever that person is. More waste of money and again, no accountability. In the meantime, I am without supplies AGAIN. I am still waiting for my other orders and I still CANNOT get steel. The district purchasing agent Mr. Carson* keeps giving me a run around by constantly giving me names of these new and never used companies/vendors that have nothing to do with what I need. All he is doing is wasting more of my time and everyone else's. It makes me wonder why all of a sudden this year I am NOT allowed to purchase materials needed for my classes from vendors I have dealt with for

years? Something doesn't feel right. I asked him to send me a copy of these NEW vendors' state contract numbers that they are supposed to have in order to sell anything to a school district. Surprise, Surprise, I never received anything. He must be an ex-student of JFK. It is obvious he's ignoring me too.
How many other teachers in my school and throughout the entire district have these same problems and had their supplies lost? Who is going to use MIG WELDING WIRE? There are only two metal shops in the entire Paterson School District and I am the only one with a mig-welder. I bet someone will take the spool of copper wire and sell it as scrap metal.

**Nov 24** - UNBELEIVABLE, it was pep rally day. It might as well have been anybody can go and do whatever they want even more day. You would think of all days the administration would have enforced the rules of students having to wear their ID cards. But no, no one had them on and the building was FILLED with so many "INTRUDERS" who were constantly walking in and out of the building. All the administrators did was stand there like talking mannequins telling students to move, get to class. The students just ignored them, still did what they wanted and so many of them just yelled shut the fuck up. It was disgusting. I am talking 100s. In herds, no gangs of students not listening, arguing, yelling, screaming, swearing, running, wrestling, boxing, jumping up trying to knock the ceiling tiles down, punching and kicking classroom doors and windows, rolling all over the floor, pushing shoving, it is out of freaking control. THIS is NOT a school! How can you call any day here at JFK EDUCATION and taxpayers have to keep paying more and more for it?

All we hear are excuses. It's a big school. What do you expect? We have so many Special Ed students. We can't do anything about it by law. First of all, it is *NOT ALL SPECIAL ED STUDENTS ACTING UP!* Secondly, if these students were acting this way outside of school they would be arrested. I don't understand why or how it is allowed BY LAW to act up this way in school? Every administrator has their reply memorized. They keep telling us teachers, "Well that's the law, I don't see why you should get all upset?" I would reply, because I pay taxes and I am tired of seeing the education aspect of my yearly taxes increased for a school that allows students NOT to go to class and to witness the continuous out of control behavior where students can go berserk all day, day after day, year after year.

I just wanted to get the hell out of here and go home.

**THEN** one of my students (name omitted) in my 3rd period, told me he will be dropping my class and another class, I think it was English. Reason is because he's failing. So his social/case worker assigned him other classes? This is what they do here. They remove students from a class or classes that they are failing, especially if they have poor attendance. They will place them in another class or classes and will start all over again fresh with a NEW SLATE. He will start his new classes with no absences, no cuts, not lateness's and NO FAILING grade. Meanwhile it is already three months into the school year. The administration WILL do this again and again in a course of a year in order to have students pass and or graduate. It is NOT about education. It is NOT helping the student. It shows the administration WILL pass you one way or another and you don't have to do anything to improve or better yourself. You'll be taken care of, graduate, receive a diploma even though you're illiterate.

**Dec 1** - 1st floor boys' room sink was pulled out of the wall. The pipes were exposed, still connected to the sink and amazingly NOT leaking. A VP was concerned and trying to get the head custodian to fix it before the kids end up breaking the pipes and causing a disaster/flood. Not worried or concerned about what can be done to stop this. Sadly, there's a security guard who sit a few feet from that bathroom.

**It's now 9th period.** It finally happened the pipes were deliberately broken. Water is all over the place. Where was security? You would figure they would have closed off that facility and tell security not to let anyone in. Or at least have each student sign in. I don't get it - doesn't any one of the administrators have leadership qualities and takes charge in getting something done before something happens?

**Dec 3** - the administration is trying to keep this a secret. It seems someone called the Paterson Police Station giving a description of a particular student and claiming that they have a gun. There has to be a record of the call and what was said.

**Dec 14 - 3rd period,** the home economics teacher told me about a big fight that erupted on the 3rd floor. Kids came into her room and attacked one of her students. One of the kids involved is from my 1st period class. Mind you this teacher is about 5 foot 3, a little lady. She tried her best to stop the kids from fighting and followed them all out into the hallway. A VP was standing out there. Another teacher was scared and concerned for this little lady and just knew a fight was going to erupt. She kept telling this teacher, don't get into it, don't get into it. Unfortunately, as hard as this little lady tried to stop it, a fight erupted. The other teacher screams for security the VP who is standing there and has a walkie-talkie all the time finally calls for help. Four policemen come running up.

**Dec 21** - ONCE AGAIN as I go to leave to go home, kids are up against and have their book bags on my newer car. I noticed there was graffiti written all over the hood in pen. Made and filled out a police report, a vandalism and violence form and will be filling out a grievance. All copies will be given to the principal, my VP, and PEA President. Let's see what happens now.

**At the end of 8th & definitely 9th period** security was extra tight. They were NOT allowing students in the hallway and escorting them right out of the building. Everything was a no nonsense no BS approach. There was a meeting in the auditorium with all administrators. What was it all about, I do NOT know. I think the superintendent was in and that is why the dog and pony show.

**Dec 22** - while I was in the weight room during 4th period, a phys-ed. class was acting up. No rhyme or reason on anything athletic. However, there was a young lady sitting in a chair in the back room where the stair-masters are. There was a boy straddling this young girl with his crotch/penis (NOT OUT) in her face as he was jumping, humping up and down on her. I grabbed the gym teacher and showed him what was going on. He went over and threw the boy out of the weight room. All the while this boy is being escorted out, he kept acting up, yelling why, what did I do wrong, what is this, this is wrong, you can't do this and on and on? Sadly, this young girl never once said anything or complained as if the boy was doing anything wrong or inappropriate. I am so freaking confused when I'm here. Once again, nothing was done about this boy, his behavior and this is why none of this ever stops.

**January 3, 2005** - first day back from the Christmas vacation, UNBELEIVABLE, FIGHTS breaking out everywhere all day long. Really bad and all gang related. Hallways were filled with 100s of students screaming, running, pushing, shoving, wrestling and swearing at the top of their lungs. Nothing you could ever imagine that would go on in any school AND was allowed to continue all day long. Massive fights, even with girls fighting in gangs. One big fight that erupted several times was from the week end, brought in from the streets and into the building. This fight went on all day long and continued after school outside the building and back out into the streets.

**Jan 4** - fights all day long AGAIN and especially after school. Kids' bodies lying all over the place, police are running all over the place because there is so much going on inside and out. Once again gangs from Eastside, Kennedy and Passaic Tech are all converging outside JFK and fighting. There were soooo many students arrested. So much for ZERO TOLERANCE TO VIOLENCE! I know I've said it before, but it IS the worse I have ever seen.

Today one of my students comes to class with his social/case worker. For whatever reason, and I have NO IDEA, he wants to leave the class and take art. I asked the social worker, what is going on? Who runs the school? When students want to leave a class/course to take another class because they want out how can the administration allow this and especially when almost half the year is over? Schedules are supposedly made specifically for each student in order to satisfy their requirements. Not us satisfying their likes and wants. I said, "This is unacceptable and disgusting. Then when they want their classes and schedules changed again, you're going to accommodate them? Are you freaking kidding me?"

**Jan 5 -** is the first day of midterm exams. Another disaster once the day resumes to what is supposed to be a normal schedule. 9th period approximately 1:36 fire alarms go off. Another false alarm! This is due to students in hallway. It is also my time to leave. I decided to get the hell out of here as quickly as I can before I am blocked in. However, as I am leaving a fight is brewing, the kids won't move and it is escalating. I finally wormed my way out and left JFK behind.

The next day a security guard told me the alarm was set off because kids on the 2nd floor placed a lit sparkler to the heat sensor. They caught one of the kids involved but NOT the actual kid. However, the principal said he was expelled and had him arrested. What is being done about it NOT happening again? NOTHING! The administration still allows students in the hallways instead of going to class.

**FIGHTS AGAIN** all day, even a policeman was injured. Today a student who didn't belong in a friend of mines classroom just walks in. The teacher tells him that he doesn't belong in here and has to leave. This punk yells back at the teacher; you can suck my mother fucking dick. Later I found out that this punk - I do NOT have his name - is on parole. So, because he is on parole and this incident would violate his parole what does the administration do? They suspended him! They gave him a five-day vacation. Gee he learned his lesson and will never do that again. There are many other students here on probation and parole and it is about time the administration start setting a standard, on how to act and conduct oneself properly? There is NO common decency in here. Later, I spoke with my friend and he told me this punk came back and said that he was going to come back and stab him. This kid was arrested.

Later that day I was speaking with Mr. Class* a TAP and he told me that Ms. Ives* told him there were so many kids in the hallway during one of the cabinet meetings that it was agreed as long they're NOT doing anything, were (the administration) just going to leave them alone. The next thing they said was, well, what is it we want to do? What can we do? Where are we going to put them?

This just proves that the administration is ignoring, teaching, reinforcing and creating problems.

**Jan 6 –** 9am, we had to evacuate the building. Someone with an accent called up, was very specific about a bomb going off, when and what it would do as well as time. The entire school had to walk to a different school for evacuation. Most kids just took off and left. As usual all the threats of punishment went out the window and those students were marked absents. We came back about 11. Then the rest of the educational day was shot. There were actually thousands of people in the streets because of the evacuation. There was no media coverage about it? Once again it was all hushed up!

**Jan 12 -** Fire alarms went off at 12:20. False alarm again! They called the fire department, but it was too late. I heard the fire trucks coming. Then at 12:55 fire alarms go off again. False alarm again!

As I was walking to the cafeteria, kids were throwing food in the hallway. Security did nothing. The place was a filthy disgusting mess. It looked like a dump with food, paper and even MILK, everywhere. As I walked out to go back to my classroom I was hit in the head with a baked potato. In fact, the entire hallway between the two cafeterias was filled with baked potatoes because the kids were throwing them.

This is what they do with FREE lunches. However, when I was hit I stopped and yelled (some very choice words), hey whose (more choice words) the tough guy, come on tough guy, do it now. All of a sudden, the entire hallway that was filled and I mean packed with screaming, yelling students all stopped. I guess they were shocked that someone was taking a stand. I was pissed. I said I will, (using some more very choice words) to who threw it. This is the only thing these kids understand VIOLENCE and threats. After about 15 seconds the students went back to being out of control. I told one of the administrators and you could see she was disgusted. I told her if I caught the kids, I don't know what I would have done. I had a big welt on the side of my head.

**Bottom line -** Both cafeterias are and were a disaster. In any direction, all over the floor, and on top of tables there was nothing but food, drinks, wrappers, cans, milk and milk cartons everywhere. The garbage cans were cleaner.

**Jan 18 -** it was freezing in school and especially in my classroom. The new heating system is not working.

**Jan 19 -** Midterm exam day. Not even 2 minutes into the school day a fight breaks out in the center hallway with girls SLUGGING it out. Police and security were trying to break it up.

**It is so cold**, absolutely freezing again in school/class. Another day without heat. So much for the new 10 plus million-dollar heating system! I had to wear a coat and hat today to try to keep myself warm. I allowed students to do the same.

**I was in the men's room** in the custodian's office. All of a sudden Doll* the security guard came in and flushed the toilet. She apologized and said she had to flush the cocaine she found. She said the gym teacher has been finding it in the gym and brings it to her. Doll* said, I don't know why they bring it to me, why don't they just flush it themselves. She also said this is going on every day this week.

*This is about my grievance and vandalism form.* My union delegate told me the principal is deliberately sitting on (holding up) my Violence and Vandalism Report as well as my grievance pertaining to the vandalism to my car by not filling out his portion. He is trying to keep it from being processed. I guess he is trying to hush it up, squash the paperwork/paper trail on what is going on here. Once again, the administration working harder because they are never proactive just reactive!

Excellent example why are students allowed to congregate outside the school all day without supervision? My union delegate said the principal has many excuses why he doesn't want to meet, one in particular is because I park in a non-assigned area. Other schools have to park in the street. I replied what does that have to do with anything? Students are outside the building during school hours, vandalizing teachers' cars which are on school property. Apples and oranges. I am ON school property. The damage was done on school property. My union delegate also said that even he is not getting much support from the PEA and in particular the vice president. So much for my union and union dues! This is the THIRD 3rd time this has happened to me. This has happened to other teachers as well.

**Jan 20 -** still no heat! I wore my coat & hat all day and allowed students do to the same. It is absolutely freezing in here. Why don't they let us go home? It is so uncomfortable.

**Also,** was told the new music band teacher is leaving for Ridgewood. She is not happy with all that goes on and is allowed to go on here. It seems her tires were slashed, and she has an assigned parking spot.

**Jan 21, 22, 23 -** *STILL NO HEAT* until 1pm January 24.

**Jan 24** - 9th period fire alarm goes off. My first reaction was another false alarm. Security guards come running in my room. They ask me what I have on. That's when I realize the alarm went off because of my room. I said you have to be kidding. They said NO, what is on? I said NOTHING. They asked if I had the furnace on. I said NO, I wouldn't turn that on without the principal's permission because that sets off the alarm. Bottom line, it was because my back door was open and there was a change in temperature.

**Jan 25** - a fight broke by my classroom in Mr. Lance's* office between a mother and daughter. Ms. Sweetness* called the mother because her daughter was being difficult and excessive foul language. The mother came in and the daughter belted her. Cops, security, vice principals, everyone rushes into the office. Never heard anything more after that. It was HUSHED UP!

**Jan 28** - 2nd period, the fire alarms go off AGAIN. All the teachers *including* myself all look at one another and ask, "WHAT DO WE DO? DO WE EVACUATE?" Now we don't leave until we get the word from a VP or security guard because there are so many false alarms. We try to hold onto our students for as long as we can before we lose them during the evacuation, and it gets too bizarre in here.

**Feb 2** - one of my male students was telling me he can hit me, and I can't do anything about it because he is a minor. I told him I will smack him back in self-defense. He kept insisting, NO, I can't because he is a minor. I can't touch him no matter what he does, or I will go to jail and get fired. I have no idea why this conversation even came up. But that is the mentality here. Students think they can do whatever they want, but teachers can go to jail. That is why things are the way they are here.

**Feb 3** - Spoke with one of the security guards. She was just shaking her head saying, the violence around her is ridiculous. She said there was a fight in rear parking lot by the buses. She breaks it up, brings the students to an administrator. The administrator tells her to bring them to the department chairperson for Special Ed. The security guard is now told to bring them to another administrator. Then that administrator tells her to bring them to another. Not one administrator took charge, wanted to be bothered and kept making excuses and passed the buck onto someone else. So the poor security guard said "F" it and let the kids go. What do you think happened? The kids went in front of the building and commenced beating the crap out of each other again. The next day this security guard told the principal the whole story. Still NOTHING happened.

**Feb 4** - I am still waiting to meet with the principal from December about the vandalism to my car.

**Feb 8** - I was talking to my union delegate. I said all I want to do is to let the principal know it is NOT personal, it is just business. The union delegate said, he knows; however, the principal is taking it personal, an attack against him. Later that day the principal said to the union delegate what more can I do? I already have a security guard out there all day. I replied, then why are there still students outside and allowed to congregate around the building all day in the first place? It is a recipe for problems, trouble and disaster?

The union delegate said the principal told him I should tell my supervisor a VP to do his job. Think about it. The principal of the school tells a union delegate to tell me to tell a VP to do his job?

**Mr. Madjar** told me they are now processing kids who have well over 100 CUTS. It is so out of control the cut office is having difficulty handling all of the paperwork.

> ### PREPARING FOR MARCH STATE-WIDE EXAM AGAIN
>
> I find it very funny during those three days the administration will have full control of the building. No student is allowed any place other than being in their classroom testing.
>
> You would think every day would be more important and every reason for students to be in class. After all taxpayers are already paying for students to be in class Monday – Friday. But *no*, the administration would rather have students come in on weekends, pay teachers overtime to use old tests and booklets as a study guide to prepare students how to take the exam. *Unbelievable!* If the administration were doing their jobs by NOT allowing students to run amuck all day long, they would be able to pass the test.
>
> Then even if a senior has failed a class or classes, has 100 days of absences, as long as they passed the state exam or something within its place they will pass and graduate! Anyone can get a diploma here.
>
> Meanwhile the School District of Paterson, NJ, is STILL under state control.

**Feb 8** - coming back from making her rounds, Doll* the security guard was upset, yelling that the 2nd floor especially between classes there were no security guards to be found. Hallways were filled with kids long after the bell to start class. Her exact words, 2nd floor lost! Meaning OUT OF F'n CONTROL!

**Feb 9** - 9th period VPs Ms. Ives* & Mr. Fonda* were in the main office complaining about how bad the 2nd floor is. Ms. Ives* said Mr. Class* and someone else is supposed to be there. There was no control all day and especially between classes to get students moving to class. Meanwhile, both VPs have been in the center hall by my classroom so many, many times and did NOTHING.

Are you kidding me, all of a sudden they are concerned about the school being out of control?

Dave* the security guard said the same thing to me about the 2nd and the 3rd floors. He is upset because the outsourced security people that are supposed to be there are not doing anything. He was upset with a security guard whose has a daughter here. All the daughter does is stands by her mom with her friends and talk all day long instead of going to class.

**Feb 15** - I heard blood curdling screaming from a girl. It seemed to be coming from the cafeteria area. It went on for quite a while. Then I saw two boys run out of the building into the street. Close behind were two police officers, followed by two security guards. I do NOT know what happened.

**Feb 16** - something is wrong today. The security in the building is very tight. They are questioning everybody. I have no idea why. Maybe about yesterday?

A boy who is on probation came back to school today. I do not have his name. Anyway, by the afternoon, he was going to kill some student and that person was going to kill him. The boy on probation was taken out of the building. What happened afterwards, if it was written up, I do NOT know.

**Feb17** - a secretary told me today is the first day EVER any principal had to go to court hearing downtown for expulsion of a student. It seems this kid pushed or hit the principal. So he pressed charges. If the kid said he was sorry the principal would have dropped the charges. The kid refused. NOW how about when this happens to a teacher? Many teachers and janitors have been laid out. Yet this is the first time in JFK history for a student to attend expulsion hearing and charges pressed? Why, because it was the principal? I guess anyone other than a principal is a punching bag via verbally & physically. After all it's the principal fault students act the way they do here.

**Feb 20 - CORRUPTION & DE FRAUDING.** I have newspaper articles from The Record & The Herald News with information and indictments pertaining to everything I have said for years. Yet I hear nothing about the superintendent who was forced to resign. No one has ever seen his contract with all of his perks and benefits. I guess that's why? However, rumor has it even though he resigned he still will be paid.

**Feb 24 - 9th period, fire alarms go off.** False alarm AGAIN! However, this time the fire department arrives. The administration didn't have time to call and say it was a false alarm. A few minutes after the alarm was set or supposedly set, it kept going off. Only one person has a key to reset the alarm. Next, is what I was dreading. A VP makes an announcement; if the alarm goes off please disregard. When the alarm originally went off, NO ONE knew what to do. Everyone stands around and NOW waits.

**Mar 7** - before the school day even started, gang wars going on outside We had nothing but gang problems all day long inside here and after school. There were so many extra police in and around the building today. It seems it was mostly the 5th Avenue gang.

**Mar 8** - beginning of 3rd period a HUGE fight/brawl in hallways.

**Mar 9** - 8th period, a fight erupts in the cafeteria. Security and police are all running. I can hear yelling and screaming and all of the noise from the by standers. It was two girls fighting. One girl just had a baby.

**Then** a HUGE brawl broke out on the 2nd or 3rd floor. Cops, security, and the principal went flying through the hallways trying to get to the commotion. This place is so freaking bad. It wouldn't be if students were made to be in class!

**Mar 14** - 9th period false alarm again! Everyone is standing around not knowing what to do. The principal starts yelling even at the head of the Phys Ed Department to have everyone evacuate the building. This is what I was talking about for years; no one takes the alarms serious anymore. Then to top things off, the principal goes onto the elevator. Absolutely ridiculous, everyone knows when the fire alarm is sounded you NEVER get on an elevator. Obviously, he does not take the alarms serious either.

**Mar 21** - 9th period a fight breaks out. A teacher gets hit. Another male teacher jumped in attempting to break it up. In fact, the head of the English Dept. was screaming there was no security. Then one of the security guards started arguing with her. I understand the student causing all of the problems has NOT been in school all week. What a freaking place!

**Mar 22** - 3rd period 9:16 false alarm. 4th period 10:05 false alarm again. 6th period false alarm again. 7th period 1:01 false alarm again. We had to evacuate building each time. Meanwhile the administration still allows students to hang out all over the building instead of making them go to class.

**Mar 23** - CAREER DAY, WHAT A JOKE. For two periods the majority of the student population had an excuse to walk in and out of classrooms they don't belong in, roam the halls and hangout all over the building. Once it was over the rest of day was shot. Students remained in the hallways doing whatever they want, defiant and NOT listening to security. It's just an indoor street corner and it's allowed.

**Mar 24** -fights all day long. Gang fights, girls fighting, Bloods vs. JSP = Jasper Street and no one was suspended. They just kept breaking them up. OUT OF CONTROL ALL DAY! It was what you would expect to see in a movie and not believe it. It seems that every student was is in the hallways. Ms. Ives* a VP had a bunch of boys in my room talking with them trying to keep a fight from escalating. Meantime, all of the commotion going on right on the 1st floor, center hallway was unbelievable. Other than Ms. Ives* being in my room, I did not see one other administrator. Shortly afterwards I finally saw VP Mr. Costello*. I yelled to him that I need help because kids were walking in and out of my room that didn't belong. I had no idea what was going on or what was going to happen. I knew they were looking for trouble. So, I yelled to him again, let's get the kids moving. But as usual they ignored him.

**Apr 4** - first day back from Easter vacation. We had so much rain over the holiday. Many areas throughout the state suffered major flooding and water damage. New Jersey received 30 million dollars in aid. However, around the same time the Paterson Public School District, which is still run, controlled and operated by the State of New Jersey, lost 50 to 60 million dollars. Twice the amount the State of New Jersey received in Federal Aid for the floods and hurricane damage in all of New Jersey for 2004 – 2005. Meanwhile the ex-superintendent is still receiving his salary.

All of these STATE APPOINTED superintendents will never be held accountable. All of the money was lost, stolen embezzled, "MISSAPPROPRIATED" (which was one of the reasons why the state took over the district) and whatever else that is done with the money. Paterson schools are a money pit. These superintendents have no stake and no responsibility and are not even from here. They are carpet baggers going to state to state looking for a superintendent's position. It is NOT a business; it is not run like a business and most of all it is NOT THEIR money.

**Apr 4** - first day back from Easter vacation, 5th period, 11:14 false alarm, evacuate building again!

**Apr 5** - 4th period, 10:05 false alarm again. Evacuate building again.

**Then,** 9th period 1:40 false alarm again. Evacuate building again.
Nobody knows what to do anymore. Everyone stands around waiting to be told to evacuate.

**Apr 6** - 9th period 1:44 false alarm again.

**Apr 7** - 9th period false alarm again.

**Apr 8** - 7th period false alarm again. This time the administration forgot to call the fire department. Once again everyone is standing around, asking what do we do? VP Ms. Ives* replies unless otherwise instructed, evacuate the building. Finally everyone attempts to evacuate. In the meantime, and as usual with every time the alarms go off, the kids think it's a joke and are running around, screaming, yelling, pushing and shoving everyone, as if it's a game. Then the rest of the day is a disaster, shot!

**Apr 11** - 4th period, I was speaking with Mr. Madjar. He was saying how the cut office is going crazy. I asked how many cuts have you processed? He laughed and said that they have almost gone through two boxes. Each box holds 10 reams of paper, 100 sheets to a ream, and three cut slips to each sheet, a total of 30k cuts per case. In total almost 60K. He said the freshman and sophomores are terrible. Everyone has cut and most have cut 60, 70 and up to over 100 plus times. Many have 300 - 400 cuts written down in their folder. I said that's why the fire alarms are always pulled. He laughed and said, "ABSOLUTELY." He said he cannot go by the rules and regulations governing students and cut policy. If he did more than 100 students would be suspended. He said it is so out of control. The students don't want to go to class. Mr. Madjar said that's one of the main reasons why we're supposed to be going to block time, to cut down on the cutting. I replied, soooo, I guess that the central office knows of the cut situation here and the block scheduling is the cure? Well if it is a cure then why doesn't it work at Eastside? He just laughed. I said as always the children and especially the taxpayers suffer!

**Apr 15 -** 7th period 12:19 false alarm, AGAIN.

**Apr 20 -** 3rd period 9:45 false alarm - It is now 4th period, time 10:10 halls are still filled with students going absolutely berserk because of the false alarm interruptions.

**6th period 11:45** fire alarms go off again. Another false alarm! I can't understand how people with a minimum of a Master's degree allows this out of control, nonproductive, chaotic behavior to continue day after day, all day, all year and for years when this is a State Takeover Run and Operated School District?

Speaking with another teacher, Mr. Allen* when one of my students walked by. He says to me, I hate that kid. He tells me one-day last year C, as he is called, was playing with a very large knife. He kept throwing it in the air. The teacher had security bring C to Mr. Lance*. When the teacher went to speak with Mr. Lance*, he was told C doesn't have a knife. The teacher was confused and said he had it in class. He asked are you sure? The teacher replied, yes. Mr. Lance* says, well there is nothing we can do about it if he doesn't have it on him now. The teacher said Mr. Lance* was more upset with him. I said, I bet he is or was told to hush it all up, squash it. Think about it, he had the knife in class, security brought him to the administrator's office, and NOW he doesn't have it. He's lying!

**Apr 21 -** 7th period 12:16 false alarm AGAIN! I'm so sick of this. Don't these administrators have kids of their own? Would they allow their children to attend the very same school they work in?

**May 2, 3, 4 & 5 -** the building is so freaking cold and damp. My room is unbelievably freezing. I caught a cold by mid-week. All teachers are complaining. Yet the blowers are still blasting cold air in the classrooms. This is the new system the taxpayers paid for.

**May 2 -** a kid was running in hallway. VP Ms. Ives* tells the kid to stop. He says no and keeps on running down the hallway. She turned to me and said, when he falls, he will sue. I just shook my head. What's the point of having supervision in the building? It was no surprise to me hearing him telling her no as he kept running. Typically, the VP did nothing.

**During 6th period,** one of my female students told me that she is 18. She failed her freshman year at Eastside, transferred here, passed her freshman year and was promoted to be a sophomore. However, she has lost credit for this year which will make her a sophomore again. She is going to go to a program called, "DAY LIGHT PROGRAM." With this program, she will be paid $50 a day to attend school and will graduate as scheduled, even though she has been left back and lost credit.

**May 3 -** 7th period, 12:47 false alarm! School was a disaster with kids, 100s of them in hallways all day. This is due to the health fair in the gym. Now they have some place else to go, hangout and cause problems, instead of going to class. They're throwing around all the stuff they got for free. What a mess - candy, paper, buttons, condoms, and stress balls that are filled with sand all over the place. Plus, they are arguing and fighting over all of this free crap. Our students need regimentation and not getting it here. We cannot have these breaks within the school schedule; otherwise the school day is lost. Today is PROOF!

A girl in my 8th period class is 15 years old and has a baby. The father is 14 and in my 6th period class, although he hardly shows up and does absolutely nothing.

**May 6** - The RECORD front page, "Poor schools paid for posh travel," continued page A-20. Will taxpayers be reimbursed? Is anyone held accountable? If this can go on, then what's the purpose of the State of New Jersey taking over the Paterson School District in the first place?

**May 11** - we had a meeting for block scheduling. I made a comment to a VP stating the REAL reason for block scheduling is *only* to stop the cutting which would cut the suspensions. NOT for the better educational process. She said 85% of suspensions are due to cutting. 2% is Violence. NO way, I do NOT believe that. Look what I have been documenting and this is ONLY what I know. You can guarantee the only reason why the violence percentages are low is because the administration hushes it all up and the paperwork is NOT being submitted. Administration feels this is NOT falsifying records.

**May 13 - FIGHTS** big gang fights, gangs of students taking over the entire wing. It was Dominicans against Arabs. This did not happen once or twice it went on all day long and nonstop. You would think the administrators would have gotten rid of these students right off the bat or even by the 2nd time. BUT NOOOOO all day long fighting, attacks, gang/mob fighting right here in the building and in one wing in particular. The school day and building were lost, not to mention the building was a dangerous combat zone. I understand according to a VP, they got a bus to take 10 kids out of here, or how he put it - to deport them.

Speaking with a secretary on Monday, May 16, she said all of the violence, fighting and attacks were all over some one throwing a ball and the wrong person was hit. Remember 5/11, the vice principal said, only 2% is violence, give me a break!

**May 19** - 7th period, 12:37 false fire alarm again! Fire department arrived at 12:43.

During our departmental meeting a VP said it is getting to be a real problem now because when the alarm is pulled all of the Arabic students don't stay with their teachers and go out the back door to fight.

A VP also told us that he is busy at least an hour or so every day with two girls who are constantly fighting. They not only fight in school, but their entire episode is brought in from the streets. Their mothers are also fighting and allowing the girls to fight in their presence.

**A teacher's daughter** was substituting today. The students were so disrespectful, vulgar, defiant and basically so bad to her, that she had to remove herself and was out in the hallway crying.

**We** received the April edition of the union's newsletter "The Advocate." It is funny because everything I said about the state-run district is NOW in this newsletter. To be used as a reference for my book. It says, if appointed, Glascoe would lead a district of 26,000 students that has been under state control since 1991 because of prior mismanagement and deteriorated facilities.

**Jun 1** - I was told a bus driver beat up a student really bad. It was a mess and blood everywhere.

**Also,** a VP told me he's being sued by the person who runs the Zone program because he suspended his son. The father is claiming because his son was suspended it's infringing on his rights to an education. From what I understand the boy was suspended because of firecrackers going off in the building.

**Jun 6** - I CANNOT believe all the students who lost credit got their credit back. They all exceeded the total absentee days out allowed. Another one of my male students was thrown out of Eastside because of poor attendance. He comes to JFK, lost credit again for poor attendance and now June 6, he receives his credit back and has NOT made up any school or class time or schoolwork. He is NOT the only student.

Another one of my male students came to my class *maybe* 10 times. He too has his credit back. I have the documentation and actual paperwork from the school.

**Later that day,** a social worker for another one of my students came in. I showed her his grades, record of absences, cuts and lateness to my class. She replied, "OH NO, he doesn't deserve it." Well, he got his credit back. Anyone can pass here and get a diploma. You just have to show up once and awhile. So much for state requirements where students have to be in school so many days a year!
I guess that's what's meant by *no child left behind!*

**Bottom line -** If I were a student, I would make sure I was classified, I would do nothing, receive the same credit and high school diploma as a college prep student & the VALOR VICTORIAN.

**Jun 8 -** 4th period, Mr. Costello* a VP told Ms. Conscientious* and I to evacuate the building before the alarms go off. At 10am, the fire alarms go off, a bomb scare.

**Again** 9th period 2:03, fire alarms go off. It seems the sensors in the TV room were triggered.
Fire department arrived at 2:10.

**Jun 9** during an In-service in room 234, we were told about SLC's (Small Learning Communities) and how they will be implemented by 2008. Key phrase, "WILL BE."

Many areas of topics were discussed. One in particular originated from one of our superintendents Dr. Conrad* who came up with the 10R plan. His idea is to have students who cannot pass the HSPT (state exam) placed in 10R, (meaning repeating sophomore). Only those students capable of passing the HSPT will take the test. In order to select these students, they would have to pass all facets of their math requirements and only then they will be allowed to take the test. This way the scores and percentages would be higher. Once again, the district superintendents are deliberately, manipulating the testing system by allowing less and only certain students to take the test to make the district look better as to give the *appearance* test scores are improving. ALL SMOKE & MIRRORS!

**Jun 10** – 7am, I pulled into the parking lot the alarm was already going off. 7:06 the fire trucks came.

**Approximately 3 p.m.** another gang fight and a shootout. A girl came running into the building all upset. The administrators thought it was because a wire was down on the street and sparks were jumping all over the place. She actually came in seeking help because a student (name omitted) was shot in the leg.
This entire week was a disaster, nothing but fighting all day, every day and everywhere.

## SCHOOL YEAR 2005–2006

**September 1, 2005 -** 1st day of school for teachers; we were told the principal retired. He has had enough and a VP is acting/interim principal. So far, I think she is doing a good job.

**Sept 21 -** watching TV NJN NEWS at 9 pm they said, $50 MILLION in extortion from the Paterson Public school district via director of facilities! I had to laugh because he said his lawyer will fight & he will be found not guilty. Another reason why I laugh is because I knew someone who was carrying a wire and has everybody on tape. *Plus*, I know that many are so high up the political chain that a deal will be made so the big shots will get away with it and it will all be hushed up. The $50 million are not just taken away from the children of the school district but the taxpayer once again got screwed. Think about it, last year NJ had flooding where $30 million of federal disaster money was needed because the ***ENTIRE STATE*** was considered a disaster area. Meanwhile the State Takeover Run and Operated School District of ***Paterson ALONE*** was swindled out of $50 million?

**Fire alarms** have been going off. They are being triggered by a faulty electrical system. So far, this year seems to be under control. I have seen several students already being taken out of the school in handcuffs. It seems the interim principal is not fooling around. She's utilizing the 3 F's - Friendly, Fair, but Firm. I hope this continues.

**Oct 12** - Mr. Madjar from the cut office said it is a disaster already here. They are already so far behind processing all of the cuts. He doesn't think they will ever get caught up.

**Oct 14** - a student who is hardly in class asked if he could go to the nurse's office. I asked why? He said he has pains in his chest. I asked what kind of pains. He snaps at me and says I don't know, pains in my chest. I asked a teacher to get a security guard to escort a student to the nurse's office. Instead, she contacted the nurse's office directly to have a nurse come with the wheelchair. Now the interesting part! I was standing by her when Mr. Lance* a TAP told her not use the walkie-talkie to do that.

**Bottom line** -The administration doesn't want anything that can be heard by others over the walkie-talkie. Another way of keeping things quiet.

**Fire alarms** are still NOT working properly. Every day since the beginning of school the principal goes on the PA system telling everyone to please disregard the alarms until further notice.

**Oct 17** - the new faulty fire alarm system is going off all the time. However, between periods 8 & 9, the fire alarm was deliberately pulled. It was pulled out by the trailers. Fire department arrived.

**During** 9th period everyone was trying to find out who pulled the alarm. I saw about 10 students being escorted to Mr. Lance's* office and the principal said, I don't care, they know who did it, suspend them all. She is the first principal who is actually taken a no-nonsense position here. It is nice to finally see someone actually taking charge and setting things rights as well an example.

**Oct 18** - between periods 7 & 8 two female students were arguing in the center hallway directly in front of my room. Students started gathering around and instigating the girls to fight. I am trying to get the kids to move & disperse. Eventually there was a circle of 100 plus students. They would not move and eventually the two girls started to throw hands. I got in the middle of it in attempts to stop it. I was afraid being that these were female students & I am a 53-year-old man. I did the best I could in keeping them from actually tangling. There were no security, police, administrators, no one but me. Luckily, Mr. Lance's* office was right there. He came out and grabbed one young ladies and the other went immediately to the wall. Even at this time students would not disperse. I immediately walked up behind Mr. Lance*, placed my hand on his back to let him know I was there and had his back so no students would take a cheap shot. Even with the TAP and I yelling for the students to move, they kept swarming in. Another female teacher made her way to help and gave support. Eventually security & police were on scene. It's a wonderful place here.

**Oct 22** - fire alarms went off around 10:00. They go off for no reason. Well, in reality there is a reason. The brainiac engineer placed the sensors where there is heat or a major change in temperatures which makes them go off. EXAMPLE: Cafeteria ovens, refrigerators and my room directly over three furnaces.

**Oct 25** - false fire alarm again. Students are running wild going crazy all around the building. Riot like atmosphere here. Nobody is stopping them. Not one administrator or security guard present.

**Oct 26** - between 4th & 5th period a BIG FIGHT breaks out on the 1st floor by the vending machines, with four girls. It was unbelievable. The hallway was a disaster. 100's of screaming and yelling students gathering around. Kids were coming down so fast filling the entire hallway up like ants on a crumb. I couldn't get through to break it up. Doll* the security guard & me finally got through. The situation became worse and extremely dangerous. I hated to leave but I knew Doll*and I needed HELP. I fought my way through the mob again to summon police. It was so difficult to get through because students were deliberately blocking me. I went with another teacher and kept my hands on her back to let her know it was me and that I was behind her. On our way through the mob I was suckered punched. Finally, the fight was broken up by police, but the hallway/school was a disaster for the rest of the day.

**During 8th period,** my supervisor asked me to contact a student's parents to inform them of their child being a habitual cutter. I had to laugh because that would be most of my students.

**Oct 27 -** 7 am, speaking with the acting principal about yesterday's fiasco/fight in the hallway when I was suckered punched. She starts saying how do we teach children not to fight, when their parents come here & fight amongst themselves right in the office. They actually start way laying, slugging it out between each other. She started telling me two parents were called in and actually went at it in Mr. Lance's* office. Then she said she called in one of the city councilmen to come in and help with the situation and then he too witnessed these parents going at it AGAIN.

**Nov 1 -** a fight breaks out between two of my students at the beginning of homeroom outside the building. Shortly afterwards, one of the student's mothers came into school. All of a sudden she was screaming, cursing as she went to attack someone and had to be subdued by police. These are PARENTS?

**Then shortly after that** another brouhaha broke out and a police sergeant had to grab a kid because he was so out of control. Once again, if there are NO consequences for your actions, how does anyone learn?

**Nov 16-** speaking with the acting principal, I was explaining between 7th & 8th period the hallways are a disaster. Other than another teacher and myself, there is so no one here for supervision. She appreciated the info and was upset security is never around. I said, well in their defense, there is so much going on all the time security is always busy. She said it's the same on the 2nd floor. I told her that it is a disaster here. I said several times I had to call her office, spoke with a secretary to get security, police, anybody here because it is so bad here and especially after the bell rings to start 8th period.

**WELL, at 8th period a fight breaks out.** This time the principal was present. It had to be going through her mind what I had just told her this morning. Same situation, no one was around. Disgustingly as much as I tried to get through to the other end of the hall where the fight was, it was impossible. I stopped and went back to the safety of my room. I was not going to get sucker punched again or worse.

**Nov 22 -** Mr. Pardine and Mr. Kott told me the cut office has processed more cuts than this time last year, over 17K. Over 5K, in the last three weeks and it's getting worse. They said they cannot even keep up with the processing of cuts being turned in. They said the kids that don't usually cut are now cutting knowing that they can get away with it.

**Nov 23 -** speaking with a SRA (Senior Review Assessment) teacher, she told me she had a student (some years ago) who cut her class every day. He told her that he will continue to do so, he will pass, go to college and she can't do anything about it. She said she continually wrote cuts on him. Then finally one day she was called to see a VP. The VP asked the teacher why he is failing. She replied because he cuts class every day and you excuse him. The VP said I didn't know he was cutting your class? The teacher replied, I don't know how you didn't, why would I be writing cuts on him then?

**Bottom line -** He passed, grade was changed, was accepted to college with a football scholarship.

Then when he saw the teacher in the hallway, he looked at her with a smirk and said, I told you I will pass, get a scholarship to college and you can't do anything about it. *It is still the same here.*

**Dec 1** - in-service day. What a joke. It was about all of this money (TAXES) and changes to ONLY the ABBOTT DISTRICTS in NJ. The politicians and district want to place *more* responsibility on the schools and especially the teachers, because parents *(not all of them)* are not doing their jobs.

**Dec 2** - nothing but fights and chaos all day right from the very start this morning. It has been unfreakin' believable. In fact, one young man came out of the office screaming cursing and his mother couldn't even control him. In fact, she says, "This is ridiculous, I keep having to come here. What am I supposed to do? He is not going to listen to me." ARE YOU FREAKING KIDDING ME! This is a parent? She was actually annoyed. That is the mentality. Just drop him or her off and let us deal with it. Parents must be held responsible and take control of their children. Mr. Madjar told me this boy is either on parole or probation and he doesn't seem to care because he is constantly cutting. Anyhow, the mother went to see Mr. Lance*. However, Mr. Lance* didn't want to hear anymore excuses and crap from her. So the mother went to another administrator and pleaded not to have him suspended, because it would be in violation of his parole or probation and will be locked up.

**Bottom line** -They didn't suspend him so he wouldn't go to jail. However, he wears an ankle monitoring bracelet. Shortly afterwards he was involved in another fight.

Obviously, this kid doesn't care. The best thing they could have done is suspended him. He VIOLATED his probation or parole. This is called TOUGH LOVE! First of all, the mother says she gave up on him, because he doesn't listen to her. The district and school does not hold him accountable for his actions. Which is really what the district and administrators really want to do because then there would be a paper trail of violence and suspension. So while this kid is attending JFK it is being reinforced that there are NO consequences for his actions and one day he is going to be involved with something really terrible and then what? The mother will blame who?

**Dec 6** - Mr. Madjar told me they have processed over 20K cuts. In the last 10 days there have been over 500. Mr. Madjar and Mr. Pardine showed me the box FILLED with cut slips. One student in particular has over 248 cuts, plus his absences, already equals 248 days out for the year utilizing the cut policy. Another student has 247 cuts and a total of 53 days absent for the year and it is only December.

**Dec 13** - between 4$^{th}$ & 5$^{th}$ periods another big fight involving girls. I don't know much more. The administrators are working harder; trying to keep as much as they can hushed up.

**During** 8$^{th}$ period one of my students tells me he only has 4 or 5 days out. I count them up and came up with 14. He says many of the days don't count because they are suspension. I replied immediately, 20 days out you fail. He came back with you can't, suspension days don't count. I said watch me, you have 5 more and then you fail. As if it really matters! He does absolutely nothing in class.

**Dec 21** - 5$^{th}$ period, 10:50, fire alarm goes off again due to the new faulty system.

**January 3, 2006** - first day back from vacation, fire alarms goes off 9:56, between 3$^{rd}$ & 4$^{th}$ period. There was a fire on the 2$^{nd}$ floor, room 235 heater. Fire department came. Nothing but fighting here all day long.

**Jan 4** - 8$^{th}$ period, 1:04, fire alarms go off. False alarm again! Fire department arrived. January 4, 5 & 6 the administration had teachers guarding fire alarm boxes instead of having students in class.

**Jan 6 -** fights all day long. It is unbelievable here. Now the rest of the day is shot. The students are in a frenzy and this goes on and on more and more. But let's blame the teachers for failing schools!

**Jan 9 -** there was a stabbing. I don't know the whole story. I couldn't get the newspaper article.

**Later,** 6th period, 11:45, fire alarms go off. It's another false alarm!

**Jan 11 - 2nd** period was held over longer while police came in and rounded up the students involved with Monday's stabbing. We have so many people in the building this morning because of the stabbing so security was extremely tightened. Usually all three floors are so chaotic and a disaster with kids all over the place However, because of yesterday and all of these people investigating the situation NOW students were in their classrooms and the administration is ACTING as if this is the typical behavior here.

NOW, because of this incident security have the wand style metal detectors. Students are now supposed to be checked before entering the building. Let's see how long this will last?

**Jan 12 -** 6th period, there was so much noise and commotion going on I went outside my room to see. There were a bunch of kids gathering around and two girls fighting. There was no security, no police, no administration, as usual NO SUPERVISION. It was a free for all. I hesitated for a minute until I seen this boy getting involved. Stupid me, I ran over trying to get everyone to stop and leave but as usual they ignored me as if I wasn't even there and continued with their frenzy. I separated the two girls and the one girl went right back attacking the other. That's when this boy grabbed her, picked her up, literally threw her into the wall face first and proceeded to grab her again. I grabbed him by the top of his sweatshirt and separated him from her. He kept telling me that she was his sister. I said yeah, sure. These kids will tell you anything-- that's my cousin, my brother, my sister, whatever-- so I said, "That doesn't give you the right to throw her into the wall." He screamed get the fuck off of me and took a swing at me. He didn't hit me, but to defend myself and to get some control over the situation, I spun him around, grabbed him around the upper chest, pulled him to the floor and held him there.

In the meantime, the kids were all over the place I was waiting to get suckered punched or worse. Finally, two TAPs came running over Mr. Lance* & Mr. Pro*. When Mr. Lance* was coming he yelled, "Let him go I got him." Then finally a few security people showed up. It was a disaster. In fact, right after that incident within a few minutes the place actually became worse and more out of control. There were more fights all day long and especially inside the cafeteria.

The next day, I told the principal what had happened. To find out she didn't know any of this. She just knew of an incident. She was genuinely upset about me being alone and in the middle of it without security or other administrators. She said I want you to press charges on the kid. I was so surprised to even hear that. Believe it or not, I didn't want to do that.

**Jan 13 & 17 -** nothing but fights and fighting in the building all day long. In fact, during 2nd period, Mr. Class* a TAP was supposed to get the chair I fixed. He couldn't because the entire 2nd floor was a disaster and so out of control.

**Jan 17 -** in today's newspaper, The Record, there was a great deal about the stabbing. I heard the student is doing well, is out of the hospital and on the streets again. A security guard told me SURPRISINGLY the administration does NOT want him back because of all the trouble he causes and doesn't want an incident to happen involving him again.

**Jan 18** - fights and out of control situations again all day. And because the building was so out of control, and having parent conferences, Mr. Class* from Jan 17 entry, still couldn't pick up his chair.

**Jan 19** - 5th period, 12:30. Fire alarm goes off. False alarm! There was a fight just prior to 6th period. The alarm went off again because students wanted to fight/revenge. Fights all day long, gangs, Arabics fighting Jasper St. & whoever else. 1:45 BIG fight/brawl in foyer, students, parents, men and woman fighting. The school day was lost. The parents broke the park bench that's in the foyer by jumping on it. The place was filled with Paterson Police.

**Jan 20** - 7th period, 12:34, false alarm! Students set off sensor in bathroom using matches or a lighter.

**Jan 24 - 27, (24)** the principal will be out on a leave of absence for a while. Since the principal's absence, the school is so out of control. It hasn't been this bad all year. There are so manymore kids in hallways.

**Jan 26** - it has been unbelievable all day. It is so freakin' out of control with all of the fighting, kids in hallways and every place else all day long. I knew sooner or later something was going to give. Fights all day on the 2nd floor between Dominican and Arabic students. At 12:08 just before the end of 6th period, fire alarms go off. We evacuated the building. Students piled paper up in a garbage can in the gym's boy's locker room and set it on fire. What do you expect when students are allowed to roam the building?

In fact, a student (name omitted), has *not* been in my class since before Thanksgiving. However, he has been suspended but not that entire time. He walks the halls all day long every day. I saw him yesterday and he basically laughs in my face.

**REASON** - He knows that I cannot do anything about it. If I call him, he will ignore me and will not suffer any consequences. Today during homeroom, he was in the center hall. I yelled for Mr. Pro* to grab him. I asked him to bring the student to the cut office. He does and asks the kid his name. The kid gives Mr. Pro* a phony name. I told Mr. Pro* he's lying. I said his name is (name omitted) and has not been in my class since before Thanksgiving. Mr. Pardine turns around saying I don't want him, get him out of here. I don't want anything to do with him. So, the student walks out and is back roaming the halls. Meanwhile, I am stuck still having to do paperwork, cuts every day because no one wants to stop this kid from cutting. It is not like he is cutting school. In reality he is BUT he is in the building ALL DAY LONG, hanging out. Sooo if he is truant, the school is allowing and encouraging him to cut.

**Jan 26** - fire alarm goes off again at 12:49, students wanted to fight so they pulled the alarm.

AGAIN 7th period, 1:23, the fire alarm goes off. Nobody knew whether to evacuate or not. Everybody was confused, standing around like zombies asking what to do. Sooner or later, there is going to be a real tragedy. Especially for those students in wheelchairs who are on the 2nd and 3rd floors. They cannot use the elevator, the hallways, stairways are filled with people pushing and shoving one another.

**Jan 31-** before school started 6:46, alarms go off. FD arrived. Seems it was a faulty alarm this time.

I was told a student (name omitted - see 2nd entry for Jan 17) is NOT allowed in school along with several other students who have been suspended for the time being. The reason is because of the incident involving the stabbing is starting all over again. The administrators are trying to keep this from erupting and in school. GREAT, it is about freaking time being proactive!

**Feb 1** - speaking with Dave Kott one of the teachers who works in the cut office. I asked how many cuts have been processed. He replied we have surpassed the biggest, 70 THOUSAND. He said, about 1/3rd of the teachers don't even write cuts because it's a waste of their time, so you can imagine how manymore there would be. Then we started talking about cuts are the main reason for the district going to block scheduling. I said all administrators have a minimum of a master's degree, I cannot believe they cannot figure out what to do to control this nonsense of students cutting and actually being in the hallways unchallenged? He replied, "You got that right, it is absolutely disgusting here."

**Feb 2 -** a female security guard was telling a young man to get out, leave the building. He had been running around in the hallways & it's time to leave. The student was defiant and extremely fresh. He kept screaming foul language, obscenities and continued antagonizing the security guard. Eventually two police officers stepped in. The student was just as defiant, obnoxious, foul mouthed and belligerent to them. They finally had enough, grabbed and escorted his fat ass out of the building. The students kept running his mouth, get your fucking hands off me, you can't do this, you can't touch me, and on and on. He started threatening the officers, saying take your hands off me and see what happens. Finally, one cop turned to this boy and said, and what, keep it up and I'll just lock you up! The boy kept being stupid, so the cop shoved him out of the building instead of locking him up. If students act this way with security guards, and to uniformed Paterson police officers, how do you expect teachers to have any respect when this behavior is ALLOWED AND CONTINUES!

**I learned today** the same student from entries Jan 17 & 31, is now placed in home school. This is away for him, a "SENIOR," to graduate. He has caused so many problems and trouble for the school with all of the violence. He is the boy who was stabbed a few weeks earlier and now that he's back in school that incident has also come back to resurface in the building. One of the VPs was concerned about this happening, but the parents didn't want to listen and persisted on keeping him in school. So NOW, he dropped my class because I was failing him, and they want him to graduate. Like I said anyone can get a diploma here. The school and district will not back teachers, school rules or policies. And we wonder why this district is a failing district? No real life lessons are ever taught here. Meanwhile he will graduate, have diploma, but he is illiterate. Our own state is simply just pushing students through the system and out into the world unprepared and under educated. Absolutely disgusting! Our own State Officials are helping to RUIN A NATION and they DO NOT CARE!

**Feb 7 -** talking with Mr. Madjar, he told me that one of my students (name omitted) has the record for cutting now. He has a total of 235 cuts. I have a copy of his profile.

I noticed for the last week or so, security is NO LONGER using the metal detectors. Typical, the administration will wait until something happens again. I do NOT understand this place?

**Feb 8 -** this incident involves two of my students (name omitted student #1) & (name omitted student #2). Both students came back on that same day, 2/8. I sent them to office #2 w/security for a re-admit slip. The office sent them back. They didn't want them. I asked security to escort them to the cut office. However, the cut office was closed. I suggest security to contact an administrator. I said school rules say, after three days absent, no student is allowed in class w/out a re-admit slip. Security came back with a note from my supervisor saying to admit students and after class have students report to the cut office. I said, "Do they actually think these kids who have been cutting will take themselves to the cut office?" I then saw a TAP, Mr. Class*and explained the situation. He spoke with the two students. He called me about 12:30 and told me the one kid has lost credit because he has 66 days out. However, he will be reinstated because he is Special Ed. I replied, "If he has 66 days out of school how can he get credit back?"

*****Student #1,** absent from my class most of September and out since sometime in October.
*****Student #2,** absent from my class since September. However, *is* always in hallway all day every day.

**Bottom line** -Nothing was done. Suspension (which I agree), is not an answer to the problem. The only lesson learned was other students will NOW follow suit seeing what has just transpired.

**Feb 9** - nothing but fights all day long. 9th period 2:20pm alarms go off. False alarm again! I do not know why, but TODAY security was using the handheld metal detectors.

**Feb 10** - 7th period 12:19, we evacuated the building again, another false alarm. It seems students set the bathroom sensor off using a cigarette lighter or match *again*. No more pulling fire boxes, because teachers are guarding them. The students are actually smarter than all of the administrators. They realize they CANNOT pull the alarms anymore so they thought of an alternative way. Meanwhile the administration who are so educated cannot figure out how to have students in class yet! Anyway, right after we evacuated the building a big fight erupts outside. I said to the head custodian one of these days there is going to be a real fire someplace else in the city and the fire department will be here and someone who really needs help will suffer because of this daily nonsense. He said it already happened. The fire department was responding to one of our false alarms and on their way over the hook and ladder truck hit a car and killed two people. It was never in the newspaper. If it were true, then who in the hell controls the media and news?

**Feb 14** - the hallways were so filled with kids all day you would think it's the day before Christmas at the mall. You couldn't walk. The hallways were PACKED like cattle in a train car. This is not a school. It is a place to hang out and play. It's a wonder why no one has pulled the fire alarms. If this type of behavior is allowed to go on inside the building and students DO NOT have to go to class, then what is the point of this school and district being taken over, run and operated by the State of NJ?

**I received** a schedule for a new student. On this sheet of paper, it had at the bottom, "CHILDREN FIRST" These are the same people who stole, embezzled, misappropriated, whatever the catch phrase is today, 50 plus million dollars. I had to laugh.

**Feb 16** - 2nd period, 8:17, bomb scare, evacuated building! It's funny, we have 20 security guards, 1/2 dozen police, yet they still want teachers to sit and guard the fire alarms. Let's not worry about getting students out of the hallways and into the class.

**Feb 17** - 1st period, 7:41, bomb scare again! They called the Board of Ed. first. Then the Board of Ed called the school and we evacuated. However, we were back in the building by 7:54am. I think that's awful quick for a bomb scare? Someone said they were doing a hallway sweep way before we were TOLD to evacuate the building and that's why we came back in so fast. This doesn't sound right to me. If this was a bomb scare where were all the added police, fire department, bomb squad, and bomb sniffing dogs, as they always have shown up before?

**Feb 27** - Dominican Independence Day. Just another excuse to act up here and *NOTHING* was done about it. Gangs, and I mean gangs of kids, in the hallway all day screaming yelling, running, just carrying on and drinking alcohol while the police just watch. Do NOT blame the police, they are not allowed to do anything unless something happens. UNFREAKINBELIEVABLE! Kids were not in classes, just roaming the halls. All the cafeteria periods were a disaster. The school day is lost. Fights, food fights, students destroyed the cafeteria. No one was allowed in front cafeteria during 7th period because of all the damage and garbage thrown all over. It has to be the worse I seen all year. Kids, 100s of them all day long in the hallways carrying on looking for fights and causing trouble. What school allows this type of behavior?

**One such fight** broke out between two students. It seems they were arguing when one kid suckered punched the other student several times. The kid fell and hit his head on a desk, giving him a big gash to his head. He was taken to the hospital and was stitched up. He also has two black eyes and his face is all swollen. The school didn't do anything other than suspend the other kid. Why wasn't he arrested?

**Mar 1 -** all week long the building is *OUT* of control with students in hallways instead of being in class. It is unbelievable. Then I realize, the administration has not and never had control over anything in the building. *Example -* They do NOT want students wearing hats, head gear, listening to music, etc. and etc. while they are in the building. Yet, students still do. Soooo, if they cannot control students of the simplest of rules, how in the hell would we expect them to have control of the very building they are supposed to be in charge of and supervising? It is 12:29 and the hallways are FILLED with students.

**March 7 & 8 -** I have never seen it as bad during testing. On the 7$^{th}$ many students were thrown out of HSPA. Both days students were to begin testing at 8:20. 8:45 students are still entering the building. We are not teaching the importance of being responsible for being on time. Once again, it is *just* about passing a stupid test that means *nothing* in life. Being on time is MORE important. That's if you plan on working.

This is the worse state-wide testing day I have ever seen. Usually six days a year during the testing periods is the *only* time the school is somewhat under control. However, today, kids are all over, in hallways, stairwells, hanging out in bathrooms, walking in and out of classes they do *NOT* belong in and just walking in and out of the building as if it is a regular day. A fight breaks out during 9$^{th}$ period. Students are running around as wild as can be even with the principal standing right there watching all of them. He is yelling for them to stop and go to class, but the students are ignoring him. They do this because they know there are *NO CONSEQUENCES*. How does anyone learn not to touch something hot unless they get burned? Here you can do whatever you want, and you are just told, don't do that, over and over and over. It is sickening. Other students who *did not* or never acted up are now acting up because they know nothing is going to be done other than being told ***don't do that again***. Meanwhile, ***nothing*** changes. All of the situations and problems just go on and on, and on.

**March 14 -** some kid (don't know if he's a student or trespasser) taken out of the building in handcuffs. I am sure it has to do with all of the fighting going on all day every day here. A short time later a fight breaks out by my room with one of my male students and a girl. School rules state 10 days ***mandatory*** suspension for fighting both parties. They get ZONE another program that's a waste of taxpayer's money.

**March 15 -** 5$^{th}$ period 10:50, fire alarms go off. Cafeteria sensor was tripped. With the alarms always going off no one knows whether or not to leave the building or takes the alarms seriously. Kids are running around going wild. I fear for the wheelchair and all of the handicapped students.

**Bottom line -**Between false alarms and sensors we are constantly evacuating the building. Sadly, since I've been here, this is the 2$^{nd}$time the school purchased a new fire alarm system.

During the evacuation time outside the kids were acting up as usual. Not all. One kid in particular jumped up on and punched a car. I watched a history teacher Mr. Kott and the history department head (name omitted), approached the kid. Instead of denying it or apologizing because he was caught, he started acting up and carrying on more with all that street BS. Whatever was said, Mr. Kott told him he was lying. The kid in an act of intimidation got right into Mr. Kott's face. The kid kept screaming, swearing, cursing and threatening Mr. Kott but was also trying to get away. When his previous acts of intimidations didn't work the kid jumped up and got so close to Mr. Kott's face you could barely squeeze a piece of paper between them once again all an act of intimidation. Mr. Kott did NOT back down, and the kid started yelling yeah, yeah, what you going to do you can't do nothing…I'm a student. The history department head chairperson told me to hurry up and get a security guard. THAT SAYS IT ALL! Where did he learn this? HE LEARNED IT RIGHT HERE AT JFK HIGH SCHOOL IN PATERSON, NJ! Furthermore, the kid was right, *NOTHING* was done about it.

**Mar 16 -** gang fights all day and I mean exactly THAT! One of my students (name omitted) was attacked by a kid with a bat. THIS IS ALL GANG RELATED - BLOODS & CRIPS. There are so many people inside the building that do not belong here. This too would never happen if the school followed the ID card policy. The district pays thousands of dollars for IDs but students do not have to wear them. 12:30, I saw two students being escorted out by police in handcuffs. This nonsense is still going on. Students with baseball bats including many who do not attend the school were roaming the halls walking in and out of classrooms looking for who and whomever.

**Bottom line -**Why is any of this allowed to go on and continuously being hushed up? It is so dangerous here. This is supposed to be a school. Does this sound like a school to you?

**Mar 17 -** teachers were coming up to me one in particular (name omitted) about the hallways during 2$^{nd}$ period & homeroom with kids 50, 60 or more just roaming around. No guards, no police, no supervisors, nothing. *Scary!* Later, I was talking to VP Mr. Loc* and he said the same teacher told him the same thing. I said this is not good especially on what was happening and going on all day yesterday. We all fear it is about to erupt here because of yesterday. He said he was going to get on it right away. I have never seen it this bad. Kids, gangs in hallways all day long and allowed to go about their business as if this is normal. Plus, the cut office is working overtime (at taxpayers' expense) to process all of the cuts. The district administrations answer, BLOCK SCHEDULING. Meanwhile it is all hushed up.

**March 20 -** fights all during 3$^{rd}$ period, with girls and one ended up hitting a cop.

**Later,** another fight with students and a security guard.

**Then,** 7$^{th}$ period, 12:15, Fire department was here? Found out there was a 3$^{rd}$ party bomb scare, whatever that means. We never evacuated the building.

**Mar 22 -** CAREER DAY, what an F'ing disaster. It's just another excuse for the kids to roam the building, go berserk and unchallenged. More nonsense to take away from any type of positive means of education for those who want to obtain an education so the district and school can say, we have career day. It's a JOKE. All that's going on today is students coming and going, walking in and out classrooms as they please as if they were saloons. If they do not want to be where they are assigned, they tell us they don't want to be here, walk out and go where ever. The halls are jam packed with students.

**CAREER DAY-** most of my students who are 15, 16, 17, 18, 19 and 20 years old do NOT have a job. Nor do they want one. However, there are those who want to learn, want to further their education and don't just want a job but a career. Unfortunately, with the 100s of students in this building that do NOT want to do anything positive and productive take away *ALWAYS* and ruining everything for those who do.

**Mar 22 -** had a meeting in the library pertaining to restructuring/block scheduling. It turned into another bitch session. However, (name omitted) the presenter did try to keep on track and stick to the point of the meeting. Unfortunately, the teachers who acted like the very same students they complain about kept complaining. I did learn something to ask and write later on. With this change (the third one) and now it is for block scheduling, what will happen to the people who are here now saying this is great stuff and it will work? We've had two other organizations here already and they both left. Today, we have **Larry Green Bush with the Center for NJ Center Coalition of Essential Schools.** Basically, three organizations have been here to help with restructuring and God knows at what cost to the taxpayers. How long will these people last?

**Bottom line -**All that is needed is discipline, have students follow and obey rules and have control of our schools instead of the inmates running the asylum. This district just wastes taxpayers' dollars.

**Mar 23 -** FIGHTS ALL DAY LONG. One of my seniors (name omitted) from 7th period was thrown out of school. I don't know the reason why. Then about 2:25 a big brawl broke out. When I walked out of the building, I saw kids sitting and standing on teachers' cars. I recognized one of the cars and who it belonged to. By the time I got ½ way to the car the kid jumped off and ran. As I was walking to my car, more and more kids started gathering around then all hell broke loose. Two police cars pulled up with sirens on. I attempted to pass through this massive mob of students as they were still carrying on and defiantly keeping me from getting through. The police and security were just watching doing nothing because they can't do anything until *after* I get hit, hurt or worse. Then they can do something!

**Mar 20 - April 3,** every day, I have been taking walks during and 4th period to the 2nd floor, just to see what everyone is talking about. NOT one student is in their classes. The hallways are PACKED, filled as if you're at Times Square on New Year's Eve. You can barely get through and anticipating getting wacked. Once the principal came back from sick leave, she jumped on it right away. It is disgusting and to think, block scheduling is to help. Oh my God, are we in trouble!

**Apr 3 -** I saw a number of students escorted out of school by police in handcuffs today. With everything that has been going on inside and around JFK nothing is on TV, radio and or in the newspapers.

**Apr 3 – 6 -** nothing but FIGHTS all day long every day, boys and girls. The lunchrooms/cafeterias are a disaster. It is unbelievable. **Thursday, April 6, 2006,** there was such a brawl and several of them at the same time in the front cafeteria, that they could NOT open up on time because the commotion and fighting going on. They needed to clean up of all the mess. The place is always messy but NOT like this. It was filled with food, milk cartons, bottles of all types of drinks, paper, wrappers, textbooks, notebooks, pens, pencils everything you can think of and could be thrown was all over the place. It is a garbage dump inside this building. I do NOT understand why the administration continually allows this behavior to go on. It is progressively getting worse and the police have to stand there and do nothing UNTIL it finally erupts then they are allowed to get involved.

**Apr 6 -** a student's mother came in. The first thing she said, "I don't like the fact that you told other people that my daughter is a bad influence." I said, "Yes I did, and your daughter is a bad influence with everybody." I told them ever since their daughter started hanging out with your daughter she has been cutting and getting into trouble. Once again, their defense is to always try to put the teacher on defense. It didn't work with me. I had to laugh. She brings her mom in attempts to intimidate me and saying I am picking on her. Just a few weeks ago, her daughter was screaming how much she hates her mother and hope she F'ing dies. I want to kill her. I hate her that F'ing bitch and on and on in my class in front of all the students and at the top of her lungs. June 19, 20 & 22 entries are a continuation to the above student.

**9th period**, fire alarms go off. There was a fire on the 2nd floor boy's bathroom by room 217, (History/Social Studies Wing). Just as I predicted no one knew what to do. Meaning, no one believes it was real and should they evacuate the building. The entire hallway/wing area was filled with smoke. Mr. Loc*, a VP, asked me to go up to the 2nd floor and get the student in the wheelchair. However, when I got up there, I did not see or find any student in a wheelchair. I got a security guard's walkie-talkie to let Mr. Loc* know right away. SCARY! Later, I happened to be standing next to the principal when she was talking to Mr. Loc*. He told her Mr. Bonora called and said there hasn't been any toilet paper in that bathroom. She said "well, there won't be any toilet paper in that bathroom for now on." That's because toilet paper was used to start the fire. Nothing was on TV or in the news?

**Bottom line -** I do not blame her, but the bad kids always spoil it for all of those good kids. *AGAIN!* If students were not allowed to be in the halls this would NOT happen or as much. This place is getting worse and worse. It is actually very dangerous. I am a little skeptical being in the hallways at all now.

**Apr 25 -** during HR 9:07 fire alarms goes off again. We had to evacuate the building. False alarm again! Students wedged something into the sensor to set the sensor off again.

**Apr 28 -** 8th period, 1:29 students deliberately set off sensor again in the boys' bathroom by cafeteria.

**May 1 -** there was a stabbing out by the trailers. There was *nothing* in the newspapers, on TV or radio. I believe everything is hushed up because this is a State Run and Operated School District.

**May 2 -** I was absent May 1st and didn't know about the stabbing until today. I realized something happened because security was checking students with metal detectors. Once again, only AFTER a situation happens. We will see how long this will go on. More than likely it will end today.

Mr. Madjar told me they have processed over 60K cuts. And the bin, where teachers place the slips to be processed is constantly full all day long.

**May 9,** 4th period 9:59, fire alarm goes off. We evacuated the building. There was a fire in room 235. Fire department came. Someone placed a pepper filled with lit matches behind the heater.
While we were all outside during the evacuation, it was so bad. The students were out of control.

**May 11 -** what a disaster, kids are all over the place. They do NOT go to class on time if at all. In fact, the principal asked three girls to come on and get to class please. They just ignored her. I waited about a minute and I asked them. In fact, a young man joined them and they (all 4) ignored me. I asked them again followed with a please. It was if I said nothing. The principal then said again for them to move on and get to class. Once again they ignored her. I say it again, if students ignore the principal and get away with it, how do you expect teachers to have any authority? Furthermore, if students can act this way in the hallway with the PRINCIPAL of the entire school what do they think goes on in the classroom.

During 8th period Mr. Pro*, a TAP, came running in, right through my room and out my back door. Later that afternoon, he explained he saw some kids walking out the building towards the buses with a baseball bat on the video monitor in security office. He realized my room has a back door and was the best way to get out there in a hurry. He ended up running right into them. While I was waiting to sign out, I saw four kids handcuffed and escorted out of the building by police with one officer carrying the bat. THANK YOU somebody didn't go to the hospital or the morgue today.

**May 12 -** 9th period fire alarms went off. This time smoke smell was emanating from the elevator. I went downstairs to shut the power off to the elevator. When I came back up, VP Mr. Loc* asked me to go up to the 3rd floor and help him remove one of the wheelchair students. However, I was not allowed to bring the student down. The VP said we have to follow procedures and have the fire department ONLY bring him down. This is ridiculous because by the time the fire department arrived and got to the 3rd floor, it was a good 10 minutes maybe longer.

You're going to tell me an administrator would say ok, check on my child and wait, we have to follow procedures? What procedure allows students to roam hallways, stairwells, hang out in bathrooms and not have to go to class, all day, and every day, all year long?

I told them if it was a really bad situation, I would have done everything in my power to get that child and any child out as quickly as I can. I do NOT want a child's death on my hands or conscience because of someone who doesn't work here and or ignores what really goes on here because this scholar wrote a procedure! I later learned from Mr. Pro* a TAP that this is DISTRICT POLICY.

**May 22 -** just as I walked in the building 6:58 the fire alarms went off and everyone who was already here had to evacuate. I found out it was the sensors in the cafeteria. The secretary called the Fire Department, but they were already in the building by 7:04 am.

**FIGHTS, BRAWLS** all day long. I haven't been writing them down. I am so disgusted cannot believe this just goes on and on every day and getting worse. Everything is hushed up.

In 8th period, I received a new student. I asked him what school did he come from. He replied Eastside. I found out he lost credit at Eastside due to fighting, suspensions and too many days absent. I don't understand, how he is allowed to come and attend JFK? Eastside & JFK are in the same school district. He fails, gets kicked out of one school, walks a few blocks and goes to another in the very same school district and starts NEW! It's almost JUNE and he gets a clean slate after 9 months of school is completed? There are only a few weeks of school left in this year! Are you freaking kidding me? How can this happen and keep going on? Where is the punishment, the teaching of following rules and consequences? This too I assume is part of no child left behind?

**May 26 -** is the senior picnic day. UNFREAKINBELIEVABLE, who walks in? The very same student from entries, Jan 17& 31, Feb 2, who was kicked out of school, forced to be placed on bed side because of all the problems he caused, with fighting, gangs, being stabbed and all of the VIOLENCE he constantly brought inside the building. And after all that, he is allowed to attend the senior picnic? As always, NO LESSONS LEARNED. That is why things never change and just keep getting worse here.

**6th period** kids throwing firecrackers in the cafeteria. No one does anything about it. No one was caught? How can that be when there are so many security people and a VP in the cafeteria at all times because it's so bad? First of all, firecrackers are AGAINST THE LAW IN NJ! I know the philosophy here. There are only a few more days left of school, just ignore it!

**6th period** again another BIG FOOD FIGHT. Kids running out of the cafeteria carrying on, screaming, swearing, cursing, pushing shoving and throwing stuff all over. It is now escalating throughout the entire hallway. And to think this is just a ½ day of school. This place is so disgusting.

**Today** I received a 3 or 4-page handout, Titled: "CREDIT RESTORATION." It's a list of (62) students (names and grades) who lost credit and will now have their credit restored. Many are my students who are constantly absent, suspended and do nothing when they are here.
*Questions:* Why did they lose credit in the first place? What did they do to earn or get their credit back?
*Obviously*, they did NOT earn my credit back. I don't know of any program or necessary qualifications that were met. They can still receive an F for a final grade to their classes. However, that means NOW they are eligible not only to get credit back but to attend summer school.
*\* If they can't pass the course in 10 months and did absolutely nothing, how can they pass a course an accelerated version in 4 weeks in summer school?*

**Bottom line** -Like I always say, *ANYONE CAN GET A DIPLOMA HERE!*
You don't have to earn it, or deserve it, but you will get it and especially Special Ed students. When I say especially Special Ed students, I mean those who are classified because they are constant discipline problems, habitual cutters, who have poor attendance, DO NOTHING but cause problems, start fights and are major disrupters. The district allows this to go on.

**May 26, 12:10** - 8th period fire alarms go off. It was pulled by post 11 & 12, Social Studies wing, next to a security guard. Everyone had to evacuate the building. Fire department came. **Approximately 12:35**, 25 minutes later I was asked by VP Mr. Loc* and Dave* the security guard to assist bringing a wheel chaired student down from the 3rd floor. I couldn't believe it, students and teachers where still nonchalantly leaving the building. This is so dangerous. I hope I'm NOT here to be a witness or become a victim.

**May 31** - we had a meeting in the auditorium at 3:15, with an assistant superintendent and the superintendent to fill out a form on what we think they should be looking for in a new principal at JFK? I had to laugh. All we need is anyone who is allowed to do their job and to have all of the students follow the rules in the teachers and student's handbook. Just a waste of time with another BS meeting!

**Jun 1** -kids throwing firecrackers and smoke bombs all day on 2nd floor. No one is ever caught.

**7th period 12:35**, fire alarms go off, pulled in basement. Everyone had to evacuate the building. However, some on the 3rd floor never left and stayed in class. Fire department came. False alarm again! It just continues day after day WHY?

**Jun 2 - 8th period 1:13,** fire alarms go off again this time out by TCUs (trailers). Still had to evacuate the building again. Fire department came. 10 minutes or better after the alarms first went off teachers & students are still strolling out talking as if they are leaving for the day.

**Again, between 8th & 9th** periods, fire alarm goes off. We evacuated the building AGAIN! False alarm again! It was pulled down in basement by the auto shop again. Once everyone is back in the building it is nothing less than chaos. No student is in class. Hallways are filled with students walking and running around playing. Teachers, security and administrators are telling students to go to class. Think about it, WHY would they go? It is just words; there are no consequences, so they do NOT care. Which brings me to write this; after a few more minutes all you hear is nothing but firecrackers going off. The hallways are filled with smoke and the rotten scent of stink bombs going off all over the 2nd floor.

Speaking with Ms. Conscientious*, I learned there is already and again serious MONEY PROBLEMS. This superintendent supposedly has the district in a shambles already. Millions are already missing and to think the new superintendent has NOT been here a year. Governor Corzine refuses to give Paterson Board of Ed anymore money. I asked her, why isn't any of this in the newspapers. She laughed. Isn't the state running everything? How can people NOT know and allow this to go on?

**Bottom line** -The state took over this district and has made it worse in *every capacity*. They want to get rid of teachers because of the money problems yet hire more people to work in central office?

**Jun 5** - kids setting off firecrackers a pack at a time. The place is filled with smoke and the smell of stink bombs going off all day on the 1st floor. Meanwhile the administration still allows kids in the hallways.

**June 6** - approximately 12:15 smoke/stink bombs. It's the same crap as yesterday. However, I happen to overhear the principal and a TAP discussing the situation as hundreds of students are all running around, screaming, yelling and acting up right in front of them. The TAP says to the principal, all the Special Ed students were all given their credit back and so they are NOW acting up.

**Jun 12 - 16 WEEK OF FINAL EXAMS**. Each class is 120 minutes long. It is a joke. Kids are in the hallways instead of taking their exams all period. It doesn't matter, they will still pass. I am watching the principal standing there telling students to get to class. On several occasions she called students to come over so she could speak to them, basically just to ask them where they belong. Only for them to turn their backs, walk away and be ignored. While others were making rude comments and remarks, such as yeah, why don't you go to hell, shut up, you're not my mother and if they are further down the hallway, yell 'F YOU, etc.? Even my students said Mack, why don't you go out there and help her. I said what for? If they don't listen to the principal, why would they listen to me? The kids said she heard me and gave a dirty look. I said back to the kids, well, it's the truth.

**Bottom line-**Final Exams are 120 minutes which is a joke! Students don't go to class which is only 40 minutes? If administrators want to pass a kid, they pass them especially if they're a senior and passed the state exam.

My question is this if you don't have to do anything and still can get a diploma, why are there so many students dropping out of JKF? As I said before, we graduate approximately 300 students each year. Even that number is fixed, and deals are made. Meanwhile every September we get approximately 1000 new students (freshman) each year. That is NOT including repeating freshman. So we are talking about 70% plus dropout rate.

The State Takeover, Run and Operated School District has been here for 15 years and the dropout rate, failing students and low graduation rate hasn't changed but they hand out high school diplomas as if it's candy on Halloween! So, the next time you ask yourself how did they graduate high school and they don't know anything, now you know!

**Jun 19** is a ½ day session. Students are supposed to attend class, but they don't. They are in the hallways playing around. Security, principals, teachers are telling them to move, go to class, and they just ignore, talk back, curse at them, give them the finger and continue to gather around more in defiance. Only a few of my students showed up and not one was a senior. Students think the cut office is closed, but it's ***not.*** Teachers refuse to write cuts anyway knowing darn well nothing will be or was done about it. I'd like to know why there's a week of school left, and students don't have to show up and ***nothing*** is done about it? So much for school having to be in session for 181 days for students!

Talking with a Home Economics teacher, she was telling me about a student she had last year and passed. He was placed in her class again this year late into the 3rd marking period and he didn't do well either. The teacher was quite upset and concerned. However, she ended up giving him a D for his marking period grade. She went to the student's guidance counselor to see what grade this child had the other marking periods so she could calculate his final grade. The teacher was instructed to just pass him. Even the teacher said what did this child learn? A student can have problems with a teacher, leave a class they are failing late into the 3rd marking period, be placed in another class, fail that class too, and will pass for the year, because the teacher is now *told* to pass him for the year? She was confused, upset and couldn't stop shaking her head. We both said anybody can get a diploma here. She said what can I do, but do what I am told. I told her this reminded me of a student I had years ago. The very same thing, a failing senior left weeks before the end of the school year to have a baby and was placed on bedside and voila, she graduated! Failed my class all year and in a few weeks on bedside not only passes for the entire school year, (meaning my grades were changed) she also graduates. WONDERFUL! I now wonder what will happen with two other students I have this year. Now because of what happened with this teacher I decided to check.

**The notes below are from the student in April 6 entry and an excellent example how we reward poor and unacceptable behavior.**

### *FIRST MARKING PERIOD:*
Absents (13)    Cuts (0)    Lates (1)
- Had 14 assignments and did only one.
- Four tests/quiz, passed only one

1st Marking period grade (D- a gift)    End 1st Marking period.

### *SECOND MARKING PERIOD:*
Absent (16)    Cuts (6)    Lates (9)
- Had 11 assignments and did only 1.
- Three tests/quiz (including Mid-term) failed them all.

2nd **Marking period (NC) = No Credit. Student lost credit for the year for all classes.**

### *THIRD MARKING PERIOD:*
Absents (21)    Cuts (5)    Lates (8)
- Had 14 assignments and did 1.
- One test / quiz and failed it.

3rd **Marking period (NC) = Receives no grade.**

### *FOURTH MARKING PERIOD:*
Absent (4)    Cuts (1)    Lates (6)
- Had 3 assignments and did none.
- May 2nd signed out of my class and went to Spanish
- **As of May 2 a grand total of Absences (54)    Cuts (12)    Lates (24)**

The above student was 11R, meaning a repeating junior and had lost credit back in February for poor attendance and cutting. She got her credit back and lost it again. She got it back again. She lost it again. This went on all year. Guess what happens, all of a sudden in June, she is a SENIOR and graduated.

**Jun 20** - I checked the computer to see what final & overall grade she receives for the year. She received an **A** for the *4th marking period*, **F** for the final exam because she did not show up and a **D** for overall grade for the year! Is this what is meant by *NO CHILD LEFT BEHIND?* How can anyone fail 3 and ½ marking periods, get transferred in **May** and pass for the entire year? I spoke to her guidance counselor and she said her Spanish teacher was *told* to give her a **D** for the year? They *are* going to let her graduate too. I spoke to Ms. Queenie* who approved this. Her reply/remarks were, it's the in best interest of the school, and we got her out of here. I screamed at her, are you out of your mind? How is giving her a high school diploma and especially if she didn't complete her courses, didn't do any work, has all these days out of school, cutting all of her classes is in the best interest for the school? The school is paid by TAXPAYER'S. You just screwed over the taxpayers. This is wrong and you are allowing this to happen. What is wrong with you people and walked away. Only to find out that Ms. Queenie*, did the same thing to many other students that very same week.

Every day she was in my class it was a disaster. She was a problem with all of her teachers. She did not want to do assignments/projects, constantly wanting to leave, refusing to put away her cell phone or playing with other toys, such as a yo-yo, blowing up condoms, constantly asking for tape, magic marker that she didn't even need, beyond excessive with foul language, to me and everyone, nasty dirty, disgusting remarks and hand gestures, over the top bad attitude and behavior, anything and everything she could do to interrupt, distract my students from doing their work, telling me what I can and cannot do, she doesn't have to listen to me or do what I say and it went on the entire time, every day and all period.

**On Jun 22,** her guidance counselor told me that she ***demanded to graduate***. She was absent from school over 80 days and was complaining that she has Drs. notes. First of all, 20 days absent is the school policy limit. Not 20 days absent PLUS doctor's notes. We found out that she altered the notes. The counselor said she changed it to say 25 days. The counselor herself was very upset and talked to Ms. Queenie*, an administrator for Special Ed, saying, "What kind of message are we sending? Other kids will do the same. Nothing is being taught or learned here. This is another way of encouraging poor social behavior." She said the exact same stuff I said to Ms. Queenie*. However, Ms. Queenie's* asinine remarks were, "she is not getting away with anything, life will take care of her and it will be always difficult. We (meaning the school) have many kids who are sophomores and above that are Special Ed and are 20 years of age. We (meaning the administration) want to get them out instead of keeping them here longer, disrupting classes and the school in general." I said nothing. I looked at her and just shook my head and under my breath I said unfreakinbelievable!

I was also told today by one of the principal's secretaries, that every student and parent that complained to the principal because they were NOT going to graduate, for whatever the reason, is NOW graduating. The Paterson Public School system is wasting taxpayers' dollars and killing society with graduating so many students who are not prepared and so undereducated, just for the sake of statistics.
***WE ARE RUINING A COMMUNITY, A STATE, AND AN ENTIRE NATION!***

**On July 26,** I was driving and saw the auto-shop teacher, so I stopped. He informed me about the above student. He said a social worker came to see him at the end of the school year and wanted to know if he would change her grade (he had a great deal of problems with her too). He said, "NO!" He said the social worker said good and that she was only following orders from Ms. Queenie*. He said the student came to class in September, started to cut in October, in November she never came back until around April and then went missing again for the rest of the year. He said, NO, NO WAY, will I change her grade. I found out they changed her grade and without his permission!

In the meantime, one of my female students (name omitted) was NOT allowed to graduate or even walk with her class because she was shy a couple of points with her SRA (Senior Review Assessment). According to her, a teacher didn't tell her that she had to take a test over in order to graduate. Last thing I heard about this student was the day before graduation, the principal said NO, she could NOT even walk with her class because that's the law. Can you imagine? That's the law! Isn't being out of school more than 20 days a year against the law? Isn't passing your classes in order to be promoted and graduate the law? Isn't changing a student's final grade without having written approval and signature of those teachers against the law? All of a sudden, the principal wants to *"FOLLOW THE LAW!"*
What went on inside this building all day, every day, all year, wasn't this all against the law?

**Jun 22** - 144 students are graduating because of SRA. If 300 students are graduating that's between 47% & 48% because of SRA, NOT the state exams.

Gangs of kids all over the school grounds, the park and side streets starting trouble. Several students who are on the soccer team were in the park practicing were jumped. I called security, cops, the principal and Mr. Madjar their soccer coach. I had the kids stay with me in my room. Later a cop brought in one of the kids who was jumped. The kid was alright, but you could tell he was really ruffed up.

***GRADUATION DAY!*** The superintendent of schools showed up for graduation ***45 MINUTES LATE***. What kind of message does that send to ANYONE? Plus, he has a driver/chauffer?

**Jun 23** - last day of school, Mr. Loc*, a VP, asked if I wanted to attend some sort of meeting or conference pertaining to (I think) block scheduling. Point is-- can you imagine--last day of school we are asked to send two people from each department to attend this meeting? You would think a little more planning on their part would be in order, especially when the last day of school many teachers have already made plans for the summer. I believe the district does this (only guessing) to say later on, well we (the district) asked but the teacher didn't want to participate. No one wants to go to a meeting in the first place. Lastly what's the point? You can train me and other teachers on what to do, but the district is still going to do the same thing. It is just a show!

**Jul 26** - Headline-Channel 12 News, "Schools in NJ are Safer," Less Violence, Vandalism, etc. *Not true*. I realize they are only reporting the information they receive but I can tell you it is all false.

**REASON** - The administration does under reporting. This is where the hushing up of everything comes into play. Keep it quiet; do NOT write anything up, no paper trail less violence, less vandalism, no suspension for any of these infractions equals false information. They may be filled out however, if nothing comes of it, eventually they're lost. Old military rule of thumb, if it isn't written down, it never happened! If all the incidents that go on inside here were reported they would shut this place down, but they can't because the Paterson Public School District is Run and Operated by the State of New Jersey. If the actual documentation and paperwork were filed, you can guarantee their "STATISTICS" would be off the chart! QUESTION, isn't pulling of false alarms and bomb scares considered VIOLENCE?

**Aug 8** - Interesting in less than two weeks after Channel 12 reports, "SCHOOLS IN NJ ARE SAFER," the HERALD NEWS reports, front page "PATERSON BEARING ARMS." About how students carry weapons to school because it is dangerous. Statistics are questionable, because as I just said above, the administration does not report *ALL* the violence and vandalism. (Newspaper article is on pages 43 & 44).

**Aug 16** - one of the secretaries told me that many teachers like myself were complaining to the principal about students having their grades changed without their (teachers) permission and that it is illegal. I was also told that the principal changed them because the dropout specialist was complaining the students and their parents are all upset because they were NOT graduating. AND it would NOT make the dropout prevention program look good. You can't make this stuff up!

## SCHOOL YEAR 2006–2007

**September 1, 2006,** first day of school for teachers. The morning started with a video from the Superintendent. In the video he mentions a "LEADERSHIP TEAM." They will be involved with, Curriculum, Safety & Finance. I find this funny, actually disgusting. It's the same thing but a different name. *Safety, JFK, is a disaster. Rules are never enforced and everything that happens inside here and especially is hushed up and goes unreported. *Finance, this is sad. Remember the following entries? February 20, newspaper article, "Corruption & Defrauding," April 4, millions missing and more than what the entire state of NJ needs because of flooding and June 2, more money problems. Plus, this is the 2nd year we have not had a principal. Last year our principal retired, and a VP became acting principal. Unfortunately, she was injured and was out for several weeks. The retired principal became a substitute principal until the interim principal returned. From what I understand he was paid $500 a day.

We still do not have a new principal. So, our substitute principal last year will continue to be principal until they find a "SUITABLE PRINCIPAL." In 2 years, the superintendent and all of the assistant superintendents cannot find a principal? We still only have one VP and short three. So, the district is not

paying (saving) for a principal and three other VPs and their benefits. I am starting to see a pattern here. It looks to me, (only guessing here) as if it is planned to make up for lost, missing or the lack of FUNDS?
(Continues on September 5, 2006, first day of school for students.)

### *Continuing from September 1st*
During our meeting in the auditorium, Ms. Gerace* an assistant superintendent was telling us that things are to change here in Paterson and JFK. Oh, I have never ever heard this before. She said there will be higher standards to be set, met & raised. And that NO student will just be passed and moved on or to graduate. In fact, her exact words were, "if they were my child I would not accept" mediocrity. This is disgusting, especially when this very same administration deliberately arranged and changed the grades of so many students at the end of the year so they would not only pass, but be able to graduate and receive a High School Diploma to make themselves look good statistically. The BS is already flying?

Next, she says there is "NO MORE WHOLE SCHOOL REFORM." I can't even imagine the amount of money that was spent and now wasted. It has to be astronomical. Once again, taxpayers get screwed.

Another comment she made was all high schools throughout the entire country have the same problems. BS! There is no way I will believe that. If they were, then why are we LAST when it comes to ranking?

**September 5, 2006,** first day of school for students and already we have problems because students' schedules were not ready.

Today students were originally supposed to go to HR for 2 hours and 8 minutes then follow a simple schedule for the day. However, because students did not have their schedules other than lunch, they remained in HR all day.

Getting back to FINANCE, because there is still no principal, we have the substitute principal and the assistant superintendent both here as principals. Also here were the superintendent and it seems every supervisor from the district. Due to poor planning, all of these supervisors/administrators are NOT at their regularly assigned place of work. So much for having a "FINANCE COMMITTEE." On top of that the students were out of control. It was shear chaos here. Already the building was lost.

To make things worse, students will not receive their schedules again tomorrow. Once again students will remain in their homerooms. However, department heads will make arrangements to have teachers come in and teach *GENERIC* lessons. This too is BS. This is so the administration can say there was school, and classes were conducted. Adding to the problems, many of our kids need to take the bus to and from school. In order to get on a bus, they need to have bus tickets. However, students CANNOT have bus tickets unless they show their schedule. Soooo, students still don't have their schedules and will NOT receive a bus pass/ticket. Not only are the student inconvenienced so are their parents. Number one priority for the first day of school is to be READY. That's what every teacher would say to their students. This is INEXCUSABLE, not to be ready, prepared on the first day of school for the reception of new and returning students! Furthermore, the administration does not know *when* the schedules will be completed.

**NOTE OF INTEREST:** -September 1, 2006, the first day back for teachers and *our* schedules weren't ready. However, we did receive them later that day and the majority of them were all fouled up.

**Sept 6 -** no change, no schedules, no classes.

**Later today,** students finally receive a schedule. However, it is NOT for block scheduling. It is the same type of schedule as last year, which was completed in (4) days! The administration just threw anything together as a schedule so students can start school. Sadly, there are still so many students that do not have a schedule while others have an absolutely ridiculous one. One student, a senior, a good student with good grades showed me her schedule. She has a 10-period day. She starts at 7:30 and gets out at 3:10. She has passed all of her necessary courses including HSPA. She should have a shorter schedule and or placed in a work study group because this young lady works after school.
**And it starts,** today, two students were arrested for mugging and stealing a student's cell phone.

**This evening** there was segment on Channel 12 News about JFK, titled "NO SCHEDULE." They reported, students were to stay in homeroom all day and did nothing. Supposedly some teachers tried to conduct a generic class unfortunately it was a disaster.

During the interview, the superintendent said it is a scheduling SNAFU. (SNAFU means, Situation Normal All "Fed" Up). He said it was because of electives being scheduled. NOT TRUE, the scheduler asked for help long before the end of the last year school. The superintendent said he apologizes for any inconvenience. He is the one responsible for all of the problems. However, today the school was so out of control. Students were already hanging out all over the building instead of being in class.

**Sept 7** - students and teachers have yet to receive updated schedules. However, by the middle of the day, we shop teachers received a mock schedule. It's the same schedule as last year's. We were told it will be used only for the 1st marking period. Hopefully by that time administration will have the schedules completed. Think about it, kids are without any type of regimented schedule and accounting for their attendance. These days give more reasons for students to cut, not to come to school and because they are not in school more reasons for them to get into trouble, injured or god forbid worse.

The scheduling officer needed and asked for help last school year only to be ignored. And the Superintendent says it only a computer glitch? The scheduling officer worked his tail off and was coming in and on his own free time (no pay or compensation because district administration refused to compensate him) trying to fix and figure out how to get things running and working. This is an EXCELLENT example of poor leadership, support, and management by central office.

Bottom line - staff and students lost a full week of school. In less than a month we will be administering the HSPA. So, if students do not do well, and especially if it's by a few points how do we know by losing this time did NOT have an impact or an effect on their score? Parents should be complaining. Friday students were outside protesting and not about having no schedules or just sitting around doing nothing. They were protesting and more concerned about the school lunch. The seniors have last period lunch and by the time they get to cafeteria there is very little left to offer and what is there is crap and cold.

**For the last 2 years**, the district was supposed to be preparing for this day which has turned into a lost week so far. The district spent millions bringing in guest speakers, setting up in-services, training, workshops, sending faculty members (with pay during summer months) and administrators all over the state and country to visit other school, setting them up with hotels, food vouchers, printing papers & pamphlets etc. etc. and not to mention those who were supposed to come in assist and help with the smooth transition into block scheduling.

It has come to my attention that the scheduling officer and principal documented and kept records every time they contacted the superintendent about needing help with scheduling only for it to fall on deaf ears.

**Sept 11** - one of my students from last year came to see me. We were laughing and talking then he said, I don't understand it Mack, I passed. I did absolutely nothing, cut classes and they still passed me. He also said that's nothing a friend of his never went to class after the 2nd marking period. He would come to school but never go to his classes and he too passed. I asked for his name, but he wouldn't tell me.

**Sept 12** - Mr. Pro*, a TAP, was telling me about one of my students. He said he had over 100 cuts and very seldom came to class. I asked if he passed. He said he didn't know, but they gave him his credit back because he is special ed. I just shook my head and laughed.
**There are still** 100s of students without schedules. The students whose parents came in to see what in the hell is going on seem to get things straightened out right away. I wish more parents would get involved and maybe the superintendent wouldn't allow JFK high school to be so out of control.

Nevertheless, kids are in the hallways, screaming, yelling swearing, and running around, playing all day. Think about it, Ms. Gerace*, one of the assistant superintendents, is here at JFK overseeing everything and witnessing the out of control, unacceptable behavior going on and does nothing! So OBVIOUSLY, the superintendents are all aware and tell the administrators here at JFK to allow this behavior to go on. I have to guess that the commissioner of education and the Governor are also aware?

**Sept 13** - 8th Period, 1:22, fire alarms go off, evacuated building. False alarm pulled in science wing.

**Sept 18** - 10th period, 3:00, I had already left, however, I found out the school received a bomb scare and evacuated the building. A policewoman called it in. The school was trying to keep it quiet.

**Sept 19** - 7th period, it is so bad here. Kids in hallway, yelling, screaming, swearing up a storm at the top of their lungs. This place is already out of control and all the BIG SHOTS are here and they too are allowing this behavior to go on and to continue every day. The noise from the cafeteria is unbelievable. I am about 60 or 70 feet away and around the corner. The noise is like one of those documentaries on TV about prison/Pelican Island. It is unfreakinbelievable. Fights are breaking out. Police officers felt they had no control and had to use mace. Now all the kids are in the hallway because of the smell.

**Found out** today Governor Corzine sent a team to Paterson Public schools to audit the entire district & Superintendent Glascoe. It is so bad here; they are hiring all of his friends and giving them administrative positions. I was told (not sure if this is true) they're to have cars and credit cards with an expense account. What are they going to do, shut down the school district, which is run and operated by the State of New Jersey already? So they keep pumping more and more money into this system. This is just a money pit that the taxpayers keep on paying for. Furthermore, JFK still does not have a principal. However, until the superintendent acquires one, they have the retired principal as a substitute. Think about it, the principal retired August of 2005, is receiving his pension, is also supposedly hired and being paid as a suspension hearing person and now part time principal. My opinion, GOOD FOR HIM! WHY NOT? It is about working and earning a living, a virtue, a goal, and a discipline that is NOT instilled here at JFK during any school year. However, the real question is why can't the superintendent find a principal? We have so many people within our own district who are qualified? My opinion is they are probably looking for or already have a friend in mind and are waiting for him to make the necessary arrangements so they can leave and come work here.

**Sept 25** - 7th period, 12:22, fire alarm goes off, evacuate the building. False alarm!

**Sept 27** - it is soooo bad, the school is totally out of control and it is only September. All the Deans do all day long is take care of constant discipline problems. A boy was arrested for trespassing.

**Sept 28 -** I yelled, forget it, it is no use, I have tried myself, while Miss (name omitted) a child study team counselor was asking (key word "asking") and attempting to get students to move. They refused and basically ignored us. One kid came out of the janitor's closet as I was standing right next to it. When I confronted him he denied he was in there. We have no power authority and the students know this and do whatever they want. That includes vandalism, fighting, uncontrollable cutting, walking in and out of classes they do not belong in AND PULLING FIRE ALARMS.

**ALSO TODAY** I spoke with Mr. Madjar of the cut office, as of yesterday, September 27, the cut office processed **3200 cuts**. Just yesterday alone, (only one day) they processed **1150 cuts**. September isn't even over yet. Yet BLOCK SCHEDULING will solve everything. All it is doing is dumping the mess onto the teacher's lap and will blame them for any and all failures.

**Sept 29 -** here we go…a big fight breaks out in back cafeteria. Now listen to this. Caf periods are for lunch. The fight broke out at 10:30. Caf had already been in progress for about 30 minutes. Meaning LUNCH for some students is 10:00. Many students show up for school at 9. This is absolutely ridiculous.

Back to the FIGHT, three kids were fighting. They each receive four days of ZONE. The handbook says, 10 days MANDATORY SUSPENSION. Well they were taught a lesson!

*So Many Students Still Do Not Have a Schedule.* Many students are forced to take classes they don't need. Many students don't have the classes they do need. This includes and especially with seniors. *Where are these children's parents?*

The students that don't have schedules just walk around the building all day aimlessly. No one should be in the hallways at all without a pass *and* it is the end of September, why don't students have a schedule?

**AND when schedules** are changed, teachers are no longer informed. Once again, teachers are in limbo and have no idea what in the hell is going on here anymore.

**Oct 4 -** you would not believe the kids in the hallway. It as if all three floors are on the first floor. Mr. Pro* and Mr. Lance*, our TAPs, are always either in their office or out in the halls trying to take care of all the discipline problems. It is NON-stop. They are beat, exhausted already, and school has only been open a month. It is a disgrace.

**OUR** students still don't have their schedules, or the necessary changes made in order to move onward. **During,** 3rd period, 9:40, fire alarms go off, evacuated the building. False alarm. Pulled by Cafeteria.

**Oct 6 -** security was tight today. There was a gentleman in the building this morning that had something to do with security. The atmosphere here seems to be a little better. Even the cops were moving kids along. However, once he left forget about it, the building went berserk and back to shear chaos. I feel sorry for whoever is finally chosen to become principal because JFK is already too far gone and so out of control.

**Oct 11-** BOMB SCARE, 2nd period, 8:23, evacuated building. Whoever called also-called the state police.

Big fight in caf again. Ever since we came back in from evacuation this place has gotten worse. It is a joke what goes on. You walk by the cafeteria and all you smell is cigarettes. There is NO way you CANNOT smell it. The entire caf-hallway stinks of cigarette smoke.

**Here is an example** of stupidity and how it is ignored. A kid holds onto another kid runs and then runs up the side of the wall. Mr. Costello* a VP is standing right there and all he said was "hey knock it off, what's wrong with you." The student just laughed in his face and did it again. This is why the kids act the way they do. Bottom line, NOTHING is done about ANYTHING here.

**Oct 12** – 8am, a BIG FIGHT starts. The secretaries were all amazed because they never realize what goes on throughout the rest of the building. They hear all about it but never witness any of this.

**Oct 13 -** Dave Kott, one of the cut officers told me they have processed over **9 thousand** cuts. He also said many teachers are NOT writing them so there should even be more. They feel it's a waste of time when the administration continually allows students to be in the hallways, stairwells, bathrooms, any and every place instead of being in class and nothing is being done about it? I spend at least 30 minutes each day writing cuts. Even with the cuts I have written was a waste of time. Ms. Conscientious* even said she has to write cuts for her class (SRA) and most of them are seniors who need the SRA program in order to graduate. They don't care. *THEY MEAN THE ADMINISTRATION AND THE STUDENTS!*

**The violence** today is the worse I have ever seen it. All day long there were fights, non-stop. The cafeterias were a disaster. Many kids refuse to go to the cafeteria because of all the craziness and fighting. Bottom line nothing is being done to stop any of this. It just keeps getting worse and worse.

**Oct 17 -** 5th period, 10:48, fire alarms go off, evacuated building. Alarm was pulled by auditorium, art wing side. Another false alarm! All day long kids just walking all throughout the entire building, in and out of my and other classrooms. Since the end of 8th and the beginning of 9th the entire hallways were filled to capacity with students yelling, screaming, cursing, running around, wrestling, and just hanging out playing. One of the security guard was screaming telling students to move. He was soooo angry. I have never seen him ever like this. He is usually so mellow and calm, a real nice guy. Yet the kids just ignored him. Ms. Conscientious* and I just looked at each other. Each day is worse than the last here. The school is lost. I ask cops every day if they want to send their kids here. They all laugh and say fuck no, (plus more) this place is a joke. We still have no principal. It's not as if it will make a difference?

**Oct 16, 17 & 18,** *No Absentee Sheets.* I went to office #2 to ask why we don't have them. I was told because the computers at central office are down. I replied that doesn't make any sense, we make and print them here in the building. She said again the computers are down. I believe this is a way to stop or at least slow down the documenting of cuts and all of this poor attendance. It's bad enough I spend 30 minutes a day to write cuts and lateness, but now if I do get the absentee sheets it is going to be hell to play catch up. I believe the administration wants teachers to become frustrated so they will not backtrack and do their attendance. Me, I am going to do it no matter what.

**Oct 19 -** I hadn't seen a certain TAP for quite a while, so I asked (at different times) a secretary and Ms. Conscientious* about this person. They told me this person has been out and hospitalized because of High Blood Pressure. I replied that's because all they deal with is discipline problems, problems associated with this school and all of the nonsense that goes on here all day long, every day and works their tails off keeping it HUSHED UP. It finally got to this person. They both said, yep!

**During 6th period,** fire alarms go off. False alarm again!

**And at the same time a** big fight erupts in Cafeteria. NOTHING was done about it.
Bottom line, it is disgusting here, it is just getting worse and we see no end in sight.

**Oct 24 -** *Fights All Day Again!* It is unbelievable here. No one was suspended. We wonder why students have weapons, to protect themselves?

**One of the incidents**/fights - TAP Mr. Pro* was walking a young lady, (I am using that term lightly) by the hand and all the time she is screaming and cursing at him at the top of her lungs, "FUCK YOU, GET YOUR MOTHER FUCKING HANDS OFF OF ME, YOU CAN'T TOUCH ME MOTHER FUCKER, WHO DA FUCK DO YOU THINK YOU FUCKING ARE, GET THE FUCK OFF ME YOU MOTHER FUCKER," and on and on. As they were getting closer to the security office she started to resist more and pulling away from him becoming combative, hitting, swinging with all of her might, trying to kick him and actually striking Mr. Pro* with intent to hurt him. Still yelling, cursing at him saying you can't touch students that's when the police finally stepped in to assist Mr. Pro*.

**Oct 24 – 25 -** security is tight in the morning. Security guards are using metal detectors. WHY? You know it has to be reactive, NOT pro-active. The rest of the day was a disaster. Kids in the hallways all day long! TODAY, 10/25, I received some video of 9th period. It only had sound, NO video. Also, when the fire alarms went off and we had to evacuate the building.

**Oct 25 -** Mr. Kott, a history teacher told me on **10/24,** they confiscated 24 knives and 1 *loaded* handgun. I asked if he knew the names. He said he did and won't mention them. However, the student with the handgun was Special Ed. And all of this is kept hushed up. Parents have the right to know.

**FOOD FOR THOUGHT-**They confiscated 24 knives and one loaded handgun. How many other weapons were inside here that were not accounted for and they did not know about? There should have been a "LOCK DOWN!" I wonder if this had something to do with the metal detectors *yesterday?*

**Oct 25 -** 9th period, 1:50, fire alarms go off, evacuate the building again, was pulled on 3rd floor. Fire department came. It's another false alarm.

**Oct 26 -** 8th period, 1:33, fire alarms go off, evacuated building. Fire department came. False alarm again!

**Oct 27 -** 7th period BIG FIGHT in cafeteria involving one of my students (name omitted) and some other girl. They both got ZONE. They're supposed to be suspended.

**9th period**, 1:43, fire alarms go off again. False alarm again! **Then approximately 1:55** police, security and everybody running through the hallways and out the front doors. Obviously, there was a fight or some other terrible incident going on AGAIN. It is an absolute disaster here.

**I heard today** Ms. (name omitted) was fired, because she did NOT evacuate the building. I understand her reason. She is a big woman, has a great deal of difficulty walking and with all of these constant false alarms, having to walk up and down the stairs, this time she decided to stay. I feel bad for her. This would have never happened if the school was under control.

**Nov 1 -** 6th period, 11:32, Fire alarms go off again, evacuate the building again, false alarm again! Also a student was sent home/suspended for having a steak knife. Why wasn't he arrested?

**Nov 2 -** 2nd period, 8:40 fire alarms go off, evacuate building, state police were here, bomb scare again! They called the state police again.

One of my students comes back to class escorted by Mr. Pardine of the cut office. He is back from suspension (so I thought). When I went to pick up my mail in the office, there was a returned cut slip with

that student's name on it stating he was in ZONE (10/30/06). Also written on that very same cut slip was the word, **"WEAPON."** Obviously, he was one of the kids that were caught having weapons on them on 10/24/06. See my Oct 25 entry.
According to the administration who wrote the student handbook any student/s caught with weapons on them are to be ARRESTED. ARE YOU FREAKING KIDDING ME!

**Nov 3** - BIG FIGHT, between 5th and 6th period. It was absolute chaos. No one could get through to break it up. I was going to try, but I said what for, no matter what happens I would be blamed for something. Eventually security guards arrived but stood there and did nothing. Then out of his office came Mr. Pro*. He barged right through everybody, got into the middle of it and was trying to stop and gain control of the situation. He had NO CHOICE but to plow through. The students were deliberately keeping anybody from getting through. Then police officers arrived. Students were still defiant and refused to move. A little 5' 4" woman teacher Ms. Conscientious* is now standing in the middle of the mess yelling for everyone to move, leave, but the students just ignored her. Each day here is worse than the last.

**Nov 6, 4th period, fire alarms go off again.** Evacuated building again. It seems students set the alarm off by placing a lighter or a cigarette up against a sensor in the bathroom. Fire Department was here. They said they caught the boy and he is being arrested.

**New principal** came in today. Rumors are circulating. First of all, he did say he's originally from Georgia and came here via Baltimore school system. Now the rumors! He was supposed to be here last Thursday. However, it is being said, he did not come because several of his requests were not met. **SUCH AS -** He wants a car, wants a home in the area, wants a personal assistant, wants Amtrak tickets paid for so he can go back and forth to Baltimore. If this is true, why is he being treated as if he is "ROYALTY," with taxpayer's money! **My thought is why is he here?** Why is there no one from the Paterson school district who is qualified? What were the superintendent's requirements to become a principal? However, it did turn out that the superintendent and the principal ARE FRIENDS! What did I say a few weeks ago?

**Nov 7 -** we have a new principal; however, he doesn't start until next week? The school is getting worse.

**9th period approximately 1:43**, fire alarms go off. We evacuated the building. Alarm was pulled in the basement. **10th period approximately 2:23,** fire alarms go off again. False alarm again! Alarm was pulled in a TCU. Fire department came both times.

**Nov 8, 11:18, 5th period,** I saw fire trucks and more police outside the building with all of their lights flashing. It seems someone called the State Police again with a bomb threat. It was supposedly extremely specific/descriptive. We did NOT evacuate the building. Who makes the decision not to evacuate?

**Nov 15 -** new principal is here. He seems to be a nice guy. We will wait & see if things change?

**Nov 16 -** new day nothing changes. Kids are all over the place. Like I said, meet the new boss, same as the old boss. These guys (principals) are puppets. They too are NOT allowed to do their job. Everything is hushed up and seems to remain hushed up. We CANNOT even get absentee papers on time or not at all. I believe (I do NOT know this to be a fact) because they are trying to curb the teachers from writing cuts.

**TODAY** some JFK students went to Eastside for a college day/fair. It ended up Eastside students trying to attack JFK students. In fact, when JFK students were on the bus to leave to come back to JFK, they were attacked by Eastside student who were throwing bottles at the bus. Police, security and administration were out there trying to stop this. And none of this is in the newspapers, on TV or radio.

**Nov 17 -** two boys were escorted out of the building in handcuffs first thing this morning. I have no idea what happened because so much happens here all of the time.

**LATER,** I was talking to Mr. Lou Bonora, a history teacher. He was upset because one of his female students (name omitted) became a senior. She had failed several classes last year, 2005 - 2006, including Mr. Bonora's class. She passed because the acting principal changed her grades. Mr. Bonora said she attended summer school and was giving teachers a bad time. She was going to be thrown out of summer school. This student made a comment to another history teacher, Mr. Dave Kott saying, if they (the teachers) don't stop messing with me, I will go downtown (meaning the Board of Ed Office) and get this straightened out too. Mr. Bonora was quite upset because all she did was curse teachers out, did not do any schoolwork, had 80 days of absences, had over 75 cuts, was promoted and became a senior.
I guess that's what is meant by "NO CHILD LEFT BEHIND."

**Nov 20 -** 7th period, 12:10, a riot breaks out in the center hall/foyer. It was unbelievable, guys fighting guys, girls fighting guys, just ridiculous absolute chaos. Fights were going on all over the building, including and especially inside the front caf. It was just a disaster. The entire building was a riot.

**Approximately** 12:34, two students were escorted out of the building in handcuffs by police. **Later,** two more kids were escorted out in handcuffs by police. I think one student was from my 3rd period class.

**Nov 21 -** another day of disaster. Kids, running in and out of my classroom who do not belong in my class, swearing and cursing at me. They are doing this to other classes throughout the entire building. It is absolutely out of control here and the administration does nothing to stop it.

**PLUS** our new principal is NOT in the building today. He went to some stupid meeting. He is needed here to get this place straightened out. I hope the meeting was about gaining control of the school!

**During 9th period** I dropped off cuts and spoke to Mr. Madjar about several of my students who cut class every day and nothing is being done about it. He replied one of my students (name omitted) was suspended today. I started to laugh and said that isn't going to solve anything, and they know that. They don't have to go to class or do anything and will still be passed onto their next grade or graduated. Mr. Madjar said that's not true. He said speaking with Ms. Queenie*, she vowed to him in front of many others that if a Special Ed student lost credit they will not get their credit back. I laughed, because she said the same thing to me about so many student's year after year. I asked if he got that in writing. He said no. **Then I asked Mr. Madjar** how many cuts have been processed? He replied as of 11/20, **23 thousand.**

**Nov 21 -** today the school newspaper (Vol. 42 No. 1 November 2006) was distributed. It's filled with all sorts of problems that I have been writing about. Now everything I have been saying at least for this year is documented in the school paper and written by students. Such as violence, fire alarms, no books etc.

**At 9:47,** student escorted out of school by police in handcuffs. There must be an epidemic going on.

**Nov 22 -** Pep Rally day. OH MY GOD, what a disaster. School is so bad here on a daily basis and today was worse. It's exhausting trying to explain everything and having to relive all of this again. It's as if I am still there. It is so freaking dangerous here. Martial Law should have been declared.

Dave*, a security guard, told me they're installing video cameras throughout the building. I kind of knew when he asked last week if I knew this kid. It was one of my students. Now if there are security cameras in the building obviously they HAVE to see what is going on in the hallways. Meanwhile students are still all over the building hanging out causing chaos.

**Dec 6** - students set fire to the 1st floor boys' room by rooms 117. They busted the lock to get in and set a fire. You can smell the fire throughout the entire 1st floor. I find it interesting because yesterday VP Mr. Costello* made an announcement about disregarding the fire alarms because they are being worked on. Point I am making, these alarms and sensors are real sensitive and when the fire was started, the alarms did NOT go off. Mr. Pro* asked me to fix the door so no one is able to get in without a key and permission from an administrator. The next day, my students and I did as requested.

**Dec 14** - between 6th and 7th period, girls set the bathroom on fire by the cafeteria. The fire was put out almost immediately, but the hallways by the cafeteria and the front of the building were pretty intense with smoke, screaming and running students. I helped to get and connect fans to get the smoke out of the building. Nothing was ever done about setting the fire. It was as if this is normal and accepted behavior here. Fire alarms didn't go off, fire department didn't come and we did not evacuate building.

**Dec 18** - 8th period, 1:23, fire alarms go off, first time in a while. We evacuate the building. False alarm!

**Dec 19** - I learned today yesterday was NOT a false alarm. It was a bomb threat called into the office. The principal decided to have us evacuate because teachers complained when the girls' bathroom was on fire and the area was filled with smoke. They felt we should have been told to evacuate the building because of its severity. So that is the reason why we were told to evacuate yesterday.

### INCIDENT REPORT:

**DECEMBER 20, 2006.**
Approximately 12:00pm, there were students standing in my doorway.

One or two of them were my students. I told them to get out of the doorway and the others who don't belong in the hallway to get out of here.

One young lady, wearing a pink coat started to curse at me saying, "Fuck you, I'll come in there and fuck everything up in there."

I started to walk over to my door saying "I don't know who the heck you're talking to, I am NOT your mother and father, and you're not going to talk to me like that."

All of a sudden, this young lady continues to swear saying, fuck this, fuck that, fuck you, I'll fuck you up, you don't talk about my mother.

She came flying at me and shoved me, I yelled for security, and no one was in the hallway. I was yelling at her to get the heck out of here. Eventually a security (woman) guard came attempted to subdue her. Then other security people came. This should have never happened. No student should be in the hallway at any time without a pass. She verbally attacked, shoved and threatened me.

No student for any reason should talk, threaten and or shove any teacher or JFK personal at any time.
Mr. Lee E McNulty (Room 114)

A copy of this will be forwarded to:
(I omitted the names)
- Vice Principal
- Assistant to the Principal

- Assistant to the Principal
- Security

***Guess what? Nothing was done about it. Poor unacceptable inappropriate, dysfunctional and illegal behavior is acceptable here!***

**Dec 21** - about 10 minutes into 4th period, I went up to the 2nd floor to see about securing overhead projector to a table. Oh My God, the hallways were jam packed with students not going to class. I asked the English teacher if this was a bad time. He said no, it's like this all the time. It was a disaster. He also said poor Mr. Calmete*, a VP, is going to have a heart attack. He tries to get control, but he can't. He's telling the kids to go, move, get to class and they ignore, yell, curse and swear at him then go about their business. He is all alone and has no help. I wish I had my video camera. No one would ever believe this is going on let alone being allowed to continuously go on especially with a new principal.

**Dec 22** - approximately 12:15, one of my male students (name omitted) comes into my room and says, "Mr. Mack, I just saw something fucked up. As I was going up the stairs there were two kids in front of me. One tripped and looked like a gun fell." I immediately contacted a VP. The VP came to my room and started talking to the student. He tells the student to tell a TAP. The kid goes out in the hallway and starts telling the TAP and a cop. All of a sudden, the TAP & the cop started talking to the student as if he did something wrong. They were rude and obnoxious, raising their voices, questioning him, more like interrogating him and asking him questions like, "What were they wearing?" The student replied, "A black hoody." The cop says well, that's a good description, no one wears that. He was being a wise guy because it typical of what the kids wear. Then they bombarded him with more questions; "Do you know them?" "Do you know where they were going?" I felt like screaming at them and saying NO he doesn't know where they were going, who they were or what they were doing with the gun either. But I kept quiet to see where they were going with this. Then the cop asks. "Was he Black, White, Hispanic," and then the TAP says "GREEN?" They were actually treating and talking to him as if he was garbage. I had enough, walked out of my room and went up to both of them saying, "Excuse me, hey, I told him to go talk to you guys." They stopped, quieted down, said no more and left the kid alone. I was furious. The both of them treated him as if he was a criminal.

ARE YOU FREAKING KIDDING ME!First of all, just with that little bit of information the kid gave them, there should have been "A LOCK DOWN!" I have an interview video with this student taken 1/8/07, along with info about a student having marijuana and NOTHING was done about it. So much for having LAWS about no drugs within 1000 feet of a school and ZERO TOLERANCE TO VIOLENCE!

**NOTE OF INTEREST: #1 on the above incident** -January 23, 2007, I was speaking with a teacher about the incident. He just shook his head and laughed. Then said, they want to keep it all hushed up, because if I pursued it the administration would have had to lock down the school, which is proper procedure and protocol and file a Vandalism and Violence report to the state. Then the district would be cited for being a dangerous school.

**NOTE OF INTEREST: #2, to the above incident** -Sadly, on April 16, 2007, a Virginia Tech student shot and killed 33 people. I find it IRONIC the media was saying that the college didn't follow procedures fast enough or properly. However, on December 22, 2006, a JFK student tried to be proactive and report students with a gun, and they gave the kid hell.

**Then at** 7th period 12:40, another massive fight erupts all throughout the building. It was if there was a riot going on all over the place. Police, security running outside of the building, in the cafeteria, up to the 2nd & 3rd floors, then back outside the building. You can't even imagine what it's like here today! It was a disaster. Kids were all over the place adding more fuel and confusion to the situation. It looked again like one of those documentaries where they're inside a prison and all hell breaks out. Kids all over the place in gangs. It is a disaster and dangerous here. One of my students said a student was stabbed. I do not have confirmation on that. I have him telling me that on my phone video. I have other video of that event, but when I placed the phone in my pocket it was pointing up and all I really have is sound.

We have a new principal, but nothing has changed, it is actually much worse and MORE DANGEROUS.

**THE BEGINNING OF JANUARY 2007**

**Next is a newsletter, "Pete's Pitch," notice the following:**
- 10 Million spent in 2 years for a literacy program
- Unclear on what 12,437 assistant superintendents, directors and supervisors do
- Teachers have a difficult time validating why they want to take students on a field trip.

## Pete's Pitch
*by Peter A. Tirri, President*

Ask just about any educational expert to talk about the purpose of education, and some time during the explanation the speaker will touch on the word "experiences", as in "one purpose of education is to provide the children with a myriad of experiences that they have not had." Education should open the "doors of wonder and amazement" to children. Although I am certainly not an educational "expert" I would add "to let children come into contact with a wide variety of experiences which open their minds to the whole world, rather than just the world they see every day."

We in the Paterson Public Schools have a greater challenge because our students often have limited experiences. Seeing, or touching, a pony. Going to the beach and encountering the ocean. Feeling the salt air on their faces. Viewing the Constitution, or the Liberty Bell, or getting a first person understanding of the conditions at Valley Forge or Gettysburg. Visiting Edison's laboratory, or picking pumpkins, or staring in wonder, and awe, and maybe even fear at a roller coaster.

Environment and economics often deprive our kids of these experiences. Experiences that stay with them throughout their lives, making them better rounded, and better educated individuals. Yet, this administration, who proudly declares their motto of "Children First", consistently deprives our students of these wonderful sources of knowledge.

Field trips are not only rejected, but almost frowned upon. In order to take students on a trip to the Liberty Bell, staff members have to submit reams of paper JUSTIFYING the visit. To the Liberty Bell! Puh-lease!! Even when this exhaustive and time-wasting exercise is completed, the trip will most likely be rejected because the Liberty Bell isn't in New Jersey. I've been told that the rationale is that there a plenty of things to see and do in New Jersey, so no trips outside of the state are permitted.

Hello! Does our world stop at the Jersey border? Does Governor Corzine have to steal Constitution Hall from Philadelphia, and then move it to Cherry Hill so our kids can visit it? Does Commissioner Davy have to tear down the Lincoln Memorial and rebuild it in Newark for our kids to be given the opportunity to see it?

Look, I know that we are awash in testing. NJASK3, NJASK4, GEPA, ELAS, Dibbles, DAR's, benchmarks. In the deified name of accountability we must test, and retest and test again until we sure that what we know is really true. But in "preparing" our students for all of these tests, we are forgetting, or worse, ignoring that children have to be educated, not just taught.

Education is more than testing; more than accountability. Education must not be drudgery or the imprisonment of the mind and soul. Children must be allowed to spread their wings and see, "up close and personal", the wide, wonderful world in which they live.

Yet this district does just that. Imprison children in their classrooms, condemning them to the four walls they see every ... single ... day. Day after day ... from September to June, because there is no money for field trips, or no money for substitutes, or no money for buses. Because there is not adequate educational justification for the trip. Because the documentation isn't there. Because the Governor imposed a flat budget on us.

BULL!

The money isn't there because it's been spent elsewhere. $350,000 this year for a swipe system so the administration will know if teachers are in school! $350,000 to replace $2.50 sign in books because this administration is hell-bent on catching all of the miscreant teachers who run out of school early, leaving their classes unattended.

Or because their paying salaries to 12,437 Assistant Superintendents, Directors and Supervisors whose job is to check up on each other, on the building administrators, and us. Or for the "super cop" hired to spy on staff members who have been injured on the job. Or for a new $5 million literacy program to replace the year-old $5 million literacy program purchased from the same book company.

You go on the trips to learn, to experience, and, to have some fun! That's the purpose. That's the rationale. If the District would stop paying to feed their own paranoia and insatiable need for more administration, there would be plenty of money to pay for field trips for kids.

To experience. To learn. To become educated.
"Children First!

*Peter A. Tirri*

---

P.E.A. *Advocate*     January, 2007     Page 2

---

**January 2, 2007** - Mr. Lou Bonora, a history teacher, told me he is still quite upset and disgusted on what happened with a student he had last year and how administration changed her grade without his permission/approval. (**See reference Nov 17, 2nd entry "LATER"**) He said he went to scheduling to see the grade change card. He noticed his name was signed to it but it was *not* his signature. This made him even more upset asking, "Who would do such a thing and allow this to happen?" I laughed, and said you know damn well administration would and did. He snaps back, "I wonder how many other teachers don't even know that their grades were changed and had their signatures forged on the student's card?" Mr. Bonora asked the scheduling officer who authorized this change. The scheduling officer said it came from an assistant superintendent, Ms. Gerace*. So, Mr. Bonora called Ms. Gerace* and she said she did *not* authorize the grade change.

**Jan 16** - what a day, nothing but turmoil and out of control chaos! Fights, smoke/stink bombs, kids in the hallways all day long! **3rd period 9:40,** fire alarms go off, bomb scare. **4th period 10:12,** another bomb scare. **5th period a big fight**, among girls in center hallway. **8th period1:04,** fire alarms go off again. We evacuated the building each time. The fire department came each time and they are NOT happy, because we take too long to exit the building.

**Jan 31** - Mr. O'Malley* told me that VP Ms. Princess* told him to change a student's grade which was originally NC = NO CREDIT, from an F to a D. Even though this student has *never* shown up for class.

**Feb 1** - speaking with my supervisor Mr. Calmete* 5th period. I was telling him about a student who is heavily sedated with prescription medication, and all she does is sleep. I called the mother several times and she does nothing. I contact her case social worker (name omitted), she did nothing. I spoke with another teacher Roberts*.He too is concerned, has been contacting everyone to no avail. I even went to the nurse, but nothing is being done. All this kid does is sleep. She sleeps so hard I literally have to shake her to wake her up. I said to Mr. Clement* I feel bad, because she is failing life, so I don't have the heart to fail her. I just pass her, but she does absolutely nothing. She is OUT COLD.

He said I should fail her. This way it is all documented. He said he had a student in summer school who was acting up, doing nothing causing problems and disrupting classes. Eventually, he had him thrown out. Only to be told he can't do that. The student is Special Ed and can't be thrown out and has to be readmitted. The kid did nothing, passed summer school, and got away without any type of disciplinary action. Then he said, well at least now there is a record of what happened and I'm clear.

**Feb 1** - I heard on the radio coming home from work that Camden, another state run and operated district is under investigation for writing and sending checks to dead employees for quite some time. Also on the news, Paterson school district, which is still under state control, is under investigation again for misappropriation of funds- TWO MILLION DOLLARS.

**Feb 2** - I collected and have in my files the profiles of 21 students. One in particular (*initials only*) ML, who was hardly ever in school for the last 4 YEARS, is a senior and will *graduate*. When I read their profiles with the days absent, cuts, and reasons for suspension all I could say is, *Unfreakinbelievable!*

**Feb 5** - Mr. Madjar of the cut office told me they processed **41,000** cuts. He said this is going to be the worse year for cuts ever by far.

**Feb 8** - we haven't had any heat in school all week. Today at the end of 5th period, 11:30am, students were allowed to leave the building because it was too cold and unhealthy for them to remain. However, the staff had to stay for the rest of the day. The ONLY reason students were dismissed was because someone called the newspapers and the Board of Health. Basically, the superintendent was embarrassed and forced to make the students leave or they would have had to stay in the cold building all day too. AND today was NOT as bad as the last few days. However, as soon as the students were dismissed, it became an actual riot inside the building. It was so out of control and dangerous. A minute or so after dismissal the students pulled the fire alarms (another false alarm).

**Feb 9** - the newspaper, HERALD NEWS, OUR TOWN SPORTS SECTION Front Page, *"Paterson brawl cancels girl's showdown"* continue B5Same newspaper, page C6 *"Lack of heat means early dismissal at JFK"*

Just what I have been saying all along. However, it states student and staff at John F. Kennedy High School were dismissed at 11:30 on Thursday, because of cold weather and the school's malfunctioning heating system. Not true, staff had to stay the entire day.

> **Lack of heat means early dismissal at JFK**
>
> Students and staff at John F. Kennedy High School were dismissed at 11:30 on Thursday because of cold weather and the school's malfunctioning heating system.
>
> Parents and guardians were notified of the early end to the school day with messages sent home in English and Spanish using the district's automated telephone system, said Laura Constable, district spokeswoman. Additional information was put on Channel 76, the local access educational channel, she said.
>
> The problem was caused by a failure in the control system software, Constable said. While the system was reloaded and repaired by 11:00 a.m., it takes some time to reheat. District facilities staff checked the building room by room and, as of Thursday afternoon, school was planned for today, Constable said.
>
> About six classrooms in the school were too cold for students and teachers on Wednesday, so the classes were moved to other locations, Irby Miller, JFK's principal, said Wednesday.
>
> "It was so cold, to the point where you couldn't do any work," Kesira Smith, 16, a Kennedy High School junior said. She said she wore her hat and coat all day Wednesday.
>
> Sweat was building up in the high school gymnasium, despite the heating problems, as Kennedy took on Eastside High School in a basketball game. Administrators watching the game said heat had been restored in the late afternoon.
> — *Danielle Shapiro*

A few years ago, JFK had all windows and outside doors replaced. They were not sealed properly. You can see daylight coming through. How many *millions* of taxpayer's dollars were wasted on this project?

Feb 9 - it is so bad today, meaning being out of control. Many of my students said it's so ridiculous here that they actually thought it was fun!

Feb 13 - BIG BRAWL in the cafeteria. Everybody, security, teachers, police were running into the caf, and dragging out students who continued swinging, kicking, yelling, and cursing on their way to the security room. In a matter of seconds everybody comes flying out, tripping and falling because the brawl overflowed out the door into the hallway.

Feb 13 - have video during homeroom. From 1st floor to 2nd floor. The only administrator I saw was a VP.

**Cannot conduct class today**. Students are too interested in what is going on in the hallways. The building is lost and so out of control. Not one administrator present. Students are constantly yelling out of my classroom to all of the students in the hallways that should be in class. I have to constantly stop what I am doing, tell students who don't belong in my class to leave, get out of the doorway, get out my class, you guys don't belong here. I am either ignored or as I approach some students they run to the back of my classroom, run around taunting and wanting me to chase them, while others who refuse to move from my doorway are cursing me out, telling me to shut the fuck up, mind my own fucking business, you can't tell us what to do, get the fuck out of here before we fuck your ass up.

**As I was walking in** this morning a science teacher who also works in the cut office gave a security guard a packet/bag of drugs. He told the guard he found it in the parking lot. This is so common here. A while back I found drugs on the 1st floor hallway. I gave it to a security, and she flushed it down the toilet. Everything is, has been and remains to be HUSHED UP. I wish some big shot would walk into this school unannounced and undercover to see and hear what actually goes on.

**Feb 21** - FIGHTS first thing this morning before school even started. Then there were fights all day long. *Nothing* is, was or will ever be done about it here, because administration wants everything hushed up.

**Feb 22** - Mr. Madjar showed me a student's record (I have the print out). The (student's name is omitted) a senior and 20 years old. He has 89 days absent. 5 of them excused. He has the following classes, and corresponding grades. (Mind you this is for the 2nd marking period).

| | |
|---|---|
| **Intro. to word** | F |
| **Phys. Ed IV** | NO GRADE |
| **Eng. JS 7** | D |
| **Arts Found II** | F |
| **Math JS** | C |
| **Phys Ed III** | NO GRADE |
| **Health III** | F |
| **Health IV** | F |

Notice he has two gym and health classes. He is supposed to be making up for past failing classes. You want to bet he will graduate? NJ STATE LAW STATES, no more than 20 days absent.

**Mar 2** - speaking with Mr. Madjar of the cut office, he informed me with the information he has and documented, 45% of the entire school population exceeds the state mandate/guide lines for student attendance and it is getting worse fast and by the day. Like I have said all along, now good kids who would never cut or was late to class are now cutting and deliberately coming to class late.

**Mar 6** - 2nd day of HSPA, state exam. Testing begins at 8:25. However it's 9am and I'm watching students still moseying on into the building with coffee and bags of Dunkin Donuts as if they have no place in the world to be or as if time does not matter and continue to do whatever they want. Students fill the hallways, running, screaming, swearing, cursing, doing anything and everything but going to class or testing. I have never ever seen testing conducted like this. Usually on testing days - which are six days a year, three in the fall and three in the spring - there's never anybody in the hallways. The building is always under control. However, this time, there is absolutely no control in this building. The kids are just running wild and there's nothing but fighting going on all during testing. This is a day where security is usually and supposed to be extremely tight. There is no way anyone would think that this is actually even a school. Some students are hanging out in the stairwell in the principal's wings. What does that say about who runs this building?
Is this what the superintendent and the entire district administration were waiting for so long in obtaining a principal? Geeeeeeeeeee GREAT CHOICE!

**Mar 7 -** Mr. Madjar confirmed 50K cuts have been processed. He also told me the State of NJ mandates any student who has 10 straight days of absence without an excuse is to be cut from roll and we are NOT doing that. We have between fifty and sixty kids who are in or have exceeded that category. In fact, a student left JFK over a month ago and a day or so ago a school in Georgia called asking for his records/transcript because he has enrolled there. Meanwhile, JFK still had him on roll here. Is this NOT manipulating the numbers and school's statistics? The principal said get him off roll along with all the others. They took care of it, only to be told by VP Ms. Princess* to put them back on roll. Everything the principal does or says, Ms. Princess* contradicts and either says or does the opposite. She does this at staff meetings in front of the principal. It's bad enough students run the building, but as for us teachers, I ask…who is the boss here the principal or the vice principal? We have over 50% of the school population with over 21 days absent, not including suspension and cuts.

**Mar 7 - 8:50,** during HSPA testing, a fight erupts out outside the school. Some kid was knocked out. Other kids carried his lifeless body into the building for help. I have never ever seen such nonsense, bizarreness, chaos and blatant disregard for the testing session. Kids are fighting all over the place. It is so out of FREAKIN' CONTROL AND DANGEROUS HERE.

**Mar 8 -** 9th period 12:57, time change due to testing. Fire alarms go off, evacuated building. False alarm!

**BIG FIGHT, actually a RIOT.** I have never seen so many cops and cop cars all over the place. **I have video**. The fight started inside and moved very fast outside in the front of the school. It was all girls, including their mothers. *UNFREAKINBELIEVABLE*! This nonsense had been going on all day with these same girls since the beginning of the school *testing day*. Nothing was done to prevent this. The administrators ignored and left it alone until it finally boiled over and erupted into a brawl. After it was finally broken up, these same girls are back in the hallway carrying on, screaming, yelling and swearing as they reenact the situation. No one tries to break them up or to get them moving before it erupts again. All the while teachers (me included) security, police, administrators including the principal just watched on as if nothing was wrong and this is normal. And it was all HUSHED UP!

**Mar 13 -** teachers were telling me last week, a student (name omitted) stole and took home Mr. Bill* a teacher's personal python snake. Mom told him to get rid of it. He placed it in a pillowcase and put it outside where it froze to death. The school isn't doing anything. Why wasn't he arrested for grand theft, breaking and entry? Why wasn't the ASPCA contacted about the cruelty to this snake? I learned he stole a smaller snake a few days prior to this event and the school knows about this too.

**NOTE OF INTEREST: with the above student.** I found out he is *only* getting 5 days suspension as punishment. He receives a freaking vacation which does not count against his attendance. PLUS I understand he had stolen money from the principal, the principal's secretary, and others. Why wasn't he expelled? From what I understand he spent a night in JV shelter?

**Mr. Madjar** told me to speak with Mr. Kott about one of his students who went to him about being raped or attempted rape in the school. It was all hushed up. If it wasn't for Mr. Madjar, I wouldn't have known about it.

**12:55, beginning of 8th period** fire alarms go off. We evacuated building. False alarms!

**Mar 14 -** Superintendent held a meeting in the auditorium about everything that has been going on here. The staff brought up concerns such as cutting (now over 65K), violence, unsafe school, chaos and etc. If nothing changes, it should now have been known, written down and documented! The local media and

DYFS should have been called in to hear all of this which is NEGLECT by administration and to have it all officially documented. I will bet a year's salary NOTHING will change.

**Then** 7th period, a BIG fight in caf. Security and police are dragging a kid out by his leg into the security office. A few minutes later another fight breaks out and a student from my 5th period class was dragged out. All day long nothing but fighting!

**Mar 15** -another BIG FIGHT in hallway. Yet administration still allows students to remain in the hallways causing problems long after the bell to be in class. I just don't understand them!

**In reference** to entry 3/13/07, I called the NJ SPCA 1-800-582-5979 to report the theft and death by freezing of the Python. It bothered me so I called. Someone had to speak up for snake.

Mr. Madjar told me they have processes over 65k cuts and they are not even close to processing all of them yet. They're pouring in by the 100s every day. Nothing but fights here all day long. Even my students were unruly. Something I haven't experienced much at all this year. However, with all that is allowed to go on all the students are now acting up. This school is like a jail/prison where you go in and then come out with all of the wrong things learned.

Mr. Kott a history teacher told me about a young lady. He would not give me her name but told me she was attacked in an attempted rape. He said a few days ago, she was in class and was very upset about something. So he had her escorted to the security office. For whatever reason, she walked out of the office and ended up in the back cafeteria? That's supposedly when two boys, one which was a friend of hers who she was just talking with, attacked and tried to rape her. Mr. Kott said she didn't tell him until Monday, March 12. She never revealed who the boys were. However, according to Mr. Kott she did have a BIG bruise and he pointed to the right side of the chest & throat area. Mr. Kott said he spoke with Mr. Pro* about this and learned this has happened before. Guess what? It was all hushed up. Think about it; students aren't even *safe* with THE STATE RUNNING THE SHOW HERE!

**I decided to** take pictures of all the textbooks that were thrown out of the windows by students. Then they'll say they were stolen and can't do their work. I should have taken pictures all year along. This goes on daily. Students are not held responsible for their textbooks. They don't even cover them. It's ignored and the administration doesn't care. Meanwhile, the schools and district want more and more money but no one is held responsible for allowing this waste of taxpayers' money.

**Received video** of another BIG fight. Students kept coming down gathering, instigating more problems and actually trying to prevent security and police from getting to the situation. Not one administrator present.

**Mar 19** - fire trucks were outside, I learned someone called a bomb threat. We never evacuated. A TAP, Mr. Class* said there is nothing we can do about it. The *superintendent* doesn't want us to do anything. This is what I mean the school administrators have let it get so out of control here and now they don't know what to do. For almost 90 minutes I wrote over 50 cuts. It keeps getting worse here by the day.

**Mar 30 - 5th period, 11:24,** fire alarms go off. We evacuated the building. I have pictures and video. Once we came back into the building the school was as if a riot was going on. After a minute or so another BIG fight erupts in the center hallway, all girls. Food and garbage is thrown all over the place. **UNBELIEVABLE DAY.** It was the most violent and destructive day I have ever seen. My colleagues said the same thing. Throughout the entire building there was nothing but fights all day long. Students run right out of the classrooms to either go see or get involved. Nothing, I mean nothing, is being done about any of this unacceptable, inappropriate and out of control for any place in the world behavior.

***FIRE ALARMS GO OFF AGAIN*** 5th period, 11:39. We evacuated the building again. Fights all over the place again inside and out! I received photos and video. Video shows even after we came back in how bad it was. It was worse than the last time we came back in from evacuation just a few minutes ago. You see the same kids just roaming, running around, dancing, screaming, and not going to class. Not one administrator present. You see cops running up the stairs and security running onto the elevator to go to the 2nd floor. Then another fight breaks out in the cafeteria. Tables thrown all over the place and in the air just like you see on a TV documentary about prisons. This place is exactly like that. Then it carries out into the hallways. I witness one of my students (name omitted), who is constantly causing trouble, problems and fights in the building all the time, in the middle of all of the commotion. He would not listen, would not stop, and just carried on acting up, fighting and being defiant. That's when Mr. Pro* went to speak with him and this student decided to take a swing at him. Mr. Pro* had no choice but to bring him down and pin him, yelling at him, "are you crazy, are you crazy!"

**Also today,** I had submitted a referral indicating the same students above has come to my class late for the 70th time. He also has 32 days of absences and 15 cuts just from my class. He should have lost credit with his attendance alone. But nooooooooooooo the administration just keeps allowing him and 100s of other students not to attend class and hangout throughout the building doing whatever they want.

I find this is funny. During 3rd period in the auditorium there was a "UNITY" meeting/program to stop violence. In the meantime, a fight breaks out in the auditorium. All that's needed is to have every student in their class, every period, the entire time, *all* day.

**NOTE OF INTEREST: -** I was absent April 2 & 3. I was back on the 4th and learned the above student wasn't even suspended. However, as we speak, he is still acting up in school and cutting classes.

**During 6th period, another fight erupts.** Security and police are scrambling again up to the 2nd floor. You can hear all the commotion over the walkie-talkies. **Then during 7th period,** I wish I recorded it so you can hear the announcements. The principal came over the PA system telling teachers, NOT TO ALLOW ANY STUDENT TO LEAVE THE ROOM FOR ANY REASON. There will be a sweep of the building and anyone found in the building that does not have the proper credentials will be arrested. Obviously, gangs have infiltrated and there are weapons are in the building. My students told me that kids have guns on them. The school only uses metal detectors when they hear of trouble or after a situation. I still see students roaming the halls as security, police and administrators do *nothing*. What was the point of the announcement? I shake my head in disgust while my students just laughed.

**Apr 2 -** student had a knife and supposedly a (hidden) firearm. Here is the report.

```
                                                               APR 19 2007
                    OFFICE OF THE DISTRICT SUPERINTENDENT
                          PATERSON PUBLIC SCHOOLS
                              Paterson, New Jersey
                                                        DATE   4/02/07
    SCHOOL    Kennedy
                              SUSPENSION REQUEST
    CODE NO.  ████ 4    HR NO. 223   GRADE 12   DOB 7/██/89   AGE 17
    NAME   ████████ █                TELEPHONE NO. (973) 924-████
    ADDRESS   91-████████ Avenue              ETHNIC BACKGROUND
    NO. OF DAYS SUSPENDED   10      SEX         WHITE_____
                                                BLACK    X
    STARTING DATE   4/02/07         MALE  X     SPANISH_____
                                                OTHER_____
    ENDING DATE     4/23/07         FEMALE
                                                CLASSIFIED_____
    RETURN DATE     4/24/07                         (IE, NI, PI)

    COMPLAINT AGAINST STUDENT   Possession of a weapon (knife),
        allegation of possession of a gun

    DATE OF HEARING    4/02/07
    NAMES OF THOSE PRESENT AT HEARING  ████████ █, Mr. ████████
        and Ms. ████████

    RESULT OF HEARING   10 Day Suspension

    INDICATE ANY REFERRALS MADE AS A RESULT OF THE HEARING:
        Ms. ████████  Guidance
        Mr. ████████  Administrator
    CONDITIONS FOR RETURN TO SCHOOL    Must return to school with a
        parent

    PARENT WAS NOTIFIED OF SUSPENSION BY:   Ms. ████ - Teacher
        Assistant to Principal

    COMMENTS:

    TO DATE: TOTAL SUSPENSIONS   3
             TOTAL DAYS         30
```

**Apr 3 -** IMPORTANT I was out sick, so one of the secretaries called me at home. I learned on Mar 30, all after school activities were cancelled because of violence. She also said six students were arrested for having *weapons* on them in the building. I replied how can the newspapers not know about this?

**7th period** fire alarms go off again, evacuated building again. False alarm again! I was absent, but students and faculty told me.

**Apr 3, below is a narrative of** supposed to be going on tomorrow, I went to the public library and wrote an e-mail to Governor Corzine Then I sent a copy to THE STAR LEDGER, via jwillse@statrtledger.com, & NEWS CHANNEL 12 via ITEAM@NEWS12.COM, informing them that I sent the same e-mail to Governor Corzine, asking all of them for help.
I also sent a copy to myself.

IMPORTANT MESSAGE BELOW:
The thing that is so damned disturbing is, with all that is going on, that has happened, the weapons confiscated and those who were arrested that had them, not knowing how many others have weapons, the administration still allows students to roam the halls freely all day long.

**Apr 3, below is a narrative of an e-mail I sent to the Governor, Star Ledger and News 12 I-Team**
We are in great danger here at JFK high school. The students run the school. They are in the hallways all day long. They are pulling the fire alarms continually. Fights occur during, while and after the fire alarms are pulled. They are gang related. Kids do not get back into class after a good 20 minutes or better. Nothing is being done. Kids are not being suspended. Violence is rampant. What happened to zero tolerance to violence? We have processed over 70k cuts. We have only 2500 students. March 30 was filled with violence so bad that all after school functions including the talent show was cancelled. Guns were confiscated on Monday and students were arrested. Why isn't the public aware of all of this? Why aren't the parents aware of this? Why is the media kept quiet of this? There is to be a big shoot out tomorrow, at John F. Kennedy high school, in Paterson, NJ Thursday, April 5, 2007 between Bloods and Latin Kings. I did not become a teacher to work in a war zone. If I did, I expect combat pay. There are no administrators in hallway moving students. Police do nothing but stand around and watch what goes on and have to wait until an incident happens. Good students are now turning bad. Falsification of school records and documentation is rampant. IS THIS WHY WE HAVE 7 ASSISTANT SUPERINTENDANTS FOR THE DISTRICT? The state was supposed to help and make things better. There is no education going on. I am scared. I am not the only one. I have been and continue documenting all of this and for years. I am looking to start a class action lawsuit against the district and the state of NJ. This is the biggest waste of taxpayer's money.
HELP, before someone gets killed.
WE NEED THE MARINES HERE          HELP US PLEASE
I have to remain anonymous because I and other teachers all fear for our jobs and now our lives.
ZORRO

*** END OF E-MAIL ***

**Apr 4** - 4th period, 10:01, fire alarms go off. We evacuated building again. They pulled the system off the wall screwing up the sensor again by the 2nd Floor Social Studies Wing. It took a while to rest the system.

**Apr 5** - with all that's been going on this week and especially these last days, things inside JFK are worse. Students are still allowed to go wherever and doing whatever they want. There is *no control, no discipline here and obviously no supervision*. With the threat of gun fight today you think things would be more secured and locked down. No it is worse. It is so dangerous here.

**Then** during 7th period, I am walking out of caf with two of my female students. We are watching kids standing, jumping on tables, milk dripping off kids' heads, and realized we have to get our asses out of here because a food fight is going to erupt. As soon as we got to the door all hell broke loose. In a blink of an eye students inside the caf got up running, plowing through one another making a bee line to get out. Here's the best part, no one was caught, no one saw anything, and *nothing* was done about it other than janitors having to clean the mess. These disgusting antics go on and on every cafeteria period.

**During** 8th period 12:58, Fire alarms went off. Evacuate building again.
**Received 3 photos &video of chaos long after we had come back into the building.**

**Also during** 8th period, either a food fight or just another fight in cafeteria. A cop brings out a kid in cuffs to security. Received video.

**Shortly after,** a big commotion erupted, kids running in hallway - I turned on my phone video when several kids start running. I let them know I had them on video just in case if something bad happened. Right after that, the principal caught one of them and the kid was giving him BS excuses on what he was doing. *Again nothing was done about anything!*

**At the end of the day,** I was talking with Ms. Conscientious* we were discussing how bad it is here and why is this allowed. She said the superintendent made a comment in the newspapers last week that the culture in Paterson is disgusting. I have to find that article and the exact words.

**Apr 17** - student having possession and the use of firecrackers. Here is the report.

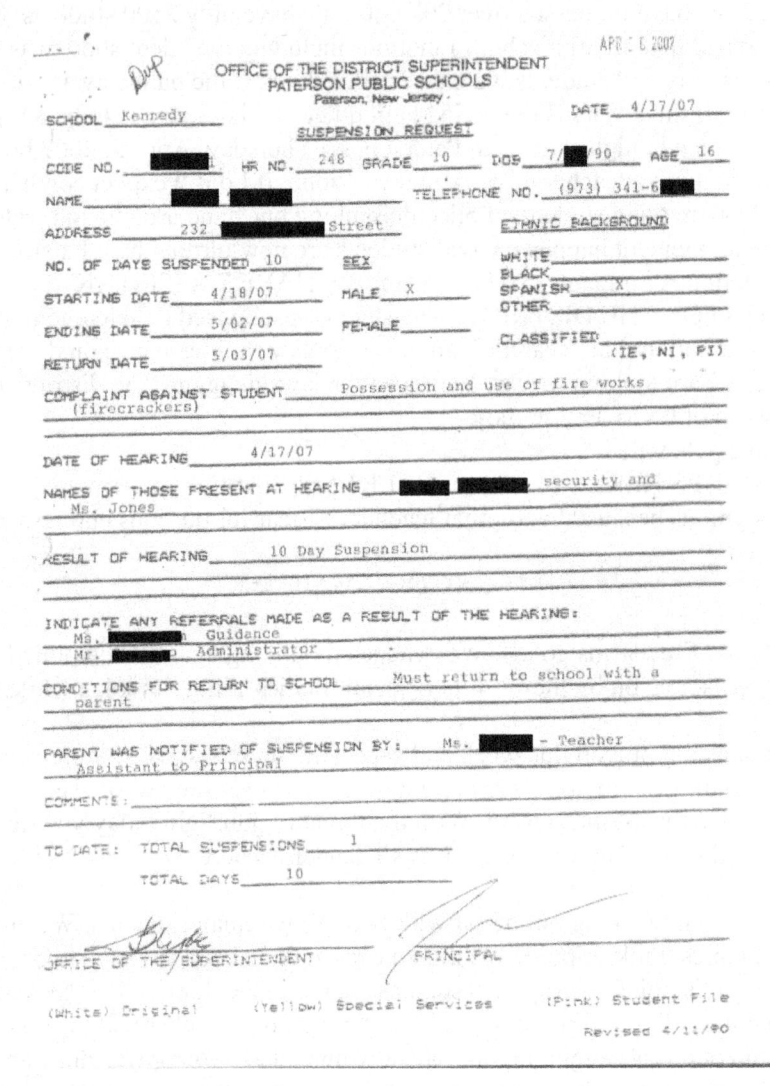

[Suspension Request form from Office of the District Superintendent, Paterson Public Schools, dated 4/17/07, Kennedy school. Grade 10, age 16, male, Spanish. 10 day suspension starting 4/18/07, ending 5/02/07, return date 5/03/07. Complaint: Possession and use of fire works (firecrackers). Result of hearing: 10 Day Suspension. Conditions for return: Must return to school with a parent.]

### IMPORTANT NOTATION
I asked several administrators why is out of control behavior, cutting, lateness, kids everywhere except in class allowed and no consequences? The answer was, if we did everything the way we are supposed to, there would be no students in the building. What in the hell does that mean? What in the hell does that say about everything I have documented? In other words, do *nothing*. Let it be. It is what it is. This is *not* education? This is *disgusting*! And this is a state takeover, controlled, run and operated school district!
*****************************

I don't have the exact times for Tuesday because I was absent. However, the fire alarms were deliberately pulled and everyone had to evacuate the building, *again!* I was told once everyone came back inside; the principal made an announcement and was upset about the nonsense of pulling the alarms. Once he was done with his announcement the alarms were pulled again. If you do not want the alarms pulled *you cannot have students in hallway walking around as if they are in a park or the mall all day!*

**Apr 23** - first day back since April 5th because we were off for Good Friday, Easter week, and flooding.

**6th period, 11:27**, fire alarms go off evacuated the building. We were outside for at least 20 minutes. I received three pictures and two videos. The 1st video documents when the alarm went off showing the clock, the day's newspaper as well as evacuation. The 2nd starts shortly after we came back in showing all the chaos and how long it takes to get somewhat settle down here. Shortly afterwards, you hear the principal's announcement saying there was a malfunction and that is why the alarms went off. The malfunction was students destroyed the alarm on the 3rd Floor Science Wing Boy's bathroom.

**Apr 24**, - I learned the *malfunction* was due to someone ripping the flashing light portion of the alarm off the wall making a circuit to set the alarm off. This is why no one knew what or where the problem was. The head custodian said there was another one ripped off and they can't find it. Dave* the security guard said kids are taking them because the strobe lights are used to put on their cars for show.

**Apr 25** - 8th period, fire alarms go off, evacuated the building. The entire day *was out of freaking control!*

**Apr 26** - 4th period, 10:01 fire alarms go off, evacuate the building. False alarm! The alarm was pulled off the wall on the 2nd floor Social Studies Wing screwing up the sensor again. Received 3 photos and video.

**Apr 27** - first thing this morning, *not* even 7:30, fights with girls. This has been going on day after day and no one gets suspended.

**Fire alarms went off**. We evacuated the building again. False alarm again! Once we came back in and the building somewhat settled down, the principal made an announcement. He was upset about the nonsense of pulling the alarms. Once he was done with his announcement, the alarms were pulled again.

**I notice two** of my students or should I say ex-students are constantly in the hallways all day long especially during 6, 7 & 8th periods. It seems every day during 7th period there is an incident in the hallways, fighting, screaming, yelling, arguing, cursing and on and on and it involves (names omitted), one of the two students. Why shouldn't they act up? The administration continually allows students to do so all day long. These kids are learning to be problems for society right here in a place of education that is supposed to be preparing students for their future in being responsible and knowing how to act in the *real world*. Can you believe this? It is the end of APRIL and the administration asks me is there anything I can do to help them with their grades? In reality they're asking me, will I just pass them? I was so disgusted I said, "NO, it is up to them to be here, to do their work which is not hard or a lot and *not* to cut class. They're even late to school every day." So what does the administration do? They removed them from my class because they are failing. Where are their parents who should have received 4 warning notices, one for each marking period plus 3 report cards? Do you believe this school is under STATE CONTROL?

**Apr 30** - between periods 7 & 8 a fight breaks out. It was going on for quite a while before a student could video it. He did not get any of the fight but caught a great deal of all the commotion including how long it took for it to break up, including *no administrators, no security, no nothing and how dangerous this place is*. You can tell by the time on the recording how long until Mr. Lance* and Ms. Princess* showed up. Kids still went about their business which was disruption of the school. Received video.

**Have copies** of the school newspaper, "TORCH," dated March 2007 Volume 41 No.3
Front page bottom, "NOVA NET helps seniors recover credit for June Graduation."
**BOTTOM LINE** -when a student has 100 days absent from school, is still on roll and able to graduate without making up any time, all of this is a JOKE! How many tens of thousands of dollars did this program cost the TAXPAYERS, only to graduate students to satisfy a quota system/statistic?

**May 1** - 6th period, 11:33, fire alarms go off, evacuated building. Another false alarm pulled in Social Studies Wing. Received 3 pictures & video.

**Student has mace**, is making threats and has assaulted some students. Here is the report.

*[Suspension Request form from Office of the District Superintendent, Paterson Public Schools, Paterson, New Jersey. School: Kennedy. Date: 5/01/07. Code No. 1021319, HR No. 336, Grade 9, DOB 2/__/91, Age 16. No. of Days Suspended: 10. Sex: Male. Ethnic Background: Black. Starting Date: 5/02/07. Ending Date: 5/15/07. Return Date: 5/16/07. Classified X (IE, NI, PI). Complaint Against Student: Possession of mace, threats, possession of stolen passes, simple assault. Date of Hearing: 5/01/07. Result of Hearing: 10 Day Suspension. Referrals: Ms. ___ Guidance, Mr. ___ Administrator. Conditions for Return to School: Must return to school with a parent. Parent Notified of Suspension by: Ms. ___ -Teacher Assistant to Principal. Comments: Transported to Juvenile. To Date: Total Suspensions 2, Total Days 11. Revised 4/11/90.]*

**May 3** - 9th period I was in the office and heard Mr. Lance* tell security to look for a (name omitted) female student, she maybe in the girls' room. On 5/4/07, a secretary told me the reason why they were looking for her is because she made terroristic threats, saying she is going to bring a gun to school tomorrow and kill people. She **was** arrested.

We see and hear about this stuff happening in other schools from all over the country all the time on TV, radio, newspaper. However, here in Paterson I don't know how they keep it all hushed up.

**Student threatens to bring in a gun** and take care of a couple of people. Here is the report.
My guess it's the girl from the May 3 entry.

```
                    OFFICE OF THE DISTRICT SUPERINTENDENT
                           PATERSON PUBLIC SCHOOLS
                              Paterson, New Jersey
    SCHOOL   Kennedy                                         DATE   5/03/07
                              SUSPENSION REQUEST
    CODE NO. [redacted]    HR NO. 341   GRADE 11   DOB 9/__/88   AGE 18
    NAME     [redacted]                TELEPHONE NO. (973) 851-[redacted]
    ADDRESS     31 [redacted] Avenue           ETHNIC BACKGROUND
    NO. OF DAYS SUSPENDED   10       SEX         WHITE _____
                                                 BLACK _____
    STARTING DATE   5/04/07          MALE ____   SPANISH    X
                                                 OTHER _____
    ENDING DATE     5/17/07          FEMALE  X   CLASSIFIED _____
                                                           (IE, NI, PI)
    RETURN DATE     5/18/07

    COMPLAINT AGAINST STUDENT   Threats to bring a gun to school and
    take care of a couple of people

    DATE OF HEARING   5/03/07
    NAMES OF THOSE PRESENT AT HEARING  [redacted], Ms. [redacted],
    Dr. [redacted], Mr. [redacted] security and Paterson Police

    RESULT OF HEARING    10 Day Suspension

    INDICATE ANY REFERRALS MADE AS A RESULT OF THE HEARING:
    Ms. [redacted]  Guidance
    Ms. [redacted]  Administrator

    CONDITIONS FOR RETURN TO SCHOOL    Must return to school with a
    parent

    PARENT WAS NOTIFIED OF SUSPENSION BY:   Ms. J[redacted] - Teacher
    Assistant to Principal

    COMMENTS:  V&V filed

    TO DATE:  TOTAL SUSPENSIONS   3
              TOTAL DAYS   20

    [redacted]                        [redacted]
    OFFICE OF THE SUPERINTENDENT      PRINCIPAL

    (White) Original   (Yellow) Special Services   (Pink) Student File
                                                   Revised 4/11/90
```

**May 4 -** student threatens to stab and cut up a student. Here is the report.

```
                OFFICE OF THE DISTRICT SUPERINTENDENT
                       PATERSON PUBLIC SCHOOLS
                           Paterson, New Jersey            DATE  5/04/07
   SCHOOL  Kennedy            SUSPENSION REQUEST
   CODE NO. ████         HR NO. 219  GRADE 9   DOB 10/██/92  AGE 14
   NAME ████████████                  TELEPHONE NO. (973) 790-4███
   ADDRESS  441 ██████ Avenue                 ETHNIC BACKGROUND
   NO. OF DAYS SUSPENDED  10       SEX         WHITE _____
                                               BLACK    X
   STARTING DATE  5/07/07          MALE ____   SPANISH ____
                                               OTHER _____
   ENDING DATE    5/18/07          FEMALE  X   CLASSIFIED _____
   RETURN DATE    5/21/07                              (IE, NI, PI)
   COMPLAINT AGAINST STUDENT   Threatened to stab/cut a student

   DATE OF HEARING   5/04/07
   NAMES OF THOSE PRESENT AT HEARING  ████████  police and
    Ms. Jones

   RESULT OF HEARING    10 Day Suspension

   INDICATE ANY REFERRALS MADE AS A RESULT OF THE HEARING:
      Ms. ████   Guidance
      Mr. ████   Administrator
   CONDITIONS FOR RETURN TO SCHOOL   Must return to school with a
    parent

   PARENT WAS NOTIFIED OF SUSPENSION BY:   Ms. ████ - Teacher
    Assistant to Principal
   COMMENTS:

   TO DATE:  TOTAL SUSPENSIONS   1
             TOTAL DAYS   10


   OFFICE OF THE SUPERINTENDENT            PRINCIPAL

   (White) Original    (Yellow) Special Services   (Pink) Student File
                                                   Revised 4/11/90
```

Remember, this is ONLY what I know and was able to get the information for.
Can you imagine how much is going on that WE DO NOT KNOW?

**May 10 -** the rest of the crap is still going on inside here. In fact, I have an *actual* school suspension list. The first student has 80 cuts, next 66 cuts, then 117, 86, 64, 160, 30, 47, 67, and many of the other reasons for suspension which verifies what I have been saying.

Mr. Madjar told me someone in school administration is changing school documents/records. They're changing student's birth date making them younger so they *cannot* be kicked out of school.

**May 15 -** 6th period, 11:31, fire alarms go off, evacuated building. Mr. Pro* called me back into the building to get him an Allen key to reset the alarm. False alarm again! Alarm was pulled on 1st floor by loading dock. They supposedly caught the kid via the cameras. Received video & 2 pictures.

**Shortly after** we came back in from being evacuated the alarms go off again. Evacuated the building again. Then a fight broke out between 2 girls. Actually, one girl snuck up and cracked another from behind and she went down. Received a video and you hear a kid telling me how the girl hit the other girl. You see the riot like atmosphere and how long it takes for it to settle down. It never settles down.

**May 17** - students are all over the hallways, worse than ever. REASON - because they are *not* allowed in the cafeteria without their ID cards. So the kids are made to and allowed to roam the halls. There has to be something very wrong mentality with the decision-making process with administration especially with all that goes on inside here? Think about it, the administration checks students for having their ID cards to enter cafeterias but does NOT check ID cards when students enter the *building*! Isn't that back as swards?

**6th period,** a big food fight in cafeteria. Janitor and security are cleaning up, not one student. This is what happens way too often with free lunches. They didn't pay for it so it is now a weapon or something to play with. *No* student is held responsible for their behavior and that's why it keeps happening.

**May 18** - I heard from many teachers during 9th period there was a lock down. Somebody was coming here with a gun! Cops were all over the place inside and out. Bottom line, I knew nothing until 1:55. The lock down was in place supposedly 8th period? Everything is always hushed up! In fact, it wasn't until today, I found out there was a lockdown yesterday. NO announcements were made either day. Lock down or no lockdown the hallways and stairwells were still filled with *whoever*!

**May 21** - nothing different, kids all over the place. However, **during 7th period**, I hear a scuffle right outside my classroom and I hear a little more than a whisper saying, don't fight us, don't fight us, stop resisting. This went on for about a minute. Finally, I decided to see what's going on. It was 2 cops with a kid's face down on the floor being handcuffed and finally escorted to security office.

**May 22** - newspaper article from THE HERALD NEWS, "OPINION" SECTION, Editorial by Superintendent Glace, crying$26 million are missing and it must be from the last administration. *UNFREAKINBELIEVABLE.*

Why hasn't anyone made a comparison in the number of administrators as well as the increase of cost to the NJ taxpayers yearly since the state of New Jersey took over this district?

**May 25** - Ms. Conscientious* was so upset, because she had to write a letter explaining why so many *seniors* failed SRA. Why doesn't the administration ask the students and most of all their parents why their child failed? I asked how many failed. She said 86 seniors failed because they did *not* do what they were supposed to. Now 86 seniors out of 240 failed (approximately 36%). I can't wait to see what kind of razzle-dazzle or hocus-pocus the district is going to use to increase graduation numbers?

**May 29** - 8th period a VP came in to see me. He said if I see any suspicious people or anything out of the ordinary to report it right away. Later I found out we were in a lock down *again,* because of another gun threat. Meanwhile the administration still allows students to continually be in the hallways instead of being in class!

**May 31 - 4th period, 10:06**, FOOD FIGHT cops pulling kids out of café and into security office. One cop was yelling at a kid; you're going to JV for assault on an officer. 10 minutes later that boy was in handcuffs & being escorted out of the building to an awaiting police car. YEAH, FINALLY!

**5th period, another food fight,** the third for the day. Each one is bigger than the last one. However, no one is disciplined. It's happening almost daily and every cafeteria period.

**A few minutes later a fourth food fight.** The administration considers this normal behavior!

**Jun 11** - 9:35am, I asked a student Eugene*, who was hanging outside my door talking, to come inside and Charles* from my 8th period class to get out of the hallway. I am met with an immediate barrage of foul language and threatening remarks by Charles*. He picked up and throw a wooden door wedge at me. As I came outside, he raises his hand to hit me telling me to come on. Dave* the security guard came over and intervened. However, Charles* continues to jump up and down as if he's a boxer telling me to come on with his fists in a striking posture. I told Dave* I wanted him arrested. Charles* continues with his threatening remarks and how I backed down from him. He was brought to the security office. Dave* came out of the office and Charles* continue with his threatening remarks saying how nobody, no teacher will walk up on me, I don't give a fuck and took a threatening posture again.

**2/9/07** was the first day Charles* came to my class this year and from that day forward he has **Absences (65), Cuts (29), Lates ().** I obtained a copy of his school attendance profile which shows to date he has **24 Days absent from school and 30 Cut Policy Days.** Cut policy is **5 cuts** = 1 cut policy day. This means he has a total of **150 Cuts.** These are only what were turned in. So many teachers don't bother because it's a waste of time. He also has **34 Suspension days and 24 Tardy days.**

I have a copy of his grades and cannot believe with his attendance some teachers are still passing him. October 27, 2006, he was suspended by Mr. Pro* for 10 days for pulling a false fire alarm on 10/25/07. June 11, 2007, suspended again for 5 days but changed to 4 so he can be here on the 15th for final exams.

Just like I have been saying all along, what goes on inside here anybody else would be immediately arrested any place else. Pulling a false alarm *is against the law* not to mention dangerous. Not at JFK!

**June 19** was 8th periods final exam day. To my surprise Charles*, even though he was late, showed up. I was extremely polite and spoke to him softly saying, you haven't been here all year, you're not going to know any of this. He too was quite reserved and spoke back softly and kindly saying I know, but my guidance counselor said they will overlook my great many absences as long as I pass the final exam.

That afternoon I confronted the person in charge of guidance. I told him what my student said about passing the final exam. He said no way, that's ridiculous and would speak with his guidance counselor. Later that day he told me the counselor never said that *and* my class does not matter for him to graduate.

All this running around, added work, paperwork, documenting everything and stress placed on me and other teachers because of this as well as so many other students just to say that my class doesn't matter. I don't believe him. I think he's BSing me because I confronted him, and he had to come up with something. I believe they will change his grade no matter what I say or do. Obviously, my documenting everything means less than my students doing *not a thing*!

Later I saw Ms. Queenie*, and said I hope you don't change any of my students' grades again, like you did last year. She tells me she never changed any of my students' grades. I said yes you did and you even told me. I mentioned the student's name. She said I never changed her grade. That came from higher up. I said no Ms. Queenie*, now you're lying. You even told me you did and said this was the best thing to do. She replied, well how old was she? I said what in the hell does that have to do with it? Quit making up excuses and things as you are going along in trying to get out of what you did last year. I said she was a repeating junior who lost credit over and over the entire year, then became a senior and graduated all in a couple of weeks. Then she went off on a tangent saying well, I better have good documentation to back up my grades. I snapped back at her saying my documentation is excellent. It's *you* who better have excellent documentation compared to mine. *See entries April 6, June 19, 10, 22 & July 26.*

**Jun 12** - No need to write anything. Nothing changes, I am tired, disgusted and want to go home.

**Jun 19** - I have a copy of the newsletter, "ADVOCATE" Vol. 34, No.4, May 2007. It verifies everything that I have been saying and documenting all along.

**Final exam day**, approximately 2:10, fire alarms go off, evacuated building. False alarm again!

**Jun 18 & 19** - are final exam days. Exams start at 8:20. You *cannot* believe all the students entering the building at 9am. I had a student show up at 9:32 and all he did was play and talk. Like I said, they do *not* come here to learn, it is a place to play and meet with friends. Meanwhile the hallways are filled to the max with students during the exams. There are 3 more days of exams. So much for teaching punctuality!

**Jun 25** - 9:00, the end of 2nd period the bell rings to go to homeroom. A BIG FIGHT erupts with girls **slugging it out in front of my classroom.** I guess the bell meant to start the fight!

Received a video of students in the hallways *loooong* after the bell rang to start 3rd period hanging out, running around, screaming, JFK is nothing more than a place to play. Not one administrator out here supervising. Later *one* lone female security guard was trying to get the kids moving to no avail. I have no idea why final exams were scheduled and finished DAYs before the end of the school year.

**June 25 – 28** - I have copies of John F. Kennedy High School Attendance Office - Credit Notice stating, "Please be informed that as of (Date is on the form) the above student A big check mark next to it, *will receive credit* for all courses with a final passing grade for the school year 2006 – 2007."

I have kids with so many absences and cuts and they get their credit back? What's the point of the attendance, cuts and tardy policies? What's the point of having a cut office with all those teachers working in there all year 12 plus hours a day? I have the *profiles* on all of the students that received their credit back. Their attendance is *horrible*? *How and why are they allowed to graduate?*

**Jun 27 - WHAT IN THE HELL IS GOING ON HERE?** We had a meeting in the auditorium. The principal said because he had put cameras throughout the building we have no more deliberate false alarms. However, he did say because of the cameras the last two times, they caught the kids. They were kicked out of school and parents were fined $1,000. I find that ODD, according to entry 6/11/07, student was *just* suspended for pulling a false fire alarm. **And now he is *GRADUATING!***

Received a video today showing all of the students who are *not* in or going to class. Unlike Monday, there were hardly any students in the building. A few were walking around. So much for students having to making up snow & flood days! Students are required to be here, but they don't.

**NOTE OF INTEREST:** - The last day of school, I went to look through the folders on a couple of seniors. One senior was 20 years old. I had to laugh. The folders were all already thrown away. The reason why I laughed, teachers have to turn in their roll books for documentation. However, the school throws out the actual documentation, student folders that have all the information and everything pertaining to students.

## SCHOOL YEAR 2007 – 2008
**MY DIARY for this section picks up the next day after BLOCK SCHEDULING and RIOT.**

**Oct 23** - as soon as I walked in this morning, I noticed security guards using metal detectors. The only time they use them is after an incident happens. In a few days they will be put away.
I was told to check a video on YouTube. It was removed. Think about it. NOT ONE TV station reported what went on here yesterday even though their helicopters were flying over JFK all day. I believe the

State of NJ is controlling the media because this happened at a school in a district under STATE CONTROL! Furthermore, the administration just doesn't care. Even after all that went on yesterday, they still continue to allow students to hang out throughout the entire building instead of going to class. Other than a new date on the calendar nothing else has changed. Meanwhile the only concern the administration has is THEIR image and work so damn hard in hushing everything up that they have caused and are never held accountable.

Mr. Madjar said, the cut office is getting 500 cuts every day. Many are for block periods, which means they are double (2) cuts. AND to make things worse, there is no record/documentation of them on the computer for attendance, other than in that student's personal folder. The cut office is so busy they haven't had the time to process lateness. Mr. Madjar said most of the teachers are so frustrated, disgusted and fed up because it's a waste of and takes too much of their time they aren't even bothering to write cuts or lateness anymore.

UNBELIEVABLE, *both* school elevators are NOT working. One of the elevators is for wheelchair and handicapped students only. *This is extremely dangerous and against the law*. We need the elevator in case of an emergency. What if the nurse or paramedics need to bring someone down from the 2$^{nd}$ or 3$^{rd}$ floor via a wheelchair or stretcher, and in many cases here used for emergencies? You can bet if this was a place of business and the handicapped elevator did not work, they would be fined and sued.

One of my old students is an Army National Guard recruiter and stopped in to visit me. The first thing he says was WOW, this place is a mess it is so out of control. Why is this like this? I can't believe it. I replied it is disgusting. He replied absolutely that is the best word to describe it. He said he was only here for a short while today and saw two students at different times being arrested and taken out of the building in handcuffs. One was a girl from Eastside who was trespassing, and the other was a Hispanic male and didn't know the reason why.

**7$^{th}$ period, 2:15,** Fire alarms go off, evacuated the building. School is so out of control. They still allow kids to be in hallways all day long and it is worse than yesterday. Why is the administration allowing this? Meanwhile the fire alarms keep going off. Who is paying for the fire department, the police, riot squad and sheriff's department to keep coming here? Received video & 3 Photos.

UNBELIEVABLE and it's getting worse. You would think with all I write down basically on a daily basis, how can it get worse? Sadly, it is and nothing is being done about it. Nothing but fights here all day long everywhere and I bet there is NO documentation being submitted! The administration doing what they do best, hush it all up!

**Oct 24 - 12:05,** coming back from lunch, the building was evacuated, the fire alarms were going off, the fire department and more police were already here. This has to cost the taxpayers plenty, AGAIN!

**12:25** coming back in from evacuation, a big fight broke out on the 2$^{nd}$ floor. As usual it was Blacks vs. Dominicans. Police and security are running all over the place in attempts to get to the commotion. However, it is difficult for them to get through being the hallways and stairwells are filled, jammed packed with out of control students.

A few minutes later more fighting breaking out all over the place. It is basically another riot inside here. I think administration is trying to contain this by keeping it all inside the building. They do *NOT* want any of this happening outside again. Received a great deal of VIDEO showing what was going on inside here once we came back in the building.

**1:24, another big fight** breaks out this time in the gym room. See a girl being escorted by police to Mr. Pro's* office in handcuffs. **This school is run by thugs.**

**Speaking of *thugs*,** while I was online to swipe out to go home, all you saw were kids walking back and forth looking to fight. Yet with security all around including the principal no one tries to stop them. Then we heard a metallic sound hitting the floor. When we all turned to look we just saw kids running. It was a metal bat or pipe of some sort. One of the VPs picked it up. Why didn't he grab the kids? It is just like a movie. The only thing this is for real, this is every day, this is getting worse, and this is DANGEROUS.

Speaking of weapons and bats, I understand security opened up a locker and found a metal bat in it. A teacher asked me, "How do they get into the building with it?" I said, "Easy, students come in and out of the building all day long. They come in when security isn't around or stick something between the door and jamb so the door never closes. This the same way gangs and other trespassers get into the building. That's the reason for students having to wear & have their ID cards visible. So, staff, security and police all know if you belong in the building or not." But nooooooo, the administration cannot and obviously will not enforce that safety rule either.

As we were lining up to leave, we heard the chief custodian say to the principal, that the kid took out and emptied 2 fire extinguishers and urinated in the lockers the extinguishers came out of.
- Does this sound like a safe environment?
- Does this sound like a place of education?
- Does this sound like a place that is under control?
- Why is this allowed to go on continually daily all day, every day?
- Why aren't the superintendent and the principal under arrest for allowing these unsafe and illegal actions to continuously go on and *not* correct it?

Yesterday security was using metal detectors. As expected, *today* it stopped. They are only used after something happens. Don't you think the students and the *thugs* who do NOT belong in here realize this too?

**Oct 25 -** 9:38, Mr. Pro* and a nasty police officer wanted one of my students (name omitted), to retrieve a student in room 348, who was involved with yesterday's gang violence (Blacks vs. Dominicans), and was also threatening my student. According to my student this young man (name omitted) supposedly knows all the kids involved on his side (meaning the black kids). Mr. Pro* was telling my student to be careful and stay away from all of those guys because yesterday, they picked up and arrested 3 kids by the bridge, (bridge, corner of Wayne and McBride Ave.) for weapons. The weapons they had were brass knuckles, knives and he used the words "ROUNDS," meaning "GUNS."
**Around 10am, I asked my student if I could interview him on camera. I have the interview.**

I interviewed the above student again about the metal detectors. He was telling me how the metal detectors really don't work, and the security personnel aren't doing anything other than just passing the wand around the kid's bodies and letting them in. When the light and sound goes off, the kids just say, "Oh, it is my belts, keys, change" or anything as simple as that. He also said, and I have it on video, the kids hide knives and other small weapons inside their shoes / sneakers and security guards don't check that with the metal detectors. **BOTTOM LINE, THIS PLACE IS SO DAMN DANGEROUS.**

**11:30,** I watched **two** kids walking around by one of the back doors when a young lady from the inside opened it up allowing them in. I have never seen these two kids before. I tried to bluff them with my cell phone camera saying I am videoing them, but they didn't care. I wished I did videotape them now especially if they were intruders/trespassers. How do we know who belongs in the building until something has already happened and *if* they are caught? That's why everyone is supposed to wear ID cards! Why does it have to be always after something happens before we do something?

**6th period 1:06,** fire alarms go off. We evacuated the building again. We were outside for quite a long time. A fire was started again in one of the bathrooms. Approximately 2:20, I noticed the Arson Squad was in the building. Received video & 3 photos.

**(BRASS KNUCKLES),** during the evacuation, I confiscated brass knuckles from a student in my 6th period class. I gave them to the principal around 2:30. He wasn't even concerned. He laughed and said, these kids are really something. I replied, well that's one set of brass knuckles off the street any way. Have a video and photos of the brass knuckles sitting on today's newspaper as a reference.

**Oct 26** - nothing's changing. All week, 10/22 - 26 we haven't had an attendance sheet. Teachers have no idea who is cutting, absent or anything. Even when there are attendance sheets, teachers are *not* getting them because Ms. Princess* says, there is NO PAPER! However, there are *flyers* plastered all over the building for NOVA NET? We wouldn't need NOVA NET if students were made to be in class! The ladies in office #2 told me the reason why there hasn't been an attendance sheet is because of all the evacuations. They haven't had the time to finish and catch up from the days before. I cannot accept that reason. I believe it is another way for administration to adjust basically falsify the actual attendance records. If we are having all of these evacuations, students are leaving school and more students are cutting now more than ever. By keeping the attendance sheets from being distributed this keeps teachers from turning in more cuts, marking students absent which would definitely show a huge spike and now having a paper trail to verify it all. One would think all the more reason to gain control of the school. The administration is supposed to be supervising; making sure students are receiving an appropriate education.

**6th period 1:15,** fire alarms go off. Evacuated the building *again.* We lose more time with our 6th & 7th period classes *again!* Approximately 2:20, the Arson Squad is in the building *again.* Obviously, there was a fire *again!* Received video & 3 photos.

**NOTE OF INTEREST:** -With all that's been going on here and especially on the 1st floor you have to ask why? How can this be when we have the principal, **(4)** VP's and a TAP, a total of **(6)** administrators who each have an office on the 1st floor? At the ringing of the bells for each period, there's supposed to be an administrator on each floor covering the hallways. One of the VPs who is in charge of student's attendance, tardiness, and cutting most of the time stays inside her office and closes the door!
1. Teachers have never had a child *drop* or *admitted* to class without receiving a drop take slip.
2. Teachers have no idea who is actually supposed to be in our classes anymore.
3. We always had updated sheets informing us who is assigned to our classes. ***But not this year!***

This is all unacceptable and a sorely lacking any type of leadership. I would also like to know with everything that has gone down all week here *why* is none of it in the newspapers or on TV and radio? I am totally convinced because this is a State Takeover, Run, Controlled and Operated School District, they control the media. **For example**, the other day on television **NEWS 12 NJ,** had a story that happened in a small rural town in NJ. A 9-year-old boy was suspended for drawing stick figures of his friends and himself. Over their heads he wrote their names. He portrayed himself shooting his friends, but with a water pistol. The reason for his suspension was "ZERO TOLERANCE TO VIOLENCE!" I would love for that superintendent, and principal to come and spend an HOUR here. Then they will see what *violence* is and their heads would explode!

**Oct 29** - the principal made an announcement over close circuit TV at 10 a.m. and again at 1 p.m. He was asking for help to stop the pulling of false alarms and setting fires in the boys & girls's room. Meanwhile he still allows his hallways to be filled with students all day. Then he tells the entire school population how the fires were set by sticking lit cigarettes and starting small fires within the smoke detectors. So now *every kid knows what to do*. And the kids know they cannot put cameras in the bathrooms. He might as well have said, go ahead start fires and leave it at that? Then he tells students there's a $500 reward if they see someone and they are caught for setting fires or deliberately pulling fire alarms. How long do you think someone would last if anyone squeals or is even accused of squealing?

**Oct 30 -** HERALD NEWS, Tuesday, October 30, 2007, Front Page, "Dropout Factory tags city schools," Eastside & Kennedy make national list. By Nancy Zuckerbrod.
That explains it. This is WHY, the administration is allowing students not to go to class, hangout anywhere and everywhere in the building all day every day, passing them and graduating them. It's about NUMBERS and STATISTICS.

**Nov 11 -** out of chronological order, is a rebuttal to the above article.
HERALD NEWS, Sunday, November 11, 2007, Pg. B12,
"Schools as dropout factories" PUHLEEEESE! By Roselyn O. Rauch, Ed.D. Special to the Herald News.

Dr. Rauch is a teacher at John F. Kennedy High School.

*[Handwritten: Will be published Sunday! Herald News - Op Ed page]*

### DROP-OUT FACTORY? PUHLEEEESE!!
By Roselyn O. Rauch, Ed.D.

Funny, but I don't remember taking any course, *Dropout 101: How to prepare your students to be bums, vagrants, drains on society, or worse*. Was I absent that whole semester?

How dare these powers-that-be lay the blame on teachers! Have these ivory-towered individuals ever taught, or even been in, these so-called "drop-out factories"? Have they seen the teachers lounging around? Have they seen/heard the teachers encouraging this behavior? Is this a valid analysis by the U.S. Department of Education conducted by Johns Hopkins ('Dropout Factory' tags city schools; *Herald News*, 10/30/07)?

You don't have to be a teacher to have heard the popular myth that teaching is an easy job: Go to work for 7 hours, summers off, lots of holidays. My response to these cynical critics has always been: "How many kids of your own do you have? When was the last time you spent even one hour in meaningful engagement with your own kids- over any topic- before someone lost interest?"

Think about it.

Teachers have to be engaged for an entire day, often with thirty students, and keep the pace going; and they do! They have to prepare lessons before classes, (often using their own monies for supplies), teach during the day, and then stay after the kids have left to mark papers, or take the papers home. Evening hours may be spent on the phone contacting parents and/or working at a second job because teacher's salaries are not commensurate with those in the public sector. Those critics could have gone into education, too, if they thought it was such a cushy job. My contention has always been that parents/all adults should be required to participate in schools and that the corporate world should have to allow paid leave to the workforce for this purpose. But, I digress.

Let's get a real-world view of what's going on in American schools.

Many individuals still have the antiquated vision of the stereotypical teacher standing in front of the class while the well-behaved, well-manicured/coifed/dressed students sit respectfully and attentively absorbing all that is presented to them. Look again. Unfortunately, many of these failing schools have no home support that encourages education. These kids have no view of future life, only the here-and-now. Believe me, the teachers, guidance counselors, and all staff, preach the same gospel: you need an education to put money in your pocket. But, too often, it falls on deaf ears.

Rather, than using the teachers as scapegoats for all of society's ills, the critics should look around and see what is happening in American culture. Look at the movies, the video games, the thug athletes, the music culture that is so counter to quality, enriched lives but is so pervasive in undermining the pursuit of academic success. Who are the role models? Where are the heroes?

I have taught in the urban inner city for over 22 years, and am now in one of those so-called dropout factories. I am highly insulted, and even enraged, maybe sickened, that those on the outside could even believe that the schools and the teachers themselves foster such an environment. Come into the building. See who is rushing from class to class carrying materials for "meaningful engagement". (BIG HINT: It ISN'T the students!!!!!)

Listen to the conversations in the teacher's lounge and hear the frustration of the teachers as they talk: About kids who just don't care. About families that you cannot contact. About kids already in the juvenile justice system who are just waiting out their "sentences" wearing tracking bracelets to school. About the cuts and absences of repeat offenders who just don't care that they may lose credit and not graduate. About those who work at night and sleep in class during the day. Calling the schools "dropout factories" infers that the teachers and staff encourage these behaviors. Puhleeeese!

Students are in school for approximately seven (7) hours a day. Who is responsible for what these kids do the other seventeen (17)? Have the families no influence on their children's actions or have they delegated the raising of their children, as well as educating them, to the schools?

The pity of it is that these schools do not have to be "dropout factories". There are many kids who want to learn. Many kids. But unfortunately so much teacher-student contact time is lost dealing with the behavior issues. Let's stop slapping these behavior problems on the wrists, put them into alternative schools, and get back to the business of teaching to those who value education and want to learn. Then, and only then, will the drop-out factories evolve into the halls of academia of which this country can be proud.

And please, stop blaming the teachers.

Dr. Rauch teaches at John F. Kennedy High School in Paterson.

*[Handwritten: Please save copies! Thanks]*

**Oct 31 - HALLOWEEN DAY,** students were told *not* to come to school with costumes. Guess what? Most of the students came to school wearing costumes anyway. A few were really so bad, too provocative and in such bad taste they were sent home while the rest were still allowed to come in. What leaders we have here in administration. Each day they prove they have no control over anything. What makes it worse now the students have an *excuse* (as if they really need one anyway) to be all over the hallways taking pictures, screaming, yelling swearing, cursing, walking in and out of my classroom and cursing at me and giving me the finger. This place is an absolute disgrace. If I complain I'm a trouble maker and all they will do is tell the kids, OH, that wasn't nice, don't do it again and as soon as they leave the kids continue. It is so hard for me to believe that any of these administrators even have children. How do they allow all of this to continually go on inside the very school, they are supposed to be supervising?

**Nov1, UNBELIEVABLE,** kids all over the place, not one administrator in the hallway including and especially the VP Ms. Princess*. The door to her office is not even 10 feet away. Yet, I have students walking in and out, refusing to leave, cursing at and giving me the finger. This has nothing to do with the amount of money someone makes. It is not about poverty. This is about losing control of the school, not following rules and LAWS, lowering human standards decency and blaming it on the community. Being poor does not give anyone an excuse or a reason for poor or inappropriate behavior or bad manners. That also includes not following rules and laws!

I would also like to coin a phrase here "IN HOUSE TRUANCY." That is what this school is; a place where students can be truant and get away with it! Students don't have to cut school and be on the streets. The streets are right here in our hallways.

**ALSO,** Mr. Lou Bonora a veteran Social Studies/History teacher was attacked and assaulted by a female student who did not belong in his class. While she was being apprehended and subdued, she continued swearing and threatening everyone in room 203 telling them she is going to get everyone of you one day. *"Zero Tolerance to Violence."* Words that don't mean a thing here at JFK.

**Both elevators are still not working** and because of that our handicap students still cannot go to classes on the 2$^{nd}$ and or 3$^{rd}$ floors. Meanwhile the office of VP Ms. Princess* is still being remodeled.

Below is a narrative e-mail that I sent to Governor Corzine;
http://www.state.nj.us/cgi-bin/governor/govmail/govmail_1.pl

I explained we have two elevators inside JFK. One is for all staff, including sick, injured and our handicapped students which operates from the basement up to and including the 3$^{rd}$ floor. We also have a specially installed handicapped elevator which operates from the 1$^{st}$ floor to the gymnasium.

### NEITHER ELEVATOR WORKS! WHY? THIS IS AGAINST THE LAW!

October 28, 2007, the fire department had to come because several of our handicapped students (wheelchair), were stranded on the upper floors and has been happening since the beginning of this school year.

This is against the law and is considered child abuse as well as neglect. Not to mention extremely dangerous and goes ignored.

Two weeks ago teachers were stuck between floors and the fire department had to be summoned. However, an administrator has been utilizing school/district funds for her personalization of her office. Just this week sound proofing, sheet rock, hardware installed, painting and the man hours to do the work.

Is personalizing an office more important than the educational needs of our school and students?

This is a very dangerous school. If I were a parent of one of these handicapped students, I would SUE everyone including you, especially being that this is a STATE RUN and OPERATED DISTRICT AND YOU ARE IN CHARGE.
I will tell the same to all parents on back to school night.
END OF E-MAIL

**Nov 2 - 6th period, 12:50,** fire alarms go off again. Evacuate building again. Fire department came again. Supposedly, it costs $1K every time our school has a false alarm. The school district (really the NJ taxpayers) had to pay $14,000 in the last two months? Supposedly they have caught the culprit?

It was *cold* in my room today. I asked the head custodian, if he can do anything with the temperature? He said, "NO!" He said, he was told from the superintendent's office not to turn the heat on, because they are trying to save money. Meanwhile, we still have the two elevators inoperable and Ms. Princess* is having her office remodeled!

Because we had no heat, below is **another narrative e-mail** I sent another to Governor Corzine.

We have NO heat here at JFK. When we ask the head custodian why there is no heat, we are told the Office of the Superintendent doesn't want it on in order to save money. Meanwhile the same administrator is having an elaborate addition to her office consisting of metal studs, sheet rock, screws, tape, WINDOWS (2), door, spackle, primer, paint and let's not the forget labor.
What about our student's needs?

The hallways as I write this e-mail are FILLED with students not in class. WHY? This is in house truancy.This is allowed? This is DISGUSTING.

*WE SHOULD BE GETTING COMBAT PAY TO WORK HERE!*

Get your tail over here now and see for yourself. It is cold in this school
END OF E-MAIL

Mr. Madjar told me so far the month of October was the worse for cutting. They processed **8900 CUTS.** They were processing 400 to 500 cuts a day. One day during the month of October they actually processed 800 cuts. They are all over worked and said thank God NOT every teacher is writing cuts. The cut office estimates only **20%** of the teachers are writing cuts. The others teachers are all so F'n fed up.

NOTE OF INTERST ON BLOCK SCHEDULING -
Students have a 20-minute lunch. Then they have a 20-minute study. Rule of the school - no teacher is to allow a student to leave the classroom in the first 10 minutes and the last 10 minutes of a class. WELL, if the class is 20 minutes what are we supposed to do? Granted some kids will take advantage, however, some kids do need to utilize the facilities? There is no thought in any of this block scheduling at all.

**Nov 6 -** I sent an e-mail to Mr. Wills and Mr. Whitmere editors at the Star Ledger. I was trying anything to get help. How can I trust government when the State of NJ has already taken over and is in charge of the Paterson Public School District? I used a pseudo-name, "Wolfgang Mackadamian.
As with all e-mail I have the originals. Below is a narrative of what I sent.

- I was asking for your help because the school is so out of control and dangerous here.
- Students don't attend class, in the hallways all day long and basically not getting an education.
- Teachers are NOT given an absentee sheet and my reasons.
- Cut office has process 8900 cuts just for October and most teachers are not writing cuts anymore.
- Falsification of student's attendance records.
- The elevators and handicapped children.
- Fire Department was summoned to bring handicap students down from the 2nd & 3rd floors.

- Last week we were without heat and the districts reason why.
- We evacuate the building 14 times because of false alarms this year.
- A VP is allowed to district funds to remodel her office.
- Hope you will investigate right away
- And how I didn't get into all of the violence yet.

**Nov 10** - I received a reply from Mr. Whitmere of the Star Ledger.
Thank you for the information. I am copying another editor on this note as my way of asking he have a reporter get in touch to learn a little more about the situation. Best regards, Kevin Whitmere.
END

**Nov 13** - first day back from a long weekend. What a mess, kids going absolutely berserk. Security are going crazy running all over the place inside and out because of the nonsense going on here all day. I said to my 1st periods students watch they are going to pull the fire alarms. My students said no. At 1:44, 7th period, fire alarms went off; we evacuated the building. Came back in at 1:57, still 7th period the fire alarms go off again, we evacuated the building again. Once we came back in forget about it, the period was LOST, kids all over the place acting up going crazier than before. Received video and 3 photos.

**Nov 14 - 12:26, 5th period,** fire alarms go off. We evacuated the building again. Fire department came. Students showed me their videos, you will see no one including myself taking this serious because this is happening all of the time now. This makes it even more serious and dangerous. We came back in and started the video again.

The video documents the following -- It was nothing but shear out of control chaos, berserkers and there was no supervision. There is no resemblance of a school or any type of educational atmosphere here. All of a sudden, a big fight erupts in the cafeteria. Security and police as well as the students are all running. A policeman in a white shirt escorting a young woman who is cursing and swearing up a storm, followed by two other girls being escorted into security. One girl is wearing a yellow top. Meanwhile the hallways still remained packed with students refusing to go to class.

**All of a sudden the fire alarms go off again, (12:44)** you can see the kids yelling and jumping for joy; they are acting up even more like sharks in a feeding frenzy. We evacuated the building again. JFK HIGH SCHOOL was *never ever* like this until the state took over the school district. It is November and we have had to evacuate the building 19 times.

Once we came back into the building it was *worse*. This place is nothing less than a building where it contains kids where they could do whatever they want. There is not one administrator or anyone of supervision trying to restore order or attempting to tell students to move and get to class. The hallways on all 4 levels were just *packed* with screaming out of control going wild students. In one of the videos, I received students are talking about all of the different fights going on outside during evacuation. There were cops all over the place spraying mace on everyone. You even hear some students complaining because they were sprayed. You see Mr. Pro* one of the TAPs take charge and attempt to get the kids moving all by himself; no one else, no other administrator. It was basically another riot here and I guess administration philosophy is as long as it stays inside and doesn't go outside everything is ok. Keeping up the *good* school image is important? Also, in the video police talk about locking the school down. They were NOT going to go through this again. Meaning having another riot on their hands and allowing it to finally fester and spill out onto the streets. Meanwhile the hallways remain filled/packed with students and will not move. You'll see some students with backpacks, but most students don't and are not carry **books which made me extremely concerned and heightened my sense of awareness. The building** was filling up with added street/beat cops. Meaning not the regular officers who are here every day working their overtime gig. These are officers who have been on their beat and were summoned because of the riot like condition here again. It looks as if the entire police force is here. Now who is paying for all of this and their time being pulled away from other police and the city of Paterson's duties? Eventually, you'll see the principal at the end of the hallway. He is *LOST* and it's his own fault. He allowed this to happen. The student taking the video was right next to me and you can hear me talking with others saying all of this nonsense makes me exhausted. It is because we are so wound up and on guard all the time. We have to be on a constant watch, listen, anticipate for everything, anything, something to happen and be constantly vigilant, on guard, ready or we will get hurt. THIS PLACE IS A COMBAT ZONE. We teachers are wired tight constantly. We cannot do our jobs because of all of the distractions. The noise here alone is so taxing. It is terrible. This is why many teachers are being taken out of here. It is leading to and causing high blood pressure due to stress, PTSD! Our senses are working overtime just having to constantly be alert. We are constantly listening and watching for anything and everything. To think and feel all of this and we have only been here two days.

**Nov 14** - there was a serious threat of firearms in the building, but the school did not lock down, WHY? Watch tomorrow, the security guards will be using the metal detectors. What an "F" joke. All because the school does not want to write up a report and have a paper trail.

**I have a report on a student, (name omitted),** 13 years old, fractured his arm during a food fight in cafeteria. He has been out of school since November 15. He returned, November 20, with right arm in a cast & sling. Student is RIGHT-HANDED.

**Nov 15 - OH MY GOD**, it is absolutely horrible and out of control here. It is the worse. Kids are all over the place and not one administrator telling them to go to class. Never even saw the principal. However, we heard him during morning announcement approximately 7:30, asking teachers if you do not hear this announcement PLEASE call the office to let him know? No, I didn't make a mistake. I burst out laughing. I couldn't believe it. That's what he said, and he said it several more times.

Something had to be going on because today, security was carrying wand type metal detectors. Meanwhile, the hallways were still filled with students *and* there was nothing but fighting all over the place all day long. The students themselves were taking videos of it all today.

Never ever saw (or heard) the principal with exception of early morning announcement asking teachers if you do not hear this announcement PLEASE call the office to let him know?

The idea of the principal making an announcement asking teachers if you didn't hear this PLEASE call the office to let him know is FUNNY and shows how ridiculous this place is.

Unfreakinbelievable, if you didn't hear it how can you let him know?

**#1.** I have a video that's 11:16 minutes long; started several minutes after the bell rang to START class. I went up to the 2nd floor and kids are everywhere instead of class. How can anyone be passing any classes? They are all cutting. Throughout this video you see Arnie*a security guard. Later you'll see another security guard, a tall guy with a beard. I walked all 4 wings of the 2nd floor. Kids are blatantly and deliberately giving me the finger. They know *nothing* is going to be done about it. Eventually I go down to the 1st floor by the art wing. You will hear and see students in the stairwell and door giving me wise remarks and threats knowing they can and will get away with it. You will not see an administrator.

**#2. Video is 3:24 long,** during 5th period at 12:40. Once again WHY are the hallways, stairwells and bathrooms filled students? One kid starts swearing at me in Arabic. Not one student has a pass or their ID card. Some students show their attitude and contempt when they realize they're on video and not in class.

**#3. Video is 7:08 minutes long,** during 7th period. No one should be in the halls however students are threatening me (on video) because I show that they are not in class. With these 3 videos I showed **21:48** minutes of students not in class. Proof the administration is falsifying records with attendance, cutting and lateness's. Why we have false alarms, building evacuations, fires, fighting and other acts of violence, students walking in and out of classrooms they don't belong in, starting situations and causing problems.
    My questions are why is this allowed?
- Why is this still allowed to go on day after day, every day, all day, all year?
- Why aren't students made to go to class?
- Why isn't this considered in school truancy?
- Isn't this considered abuse, neglect via the administration?
- Why isn't the administration held responsible?
- How do so many even graduate from this school, when they do not attend class?

**Nov 15** - I was told by Mr. White*, Mr. Pro* and Dave* the security guard that every student that is suspended, the next day the assistant superintendent Ms. Gerace* tells the principal to bring them back / rescind them. This is the same person in my September 1, 2006, 4th paragraph entry, who said she "would not accept mediocrity." Bottom line there are no laws enforced, no discipline, no rules obeyed, and no recourse for inappropriate, poor and illegal behavior. It is a building where lawlessness exists is nurtured and enforced. Students are never held accountable for anything especially not going to class. Many should be expelled and more should be arrested, but nooooooo all of these very wise and so educated superintendents will not allow it because it will ruin *their* image!

**Nov 16** - Mr. Pro* caught several students urinating on the floor in the hallway yesterday.

Both elevators are still inoperable. Rumor has it that the elevator company will not come because they have yet to be paid for the past repairs.

**10:32, 3rd** period, have video **9:37** minutes long. Went up to the 2nd floor hallways were filled with screaming, yelling, cursing, and just hanging out students in all four wings. I cannot even describe it because this is supposed to be a school and I cannot comprehend why this is allowed. About 8 minutes, I decide to go down to the 1st floor and you still see students in the stairwells. You will notice not one student has their ID card, (waste of taxpayers' money); hear the continuous barrage of foul language and see no one going to class. JFK is nothing more than in school truancy and an indoor street corner.

**Nov 16** - during my lunch there were so many security and police scrambling all over the place. Obviously, there was *another* fight. A few minutes later I see several boys being pulled and dragged into the security office. The students are screaming, yelling, swearing, and threatening everyone as they are brought into the security office. Here's the best part, not even 10 minutes later they were walking out.

**7th period 1:56pm** class has already started. Have video **10:58** minutes long, taken on the first floor, same crap different day, no security, no administrators. Ms. Princess's* door is open, but she never came out to move the students. Hallways filled with students, no IDs and we don't know who belongs in the building? You hear students in the hallways and threatening me, because they are caught cutting and hanging out instead of being in class. Some students get an attitude because I'm the only one doing a job of monitoring who is in the hallway. The foul language and threats to teachers (me) go on as if it is normal. In a way it is, because nothing is done about it. It goes on continually, so you tend to expect it, become thick skinned and eventually it is normal because it happens all day long every day. That is what I mean when I am inside this school, I have no idea what is right and wrong anymore! All of us teachers should be getting combat pay to work here. One of my students came up to me telling me he was absent today. I said to him quietly, you're not supposed to be in the building if you're absent, this is considered trespassing. He said he had to speak to a teacher. I said ok, get out of here before you get in trouble. Have a nice weekend and I'll see you Monday. When I got back to my room, you can hear the principal making an announcement over the PA system calling for me. Shortly after I stop videotaping and went to the principal's office. See my notes about my conversation with the principal.

### *** PRINICPAL'S CONVERSATION ABOUT VIDEOTAPING ***

**Nov 16 -** I was summoned to the principal's office. I have to say he is VERY much and an absolute gentleman. He said people have been complaining about me videotaping. I told him I didn't believe it and for anyone to complain is because they were afraid of the truth coming out.

He said, "It is against the law." I said aren't you videotaping the 1$^{st}$ and 2$^{nd}$ floors, taking students photos for ID cards, and there are cameras outside the building? He replied, "Yes, but we are taping it." I didn't understand what that meant and foolish me, I didn't question what he meant by that. I think, he made a mistake and was trying to cover up what he had almost said by dropping that part of the conversation.

I said, "What's the difference? You're videotaping everything and still allowing this school to be *out of freaking control* and not using the videos to show or prove it all." I will! However, the principal did say in today's technology, people can take a picture, crop it, then place it anywhere to be placed in YouTube, MySpace, etc. I replied, I know, but I never ever thought of that. I am not like that. The principal replied, I know, but I just wanted to give you a scenario why others are concerned. The district's lawyers were concerned when I was videotaping during the chaos. I said then why didn't they have me arrested?

The principal did *not* say chaos. I wrote that because I don't remember his exact word. However, he was referencing to the day of the riots and they wanted to come after me. (Once again, those are **not** the principal's words) However, in my mind I was thinking, if I was doing something illegal and that was what the principal said, then why didn't they come after me then, almost a month ago? I think they are worried that I have a great deal of documentation on what really goes on here at JFK.

I even made a suggestion. I asked him on Monday, after **home room** when the next class has already started, to take a walk up onto the 2$^{nd}$ and 3$^{rd}$ floors. I then asked if he was familiar with the local malls. He replied, "Yes." I then said, that is exactly what the hallways are like, long after the bell rings to be in class. OUT OF CONTROL! I said, "You promised that supervision and all administrators will be present. I said there not anywhere. The students are in the hallways loooong after class has already started. WHY? The principal said, "How can that be? I was up there today right after homeroom." I replied, "Right after homeroom? No way, I was up there and didn't see you. Do you want to see the video?" He quickly snapped back, "NO, NO, I don't want to see the video."

Then I realized he would have to admit to what he saw. However, throughout the entire conversation the principal was every bit the consummate gentlemen and kept saying, Mr. McNulty, you are a professional as so as I. I cannot tell you what to do, BUT I suggest you think about it over the weekend. Like I said, several teachers have complained about you taking their picture. I replied, "I am not taking any one's picture. I am videoing what is going on." He replied, "But they are upset with it." I replied back, "Who are 'they,' because I know it is *not* teachers."

I asked the principal for permission if I may speak directly. As the perfect gentlemen he is, he said yes, please. I said I'm not a politician. I'm just a simple man who talks straight. You know in 21 years I have never felt like this being here. It is so bad here; it is absolutely dangerous and I do **not** feel safe here.

The principal replied, "Do you really think it is that bad here? You have never seen it like this before?"

I almost fell out of the chair. I said NO, this is the worse I have ever seen it in 21 years. I fear that something is going to happen here. I actually fear I am going to get seriously hurt here. I feel like I am still in service and on guard duty. Then I said, "Even as I am talking to you, sir, I am listening and paying attention to my surroundings because I don't know what is going to happen and I want to be ready. It is a horrible feeling." I added, "Because of all of that, I am worn-out when I leave here. I am actually exhausted."

Dr. Miller replied again, do you really think it is that bad?

I said yes and I am not the only one. I asked if I may I make another suggestion. He said yes. I said, next week as you know is the annual pep rally. With all that is and has been going on here it is going to be even more dangerous here.

That is when the principal said, he is thinking of an alternative plan. NOT to have the pep rally and to have it at a later date because of the situations going on.

So, what does that tell you? It tells me he really knows how bad it is here.
Once again, I like the principal. I think he is a good and honest man. Somewhere along the line he got screwed into coming here and allowing all of this to continually go on where education is not a concern.

I said to the principal, "Sir, this place is so dangerous and out of control." I reminded him of the very first day of school when he gave a presentation on where's the cheese, which his message was about being on time. To be followed by Ms. Princess* who said we are allowing students 14, 15 or 16 minutes to be late before it is a cut, which is the complete opposite of what you said. Then he interrupted me (politely) and said we changed that policy. Whatever that meant? I asked changed it when? I asked what policy, there is no policy. There is no documentation of students cutting class other than their folder. WHY? Students are not in class how can they graduate being in the hallways all day long every day? Eventually we both were just repeating ourselves, but not in animosity. The principal said just think about it, ok. I said "Thank you, sir, I will."I shook his hand and wished him a good weekend as he did the same with me.

FOOT NOTE
Before I went to the principal's office, one of the teachers stopped me and said, tonight watch Channel 12, we will be on TV. At 7:05 and about 7:45, JFK was on about the violence in the building, along with interviews from students. That evening while watching Channel 12 news, they said (THEY = the news people) spoke with Dr. Miller. He said it isn't really as bad as all that, everything is under control. He's lying again. Well, if it isn't as bad as all that, then why would he be changing the pep rally which has been a tradition here at JFK if it isn't so dangerous? Obviously, he does realize and knows how bad it is here. Then I realized if it is ok, it's under control, it is not that bad, if it is a safe place, why have so many teachers been assaulted, attacked and there is still one teacher out because of the injuries sustained by students. Meanwhile the administrators are still allowing students to continually hangout throughout the entire building, not having to go to class, all day and every day.

**I just learned today** there was a student who brandished a gun in the cafeteria last Friday. That's why the students ran out of the cafeteria. I have no idea what was done with the student. I did not see anyone that day being arrested or escorted out in handcuffs. Why wasn't the school LOCKED DOWN? Why was it HUSHED UP? If I didn't know about it, how many others in the building didn't know about it? What about the parents who have the right to know and still don't?

**I received an e-mail from a Mr. Ben-Ali, Russell of the Star Ledger:**
Very interested in talking to you about this. Please give me a ring at (201) 646-3xxx at your earliest convenience or email and let me know when you're free to talk. Many thanks.

I replied to Mr. Ben-Ali, Russell the same day. My reply was quite lengthy. It was a combination of my e-mail to Mr. Whitmere and Governor Corzine. I made one request and that was I must remain anonymous until we finally meet. I thanked him and said I hope he can help.

**Nov 21 -** today the principal made an announcement because of the ongoing situations within our school. He felt for *safety reasons* that the Pep-rally will be postponed to a later date. All along he has told the newspapers and the media, that it is *not* that bad here at JFK. Well, if it is so, then why did he postpone the Pep Rally and *admit* it is unsafe? I have the principal's announcement on video about no pep rally. So much for the Channel 12 interview on things are not that bad here!

Mr. Madjar of the cut office told me they have processed 16,000 cuts. Mr. Madjar also said that is *not* the exact number of cuts. It is only the amount of cut slips that have been processed. Lately so many teachers are turning in cuts with multiple dates. Meaning more than one cuts on a sheet. I know, I personally have sent in many cut slips on a student who has been cutting almost an entire month. The approximate number of cuts would be and I am quoting Mr. Madjar, possibly 25,000.

With all of the nonsense and violence going on with the prospects of greater violence that would coincide with today's pep rally or lack of pep rally, students are all over the hallways as if it is Black Friday at the malls. JFK is and has been under *siege*. I have video which is 3:32 minutes long. I am taping this through my class window. I am keeping my door shut because I do not know what is going to happen today and I am not going to be a victim.

**Nov 26 - 6th period 1:23 the fire alarms go off**, as we were getting ready to evacuate the building the principal came over the PA system and told us to disregard the alarm. He said the alarm went off because they were working on it. This doesn't sound right because he has always come over the PA system to warn us about the possibilities of the alarm going off because or repair and etc. Also I heard over security's walkie-talkie that a man with a blue jacket or shirt has pulled the alarm! I will check into this a little more by asking one of the security guards and the head custodian.

**At 1:26, fire department came and entered the building.** So obviously it was a lie about working on the alarms. If they were supposedly working on the alarm system, they would have called the fire department for a heads up in case the alarms accidentally go off?

**ADDED to above entry -** November 30, I was speaking with a secretary from Office #2about the fire alarms on 11/26. She said when she was coming back into the parking lot from lunch, she saw a young man with a blue jacket running like hell as if his life was depending on it. I replied obviously he must be the guy. My question is: didn't the 1st & 2nd floors and outside cameras work? It's because of people like him entering the building that do not belong in here and the administration by not enforcing the rules and consequences with students not wearing their ID cards makes it dangerous for all of us.

**Nov 26 - 7th period 1:52 the fire alarms go off again** within a few seconds, the principal came over the PA system again and told us all to stand by for further instructions. I don't think he knows what to do.

**Have video** (1:14 minutes long) of my room so I can hear the principal say over the PA system in the next few days all students will have to display (wear) their ID Cards because of security reason.

**Nov 27** - spoke with the head custodian today. He confirmed exactly what I suspected. The principal lied about the fire alarms being tested/working on. They were pulled, not twice, but *three times*. Reason, because he said they were working the alarms, so students realized, hey what the heck, no fire department. So, they pulled it AGAIN & AGAIN. Bottom Line, the principal was covering it all up. This continues to make everything worse here. First of all, no one feels safe here. Even when there were several real fires, staff & students do not take them seriously. Sooner or later, it is going to be serious. And who will be held responsible for this? It just makes JFK a more dangerous of a place.

**ADDITIONAL INFO -** I spoke with the head custodian today, **11/29/07,** and asked him if the alarms were turned off? He said, NO and that he explained to the principal, he will not do that again. He does not want to go to jail. He said the principal told him that he would take responsibility for it. The head custodian said, NO, he can't take a chance especially if something God forbid should actually happen!

**Nov 28 -** approximately 12:24, police and Mr. Pro*, a TAP, brought a student inside security. All the while you can hear all this commotion of things being knocked over and pushed around along with the kid cursing and screaming, "Get off my fucking shirt." I wouldn't mind, all he was wearing is what all the kids wear every day no matter how cold it is, a T-shirt. I guess they hushed him up, because I never seen or heard of him again that day. Obviously, none of the big shots saw this.

UNFREAKINBELIEVABLE. I could not figure out why all the VPs were dressed up. Why they were in the hallways starting in the late morning telling students to move get to class, don't stand here and on and on, really putting on a show. This continued as I was leaving to go home at 2:20. It was a dog and pony show. The superintendent, assistant superintendent and a few others central office big shots were walking around, and they were all with police escort. If it's so safe here, then why would they need a police escort? These fools have to come here unannounced to see what is really going on, what it is really like. I bet the fire alarms were turned off. I will find out tomorrow.

**Nov 29 -** I spoke with the head custodian and asked him if the alarms were turned off yesterday. He said, NO. He said he was asked to again. But he refused and made it clear he will not turn them off again.

**12:20** a big food fight again in cafeteria. Not one student was brought out and into security. Wonder why this goes on every day? Why didn't the state superintendent eat lunch in cafeteria yesterday? They should see what it's really like here and what the food is really used for. Then they would need their escort.

**Approximately 12:30,** a math teacher, watched a young lady/student go into an epileptic seizure. No security to be found, no administrators to be found. However, he did see the head custodian and someone from PEOSH. The gentleman from PEOSH utilized his cell phone to call for help. There were no phones that were operable (classrooms) where the young lady went down. The ambulance came but the elevator is still *not* operable, so they had to carefully wheel the young lady down from the 3rd floor via the stairs. Luckily, she was a little girl, not some of our bigger students. Not one administrator came.

**12:34pm**, Mr. Pro* & VP Ms. Lady* were in the center hallway telling students to go to class, which started loooong ago. Some students may move a few feet, but basically ignoring them both. It's now 12:45, Mr. Pro* and Ms. Lady* just left and the students stayed. Now there are NO administrators.

**Nov 30 -** I cannot believe it is getting worse. How in the hell can this happen? During 5th period, two classrooms, room 210 from world language & 212 social studies were destroyed. Everything in the rooms were tossed, broken, destroyed, and thrown all over the floors. First of all, this goes to show how bad it is when students can act like this and have no fear of getting caught! What makes it worse is supposedly no one knew or heard anything. Why? *How*? Me, I don't believe that. I believe people are just afraid and what's a teacher going to go other than get F'ed up! Where are the administrators? I know where, staying away from the students because they run the school. This building is under siege. Students all day long are all over the place like ants on food at a picnic. Even the principal took the day off. Truthfully, I can't blame him. Bottom line two classrooms trashed, and these rooms were from different wings and on opposite sides of the floor.

I was so embarrassed. I saw several sets of parents in the hallways. One could not speak English very well and attempted to ask some students for help. She was harassed, laughed at and made fun of her until a young lady walked over and helped her. Others were walking with their child and the hallways were just filled/packed with students all swearing, fuck this, fucking bitch, I am going to fuck this one up, fuck her and on and on. ABSOLUTELY DUSGUSTING! There was not one administrator. I could see by the look on their faces they were wondering why aren't these students in class? What the hell is going on in here? It was obvious they were scared and just as disgusted.

**I have video 4:50 minutes long.** It is definitely not getting any better. I started right after the bell rang to begin 3rd period. After 10:30 I went up to the 2nd floor. There was no security. There was one lone VP in the middle of it all in the center hall. Hallways were filled with students. When I left it was still filled and so were the stairways. I felt it was time for me to get the hell out of here before something happens and to me.

**NOON**, I am trying to walk to office 1 to pick up my check. The stairwell between office 1 & 2 was FILLED with at least 60–70 students. This is the principal's wing and close to his office. They were screaming, yelling, cursing and swearing up a storm. There was no security or administrators, just the teacher whose classroom is right across from the stairwell and little tiny English teacher. They were both calling for help/security. A few seconds later I see a security guard burst through with a kid. He had him by the back collar of his T-shirt. The kid is swearing fuck this, fuck you, get your fucking hands off of me you mother fucker, I'm going to fuck your ass up, fuck that, I don't give a fuck and on and on all the way to security office. I finally made it to the office and one of the secretaries was calling for security because she was getting so many calls over the walkie-talkie for help. She tells security to go to the library and then to go back to right where I was a few seconds ago, between office 1 & 2 and stairwell. You would think none of this would ever go on next to the principal's office? That's how bad it is here. Students don't care, not afraid or have respect for anyone and that is what I mean, this place is so out of control and DANGEROUS. Then, there was another big brawl. This behavior and out of control is hurting the teachers in the classroom, because if students can act up in the hallway with impunity, what in the hell do you think they do, will do and say to a teacher in the classroom? Meanwhile, the hallways all day remained out of control. It is so dangerous here. I TRULY DO NOT FEEL SAFE HERE!

One of the brawls today was five boys attacked another boy (name omitted) and beat the hell out of him by the library. They did apprehend two students. As far as I know, not one kid was suspended for the fight. As of today, 12/5/07, this boy's right side of his face and eye is still swollen and all black and blue.

**NOTE OF INTEREST: BLOCK SCHEDULE SCREW UP-**
I just realized how screwed up this block scheduling is. 11/19/07 was the last time I had my 1st period A-Day class, until November 29, 2007. The next time we were to have A-Day would be Wednesday, the 21st, but we had early dismissal and that means *no first period*. Then we had two days off for Thanksgiving and two days off for the weekend. Monday, November 26, was a B-Day. Tuesday was an In-Service, so once again early dismissal for students and again, *no first period*. Did not have 1st period, A-Day students

until Wednesday, November 29, 2007, a total of 9 days later. Now what about all of the other classes and courses that lost all those days of instructions? Doesn't anybody do any planning?

**Dec 5 - OH MY GOD,** it is so F'ing bad here. Fights all day long. Food fights all day long. Hallways are filled with out of controlled students. Today, I finally started videotaping students walking in my class who don't belong. You see how they just ignore me and continue to stand in the doorway. All students are to be in CLASS! I do not understand why this is allowed?

Also, Mr. (name omitted), was verbally attacked and threatened by a student. A policewoman wanted to place the student under arrest and couldn't. You know why? She was *not allowed*! On his schedule there is an asterisk, meaning he is Special Ed and cannot be touched. ABSOLUTELY UNNACCEPTABLE! My reply was if he acted like this at the mall the asterisk would mean nothing, and he would be arrested. The teacher who was threatened said absolutely.

The administration comes up with so much BS excuses for students NOT to obey rules and laws. They are preparing these students for a life of failure. Nothing is ever fixed or changed it is always allowed to be left alone unless it is another excuse to pass students for doing *nothing!* It is spreading and we are not cutting out the infection! This entire building needs a massive amputation! While on line to go home, you can hear teachers talking how they are **not** going to be in the hallways anymore unless it is absolutely necessary because it is too dangerous.

**I had such a headache**. I am sure my blood pressure was up. I am absolutely exhausted all because I am constantly wired tight. I'm commuting to war every day when I go to work. I bet the stress level here is the same that any prison guard endures when they are at work! When I got home a little after 3, I sat in my chair and literally passed out, fell asleep, "DIED!" The next thing I knew it was 6. I slept for three hours in the afternoon all due to stress. I have no idea how the security guards at JFK do this all day long every day. They are in the middle of it all, all the time and catch hell from every side, administration, the students, parents and teachers. It's a rough job, with no reward, little money and with a *big* turnover.

**Have video 4:13 minutes long** of the principal making announcement over the PA system, for tomorrow's multicultural meeting. Bringing it to the next level and on and on about this forum, but NOTHING is changing in the hallways or this building. This is all BS. To take back the school is to enforce the rules and have consequences. Grownups are to run the school, not the students!

During the afternoon, Mr. Pardine was trying to get a hold of a kid/trespasser he would not stop. He kept walking away. Mr. Pardine summoned security. The kid ignored them both and kept walking. When finally confronted he still tried walking away. Mr. Pardine and the security guard were asking for his ID Card. This kid was noncompliant and kept walking. Guess what? Nothing was done about it. He was left alone, and everyone went about their business as if this was normal. So much for safety and security! While this was all going on security guards and police were bringing a load of kids into security office. One kid tried smashing the door window. This is what I mean. Nonstop action, tension, violence and it is *not* getting better. It is all allowed to continue. This is supposed to be a school, yet you wouldn't believe it even if you see it for yourself! Not one administrator to be seen. Not even the principal.

**I sent a letter to the President of the PEA Pete Tirri via my union delegate.**
December 5, 2007
Lee E McNulty (Teacher)
John F Kennedy High School
61-127 Preakness Avenue
Paterson, NJ

Dear Mr. Pete Tirri, PEA Officers and all Associates,

On November 16, 2007, I have informed Principal, ▇▇▇▇▇▇▇▇, that I do not feel safe here at John F. Kennedy High School.

I am writing this letter in which I would like to have on file as documentation in case something should happen to me.

I, Mr. Lee Edward McNulty, a teacher at John F. Kennedy High School, do not feel safe here at John F. Kennedy High School. John F. Kennedy High School is out of control and the students are running wild. There is no sense of order or discipline here. Violence is a constant, all day, everyday occurrences here inside and out. I never know when I am going to be attacked.

Every day, it's a constant nightmare to remove students from my classroom who do not belong or are not assigned to my class.

I am ignored, met with verbal threats, a barrage of foul language and inappropriate hand gestures. Many times students standing in the hallways and by the door of my classroom will throw objects at me, my students and just into the classroom, as well as walking in and stealing. All of this makes the working conditions here nauseating, tense, mentally and physically draining, and extremely dangerous. Every student has an assigned classroom.

However, students are continually allowed to gather and hang out in the hallways, stairwells, all entrance and exits to the building.

Already several of my colleagues have been attacked because of the very same situation I have just described. What makes it worse, is that these trespassers, aggressors, attackers of my colleagues go unpunished and without fear of being arrested.

Adding to the chaos here at John F. Kennedy High School, our security personnel are NOT allowed to do their jobs. They catch and apprehend violators, bring them into security office only to be told to let them go. Many of our security personnel have also been assaulted.

Are there a different set of laws, behavior, and standards here at John F. Kennedy High School that the rest of us in a civilized law-biding world have to follow and obey?

When I leave John F. Kennedy High School to go home, I have a headache, upset stomach, mentally and physically drained. All because I am continuously wired tight waiting for something to erupt as if I am in the military on constant guard duty.

I would like to request a lawsuit to be filed for being forced to work in this type of environment where the administration via the district superintendent's orders has caused and continues to be implemented.

This is absurd. This should not and never be happening with in the walls of a SCHOOL.

During contract negotiations, combat pay must be a priority.

LET IT BE KNOWN THAT, ONCE I ENTER JOHN F. KENNEDY HIGH SCHOOL, I NO LONGER HAVE ANY CONCEPT OF WHAT IS RIGHT OR WRONG

I thank you for your time and most needed assistance.

Sincerely & most respectfully,

Mr. Lee E McNulty

**Dec 7** - OH MAN, where do I begin? All day long fights and fighting on every floor continuously. Security brings them into the office and shortly they are released. I have no idea what happened to 10 days mandatory suspension if you fight. Nowadays, here you're attacked. It is so out of control here. There was a huge fight during the beginning of 3rd period. Security, police were flying all over the place. You can hear screaming and panic over the walkie-talkies that they need a nurse, bring the wheelchair. I don't know if this has to do with the fight but as the police and security where trying to get control and catch the attackers, someone jumped into the river. Was it to get away? I don't know. I cannot make this stuff up. It is BIZARRO WORLD HERE!

Parents were coming into the building between 3A & 3B periods, because of the report of weapons (GUNS) and fights. Meanwhile with all that is going on inside here it is somehow and miraculously still all hushed up? I want to know why there wasn't a "LOCK DOWN." Is lying, covering and hushing up, stopping any type of paper trail on everything that goes on inside here more important than the safety of all the children and staff inside this building? Really would anyone from administration actually send THEIR child here? I say it again, I smell a BIG CLASS ACTION LAWSUIT HERE!

**Dec 10 -** I received a copy from the Internet of a newspaper article, THE HERALD NEWS "Paterson community goes to work" Sunday, December 9, 2007, written by Michael E. Glascoe. *Unfreakinbelievable,* it is all lies. And I quote, "Kennedy High is back on track and 'incident free' for over two weeks. Indeed, we are pleased to see this school's resolving problems that have hampered its progress for some time." That's because the administration is covering everything up. They are working harder covering up problems instead of stopping them. They allow them to happen by having the school continuously being *out of freaking control*! Just Friday, December 7, 2007, it was one of the worse days in history, *fights all day long*. Arnie* the security guard had a knife pulled on him. The student only got four days suspension. Can you believe it, not arrested! Remember this is a State Takeover, Run and Operated School District. It is obvious they can do whatever they want and that includes lying to the PRESS.

**Today students set stairwell #15, on fire**. Supposedly they caught the kids on video? So much for on track and without incident!

AND at 12:40, another fight in the cafeteria. A young *lady* being escorted out by security.

I learned today for the 2006 - 2007 school violence and vandalism reports for the entire school district was 98. More lies, cover ups and not filing reports. I bet I have more documentation than what was reported, and they are saying for the entire district! In fact, we here at JFK High School have surpassed that this year already. It is impossible. Between Eastside and Kennedy, the numbers would have to be in the thousands. There are fights every day here. This is major falsification of records and documents. Remember, everything you are reading is *only* what I know or found out. Can you imagine all that is going on that I do not know? Think about it, most of the time security is telling me what has happened. Meanwhile the report say 98 reports were filed for the *entire school district*. I can take this anymore. It is absolutely disgusting. This school district is run by the State of New Jersey, do you actually think I can trust Government at all knowing and seeing what all goes on inside here?
*If there haven't been any incidents here in weeks, then why are parents taking their children out of here?*

**Dec 11 -** it just doesn't stop. Students are all over the building all day long. All you see and hear are students running, pushing, screaming yelling cursing, swearing at the top of their lungs, jumping, knocking people over and on purpose. During 6th period, at approximately 1:50 pm, it was so bad I called the principal's secretary and told her to let the principal know the hallways are filled jam packed and out of control. It was unfreakinbelievable shear chaos. All I can think of is here we go again, another riot. The Police just stood there. It is not their fault. They are following orders to do nothing until they are told to get involved by administration. Security is running around all over the place like chickens with their heads cut off because of all the fights going on all over. Later that day security was on the 2nd & 3rd floors cutting locks off of lockers that did not have a school lock on them, AND what do you think they found, "WEAPONS, PIPES." Yes, JFK is on track. There hasn't been an incident here in over two weeks. I know what he means now. He is playing on words. There hasn't been a fire alarm pulled in 2 weeks. However, that too is a lie; I just check my fire alarm records.

**Approximately 6:09 pm,** I received a taped message from the principal, about students having to wear ID Cards and the school will be enforcing this policy AGAIN! Why wasn't it enforced back in September is beyond me? Anyhow NOW, all students must have an ID card and wear it around their necks on a lanyard. When asked by any adult in school to see it, students must display it. YEA RIGHT!

**Dec 12 - 11:03,** a fight in cafeteria. Students are all standing on the tables. Security goes in and brings out one kid. This kid is cursing up a storm. He is one of the kids who is always in trouble and always starting problems. No surprise here. However, he is yelling some black kid was choking me, what am I supposed to do? But no black kid was brought out? I have learned from being here so long, that I don't believe what anyone says. As far as I am concerned everyone is a liar and guilty until proven differently. It is absolutely the opposite way of thinking here. That's how F'ed up things are here.

**12:33, another fight** in cafeteria. Security brings out three kids. So much for Glascoe's report there are **no** incidents here! **At 12:42 the very same three kids** that were brought into security were released. The administration refuses to do anything and ignores everything so they do not have to write, document, file and submit violence and vandalism reports as if nothing happens. That is what is meant by **no** incidents.

**Dec 13 - no change, it's a catch and release program.** I am watching fights all day long. Students being brought into security by security personnel and police and a few minutes later released to go and continue with their fighting and other chaos here. In one incident, I was very loud yelling, "It doesn't matter, they don't have to go to class, they don't have to do anything, but they will get a diploma."

**Tried to take a video today just as homeroom started, once again, I screwed it up**. You would have seen the 1st and 2nd floors filled with students. It was so loud and noisy you couldn't even hear the pledge of allegiance and announcements being made. All the while students are hanging out all over the place. I waited and started as soon as the bell rang to start 2nd period. It was if nothing changed. Several of the kids were angry because I was taking video. Then I realized it's because they're the students who are constantly and continually in the hallways all day long. These are the students who cause most of the problems, do all the complaining and get away with everything. Even as I was leaving the hallways were just packed. How does any one pass a class and not get suspended for cutting? The administration still allows this to continue. **The video is 5:25 minutes long**.

**9:23, a big fight by ID room.** The girls wouldn't stop. I summoned a VP but he just watched. Finally, several security and police arrived to finally break it up. They didn't bring them to security. Once again *catch & release.* No suspensions for fighting? It is *100% Tolerance to Violence!* These same kids will fight, and cause fights all day now because they know nothing will be done about it.

**10:05** - a female student (name omitted) is being taken out by police in handcuffs? A few hours later, I saw her back in school?

**It's 11:10,** the hallways are still filled jammed packed with screaming out of control students. No one is moving. There is no administration and no security present. Once again, security is way undermanned because of all that is continually going on all over the place and are more than likely running around with all the other nonsense throughout the entire building. They *cannot* be everywhere. Nevertheless, on the 1st floor in the center of the hall all you see are boys wrestling and tackling girls, boys and girls slap boxing, swearing, cursing, pushing, running, deliberately tripping other students, and you do **not** see one administrator. Is it, if I don't see it, I don't write it, IT never happened! There is no schooling going on here. If students fail so what, they'll just blame the teachers! This place is becoming more and more dangerous by the day here. I am wired tight! To make things worse, the hallways remained the same jammed packed with out of control students even when I walked out of my classroom which was 11:35, to look for someone to get these kids moving. I found no one. Where are they, hiding in closets!

**Dec 17** - a few minutes after I walked into the building this morning, 7am the fire alarms go off. I immediately went to the janitor's room to read the electronic panel. It said Auditorium. Fire department came. I took video from my room and you can see the red flashing lights. The head custodian went outside to tell them that it is a false alarm, an electronic problem. YEAH RIGHT! It is obvious someone told him to say that at the last minute. If it was an electronic problem don't you think they would have called the fire department right away before they came? What was really disgusting and scary was everyone walking around asking, do we evacuate the building. No one knows what to do. No one takes the alarms serious anymore, including me.

**5th period,** I went up to the 2nd floor to see the president of the PEA. I did not realize that NJEA UNI-SERV was also present. They were seeing for themselves what it is like in the hallways. There was nothing but kids all over the place. Sadly, many teachers were wrong and very disrespectful to the president. Also they were passing the blame on to security. Obviously, they are all frustrated and feel abandoned in having to work in a place that is absolutely out of freaking control and dangerous. Anyhow and unfortunately, no one saw any security. At that time there were two kids wrestling right in front of us, by a glass showcase. Luckily, there was no glass in the showcase because it was already broken out. I said to the PEA President and the NJEA Reps watch this. I asked the kids to stop. They kept it up. Now I yelled for them to stop. They went on as no one else was around. I screamed louder to make my point and as expected and was demonstrated, the kids just kept it up and ignored me. I then said, "See what I mean, it doesn't matter." I also said there has to be a class ACTION LAWSUIT FILED!

**2:20pm,** something is going on and happening right now. A few seconds later paramedics and more police officers arrived, enter the building and went into security. Kids were all over the place, jumping, wrestling swearing screaming just awful outrageous and uncontrollable behavior going on. Absolutely sickening especially knowing that the State of NJ is running this school and entire District! There were two parents standing by the security entrance door. They were looking and shaking their heads. The woman said to the man, "This place is disgusting, this place doesn't have a handle on anything here." They were shocked. Doll* the security guard came out and started talking with them. They were talking about an incident and a police report. Obviously, their child was involved in something here.

*STUDENT WANTING TO LEAVE KENNEDY BECAUSE IT IS TOO DANGEROUS.*
*SCHOOL ADMINISTRATORS SAID NO?*

**Dec 18** - I was talking with a student of mine, (name omitted), HR 238 and is a sophomore. He told me on Monday, December 10, he came here with his mother to get signed out. He wanted to go to Paterson

Catholic. He and his mother were told NO! I asked him whom did he speak with? He replied, Mr. Lance*, Ms. Princess*, a Mr. (name omitted) a teacher, Dave* the security guard and Ms. (name omitted and I don't know who she is?). His mother made it clear that she doesn't want her son to attend JFK anymore and wants him to attend Paterson Catholic. According to my student all of the above said NO, HE CANNOT GO. I asked why he and his mom didn't speak with the principal. He said Ms. Princess*said he was on the phone. He also said his mom wants to sue the school because other parents took their children out of JFK because it was too dangerous. I asked who? He told me, (three students' names omitted) and there were a few others but didn't remember their names at that time.

**Dec 19** - today was even worse. I was going to go take some videos of students all over the place but decided not to because it doesn't matter. What I have is really what goes on here every day. Anyhow, if necessary, everyone who works here if subpoenaed would have to testify and tell the truth. After all there are over 300 staff and teachers here. SOOOO, I decided to do something else. I went to every BOYS' ROOM/BATHROOMS in the building. I have 6 videos. *Unfreakinbelievable!*

1.     **2:06 minutes long.** 2nd floor - middle of the building above the art wing. I said December 20, but I meant to say was the 19th. It shows the date to the video as December 19, 2007. Bottom line, disgusting, I show and talk about everything, graffiti, no soap, soap dispensers tore off wall, dirty and you can see where they set the fire alarm on fire. The heating system is completely destroyed.

2.     **1:55 minutes long.** 2nd floor, front side of the building, underneath the Science department office. No toilet tissue in either stall. No soap dispensers because they are broken off. DISGUSTING

3.     **2:03 minutes long.** 3rd floor, across from room 348, filthy, graffiti and three places where soap dispensers were. No heating system at all/removed. Ceiling all loaded with either a combination of stains and mold. Open electrical box with wires exposed.

4.     **0:43 seconds long.** 3rd floor, home economics wing, across from room 319.
**All of a sudden, the camera malfunctioned.**

5.     **1:17 minutes long.** Started about 10 minutes later, bottom line, same as above & filthy.

6.     **2:21minutes long.** Bathroom across the front cafeteria the floor is filthy. Floor had large puddles of water everywhere. Soap dispenser DOES WORK. No heating system. The toilet is disgusting. The ceiling has holes and is disgusting. The fire alarm/smoke detector is black from where the kids set the fire alarms off with cigarettes or lighter. It's destroyed and has to be non-operable. This too may be a safety concern especially with all the non-stop smoking that goes on and is allowed to go on every day all day long here. The place itself just stinks like a filthy dirty old ashtray.
THEY WERE ALL DISGUSTING AND NOT CLEAN AT ALL.

**Went to office #1.** All the while the hallways and especially the hallway adjacent to the principal's office were filled jammed packed with students swearing and cursing. Other than the date nothing changes. We have visitors, parents and whomever else that comes into the building and office 1 seeing and hearing of all of this. But nothing is done about it. This is the principal's wing and where was he?

**January 2, 2008,** first day of school in the NEW YEAR, and *NO CHANGE*. Students are all over the place, not in class, walking in and out of my classroom giving me the finger and yelling FUCK YOU. Wonder why people, children, students, teenagers are and act so dysfunctional? It is because improper behavior is allowed to carry on in this school without consequences. Why would any child be allowed to tell a grown up, a teacher, FUCK YOU inside a school and know that NOTHING will happen to them?

I sent an e-mail this evening to the president of the PEA informing him I have the videos ready for pick up. I told him the NJEA is coming tomorrow to pick up their copies.

**Jan 3** - pretty much the same as 1/2/08, It seems there were more students absent yesterday so there are more students in the hallways and in my classroom that don't belong here today.

Mr. (name omitted) of the NJEA picked up the VHS videos and two CDs that I have on everything and all of my information documented. I also gave him a breakdown on everything he was receiving. Such as
- Received VHS Tape
- 2 CDs from cell phone videos
- Updated JFK Video 2006-2007 VHS & cell phone list
- Will send via e-mail updated documentation pertaining to all JFK boys' rooms & their conditions
- A memorandum we received about the "Conscientious Employee Act Whistle Blower Act."

*FROM THIS POINT THE NJEA & PEA HAVE COPIES OF EVERYTHING*

**Jan 4** - FIGHTS all day long, especially during the afternoon. SUPPOSEDLY it is to be better starting Monday with *Zero Tolerance* for students *not* having their ID cards. The principal came over the PA system "AGAIN," warning students that they WILL need their ID Cards to even get into class? Gee, WE never heard that before!

*\* The next three entries 1/4, 1/11 & 1/17/08, I kept together. Then the dates continue chronologically.*

**Jan 4 - SPEAKING OF FIGHTS,** I was in the cafeteria around 11:30. The police ran out and all I heard was them yelling, let's go, fight, fight. It wasn't until later this afternoon, I found out after speaking with Mr. Pro* that some student actually had the balls to punch him in the mouth. I can see the poor guy's mouth/lip was swollen and still see blood on his front teeth from his bleeding lip. I asked if he pressed charges, he said yes. Now, I find that funny, because when a student attacks a teacher, they are hardly ever suspended. I asked if the kid was suspended, and he replied, "OH HELL YES!" He told me VP Mr. Nickels* said he will sign off on the suspension and that this kid (name omitted) HR 250, a 9th grader is suspended indefinitely. INTERESTING, try to get backing by administration if you're a teacher?

I personally find the situation with Mr. Pro* terrible. He is a GOOD GUY. He's a good-hearted guy. He looks and is built like a professional football player. You would have to be out of your mind to even think about hitting him.

**Jan 11 - I was told by Mr. Pro\***, that this student's mother knows one of the superintendents and NOW assault charges have been filed on him by her. What makes this all disgusting, whether you're a teacher or not, is that the principal as well as the district administration is *not* supporting him.

**Jan 17** - I was told this morning Mr. Pro* has to leave JFK and report to Personnel? I don't know if it's for reassignment, suspension or whatever? However, it all has to do with the boy who smacked him in the mouth. This is why I fear working here. Now if students can assault a VP/TAP and not only get away with it, is backed up more by the administration what do you think would happen if it was a teacher? Like I have said over and over, everything here is backwards. What's right is wrong. What's wrong is right. I don't know the difference anymore when I' here. Most disgustingly, what kind of message is the administration sending to students on what they can do and get away with?

<u>**Continues Chronologically.**</u>

**Jan 4** - there were some big shots in the building today. I noticed for the first time in MONTHS that the principal was in the hallway (about 11 am) telling students to walk and talk. Then once the dog and pony show was over, all hell broke out. *Absolute chaos!* The students run this place. Nevertheless, the rest of the school day was a disaster. Listen to what I said, "SCHOOL DAY!" There hasn't been a school day here in years and it is the worse this year which is only 4 days old. This place is disgusting; lies are constantly told & reported on how safe & wonderful this place is.

**Jan 5** - Saturday, received ANOTHER phone call from the principal via robot phone service stating that January 7, 2008, ZERO TOLERANCE to students ID will be enforced. SURE!

**Jan 7 approximately 9:35** - I went upstairs to give a teacher a package that has all of the videos. She is delivering them to the president of the PEA. The hallways were packed with students like bees on honey. They would walk into a classroom, a few seconds later walk right out. Then do the same to the next classroom and the next and the next as if they were at a party. It looks as if most of the students were not even in class. Some are students I had last year who had over 90 cuts and close to 100 days absent and were promoted/moved up to the next grade. This is what goes on if you're a student and especially if you're Special Ed at JFK.THAT'S NO CHILD LEFT BEHIND!

**Later,** I was in the cut office when a female teacher told us that a male student told her "Do not raise your voice to me, "YOU FUCKING TRICK!" Guess what, and *NOTHING* was done about it.

**A student told me** as he and other students were coming into the building, security was asking to see IDs. Students just ignored them. So much for enforcing *Zero Tolerance for students wearing IDs*!

**ALL DAY** students were all over the place and not one student has their ID. Remember all of the announcements, phone calls and today a bulletin from the principal stating the enforcement of, reasons and the consequences for *NOT* wearing ID. Was it enforced? NOOOOOOOOOOOOOOOO. I went upstairs the hallways and stairwells were filled with students. And to think taxpayers are paying for this. You can hear security yelling get out of the hallway, but they are ignored. I have 6:39 minutes of video.

**Have video** during my lunch period, 1st floor hallways no different, no change and no control!

**Jan 8,** speaking with Mr. Madjar &Mr. Pardine of the cut office. <u>*Note the following --*</u>
- As of yesterday, they processed over 30,000 cut slips. *That's cut slips!*
- (Name omitted) HR 253, 129 Cuts says he shouldn't be suspended, give him detention.
- (Name omitted) HR 216, 180 Cuts, is a senior!

Have video. Bottom line all the same crap. You will see Ms. Princess* eventually just walk on by and ignore everything as if everything is fine. You will not see any students wearing ID cards.

**Jan 9** - we have a new PA & bell/horn system. At 10:03 the bell/horn went off. Students left classes. It was not the right time. Between 10:07 and again at 10:10, the principal made an announcement that the alarms went off in avertedly. Teachers are not to allow students to leave and to get students back into their classrooms. Yeah Right! You have to be kidding? What planet is he from? Students do not listen to him; they will never listen to teachers. After all, why are students in the hallway all day long in the first place? I am not fooled because today we have visitors. Soooo, the principal and all the administrators are putting on a dog and pony show. Now the teachers are left again to go crazy cleaning up their mess.

**Jan 11** - a few minutes into 2nd period, I went up to the 2nd floor. What a disaster, I started to record the hallways that were just filled with students. The only administrator present was Mr. Arthurs* a very well mannered, refined and distinguished gentleman. You will hear him saying come on students get to class.

But the hallways were getting worse and worse by the second. I walked all over the 2nd floor and down each hallway. Then all of a sudden, a fight broke out between two girls right in the center hallway. Once again, no security, no administrators! The one girl was actually picked up and thrown into one of the showcases. It is a good thing that the glass was broken before and not in place. This young lady would probably been cut in half. Students, 100s of them, were circling them like a pack of hungry wolves and antagonizing the fight even more. It was really scary. I thought the entire floor was about to erupt into one big fight. It went on for quite a while until two male teachers broke it up. Unfortunately, being girls fighting, we as guys are afraid to do get involved in breaking it up especially knowing the possibilities and problems that could and most likely would happen afterwards. I decided to keep walking around some more. It just kept getting worse. Kids were actually hanging by classroom doors, disrupting the classes inside by banging on the door or glass, talking to someone by opening the door partly and talking through the door. The school is so out of control and it is *not* getting better. It is more dangerous now than before we left for Christmas break. I finally had enough and decided to go back to my classroom. You can hear student threatening me for taking video. "THREATENING!" That is how brazen these punks are. Once I entered my classroom, I took a picture of the clock in my room **(9:40)** and of today's newspaper. The situation in the hallways is happening every day all day long. And to make things worse I found out that neither of the girls were suspended? Names are omitted however, one girl age 16, received 5 days in Zone and the other girl received 3 days in Zone. Ten-day suspension is mandatory for fighting. However, the school and district does not want to fill out, document and submit everything to the state showing how bad things really are here. In reality administrators are lying, covering everything up to protect the so-called image of this DUMP! It is all smoke and mirrors. As far as I'm concerned by not writing up and sending all of these incidents reports in, it is still falsifying records.

**Jan 15** - I haven't bothered to write anything in the last 2 days because it really doesn't matter anymore. I'm so tired, disgusted and confused. Don't understand how any of this is ALLOWED to go on in a school and especially from a district that was taken over by the State because it was operating so poorly. Today a bunch of girls during 7th period just wouldn't leave. They kept banging on the door, yelling obscenities, and swearing as if they were all out in the streets. DISGUSTING! It doesn't stop!

**Jan 16 -** I learned today that Mr. Nelson*, a gym teacher, was attacked yesterday. He is pressing charges. This too is hushed up. Let's see what happens? What makes things even worse, he was supposedly attacked by a 19-year-old freshman who is on parole. Unfortunately, that's all the info I can get.

**Jan 17, 11:37, fire alarms went off today.** We evacuated the building. Fire department and more police came. We came back in at 11:53. It was another false alarm, pulled in basement post #14. In fact, a fight started to erupt. One teacher was trying to break it up, when Mr. (name omitted) a Math teacher, walked over and grabbed a kid and pulled him away to talk with him. What happened after, I have no idea. **Received video and some photos.**

**Jan 18, about 12:10 -** there was a big fight on the 2nd floor "Dominican Wing." Seems the "West Side Gang," jumped this little Mexican Kid and for no reason. As far as I know, nothing was done about it. This poor kid really took a beaten.

**Jan 22** - it is getting worse. There are more kids than ever in the hallways. I know I keep saying that, but it's true. Eventually there will be NO ONE in any classes. Most students should be receiving F's for this marking period. This school is nothing more than an indoor street corner for in House Truancy.

**A Spanish teacher** asked a young man who did not belong in her classroom to leave. He refused. She went to summon security. He violently threw her up against the wall. She fell and her face hit the floor cracking her tooth. The Spanish teacher went to the school nurse. However, from what I was told the nurse refused to check her out *until* she received a report? I couldn't believe that. It didn't make sense. This is what I said and warned what would happen. Being that Mr. Pro* was assaulted, removed from JFK, transferred to another school, students now think they can definitely do what they want and get away with it. This is NOT a school. This place is getting more and more dangerous by the day. It is scary here.

**Jan 23** - I was told the following. While the teacher was on the ground another boy was trying to set her hair on fire with a cigarette lighter. I confirmed this to be true with the documentation I received. It is written in the section or page called -
**PART II - TO BE COMPLETED BY BUILDING ADMINISTRATOR.**

**On February 6, 2008,** I received seven pages of documentation on the attack. I sent copies to the PEA & the NJEA. Speaking with one of the secretaries, I learned the Spanish teacher is not pressing charges. It seems the father of the student who attacked her is in jail for murder. The father is *supposedly* in the Latin Kings. So, the Spanish teacher is scared. Can you blame her? However, I can and do blame the school district for *NOT* pressing charges. All because of the assault, I was told the teacher had surgery the other day.

**MY COMMENTS -** If you think about it with what had happened and how it happened including the outcome, NO ONE, not even one student from her class came to help her. They sat there and watched their teacher not only being assaulted by a 17-year-old freshman, but as another boy attempted to set her hair on fire. What does that say about the climate and mentality of this school? The more and more I think about I wonder if any teacher would have helped. Everyone is afraid of doing anything, because of possible repercussions and firing. That is how screwed up everything is here. Like I say over and over, nobody knows what is right and wrong anymore while we are here.

From what I understand the district/superintendent wants the teacher to be transferred? Once again, let's protect the child/the CRIMINAL! What is going on here and in society? This is exactly what I have been saying all along. The inmates (students) run the school and this is a State Takeover, Run and Operated School District. Furthermore, all of this was *HUSHED UP*. None of this was in the newspapers, on the radio or TV. How can that be? This was a **CRIMINAL ACT!**

*HERE ARE SOME DOCUMENTS OF THE ATTACK*

## Paterson Public Schools
### John F. Kennedy High School
### Office of School Safety
### OFFICIAL REPORT

Date: 01/22/08
Time: 1:45 pm
Location: Room 209
Incident: Aggravated Assault
Submitted By: Sgt. ███████, PPS █6█
File No. PPS-012208-2

Narrative:

On 01/22/08 at 1:45 pm, Mrs. ███ ██████, the teacher in room 209 states that ██████ ██████ pushed her out the classroom door causing her to fall on the floor. In the course of her falling on the floor Mrs. ██████ hit her head and cracked her tooth.
The teacher stated that ██████ did not belong in her classroom as he was not her student. ██████ was apprehended by security and taken to the security office for questioning.
██████ admitted that he did not belong in Mrs. ██████ class and that he pushed her and the door to leave the classroom.
A police incident report was made although the teacher declined to press charges against the student.
Ms. Van Hoven is handling the discipline in this matter.
This matter is currently pending further investigation by this office.
End of Report.

(see attached medical report)

PATERSON POLICE DEPARTMENT | NARRATIVE | FILE CONTROL # ▓▓

While working an off-duty assignment at JFK High School on 1-22-08, this officer was advised by school security that a teacher, Mrs. ▓▓, was assaulted by a student, ▓▓ ▓▓.

Mrs. ▓▓ states that the student was in her class room and did not belong there. She told the student to stay in the class while she contacted school security. As she looked out of the class room door for school security, the student pushed her out of the way of the door so he could leave the room. After being pushed Mrs. ▓▓ fell onto her front on the floor. The student then fled down the hallway.

Mrs. ▓▓ informed school security who the student was and they found him in his class and brought him to the school security office where he positively identified ▓▓ ▓▓ as the student who pushed her down.

Mrs. ▓▓ did not suffer any serious injuries from this assault. He was advised of her rights and stated that she did not wish to sign complaints at this time.

School security advised that they would further handle this matter in school.

---

Note, "They" (meaning the school and districts administration) would further handle this matter in school. The administration is only concerned about the PERCEPTION of the school not what truly goes on within it. The school & district which is a State Takeover District wants it all kept quiet, hushed up.

**PATERSON PUBLIC SCHOOLS**
**EMPLOYEE INCIDENT/ACCIDENT REPORT**

Received by Risk Management: stamp_____

PART I – TO BE COMPLETED BY EMPLOYEE (IN PRESENCE OF ADMINISTRATOR)

1. Last Name: ███  First Name: ███  Middle Initial:
2. School Phone #: 973-321-8500   Home Telephone #: 973-720-8███
3. Street Address: 69 ███ Ave. Totowa, NJ
4. City:   State:   Zip Code:
5. Date of Birth: 4-█-40   Social Security Number: 066-██-████
6. Date of Hire: 4/█/1985   Sex: M (F)
7. Occupation/Job Title: Spanish Teacher
8. Marital Status: Married
9. Annual Wage Rate/Specify 10 or 12 month employee:
10. School/Building Location Where Employed: JFK HS
11. Date of Injury or Illness: 1/22/08
12. Time Employee Began Work on Date of Injury or Illness: 8:15 AM  3:10 PM
13. Time of Injury or Illness: AM  2 PM
14. Name of Administrator to whom employee reported injury/illness: Mr. ███
15. Date Employer was Notified of Injury or Illness: 1/22/08
16. Specific Location Where Injury or Illness Occurred: Rm #209
17. Specific Activity Employee was Engaged in When the Injury or Illness Occurred: Teaching Class
18. How did the injury or illness occur? Describe the sequence of events and describe any objects or substances that directly injured the employee or made the employee ill:

## PART II – TO BE COMPLETED BY BUILDING ADMINISTRATOR

1. Name of School Employee In Charge at Time of Incident: ▓▓▓ Phone #: 973-321-0500

2. First Aid Given: (YES) NO
   By Whom? ▓▓▓ s RN
   Ambulance Called? YES (NO)

3. a. Nature of Injury or Illness (As Reported by Employee): Teacher states was thrown against the wall by a student. She states ① frontal forehead than fell to floor and was kicked on ② hip. States her whole body hurts. Upset and very anxious during assessment. BP 146/70. While interviewing ① molar/connected to bridge broke off. Orasol applied to tooth. Also states that another student was trying to set her

   b. Nature of Injury or Illness (As Reported to the Administrator by School Nurse): hair on fire with a lighter.

4. Nature of Visible Injuries or Conditions Observed by Administrator:

5. Reported Injury or Illness Investigated By:
   Name:                          Business Tel. No.

6. Findings of Investigations: (provide separate sheet if necessary, and include copy of report to facilities, if any)

I CERTIFY THAT THE FOREGOING STATEMENTS MADE BY ME ARE TRUE. I AM AWARE THAT IF ANY OF THE FOREGOING STATEMENTS MADE BY ME ARE WILLFULLY FALSE, I AM SUBJECT TO PUNISHMENT.

ADMINISTRATOR SIGNATURE: _____ DATE: _____

ASST. SUPERINTENDANT: _____ DATE: _____

OFFICE OF THE DISTRICT SUPERINTENDENT
PATERSON PUBLIC SCHOOLS
Paterson, New Jersey

SUSPENSION REQUEST

SCHOOL: JFK
DATE: 01/23/08
CODE NO.: 1166710   HR NO. 105D   GRADE: 9   DOB: 12/██/90   AGE: 17
NAME: ███████
TELEPHONE NO.: (973) 519-3███
ADDRESS: 86 ███████ AVE, PATERSON, NJ 07522
ETHNIC BACKGROUND: SPANISH
NO. OF DAYS SUSPENDED: 10
STARTING DATE: 01/23/08
ENDING DATE: 02/05/08
RETURN DATE: 02/06/08
SEX: MALE

COMPLAINT AGAINST STUDENT: ASSAULT ON A TEACHER

DATE OF HEARING: 01/22/08
NAMES OF THOSE PRESENT AT HEARING: STUDENT, MS. ███████, OFFICERS R███████ AND R███████ N, ███████

RESULT OF HEARING: 10 DAYS SUSPENSION

INDICATE ANY REFERRALS MADE AS A RESULT OF THE HEARING:
V & V Report, Police Report, Employee Incident Report

CONDITIONS FOR RETURN TO SCHOOL:
PARENT MUST ACCOMPANY STUDENT FOR RE-ADMIT

PARENT WAS NOTIFIED OF SUSPENSION BY: ███████

COMMENTS:
TO DATE: TOTAL SUSPENSIONS: 3
152  TOTAL DAYS: 25

OFFICE OF THE SUPERINTENDENT        PRINCIPAL

(White) Original   (Yellow) Special Services   (Pink) Student File

---

**Jan 23** - I received a profile of a 17-year-old male student, name omitted, who has a total of **139 cuts!** How does any one pass? It is NOT about students being educated or if they have earned and satisfy their educational requirements. It's ONLY to make it look as if the graduation rate has improved. This is all allowed to continually go on by a State takeover and controlled school district.

Below is his profile. He is only one example of the 100s of students with rampant cutting.

321

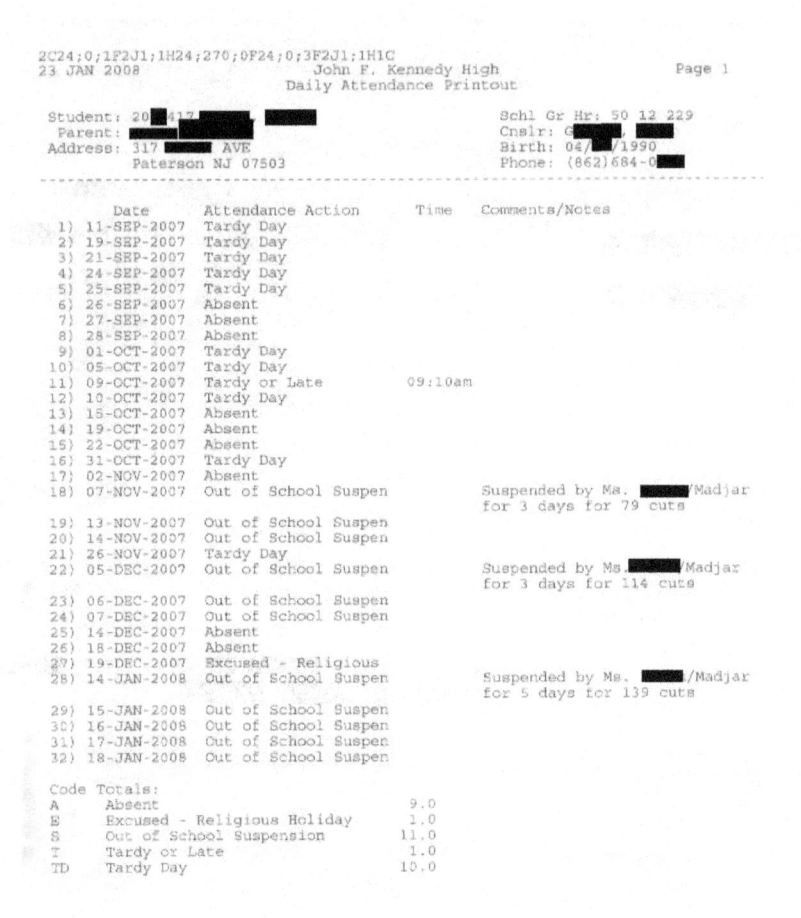

```
2C24;0;1F2J1;1H24;270;0F24;0;3F2J1;1H1C
23 JAN 2008                    John F. Kennedy High              Page 1
                              Daily Attendance Printout
     Student: 20█████ ███████            Schl Gr Hr: 50 12 229
     Parent:  █████████                  Cnslr: G█████,█
     Address: 317 ██████ AVE             Birth: 04/██/1990
              Paterson NJ 07503          Phone: (862)684-0███
     ------------------------------------------------------------------
          Date        Attendance Action    Time    Comments/Notes
      1)  11-SEP-2007 Tardy Day
      2)  19-SEP-2007 Tardy Day
      3)  21-SEP-2007 Tardy Day
      4)  24-SEP-2007 Tardy Day
      5)  25-SEP-2007 Tardy Day
      6)  26-SEP-2007 Absent
      7)  27-SEP-2007 Absent
      8)  28-SEP-2007 Absent
      9)  01-OCT-2007 Tardy Day
     10)  05-OCT-2007 Tardy Day
     11)  09-OCT-2007 Tardy or Late       09:10am
     12)  10-OCT-2007 Tardy Day
     13)  15-OCT-2007 Absent
     14)  19-OCT-2007 Absent
     15)  22-OCT-2007 Absent
     16)  31-OCT-2007 Tardy Day
     17)  02-NOV-2007 Absent
     18)  07-NOV-2007 Out of School Suspen      Suspended by Ms. ██████/Madjar
                                                for 3 days for 79 cuts
     19)  13-NOV-2007 Out of School Suspen
     20)  14-NOV-2007 Out of School Suspen
     21)  26-NOV-2007 Tardy Day
     22)  05-DEC-2007 Out of School Suspen      Suspended by Ms. ██████/Madjar
                                                for 3 days for 114 cuts
     23)  06-DEC-2007 Out of School Suspen
     24)  07-DEC-2007 Out of School Suspen
     25)  14-DEC-2007 Absent
     26)  18-DEC-2007 Absent
     27)  19-DEC-2007 Excused - Religious
     28)  14-JAN-2008 Out of School Suspen      Suspended by Ms. ██████/Madjar
                                                for 5 days for 139 cuts
     29)  15-JAN-2008 Out of School Suspen
     30)  16-JAN-2008 Out of School Suspen
     31)  17-JAN-2008 Out of School Suspen
     32)  18-JAN-2008 Out of School Suspen

     Code Totals:
     A     Absent                          9.0
     E     Excused - Religious Holiday     1.0
     S     Out of School Suspension       11.0
     T     Tardy or Late                   1.0
     TD    Tardy Day                      10.0
```

**Jan 24 - FIGHTS ALL DAY LONG.** Looks as if every kid is in the hallways and this place is absolutely worse than yesterday. I *have* to keep my classroom door close. Even doing that, students who do NOT belong in my class are banging, kicking, tapping on the glass on the door, yelling, screaming, cursing, giving all sorts of vulgar hand gestures, anything and everything in defiance and or just trying to contact another student and distract my class. They are not deterred or scared of me or care. Actually, they challenge and threaten me when I do go to the door to tell them to leave.
I am watching students walking in and out of the building all over the building and especially via the back doors. They are coming back in unchallenged, with Chinese food, pizza, food and drinks from Checkers. So much for the school being safe and improving the security with ID cards.

This goes on continually every day, all day long; there is no way the administration nor any of us know who is a trespasser or not. That's the point of having and wearing IDs! In the meantime, students in defiance are not wearing them or don't even have them. However, I have to admit, that when Mr. Lance*, one of the TAPs, catches students not having their IDs he says I'm following the principal's orders and have been suspending them. The students are kicking up a fuss and carrying on, swearing, you can't do this, this isn't right, you can't make me wear an ID, I don't have to have an ID, and on and on. They have been warned and warned over and over. Nevertheless, I bet if every student was checked and challenged for ID Cards, most of them would be sent home. The administration is not going to do that for the same reason they allow students to be in the hallways all day long and I don't know what that reason *IS!*

**Jan 24** - as we were lining up by the office to go home, you should see all the kids, I mean hundreds are just filling up the hallways to sign up for "NOVA NET." What a JOKE. Most of the kids I see are kids that are in the hallway all day, every day, since September. Another added expense to the taxpayers because the administration continually allows students to be in the hallways instead of being in class and now, they can make up their time by signing up for "NOVA NET." One student was assigned to me last year. The reason I say assigned, is because out of the entire school year, maybe he showed up in total a WEEK. He was always in the cafeteria and hallways all day long. AND, I am really stretching the word, "WEEK."

**Jan 28 - have video 6:09 minutes long, started at12:16.** Each day is worse than the last. Nothing changes with exception of the kids who refuse to go to class yelling I CANNOT take videos. That's how defiant they are. If they were in class, the NJ taxpayers wouldn't have to pay the added BIG BUCKS for them to sign up for NOVA NET.**PLUS.** NOVA NET costs the taxpayers more than it cost for summer school. So many students are not failing just one class, but as many as 7 and 8. I have the documentation.

Have a memo from Dr. Miller stating, "Effective immediately, all serious incidents must be reported to me immediately. Serious incidents include but are not limited to the following: weapons, assaults or threats, staff on staff assaults, students on staff assaults, staff on student assaults, rioting, false or real fire alarms, serious student altercations, terrorist threats, arrests of students or staff and physical harm to students or staff because of an in school incident.

Please get the preliminary information and do the investigation. However, do not wait for the investigation to be completed before notifying me. **I must be notified immediately so a preliminary "Heads Up" report can be submitted to Ms. Gerace* an assistant superintendent."**
I would like to know what does **"Heads Up,"** mean.

If I am off campus at the time of a serious incident, the incident must be reported to the lead Assistant Principal in charge. The lead Assistant Principal will be responsible for contacting Ms. Gerace* at 10790 and me via my cell phone at 443-994-xxxx.

As your principal, I thank you for your continual support as we transition our school from a Good School to a GREAT SCHOOL."
What B/S and lies. Please explain, "How is this even considered a 'Good School'!"

**Jan 30 - 3rd period, 10:40** - fire alarms go off, evacuated the building. False alarm! Fire department came. The fire alarm was pulled in stairwell #14, in the basement. I sent video & 2 pictures to the NJEA.

*THE OFFICIAL JOHN F. KENNEDY HIGH SCHOOL IDENTIFICATION POLICY.*

## JOHN F. KENNEDY HIGH SCHOOL
## IDENTIFICATION POLICY

For the overall safety, welfare, and security of the John F. Kennedy High School community, ALL STUDENTS are required to have and wear an official John F. Kennedy High School ID. With a student population of our size, staff members cannot know all students by name. Therefore, because of safety and security concerns, students are to correctly identify themselves by presenting their ID.

The ID must be worn in an appropriate and visible location (at waist level or above). Students are required to wear their ID badges with the picture side visible to enter the following areas: the building, the cafeteria, classrooms, the library, to ride the bus, and to enter any athletic event on or off campus. **ALL STUDENTS MUST PRESENT THEIR ID BADGES WHEN REQUESTED BY SCHOOL ADMINISTRATORS, TEACHERS, SECURITY PERSONNEL AND ANY OTHER ADULT STAFF MEMBER ASSIGNED TO JOHN F. KENNEDY HIGH SCHOOL.**

Students must not change, alter, or deface their IDs, nor should the ID be worn by anyone other than the student whose name appears on the ID. The first ID badge is issued early in the year at no charge to students. Additionally, all newly assigned students to John F. Kennedy with a schedule will be issued an ID at no charge. Students with no ID will be sent to the **School Security Office** and be given the opportunity to secure a new ID for a fee of $ 5.00. Students who repeatedly violate the ID Policy are subject to the following disciplinary actions:

| VIOLATIONS | PENALTY |
| --- | --- |
| 1ST Violation | A one time temporary ID will be issued for the current day violation. Parent notification. |
| 2nd Violation | 1 Day Suspension from school. Parent notification and phone conference for reinstatement. |
| 3rd Violation | 2 Day Suspension from school. Parent notification and parent conference for reinstatement. |

The proper use of wearing your ID will help to foster a safe and secure environment where optimal learning can take place. Finally, a student must surrender his/her ID badge upon transfer or withdrawal from John F. Kennedy High School.

January 3, 2006

*Next is an updated 2007 – 2008 Drop from Enrollment List.*
*Notice the ages of 9RR's and the 9RRR's.*

**John F. Kennedy High School**
**Drop from Enrollment List**
**Grade 9**

| # | I.D Number | Student Name | Grade Repeated (R) | Homeroom | Absences | Cuts | Tardy | Failures | Credits | Age | Att. Letters | Att. Contact | Truant Visits | Hearing Date | Hearing with | Reinstate yes / no | Reinstate Date |
|---|---|---|---|---|---|---|---|---|---|---|---|---|---|---|---|---|---|
| 1 | 12▮661* | ▮ | 9R | 336 | 84 | 23 | 15 | 7 | 0 | 16 | 3 | none | 1 | | | | |
| 2 | 13▮141* | ▮ | 9RRR | 336 | 25 | 131 | 22 | 11 | 25 | 18 | 2 | 11/27/2007 | 2 | | | | |
| 3 | 10▮861 | ▮ | 9RR | 404 | 60 | 54 | 9 | 15 | 28.8 | 18 | 4 | none | 2 | | | | |
| 4 | 12▮217* | ▮ | 9R | 109 | 98 | NA | 3 | 13 | 1.25 | 16 | 2 | none | 1 | | | | |
| 5 | 10▮884* | ▮ | 9RRR | 336 | 96 | 38 | 6 | NA | 15 | 17 | 3 | none | 1 | | | | |
| 6 | 12▮205 | ▮ | 9 | 222 | 45 | 165 | 2 | 11 | 11.3 | 16 | 4 | 1/8/2008 | 2 | | | | |
| 7 | 11▮553 | ▮ | 9 | A4 | 46 | 91 | 13 | 8 | 5 | 16 | 4 | none | 3 | | | | |
| 8 | 20▮667 | ▮ | 9R | 213 | 32 | 140 | 30 | 11 | 30 | 17 | 5 | 1/9/2008 | 2 | | | | |
| 9 | 13▮468 | ▮ | 9 | 106 | 38 | 182 | 45 | 11 | 0 | 16 | NA | none | NA | | | | |
| 10 | 10▮040 | ▮ | 9RR | A4 | 46 | 55 | 22 | 8 | 43.8 | 16 | 4 | none | 2 | | | | |
| 11 | 20▮180* | ▮ | 9R | 213 | 41 | 87 | 15 | 10 | 10 | 16 | 3 | none | 1 | | | | |
| 12 | 20▮204* | ▮ | 9RR | 250 | 66 | 53 | 3 | 8 | 25 | 16 | 3 | none | 0 | | | | |
| 13 | 11▮783 | ▮ | 9RR | 213 | 30 | 96 | 19 | 13 | 5 | 16 | 2 | none | 1 | | | | |
| 14 | 11▮471 | ▮ | 9R | 220 | 48 | NA | 10 | 8 | 15 | 16 | NA | none | 2 | | | | |
| 15 | 1▮007 | ▮ | 9RR | A3 | 96 | 12 | 1 | 13 | 0 | 16 | 3 | none | 1 | | | | |
| 16 | 20▮561 | ▮ | 9R | 222 | 37 | 91 | 5 | 14 | 5 | 16 | 4 | 1/23/2008 | 2 | | | | |
| 17 | 20▮393 | ▮ | 9RR | 210 | 27 | 100 | 23 | 12 | 18.8 | 17 | NA | none | NA | | | | |
| 18 | 14▮135 | ▮ | 9R | 200 | 45 | 243 | 10 | 16 | 10 | 16 | 5 | none | 2 | | | | |
| 19 | 20▮445* | ▮ | 9RRR | 219 | 55 | 35 | 25 | 14 | 25 | 17 | 5 | none | 1 | | | | |
| 20 | 10▮251* | ▮ | 9RRR | 210 | 79 | 60 | 24 | 11 | 15 | 18 | 2 | none | 0 | | | | |
| 21 | 11▮927 | ▮ | 9R | 311 | 55 | 171 | 4 | 17 | 5 | 17 | 3 | none | 1 | | | | |
| 22 | 11▮795 | ▮ | 9RR | 327 | 53 | 177 | 8 | 18 | 1.25 | 16 | 3 | 12/8/2007 | 1 | | | | |

Grade 9
Spec Ed  8
Reg. Ed.  14
Total  22

Grade 9 = 1 year
Grade 9R = 2 years
Grade 9RR = 3 years
Grade 9RRR = 4 years

Letters Mailed  22
Appealed
Reinstated
Not reinstated
No reply

**Feb 1** - have video starting approximately 12:30. No change other than the date and day on the calendar.

**Feb 2 - Received an e-mail from the PEA           Subject: Fwd. Keep Dr. Glascoe**
Some of you may have seen the email that Irene Sterling sent out to try to continue her battle to retain Dr. Glascoe. It is clear that she, Sayegh and Hodges, plan to keep everything focused on Dr. Glascoe and not on trying to turn the Paterson School District around. While she plays these games, Kennedy just gets worse (3 more assaults on staff in the past couple of weeks), there still are not sufficient supplies and materials in the schools and none of the issues that must be resolved in order for our students to get a thorough and efficient education are being addressed.

I'd like to suggest that you do as she asks, call the number (609) 777-2510 and send a simple message.

Commissioner Davy did the right thing in accepting Dr. Glascoe's resignation. Don't let a few of his supporters try to convince you otherwise. This district needs competent, educationally sound, fiscally prudent leadership, and that's where our attention should be focused.

Once you've called, please forward this to as many staff members as you can.
Thanks.
Peter A. Tirri,
President
Paterson Education Association

**Feb 4 - Fire alarms went off at 11:05.** Evacuate the building AGAIN. I received a great deal of video. It is all NOT GOOD for the school. However, the fire department arrived. It was a false alarm. It was pulled in stairwell #16, basement by the Teen Center. After we came back in I decided to video to see how long it will take to clear the hallways. I ended up in an argument with a security guard and shut the camera off. However, after a short period of time I continued. I have approximately 30 plus minutes of video, with students all over the place and NO ADMINISTRATORS. Security are busting their asses and are all over the building trying to get some sort of order inside here, not to mention dealing with all the BS that is now going on in the cafeterias. These poor security people take so much crap from administrators because they say they are not doing their job. This is BS, because administrators will NOT allow them to do their job. Then security also gets crap from the teachers and to make it worse they get crap from the students.

**Feb 4, 5 & 6 -** A security guard was pulling out video recording cable as the two wood shop teachers and their students were installing *new* cable and cameras. Now, if the students are in the hallways, they are still pulling fire alarms, you have video cameras and now they are breaking them, why are we still leaving /allowing students to roam the hallways? Shouldn't it all be caught on camera? Bottom line, if students where in their classrooms, the violence, vandalism, fights, assaults on teachers, pulling of fire alarms and starting of fires come to an end or drop CONSIDERABLY? Lastly what happened to the principal with all of his announcements and calling home saying all students WILL have to wear ID cards? *THE ONLY CONTROL HERE IS OUT OF CONTROL!*

**Feb 4 -** Mr. Madjar told me a young lady held up three students for money, 75 cents. I don't know if the amount is true, but I will find out because according to Mr. Madjar, one of the students (name omitted) is in my 7th period class. I will ask him on Friday.
I have omitted the names of the three students that were held up at knife point.

<u>*Addition to above notes:*</u> **as of 2/8/08,** I spoke with my student and he confirmed it was over 75 cents. I said I was surprised he didn't break her jaw. He said he wanted to but was afraid of the knife. I asked him if he and the others are going to press charges, he said, "NO." Only guessing but knowing this student, he will take care of it at another time and hopefully place. Anyhow, this incident may have happened on 1/31/08. Reason why I say this is because I have her (name omitted) profile. She is 15 years old and it shows 10 days' suspension for armed robbery with knife. Gee what a coincidence!
Can you believe she only received 10 days of suspension? A vacation for armed robbery!

<u>*Next page has her profile.*</u>
- Notice her grades for the 1st & 2nd marking periods.
- Why wasn't she arrested?
- Did the district press charges?
- What happened to "ZERO TOLERANCE TO VIOLENCE?"
- Why was it hushed up?

If this was any other school district, it would have been on TV, radio and newspapers.

Once again, this state takeover run and operated school district and the school administration just told the student body, it's ok to rob someone at knife point in school. You'll only get 10 days suspension. I may not know right from wrong while I am here, but it is *STILL AGAINST THE LAW TO HOLD ANYONE UP AND ESPECIALLY AT KNIFE POINT!* Why is this allowed to go on inside this school?

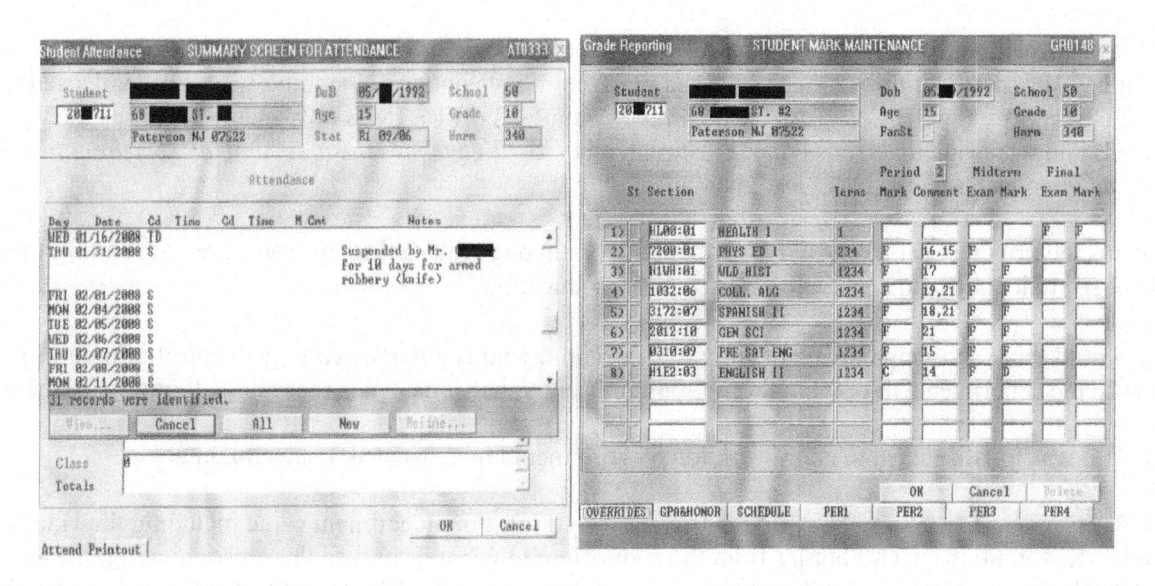

Feb 5 - 5th period fight in cafeteria between another two girls, (names omitted). No one was suspended.

### *New Meeting with Principal, Two Union Delegates About Me Videotaping.*
**Feb 6** - around 1:15pm, I was asked to report to Principal's office. When I arrived, Mr. Most* & Mr. Hull*, two union delegates were speaking with the principal. Shortly afterwards, I was called in. The principal says to he received reports of me videotaping. Then he said, I thought you (meaning me), wouldn't do this anymore. When he was finished speaking, I replied calmly and politely just as he spoke with me, I said, in November you and I spoke about you were receiving complaints about me videotaping. You told me I'm a grown man. You do what you think is right. I am NOT telling you what to do. But I want you to think about it over the weekend and I said I would think about it. However, I reminded him I never said I was going to stop. I also reminded him in our conversation I told you I do not feel safe here at JFK. That was in November, the situation here is worse. I have to protect myself. I have not done anything with the video. The principal said he has reports that others have seen the video. I then replied I have not given the videos to anyone. However, I have given a copy to the PEA & the NJEA. He said he knew. Then all of a sudden, a big disturbance/fight broke out right outside his office. Mr. Most * had to physically take control of a student. It was an ugly terrible scene. Mr. Most* felt terrible in the way he had to gain control. He had no choice on what had to be done because this student was out of control / berserk.

It seems this situation involved a young lady who was not supposed to be in the BUILDING (trespassing). Once again, so much for ID CARDS & SAFETY IN THE BUILDING! Just killing any creditability or argument for the principal saying how safe this school is! If I was the principal and this happens, I would have been mortified. Almost all day long every second of the day, there is some sort of crisis or problem going on inside here. Once everything settled down in the hallway, the principal and the two union delegates agreed to continue this conversation tomorrow. However, I asked to speak with the principal for 90 seconds and he obliged.

I assured him, that I have NO ILL FEELINGS TOWARDS HIM. I asked him to look into my face and watch me speak to see that I was sincere. He said, I am asking you to not videotape anymore. I said I am a very honorable person. If I say something you can take it to the bank. I said I will not take anymore videos. He did say if you see something (meaning of violence) by all means to do so. I replied, OK, I will do whatever you ask of me. However, if you do NOT get control of this school, I have no choice but to document it. What is going on inside this school building has to be criminal, against the law and it is all being hushed up. I will now have the proof, especially if something really bad happens, and I feel it is just a matter of time. I then reassured him, that I have not done anything with those videos other than given a copy to NJEA & PEA. Then I walked out of his office. I was only out of his office a few seconds and went right back in saying, I just remembered, *"I gave my cousin a copy of everything just in case anything should happens to me"* then left.

It seems the principal is more concerned about me or anyone videotaping, instead of having control of his school so students would be able to obtain a proper education.

You would think a principal in a large urban high school who is not *allowed* to get control of their school because the superintendent or whomever, would be happy that someone is recording all of this for them!

**Feb 7** - I was too disgusted to go to work today. I am mentally exhausted. I stayed home.

**Feb 8 - 4th period 11:35** - once again the fire alarms go off. Fire department came including the Hook & Ladder. Kids took two CO-2 bottles from the auditorium lobby and sprayed the sensor, making the alarm go off. The head custodian said it cost approximately $80 for a new CO-2 bottle, plus the damage the CO-2 has caused to repair the sensor and the chemicals needed in order to pick up and confine the CO-2 for disposal. Let's not forget the cost for the false alarm/s. It just gets worse here every day.
The administration just ignores and hushes it all up.

**Feb 13** - the school newspaper, The TORCH, dated February 2008, Vol. 41 No. 2. It shows the top ten students. I have to laugh. They ARE good students. However, I have said this over and over before. These students do well, work hard, and are conscientious, which is also a miracle with all of the distraction they have to endure just being here at JFK. They deserve and should get credit and positive reinforcement for their work. HOWEVER, and unfortunately, they would not do well in any other school or school system outside of the Paterson. I have already seen this with a few students. One in particular moved and went to Fairlawn High School. This student was doing so poorly yet was a straight A student here.

**Feb 19, 6th period, 1:03**- fire alarms go off again. Evacuated the building again. False alarm again! Fire department came again. Alarm was pulled by stairwell #16 again. ONLY this time they caught the student with the security cameras. Once again, the cameras are only used AFTER SOMETHING HAPPENS. My question is, why aren't these cameras used to get students out of the hallway, stairwells, bathrooms and every other place where they are hanging out in plain view instead of going to class? This shows me how corrupt, defiant and obstinate the Paterson Public School District, which is still under state takeover and control, is and has no interest or concern about student's education.

**Feb 20 - Front page of the HERALD NEWS,** "JFK teachers say school is out of control, file complaint with the state, citing assaults and profanity." Continues page A4. By Danielle Shapiro
Complete article on page 45.

**2nd period, 9:37** - fire alarms go off, evacuated the building again. Fire department came. It was freezing cold and we were outside for at least 30 minutes. So many kids were without their coats. These poor kids will end up getting sick or coming down with pneumonia. There was actually a fire, 2nd floor, by room 230, English wing. One of my students (name omitted) was telling me about the fire. He said he was trying to get someone's attention, and NO one would believe him. I asked if he saw the fire. He said, NO, but did see a great deal of black smoke coming out of the boys' bathroom. I asked him if the boys' bathroom was broken into. He said NO. It was opened last week. I then said, according to the principal and his announcement after we came back into the building from evacuation, he said (paraphrasing) someone broke into an area that was locked and caused a serious situation. I do have it on video. Bottom line, the principal said it was a LOCKED AREA. However, my student and many other students said it wasn't locked! He also said VP Mr. Calmete* pulled the fire alarm. I find the principal's announcement stupid and insulting. He started talking how serious it is and dangerous. I believe he said that because of today's front page on the Herald News about how dangerous it is here. There must have been guests in the building and was trying to make it look good. Just as I thought around 12:15, I noticed one of the assistant superintendent's in the center hallway. Then at 12:20, I noticed the principal and another assistant superintendent in the center hallway along with some of the school administrators telling students to move, get to class. Where's your ID? Putting on the Dog & Pony Show! I received video & pictures.

**Later,** a student was taken out in handcuffs.

I noticed the retired Paterson police captain (who is now in charge of the entire school district's security) was here. He was taking charge, having students move along all in attempts in gaining some sense of order and control here. Spoke with him and he said he is going to tell the principal what to do. I was really happy to hear that and hope things get straightened out here.

**More assaults.** It seems the little Mexican kid who was assaulted a few weeks ago was jumped again. If students were made to be IN CLASS and trespassers were NOT in the building, all of these assaults would not be happening. I have to think (guessing) that the parents of this poor kid that was assaulted again may be illegal immigrants. They're keeping quiet and that is why nothing is being done about it. I feel terrible for them. How can they send their child back here again?

**Feb 21** - police escorted two students out in handcuffs. I do not know why. Speaking with head of security an ex-police Captain, he said there are going to be more. He is not going to let this behavior continue.

**Feb 25** - UNBELIEVABLE, with all the newspaper and publicity on how bad it is here, TODAY, *it is still business as usual, meaning out of control chaos!* I guess the big shots feel the newspapers and bad publicity has blown over. Hallways are filled with kids, screaming, yelling, cursing, hanging out all over the building, walking in and out of the building, *NOTHING HAS CHANGED!*
However, I found it funny as soon as the retired Paterson police captain and now district head of the Security walked into the building. I saw the principal all of a sudden come out into the hallway.

**Last night** I received a quite lengthy recorded message from the principal stating starting tomorrow, 2/26/08, there will be major changes in attendance policy. He talked about absenteeism, cutting, being late, and etc. Basically, reinstating last year's policies. Bottom line, it's just *talk!*

**Feb 26** - 8:49 a big FIGHT! Then there were fights all day long. No change, same crap different day. However, I did see the principal in the hallways moving students and bringing them into the security office. Only for them to come out and go right back to the street corner this place is.

**Feb 27** - 6th period, the principal came over the PA system telling everyone how tomorrow there will be a change and students will report to the auditorium for study instead of their respective classrooms. Anyone walking the hallways without a pass and ID will suffer consequences. I have it on video because it was the only way I could record his announcement.

**The Record, page L9,** "What's needed when school is a war zone," by James Ahearn.
It is still not everything that goes on here at. However, typically the blame is being passed down on to the teachers. Not to mention the superintendent says he **had no idea it was this bad**. Doesn't he view the school's surveillance videos?

**Feb 28** - 3rd period 10:46, fire alarms go off, evacuated the building again. False alarm again! The alarm was pulled in stairwell #14 in the basement again. It was brutally cold again. However, several students told to me it seems the seniors were upset and rumors were flying about their prom, year book, graduation and the whole deal was to be canceled. However, the principal come over the PA system approximately 9:30 - 10 saying it is not true and he assured everyone, especially the seniors, it is all rumors. Later, several of my students (names omitted) told me some students (names omitted), contacted NJ News 12 and told them the fire alarms were turned off. My question was how would they know? She said because students pulled the alarm, and nothing happened. Received video and 3 pictures.

**NOTE OF INTEREST: -** With all that is going on I find it funny, (meaning sarcastically) this is black history month. Every Sunday I've been watching a great deal of documentaries on Civil Rights in America during the 60s & 70s. In particular how the Black people wanted their children (and the children wanted) to receive a good education. *Example:* The horrific treatment in Boston with busing. I don't know in my heart how parents sent their children off to schools in search of a better education knowing there was a good chance their child or children would be killed. It was absolutely horrible. People (if you want to call them people) were throwing Molotov cocktails at the school buses filled with children. The key word is "*CHILDREN,* how horrible is that? Now 35, 45 years later look what's going on right here in Paterson, New Jersey, and what is allowed to go on by a State Takeover Run and Operated School District, where the superintendent and the majority of the assistant superintendents and administrators are black. Did they forget how hard these parents fought and how many of these little children were killed just in BOSTON, MA, and all the other Jim Crow states just so their children would receive an education and become "EDUCATED?"

**Feb 29 - have video for audio 2:25 minutes long,** of the principal making an announcement saying they caught one student who pulled or was involved with yesterday's false alarm. There is supposedly another culprit involved. As you will hear, all of a sudden, the principal is concerned for our handicapped students. Then he says this act will not be punished by 5 or 10 days suspension. How many times has he said that this year? It's a dog and pony show because of all the big shots are in the building and the pressure of news article about JFK being out of control. There is *no way* the superintendent and the assistant superintendents did NOT know about any of this?

**Mar 4 -** I was assigned to room 219 for HSPA testing. As I entered and looked around I noticed the walls were all kicked in, large holes in the walls, some were actually going through to the next room or out to the hallway with many patch jobs already to these walls. There were two fluorescent lamps not working the entire time testing, live electrical wires hanging that were still plugged in and exposed. I couldn't stand it so I unplugged and removed them. The room and floor was absolutely filthy. The cabinets were filled with mold, rust, dirt and mice feces. The place was disgusting and to think it is not only filled with students every day the administration also sees it fit for the next three days to be utilized so students can be administered the HSPA exam (State exam). The 3:42 minute video of the room explains it all.

I decided to go next door to room 220. OH MY GOD. You have to see the 3:17 minute video. It is disgusting and embarrassing. You would not believe the size of the holes in the walls. You can smell rodent feces. There was graffiti all over the place. The floor was filthy. No child should have to go to class / school with rooms like this. Same photos from pages 12 & 13.

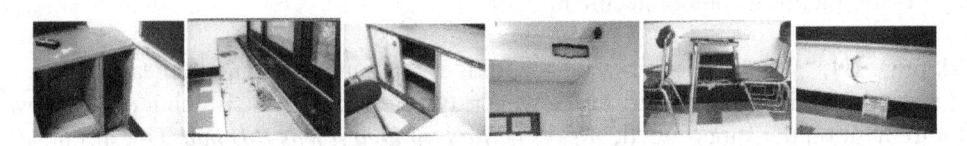

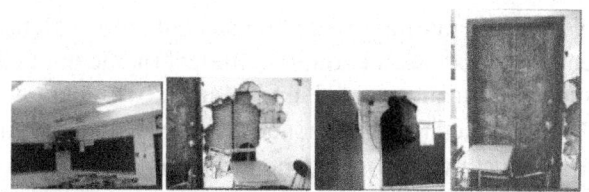

Does this look like a school that is under control?

## *NOTATION ON THESE TESTING / CLASSROOMS*

The battle cry is "No Child Left Behind." The superintendent's battle cry is "Children First." How insulting. My parents did not have a lot of money and things were always tight and scary. However, they made sure we were clean, fed, and clothed. Bottom line, they did without, so we had the essentials. However, our schools in Paterson and especially JFK, too many classrooms do not have heat, all the lights don't work, no phone (which is important for security and health reasons) and the classrooms are filthy. The students' bathrooms are as bad as any gas station or Port of Authority bathrooms. I bet the superintendents all have phones, lights, their offices are cleaned daily, they have clean and proper bathroom facilities, are not susceptible to rodent feces, mold, mildew, rust, deteriorated heating, disgusting cabinets, holes in their walls and have unlimited supplies. Like parents they should be doing without, so the children of Paterson do not have to attend school/classes in this condition.

**Mar 4** - we had a staff meeting for the first time this year. It was about the situations and violence here at JFK. We received a 4-page handout outlining the changes to be implemented to secure our schools. The principal sent out letters to parents whose child has horrible attendance. Only to find out all the students who were dropped from roll were all reinstated that evening by a superintendent. Have video sound only of the meeting. (46:31 minutes long).

Mr. Madjar told me, and it was confirmed later with the principal's speech during the faculty meeting about an incident and how it was handled properly. A female student (name omitted) has assaulted several teachers. She was removed from all of these teachers' classes and was placed into another teacher's class (name omitted). Now and again, she went after her new teacher and another teacher, threatening them both. Meanwhile she is *still* allowed to remain in school. According to Mr. Madjar and Pardine, she has threatened 3 to 4 other teachers and NOTHING was ever done about it.

First of all, there is something very wrong mentally with a student like that. Secondly there is something very mentally wrong with the superintendent, the administration, the principal and all of the administrators for allowing this child to continuously act in a violent and threatening manner without consequences. Lastly, why didn't the district pursue charges? I do understand why the teachers didn't!

I saw Mr. Whalen* who was attacked on 10/07/07 and Mrs. (name omitted) the Spanish teacher who was attacked on 1/22/08, today at school. Rumor has it they were **TOLD** by the superintendent's office to come back to work.

**Mar 5** - I understand another teacher was assaulted today. So much for yesterday's staff meeting on how things were going to change and especially the principal's commitment to **ZERO TOLERANCE to VIOLENCE!** Let's not forget about the phone calls we received on **3/3/08 & 3/4/08** telling parents and teachers how things will change and zero tolerance to violence and poor attendance will be implemented on **3/5/08.** It seems nothing is going to change. I don't understand! Then what is the POINT of this school district being taken over, run and still operated by the state of New Jersey?

**Mar 6** - HSPA testing. First thing this morning a fight breaks out in the cafeteria. **Around 1 p.m.**, another fight, 2nd floor, Science wing between two girls. Student (name omitted #1) whose face and eyes were really messed up by student #2 (name omitted aka "Maggie"). Student #1 spent a great deal of time in the nurse's office. On 3/7/08, I looked to see if these girls were suspended or in ZONE. NOTHING! However, student (name omitted #1) was absent, meaning *not* suspended or in Zone. Reason why they were fighting? Someone bumped into the other.

**After school** a big gang fight, about 20 - 30 kids and nothing in the media. Everyone hushed up!

**Mar 7** - first thing this morning a fight in the cafeteria involving all girls, threatening to KILL one and other. A large mass of students gathered around trying to get a cheap shot in, instigating more problems and for others to get involved. When told to move students were defiant. As security tries to move them, they start screaming, "Don't fucking touch me, fuck you, you can't fucking touch me," and remained defiantly and will not leave. Then there was nothing but fights all day long.

**I have video 1:56 minutes long** when I took a walk into the auditorium. I went to the entrance and couldn't believe it. The place smelled and reeked of urine. As I walked around, I realized students are NOW utilizing the bathrooms because the so-called study periods are being held in the auditorium. As I walked by the boys' and girls' bathrooms, I noticed there were **NO FIRE EXTINQUISHERS**. The lockers were empty. How can this go on knowing students have already set several bathrooms on fire?

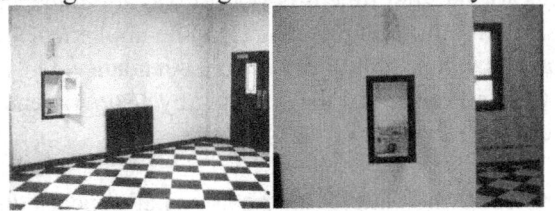

**Have video 3:14 minutes long,** I went up to the 2nd floor by room 224, you will notice several emergency lighting systems broken, panels missing and ceiling tiles missing with expose asbestos. Went down the stairwell broken glass in fire door, filthy as hell, paint just sloppily painted and just caked on, floor is absolutely FILTHY, see heating system almost torn out of the wall, dust and or spider webs overhead. DISGUSTING!

**Mar 10** - NO HEAT AGAIN IN SCHOOL. IT WAS SOOOOOOOO COLD IN HERE. One of my female students (name omitted) called NJ 12 news and told them. I don't know if anything became of her call. I bet the superintendent and all of them had heat. So much for **"CHILDREN FIRST"**

**The week of March 10 -14** -supervisors from central office, many whom I have never seen or met before are in the building. They are here to "**MONITOR**" the situation. I have to laugh. It makes no sense. If the district is corrupt and the superintendent and his staff are covering up what really goes on NOT just here at JFK but throughout the entire district, how can anyone say well it will be better now because **"WE"** are monitoring it? RIDICULOUS! You cannot have the people who are deliberately covering things up, lying, falsifying records, and denying that they know about the situations that are going on at JFK to the new papers, MONITOR the situation. IT IS ABSURD! All you see are these highly paid "SUPERVISORS" with a bottle of water or a cup of coffee in their hands walking around and talking as if they're out for a stroll. In the meantime, students are still in the hallways and not going to class.

**NOTE OF INTEREST: -** I realized with all of the media coverage we've had the last couple of weeks, not one politician, especially the governor and the commissioner of education, came here to see what in the hell is going on. UNFREAKINBELIEVABLE, they're more worried about their careers than the people and their children they're supposed to represent by making sure they are being properly educated by having the state of NJ running *this* school district!

**Mar 13 - have 2:55 minute video from the 2nd floor**, a set of lockers are ripped right out of the wall, ceiling tiles missing all over the place, cable wires exposed, because their covers are ripped off.
**AND I have video from room 222, 3:09 minutes long,** heating system grating down, wires exposed, patch jobs from holes put in walls. Walls cracked, holes all over the place, exposed cable wires, black board loaded with graffiti, no phone, ceiling tiles missing, stuff (tar?) dripping from pipe, cabinets / lockers in the room are filthy, the room is absolutely disgusting. So much for "CHILDREN FIRST"

**Mar 14 - have 1:20 minute video, 2nd floor stairwell #9, far corner heating system, DISGUSTING!** Heating system cover is missing, filthy, covered with dirt. We see this stuff every day and we come to think this is normal. It is NOT normal or acceptable. Nor should it be acceptable. Years ago, the district got rid of all the janitors and hired an outside company. Since then this building has not been cleaned properly. You can guarantee the superintendent would not allow this to go on at central office. I bet they would NOT send their children or grandchildren to this school. In the meantime, all of these problems are getting worse because they are not being taken care of properly and in a timely manner. In the long run, it will cost the district and ultimately, the taxpayers MORE! This is poor management. Actually, this is NO MANAGEMENT. See photos below.

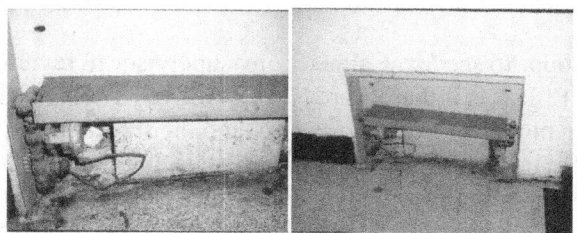

These are still the same in 2014.

**Mar 25 -** first day back from Easter recess. I would like to know what Zero Tolerance means. I know what it means, but I want to know what the superintendent and administrator's version means?
**ALSO, over the Easter Recess,** the library was broken into and approximately five computers were stolen. It looked as if they were going to take more by the way they were all stacked up. They also took a TV. The school administration wants to blame it on students. NO WAY, I don't believe that. To take a TV off their stand which is mounted about 7 feet from the ground, students would have to bring tools and not just regular tools but Allen wrenches. Students don't carry a pen! How would they know what size because sadly, most students can't read a ruler or understand fractions?

**Mar 26 -** Mr. Madjar, told me as of the last day of school before Easter recess, they processed 60 thousand cuts. He made it very clear that is the number of *cut slips only*. Most of the cut slips received have a week or more on one slip. Then Mr. Madjar said, "conservatively 180 thousand cuts and most likely MORE!"

**First thing** this morning there was a John F. Kennedy High School Drop from Enrollment List Grade 9, in my mailbox. Obviously, someone wanted me to have this. There were students who are in their 4th year at JFK and are still only a FRESHMAN, with 79 & 96 days absent this year, along with so much more information. I sent it to the president of the PEA, the two NJEA Union Reps. and Mr. Hull* a fellow teacher and a PEA union rep/delegate.
I showed Mr. Hull* the structural concerns I have in the schools' basement. I also showed the head security guard and Mr. Pro*. They brought the principal to see. I said, it is a serious

structural concerns. Only to find out that the security guard said it is nothing to worry about. It is just the building settling as we would have in our home and basement. I laughed and said no way. No one would allow this to happen in their own home. That cinderblock wall shakes when you put the least amount of pressure on it, plus you can see straight through to the outside because all of the cement is gone. I brought this to the principal's attention we had a few years ago only to see there are more stress cracks and in other areas as well. However, Mr. Hull* said he was going to follow through with PEOSH? Let's see what happens when they inspect?

**Mar 31** - Once again, it was freezing in the school. I had to keep my coat and hat on for several hours. The hallways felt worse than actually being outside. It was absolutely terrible. I bet the superintendent and all of the other superintendents weren't wearing their hats and coats in their offices!

Received a copy of the PEA NEWSLETTER, "ADVOCATE. **"February 2008.**
Inside it has everything I have been saying and writing all along.

**Apr 1** - Mr. Madjar gave me a copy, both sides, of a "SUSPENSION REQUEST" for a student who is #1 in cuts as of 3/27/08. She has a total of 238 cuts. He said the cut office received two more cuts now making her total 240. Mr. Madjar also said nothing has changed since the supposed "ZERO TOLERANCE POLICY" has been put into effect and they are processing cuts &tardiness just as much as before.

**Apr 3** - I went up to the 2nd floor to see Mr. Calmete* my supervisor to review my yearly evaluation. UNFREAKINBELIEVABLE! It was if there were NO CLASSES. The hallways were filled with students (SRO). Security were yelling move, go to class, let's go, and the students were ignoring them and kept going about their business. Security was blowing their whistles, but the kids still refuse to budge. Even Mr. Calmete* said he is NOT going to get involved or say anything. He had students go off on him, cursed him out, threatened him, and NOTHING was done about it. He said, he too can't take it and it is not worth getting upset over it because the administration, meaning the principal and above will not do anything about it.

6th period BIG FIGHT, OUT OF FREAKIN' CONTROL. Then again **approximately 2:15 - 2:20pm**, another BIG FIGHT ERUPTS in the stairwell 2nd floor between office #1 & 2. Rumor has it that a cop was shoved down the stairs. Found out that was *not* true. It seems the officer slipped as he was escorting a student who was under arrest and in handcuffs.

NOTES OF INTEREST FOR THE WEEK OF MARCH 31 - APRIL 4 -
I am tired, depressed, burnt out, and stressed out. I'm just a teacher who works where the stress and anxiety level is so high, because I am in a COMBAT ZONE, that's supposed to be just a high school. All because the superintendent, all of the assistant superintendents and principal allows chaos, extreme out of control behavior, lunacy, in house truancy, and nonstop violence to continually go on within a *school*! I am *not* the only teacher that feels this way either.

**Apr 7** - it's the principal's first day back since we left for Easter Break. The school is worse. There is NO such thing as ZERO TOLERANCE to anything. There is no control, no discipline, nothing but out of control chaos. The principal is a lame duck, useless, has as much leadership quality as a used napkin. Approximately 10am I watched a young man being escorted out of the building in handcuffs by police. About 9:45 I was on the 2nd floor speaking with Mr. Hull* a teacher. The hallways were filled, packed tight with screaming out of control students. We both just shook our heads and shrugged our shoulders. I said, "It is unfuckinbelievable here." He replied, "You got that fucking right," and we both left.

**Week of 4/ 7/08 - 4/11/08 -** No change! The cut office is packed, overflowing with students waiting to be processed. Dozens of students have to wait in the hallway because there's no room in the office.
**EXAMPLE -**April 11, everybody in the cut office was telling me about a student, (name omitted), a 17-year-old 10th grader who will be suspended starting Monday, April 13 or 14, for 5 days for cutting. He has *over 300 cuts!* This is "IN HOUSE TRUANCY! Yet the administration is not held responsible! I have scanned & saved the above students document on diskette.

**Apr 14 -** beginning of 6th period, 12:45, fire alarms go off, evacuated the building. We were told after we came back in by the principal it was a malfunction?? **Have 2 photos.**

**Apr 18 -** went to the 2nd floor at 10:30 to speak with my supervisor. UNFREAKINBELIEVABLE! The entire floor was filled with students. Security is yelling trying to be overheard over the students telling them to move, go to class, blowing the whistle but the students ignore them. The place is so out of control. Speaking with my supervisor, he said what can we do, the students won't go and they don't listen. There is no type of punishment or actual rules in plan to be enforced. There is no detention. Even when students are assigned a Saturday detention, they don't show and nothing is done about it. The cut office is already overburdened. Too many teachers are NOT writing cuts and lateness and this is what we have "CHAOS!" Nothing has changed. I don't even know if the jerks from central office are still in the building. I had to laugh because he blamed the teachers for not writing cuts & lateness slips!

**Apr 23 -** spoke with Mr. Madjar of the cut office. He and the rest of the people in the cut office are so disgusted and cannot keep up with the work. They have processed conservatively 70,000 cut slips. That is just pieces of paper/cut slips. Mr. Madjar said the # of cuts is a minimum of 240,000. There is no leadership here which equals to no control here. This is the worse I have ever seen it. I just don't understand!

Spoke with the Journalism teacher. She is doing an article about my students and especially (name omitted student #1) on how we adapted a wheelchair for one of our handicap students. She was so happy. She said we have nothing good to put in our paper. It is all negative. This is great because now we have something positive to print about our school. She also said too many things she will not print, because she's afraid of retaliation. This is a school newspaper written and produced by the students. However, the teacher feels she must keep a lot of the articles the kids want to write about OUT!

**Apr 23 – May 5 -**so disgusted, exhausted, worn and burnt out. The same crap every day, it is NOT about education here. It is all BS equaling "NOVA NET!"

**May 5 -** one of my 1st period students did not come to school. However, around 2:20 I saw him. I spoke with him the next day about writing a cut. THIS IS GOOD. He tells me I can't write a cut. I wasn't in school today. I replied, then I didn't see you, I'm lying? He said NO, I wasn't in school. I never went to homeroom. I only came in for NOVA NET. I remarked oh no, this can't go on. You can't come to school, but you can come in for NOVA NET? Absolutely disgusting! If a student is absent, they are not allowed to play a sport or go to practice that day. However, they can come in for NOVA NET! Then why don't we just shut the school down and just have NOVA NET? It would save taxpayers millions of dollars. In reality that's what's going on any way. Kids refuse to go to class, hang out all day in school, or they don't come to school at all, UNTIL it is time to go to NOVA NET!

**May 7 -** I cannot believe this, Ms. Princess* is in the hallway directing students, telling them to take their hats off, radios off, clearing the hallways attempting to move students. Then I realized the superintendent and an assistant superintendent were in the building. It was an act, another dog and pony show.

I learned today a female teacher (name omitted) was threatened by a student. He wrote a threatening note to her. And guess what? NOTHING was done about it!

**May 8** - BIG FIGHT IN THE AUDITORIUM, students were arrested, including students who wouldn't stop taunting the police after they were warned several times. Students figured as long as we're in school the cops can't do anything to us? Bottom line, nothing new, fights all day.

**May 9** - long after the bell rang to begin 2nd period, I went up to the 2nd floor to speak with my supervisor. Only to find out he wasn't absent. The hallways and especially the center hall were filled, and I mean to overcapacity, with students just hanging around talking. I could barely get through to get back down to my classroom. Not one administrator around! What a waste of taxpayer's money. Let's blame the teachers for failing students and being the main reason for DROP OUT FACTORIES!

**1st floor absolutely ridiculous**. The hallways were filled, and I mean packed with students. It is as bad as it was when I was on the 2nd floor earlier. No administrator present. It was a free for all. I had no choice other than to take **video, 4:38 minutes long.** Found out today it was because the lunch bell rang early in the auditorium and not in the cafeteria. Students will use and abuse any excuse *not* to go to class and remain defiantly in the hallways. This is supposed to be a school, a place where order, discipline, structure and a rigorous education. NOT HERE! To think the district's motto is "CHILDREN FIRST!"

**May 13** - there was a fire today inside JFK, around 10:40-10:45. It was set inside a stairwell, between the 1st and 2nd floors. What makes it more sickening is the fire was in the principal's wing stairwell, a few feet from his and across from the guidance counselors' offices. Students set newspapers on fire. It gets better. The fire alarms never went off. The 2nd floor was filled with smoke. Teachers wanted to leave but were told to go back into their classrooms, close the door and open the windows. Are you freaking kidding me! Everyone knows if there's a fire you NEVER open a door and or window. By doing this you would be feeding the fire more oxygen and making it worse. This is not just unacceptable but absolutely dangerous.

Who makes these decisions dealing with children and other people's lives? Sadly, unless students tell their parents what happened today, they will never know. What's even worse, many of us (students & staff) didn't know ANYTHING about this! I believe the administration deliberately turned off the alarms in attempts to hide, cover/hush up the fire because they are AFRAID of the bad publicity and the TRUTH, about the fire/s and everything else that's happening inside and around JFK High School. The newspaper company would be doing a *big* service for the students, their parents, the entire community and especially NJ taxpayers if they had an office right here at JFK. Maybe that's what's needed so schools can't lie, falsify records and not be out of control!

I sent an e-mail informing the NJEA & PEA about the above incident and never received a reply.

**May14** - I heard there was another fire today on the 2nd floor. Once again, NO FIRE ALARMS!
How many other students and staff are not aware of this a*gain?* Here's a better question. How many other fires have there been when the fire alarms didn't go off that we don't know about?

Picture was taken on 5/14/2008, before school was open.
I took this picture to document what a joke this place is.
The poster is like everything else around here just meaningless!

**May 16** - here we go again, fights all day long. It is so disgusting here. Hallways are jammed packed with screaming, swearing, cursing at the top of their lungs, out of control, defiant students. It's unfortunate. We teachers are not allowed to do our jobs. However, we are held responsible and blamed for *everything* that goes wrong.

History teacher, Lou Bonora was assaulted AGAIN today. This makes three times this year. Not to mention being continuously threatened and cursed at. This is a school. Can you believe it?

**May 22** - The President of the Board of Education was in the building around 2:25pm. Hallways were filled with unruly, out of freaking control defiant students, all running around, screaming, swearing and refusing to go to class. Several of my colleagues and I watched him walk around like he was lost, didn't know what to do, said nothing to anyone, then just walked out of the building. I am so confused!

**May 27** - No change. Nothing more to write, it is the same every day. I am so tired and exhausted. The constant screaming and all around noise alone is wearing me out.

**May 29, 1:49** - 7th period fire alarms go off. We evacuated the building. Fire department came. The sensor was deliberately set off in stairwell or exit #5. This happened even with the student population being light today because the seniors were out on their senior picnic. **Received video & 2 photos.**

*FIGHTS ALL DAY LONG.* A girl was jumped by four other girls in the auditorium that was filled with teachers, several VPs and the principal himself. Here's the best part, this young lady was by herself, jumped, had to defend herself and she gets suspended. I don't know what happened to the other girls.

**May 30 -** *HSPA TEST SCORES ARE IN!* They have been in for two weeks but guidance was *not* allowed to give them out. I don't know the reasons. I understand the numbers/percentages are NOT GOOD. Do you think this may have something to with students being continuously allowed by the administration to be every place and anyplace all day, every day, all year instead of being IN CLASS? If I was a parent and I found out about all of this, there would be a MAJOR LAWSUIT!

379 Students took the HSPA.
This includes SRA and Special Ed students. I am sure this is where they will fudge the percentages.
This is what I received from counselors.
- 98 students         passed Math & World Language
    This equals 25.85%
- 173 students        passed Language Arts.
    This equals 45.64%
- 117 students        passed Math.
    This equals 30.87%

> **IMPORTANT NOTATION -** I truly believe these out of state superintendents are brought here on purpose. This way when they fail, leave or not rehired (fired) the next one can turn around and say, look what the other guy left for me to fix. They just keep passing the buck, while stealing many bucks. GOVERNMENT is the real culprit of the failing public education system. Look at everything that has the word, PUBLIC in front of it. They are a disaster. After 18 - 19 years where are the improvements, what does the City of Paterson have to show for the state taking over their school district other than millions upon 10's of millions of dollars "MISSING" and "UNACCOUNTED" for? Meanwhile there is so much violence in this school, students are continuously allowed to roam the building instead of being in class and are just pushed through the system.

Only a few students came to get their scores. Obviously, they didn't hang out in the hallways and went to class every day. But majority of the students did not come and DO NOT CARE.

**Jun 3 - 12:54, 6th period -** fire alarms go off again. Evacuated the building again. Fire department and added police came again. Fire alarm was pulled in stairwell #13. Received 2:07 minute video & 3 photos.

Received a memo dated May 30, 2008, from Ms. Princess* To Cut Office about Student Graduation Status, Grade Level Status, Enrollment Status.(See memo next page.)

> PATERSON PUBLIC SCHOOL DISTRICT
> **John F. Kennedy High School**
> 61-127 Preakness Avenue, New Jersey 07522
> Office: (973) 321-0500 ext. 50258    Fax: (973) 321-2204
>
> *Beyond...Excellence in Education*
>
> To:      Cut Office Staff
> From:    ▓▓▓▓▓▓ Assistant Principal ▓▓▓▓▓▓
> Date:    May 30, 2008
>
> **Student Graduation Status / Grade Level Status / Enrollment Status**
>
> Please be reminded that the professional responsibility of informing students of their graduation status, grade level status and / or school enrollment status is assigned to the Supervisor of Guidance, Guidance Counselors and the Child Study Team Case Managers. This information is then reported to the building principal and a protocol is established to inform students and their parents/guardians.
>
> I am requesting that during your interaction with students and / or their parents/guardians for the review of cuts, lates, attendance and readmit conferences that you specifically refrain from any conversation that may be misunderstood as suggesting, commenting on and / or referencing to students as being in jeopardy of not graduating, in jeopardy of not being promoted to the next grade level and / or that may not be returning to John F. Kennedy High School for the upcoming school year.
>
> If students and / or the parent / guardian present you with an inquiry about graduation status, grade level status and / or enrollment status, please refer them to either the Guidance Department or the Child Study Team Office.
>
> Thank you.
>
> c: ▓▓▓ Principal
>    Assistant Principals
>    Department Chairpersons

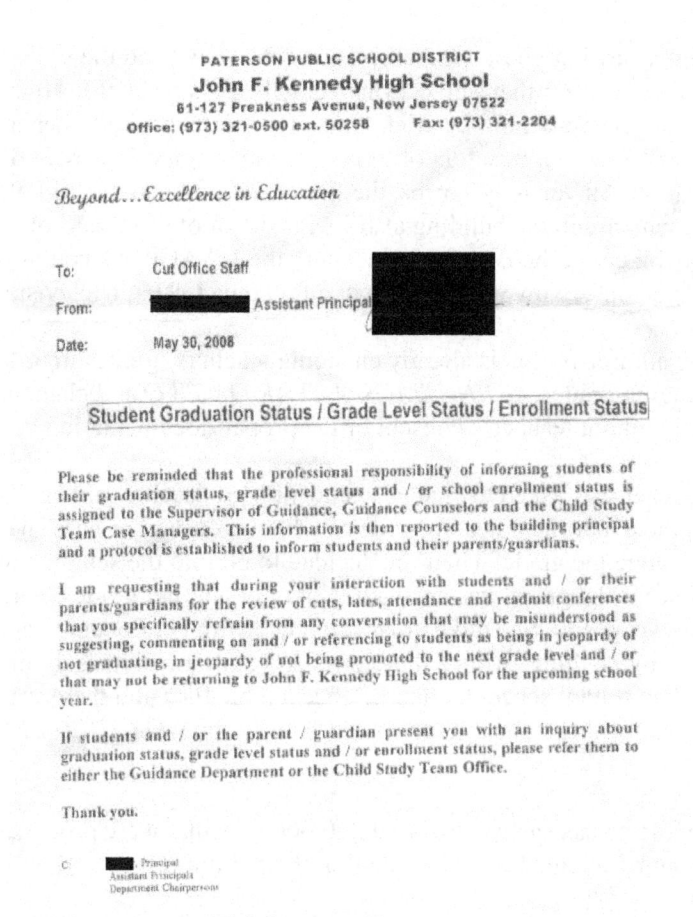

This is something new.
Another way for Princess* to manipulate and make changes in order to increase graduation numbers.

**Jun 5** - 8:52, first thing this morning a *BIG FIGHT*, girls, major pandemonium. Place was out of freaking control. This school environment is blood thirsty and no one would care (students) if someone was stabbed or killed in front of them. They thrive on it like sharks around blood. Then they feed off of it and the rest of the day is filled with more fights. All because the administration ALLOWS IT! The hallway was absolute chaos. The police couldn't get through. While the police officers were attempting to get to and break up the fight, the nasty instigating MOB of students were arguing, yelling and cursing at them. Now they're complaining that the police were pushing them. The police had no choice. These instigating defiant thugs refused to allow police through by deliberately blocking them, refused to move in attempts to keep the commotion going and now trying to turn everything around and start more chaos by blaming the police officers. When the police finally got to the scene, the girls wouldn't stop fighting. One of the girls was cursing and screaming at the police to let go, get your fucking hands off of me you mother fucker, you can't fucking touch me, get the fuck off, get the fuck off of me, on and on and on. If this was any place else other than being inside JFK, this person would have been maced, put to the ground face first, handcuffed and arrested. But nooooooo, the law does not matter in J. F. K. High School. This is a land of lawlessness. This young lady was defiant and she knew nothing was going to happen to her so she kept it up putting on a great show teaching other students you can do this too, nothing will happen to you either, WATCH! There were large clumps of hair all over the floor. This was REAL HAIR not phony weaves.

**Jun 6** - *A THOUGHT CAME TO ME.* I gave all those videos, photos, and documentation to the PEA and NJEA. The PEA has a televisions station. So why didn't the PEA & NJEA utilize the videos while they were talking and interviewing guest speakers? They could have had the videos playing in the background so everyone can see for themselves what actually goes on at JFK High School that is in a State Takeover Run and Operated School District. And have guest speakers such as the Governor Corzine, Congressman Bill Pascrell, Senators of Passaic County, Superintendent of the county, NJ Commissioner of Education, Mayor Joey Torres, the fire chiefs and marshal of Paterson NJ, the Paterson Police Chief, the police who are in the building at JFK, President of the Board of Education, Council members, any and all members of the Board of education, the NAACP, as well as the local community leaders of the City of Paterson?   Now that would make for some GREAT television!

**Jun 13 -** I found out the administration is already changing teachers' grades in order to get kids to graduate. *NOT* just changing grades, *GOING BACK A YEAR OR TWO* and changing grades without authorization. (Meaning without teacher's consent or the proper documentation being submitted)

Example - A science teacher was asked to change a student's grade. She said no. This was from the previous year. She told the department head of science what was asked of her. The department head said absolutely not, do not change the grade! Then she decided to go into the school computer system FUSION, to check and see if the grade was changed. Not only was her grade changed but grades were also changed from a few years ago. She did a cross reference with her documentation and found other grades were changed. To make things worse, there were *NO* authorizations submitted for the change. So, Mr. Madjar went to see the school scheduler and he checked his files and there was NOTHING authorizing grade changes for this student. Is this what's meant by *NO CHILD LEFT BEHIND FOR ABBOTT DISTRICTS?*

Mr. Madjar said the cut office has easily surpassed 200,000 cuts that were processed for the school year. On an average that is about 100 cuts for each student in the building.

**Jun 16 -** fights all day long again and mostly girls. Many of them are being escorted to the security office or taken out of the building in handcuffs. Then around 2:30 something was going on outside the building. Eventually police and security guards brought a young lady into the security office in handcuffs.

**Jun 17** - 8:31 kids still just moseying on in the building. Final exams started at 8:20. They come in with coffee, donuts, soda, chips, sandwiches etc. and hangout in hallway BSing. Meanwhile no one tells them to go to class and it's final exam time. First of all, they shouldn't be allowed to just come in late without going to the attendance office first. It is now 8:45am, students still moseying on in still hanging out. No desire or ambition to go to class. Why should they? They all know whether they take a final exam or not, pass or not, they will still be promoted, graduate and receive a diploma. It is now 8:55 a herd of students just walked into the building. Final exams mean absolutely nothing; they do NOT care.

Ms. Conscientious* told me why she was so upset yesterday. A young lady who was on bedside because she was pregnant never came in to take her final SRA test. Then when she had the baby and did come back into the building, Ms. Conscientious* reminded her about taking the test. She never did. In the meantime, she got into a fight and was suspended. Now she did not take the test and the deadline for taking the SRA test has passed. All the necessary paperwork had to be turned and sent in. *THEY JUST DON'T CARE!* They have been taught that the school system will just pass them, and the government will take care of them.

Ms. Conscientious* was summoned to Ms. Princess's* office along with the student, the SRA teacher and Ms. Lee* of dropout prevention.
*OBVIOUSLY, THEY ARE TRYING TO ADJUST FOR GRADUATION NUMBERS AGAIN.*

They wanted to know why she cannot graduate. Ms. Conscientious* said, she was reminded several times to make up the test. She never came in. This is ridiculous. She was stupid for getting into a fight and getting suspended. Ms. Princess* said you shouldn't say stupid. This is a tactic some administrators do; they try to place the teacher in defensive posture in attempts of getting their way. So, the teacher said ok, irresponsible, getting into a fight because someone said something about her baby. Then Ms. Princess* said, well, her hormones were kicking. That's when, Ms. Conscientious* said, this is ridiculous. So, if a woman kills her baby because of her hormones this is all right? This is unacceptable! I am not going to sit here, be talked to and listen to your excuses and walked out. If Ms. Princess* is so concerned about this student, then why wasn't she helping her all year and none one of this would be happening? Now she is running around scrambling to get as many kids even though they failed; to pass and graduate.

**Jun 20** - I decided to do my yearly statistics.
- **Year 2006 - 2007**, I serviced approximately 180 plus students.
- **Grand total:    Cuts: 1080          Lates: 962**

Year, **2007 - 2008,** I serviced fewer students compared to last year and I included absenteeism.
- As of **6/20/08,** I had the following:
- **Grand total:    Absents: 1503        Cuts: 1288         Lates: 945**

Mr. Madjar told me the total cuts processed for the 2007 - 2008 school year is **250,000**. You should hear all the fighting, screaming, yelling, bickering, arguing, swearing because kids are not graduating. I laugh, especially with many of the administrators, guidance counselors and all the other support BS personnel like dropout prevention, trying to make deals with teachers so kids could and would pass to graduate. Where were all of these people Sept, Oct, Nov, Dec, Jan, Feb, Mar, Apr, May, and now it is days before graduation? Not to mention 3 report cards, 4 sets of warning notices, letters gone home and the many phone calls home. Now the administration wants to do their job!

**Jun 23** - all classes empty. Either students have left for the rest of the day or they're just roaming the halls.

**Have video of a teacher** with bolt cutters snapping off locks from student's lockers, so he can collect textbooks. Wonder why we have no textbooks and the school spends so much money on them. Students do not turn in or held accountable for them. This goes on year after year after year.

**Jun 24** - I received a 7-page list of 147 students names, their ID # and HR that shows all of their cuts. The least amount is 100 cuts. So many students have 200 – 300 cuts and one with 420. All for the 2007 – 2008 school year. Unbelievably many of these students will still graduate this year. This verifies the hallways were filled with students and that *NOTHING WAS DONE ABOUT IT!*

*NO KIDS IN ANY CLASS.* They refuse to do make up exams or even to turn in their textbooks.

**Gang fight** (supposedly from Eastside) and a gun shoot out? Will try to get information tomorrow. Notice nothing is in the news? However, security guards are supposed to write up and file a report?

**The school newspaper**, "THE TORCH," has an interesting article that starts on the front page, "Dr. Miller says good-bye to JFK." The principal "QUITS!"

**June issue of the** "ADVOCATE" the Pea Newsletter has a great deal of information in it that I have been writing and supplying the PEA with over this last year.

**June 25** - big fight at the graduation field involving Eastside students only.

\*\*\*\*\*\*\*\*\*\*\*\*\*\*\*\*\*\*\*\*

**The following information was obtained talking to one of the police officers that works at JFK.**

This afternoon, a shot went off this was after a JFK security guard noticed a person with a large bulge (possible gun in his clothes). Also, there was an off duty undercover police officer who noticed suspicious people. He watched them get into a blazer. They came back and went into a house on Front St. Police arrested them, found two guns, drugs and a scale. The shooter or the person who accidentally discharged the gun was hiding in the closet. Some of those arrested were kids from JFK.

There was nothing on or in the news about it.

\*\*\*\*\*\*\*\*\*\*\*\*\*\*\*\*\*\*\*\*

**Jun 26, Last Day of School** - we had a meeting in the auditorium for all our retirees. The principal was not there. I was told he came into the building, gathered all of his stuff and left.

## SCHOOL YEAR 2008 - 2009

My new notes start in September on the 1st day of school up to and including September 29, 2008.
OH MY GOD what a change, what a difference having a new principal and all of the powers to be. The school is a thousand times better. There are still kids in the hallways after the bell rings to start class, but they dispersed fairly quick and organized. I was dreading coming in the first couple of weeks because of last year. This was the very first summer I did NOT want to come back to JFK. I am usually ready and anxious to get back to work by the very latest mid-August. This past summer I was so burnt out. They have really gotten things/rules in order and are enforcing all policies. In fact, we have students' attendance recorded automatically on INTRANET. We don't even have to write cuts or tardiness.

All we do is mark the student absent or late the computer automatically does the rest. It will say Cut or Tardy and make the information go automatically to the cut office and office #2 which is the attendance office. NICE!

It seems Ms. Princess* lied because I have a memo here that states the following, "District Policy Attendance & Electronic Devices. Everything VP Ms. Princess*said we were doing in the 2006 - 2007 school year was ILLEGAL, was a Ms. Princess* LIE. The principal and VP Ms. Princess* ruined the entire school for two years. Then allowed students to graduate who didn't deserve to graduate.

However, the memo from the District clearly states Attendance guidelines. Including consecutive days' absences 5, 10, 15 & 20 and after a student has accumulated 20 days of unexcused absences. It also explains if students exceed the 20-day limit, if students are 16 and older, late and cut policies, the cracking down of cell phone & pagers, and the consequences. Let's see what happens! So far so good. However, I have already seen many students taken out of the building by police and in handcuffs into an awaiting police car. It seems they are keeping things quieter this year. However, it also looks they are not accepting any BS either. For example: Sept 10, 2008, 11:55 am, police took out student in handcuffs and into an awaiting police car. I don't know why?

**Sept 29, 6th period, 11:30** - this is the first time the fire alarms went off and we evacuated the building. It was a false alarm. One of my students from 4th period (name omitted) pulled the alarm. This was during the very end of HSPA testing. I do not have any digital pictures; however, I did receive video.

**Oct 3** - Oh no, it's starting to look and feel like it is starting all over again. I hope not. More and more kids are hanging out in the hallways and longer after the bell rings to begin classes.

I just came down from the last day of testing. OH MY GOD, I feel so bad for the kids and some teacher. I left early because I have a class in a few minutes but classroom 220 was absolutely freezing.
This place is disgusting. This is the same room as last year that I took pictures and video of and it is still in the same condition. The only thing different was they plastered up the huge hole in the wall. It is still disgusting, dirty, rodent feces infested, graffiti all over the place and *FREEZING*. There is NO way this would be allowed in another school district. As soon as I came to my room, I had to put my coat on and zipper it all the way up. I guess the October rule of turning the heat on also applies to public urban schools. I hope to God it doesn't snow tomorrow or the pipes will burst. How does the superintendent and his administration get away with this? This is NOT acceptable! I felt good this morning, now watch me come down with pneumonia. This is NOT fair to the children. Where is the news media?

**7th period 12:47** - fire alarms go off. We had to evacuate the building. Fire department came. It was a false alarm pulled down in the basement. Have video and 2 photos.

**7th period, 12:49** - fire alarms go off again. Evacuate building again. Fire department came again.

**Oct 14 - 3rd period, 9:05** - fire alarms went off. Evacuate building, again. Supposedly a sensor!

**Again 3rd period, 9:19** - fire alarms went off again. Evacuate building, again. Supposedly a sensor again!

**Oct 15** - I overheard one of my students (name omitted) talking about playing football for JFK? I have to laugh. This is the same kid on September 29th who pulled the fire alarm and is *STILL* allowed to play football? In a real school district, he would be expelled and wouldn't be allowed to play football. From what I understand the only person who was punished was his father for having to pay the fine.

**Oct 16 - 4th period, 10:37** - fire alarms go off again. Evacuate building again. They're calling it fire drill. It was because the sensors have DUST in them! Now we are to disregard future alarms today unless otherwise notified. Have video and 2 photos.

**Oct 20** - before homeroom there was a big fight involving girls. Then again 6th period more fights. Both times security and police were literally dragging students into the security office. It is starting to get out of control with all the screaming, cursing and carrying on going on.

**1st period** fire alarms go off, evacuated building. We were told to disregard the fire alarms until further notice. After we came back in the alarms go off several more times 8:20, 8:56, 9:20 & 9:57. The entire day the alarms were going off and we do not know why. Have video and 2 photos.

**Oct 22 - 7th period 12:30** - fire alarms go off evacuate building. Sensors again! This system is only a few years old. This would not happen at a professional *sports arena*! This unacceptable!

**Oct 29** - Mr. Madjar of the cut office told me they are processing approximately 500 cuts a day. There are only 1600 students enrolled here this year. Students are *NOT* showing up for 1st, 2nd, 9th, and 10th period classes. It's obvious, because it's taking forever for the hallways to clear.

**Nov 13** - big mess/problem in the hallways with either MACE or PEPPER SPRAY. Kids were getting sick, can't breathe and their eyes were all effected. Don't know who did it, but it was a student or students. Meanwhile students are still in hallways long after the bell.

**Nov 17 - 8th period,** fire alarms go off, evacuated building. Fire department came. They caught the kids.

**Nov 26 - 9:01**, fire alarms go off, evacuated building. Fire department and added police came. I assume false alarm but not sure. Came back in alarm went off again. I do not know why. A few minutes later the alarm went off again, no one knows whether to evacuate or not. Nothing but chaos here! It is taking forever for these kids to go back to class. The alarms went off all day. They turned off the alarm sound, but the strobe lights kept going all day. Supposedly the fire alarm company was here working on it. *FIGHTS ALL DAY LONG.* Have video.

**Dec 12 -** 6:50am pulled into parking lot. The fire alarms were going. Don't know the reason why.

Received a phone call from a student's father. It was about his son losing his phone. I told him, I have nothing to do with that. Students are not to have a phone in school. His father said well, he had it on vibrate. I repeated students are not to have them in school. He then replies, me being the teacher, I should have kept everyone in class to find out who has it. I tried to explain, it has nothing to do with me, teachers, security guards, police are not to get involved with this kind of stuff. His next comment was what about if it was your phone? I said it doesn't matter; it has nothing to do with me. It is not about me. As I was trying to explain, he started screaming Fuck you, fuck you, fuck you, and hung up. I now know why his son acts the way he does. It is so true; the apple doesn't fall too far from the tree! Shortly afterwards, I notified my VP about the phone call.

**Dec 11 - the above student was** dropped from my class. I have three pages of anecdotal notes on him pertaining to his foul mouth, unacceptable, dysfunctional, defiant, argumentative poor behavior and attitude. Every time, I refuse to let him act inappropriately or do something wrong, I am called a mother fucker and a racist. This was the *FIRST* time I heard from his parent. I guess his father is more concerned about a phone than his son getting an education. **THAT'S PRIORITIES!**
Like I said, the apple doesn't fall too far from the tree.

**January 14 -** Mr. Angelo Bonora, the wood shop teacher, and his students were putting up another video camera in the center hallway. It seems pennants are being stolen off the walls. So, the administration wants new cameras installed in hopes of catching anyone who tries to steal the pennants again. *INTERESTING*, putting up more surveillance cameras because *PENNANTS* were stolen. But not last year and the year before with all the violence and students in the hallways all day long every day! And the money to purchase the cameras and accessories came from Mr. Banora's class budget.

**Jan 20 -** 8:02, fire alarms go off. We evacuated the building. A steam pipe broke in office #1's bathroom.

**Jan 26 -** so far this school year is so much better. *NOT PERFECT*, but this proves to me why, you do not hire someone out of the district. The two principals we had that were hired out of the district were a freaking disaster and they both wanted to be called Dr. They had absolutely no control over anything not to mention the losers we've had as SUPERINTENDENTS.

**Jan 27 -** I'm getting nervous and spoke to soon. It seems the school is starting to loosen up and slip. Students were in the hallways all day long today and this is Mid-Term Exam Week.

**Feb 2 -** oh no, the school is getting out of control and fast, especially this being a Midterm exam day. There were fights all day long all over the place.

**Feb 3 -** approximately 11:42, we received an announcement that there is no more bus AC1. It has been canceled due to excessive and nonstop vandalism, violence and graffiti.

A teacher was telling me it is really bad on the 2nd floor. She is upset with all the fighting. She said there was one last week right by the door of her classroom where a bunch of kids beat a kid up really bad. Blood was everywhere. She was so disgusted and starting to get in the despair mode as we all were last year. *WHY IS THIS ALLOWED TO START UP AGAIN?* They're allowing students to roam and hang out in the hallways again. This is not fair to students who want to learn, their parents, and NJ taxpayers.

**Feb 4** - cannot enter grades for report cards or attendance in the last two days. Computer system is down. I am always skeptical when this happens in this district.

**Feb 9** - we are losing the school again. Hallways are filled with students especially during cafeteria periods. Fights all day long, everywhere! What has happened to *Zero Tolerance to Violence*?

Talking with Mr. Cubi*, a TAP, he said about 200 students are roaming the hallways constantly. These are students who have lost credit (NC). He said it so nonchalant and as if this is what it is. I did not say this but I was thinking, I realize they lost credit and it doesn't really matter to these students, but why are they allowed to roam the halls causing problems? It is *NO DIFFERENCE* than kids hanging on a street corner. Eventually they will do something wrong or stupid because they are bored and are *NOT* in class. In fact, the cut office is not processing cuts and tardiness the last few days, because they're so overwhelmed with students' attendance and attendance policy problems. Think about it JFK has a CUT office that is open longer than the regular school day just to try to keep up in the processing of cuts. There's a full-time secretary and a ½ a dozen teachers working in the cut office instead of teaching. How can the administration allow the school to get so out of control? Now they have to pay teachers to come in on Saturdays to operate the cut office as well as to supervise for detention. On top of that, most of the students who are assigned Saturday detention *DON'T SHOW!* Talk about wasting taxpayers' money? If things do not improve soon it is *NOT* going to get better. Why all of a sudden, a BIG change and allowing the school once again to get out of control? Also, students can now register for NOVA NET so they can make up time lost and credits for classes they failed. This is BS, taxpayers are getting screwed again. And another year goes by where the students from Paterson are *NOT* getting a proper education other than learning and reinforcing what they may already know on how to get over. NOVA NET or any other program would not be necessary if students were made to go to class. NOVA NET and all of the other programs in my opinion are a joke and used only to improve the students/schools/district numbers on drop out, and the number of students graduating each year. It is a scam because the administration refuses to make student go to class and it is costing the NJ taxpayers big bucks on top of what they have already paid per student for the school year. It is soooo good that the state is running and operating this district. It proves my point how ineffective *government* is.

**I found out the caps** that were re-placed on the steps during the summer are now loose and the stairwell is inoperative and dangerous. Another job that was done improperly by outside contractors and will have to be done again. The 3rd floor stairwell all the way to 1st floor, between offices 1 & 2 cannot be used. What if there's a fire and we have to evacuate the building in a real emergency? The number one question I have is why wasn't the job inspected prior to signing off on it and being paid for?

**Feb 10** - many of the 2nd and 3rd floors classrooms for the past 14 days did not have heat! The rooms were freezing. The *average* temperature was approximately 50 degrees.

**FOOD FOR THOUGHT** - It seems everything has to be done over and over here. Nothing is ever installed, replaced or repaired properly at the beginning or the first time. Am I the only one that sees this?
**EXAMPLE** - Floors, doors, walls, windows, paint, heating system, bells, clocks, PA system, fire alarms, sensors, etc. Everything is done fast, incomplete and paid for. No one knows what to look or check for. For these contractors it is take the money and run. And that is exactly what they do. Then the district has

the nerve to cry about money. Then Dr. (name omitted) another genius with a PhD. comes into the building almost every day and is more concerned about stupid college pennants being stolen but does *nothing* about the rooms without heat. What freaking priorities and the taxpayer keeps paying and paying!

**Feb 11** - to save money they lowered the amount of security personnel in our building--laid off or fired!

**Feb 13** - I had it. It's the first time this year I started to video the hallways on the 1st floor. When I stopped the halls where still filled with students. I have a 5:05 minutes video starting right after the bell rang to start 2nd period. Wonder why the cut office is open all the time? For this to be allowed to go on and on, then there is and never was any reason for the state of NJ to take over and run this school district.

**Mar 4 - I was in room 219 for HSPA testing**. It is still a shambles as it was last year and filled with graffiti. I have video. Other than patching the BIG hole in the wall and not painted, everything is exactly the same, even the bulletin board. This would not be allowed in any other school District!

**Mar 11** - fights all day long. Some were extremely brutal and violent. One kid had to actually be taken out in an ambulance because he wouldn't calm down, wanted to fight and attack everyone in his sight, teachers, police, security other students. Once again, the administration is NOT enforcing the 10-day mandatory suspension for fighting. I truly believe the principal and the VPs are *TOLD,* directed by the superintendents to allow the school to be out of control and *NOT* to discipline students.

**Mar 12 - 9:24, fire alarm** went off. We evacuated the building. It was a sensor in *my room*. It activated shortly after I turned the fans off in my room. I had the fans on since 7:30am and turned them off to go to the office to make copies. It seems that the heater was blowing so much hot air it set the sensors off. Fire Department came. **All that money wasted on this alarm system.** I have 1:43 minute video and 2 photos.

**Mar 13** - I went to the library when the bell rang for 3rd period to begin. I couldn't believe the 2nd floor. It was jammed packed FILLED with students. It's just like last year. It was a good 15 minutes until the hallways started to thin out. I have to laugh; the administration talks about extending the school day. I wouldn't mind, but the longer they extend the day the longer the kids will be in the hallways instead of being in class! It should be easier to check which kids are constantly in the hallways because attendance, cuts and lateness's are all computerized by each teacher. OR is there someone who changes everything without teacher's permission? It's a shame I think like that. However, after what has been going on here ever since the State of New Jersey has taken over this district, how can I help it or *NOT* think like that!

**Mar 23 - 4th period, 10:19** - fire alarms go off. We evacuated the building. The fire department came. Students set the 1st floor, art wing boys' room on fire.

**Then 5th period, 10:59** - fire alarms go off. Evacuated the building again. Fire department came. Students started a fire again in the boys' room bathroom. We came back in at 11:30. Have video and 2 photos.

**Mar 24 - 4th period, 9:54** - fire alarms go off again. Evacuate the building again. Fire department came again. We came back in at 10:04. A false alarm!

**Mar 30 - 8th period, 1:35 -** fire alarms go off, evacuated the building. Fire department came. Came back in at, 1:46. Passaic county arson squad came. Seems someone lit a sensor on fire in the boys' bathroom in the basement by Teen Center. I have video 2:58 minutes long & 2 photos. AND the administration still allows the students to roam the hallways all day long.

IMPORTANT NOTATIONS:
Today March 30, 2009. I just realized while I was placing today's evacuation information and pictures on diskette that the times I have written and the times on the camera may be incorrect. This is due to the change of day light savings. I don't know how many are like this. Bottom line the times *only* are off. My records are accurate. They can be easily checked and crossed referenced via the Passaic County Sheriff's office, Paterson Police & Fire Departments and etc.

**Apr 30 -** during homeroom announcements, school bus #5 is canceled due to vandalism.

**May 14 -** I received a tardy referral slip back. When I submitted it I had the following added information on it because I was fed up having to keep filling out all of this paperwork for the same student/s.
**TOTAL         ABSENT 37              LATE 56            CUT 28**

Mr. Pardine wrote a note on the slip saying he has a *total of 122 cuts &100 lates.*

Same day, I received a memo from Ms. Queenie* with a list of students who lost credit and if I or any teacher think they should receive their credit back? The above students name was on it. I said NO and went it to great length of explanations such as; this is absolutely ridiculous, students do *nothing*, are absent, cut school and classes, suspended all year yet you want to *GIVE THEM CREDIT BACK!* What a waste to NJ taxpayers and insult to teachers.

**May 19 -** I obtained a profile (*6 pages*) on a student (name omitted) a junior and is on the basketball team.

| | | | |
|---|---|---|---|
| Arts foundation | 2 Absents | 4 Cuts | |
| Algebra | 11 Absents | 41 Cuts | |
| World History | 11 Absents | 5 Cuts | 47 Lates |
| Metal Shop | 9 Absents | 2 Cuts | 31 Lates |
| Biology Lab | 6 Absents | 5 Cuts | 14 Lates |
| Phys Ed | 8 Absents | | |
| Child develop | 7 Absents | | |
| English | 8 Absents | | 4 Lates |
| Health | 0 Absents | 1 Cut | |
| **Total:** | **62 Absents** | **57 Cuts** | **96 Lates**   and has not lost credit? |

Obviously, some teachers have not written cuts. How can he be out of class but is in school?

I obtained a profile (23 *pages* in total) on a student (name omitted) aka the "Phantom," because *if* he comes to school, he is never where he should be or is always in the hallways all day.
Below are his classes for the last *three* years and was still either a repeating 9th or 10th grader!

| | | | |
|---|---|---|---|
| Phys Ed | 73 Absents | 16 Cuts | 3 Lates |
| English | 24 Absents | 11 Cuts | |
| Math | 27 Absents | 12 Cuts | 1 Lates |
| Science | 23 Absents | 10 Cuts | |
| Employ Skills | 26 Absents | 15 Cuts | |
| History | 24 Absents | 10 Cuts | |
| Life Skills | 28 Absents | 10 Cuts | |
| Life Skills | 22 Absents | 8 Cuts | |
| English | 19 Absents | 9 Cuts | |
| History | 17 Absents | 9 Cuts | |
| Science | 19 Absents | 8 Cuts | |
| Employ Skills | 19 Absents | 8 Cuts | |
| Math | 42 Absents | 16 Cuts | |
| World History | 49 Absents | 13 Cuts | |
| Math | 42 Absents | 16 Cuts | |
| Employ Skills | 44 Absents | 13 Cuts | |
| Science | 49 Absents | 10 Cuts | |
| English | 52 Absents | 10 Cuts | |
| Life Skills | 49 Absents | 12 Cuts | |
| Health | 20 Absents | 1 Cuts | |
| **Grand total:** | **668 Absents** | **217 Cuts** | **4 Lates** |

My concern is, "This is NOT the only student. There are 100s just like this.

**June 8 -** I acquired a LIST of 66 students who had their credit restored by Ms. Queenie*.
Wonder why so many students (not all) leave JFK with a diploma and are illiterate? Many are students I had 4 years ago. They lost credit, got credit back, lost credit again, got their credit back again and this yo-yo affect goes on and on all year long for 4 years.

Several people from the attendance office said, if they threw every student out that should be thrown out it would be over 1000 students and we will be out of a job. I said so what, all we are doing is teaching the other kids now that there are no consequences, it is ok not to go to class, don't do your work and you will STILL GRADUATE? All they are doing is constantly lowering standards. Do you really wonder why students CANNOT pass the state exam, which is ALL that the school teaches to and cares about!

Ms. Queenie* said, if we don't pass them, they will end up staying here forever! "WHAT THE HELL KIND OF REMARK IS THAT?" I want this fool to send her children and or grandchildren here. Let's see how fast her attitude will change. No one is to go forward, pass, and graduate unless they meet the necessary requirements. It's obvious to me after hearing a DUMB remark like that; she doesn't want to do her job. If students need to be here longer, then so be it. It is supposed to be about students/children and their education, preparing them for life, so they can and will be gainfully employed, able to work with others, be on time and consistent for work, to know how to work hard, to continue and further their education if they choose too, and to be able to advance in life and social stature. Not to be just thrown out into the world. This behavior and attitude here in Paterson will not only cost the New Jersey taxpayers' but the entire country more and more each year as they just pass and pushed students through the System which in turn is, "Ruining A Nation!"

OBVIOUSLY, it is the end of the year. The administration is scrambling to show improvements in the graduation rate / statistics. It is NOT about the children, students or their education. It is ONLY about *perception,* making the superintendent and his administration look good.

**Jun 19** - statistics for my classes only.
### 2008 - 2009 TOTAL ABSENCES, CUTS, TARDIES & STUDENTS

| 1st Period | Absents 70 | Lates 46 | Cuts 25 | @ 7 Total students |
|---|---|---|---|---|
| 2nd Period | Absents 142 | Lates 60 | Cuts 37 | @31 Total students |
| 4th Period | Absents 140 | Lates 91 | Cuts 15 | @ 31 Total students |
| 5th Period | Absents 342 | Lates 170 | Cuts 85 | @20 Total students |
| 6th Period | Absents 627 | Lates 181 | Cuts 237 | @ 21 Total students |
| 8th Period | Absents 396 | Lates 163 | Cuts 115 | @19 Total students |
| **Grand total** | **Absents 1717** | **Lates 711** | **Cuts 514** | **@129 Total students** |

**1:46** fire alarm goes off, evacuated the building. It was a malfunction.

Students were told to clear out their lockers. They threw everything imaginable all over the floors including textbooks throughout the entire building. I don't understand why students are *not* held responsible for their textbooks? Wonder why the school does not have enough textbooks? However, if their cell phone, iPod or anything else is missing, damaged or stolen which should *not* be in school, you should hear the cussing and fussing that goes on and want to hold the TEACHER responsible. The NJ taxpayers get SCREWED AGAIN and ends up paying for everything here over and over.
**Total cut slips *RECEIVED AND PROCESSED* for 2008 - 2009 School Year was 111,752.**
I have access to all of those cuts slips.

### SCHOOL YEAR 2009 - 2010
**September 18, 2009** - 6th period, I received a new student, (name omitted). I asked him to fill out his student data card. He did but did not know how to spell Presidential Boulevard. He's a freshman in High School and CANNOT spell his address. Meanwhile the superintendent of the Paterson school district, the Governor, Commissioner of Education and everyone else wants to hold High School teachers accountable for students PASSING the state-wide exam/HSPA.

**Sept 22 - 10:55** - fire alarms go off, evacuated building. A fire was deliberately set in the girls' bathroom on the 3rd floor. Fire was extinguished by security. The fire department came. The fire marshal is investigating this situation.

**Oct 8 -** Boys and girls taken out in handcuffs. The hallways are starting to remain filled with student's looooong after the bell rings to start class. Cut office is already over inundated with cuts, and tardiness.

I have students who refuse to come to 1st period class and or come to class always late and not by a little bit, because they say class starts too early in the morning. Then guidance counselors and Ms. Queenie* will change their schedules. Our students never learn anything other than having excuses and wanting things made and changed their way. Of all things school is to prepare students to be productive members of society and that means it prepares students for the REAL WORLD OF WORK, meaning YOU MUST BE ON TIME for school. Sure, it's too early in the morning to get up when parents allow them to go to bed after midnight. Most businesses start 7am. Class starts at 7:30am. We wonder why these kids have no job/employability skills. However, school districts want to hold teachers solely responsible for passing the state-wide exams. NOT THEIR PARENTS!

**Oct 9** - fights all day long, every place, involving boys & girls. Here we go, it's starting.

**Oct 14 - 9:12 am, 3rd period** - fire alarms go off evacuate building. I have 2 photos. It *was* a fire drill. It's another day of fights and fighting all day long and everywhere in the building.

**Nov 23** - a student in my 5th period was locked up for 5 days or so. The reason, he choked his grandmother, whom he lives with. His remarks were, "well what do they expect, they know I HAVE anger management problems." There is no sense of right and wrong. Just excuses without remorse. It is everybody else's fault, NOT HIS!
**To date this is his attendance:         Absents 25       Cuts 23         Lates 16**

**Nov 24 & 25** - we are starting to lose control again, nothing but fights all day long everywhere. Believe it or not, so far it is still much better (safer that's all) than it has been in a looong time.

**Dec 3** - a Special Ed counselor came in to see me about one of my students. He said he was complaining because I give him too much work and mark him late to class. I laughed and said, he does absolutely nothing and if he is late, what am I supposed to do? Then I am told he has problems. Who doesn't have problems? If they do NOT learn how to follow rules and be on time, do their work, just being a responsible person, they will have more problems in life and so will New Jersey taxpayers. He should have been dropped from roll last year because of poor attendance and cutting.

**Dec 7** - things are still much better here. However, the above student continues to cut class and is still complaining. In fact, today his guidance counselor told me, he will be dropping my class. I asked why. He said by order of the Special Ed department. I said, Mrs. Queenie. * He replied, YES. I replied immediately, she is useless. I will guarantee my attendance will not carry over into his next class. Ms. Queenie* will give him a new slate. That's why she removed him from my class, because I DID my job, and she is allowing him and others like him to be get-overs. She and this district have taught students that they do NOT have to do anything; we will just pass and push you through the system and receive a diploma.

**Dec 16** - on my way home, School #9 Bus, 724 or 725, the kids were jumping all over inside. It looked like a fight going on with all of the kids up and out of their seats shoving, pushing and throwing jackets. At one time I thought they were going to open the back door and jump out. I was so mad and didn't know what to do. They would stare out the windows at me in act of defiance and intimidation. I knew I couldn't get out of the car. I wanted to stop the bus, make the bus driver pull over to call the cops. That's what the driver should have done. It was so out of control. So, I pulled out my cell phone and made like I was recording them. They saw me and stopped. Several of them covered their heads and faces with their jackets. On December 17, one of my students confirmed what I was saying because he saw me and asked to see the video. I said no because the principal and the police have it. I lied hoping it would get back to those punks on the bus. I did speak with the principal and one of the TAPs. Other than that, I have no idea what happened. However, the principal said he informed all bus drivers if students act up, they are to turn around, come right back to the school, let them out and they can find another way to get home. A security guard told me the buses use to have video cameras but had to remove them for some BS reason. I wouldn't be surprised the administration had the cameras removed to cover and hush up the way these punks act, behave and carry on adding to the insanity and the safety of everyone on the bus.

**Dec 21** - here we go with the food fights. There was a student dancing on a cafeteria table. The police were summoned and asked the kid to come down. The kid gave the cops a ration of BS and was so defiant and disrespectful. The police had enough, ended up grabbing, handcuffing and taking him away.

**Dec 22** - first thing this morning, girls fighting. The rest of the day fights all over the place.

**January 4 - 11, 2010** - this place is going downhill and fast. Kids are all over the place in the hallways. Cut office is filled ALL DAY LONG with students.

**Jan 12** - fire alarms go off, evacuated the building. It was cold and windy. It was *not* a drill. Fire department and added police came. The principal made an announcement saying that it was a false alarm and they caught the kid and he was whisked away by police. However, the nonsense of pulling false alarms has dropped drastically and it *IS* due to the video cameras. Still nothing in the newspapers!

**Jan 19** - FIRST DAY OF MID TERM EXAM, what a disaster. Kids are all over the place all day long. Even during 2nd period, 1st exam of the day, kids are still coming in at 8:45 am. Exams start at 8:15am.

- Later that afternoon an announcement was made about NOVA NET / CREDIT RECOVERY. Students or their parents do *not* have to pay for Nova Net. The NJ taxpayers have to pay for it, plus overtime for administrator & teachers to be present from 3:30 to 5:30. Two hours of NOVA NET to make up for an entire day and all their classes? Why bother having school?

- I hate to say this, but it looks as if the school is getting out of control again.

**January 19 – 22, Mid Term Exam week**. What a shame, it was out of F'ing control here. I don't understand why students are allowed to just walk in and out of the building as if it is a saloon. School starts at 8:15am, yet students were still walking into the building after 9am. It's the same kids who normally start at 7:30 am and are continually late and are still late. This proves they are always deliberately late. Some come in much later. It used to be if you were that late you were not admitted in without a parent. The students and obviously the administration *both* just don't care. The school district has taught students that attendance, lateness and when you come to school doesn't matter. The administration can fix, adjust, manipulate, and doctor up your attendance so you are not held accountable! Plus, there were nothing but fights all day long every day. There was a BIG FIGHT especially on January 21. The hallway was like a scene in jail house movie. Cops and security guard could not get through because the students would not allow them through. Students were deliberately holding and pushing security and police back to keep them from getting to the fight / scene.

Shortly afterwards another fight broke out in the cafeteria. They escorted a boy out. It was obvious he didn't care. He was putting on a good show screaming, yelling cursing; telling the cops and security to get your fucking hands off of me, all of you mother fuckers are dead and on and on. A few seconds later he walks away and out of the office as if nothing happened and went directly back to the cafeteria. A few seconds he is running in the hallways FULL SPEED, being followed by a young lady who too is running as fast as she can. Security, teachers, police and myself were yelling to stop, but we were *ALL IGNORED*. While running the young lady is screaming, cursing all sorts of profanity and threw 3 milk cartons at that boy. The best part about all of this, *NOTHING* was done about any of it!

**Jan 21** - I noticed one of my students being handcuffed and escorted out by police. As usual he had his MP3 player on. The teacher told him to put it away. As usual this student was defiant, ran his mouth and took his sweet time about it. The teacher was not happy with his continued defiance and especially on how long it was taking so he told him again to put it away. So in anger the student shoved the teacher.

District and school rules states, MP 3 players, iPods, etc. are *not* allowed. Meanwhile in defiance students wear them as they are walking into the building. Why don't security and the administrators confiscate them right then and now instead of having a teacher being subjected to all of this nonsense continually?

**WEEK OF FEBRUARY 1 - 5 -** school is getting bad, fights more and more every day. Hallways are filled with students loooong after the bell rings to begin class. Cut office is filled with students for cutting, being late and truancy. I have to laugh because the new governor, Christie thinks Charter Schools are the best thing since slice bread as well as Catholic Schools. However, I do believe Catholic Schools are better. That is where students get the best education and is no comparison to Public Schools. After all you don't see politicians send their children to Public Schools. The point I am trying to make is teachers are not allowed to do our jobs. Teachers and security guards here are nothing more than punching bags. All because the superintendent and administration continually allows, teaches and reinforces students to do whatever they want and to act as I have been describing throughout this book with no fear of getting in trouble or of ever being disciplined. It just doesn't STOP! What a waste of taxpayers' money!

**Mar 3 - HSPA** during testing a young man was asked to hand over his cell phone to a guidance counselor. He refused. Not only did he refuse he was extremely defiant and obscene. It was nothing but FUCK YOU, you're not getting my mother fucking phone, nobody is taking my mother fucking phone, fuck you it's not your phone, you don't pay my fucking phone bill, get the fuck away, fuck me and on and on. One of the personal aides in that class said it was so bad, unbelievably disgusting and disturbing how this kid carried on. He said he couldn't believe what he was seeing. He said to me that he had to do something, so he went up to him and quietly said, my man, I don't want to embarrass you, you're not going to win, give me the phone and I promise I will give it back to you at the end of testing. I promise, just give me the phone and I promise I'll give it back. He said reluctantly the kid gave it to him. A few seconds later the test coordinator came in. The aide said to the kid uh oh, too late. They took the phone, had the young man escorted out and was immediately suspended. The purpose of this entry is to show how defiant so many of these students are. School RULES state no phones. NO ELECTRICAL DEVICES are permitted during testing let alone in school all together. It doesn't matter what rules or laws say so many of these students are nasty, defiant and will challenge all authority, have the attitude you cannot tell me what to do, will do whatever they want when they want and just don't care.

**Mar 8 - 12,** UNFREAKINBELIEVABLE, all week nothing but fights all over the school. First thing this morning on the 9th it starts off with a bang, a fight erupts. To make things worse and contributes to the fighting and problems, is that the hallways are getting worse and are constantly filled with students. It is disgusting how students can just walk around and hangout in the hallways without penalty. The cut office is filled with students all day long processing their cuts and tardiness. It is absolutely ridiculous. *Now*, I am convinced it is definitely **not** the principal allowing the school to be out of control. There is no way he would allow this to go on in his school. I believe he is told and following orders from central office.

**Mar 29 – Apr 2, FIGHTS ALL DAY LONG** - everywhere in the building involving boys, girls and everyone. The school is so out of control again. The cut office is constantly filled with students. Mr. Pardine, Mr. Madjar and about a half a dozen other cut officers are frantically trying to get caught up processing all of the cuts and tardy slips.

**Apr 2 -** there was a meeting in the auditorium for all seniors. I found out there were 200 students who would NOT be able to take and pass the HSPA so instead they took SRA. Well, the results show out of the 200 hundred students who took the tests for SRA only ONE (1) PASSED! That is 0.5 percent. That says it all! If parents don't care students don't care. Also, if students are allowed to roam the halls, hang out in stairwells, bathrooms, not go to their classes what do you expect? You're going to hold teachers accountable? First of all, this shouldn't be happening when the STATE of NEW JERSEY is running and operating this school and district. They are allowing students NOT to be EDUCATED!

**Apr 27 - 10:22, 4th period,** fire alarms go off evacuated the building. The fire department and added police came. False alarm pulled by the gym. I have photos of the evacuation. However, it is still better here than it has been in almost 20 years.

Seems students across the state were to walk out of school to protest Governor Christie's budget cuts, attacks on teachers and teacher's union. However, as usual here at JFK, students need very little to be disruptive. So the students were walking out, causing a great deal of disturbance in the school and the streets where the police had to come and get control. In doing so, many students were maced. This is so typical here in Paterson. Soooo many of the students here have this jail house mentality and will do whatever they can to destroy, disrupt, become defiant and will continue to do anything to cause havoc and escalate a situation. It was so bad and disruptive that principal came over the loud speaker telling security and administrators to escort any student in the hallways without a pass, wearing a hat, using their cell phones, iPod etc. to the office and they will be suspended for 5 days. He made it clear he is not going to allow this nonsense to continue. For the first time in a long time I was so proud of the principal. He is the first principal in almost 20 years to try to get our school back and in control.

**Apr 28 -** listening to the radio WGHT on my way to work, they said that Rosa Park students walked out of school in protest and that they were the only school in the entire Passaic County to do so. See what I mean, what went on here at JFK goes hushed up again. If this went on here and at Rosa Parks, I can only imagine what went on at Eastside High School. I have not been keeping up with my journal because it is all the same. The cutting and students roaming the halls is too much.

**May 28 -** nothing has changed. It proves to me it is *not* the principal. He is following orders. Things have slipped so much ever since the new superintendent arrived. Remember the words to the Who song? *"MEET THE NEW BOSS, SAME AS THE OLD BOSS!"* It is so true. They pass and graduate students that have over 100 cuts and the same in absences? What is wrong with the teachers for passing them? It has to come down to the fear of evaluations. This school is nothing more than a place where poor and horrible behavior is allowed and excuses are acceptable especially with and for the Special Ed students. They are classified, re-tested once and awhile and that's it. What is the purpose of having all of these Special Ed case workers/counselors if *nothing* is done to try and change the behavior of these students?

**Jun 1 -** went up to the 2nd floor just prior to the start of 3rd period. All of the hallways were a mess, out of freaking control and loooong after the bell rang to start 3rd period. It is no wonder why the cut office is so busy all day long and overflowing with students. What makes it worse is I do not have any video or photos of this. However, many teachers were pleased that I am documenting everything. I was furious and snapped at them. I told them that they should be doing the same thing and not to expect someone else to do their dirty work. What I see and you see are different and at different times. I said we have to protect ourselves and show what is really going on in a state run and operated district and it is NOT about education. I said, you all sit around, complain and do nothing about anything. This place is getting worse and worse for the last 20 years and what have you done to change things? Then I just walked way. It is because of that attitude that the state Takeover District of Paterson, NJ has been getting away with everything. The superintendent and administration know teachers are NOT going to do anything about anything other than complain. Well, pretty soon all of this will be OUT!

**Jun 3 -** I went back up to the 2nd floor to take video just prior to the start of 3rd period. The bell rings and hallways remained out of freaking control an absolute and complete disaster. It's just as bad as it was 2 years ago. I truly believe, it is **not** the principal's fault; they're following orders from the superintendent.

I kept the video going until I came back into my classroom. I narrated it all. About 15 minutes later, the principal came to see me and wanted to know if I was videotaping? I said yes. He asked me why? I told him that I have been documenting this stuff for years. I said you know I have been doing this because I stood next to you a few years ago during a fight on the 2nd or 3rd floor. Then I said if you are worried about me placing this and the others stuff on YouTube that is not going to happen. I told him I had the conversation with our last principal on many occasions and never ever placed anything on the web. He said "as an administrator we have to be worried about this type of stuff." I also told him that I appreciated him for being direct with me. He replied we know what is wrong and are going to make changes for next year. I kept quiet and thought to myself why wait until next year? There's a problem and no one is going to do anything about it? I know in my heart it is not him. He is TOLD to let things go. I will keep my guard up. If they make a fuss, it is to try to suppress me and all of the documentation I have to PROVE what is really going on here.

ALL day long students are in the hallways walking in and out of my and other teacher's classrooms. When we tell them to get out, we are cursed at, threatened, some teachers have been attacked and pretty brutalized. What does the school and district do about it? Everything they can to keep it all hushed up!

I have no choice but to take more video. It will show and prove how the superintendent's and the administration keep everything hushed up. I will try to encourage other teachers to do the same, PLUS documenting everything. Then after showing all of our documentation on how bad things are, how things operate here and have been all the while this school was under State Control, then shove it all up the politicians' asses. Sorry, but it had to be said and said that way.

**Jun 3 - 9th period fire alarms** go off. We evacuated the building and were outside for quite a while. Then a fight erupts out by the park. All the students run to the fight just to see the show and as usual instigate more fights, making the situation bigger and causing more trouble. We came back in about 2pm. The principal came over the PA system saying the alarm has malfunctioned. However, once we came back into the building the entire school was an absolute disaster shear chaos. I have video and 2 photos.

It is a shame what is actually going on with the 2010 graduation year. *EVERY* student is walking! How can this be when soooo many students didn't go to class all year?

**Jun 28** - hallways are filled with students for summer school registration and it's almost going out the building.          Unbelievable! Students don't go to classes all YEAR and still allowed to go to summer school and will PASS in a few weeks. Why bother having school if students only need a few weeks to pass?

Students wouldn't have to go to summer school if the administration made them go to class instead of hanging out all over the place and roam the building, all day, every day, all year. Just cross reference all the cuts that were processed with all of the students for summer school. Taxpayers get screwed again!

**Jun 29 -** I was told today that most of the students ARE participating in the ceremony but not graduating. The students could NOT only pass the state test, they couldn't pass a redo, then some other BS exam, then SRA, then lastly they were allowed to take and utilize the ASVAB (Armed Services Vocational Battery) as an alternative and still DID NOT PASS.

Approximately 1000 students registered for summer school.
However, here at JFK in Paterson, NJ, summer school is FREE! I don't get it, *NOTHING IS FREE!*

Mr. Pardine & Mr. Madjar found the following information on the Internet.
In some districts summer school is per class/course and the parents have to pay-
- $340 Summer School
- $640 Advance Class
- $900 Enrichment

Let's make it $300 x 1000 students = $300,000.00, at the expense of the NJ taxpayers!
And that's *ONLY* if each student *ONLY* failed one course/class!
Then in a few weeks, what couldn't be done in an entire year, miraculously all of these students PASS!
All because the superintendent and his administration continually allowed students NOT to go to class!

## SCHOOL YEAR 2010 – 2011

**September 15, 2010, 9:35** - one of my students (name omitted) was escorted in handcuffs by two Paterson police officers and brought to a TAP's office. He was picked up for having marijuana in his locker along with 50 individual packages for sale plus other stuff. According to the police basically nothing will happen because he is a juvenile. However, if he were a grownup, he would be locked up because of the 1000 feet from a school zone law. I don't know if I believe that. Breaking the law is breaking the law!

**Sept 30** - all the money poured into this district and nothing changes. Brand new elevator doesn't work. Brand new district computer system is always down, or so slow teachers cannot enter their daily attendance. And the building is the same, still out of control.

You know what else is a waste? The first week in October the entire 9$^{th}$, 10$^{th}$, 11$^{th}$ & 12$^{th}$ graders in the Paterson Public School District were required to take the PSAT. From those administering the test, I was told each test cost the District $16. $16.00 x approximately 2000 JFK students = $32,000.00.
It took several hours to take the test, which included students having to grid all pertinent personnel info. It was a disaster. No one finished the test. Students couldn't follow direction or grid in their names properly. Unfortunately, most of our students cannot & some will not follow directions.

**Oct 14 & 15** - the principal started hall sweeps. Any student who is *NOT* in their classroom after the 2$^{nd}$ bell is to be picked up and brought to the office and disciplined. He is the *ONLY* principal in years who is trying to keep students from being in the hallways, stairwells, bathrooms and etc. If he fails and everything continues as it has been, I will now know he is being told by the superintendent of schools to let it go and ignore it all. It is obvious the superintendent is more worried about the perception, his reputation, the state and federal funding, instead of students receiving a quality education.

**Oct 15, I received the following memo from my immediate supervisor.**
    Please ensure that each teacher under your supervision gets a copy of the attached letter.

To:    JFK Teachers
From:  The Principal
RE:   Recording Student Attendance
Date:  October 14, 2010

    On Thursday, October 14, 2010 the school administration addressed a serious issue of too many students in the hallways after the ringing of the second bell by conducting hall sweeps. These sweeps were conducted to demonstrate to our students that this administration takes the enforcement of all rules seriously and that all rules will be enforced. It becomes a security and safety issue when too many students are in the hallway after the ringing of the second bell.

The first sweep at the beginning of third period resulted in sixty students being disciplined by issuing Saturday morning detention to each one. I bring up the number sixty because I wish to compare that number with the total number of lateness's that were recorded for the whole day on Friday, October 13 which was eighty. Only eighty lateness's were recorded for the entire day! If sixty students were late in one wing only during one period, then the recording of lateness's by teachers is not being done by many teachers. The failure to record lateness's and having no consequences for that action is just teaching our students that bad habits are acceptable.

I have asked that teachers make their students accountable to being on time to class. One major requirement is that accurate attendance is recorded by every classroom teacher. This is one of the required duties of every classroom teacher. There would be no need for hall sweeps if all students are held accountable by teachers. The cut office is fully operational and has my authorization to discipline students who constantly cut and come to class late.

The ensuring of having a safe and orderly school is everyone's responsibility. The administration will continue to conduct hall sweeps to instill upon our students the need to be punctual to class, and I will continue to monitor the daily attendance to see if accurate reporting of class attendance is being done.

Respectfully,
The Principal Mr. ▮

END

Even though this place has been so bad and for years, there is NO reason for not keeping accurate records on every one of our students. YES, it may have been to no avail and it was just a waste of time, a great deal of useless time consuming and repetitive paperwork; however, that's our job and I agree with the principal on this completely. After all, and MOST importantly, even though we receive a paycheck from the Paterson Public Schools, I truly believe we actually work for the parents of our students/children. Furthermore, God forbid if something should happen to a student and we were asked if he or she was in our class and we didn't keep accurate records. It would *NOT* only be wrong, and embarrassment, I believe it would be grounds for dismissal because we should be keeping ACCURATE records on ALL of our children/students all of the time. After all parents and guardians are entrusting us with their children.

**Oct 22** - for the last 2 weeks the administration has been conducting hall sweeps pretty actively in attempts to curb cutting and students being in the hallways.

**Nov 10** - what a place last week, I could not do attendance because the system was down *again*. When I came in on Monday it was still down. Today, 11/10, I attempted several times to enter the grades for the 1st marking period as well as student's attendance and the system was still down. Grades and attendance were to be entered into the system on Monday. Can you imagine what it's going to be like once the system is back up and everyone in the district is trying to enter all their information at the same time?

**Nov 12 - 4th period, 10:27** fire alarms go off evacuated the building. Student in a trailer rolled up and lit papers on fire by a sensor setting off the fire alarm. The fire department and added police arrived. THEN later an actual fire was started in room 105 and someplace else at the same time. Most of us teachers didn't even know about this. Parents have no idea what's going on inside here! Everything stays hushed up! HOW, especially when the fire department is dispatched to the school?

**The students just keep cutting.** Some students have over 80 cuts already. The cut office is opened all day long and fully staffed. The only time kids are out of the hallway is when they have a hall sweep. Students should be picked up all the time, NOT just when there are hall sweeps.

**Nov 16** - Mr. Madjar showed me a profile on a student who has over 60 cuts. Mr. Madjar also said cut days no longer count towards student's attendance by order of the superintendent. I believe the superintendent wants JFK to fail by allowing JFK to remain out of control so he can implement his plan for restructuring. He is gambling and screwing with student's education and lives for his career. Meanwhile, students, parents, the community, the state of NJ and all taxpayers are losing and paying the price for his deliberate failure. Why bother having students come to school at all if he is going to allow them NOT to go to class? Just shut the entire Paterson Public School System down and give every student a diploma. After all they're doing that already!

Oh God, here we go again. School is so out of control, fights all day long and the students are in the hallways all day and defiant to everyone. However, students **are** being removed from the building in handcuffs and under arrest. What a nice school we work in. Even one of the security guards said he feels like he is going to have a heart attack because of all of the drama going on all over the place. Meanwhile our governor blames teachers. This is a State run and operated school, so HE is the one who is "F'ing everything UP here! He is the State and is punishing children and NJ taxpayers.

**Nov 18** - *UNFREAKINBELIEVABLE, STUDENTS WERE ALL OVER THE PLACE.* In all the years I have worked here I have only heard the principal yell one time before and that was when he was a VP. I was quite surprised. I knew something had to be very wrong. He's always a calm take it in stride, guy. However, today, oh my God he went ballistic. These kids were so out of control and extra defiant. He was upset. But why are students allowed to be constantly in the hallways instead of being in class? He has to be following orders! There is no way this principal would allow this.

**Nov 19** - *IT'S GETTING WORSE.* Kids are all over the place, absolutely defiant with everyone. The way they act in the streets is the way they are acting in the hallways and it's carried into the classroom. It's not even Thanksgiving and it is already soooo out of control. There's nothing but fighting inside and outside of the building every day, all week and all day long between the Blacks & the Dominicans. What is so sickening even if they're friends with some of the people from the other side, they still attack one another with machetes. They have them in their back packs or hide them outside the building. AND we still don't have metal detectors! Just those stupid handheld wand type that are ONLY brought out and used AFTER something has happened. What is even MORE disgusting is today during our In-Service (Teachers Meetings) we were told to expect to see the worse and expect LOCK DOWNS! Meanwhile parents have no idea how dangerous the school is or made aware of any of the vicious crimes and attacks that are going on here. The administration wants and works so hard in keeping it all hushed up and is NOT reporting all of these acts of violence to the State of NJ as required?

**Nov 24** - this has been the worse week so far this year. It is so bad here, just like the days of the last superintendent & principal. I was just told by lieutenant of the Paterson Police Dept. that last Tuesday; they were so busy here. They arrested 6 students.

**Nov 29** - UNBELIEVABLE, the school is lost. It is so out of control and dangerous here. Kids are in the hallways looooong after the bell rings to start class just cursing, wrestling, playing and hanging out as if they are out on the streets. There was a young lady (if you want to call her that) screaming at the top of her lungs. It was unbelievable the way she was yelling. You would have thought that she was being killed. All she kept screaming is FUCK YOU, FUCK ALL OF YOU, FUCK THIS PLACE, THIS FUCKING PLACE IS FUCKING OUT OF THEIR MOTHER FUCKING MIND AND ALL THE TEACHERS CAN GO FUCK THEMSELVES. Then what really shocked me was when she said, "I SHOULD COME BACK AND KILL ALL OF THESE FUCKING TEACHERS" and nobody did anything. There were security guards, 3 police officers, a TAP, a several other people all standing around the security office door, while teachers, and support staff all in the hallway as this student continued cursing out profanities, carrying on and putting on a show. That also includes ME! We all did NOTHING and allowed her to carry on. So, in reality we all just told that student and all of the other students who were present in the hallway that it is OK, you CAN act this way and carry on and NOTHING will happen to you. IT IS ACCEPTABLE HERE. As for all of us teachers, we kept quiet because we all know that no good deed goes unpunished here. Like I have been saying, in here everything is backwards. There is NO sense of right and wrong. If anyone of us teachers were to get involved, we would end up in trouble. The student would have acted up more and it could or would have escalated and then the administration and even the parents would all come down on the teacher saying; why did you get involved, she was only yelling, she wasn't doing really anything wrong. It is an absolutely disgusting place and environment.

**Nov 29 & 30** - both days the district computer system was down. Could not input attendance or retrieve student data/information. **IF** the system is up tomorrow, every teacher will have three days' worth of information to input. Like I said, if this was a business, we would have been bankrupt. Ever since this district has been taken over by the state, it only proves GOVERNMENT CANNOT make a difference or change ANYTHING for the better.

**Nov 30** - many students were arrested. However, all day long students are still all over the place hanging out in the hallways, stairwells, bathrooms, walking in and out of the building, running, wrestling, screaming, cursing, threatening, pushing & shoving and on and on. This place is so out of freaking control and no one is going to class. *WHY IS THIS ALLOWED TO CONTINUE?*

I want to make it very clear, seeing this new principal having to deal with all of this out of control crap, I am TOTALLY convinced he and all of the school's administrators have their hands tied and are following orders from the superintendent.

**Dec 1** – Computer system still down?
I called the governor's office today about the computer system being down again and how the school is out of control.609-292-6000. When I went to utilize the Districts Internet Service to contact the Governor one of his web addresses was blocked, http://www.state.nj.us/governor/contact/
WHY would the governor's web address be blocked?

**Later I** received an e-mail from the district about the system being down.

Kids in the hallways and everywhere else other than being in class all day. It is so out of control and noisy here. I think it was quieter on an aircraft carrier while conducting combat flight operations.

**Dec 2** - seniors are being tested. It is only those seniors who failed the HSPA. Today the test is called AHSA, (Alternative High School Assessment), formerly known as SRA (Senior Review Assessment). Teachers had to do all the gridding (filling in names, ages, ID numbers, etc.) because these kids will *NOT* or deliberately screw it up. They have the mentality of "You do it; I don't have to." The testing is going on for a full week. Like last year, many will FAIL, and the district will come up with some other BS idea and program to let them graduate. Bottom line, anybody can get a diploma here. You don't have to do anything! If you can't get a diploma here, then there is really something wrong with you.

The computer system is still down! I understand all info (input) was lost at the main office. I find this unacceptable and suspicious/deliberate?

Nothing changes; it is out of control and bad here. One of the security guards was telling me that yesterday; FIVE students were taken out of here in handcuffs and arrested.

Next is a copy of my incident report:
INCIDENT ON THE 2ND FLOOR
December 2, 2010

Today, Thursday, December 2, 2010, I was on the 2nd floor on my way to speak with Mr. Class*. As I approached the center hallway, there were approximately 20 - 30 student, boys & girls standing around long after the bell to begin 3rd period.

I asked them to move. They ignored me. I said over and over "Ladies & gentlemen, let's go, get to class." This went on for about 2 minutes.

However, 2 boys in particular were arguing back and forth. One boy was (name Omitted-Student #1) and the other I cannot think of his name (student #2) right now. However, when I do, I will have him escorted to security office.

After several more times of me saying knock it off to these two gentlemen, they kept arguing as if I didn't say a word or existed. They continued threatening and cursing at each other. That's when (Student #1) went after and attacked the other student.

I attempted to stop him by restraining him next to me, by placing my arms out on front of him. Student #1) just shoved me away, cursing and saying "FUCK YOU, GET THE FUCK OUT OF MY WAY, FUCK YOU MOTHER FUCKER." I ignored him and once again, I attempted to keep him from attacking the other student. He did the same thing again, knocking my arms out of the way yelling "FUCK YOU, GET OUT OF MY FUCKING WAY, GET THE FUCK OFF ME", and on and on. That's when I started yelling for security. There was no security.

Several minutes later, Mr. Arthurs* made his way around the corner. I yelled to him to get security and to bring this boy to security office. I pointed and said this boy is trying to start a fight.

Mr. Arthurs* became immediately involved in the attempts to get control of this situation.

In the meantime, (Student #1), continued to threaten the other student shouting, screaming with non-stop foul language and made several more attempts to attack the other student even while being restrained by the Mr. Arthurs* and finally security.

Mr. Arthurs* yelled over to me to let me know that he and security has (student #1) and will take care of this and asked me to write up a report.

In the meantime, the other (student #2) kept antagonizing (student #1). The hallways were like being in a tank of sharks during a feeding frenzy. I kept yelling for everyone to move and get to class. It was just a waste of breath. The students just continued to hang around in the center hall trying to instigate and antagonizing each other to start more violence and fighting all the while yelling out every type of profanity at the top of their lungs and screaming just to make noise and to be disruptive.

All of a sudden, the students and I noticed the principal was standing there. The students started to move but not without more confrontation, yelling, screaming and shouting excessive obscenities.

Most respectfully,
Lee E McNulty (Room 114)

## NEXT IS ANOTHER INCIDENT REPORT

### INCIDENT REPORT IN ROOM 213

Today, Thursday, December 2, 2010, I was approached by, and spoke with Ms. (name omitted) a teacher, earlier this morning who was extremely upset and quite concerned. She was explaining to me, how students from our academy are giving the substitute in room 213, during 3rd period such a bad time. She said they are so disrespectful to the substitute and making her job not just difficult, but unbearable.

I told her I would stop up during that period.

Approximately 10 minutes into the period, as I was approaching room 213, Ms. (name omitted) the teacher who I spoke to approached me again and asked if I was going to show up.
She was quite upset and said she was just there, and the students are being so disrespectful right now to the substitute. She was upset because one student said (I don't exactly remember what she said, you can ask her but something like), "who the hell are you to tell me what to do."

Once again, I am not sure what exactly what was said. Nevertheless, this behavior is not acceptable.

Just before I entered the classroom, (students name omitted #1) and (students name omitted #2) were outside the door. They BOTH never came into class until much later.

I entered the classroom and the students were surprised to see me. Many of them stopped talking. A couple of them said under their breath, "Oh boy," realizing I was sent up because of the class actions and attitude.

I started telling them that I received reports that many of you are acting up, being disrespectful and giving the teacher (substitute) a bad time.

I explained this is coming to a halt. I explained if anyone thinks they can act up and nothing will happen they are sadly mistaken. A couple tried to test me. That's when I said, I have NO PROBLEM, assigning the entire class, Saturday Detention. This is NOT going to continue.
Several students said, I can't do that, you're not our teacher, in their attempts to test me.

I replied, try me gentlemen, I'll do it right now.

Not only will you have Saturday detention, your assignments will be, to complete all assignments you're missing for this class.

This went on for several minutes.
Afterwards, I assured the teacher, if she has any problems, not to worry, I'll take care of it for her. I said, just write their names, a little note and give it to me. I will take care of everything. There is no reason for you to be treated like this and having to go through any of this disrespectfulness and nonsense.
Try not to let them get to you and I will take care of everything.
That's when (Student #1) decides to show up and enter the classroom.

9:25am, late for class, wearing a hat and a hood. I told him to take them off. He ignores me. I tell him again. Disrespectfully and in his nasty defiant attitude, yells back, I just got here, don't tell me what to do. I replied, take off your hat again. No one is to wear a hat in school. He replies, NO, you wait. I don't have to do what you say.

That's when another student walked into class, late, a (Student #2).
Meanwhile (Student #1), continues being disrespectful and is defiant to authority telling me, I am not his teacher, his boss, you can't tell me what to do. Get out of my face man. Oh man get out of here, then starts with the foul language. All the while, he is making his rounds shaking every student's hands in the classroom. Another act of defiance - look at me, I can do whatever I want and you can't do anything about it. Typical defiant, argumentative disrespectful, nasty (Student #1).

**NOTE OF INTEREST:** - This is not part of the report. Student#1 has a reputation of continually causing trouble, defiant and threatening especially women teachers. END

Defiantly he still refuses to take off his hat. That's when I told him to come on. I was going to escort him to security office. He tells me no. I can't tell him what to do. I am not going you can't make me and on and on. I was insisting, saying come on let's go. He continues with his nasty a barrage of foul language and disruptive behavior. He is a student who acts in intimidation and tries to make you think he is going to hit you.

**NOTE OF INTEREST:** - The note of interest was NOT in the report. However, this is the same students who deliberately pulled a false alarm on September 29, 2008 and were talking about playing football on October 15, 2008. END

I walked out of the classroom and had another teacher get security.

Shortly a security guard came in. I asked her to escort him to security office.

He still refused and was defiant and continued with his foul language and talking to me disrespectfully, saying, I'm not going anywhere. I don't have to go anywhere and on and on.
Another security guard came in. Now both of them were talking to (Student #1) softly and nicely (with kid gloves). However, he continues to act up, be defiant, disrespectful, obnoxious, and still wouldn't go.

He's yelling, swearing and being disrespectful as well as defiance of authority. Finally, he gets up and he is escorted out of class but continues with behavior that is NOT acceptable any place.
A few other kids thought this was the opportune time to act up. Nothing serious but I wasn't going to leave and leave the teacher (substitute) with them all wired up.

I made it clear, this is not going to continue or happen anymore. I told them they are here to work.
That's when (Student #2) has to make noises, the raspberry sound several times trying to see what he can get away with.
I asked him if he wanted to be a wise guy. He continues with the typical street nonsense with acts of defiance and intimidation. All in attempts to put a show on and disrupt the class further.
I asked him, do you want to go too? He said, I didn't do anything and you're not my teacher. I said alright, no problem come on let's go. He now continues further with poor behavior just like (Student #1), in the exact same manner. Proving my point when one student acts up and thinks they will get away with their actions, others do the same.

He also stated I didn't do anything. I just replied, let's go. He gets up but not without acting up further and continues carrying on, telling me, I'm not his teacher, who are you to tell me what to do I don't have to go.

As he was walking to the door he continues, What, what, what did I do, you can't do anything. I kept saying let's go. (Student #2) kept telling me you wait, you're not going to do anything, I'm going to go downtown and get you fired. Yeah, you're mad, you wait and see. You can't do anything to me, because I didn't do anything. Wait until I tell them downtown how you pulled me out of class for no reason. I just kept saying let's go as we were walking to room 117. I wanted to have Mr. Angelo Bonora, the lead teacher for the CTA academy present.

**NOTE OF INTEREST:** - Room 213 is an academy class. As far as any of us from the CTA, (Construction Trades Academy), we have no idea (Student#1) & (student #2) are assigned to us? Nevertheless, as we continued walking to Room 117, (Student #2) continues, you can't pull me out of class for doing nothing and all of the other nonsense. Threatening me that I am going to be fired, you just wait and see.

We finally arrived to room 117, I asked the young man calmly and softly to sit down and relax. (Student #2) replied, I'm not sitting down. I don't have to sit and on and on. I simply replied suit yourself.

I went into Mr. Angelo Bonora's office and he was not there. I asked one of the TAPs to contact him and that it was important.

When he, arrived and as I was explaining what has happened, he had to endure all of the nonsense of (Student #2).

In a further act of defiance (Student #2) walks out screaming, yelling and cursing. You can't do anything to me. I didn't do anything. He was basically proving my point to the lead teacher.
The lead teacher and I went back up to room 213 (outside) and spoke with the security guard. The lead teacher also spoke with the teacher (substitute) in room 213.
(Student #2) was brought out into the hallway.
He continues with the same nonsense of nothing more than an act of intimidation, threatening me I will lose my job, you just wait.

Once more (Student #2) was proving his conduct again in front of the lead teacher, the security guard and whomever else that was present.

Several times the security guard, asked him to be quiet. Yet (Student #2) continues with his act and attempt of intimidation towards me.

Later that period, Mr. Angelo Bonora and I also spoke with Mr. (name omitted) the Head of the English Department.
He said he is going to speak with, (student #2) guidance counselor.
I made it clear; this is NOT to be swept under the rug.
This is unacceptable behavior for anyone.
If I were to act this way, I am sure I would be swiftly and severely punished.
These types of actions and behavior would never ever be tolerated in any other public place.
If anyone did act this way they would be arrested.
This is as school a place of learning and instilling proper behavior, not the streets. Street behavior is unacceptable.

Swift Disciplinary actions are necessary for BOTH, (Student #1) and (Student #2).
Furthermore, (Student #1) needs to be removed from JFK High School or at least places in a self-contained class.

As I said to the Head of the English Department, all teachers deserve the same respect and treatment as the principal.

When a teacher speaks, ALL STUDENTS ARE TO LISTEN AND OBEY. NO EXCUSES.
Bottom line, if the students in room 213 acted that way with me, how do you think they've been acting along with the substitute all the time, every day. UNACCEPATEBLE!!!
This just proves what is going on in class and they all think they can get away with it.
It is time for all of them to learn by disciplinary example and of consequences.
Talking is just a waste of time.

One last thing,

I am tired of being made to feel uncomfortable as if I did something wrong, because of these situations with too many of these students.

Thank you & most respectfully,     Lee E McNulty

**Dec 2 -** when Mr. Angelo Bonora and I were speaking with the head of the English Department, I called to a security guard. He came over and said he doesn't have time to speak right now. He explained someone called the Mayor's office because there was a gunshot heard either inside or right outside the school and he's on his way over here now. The Mayor wanted to know why they weren't notified what is going on in or outside the school building. I didn't say anything but thought-*why aren't the parents notified on what goes on every day here?* I also wondered why there wasn't a LOCK DOWN!

INCIDENT REPORT<br>12/2/10<br>VICE PRINCIPAL MS. NICE* BEING ABUSED:

**Dec 2 -** 8th period, the school was out of control. All day, kids were all over the place and it seems to be more than there has been in the last couple of years. A handful of kids who should NOT have been in the hallways in the first place were extremely fresh, defiant, loud, obnoxious, acting up and giving VP Ms. Nice* a very bad time. They were defiant, argumentative, MOST DISRESPECTFUL, USING EXCESSIVE FOUL LANGUAGE, and going on and on mocking, making fun of Ms. Nice* to her face, as they continued to walk down the art wing. I came out of my room to help Ms. Nice*. These students kept up with their disgusting and foul mouths, mocking and degrading her. They were deliberately being disrespectful and talking disgustingly towards Ms. Nice*, thinking this is all a big joke. Their behavior was atrocious and excessive foul language was nothing remotely acceptable to anyone at any time. These very same students are in the hallways all day, every day causing problems, with their yelling, screaming, excessive foul mouth in defiance and all without fear. As I yelled to them to knock it off they continued with their poor behavior and brazen foul language directly towards VP Ms. Nice*.

I yelled to them to knock it off again. I summoned security and wanted them brought into the office. I yelled again, what are you guys doing in the hallways in the first place, get over here.

One student in particular said something extremely foul pertaining to Ms. Nice* about fucking her up the ass. I yelled to the tall one who is the most disrespectful of them all, and said, bring in your mom and you can do the same to her. He turned and started towards me and all of a sudden turned and started to run away. I yelled to him and all of them again, get over here tough guys. You're all such tough guy when it comes to a woman, come on tough guy talk to man like that. I yelled for security to grab them and bring them to security office again.

Poor Ms. Nice* was so outraged, disgusted and upset. Mr. Jim* asked what was going on and Ms. Nice* explained. Mr. Jim* and security rounded up the students.

These student's behavior was so degrading. NO ONE SHOULD BE TALKED TO LIKE THAT, ESPECIALLY A WOMAN. THESE KIDS ARE DEFIANT AND FEARLESS TO THE LACK OF CONSEQUENCES. WHY???
I truly believe if I didn't come out to assist Ms. Nice*, these kids may have attacked her.
They were like wolves surrounding their prey.
Thank you & most respectfully,

Mr. Lee E McNulty

**Dec 8** - Computer system was down again. Halls are filled with students again.

**1:35** - student escorted out of the building in handcuffs (Arrested) again. The place is lost, and it can and will ONLY GET WORSE

**1:38** - another student escorted to security and then immediately taken out of the building in handcuffs / arrested. Students are lighting firecrackers in the building AGAIN, today by room 404 and the gym.

**Dec 17** - gym teacher was telling me that he went on an interview for a VP position. He was at a grammar school and the kids were acting up and were really wild. They asked him what he would do to keep the kids from acting up. He replied I would get control of the school first. Needless to say, he didn't get the job. He said they even gave him the reason why he was not accepted, "He was too strong!"
Can you imagine too strong! It is obvious whatever way they are using now it's NOT WORKING!

**Dec 23** - have video of boy's bathroom on 2nd floor across room 217. *UNBELIEVABLY DISGUSTING!* It's worse than last year or two when I first took video of this facility. Just goes to show what happens when students are allowed to hang out in the bathrooms, are not in class and NOT supervised.

**ALSO,** I found out today 280 students (seniors) that took the HSPA or whatever it was back in October, only 60 or 65 passed. That's approximately 23%. Now administration wants to see how they did with the test they took a few weeks ago. No matter what, the blame will be on the teachers, NOT the parents!

**January 3, 2011**- first day back from Christmas vacation as I pulled up to the building, there were teachers and secretaries standing outside waiting for someone to open the doors. All doors were locked? Period/class bells aren't working. Clocks still don't work and or have the wrong time.
No change, students still hanging out everywhere as if they are out in the streets and still on vacation. Meanwhile our politicians are more concerned on building another or new professional sports arena.

**Jan 4** - as I'm sitting in the cut office, students are coming in who were suspended for cutting. They were admitted *BUT* their parents did not re-admit them. Parents are to come in to re-admit their child. One student said no, she couldn't come, so she called. How ridiculous! How do you know that was the mother who called? For all they know the parent or guardian never even knew their child was suspended. What would happen if that child was seriously injured and the parent/guardian did NOT know their child was suspended and thought all along they were in school? Who would be held responsible? Even if it was the mother, parent or guardian who called, too bad, now they have to get involved and have to be here. That is a ***BIG*** reason why we have FAILING SCHOOLS. It is because we have failing parents. **NOT ALL OF THEM!** Unfortunately, a great many parents DO NOT CARE. The administration keeps lowering and lowering standards and making excuses NOT to follow the school/district rules, just to lower the suspension rate and increase the attendance rate. It's just smoke & mirrors. You wonder why the school is out of freaking control. Also while I was there, one young lady had 85 cuts. Mr. Pardine said, if you cut 5 more times, I am suspending you again for another 5 days. This is BS! IF that student does not want to be suspended, (I doubt it, because it is a FREE vacation) she was just told she can cut 4 more times and get away with it. With students like this young lady every time they cut their parent or guardian should be contacted and insisted they come in. The school and school district is always complaining on how do we get parents / guardians involved! Well now the parent/s or guardian has to be involved! Do you really wonder why so many students do NOT have any school and work ethics?

**NOTE OF INTEREST:**
- In reading and writing the above, I have to laugh when administration tells teachers we need to have a program to get our students to do better.

- What program allows students not to follow school rules, curse, swear, threaten people and scream profanities in the hallway or in a classroom at teachers as if they are on a street corner?

- What program allows students not to go to class, roam the halls, hangout in the stairwells, bathrooms, and walk in and out of classrooms they do not belong in inciting trouble and violence?

- What program is this State Takeover, Run and Operated School District using in allowing all of the above to continually go on day after day, all day, every day and for years!

- Schools should be a place to groom children for a positive and rewarding future. Not to have students fail life.

**Jan 5** - fights all over the place. School is so out of control. Students everywhere all day except in class just going wild. It's nothing more than in house truancy and an indoor street corner. As I always said, if students acted like this any place else they would be arrested. Do we really wonder why the cut office is open all day long with all those teachers working there instead of being in the classroom teaching? I'm convinced the principal is told to ignore everything that goes on here by order of the superintendent! If I was a parent whose child attends this school and found out what's been going on and has been continually and deliberately allowed to go on and for years I would seek an attorney and sue this school district, the city of Paterson and the State of New Jersey.

**Jan 6 - 11:54, fire alarm** goes off evacuated the building. Fire department came. There was a fire on 2nd floor. Came back in at 12:23. I would have never thought it would ever be like or even worse than when the previous superintendents were here. And to think they have Dr. in front of their name. All you see is students all over the place all day long just hanging out instead of being in class. Do you really wonder why they cannot pass state-wide exams!

**Jan 13 - 1:18, fire alarms** go off. We evacuated the building. The fire department and added police came. It was very cold, and many students didn't have anything more than a t-shirt on. Have photos. Supposedly with fire alarm went off because of a malfunction!

**FOOD FOR THOUGHT**
Supposedly the fire alarm malfunctioned. We have a new fire alarm system, clocks replaced, repaired and reset, new computer system, stairwell steps replaced, new doors, new windows which are all CRAP, still

doesn't work or work properly and costing the NJ taxpayers how many 10s, no 100s of thousands of dollars! However, the politicians and big shots feel it's time to build a NEW GIANTS STADIUM.

FOOD FOR THOUGHT PART II
We have NOVA NET/CREDIT RECOVERY Another BS scam that allows students to come to school, but not go to class, can hang out and play for 7 to 8 periods a day, every day. Then will be allowed to make up time, class credit, sign up and do NOVA NET for 90 minutes at TAXPAYERS EXPENSE.
It costs New Jersey Taxpayers approximately $12,000 a year per student to attend Public School.
*If a student at JFK attends*
- 7 periods x 41 minutes = 287 minutes = almost 5 hours.
- 8 periods x 41 minutes = 328 minutes = almost 5½ hours.
- These are class periods, NOT LUNCH

*HOW* does 90 minutes of NOVA NET even if it is every day compare to an entire school day?

**Jan 20** - another dog and pony show today because the superintendent was here with other big shots. Meanwhile, there was a big fight on 2nd floor. I still say that the superintendent should be made to have his office in the building. This way he can explain why things are allowed to go on the way they do and why everything is all F'ed up here.

**Jan 28** - it is soooo bad here. The place is so out of control and lost. There is NO WAY they can recover and gain control so it would act and perform like a real school now. Same crap, with students all over the place all day screaming, yelling, running, playing cursing anything and everything else other than being in class. It is an indoor street corner. Many of my students who eventually do show up for class are coming in late enough to be considered a cut (like that really matters to them). It is never going to stop? Unbelievably, there will be classes on Saturdays paying teachers overtime to prepare students so they might pass the state-wide exam at *another* expense to the NJ taxpayers.

**Feb 9 - today is a perfect example of no leadership, no discipline and no structure.**
One of my students is continually late or cuts not just my class but all of his classes. Then because of his accumulated cuts and lateness, he is assigned a Saturday detention. When he finally shows up for Saturday detention, he is late. Then instead of being in *detention,* he is allowed to go and participate at wrestling practice in which he was on time for. Monday comes what does he do? He *CUTS* my class and many of his other classes. WHAT A FREAKN' JOKE!

**Feb 15** - as of Monday, February 14, 2011 we no longer have police in the building.
Reason No Money! However, we still have seven assistant superintendents? WHY?AND the district just hired an additional personnel director? UNFREAKINBELIEVABLE!

**Feb 16** - so far, the entire month of February, JFK was so freaking out of control. It was just like the days of Dr. Miller & Dr. Glascoe. However, today it was a little different. Not really bad at all, and that's BECAUSE we had a state monitor in the building. The perfect dog and pony show.

**Feb 22** - it is so bad here. There's nothing more to say. It's the same thing every day. It is no wonder so many students have over 100 cuts and the same in absences. To think 100 absences but they *ARE* in the building. This is what I mean by *"IN HOUSE TRUANCY!"*

**Feb 23** - street cops all over the building today. It seems three kids were attacked, beaten and stabbed. Cops were here to look for the weapons in lockers. What a nice place to work.

**Feb 25** - a VP came into the cut office to speak with Mr. Pardine. Seems some student was suspended and has yet to return with his parent. However, he has been going to homeroom, being marked in school but not attending any of his classes. So, Mr. Pardine has been marking him absent. The VP tells Mr. Pardine he cannot do that. It seems this student may be involved with the stabbing from the other day and the administrators are worried for some reason. Bottom line the student was suspended. He defiantly comes back to school without a parent as REQUIRED by school and district rules in order to be readmitted. The administration will now just turn their heads and let it go. As I said before, how do they know that this student's parents even knew he was suspended? Wonder why the school is out of control? Meanwhile the idiots at central office are worried about too many students being suspended? There is no discipline, not one rule is enforced, just a constant lowering and lowering of standards and creating more excuses.

What's the use? Everything is the same, out of freakin' control, chaos and nobody is held liable!

**Mar 1** - the bell rang for all students to begin state testing. Students didn't care they were in the hallways clowning around. VP Ms. Nice* yelled, knock it off; you have to get to class on time today. Today the administration wants to follow the rules and MAKE students attend class for testing. Unfreakinbelievable, why aren't students made to attend class and have rules enforced every day?

**Mar 25** - it keeps getting worse and worse by the day here. Students are cutting so much more now. To make things even more ridiculous if students are assigned a Saturday detention, they might say NO, I want ABC and they get it. If they are assigned a punishment via the cut officer students will defiantly kick up a fuss, scream, yell, curse, threaten them and disgustingly, nothing is done about it. I have never seen or been in a place in the world (and I have been all over the world) where everything is all "F'ed up. There is NO right and wrong here. There is *ONLY WRONG* and out of control. Bottom line, the students get away with it all and they just keep oooooooon cutting.

Once again, for the last 2 weeks, announcements have been made for seniors to get measured for caps and gowns. They just don't care and won't show up.

I laugh because of all of this *"CHANGE,"* Obama style wording. In the meantime, students are still in the hallways. Students have over 100 cuts, with the same amount in absences and lateness. Kids are NOT doing their work, yet teachers are held responsible if they fail. What happened to PARENTS being held responsible? This district has gone downhill fast and faster each year with MILLIONS of dollars wasted on so many different programs. Then when the new school year starts, last year's program is scraped, a new one will take its place and the process starts all over again. To see this over and over for decades ever since the State took over the District of Paterson, it just makes me think somebody is getting greased, making a fortune off of this district and off of the backs of the NJ taxpayers. We don't need any programs, just discipline, rules must be followed and most of all enforced.

**Apr 6** - 11:54, fire alarms go off. We evacuated the building. The fire department came. There was a fire deliberately set in the 2nd floor history wing boys' room. We came back in at 12:23. Now the school day had to be modified to accommodate lunch periods. The administration is more concerned on making up and making sure students get 40 minutes for lunch. Meanwhile if it weren't a lunch period, that class would be not only disrupted but shorter. And none of this will make the newspapers, TV or radio.
I received 2 pictures of the evacuation.

**Apr 12** - back to school night! The worse turn out ever and brother they are all bad. Meanwhile, the Superintendent blames teachers for failing schools.
- It is NOT teacher's fault if parents do NOT attend back to school night.

- It is NOT teacher's fault if *some* parents do NOT care about their child's education.
- It is NOT teacher's fault if so many students have poor attendance, allowed to cut, are late, roam the building, hangout in the hallways, stairwells, bathrooms and basement.

Then the superintendent and administration cannot understand why students do NOT pass their classes, state exams, SRA and everything and anything else they attempt to make students pass and graduate?
- Parents ARE the key factor in a Child's education and *LIFE*.
- Children pick up their parent's habits and ways. The apple does NOT fall to far from the tree.

**Apr 14** - they're still making announcements for seniors to come for their cap and gown measurements. They just *do not care*. They feel and believe it is up everybody else to give and get them what they want and need. I have seen nasty arguments between students and teachers because the student needs a Kleenex, and the teacher didn't have any. The students feel that the teacher should always have Kleenex's for them. To avoid this nonsense, I would get a roll of toilet tissue from the janitor and keep it in my class.

**Apr 21** - last year they revamped Eastside High School by having academies. Something the district has been talking about since the state first took over the district in 1991. Took a little time didn't it? However, in the early 90s, JFK had the first academy in the entire school district called "STEM", (Science, Engineering and Mathematics) with an off shoot for freshman students called "SIPS," (Survey Introductory Procedural Skills) A GREAT PROGRAM WITH GREAT STUDENTS! Most to all of them wanted to learn and participate in almost everything the school had to offer. With success story after success story for our students and for *YEARS!* A *GREAT* program destroyed by the superintendent and administration! Starting September 2011 - 2012, JFK will have academies!

**May 6** - in 2009 - 2010 there was a total of 1500 out of school suspensions. There should have been more. However, the administration did *not* want to suspend students anymore for the MOST idiotic reason of all, because they said there are too many students suspended. Is there a number a school *cannot* go over in suspensions? First of all, in too many cases students shouldn't have just been suspended, they should have been arrested. It is not about too many students being suspended. It is about perception and BS to make it look good on paper that everything is OK here, WHEN IT IS NOT! Meanwhile the nonsense, school being completely out of control, poor, inappropriate, dysfunctional behavior prevails and continues. The students have better control and organization of the situation than anybody in administration. They're getting their way. Think about it, uneducated young children/students controlling grownups who all have at least a master's degree and some with PhDs. Now tell me, who is smarter?

**May 17** - today, I had an interview to keep my job. All teachers, secretaries and support staff has to reapply for their positions, give reasons why they should be hired, submit references, a resume, and go through an interview process to keep their jobs for the up and coming 2011 restructuring year. After 25 years, they don't know me by now? They have all my evaluations on files. This is just another BS waste of precious time and taxpayer money so paperwork will be submitted into Trenton, so the superintendent and his administration can say look what we did in making the restructuring a success.
Let's see what next year brings and the tax dollars keeeeeeep on pouring in.

I am already getting a bad feeling for next year. The administration is already saying they will *not* suspend students. They will not remove student/s from class no matter what students do. I am already anxious and nervous, and we have 3 &1/2 months before the start of the new school year.

**Week of May 16 – 20 - it is so OUT OF CONTROL HERE.** Students are everywhere and anywhere except in class all day long. The noise is deafening. All you hear is students screaming, yelling the most vulgar of profanity at the top of their lungs as if they are out on the streets. Students are wrestling, slap boxing, pushing one and other, running, jumping, doing flips, trying to knock down ceiling tiles, all the while security, the administration were right there. They just kept walking by and through it all as if this is normal and acceptable behavior. What the hell will next year be like?

**May 20, 1:20pm -** Name omitted student #1, was taken out of school on a stretcher to an awaiting ambulance. She was beaten up/jumped by some girl/s. It seems it was in retaliation because she shoved another student, into a moving bus and was seriously injured.

**May 24 - Algebra testing for freshman, in room 351.** There were seven fluorescent lamps not working. There were two sets of two lamps in each row. If the administration knew there was going to be testing why were there lights not working? Shouldn't all lights in every classroom be working properly every day? How does the administration allow students to attend any classroom where the lighting is NOT operating properly? How long have they been out? Why wasn't every room that is to be utilized for administering the test inspected *prior* to testing? Lastly, if there were no more bulbs or working fixtures, then the offices should do without. Students are and should always be our *main priority*. After all, that's why we're all here, for the EDUCATION OF CHILDREN!

I know exactly what people will say, "Why didn't the teacher report it." They do. When I reported having lights out in my classroom it took sometimes two weeks to get a bulb replaced. There were many times I had to wait even longer because I was told there were no bulbs in the entire district and if I needed a ballast, they will have to order one. So much for the District's slogan; "CHILDREN FIRST."

**May 24 -** found out the woman who started the 1st academy and most successful program at JFK, "STEM & SIP's," will no longer be in charge because the principal doesn't want it. She said to me, "it's too scientific!" What does she think STEM, stands for? "Science, Technology, Engineering & Math." It has been a successful program for 20 years and all of a sudden with a click of the pen ruins it. The students who were part of SIPS and STEM were the best that JFK had. They were continuously challenged educationally, were pushed to succeed and wanted to better themselves. In June, the majority of the students who graduated and *EARNED* their high school diplomas were from STEM.
The woman, who started SIPS & STEM, has been working in Paterson School System, for 50 YEARS!

**Jun 10 -** they are still making announcements for seniors to get fitted and pay for their caps & gowns. Since January they have been making this announcement. They said *today* is the last day. *YEAH RIGHT!*

**EXAMPLE -** Here are two of my students' information from the cut office for the 2010-2011 year

| Name: | Absent | Cut | Tardy | Tardy cut |
|---|---|---|---|---|
| Name omitted | 134 | 108 | 26 | 12 |
| Name omitted | 118 | 224 | 11 | 7 |

This is just two students with over 100 days absent with the same and twice as much in cutting.

You should see my student roll, roster and end of year records, it is *UNFREAKINBELIEVABLE!*

I have the actual school print outs and documentation on many of the students with horrible attendance.

Next is a list of 82 students with their names, Id #'s, grade level and homeroom, for the 2010 -2011 school year that has 60 to 115 cuts. The student with the 115cuts is a senior.

STUDENTS WITH 75 OR MORE CUTS 2009-2010    Sheet1

| LAST NAME | FIRST NAME | ST. NO. | HR. | # CUTS | NO CREDIT | LEFT SCHOOL |
|---|---|---|---|---|---|---|
| | DE██E | 110██7 | 12-339 | 115 | | |
| | QU██MAR | 203██3 | 9-214 | 113 | X | |
| | JA██YAH | 203██8 | 11-334 | 112 | | |
| | TIF██NY | 200██1 | 9-348 | 110 | | |
| | JO██THAN | 204██8 | 12 | 110 | X | LEFT |
| | DE██NY | 200██4 | 9-229 | 110 | | |
| | AL██S | 202██6 | 9-218 | 110 | | |
| | ST██N | 203██1 | 9-215 | 105 | | |
| | TA██AN | 203██5 | 10-212 | 105 | | |
| | SH██RAH | 100██7 | 9 | 105 | X | LEFT |
| | AL██ANDER | 200██6 | 9-255 | 101 | | |
| | AL██TY'E | 201██7 | 9-213 | 100 | | |
| | BR██NNA | 203██7 | 9-222 | 100 | | |
| | AL██S | 205██1 | 9-117 | 100 | | |
| | AQ██LLA | 200██8 | 9-239 | 100 | | |
| | IV██ | 200██0 | 10-248 | 100 | | |
| | AN██ETERIA | 200██9 | 9-215 | 96 | | |
| | XA██ER | 29██2 | 9-87 | 95 | | |
| | LU██AR | 102██1 | 9-228 | 95 | | |
| | DA██ON | 200██3 | 9-230 | 95 | | |
| | KY██RAH | 200██1 | 9-238 | 95 | | |
| | N██MI | 200██1 | 9-237 | 94 | | |
| | JA██CARLOS | 204██8 | 9-215 | 90 | X | LEFT |
| | CH██HER | 200██4 | 10-87 | 90 | | |
| | JO██ | 200██8 | 10-210 | 90 | | |
| | BA██KAH | 200██7 | 10-248 | 90 | | |
| | O██SHON | 200██2 | 9-87 | 90 | | |
| | JU██ON'T | 20██21 | 9-221 | 85 | | |
| | A██AH | 20██73 | 9-255 | 85 | | |
| | C██AR | 20██52 | 9-222 | 85 | | |
| | B██ANA | 20██96 | 10-313 | 85 | | |
| | A██ | 20██41 | 9-217 | 85 | | |
| | M██ERICK | 12██45 | 12-325 | 85 | | |
| | JO██AN | 20██54 | 10-313 | 84 | | |
| | JO██UA | 20██76 | 9-238 | 80 | | |
| | E██NUEL | 20██63 | 9-228 | 80 | | |
| | A██ | 20██57 | 10 | 80 | | LEFT |
| | S██NLEY | 20██15 | 11-352 | 80 | | |
| | G██ALDIN | 20██61 | 9-230 | 80 | | |
| | A██RA | 20██32 | 10-113 | 80 | | |
| | E██ARD | 20██38 | 9-214 | 77 | | |
| | M██SKA | 20██53 | 10-113 | 77 | | |
| | H██O | 10██84 | 10-318 | 75 | | |
| | A██M | 13██82 | 12-255 | 75 | | |
| | S██NAIRA | 12██31 | 12-234 | 75 | X | LEFT |

370

STUDENTS WITH 75 OR MORE CUTS 2009-2010    Sheet1                                    Page 2

| Name | | | Cuts |
|---|---|---|---|
| JOSHUA | 10 03 | 10-212 | 75 |
| JO N | 20 77 | 9-340 | 75 |
| S NTEL | 20 43 | 9-222 | 75 |
|  | 20 24 | 9-222 | 75 |
| L EL | 20 68 | 12-336 | 75 |
| S E | 20 40 | 9-213 | 75 |
| D ANTE | 1. 07 | 12-404 | 75 |
| C TOFEL | 20 29 | 10-313 | 75 |
| M | 10 88 | 12-324 | 75 |
| K IN | 12 22 | 10-253 | 75 |
| D | 20 71 | 9-87 | 75 |
| B INA | 20 69 | 9-108 | 71 |
| B TY | 20 63 | 10 | 71   X  LEFT |
| J GE | 20 26 | 9-87 | 70 |
| C STAL | 20 23 | 10-210 | 70 |
| A RAH | 20 60 | 10-A3 | 70 |
| E ONIE | 20 44 | 9-226 | 70 |
| R IMY | 20 48 | 9-201 | 70 |
| M NUEL | 20 49 | 9-218 | 70 |
| T HAUN | 20 33 | 9-255 | 70 |
| R | 20 20 | 9-213 | 70 |
| R IM | 20 16 | 12-307 | 70 |
| IA | 20 16 | 12-351 | 70 |
| L | 20 58 | 9-239 | 70 |
| R L | 20 20 | 9-215 | 70 |
| L S | 20 26 | 9-224 | 70 |
| L MONT | 20 36 | 9-216 | 70 |
| S UEL | 20 26 | 9-221 | 70 |
| A | 20 45 | 9-238 | 70 |
| D LCE | 20 27 | 10-338 | 70 |
| J SSA | 20 52 | 11-353 | 70 |
| O | 13 59 | 10-327 | 70 |
| Z IR | 12 11 | 11-353 | 70 |
| W LIAM | 20 72 | 9-216 | 70 |
|  | 20 18 | 9-219 | 70 |
| J HUA | 20 50 | 9-218 | 65 |
|  | 20 81 | 9-215 | 60 |

These (2) sheets are for the first (3) months of school, starting 9/7/10 ending 12/7/10.
It does NOT show their absenteeism and there's six (6) months more to go.

The administration allowed these and other students *not* to go to class, then blames teacher when they fail.
However, on the last day of this school year, we teachers received the following copies -

**CERTIFICATE OF SPECIAL CONGRESSIONAL RECOGNITION**
    From Congressman Bill Pascrell                    DATED: JUNE 15, 2011

**SENATE CITATION**  from Senator John A. Girgenti        DATED: JUNE 15, 2011

**STATE & GENERAL ASSEMBLY CITATION**
    From Assemblywoman Neli Pou                  DATED: JUNE 15, 2011

**PASSAIC COUNTY FREEHOLDERS CERTFICATE OF RECOGNITION**
    From Terry Duffy, Freehold Director            DATED: JUNE 15, 2011
    Deborah E. Ciambrone, Freehold Deputy Director    DATED: JUNE 15, 2011
        Greyson P. Hannigan        Freeholder
        Bruce James                 Freeholder
        Pasquale "Pat" Lepore      Freeholder
        Michael Marotta            Freeholder
        Edward O'Connell          Freeholder

**THE CITY OF PATERSON OFFICE OF THE MAYOR / MAYOR'S AWARD FOR OUTSTANDING CIVIC CONTRIBUTION**
    From    Honorable Jeffrey Jones                    DATED: JUNE 15, 2011

**THE CITY OF PATERSON MUNICIPAL COUNCIL CITATION**
**TO THE STAFF OF JFK H/S**
    From    Aslon Goow, Sr. Council President         NO DATE

Council Members:
| | |
|---|---|
| Veradene Ames-Garnes | Rigo Rodriguez |
| Anthony E. Davis | Andre Sayegh |
| William C. McKoy | Julio Tavarez |
| Kenneth M. Morris, Jr. | Benjie E. Wimberly |

I FIND THIS FUNNY AND DISGUSTING!
If we are such a poor and failing school, why are we receiving all of these awards?

Does anybody really know or actually care what is going on in our school? This is typical political and politician BS? They smile in your face, give you awards, then say what a rotten job teachers are doing!

## 2011 - 2012
### 1ˢᵗ YEAR OF RESTRUCTURING

I've been holding off writing, documenting and commenting on anything this year because it is supposed to be new and improved school building and school climate.
I cannot hold back anymore. Names changed, but it's still BS, lies, covering/hushing up and it is worse!

**October 10, 2011** - a female student was in the SET Academy office because of discipline problems. For whatever reason the student did *not* get her way, flipped the principal's desk over, started destroying her office and actually went after the principal in attempts of attacking her screaming, "I'M GOING TO FUCK YOU UP," and on and on!

Mr. Class*, a TAP, was in his office when he heard all of the commotion, the loud bang of the desk being flipped over, screaming of threats, cursing and at the same time a student ran into his office saying someone is attacking Ms. Nice*. When he got there the office was a mess and this large female student was going after the principal. Somehow Mr. Class* kept this young lady from striking the principal, calmed her down and brought her to his office.

Here's the disgusting part. I don't know what happed (disciplinary wise) with that student. Surprise, surprise and it seems either does anybody else in this building. More disturbing as it is required by LAW, no one knows even if a V&V (Violence and Vandalism), report was ever filed.

**Oct 11** - PSAT testing. I was a proctor in room 219. Once again, there were florescent lights not working. WHY, with all of the taxpayers' money spent on construction and alterations to the inside of JFK, do the classrooms still need light bulbs? The cabinets were absolutely filthy looking like they are covered with mold. Wait it gets better. For a week there were announcements telling students to be sure to bring in pencils and a calculator because the school and district will not be supplying them.

REASON -We were told there is NO MONEY, FUNDS, or BUDGET to supply students with pencils and calculators. I bet every superintendent or anyone who works at 90 Delaware Ave. has everything they need. Bottom-line, if they are supposed to be caring and like parents to the children, they are responsible for, why don't they do without so the students have what *they* need?

Throughout the entire time of testing the school bells were going off. It was extremely disturbing. I don't get it; doesn't anybody know how to set a clock? If testing is so important then why are there lights not working, no pencils and calculators? For over 23 years we always supplied students with pencils and calculators especially during testing and always the clocks were adjusted so students would *NOT* be disturbed while taking an exam.

Prior to testing teachers receive training on how many students are in class, take excellent attendance, be sure you have the right amount of answer sheets, be sure each student gets *their* answer sheet, etc.
It is stressed accuracy and accountability for students and testing. I go to room 219 to administer the test, by the time testing is ready to begin I now have four students who were not assigned to me or on the attendance roster that I received. I received 24 test booklets and 20 answer sheets??? There's supposed to be 24 and 24. I truly hope this is NOT the beginning of another unorganized school year.

In the classroom directly below, all we could hear was screaming, yelling, cursing, chairs and desks either being pushed or thrown around. I asked Mr. Madjar to go down there to see if he can get security to have the teacher/s get control of that class. Only to find out it was a class of Special Ed students (meaning nothing more than discipline problems kids) and four teachers just watching them. Bottom line, the noise continued. Six weeks into a new school year and a NEW PROGRAM and it is so disgusting here. No change, just a lot of taxpayers' money spent and once again wasted!

All the changes with this so-called restructuring, the millions of dollars spent, including with the increase of administration and they still won't enforce rules and basic discipline.
All this expense and discipline cost NOTHING!

**Oct 19 -** RESTRUCTURING! CHANGE! Things are going to be different, better! IT'S NOT, IT'S THE SAME! I am marking students absent for homeroom. I notice the next day, my attendance for students is changed. I wrote several emails to my supervisor about cutting, tardy, no show in attendance asking what do I do, what is the procedure, do we have forms to fill out like we had last year, before the so-called restructuring? I receive no response back. I am being ignored.

Once again, all of these highly-educated administrators did NOT think of having new forms created or even use the old forms for the time being. It wouldn't matter what date would be on them. Or is it that they do not want to document students' true attendance at all? Right now, I have two students who are on bedside. I have several students who are off my attendance roster and left the building. However, they are still on the school's master roster. If these students are still on roll will the district/school receive money funds for them? My question is, are they in another school in the district? If so, then will the district be paid twice for that one student? It's a shame I think like this, but this is what has happened after seeing all that goes on here for so long. Nothing surprises me anymore.

On the first day of school we received a folder telling us 1 minute after the bell students will be swept up, no student will be in hallways. Unfreakinbelievable, here we go again! NOTHING is done about students remaining in the hallways all day long again. However, teachers are being held responsible if students fail. Whose fault is it if students are in the hallways and not in class? Where are the two building principals? Where are the four academy principals? Where are the eight academy vice principals. Where are all of the other new and created administrators that are now in the building? Where are the two retired Paterson police officers who are supposedly heads of security?

**Oct 21** - I sent an email to the President of the PEA about no pencils for students taking the PSAT and how if they do not bring in a pencil, they will not be allowed to take the test. I did this to create a paper trail and for it to be documented.

Unfreakinbelievable, kids in the hallway all day, loooong after the period is in session. There is NOT one administrator present. The school security guards are taking a beating already with *all* of the chaos and out of control behavior continuously going on. So much for restructuring!

**Students were telling me during 6th period that the girl's bathroom by the cafeteria was set on fire.** Fire alarms did not go off. Fire Department didn't come. Here we go again as usual everything will be hushed up. WHY? Because it is restructuring, the administration will lie and make believe everything is BETTER. Parents have no idea what is going on inside here. WHY? Don't parents have the right to KNOW what's going on where their children attend school? Good God, we have "RIGHT TO KNOW," meetings every year on chemicals and even soap that's in the building. What's more important chemicals in soap or all of the fires that are deliberately set within the school, false alarms, bomb scares, violence, and etc. that goes on here. Now that's a "RIGHT TO KNOW!"

- **I have student's permission speaking about it on video.**

One of my female students told me that she couldn't even get out of the cafeteria because kids were throwing ketchup at everyone.

**Oct 24** - there is no attendance "Record Keeping" on students with 5 - 10 - 15 plus days absent. The district and or the school/academy are doing this on purpose to cover up failure of this program already. Letters are *supposed* to be sent out to parents warning them about their child's poor attendance, including cuts, tardy/cuts and lateness. It's already getting out of hand. We are circling the drain!

**Oct 25** - students in the hallway loooooooooooooong after the horn sounds to be in class. Not one administrator is in the hallway to move and get students to class. Remember according to the two building principals one minute after the bell rings to start class there will be a hall sweep. No students will be in a hallway. All you see all over the hallway floors are ketchup packets. Students are throwing them all over the place, every day, all day long. Something new and nobody does anything about stopping this. Seriously, is this normal and acceptable behavior? Once cafeteria periods start everything students get their hands on is thrown all over the place. They throw at each other, up against the walls, smashed on tables, floors deliberately making a mess and will *never* cleaning it up. Many times, students are not allowed to enter the caf on time because security and some teachers are trying to clean the place up to be a little presentable. The place is a freaking PIG STY and it *still* goes on day after day each lunch period.

**Oct 28** - we had to evacuate the building for a fire drill. It took over 10 minutes to get 3/4 of the student population back into class. Why? It should only take a minute and what about the other ¼? Because students refuse to stay with their teachers and *nothing* is done about that either! Me, if a student leaves, I write a cut. Then again being this year is restructuring, cuts are not even being processed. Already manipulating and falsifying records. THIS SCHOOL YEAR IS ALREADY LOST!

**Oct 29** - the beginning of 8th period and loooong after the horn sound to begin class the hallways were just filled with out of control students, refusing to go to class. One of the building principals was in the hallways and just ignored it all as if this is normal. Well for here it is normal.

*IT IS ABSOLUTELY OUT OF CONTROL AND IT IS ONLY OCTOBER!*

There is absolutely no accountability for student's attendance, cutting, tardy/cuts and lateness. This is restructuring? Where's the change? Plus, this is a state takeover, run and operated school district.

**Nov 1** - 2nd period marking period exam. As I am writing this it is 9:24 and there are still students in hallway, running, yelling screaming, swearing, going wild and nobody is doing anything about it. It is the same crap just a different day and it is called "RESTRUCTURING!" WHY? So much for the importance of marking period exams, but let's blame the teachers for student's failure.
I gave my 2nd period their exam. They were *all* complaining that they want to use their notes. I said, "NO! I gave every one of you the exact questions and answers, but you choose not to study." They don't care and want everything for free or you're to do it for them. They do not want to work at all. If they do this in my class, they do it in their other classes. The sad part, they will pass and still *graduate*.
HOW? THIS IS BEYOND MY COMPREHENSION!

Ever wonder why so many with High School Graduates are illiterate? The only thing the administration cares about are the NUMBERS and STATS! It's not fair to these students, their parents, the community and the country as a whole. It's also not fair to the students who do their work, earn their grades, show up for classes, have good attendance, graduate and earn their high school diploma.

As a reminder I give every student two weeks in advance a copy of the EXACT exam. Every day right up until the day of the exam we go over it in class, discussing and explaining every question and answer. Now supposedly each student has all of the answers. The exam contains multiple choice and true or false questions. Sections of the test also contains fractions, decimals, percentages and reading a ruler, all the answers were given as well as extensive review.

This year I decided to do and add something different to help give students a better grade. On the day of the exam, students were to turn in the study practice exam back to me. If completed I would *give them* **25%** credit towards their exam grade. Then students receive a NEW copy of the EXACT exam. Disturbingly, most of the students did not fill in the answers to the study sheet or it was partially completed. They already lost 25% of their exam grade. The students that did the practice, study exam did very well, OBVIOUSLY. Wonder why students *CANNOT* do well on the State-wide Proficiency Exam?

**Nov 2** - UNFREAKINBELIEVABLE, kids are all over the place, just hanging out and going wild. It is one of the worse days ever. The entire school was completely out of control. Not *one* student disciplined, asked to stop, go to class or even picked up by security. Everything is to be left alone and ignored here. It is hell here. We are teaching all the students that there is NO LAW AND ORDER HERE. That there is NO such thing as discipline and rules. You can do whatever you want.
- On the 2nd and 3rd floors students were jumping/attacking students from other academies. So now the academies are *gangs*. They are identified by the color shirt they wear.

*Explanation* - There are (4) academies; ACT, SET, STEM and BTM. Each student is supposed to wear a uniform to help easily identify which academy they belong to. Even that rule is not enforced. Another B/S problem caused by administration that they dumped onto the teachers. Anyway, now that each academy has a specific uniform, the different academies are ganging up and attacking students from other academies. This is called "RESTRUCTURING!"

**October 6 - I sent an email to the president of the PEA (Paterson Teachers Association)**

In the email I said, I wanted to meet and speak with him, because of all the money that was spent on this so-called Restructuring and the only *change* is that everything is worse! I explained the climate and condition of the building as I have been documenting. How students are NOT being held responsible for being late, cutting (which is rampant), even their attendance is being doctored. There is No Suspension, NO discipline of any type making it even more of an indoor street corner. I explained how students wear different color shirts to identify the academies they are in and because of that they are now gangs, ganging up and attacking other academies.

**Nov 8 - 7:45,** fight breaks out in front cafeteria involving two girls. School hadn't even started yet.

I received a reply back from the president of the PEA. He said he spoke with Mr. (name omitted) about my concerns and will come up to see me as soon as he can, because his workload is overwhelming.

**Oct 9 -** I am so disgusted. During the morning announcements, Principal Dickinson* says, "PLEASE be quiet during homeroom, participate with the pledge of allegiance to the flag and pay attention to the announcements." This is the PRINCIPAL IN CHARGE OF DISCILINE!

He should be upstairs walking in and out of homerooms taking notice of all of the students NOT saying the pledge of allegiance, on their cell phones, listening to music, clowning around, not paying attention to anything unless it concerns them or is happening out in the hallways. But nooooooooooooo, he's too busy chatting it up in the center hallway, drinking coffee as students are still just strolling on into the building.

**Oct 15 -** students in hallway loooong after the bell rang. There is NO supervision to be seen anywhere. Not a thing is being done about this other than allowing it all to continue and to grow. I have students already with 20 plus days out of school! Student tardiness, cuttings are all being ignored, and nothing is being done to curb or correct this. Students have an absolute free reign to do whatever they want. To think the superintendent wants to lengthen the school day. I guess this is so students can be in hallways longer.

**6th period** -*THE ENTIRE BUILDING IS SO FREAKING OUT OF CONTROL!* No administrators. Teachers opening their doors to see what in the hell is going on and then immediately closing them. KIDS in hallways looooooooong after the bell to begin class just going berserk! Key word "BEGIN!"
This boy had a girl by her foot and deliberately tried to make her fall. I yelled to knock it off. I was afraid she would have fallen and cracked her skull open. I was ignored. The place is absolutely out of control!

**October 16 - I sent two emails to the President of the PEA.**

I talked about how the district wants to increase the school day, which makes no sense to me especially when students are constantly in the hallways and not going to class. I gave an analogy - if students showed up for class on time, using just six classes as a mean, times 15 to 20 minutes each class the school day would automatically be increased 1½ to 2 hours every day without increasing the school day! And I don't have a master's degree to figure that out! I asked what the point was if the administration is NOT going to enforce school and district policies. It is NOT the teachers who are failing our students. We are NOT allowed to do our jobs and that includes security.

**Oct 18 -** the entire building is a freaking disaster. I was giving lessons on the ruler $1/8^{ths}$ & $1/16^{ths}$. This is unbelievable. This is high school and so many of my students do not even know what an even or odd number is! However, according to the superintendent students are doing better.

**Nov 18–29 -** I am not sure of the date. However, here is another police officer banned from the building for doing his job.

A police officer in the cafeteria was observing a student, who kept manhandling, pushing around a female student. Several times he told the male student to stop and knock it off. As usual the police officer was ignored. As the police officer anticipated, the male student suddenly struck the young lady so hard she fell off the bench and struck her head on the floor. The impact was loud enough to be heard over the rest of the noise in the lunchroom. The police officer jumped up and went to get the male student and the student took a stance to fight him. The officer grabbed the male student, then he and another officer handcuffed him. They were going to take the male student to the security office and an awaiting a sector car. All of a sudden one of the building principals showed up and asked the girl what happened? He kept asking her, "what happened, you are all right, you were just playing, Right?"
It was obvious the principal was coaching her. The young lady hurt and obviously confused went along with the principal as he kept trying to make this entire situation as if they were both just playing. Only to find out later, this young lady's parents told the school administration that the male students is to stay away from their daughter. The two students are NOT allowed to be together because she had been assaulted by him numerous times already and the building principal knew this. As expected in trying to keep everything hushed up and not having a paper trail the principal did not want the police officers to arrest the student. One of the police officers said, it's too late it is out of your hands.

Here's the best part. By the time the police officer finished writing his report the student was BACK and in the building. The following day when the police officer came in for work he was told he was banned and no longer allowed to work at JFK anymore. Bottom line, the police officer was punished for doing his job and the student who assaulted this young lady? Nothing was done about it.

**Nov 30** - all of a sudden, I see both building principals doing hall sweeps. They and security were picking up students that are in the hallways and bringing them into the security office. There had to be a reason for this to all of a sudden happen. I was right, they were expecting visitors. PLUS, according to one of the security guards tomorrow some people from TRENTON are supposed to be coming in for inspection. I knew it, just another dog and pony show. AT 12:30, it was back to normal, or normal for here. Not normal any place else in the real world. All you hear is screaming, yelling, arguing and cursing. No one is going to class and guess what? NO MORE hall sweeps! The part that truly bothers me is how do these administrators go home at the end of the day knowing what they continually allow/ignore to go on inside here is wrong and *ILLEGAL!* Are they going to say when they get caught, I was just following orders? That defense didn't work with the Nazis! Would they allow their children to attend school here?

**Dec 1 - UNFREAKINBELIEVABLE HERE!** The school is so out of control. I really cannot explain it. It is so loud, and students are everywhere instead of being in class. I thought there was going to be visitors from the state? There is NOT one administrator present as this place is getting progressively worse and more dangerous. A security guard told me that his wife works for or with the superintendent and the paperwork coming in is saying how smoothly JFK is running. The truth is hushed up.

Below are photos of a trailer (TCU) A-4 that is a disaster, loaded with mold, electrical boxes exposed, and furniture just thrown around. These trailers are supposed to be used as classrooms, but many are used as an office for child study team.

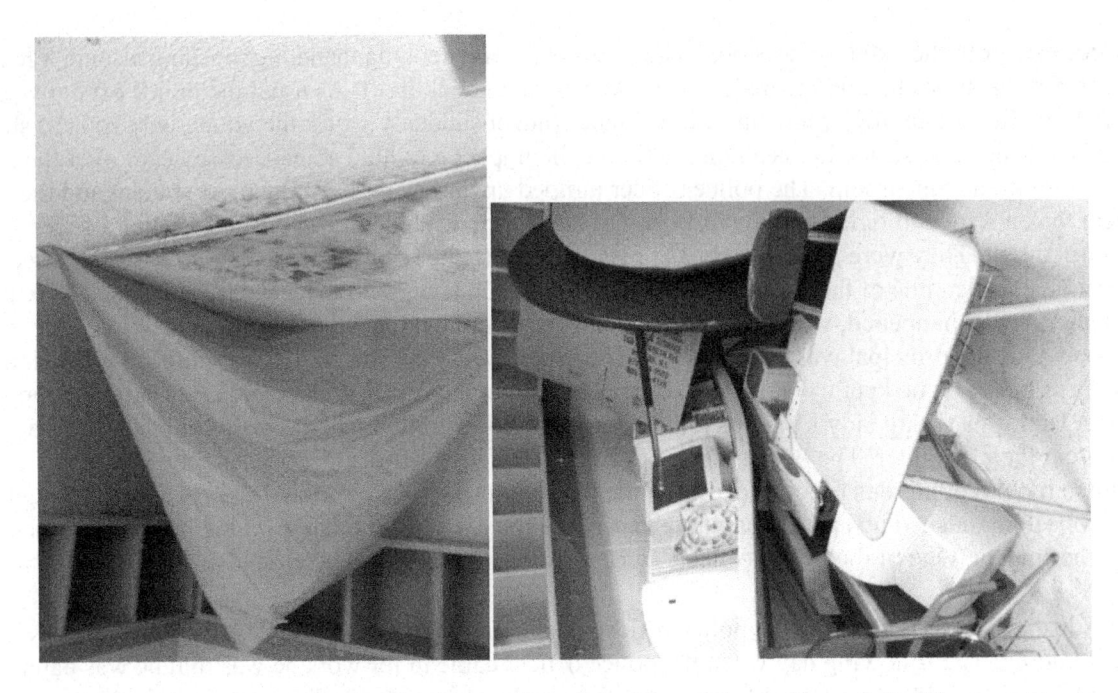

Picture #1 shows mold, and it has been there for years. No teacher will work in this room because the smell is terrible. Photo #2 shows furniture and computer equipment just thrown around.

Same trailer showing exposed wires were a phone was ripped off the wall by students.

**Dec 5 - 2:33pm**, had to evacuate the building. Do not know *why!* Fire department and added police came. Came back in at 2:52. The administration is really working hard keeping *everything* hushed up.

**Dec 7 - 12:33**, evacuated the building because the fire alarms went off AGAIN. Don't know the reason.

**Dec 5, 6, 7 & 8 -** I was assigned to room 318-B for "Renaissance Learning Star" assignment. In the last few years, students are required to take all of these different types of testing through the entire school year. Once again, students are in a room having to take an exam for four days where all of the lighting are *not* working. Why aren't lights fixed right away in any classroom as soon as there a problem? After all isn't the Paterson Public School's Motto, "CHILDREN FIRST!"

Also, in 25 years I have never ever been subjected to students whom were so disrespectful, defiant, threatening cursing, refusing to follow directions, refusing to put their food, drink, cell phones, iPod, and head phones, away, would not stop talking and can show up whenever they wanted to. If a student refused to follow any of the rules, didn't get their way, they would get up, curse and threaten me/us and walk out. The administration continues to allow this behavior not only to go on but to grow as if it is normal.

Students had to put in their ID #s to log onto the computer in order to take the test. Many students did not have their ID cards and didn't know their student #. If the teacher didn't have it or knew it, the student would give the teacher a bad time. This is what I have been saying all along. These students have been taught everything will be done for them. If they don't then the students gets an attitude and acts up. Saying act up is just putting it mildly. They *IMMEDIATELY* start cursing, berating the teacher, why don't you have my ID#, you're the teacher, you're supposed to have it and on and on. They get away with it. All students are required to have their ID card at all times. They were warned of the consequences if they do not have it. BUT as usual nothing is/was done about the students behavior. Many students are realizing this so they deliberately carry on, act up purposely to disrupt the class and entice others to join in, making the situation worse and last longer. It is an absolute joke here and a *BIG WASTE* of taxpayers' dollars.

To make things worse and add to the chaos throughout testing, (which was all day) there were 100s of students in hallways, yelling, screaming, cursing, knocking, kicking, banging and even spitting on the doors, walking in and out of the classroom that they didn't belong in. When asked to leave they would ignore me and continue walking in. They would run around the classroom, talk with students who are being tested, and carrying on with the other students that all walked in together. As the other teacher and I persisted in making every attempt to get these thugs out of the room, they would run around and away from us, curse, threaten and were Just as defiant about leaving.

These punks did everything they could to continue to be disruptive and show their defiance of authority. It was absolutely disgusting. I cannot believe how much self-control I had. I was losing it. I had enough of being talked to and threatened by street punks who were confident enough to carry on and act in this matter comfortably without any fear.

What school allows this to happen even once? This is every day, all day, for years and today I have had enough of it!

This is how a teacher ends up getting into trouble. It is so freaking difficult to work in and put up with this crap all of the time constantly, where unfortunately someone loses it and ends up grabbing a hold of one of these bums. I know in my heart, no matter what any teacher does here even if it is in self-defense, the administration would back up the student/s and leave the teacher/s out to dry.

This school is *STILL* a dangerous place. The inmates are allowed to do what they want with a free rein and fear nothing. This behavior and out of control atmosphere was allowed to go on and continued for the entire four days of testing. This type of behavior would never be allowed anyplace else in the world, but it is allowed here, in a State TAKEOVER, Run and Operated School District, where the superintendent is chosen by the Governor of NJ. It doesn't make any sense?

I want to know why none of this was seen on any of the school surveillance cameras! Either they were shut off, nobody is monitoring them, or it is all being *IGNORED*! You want to bet which one it is? I was so disgusted, I told Ms. Conscientious* who assigns teachers for testing that I will NEVER do any type of testing again. I told her if she assigns me again, I will not show up and call in sick. NO F'n WAY!

**Dec 8 -** I was speaking with Mr. Franz*. He was telling me his wife is on the **"SET" Academy Liaison Committee.** They had a meeting yesterday afternoon **(December 7)**. During the meeting, his wife Mrs. Franz* asked the director of the Set Academy, Mrs. Nice*, why isn't there a cut office? Mrs. Nice* replied, there will never ever be a school wide cut office, to track cuts, lateness, attendance, etc. anymore. REASON, the two building principals and the powers to be at the Board of Education do *not* want to generate statistics on cutting, lateness, and etc. Mrs. Franz* asked, and wanted to know how can we show that we went from over 200,000 cuts last year to *NOTHING* this year? Then she said don't you think just that alone would be a little ridiculous of a change all of a sudden? Not to mention flat out lying and falsifying of records!

Ms. Nice* said that all cuts, attendance lateness, and etc. will be handled with in each academy. If a student is a heavy hitter, (meaning many absences, lateness, cuts & etc.) that student will be assigned a ***lunch period detention***. If a student doesn't show for his detention that student will get one day suspension, which is not counted against his attendance.

**Dec 8 -** I was in my room taking a break from testing watching the substitute doing an excellent job giving a lesson on fractions. One of my students (name omitted let's call him FOOL*) not once but several times was disruptive and very disrespectful where I had to interject and finally had to remove and escort him out of my room. I brought him up to our ACT ACADEMY Office. I asked a secretary where the principal was. She laughed and said he's in a meeting. Then I asked where the VP was. She replied he too was busy.

So, I went to Ms. Daniels* another VPs office. I explained what had happened and wanted to set FOOL*, up for ISS **(ISS = In School Suspension).** She laughed and said you don't want to do that. I got annoyed and I thought I was going to be deterred because the administration didn't want to have students go to ISS anymore. In fact, to my surprise she said it is a waste of time. She said ISS is not how it used to be when students were made to be quiet and had to complete assignments. She repeated it is a joke. She said she found out about this when she had to cover ISS the other day. The kids were not doing any assignments or homework. They were all either listening to their iPod, talking on the phone, playing games, heads down on the desk sleeping, or talking with one another. She said it is a big waste. And to think with all of the extra and added in heavy weights administration in this building and within the academies due to "RESTRUCTURING" this place is worse than ever. Once again there is NO punishment, no lessons learned on what will happen if you continue to behave inappropriately. So, ISS is basically a picnic, a day off from school while being in school, where you do not have to do schoolwork, keeping up with their assignments, and NOT being marked absent from school. This is another ploy (Smoke & Mirrors) by the State Takeover, Run and Operated School District. EXPLANATION - When students are assigned to ISS that means JFK did *not* have a suspension tallied up or another student being absent from school. This only makes the district; the superintendent and administration all look good as if RESTRUCTURING is working. It is not, it is a freaking disaster. It is lying. It's falsifying records by omitting the truth. The administration is deliberately and purposely not keeping accurate records and controlling what ***IS*** to be reported.

Then she says I may want to consider some other type of punishment, such as *"Lunch Period Detention."* I laughed and said are you freaking kidding me! How is that a punishment? What lesson is that going to teach, especially when most of the time students don't even show up? Then all you guys do is reassign another Lunch Period Detention. Then when they don't show up again, you guys just forget about it.

***Explanation of lunch period detention*** - If a student has a lunch period detention the student is allowed to go to the cafeteria, eat their lunch and when they are finished (the operative word is *"WHEN")* then they are to report to the office and spend the remainder of their lunch period there.

I ended up setting the FOOL* up for early morning detention with me. Now I'm the one who is being punished and made to come to school earlier so he will have some type of disciplinary action taken. The sad thing is that everything is blamed and dumped back onto the teacher. Teachers are NOT allowed to do our jobs. How can anyone do their job when students can do whatever they want without structure and discipline? When the superintendents and administrators are more concerned about perception, making the school and district look as if is better. When in reality it is the absolute worse, I have ever seen here and it continues to get worse and worse each day & year.

This is the public education here at the now *JFK EDUCATIONAL COMPLEX.* Furthermore, I do NOT understand why the State of New Jersey, took over the school district of Paterson if it operates like this?

**Dec 9 - 12:56, fire alarms go off again.** Had to evacuate the building again.

**Dec 12 -** during morning announcements, Dr. (name omitted), whoever the hell he is – we have so many more administrators now and with doctorate degrees - meanwhile the school is out of control and he is saying today is the first day to start credit recovery period. UNBELIEVABLE!

If students were made to attend their classes by all of these administrators here with doctorates degrees, there wouldn't have to be a student recovery. WHY at this time of the year should any student need to make up lost credits? Unless the students have soooo many days out of classes NOT SCHOOL, classes, because they are continually allowed to hang out, throughout this building day after day, all day long. Anybody can get a diploma here, but too many still can't read, write or do the most basic of math.

**Dec 14 -** a security guard was beaten up so badly he had to go to the hospital. The *ADMINISTRATION* wanted to hush it up. Eventually they suspended the student because now they had NO CHOICE, knowing there will be a police report and a hospital record on this matter? I asked why he wasn't arrested. Security tries to do their job only to have students tell them to go FUCK themselves or worse, threaten them, actually stand in front of them provoking the guard/s into a confrontation which alone that should be a CRIME. But these poor security guards do nothing because like the teachers here, they know even if the student starts a fight with them and the security guard is defending themselves, they will be thrown under the bus by the administration. Think about it, just a few days ago I wrote about a police officer doing his job and because he did his job, he was removed and banned from working at JFK.

**Later today** there was a big fight in the auditorium. Now security has to monitor/patrol the auditorium.

**Dec 15 - 8:10,** the hallways are filled with students boxing, wrestling, yelling, running, pushing people around, screaming and cursing. There is NOT one administrator present let alone visible. It is an actual free for all here. I refuse to say or do anything.

**8:30am,** students come into class, flop into their desks and immediately put their heads down and want to sleep. They're exhausted. They don't go to bed until after midnight. So many tell me they don't go to bed until 2 or 3 am. I ask them what they are doing during at that time. They will say, I was out; I went to a party/club, talking to friends on the phone and my favorite...I was playing video games. What is wrong with them? Worse, what is wrong with their parents? Then when I ask them for their homework, it is as if I asked them to go slay a Dragon.

I am so sick of this place and the BS that is going on here. Nothing remotely resembles anything to being a school or a place of education. It is exactly like one of those movies about schools and you cannot believe that can happen. WELL, IT IS, and it is happening right now and all the while JFK and the entire Paterson Public School System/District is still under State Control and has been for 21 years!
**Approximately 1:45**, another BIG FIGHT in the auditorium between Blacks and Dominicans. A security guard told me Mr. Dickinson* was to have a security monitor the auditorium, but it never happened. I'd like to know what happened with the students who were caught fighting. I actually do know, "NOTHING!" If it wasn't for the security guard telling me I wouldn't have known.

**I found out today** the teacher in room 111 left. I don't know why. However, as I was walking down the hallway, I heard all of this noise and carrying. I was a good 30 feet away from the classroom. It was so freaking loud I cannot believe none of the other teachers complained or called security. Then when I got up close to the room, I heard and saw students so disgustingly obnoxious giving this female substitute such a bad time. I heard the substitute say over and over sit down, get back in here, NO you cannot leave and on and on. The noise emanating from the classroom was absolutely deafening. All the while as I was walking up towards the room all I saw were students walking in and out of that room as if it was a bar.

First of all no matter what time of the day it is, this hallway (the old art wing) is notorious for students who refuse to go to class to end up here, gathering around, hanging out with their friends, play music, wrestle, dance, yell, scream, curse, go to the auditorium and disrupt all the other classrooms that are in session. JFK is nothing more than an INDOOR STREET CORNER. Where in house truancy is ALLOWED! I want someone to tell me that this place is NOT out of control!

**December 16 - I sent another email I sent to the President of the PEA**

I told him it is out of freakin' control here. There was another fight yesterday between Blacks & Dominicans in the auditorium. And because this is an ongoing event there was supposed to be security posted in there but there wasn't. Security guards are not allowed to do their jobs. Our security guards are taking a beaten, literally. One went to the hospital the other day. Security and staff are so frustrated.
It is worse than ever before and that we need *HELP!*

**Dec 16 -** In-service day. One of the topics the principal of the Act Academy brought up is how we are all disgusted with the way things are going, the climate in the building and how we are monitoring student attendance, cuts, lateness, etc. Then he said once we get back from the Christmas holidays things are going change here. Oh, I have never heard this soooo much before!

He said this Tuesday, December 20, 2011, 2nd period there will be an ACT ACADEMY meeting with all students and teachers being present and he will tell all of us how things are going to be. As far as I'm concern that was said the first day of school. Now starting in January we're going to enforce rules? As long as I have been here actually as long as the State of New Jersey has taken over and started running this school district NO RULES ARE ENFORCED. Excuses and keeping things hushed up and quiet are the order of the day, FOR TWO DECADES.

He also told said there is NO 20-day absentee policy. The superintendent does NOT want to enforce the mandatory absences from school as 20 days, which is the law! Then he explained, if a student has 20 or more days out the first marking period yet he or she does better the 2nd, we are to grade them on that marking period.

It is ridiculous! It's all about just pushing students through the system it is NOT about education. This is proof they are manipulating the system. When we have a day off because of bad weather, then why does the superintendent and the State of New Jersey make it mandatory in making up that day/s?
Several teachers asked if the 20-day absentee policy is a state law/mandated? The principal said, it is actually less, but he is not sure? But being that the superintendent signs his check, he will do as he is told. One of the other topics that were brought up was students who leave for 2 or 3 months and did NOT attend any school while they were away. Why are they allowed to come back and pick up as if nothing has changed? The principal said the superintendent said that we have to give each student an education and it doesn't matter; they can just go back to their classes.

There's a difference in giving an education compared to giving a diploma. What is being told of us to do is not giving an education! So, for those students who do their work, go to school all year and pass and graduate, it is ok for others to take 2 or 3 months off (a vacation) also pass and graduate?

This made me think of something. We have standardized testing twice a year, yet there are no standards in this building and classrooms.

WONDERFUL, we keep going about the same road because we are all, *INCLUDING ME*, are afraid of losing our job. And I am ashamed of myself. I swear to God once I retire, I WILL bury these people and write a book telling everyone what is going on here day by day. I have said this before, what I write is *ONLY* what I know. Can you imagine with everything being hushed up how much I do NOT know?

Now, to add insult to injury, there are soooo many programs they're instituting to keep students from failing. One alone according to our principal said that the district paid $400,000 for it.

We received handouts about the numbers and statistics from the last school year. The administrators say that JFK had 100,000 cuts. That's partially true. Like I have said before in other entries, so many teachers refused to bother to write cuts knowing it was a waste of their time. While so many other teachers like myself did. However, instead of writing a cut on a student each day, we would write one slip for each student who cut at the end of the week. There would be 2, 3, 4, and 5 cuts on one slip. So YES, there may be 100,000 cut SLIPS, but there were actually over **400,000 CUTS**.

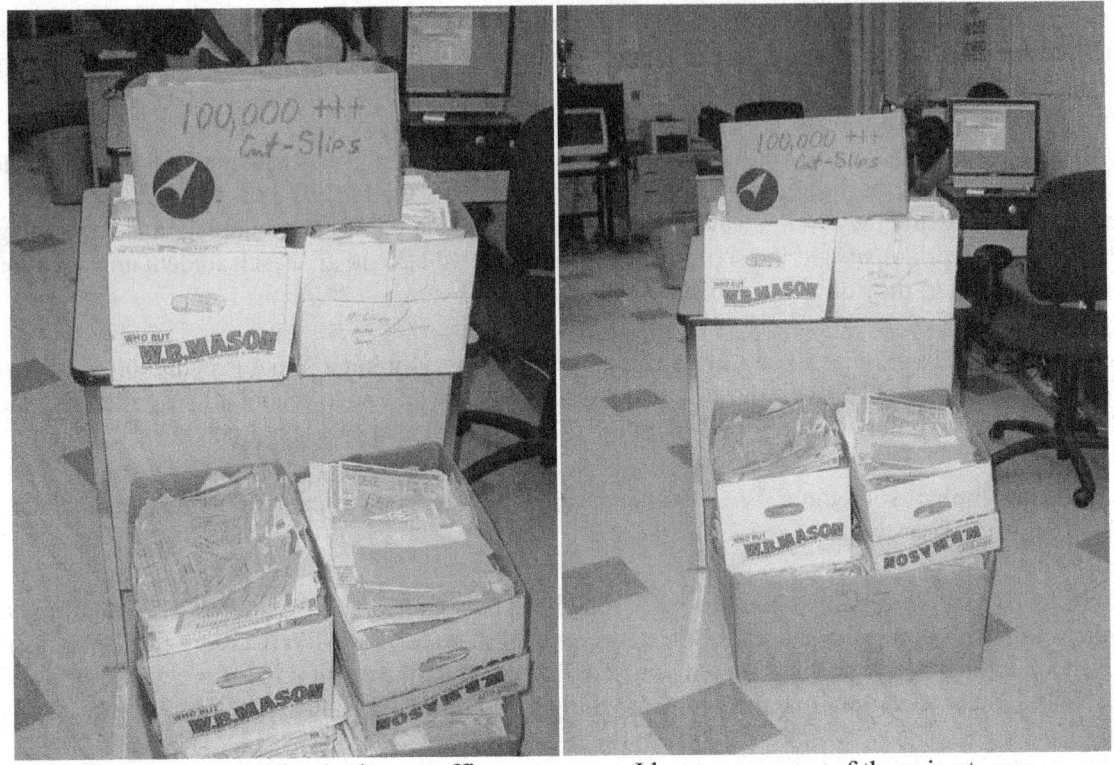

Here they are, sitting in the cut office.        I have every one of them in storage.
Notice the 100,000 + + + cut- slips written on the box.
That means most of the cut slips have at least THREE (3) cuts on one slip.

This is NOT including all the cuts slips from the school year 2009 – 2010 which was just as bad.
They too I have in storage.

Even our principal said he is pretty good with figures and knows how to manipulate the numbers.

This means starting right now, I have to more than ever start documenting everything as much as I can. This cannot continue. Most people don't even know this. When the State of New Jersey took over the District of Paterson, they were *ONLY* supposed to be here for a few years.

**Dec 20** - 3rd period. Now that there are soooo many administrators assigned to JFK because of "RESTRUCRURING," NOT one is in the hallway attempting to gain some sort of control. They all do absolutely NOTHING. Several minutes have gone by and the students are packed in the center hallway where so many administrators' offices are. Finally, I see one administrator and he just walks by and away from all of the commotion and carrying on instead of taking charge of the situation. They do NOT care.

**January 4, 2012 - 2nd day of school in the New Year**. Hallways and stairwells are packed with students. The entire building is out of control. Yet they have so many programs including after school credit recovery and starting this Saturday prep for the state exams. Who's paying for all of this? We wouldn't need all or *any* of these programs if students were made to be in class and on time. Meanwhile our politicians want to hold teachers accountable. However, here at JFK, as I walk the hallways, if I should see an administrator all they're doing is talking and drinking coffee. It is January, 5 months into the school year, the school *should* be running smooth but it's NOT because the administration STILL allows students to run wild, have a free rein to do whatever they want whenever they want. I want to know what happened to December 16, when our principal said to us at an in-service, "Once we get back from the Christmas holidays things are going change here at JFK."

**2nd day of school in the New Year continued.** There is NO restructuring here. I want someone to show me the *positive change*! It is systematically de-structuring. The teachers are taking the blame for everything going wrong and especially for students failing. You will also hear students calling me racial remarks. White ass etc. and they get away with it. If I should slip and say anything remotely like what these students can say, I would most likely be fired. This is teaching and reinforcing the most inappropriate of behavior and attitudes which are *NOT* acceptable in *any* society. You will see many administrators walking through a large crowd of students in the hallways knowing damn well they ALL belong in class and they say and do nothing. They just keep going on their merry way and ignore it all. Now you know why students openly and defiantly stay in hallways instead of going to class. I would like anyone to explain how this is the fault of TEACHERS, when we are NOT allowed to do our job, security is not allowed to do their job and the Paterson police officers that are assigned here for added security are not even allowed to do their jobs. *WHAT A WASTE OF TAXPAYERS MONEY.*

As far as I'm concerned by allowing students to behave this way and have no regards for rules and laws the administration is destroying society. You have to come here to see and listen for yourself to fully understand what is constantly going on inside JFK High School to get the full impact of the meaning when I say this place is nothing more than an indoor street corner that is allowed to be out of control and lawless. Then ask yourself why is this allowed to happen, go on?
Every parent who has sent their children to JFK High School ever since 1991 and especially since 2007 to present day, they ALL have a *MAJOR LAWSUIT/CLASS ACTION* against the school district, the superintendents, the administration, the commissioners of education and the Governor/s. Especially Chris Christie, because this is ALL happening under his watch and the Paterson Public School System is STILL under State Control, meaning he's is in charge!

**Jan 10 -** all during 3rd 6th & 8th periods there are so many students in hallways looooooooong into the period. It is the same students, no uniforms, cell phones, head phones, excessive foul language, ignoring security to move, refuse to go to class, walking in and out of classes they don't belong in, giving teachers a bad time when they try to remove them, it is just completely out of freaking control. However, the principals, all six of them, will tell you everything is going great! That's why they are never seen in the hallways. Once again, if they don't see it, it's not happening, and they consider that NOT lying!

**Jan 12 - I received photos** from 1/3/12, of a major leak pouring from the roof, 3 floors above to the floor by the entrance to the weight room. It is an absolute disaster and happens every time it rains. Nothing has been done yet to fix the problem. There has to be mold growing between all (3) floors because this has been going on for years. Which makes sense, you don't get a leak of this magnitude all of a sudden. It is from years and years of neglect. The powers to be in order to save money and increase administrators to be hired, they let go of so many maintenance workers in the district. With what is left of that department it is nothing more than a skeleton crew and with over 30 schools and a monstrosity of a building for the Paterson Board of Education, these guys are stretched real thin. If there should be a leak at 90 Delaware Avenue, it would be fixed immediately, and no expense spared. However, here at JFK and for years it will continue to be years before it is repaired. Solution? Let's just throw a coat of paint over everything, even the MOLD!

The lighting is poor because the bulbs busted and shorted out due to the water pouring down on them. As it was raining outside the water was pouring worse inside. Notice the ceiling tiles missing? They were destroyed, almost dissolved into little particles because of the amount of rainwater falling on them.

**Jan 12 - 6th period** loooong after the bell rang to be in class. There are students hanging outside a couple of classroom doors and not either going in or coming out. They stood there hanging around, eating, drinking, cursing all the while the teacher is yelling to come inside, close the door sit down, ONLY *TO BE IGNORED!* But administration will tell you that everything is much better here ever since *"RESTRUCRURING!"* They all have become politicians. They will smile in your face and tell you nothing but out and out *lies*! All of the security guards are so disgusted. All of a sudden, the security guards are getting yelled at by both building principals for *NOT* moving students to class and getting them out of the hallway. There must be visitors so the ye ole dog and pony show begins.

**<u>January 13, I sent an e-mail to my principal and my two vice principals. Below is a narrative.</u>**
Good Morning Mr. Baker*, Ms. Daniels* & Mr. Arthurs*,

Attached are my Lesson Plans for the week of January 16 - 20, 2012.

I have concerns/questions:
Students refuse to remove hats, wear uniforms, be on time, have good attendance and cut profusely.

All day long the 1st floor hallway is filled with students especially ACT Academy students.
The foul language is way over the top and unacceptable.
The other day, there were 2 parents standing outside my classroom and they were horrified.
I placed them in my room and closed the door. I was concerned and embarrassed.

When ask student/s to follow school rules, we are met with much resistance.

We are spending way too much time on those who cause problems while the students who want to participate and learn are losing out or changing their ways and becoming a problem too.

I'm at the point when a student refuses to follow any of the rules especially giving me a bad time about wearing a uniform; I am just going to send them to you. If they don't go, they will receive a cut.

Students who do not belong in my class are walking in and refuse to leave. When they finally leave, they are cursing at me and yelling threatening and racial remarks. When I close the door because of all the nonsense and noise that is going students start to bang on it, (amazing not breaking the window), yell, and curse at me in defiance. None of this is acceptable in an educational facility!

I watched Ms. Daniels*, assign detention to students for not wearing a uniform and gave them shirts. One of those students in particular, a real defiant wise guy, as soon as he walked out of the office, took off the shirt, placed the other shirt and hat back on and said fuck them, I'll do whatever I want to another kid?

I am NOT complaining where I'm not going to perform my duties or do what is expected of me. I will always do as told and expected to the best of my abilities. However, I am discouraged.

On 1/12 received note from the OFFICE to call mom, need Spanish speaking person.
On 1/13 called home approximately 9:30, Carlos interpreted for me.
It seems mom Mrs. (name omitted), wants us to take care of the discipline for her son and many other requests to do her parenting duties.
I had Carlos explain, I will inform you all.

**END**

I never received a reply or heard anything in reference to the above e-mail.

**Jan 13** - early this morning one of the building principals made an announcement telling everyone to ignore the alarms if they go off because they're being worked on. At 11:58 the fire alarms go off. Several minutes later the other building principal made an announcement telling us to evacuate the building. It ended up being a false alarm. The fire department and extra police came.

**Jan 18** - 7th period, it is so out of control here. Mr. Arthurs* one of the VPs was in the hallways actually trying to get the students to move and go to class. This went on long after the horn sounded to be in class. The kids gave him a bad time. They all should have been in class in the first place. The VP stayed by my classroom watching and eventually walked up and down the corridor by the vending machines, which was horrible and filled with 100 plus students. It was just jammed packed and they were refusing to leave. I wished he would walk with me down by the old art wing. It is soooo bad there and believe it or not much worse. All you will hear is constant screaming, yelling, cursing and commotion going on all period, all day and every day. There was one young lady whose mouth was absolutely terrible, not more than three words would come out of her mouth without it being the vilest of foul language and all at the top of her lungs. It echoed throughout the entire floor. She was doing it on purpose because she knew she would get away with it and knew she was disrupting classes. It is absolutely disgusting here. *Have video.*

**January 18, I sent the following e-mail / discipline referral to my principal and two VPs.**

DISCIPLINE REFERRAL

Lee E McNulty
John F. Kennedy Complex (ACT ACADEMY)

Metal Shop Room 114 ex. 50114
On January 18, 2012, student (name omitted) comes to a class once again and refuses to remove his coat.
I asked him again, he refuses, starts cursing, being disrespectful, giving me all of his jazz and attitude.
I replied, (name omitted) take off your jacket, we're not going to go all through this again.
He replied nastily, FUCK YOU! GO FUCK YOURSELF, I'M NOT TAKING IT OFF.
I DON'T CARE YEAH, YEAH, YEAH, FUCK YOU BALDY and it continued.

THIS UNACCEPTABLE! I AM NOT GOING TO ALLOW THIS TYPE OF BEHAVIOR OR LANGUAGE IN MY CLASS EVER!

I replied, go to the office and have the secretary contact me once you are there.

Without missing a beat, I am met again, FUCK YOU, GET OUT OF MY FACE YOU BALD MOTHER FUCKER, FUCK YOU, GO FUCK YOURSELF, I DON'T CARE, SUCK MY DICK AND ON AND ON AND ON ALL THE WHILE AS HE WAS LEAVING MY CLASSROOM.

I had not received a phone call from a secretary informing me that student (name omitted) had shown up.

To all involved.
This is unacceptable behavior and way over the top. A slap on the wrist is not appropriate punishment.
He and the other students act this way because there is NO discipline.
I am not here to be cursed out in the most vile and viscous way by a juvenile or anyone for doing as asked by my administrators.
I am not here to be disrespected or not backed up with appropriate measures in efforts to keep this type of behavior down to the lowest denominator.     UNACCEPTABLE!

If this behavior is allowed to continue without any type of proper discipline, then it leaves me choice to stop informing students to remove their hats, coats, wear their proper uniforms, and etc.
I am not going to be subjected to this behavior and be placed in this type of situation over and over.
If this type of behavior is going to be allowed, then student (name omitted) can sit with the building principal's and they can allow him talk to them that way.
Tried to call home however, phone was disconnected.

Below is his information and attendance.

Name omitted        Tel omitted         Parents Name omitted
xxxx N 8th St       DOB 11/28/93        A1 114 G 212 237 C 800 113 226
AS OF JANUARY 18, 2012,    ABSENTS (13)      CUTS (1)      LATES ()

Thank you and most respectfully,

Lee E McNulty

**NOTE OF INTEREST:** - Being that JFK is so out of control and the superintendent and administrators do not want any type of paper trail documenting what is really going on here, I am taking it upon myself to write and send email to administrators and the unions (PEA & NJEA) now creating a paper trail. Even though I am not receiving a reply back from my emails or even as much as a verbal response, I am creating a paper trail that *cannot* be deleted or denied.

**Jan 19** - I received a copy of a form from one of my students (name omitted), where he is being assigned to a program now called **"TWILIGHT 2011-2012."**
<u>*Now pay attention to what it says.*</u>
*I, (Students name is omitted), understand that my main reason for attending the TWILIGHT PROGRAM is to obtain a quality education to complete high school graduation requirements. This affords me the opportunity to obtain high school credits towards graduation and/or return to a day high school program.*

*I understand that I must adhere to the established Code of Conduct and all the rules and regulations of the school district as outlined in the Paterson Public School District's Student Handbook. These rules include "zero tolerance" or tardiness and attendance policy not to exceed three absences. Three tardiness of any length will count as one absence.*

*I fully understand that I must display appropriate behavior, respect myself, my peers, my teacher's administrator and all members of the Twilight Program.*
*I have full understanding that any violation of this agreement will result in my losing credits from the Twilight Program and my returning to no credit status for the duration 2011-2012 school year.*

Then his signature.

Are you kidding me, why weren't these rules enforced in the first place at the JFK Educational Complex? It's the exact same rules written in the students' handbook which students receive on the first day of school. It states in the second paragraph "I understand that I must adhere to the established Code of Conduct and all the rules and regulations of the school district as outlined in the Paterson Public School District's Student Handbook." So if you have poor attendance, you have many cuts and have been continually cutting, are late, you get placed into "TWILIGHT 2011-2012," that has the *exact* same rules as JFK Educational Complex and if you do NOT abide by *these* rules you cannot graduate? Am I missing something here? This is another BS program at another and greater expense to the NJ taxpayers because rules and regulation are continually and deliberately ignored by administration in the first place at JFK.

**Jan 20 - 9:56, fire alarms go off again**, false alarm again. Fire department and extra police came again. This is restructuring? With all that is allowed to continually go on, ignored, overlooked here and then to add a BS Program like "TWILIGHT" makes me wonder if somebody is getting greased?

Something is going on because all of a sudden, I see one of the two building principals in the hallways attempting to move and get students into class. However, the kids are giving her a really bad time. This shows exactly how disrespectful these students are. Furthermore, GOOD, she deserves it. After all, she, and all of the other administrators caused these problems. Now they are getting what they created and ignored plus getting a sample of what teachers have to put up with all day, every day and it is all IGNORED by them. So don't get mad superintendents, administrators you are all doctor Frankenstein and now you have to deal with the monster you created!

7th period, Mr. Arthurs* a VP came into my room and wanted me to make a list of students who do NOT have their uniforms on. Five minutes later, he came back and there was only one student. He left with the name. Five more minutes goes by and my principal comes in and gives that student a Saturday detention. I'm thinking they are finally cracking down on students who refuse to wear uniforms. Silly me, instead during our In-service that afternoon our principal said, by making students who do NOT have their uniforms on they WILL be assigned Saturday detention. This way we will now have at least 50 students for the Saturday HSPA, instead of the 15 that showed up last week. It was not about discipline, it was about manipulating the numbers and statistics.

**Jan 24** - I could not figure out why all of a sudden, security and especially so many of the administrators, were in the hallway moving students and getting them to class. Even the two retired Paterson police officers were involved. That's when I realized we are having visitors and a dog and pony show was about to begin. It wasn't until 4th period I knew for sure because I saw the superintendent walking along with one of the two building principals and eventually to be followed by the other rushing over.

Once the superintendent left the entire building went back to complete OUT OF CONTROL CHAOS!

**Jan 25** - 8th period, the building was in complete chaos. My student was telling me things, especially how the BTMF Academy wing is so dangerous. You have to realize these kids live this stuff all day long and for them to tell it so matter of fact. Even the teachers are becoming immune or desensitized from it all and are thinking this is normal. I DON'T!

**Jan 26** - 9th period, I had it. It was so bad outside my classroom. I went into the security office and had a security guard move all the kids away from my classroom and out of the area. However, just as he was moving them down and out of the corridors, they turned around and started heading back.

A few minutes later they (about 30), where all outside my room again, screaming swearing cursing, wrestling and on and on and on. That's when I saw Mr. Dickinson* turning the corner and I had it. I yelled to him, Mr. Dickinson* what is going on here? Why are all these kids in the hallway? I cannot get any of my work done. I can see he was disgusted but remained cool and polite. He told me that two programs had just ended simultaneously, and the kids are hanging around. I replied, I'm sorry, sir, that is no excuse for this, students are constantly hanging around here, all day, every day, all year.

I also apologized to him and wanted to know I am NOT yelling at him, but I am disgusted that this is going on. He replied, I don't take it personally, but please bear with me, in the next 72 hours there is going to be a *BIG CHANGE* and I'm going to need your support to back me up. I said you got it. Then I started thinking, *here we go again, gee I never heard that before*. Twenty plus years of hoping! I don't have much left. I hope they don't pass the blame now onto the security guards. The real problem is there are no consequences for student's poor behavior because the administration does more work in covering up problems and incidents than preventing them from happening by making students GO TO CLASS.

**Jan 26** - security and police opened a student's locker then arrested him. I have to laugh, all the laws about drugs and drug paraphernalia in proximity of as school is a joke. If you're a juvenile, NOTHING HAPPENS. **See September 15, 2010 entry.**

**Jan 27** - several Special Ed teachers told me that Mr. Little* an administrator of the Special Ed department told them no matter what as long as a student comes to class, even if they do nothing, you have to give them a D for their grade. So, in reality he just told them that students DO NOT have to do anything. These teachers also told me that they told several students it's time for them to be mainstreamed. The students all of a sudden woke up screaming and yelling, NO, they do too much work and I'm not going to do it, I'm not going! This is what the Paterson Public School System the State Takeover, Run and Operated District has taught these children.

Unbelievable, the entire hallway was FILLED with students. Not one administrator to be seen. It is soooo bad here. Two different security guards removed 2 girls from ROOM 106 for fighting.

However, the fighting didn't stop. Then students were taunting and bullying the teacher. It is so out of control HERE. There are supposed to be laws about bullying, yet NOTHING was done to the boy *BULLYING* the teacher. The teacher was trying to close his door and this student wouldn't let him. He kept cursing and threatening him with bodily harm. This inappropriate, out of control, dysfunctional and criminal behavior not only goes on here all day, day after day the administration allows it to continue and to spread inside JFK like a cancer. This poor teacher was taking such verbal abuse along with a barrage of foul language and threats. He was working so hard in keeping his composure, trying to just close the door and get back to teaching his students. This foul mouth punk wouldn't stop berating the teacher and wouldn't let go of the door so the teacher could close it. He kept on screaming at the top of his lungs cursing and threatening him. I really felt bad for this teacher. While I am standing there watching all of this other teachers and staff were coming up to me and expressing their shear distress and disgust with all of this. A VP Ms. Corfu* came down to see what was going on and tried to stop all of the commotion. Now the students started yelling and cursing at Ms. Corfu* She just stood there taking all of this abuse, foul language and derogatory remarks. She let it go on and on instead of calling security and having these students removed. She did say she was going to suspend the girls and the one boy who was threatening the teacher. As soon as she said that the first thing out of the boy's mouth was, "I'm calling my mother, I'm not letting some girl call me a bitch and get away with it." *I received a video of this entire incident.*

Shortly afterwards I saw security and police bring in a bunch of kids into the security office. Several minutes later several of my students told me there was a guy inside the building with a machete. Then later the girls in one of my classes were telling me there was also a boy outside the building with a knife looking for someone. Then at the end of the day, several other teachers were talking about the intruder running around inside the building with the machete. Are you going to tell me if I know or found out about what was going on inside and all around the building today that means security knew and if security knows that means the administration knew? Why wasn't there a "LOCK DOWN?" Isn't that what a LOCK DOWN is used for? So once again, in the attempts in keeping everything quiet, hushed up and not creating a paper trail of what was going on inside and around JFK, the brainiacs took it upon themselves to jeopardize the security and lives of the students and everyone else who works here AGAIN!
The entire day there was nothing but trouble going on here. You can actually feel the tension and anxiety that something was brewing, and the hunt was on. Only to find out from all of the teachers talking there was a big brawl on the 3rd floor in SET ACADEMY wing and supposedly VP, Ms. Nice* was hit.

**Jan 30 - 2:30, fire alarms** go off, evacuated the building again. False alarm again! And last Thursday, January 26, Mr. Dickinson* said things were going to change in 72 hours. Received video & photos.

I have an audio interview of my students talking about a big fight/gangs after school actually in the street of Totowa Ave. Many weapons especially machetes and knives. People were stabbed and hacked. They talked about people in their 20s to 30s involved in the attack/ fight. And all hushed up!

I noticed the same kids who gave the teacher and Ms. Corfu* the VP a bad time on January 27, were *STILL* in the building. Obviously, nothing was done about it. It went ignored and unpunished.

**Jan 31 - 9:47,** a student was escorted out of the building by police in handcuffs. Found out he had a knife on him. There are *still* BIG GANG FIGHTS GOING ON. This morning Mr. Lawrence* a TAP, and VP Mr. Arthurs* were stopping and checking every student and their back packs for weapons. I interviewed a student and he was telling me all about what is going on with the fights/gangs. REALLY SCARY! It's basically the exact same things as my other students told me.

**It's 1:15, the** hallways are filled with out-of-control students. All of a sudden, two students start fighting. There were two VPs there and all they did was separate them. Meanwhile the two students continued cursing, threatening, and still trying to attack and fight each other. I said these guys will fight again before the day is out all because you let them go. As expected, *nothing* was done about it.

Later I spoke with the VP and asked about IDs. He said all the kids don't have ID cards and refuse to purchase another. What can we do about it? I laughed and said who runs this school? After all, the principal did say on the first day of school any student without their ID they will be rounded up and placed in detention. This proves the administration will not enforce any rules.

A great deal of the fighting all day was on the 2nd floor BTM ACADEMY! A teacher told me he saw a young man attacked, knocked down and they were stomping his face. He said he was a bloody mess. It is MOB mentality inside here. It is the most dangerous I have ever seen here.

It is so out of freaking control here and it shouldn't be especially when JFK high school is in a district that is still under STATE CONTROL. If this is the best the STATE of NJ can do running this district, they need to get the ***HELL OUT***!

**Feb 1 -** so much for the building principal telling me last week everything will change in 72 hours. The building is absolutely lost, students defying everything, anything and everyone. While walking in the hallway, Mr. Camp* a math teacher was hit in the head and back with several pieces of plastic or wood. He complained and wrote up a report. It wouldn't have been too difficult to find who did that using the surveillance cameras. Instead NOTHING was done about it.

It was so bad during 6th period I went out in the hallway yelling to get the school in control. The students all laughed and cursed me while other teachers and the new Phys-Ed director just stood there looking.

**Feb 2 -** on January 31, security was checking every student for weapons prior to entering the building. The next day it stopped! However now, they are checking students again with a magnetic wand. I'm actually surprised security is doing that outside knowing how paranoid the administration is that someone might take a picture and send it to the newspapers. If I didn't have a class, I would have. Bottom Line, security is outside all morning and now we have less security in the building. It is 8:40 and kids are still coming to school. The kids just come in whenever they want.

**6th period,** what a freakin' shame. Not one administrator to be seen. The place is so bad it's short of another riot. How can there be all of these students and I mean 100s of them NOT going to class? It all has to be on the surveillance cameras!

You can't blame students for doing whatever they want. The administration has taught them, and has allowed them to. Is this what every administrator is taught in college in terms of how to have control of your school and students? Even a person without a high school diploma knows *all* children need to be supervised *not* let to run wild. Furthermore, I *cannot* believe this is allowed, especially while Chris Christie is Governor of the State of New Jersey and this school and district is still under state control.

**Feb 6 -** have video during a meeting/announcement of the building principal talking about how they're going to instill order and gain control of the school. They're admitting to it! They are going to do this by giving teachers more paperwork and added responsibilities. Then why in the hell do we need all of these administrators? All they are doing is dumping their work and responsibilities onto us giving them more room to blame teachers. The picture quality is poor, and the volume is really low. I am sure there is a way the volume could be enhanced.

**Feb 8 -** I found out students are NOT showing up for after school credit recovery. So Mr. Myers* one of the *newly* added administrators with a PhD. is taking students out of their regular assigned classes to make up other classes in order to graduate. Does anybody else see this being *WRONG* other than me?

Then at 1:38 just before the end of 7th period, he comes over the PA system telling students to see him after school to get help with the SATs and that they have programs that cost several thousands of dollars each, so students should come take advantage of this program. The money just keeps on rolling in! However, last year I wanted students to come in on Saturdays to do their work/assignments and my principal said I couldn't do that. I asked why? He said Saturday detention is for discipline you cannot make students come in to do their work. You can't punish students for not doing their assignments.

I had to laugh and didn't say anything because just a few weeks ago on January 20, he was going to classrooms looking for students who did not have their uniforms on. Any student that did not have their uniform on he assigned them Saturday detention. However, if you read the entire entry it was to *make* students attend Saturday HSPA, to get the numbers up! You can't make this stuff up!

Mr. Lou Bonora was suspended from work because he used foul language to an administrator out of frustration. He was excited because kids deliberately pushed him down in the hallways and he wanted to know WHY nothing was going to be done about it.

However foul language, cursing, direct threats made to teachers and security by students are allowed?

My question is if the districts administration and school's administrators continuously allow this type of behavior, the use of foul language and threatening remarks made by students to teachers and security, how long is it going to take for students to realize if they get into trouble in later years, they can say I am not responsible for my behavior because I was taught and allowed to act this way when I was a student at JFK? Some smart attorney will think so!

**February 9, Mr. Madjar sent me the following newspaper article in an email.**
"Concerns Grow about Violence near Kennedy High at Dismissal" by Joe Malinconico
Saturday, February 4, 2012
PATERSON, NJ - Officials say there has been a recent increase in fights among Kennedy High students near the school at dismissal time, especially confrontations between black and Dominican youths.
City police say they have had an "extra presence" at Kennedy, as well as at Eastside, for more than a month and education officials are planning a meeting among students to try to resolve the tensions. Parents and officials say some groups of students have armed themselves with baseball bats after school and there have been reports from parents and one teacher - which authorities have not confirmed -of students having machetes.

"I tried to call everybody about the situation and it's like they don't care," said Latinya Sinclair, whose 16-year-old son is a junior at the school. "If my son gets stabbed, I'm coming after the school and I'm coming after the police. Where is the protection?"
Sinclair said her son and several other black students recently were jumped by Dominican youths who she said mistook them for a group called the "Westside Boys." There were large brawls after school in the Kennedy neighborhood several times in the past two weeks, she said.

A teacher at Kennedy, who asked to remain anonymous, said the situation has created fears among students not involved in the fighting.

"It's out of control," said Councilman Aslon Goow, who represents the 2nd Ward, where Kennedy is located. The problem goes beyond racial rivalries between the black and Dominican students, Goow said. Several weeks ago, an area resident walking through West Side Park was attacked by three youths wearing Kennedy school uniforms after dismissal time, Goow said. Moreover, teens have been robbing onions and potatoes from area grocery stores and throwing them at passing vehicles, Goow said.

During the fall there had been a similar surge in after school violence near Eastside, including one instance in which several black youths badly beat members of a Dominican family at the laundromat on Park Avenue.

After the city's decision last spring to lay off more than a dozen school crossing guards, police officers have been assigned to those posts in the mornings and afternoons. That has left fewer cops on patrol at those times of day, officials said.

But city law enforcement officials say they have shifted manpower to address the problems at Paterson's two main high schools. "All I can say is we have extra presence at both high schools," said Deputy Police Chief Danny Nichols.

In response to complaints from parents, the school district is planning a meeting with students to try to curtail the problem, said spokeswoman Terry Corallo.

City Council President Anthony Davis, who represents the 1st ward, which has many Kennedy students, said he has heard about the fighting. "I'm investigating what's going on," Davis said.

Paterson Schools Commissioner Pedro Rodriguez, who lives on the city's North Side, said he doesn't think the Kennedy fighting has become as bad as the situation was at Eastside in the fall. But, Rodriguez warned, February tends to become a volatile time for the city's racial tensions. Not only is it black history month, but Dominican Independence Day falls on February 27.

"You see an increase in fights," Rodriguez said. "People show their flags and wave them in the other guy's face and then he gets ticked off and the fight starts."
END

**Feb 10** - 6th period and loooong into the period students are defiantly standing in hallway knowing they are being recorded. One large student in particular is looking for a confrontation with me. I just stood there. I said and did nothing. My point is that is how brazen the students are here. These punks will tell me what I can and cannot do. In the meantime, the students make it clear NO ONE can tell them what they cannot do, because the administration allows this MOB mentality to go unchecked.

Later I spoke with one of the building principals. She said the superintendent was not pleased with the hallways. She said she took him to all the hot spots where kids hangout and do not go to class. She just *admitted* they allow students to hangout! Then she says, she told the superintendent they need more guards. We don't need more guards! The students don't even listen to her. Sure, let's get more guards that the students won't listen to, respect, can threaten, attack and all at the added expense to NJ taxpayers.

**Feb 13** - 11:10 police escorted a student out of school in handcuffs into a police car. I don't know why!

**Feb 15** - I took video of the ceiling and the water damage by the weight room entrance doors. It is the same place as above entry on January 12, 2012. Bottom line it still has NOT been fixed/repaired.

**Feb 16 - received an email today from my principal about HSPA Boot Camp again!**
FW: ATTENTION ACT #1
From: Mr. Baker*
Sent: Thursday, February 16, 2012 11:45 AM
To: (All names in e-mail sent were omitted)
Subject: ATTENTION ACT #1

ACT #1 – As per district request, we will begin our HSPA Boot Camp today. Please excuse all testing juniors from periods 2-5.
I will forward an attendance list daily to keep you informed of which students were present.
Attached you will find the list of students identified to participate.
If you would like to volunteer during free periods to assist students with preparation…language arts will be located in room 230 and math will be in room 232.
Drop in and lets all pitch in to help our students during this last push.

12 DAYS UNTIL HSPA

I CAN'T THANK YOU ENOUGH FOR ALL YOUR TIRELESS EFFORTS.

Mr. Baker*

                    END

Standardized testing? How is removing students again, from their regularly assigned classes, periods, 2, 3, 4 & 5 every day, for the next three weeks, for the second time this year to prepare them to take the HSPA State Test *a standard?* Testing is supposed to be about WHAT students have learned (if they were made to attend class) while they were in class. That's what is meant by STANDARDS. Why bother having school at all? Just open the doors for a few hours a day for a few weeks preparing students to take and pass the state-wide exam. *Done!*

How many programs are there for students to prepare to take and pass the State-wide Exams? There were weekend programs, if students show up. There was a mandatory summer programs in August if students showed up. There were after school programs if students show up. All these programs if students showed up just like **if** they show up for classes all year in preparing students to take and pass the standardized test.

**Feb 16 - 12:13, fire alarms** go off again. Evacuate the building again. This time it was a sensor in room 117, the wood shop, because of hot saw dust floating in the air setting it off.

**Feb 17 -** 6th period the horn sounded to be in class. As far and as you can see in any direction all you see is students. They are NOT going to class. As time is going by there are more and more students gathering around just to hang out. What happen to hall sweeps? Where in the hell are the administrators? There is *not* one to be seen. What happened to January 26, the day when the principal said to me, "please bear with me, in the next 72 hours there is going to be a *big change* and I'm going to need your support to back me up?" This place is out of freaking control and a complete disaster. Students are failing because of the administrators, NOT teachers, because they continually allow students NOT to go to class and hangout throughout the entire building. Parents haven't a clue what is really going on in here!

**Feb 21 -** I sent a lengthy letter to Governor Christie and the Commissioner of Education about this place.

**Feb 22** - all of a sudden the big shots, a building principal, a TAP and about 8 other administrators come in my room to talk to one of my students (name omitted) because he had a hat and coat on. All year these fools did nothing with students wearing hats and coats. Meanwhile, the hallways are still jam packed with screaming and yelling kids including a couple of the biggest and defiant offenders who these administrators continually let go or just ignore. Now all of a sudden, they pick on one kid in my class and did the same thing in the print shop class. There has to be more to this? This is just out of the blue.

**Feb 24** - Principal Mr. Dickinson* made the morning announcements. He said, "students are not to wear hats in the building. All students must wear a complete uniform. Any student who does not follow these rules will be picked up and brought to the security office." I laughed. School has been in operation for almost 6 months. When the horn sounded, I did NOT see one administrator in the hallways. Meanwhile, the students were wearing their hats and coats in defiance just as they have been since day one.

Later that day and with their permission, I interviewed and videotaped three of my students. They were telling me about a riot going on in the hallway by the old art wing just prior to class starting. Mr. Camp* the math teachers saw it and said he will give me a copy of the video.

**Feb 27** - I made a copy of Mr. Camps* video from February 24. The date on his camera is incorrect. However, the riot like situation and all of the commotion is real.

**Feb 28** - for the last few weeks, room 113 has been receiving all brand-new wood working equipment and machinery. Twenty years ago, room 113 was a Wood Shop. It was fully equipped with the same equipment that is being purchased and installed now. When the state took over the district it was all removed. In fact, I was instructed to help dismantle all of the equipment. NOW NJ taxpayers are paying for all this NEW equipment again. In the meantime, students are sitting around doing nothing while the teachers are assembling, installing and setting up everything.

6th period, UNFREAKINBELIEVABLE, it looks as if the majority of the student population is everywhere except in their classes. How can they be passing any classes?

**Feb 29** - took video so we can hear morning announcements about the rules, no hats, full uniform, no iPods, etc. Same crap, but that's all it is—CRAP. Once the bell rings, where are the administrators? Nothing has changed. Just a lot of TALK! This place is a disgusting *joke*!

6th period, the bell rang, the hallways are the same. Not one administrator to be seen. Students refuse to go to class, hang out all over the building and do whatever they want to do every day, all day long and it is allowed. The real reason why administrators are NOT in the hallways is then they would HAVE to do something about students hanging out all over the place. If they do something, then there has to be a paper trail. THEY DO NOT WANT THAT! Meanwhile students are NOT getting an education and learning a most viable lesson, "DISCIPLINE!" All that matters here is passing the HSPA! Other than that, this entire complex is a big waste of taxpayer's money. We're talking 100s of millions of dollars.

It's obvious that something was going on. Supposedly someone pulled a knife. From what I was told, all they did was usher him out of the building instead of apprehending and arresting him.

NOW WHAT IS GOING TO HAPPEN LATER? It is against the law to have a weapon in the building. Whether it was a student or an intruder they should have been immediately arrested. Why wasn't there a "LOCK DOWN?" It seems laws do not apply to John F. Kennedy Educational Complex! It's now 9th period and the building is a disaster and nothing is being done about anything.

**Mar 2** - the hallways and the entire building is soooo out of control. It is INSANE here, sheer chaos. The two retired Paterson police officers who are supposed to be in charge of security just walk by as if they are taking a stroll in a park and as if everything is fine and running smoothly. When they are actually walking and maneuvering their way through the ever continuously growing crowd of students who are filling up the hallways in the entire building to just hang out and not going to class. However, in their DEFENSE, they were police officers and police officers follow orders. Soooooooooooo it is very possible that is exactly what they are doing, following orders to do nothing, let it go and ignore it all. In fact, many years ago when one of them was a motorcycle cop, I use to ask him, if he would send his children here? To put it mildly his reply back started with *"HELL NO,"* followed by and with *many* expletives. NOW, just like the rest of us, is he keeping quiet because he doesn't want to get fired?
I have been working in this building for over 20 years. We have never ever had two retired Paterson police officers working as heads of security until, this year with "RESTRUCTURING.
It is absolutely insane here. The place is getting worse and worse by the minute. Then two girls start fighting. Students crowded around so security couldn't even get through and kept instigating and causing more problems at the same time. It was really nothing short than a riot. The administration continually allows students to congregate and hangout all over the building instead of being in class. I guess the administration *wants* students to fight and to get hurt. I swear if parents knew what is going on here, this place would be shut down, a massive investigation would have to go on and finally hold all of the administration liable for creating and continuously allowing a most dangerous and no educational environment. It is unacceptable especially when we have all of the extra administration in this building with this so-called "RESTRUCTURING!" I hope when my book comes out, "HEADS WILL ROLL!"

Every day all day long the hallways are jammed packed with students hanging out and taking a stroll. After a while, you recognize as well as know most of them. One student in particular, FOOL*, is one of them. *Same student from December 8, 2011, entry.*

I asked Mr. Lawrence* why is FOOL* allowed to be in the hallways all day long. He said the administration is waiting to place him in an alternate program. I just shook my head. Fool* never went to the alternate program and stayed at JFK.
- ***FOOL* seldom went to classes for years and in June 2013 he graduated.***

**A personal aide** told me there was a big pow wow with administration and a few of the personal aides because there was a boy who pulled his pants down in front a female Special Ed student. I asked him to get me the kids and aides name. He said it is all hushed up. I asked if police were called in. He said, he doesn't know or think so. My next question was, does the young lady's parents know? He said it is all hushed up. I could never get or find any more info. Like he said, it was all hushed up.

**Mar 5** - speaking with a security guard, she said about 30 people were trying to enter the building by the back door next to the trailers. They all had Dominican masks covering their faces and were looking to start trouble. Shortly afterwards a student in my 1st period class was called to the office. When I spoke with him later that day, it was about what the security guard was telling me. Meanwhile I want to know what was done and what is being done to protect us all? As far as I know, NOTHING other than working hard to keep it hushed up. Many of the teachers I spoke with had no clue that this was going on.

**Mar 6** - have video of my principal talking in auditorium how the school is out of control, that there are too many intruders entering the building to start violence, create havoc and he wants to catch them.

**Mar 7 - 3rd period,** have video prior to class beginning and long after class has begun. What a disgusting mess and a disgrace this place is. To think the administration is supposed to have control of the building during HSPA. What's going to happen the rest of the day and testing days to come?

**Mar 8 – 20,** what's the point of writing anymore? SAME CRAP! I earn a living, but how much of it's being wasted on tax dollars spent here?

**Mar 21 - 2nd period,** one of my students told me he was taking a short cut home yesterday through a parking lot with two of his friends when three guys held him up at knife point. One of the thugs put the knife to him but didn't cut him. However, he did rough him up and knocked him around a little, then took his iPod. After he told me what had happened, I summoned one of the police officers to talk with him. The officer made a police report. After the police officer left, I asked my student where were his two friends? I said, something doesn't sound right, and I have a feeling they set you up. My students just stared at me. Either he just realized it now or was afraid I may say something else to the police officer. And I did!

**Mar ?-** as soon as we came back from Easter break, I asked my student if he went to the police station. He said yes and identified the kid that held him up. This thug's picture was in the system because he was picked up earlier and locked up for another crime. I was soooo happy that this story had a good ending.

**Mar 26 - 6th period.** I walked all around 1st & 2nd floor. I didn't stay in one spot. It's now 12:50 and the hallways are still filled with students. Where are the two heads of security or an administrator? I believe their philosophy is if we don't see any of this, it's not happening! Doesn't anybody view the surveillance camera tapes? I wish I had gone up to the 3rd floor too, I heard it was just as bad.

**Apr 2 -** as I was walking from the nurse's office a student was writing on the wall. The wall is right next to the building principals' offices as well as one of the *many new* administrators, Dr. Myers* office. I purposely walked between him and the wall and told the kid don't write on the wall. If you want to write on something write on your mother's kitchen table. Here's the best part, Dr. Myers* was standing right outside his door. He seen and heard everything. As I was walking away Dr. Myers* looks directly at me then turns, goes back into his office and closes the door. ABSOLUTELY USELESS!

**NOTE OF INTEREST: -** 2011 – 2012, is the first year of "RESTRUCTURING." Students went from actually working on construction sites, installing windows, doors, trim, stairs, risers, laying tile, installing shingles on a roof, putting up sheet rock, spackling, light electrical and plumbing work, fabricating large portable sheds (just like a modular home) that can be taken apart, packed on a trailer with all of the necessary tools and equipment, brought to the customer's home and reassembled. To where students are making wooden piggy banks just as they did in 1987 - 1991. Mr. Angelo Bonora the teacher and gentlemen loved by all students built this program up from nothing making the biggest POSITIVE change and advances to a Wood Shop Program in the entire school district of Paterson, using his vast knowledge and experience of construction and ingenuity was transferred. For whatever asinine reason, the students at JFK High School suffer again. In 2012 – 2014, the students now make dog and bird houses.

**Apr 2 & 3 -** recorded the last part of the announcements so you can hear a young lady say, "In the words of Principal Dickinson*, education is the key to life." How, when students are not in class?

**Apr 2 -** there were visitors from the state and county here at JFK to see and saw what is and has been going on. They were NOT pleased. Ever since then it seems that there are some administrators in the hallways and only because there are visitors here.

Even today, Thursday, April 5, administrators are in the hallway and just talking with students. It is now 9:04 and morning announcements are being conducted and the hallways are still filled with students. A security guard told me students are going to play man hunt. I said what the hell is that? She said students will be running around the building and not going to class. I said they do that every day. Bottom line this is proof students know nothing has been or will be done about them *not* attending class.

**Apr 4** - not one thing is done about students with poor attendance. I have students with over 30 days of absences and twice as much in cutting. So much for the districts mandatory 20-day attendance policy! In reality our school system is the reason for our students failing in life because they CANNOT hold a job. After all, school is a place of learning and look at what JFK has taught them. Students were taught and reinforced all bad and inappropriate behavior.

One more and *MOST IMPORTANT* thing, this is *NOT ALL STUDENTS* at JFK. Many students are good, hardworking, and conscientious and have done well here. However, even these students who did well were NOT brought up to their potential. If they transferred out in the junior or senior year, and went to another school district they would have NOT been up to par. They would be so far behind. That CANNOT be blamed on these students. However, it CAN and must be blamed on the *superintendents*, their administration, all of the commissioners of education and governors of New Jersey, ever since the state took over this district and right up to and including today.

**Apr 5** - wonder why things are this bad here? I just heard two security guards yell for students to keep walking. The students yelled back, "FUCK YOU, YOU KEEP WALKING AND MIND YOUR OWN MOTHER FUCKING BUSINESS!" The two guards just shook their heads. Why are students allowed to talk to anyone this way? How can you expect security to do their job if this behavior is ALLOWED?

**12:32 fire alarms go off again.** We evacuated building again. False alarm again! Received a video, you can hear the Fire Department, Police and Sheriff's Departments sirens, all coming to JFK and nothing will be reported in the newspaper, on TV and radio. If it was another district it would be plastered all over the place. Everything is hushed up. Thirty minutes later we were allowed to come back into the building and it was sheer chaos. You will see the same kids just walking around and around. Not one administrator in the hallway. To make it worse, there was testing going on the 2nd floor. At 1:59 someone came over the PA system asking for about a dozen kids to report back to testing. It was over 20 minutes and those students still did not show up or report back to their assigned testing place. This is exactly what I mean. I would have just failed them. But nooooooo, everything is overlooked. There is absolutely no discipline or responsibilities instilled in students and that's why things are the way they are here. The entire building is out of freaking control. Fights are breaking out all over the place.

**Apr 16 - 12:46, fire alarms go off again.** We evacuated the building. False alarm again! Students brought in water bottles and were throwing them all around, at one another, into classrooms, then decided to go outside to have a water fight so they pulled the alarm. Guarantee, nothing will be done about this. It is now 1:26 and the hallways are still filled with kids.

**Apr 30 - received video that starts just before the beginning of 6th period.** You will hear the horn to begin class. Hallways are filled with kids. You will not see one administrator. You will see a security guard attempting to bring a young lady into the security office. You can hear her yelling I want this guy fired. She is one of the biggest troublemakers and does only what she wants to do. She looks for teachers and security guards to do something she does not like and complains, yells, screams kicking up a fuss demanding them to be fired. The entire building is out of freaking control. There is a young man whipping young ladies with a belt. He will not stop. This is ALL on the surveillance cameras. You will hear the constant barrage of foul language. I do NOT understand how this insanity and out of control behavior is ALLOWED to continue nonstop, day after day all day long. On the 2nd floor, it is NO different. It too is so out of control. The very same boy from the 1st floor whipping students with the belt is now on the 2nd floor. HOW IN THE HELL IS THIS "RESTRUCTURING!"

**May 1 - UNFREAKINBELIEVABLE,** have a video just before the beginning of 6th period. You can hear the bell/horn to begin class. This place is out of control. Students are all over the place, like ants at a picnic. However, there WAS an administrator in the hallway. A tall woman in dark suit and she was telling students to get to class and let's move. However, students just ignored her. Then there was a tall gentlemen/administrator walking through the old art wing hallway and the entire wing was filled with students hanging out and sitting on the floor instead of being in class. He did absolutely nothing, just kept walking as if the students weren't even there.

If students were disciplined for doing something wrong that is supposed to be how they learn NOT to repeat the same infraction again. To talk and talk to these kids is a waste of time. Obviously if talking did any good, then why are they still in the hallways when the lady asked them all POLITELY without raising her voice to go to class? Secondly it is the month of *May*, students have been talked to since September.

**7th period,** a teacher Ms. Sweetness* called me. She was so upset. She said after I walked by she was so mad she decided to take her cell phone out to take pictures. That's when the same tall thin administrator who did and said absolutely nothing to any of those students in the old art wing hallway goes up to and tells Ms. Sweetness* she cannot take video and she is in trouble. Unbelievable!

The students can cause riots and the school is so dangerous but nooooooooooooo the administrators are more concerned in containing the TRUTH by keeping everything hushed up. Hundreds of thousands of dollars are wasted DAILY in this building by administrators allowing students NOT to go to class and get the education NJ taxpayers are paying for. I told Ms. Sweetness*to contact the president of the PEA immediately and if she was called into a meeting, do not talk unless you have a union rep and recommended a specific rep. I also told her the head janitor takes videos all the time of kids destroying and damaging school property. Then immediately calls Mr. Dickinson* to show him the videos. I have seen this myself and he has told me he does this. I also said if they want to make a big scene about this then you tell them that you *will* contact all the newspapers and will also show the governor. Obviously if they want to try to admonish you and not the students believe me, they do NOT want this info going out into the public showing what really goes on here *ALL YEAR LONG!*

**May 2 - all during 5th period** one of the retired Paterson police officers was standing outside my classroom. When, the bell/ horn rings to end 5th period he leaves, disappears. Now there is no supervision in the hallway. ALL of a sudden, all HELL BREAKS LOOSE; there's a massive gang fight. A few seconds later the other retired Paterson police officer and someone else comes running around the corner. First of all, what the hell is wrong with them? Why do they do a disappearing act as soon as the bell/horn rings to end class, especially when everyone knows that's when things really get out of hand? I cannot help but believe that they do NOT want to see anything. If they don't see anything, they don't have to get involved and no reports will be filled and once again hiding the "TRUTH" leaving the hallway a chaotic disaster. This is supposed to be "RESTRUCTURING."WE ARE RUINING A NATION!

**Our** students thought of something new to do in the hallways. Using extremely high pitch whistles they were blowing them making an awful screeching sound all day long. NOT one administrator made an effort to stop it. There is absolutely no control or anything remotely close to what an educational setting and atmosphere should be like here. After sitting back and thinking about everything I have documented there is NO WAY anybody will believe this! Like I said, subpoena all of us who have worked here.

**May 7 - 6th period,** same as always, hallways are a disaster filled with student's loooooooooooooooong after the horn to begin class Walked all through the 1st, 2nd & 3rd floors. They are absolutely disgusting. It reminded me of those movies about schools that are out of control. Now I work in one of those schools in a district that is operated and controlled by the State of New Jersey. Have video.

**May 8 - 6th period, UNFREAKINBELIEVABLE,** watching students being defiant to an administrator. GOOD, let them get a dose what we teachers have to put up with constantly. I cannot believe it; I actually see an administrator. He asked a student several times to move, go to class and remove his hat. The kid ignored him. Eventually the administrator goes over to remove the hat, the kid defiantly refuses, and you can see this kid is about to hit and start a fight with the administrator. The administrator just walks away, and the kid kept his hat on. Now this kid was just reinforced, that he can do whatever he wants, and they won't do anything to me. They cannot tell me what to do. Then this kid sees I'm watching so he tries to intimidate by staring me down in defiance. He realizes it is NOT going to work with me. Then this punk becomes defiant to Mr. Lawrence* a TAP who is really a good guy. Mr. Lawrence* says the same things, move, go to class and take off your hat. The punk ignores him. As Mr. Lawrence* is walking away this punk never moved, still defiantly standing in the same place with his hat on. Then he sticks his tongue out at him. I laughed and shook my head. There's really nothing more to say, this proves my point all along.

I went up to the 2nd floor it is the same thing, students everywhere and it is out of freaking control. In fact, the same punk Mr. Lawrence* was telling to get to class is now clowning around on the 2nd floor.

**Received a 14-minute video.** Notice students on the 2nd floor by the doorway of the stairwell. This out of control behavior does not stop. They refuse to listen to a security guard and kept on screaming and using foul language. Went back to the 1st floor, saw Mr. Dickinson*. This is the first time I have seen him in weeks. Nevertheless, he did nothing to control the students in the hallway. He walked through and acted as if this is the way it's supposed to be and the hallways remained filled with kids long afterwards.

**May 9 - 1st period, UNFREAKINBELIEVABLE!** Kids are still pouring into the building. They are all major LATE. Yet they walk in eating drinking coffee or soda and mosey around the hallways instead of being swept up for not being late but cutting. This is the end of 1st period. For all I know they may have belonged here for zero period which starts at 7:30? Bottom line the administration does not care. OBVIOUSLY, ATTENDANCE, LATENESSES AND CUTTING are not being documented. If they were, it would be off the grid even by last year's standards. However, teachers are to be held responsible for student's achievement and are questioned if students fail. Meanwhile it's the administration who allows students *not* to go to class. They would rather have students in the hallways, stairwells, bathrooms, anyplace and everyplace else instead of where they belong, which is being in class *learning*.

**May 9 -** I was told by the science teacher in room 107, she was to have a working lab. However, PEOSH was in the building today inspecting and checking out all the infractions pertaining to her room. NOW, I understand why Mr. Dickinson* was in the hallway yesterday 5/8 and going in and out of room 107. He wasn't there because of the students. He was there because of PEOSH! Let's see how he covers this up?

**9:58 -** I watched a truant officer bring in three young ladies to the security office. NOW, if there is a truant officer for students who didn't or don't go to school, then don't we need them to be here picking up students who are continuously in hallways, stairwells, bathrooms, any and every other place in this building and constantly truant to their classes?

**I sent this and the above 3 entries to the president of the PEA via email.** I have copies of all email.

**8th period -** you can somewhat see and definitely hear looooooooooooong after the horn sound for students to be in class there's a girl and boy by rooms 108 and 109 boxing. Eventually the guy picked her up and put her to the floor. Bottom line they should be in class. *THIS IS NEGLECT & TRUANCY!*
I went upstairs and it was actually pretty good. Then again it was 8th period. Many students had left. Came back down to the 1st floor and the same kids are standing in the stairwell and doorway, acting up. A security guard is leaning up against the wall telling them to go, but the kids ignore him. Have video.

**May 11 -** it is homeroom. It wasn't as bad as usual, but you'll see what I see at my desk - students not attending homeroom, just hanging out, and walking around talking in the hallway. Nothing is being done about student's attendance, cuts and lateness. You hear the last part of the announcements, "in the words of our principal education is the key to life!" Every day it's said, and every day students are in the hallways and not in class. The horn sounds for students to GO to 2nd period. 4 minutes later you hear the horn again for class to start. Typically, and as always, the hallways remained filled with students hanging out. Not one administrator is present to make them go to class. One of my students is always in the hallways and has NOT been to class in weeks. In a few weeks WATCH all of the administrators go crazy trying to do what they can so students will pass and graduate. It's coming down to crunch time and they want the numbers up for graduation. Then they will be pleading with teachers what can students do to pass? As always, I say, "NOTHING, they haven't been in class 30, 40, 50 PLUS days, same amount in cuts and if they do show up they are late." Have video.

**3rd period -** you can hear the horn that indicates the beginning of class. No one is going to class. Students fill the entire hallways. Many of them are just walking in and out of classrooms as if it is a night club. Do they belong in these classes? No one knows and no one cares. It doesn't matter; students can do whatever they want. As I was going up the stairs about 100 plus students came flying down. Either someone is after them or they were going to start a fight. This place is sooooooooooooo dangerous and out of control. *This is restructuring? This is what taxpayer's dollars went for as improvements in education here at JFK?* I finally made it to the 2nd floor and it is so out of control. Students were all over the place. Hallways were filled with students and not one administrator to be seen. As I walked down the hallway there wasn't even an administrator in their office. Where the hell can they be HIDING?

As I made my way around the corner there was a police officer. He was the only person trying to secure some type of order and especially with this one kid in particular. This punk was so fresh, nasty, foul mouth and defiant. When the officer told him to go to class and to get out of here, the kid said he doesn't have to, he's passing all of his classes, with A's & B's. I said to myself, Yeah right! If he is, it's because he probably has new teachers who don't want to lose their job for failing students. (This is just a guess but then again, if a student does not go to class how can they pass?) Then the cop said, "If I was your parent, I would beat your ass." All this time I never saw an administrator or the heads of security. Have video.

**I sent the last three entries via email to the President of the PEA as documentation.
I am sending email to the PEA & NJEA to continue creating and documenting my own paper trail.**
**May 14 –** I took a quick walk around. NO CHANGE, not as if I expected it. Kids are all over the place and NOT one administrator to be seen. PLUS, there are 3 or 4 field trips so many students are out of the building today. There is still no reason for anyone to be in the hallways. In fact, the nurse was walking by me and she said at her kid's school you don't see anyone in the hallways after the bell rings. I have been in my room for 6 or 7 minutes now and the hallway is filled with girls cursing, screaming and carrying on. What's going to happen when the results come back from the state exam and the scores are not favorable? *DOESN'T REALLY MATTER, THEY HAVE THE TEACHERS TO BLAME!*

### May 15, 2012, I sent in an e-mail to the president of the PEA.
**Subject: UNBELIEVABLE**
**DURING 6th PERIOD**, (Have video), this is absolutely the worse. The video is self-explanatory. At one point I was standing in the old art wing. I just happened to move and a bottle came flying by. If I didn't move, I would have been hit either in the head or face. I knew who did it, but with all the students in the hallways and it being so out of control I had to keep quiet or risked getting seriously hurt. I know in my heart if I said anything god only knows what would have happened. I had no support and the entire wing filled with students would have turned on me. WHY should I have to be afraid to walk the hallways in a school? Why should the hallways in a school be so out of control, dangerous and confrontational? Why wasn't this seen on the surveillance cameras? Why are students allowed to be in the hallways continuously all day, every day?

Have video. It starts seconds before the bell / horn sounded for ALL students to be in class. It starts 12:14) and stops at 12.32. For 18 minutes the hallways were still filled and students just walking and hanging out all over the place. You will NOT see any administrators. Earlier you do see and hear one of the two heads of security as he walks over to security office. Meanwhile the hallways remained filled with students hanging out, drinking and eating instead of being in class. There were bottles, food, wrappers all over the place and worse they are on the stairs where someone could get hurt or killed. I want to know how do you *know* students do not have alcohol in the drinks? There is no reason for any student to walk around from class to class with drinks or anything to eat. As I was walking up to the 2nd floor, there was a young lady getting ready to drop a bottle down to the first floor. Luckily, I saw it and it wasn't me. This is exactly what I mean about security. If the head of security was around, then this shouldn't and wouldn't be happening and it would be proactive not reactive.
I am also sick and tired of hearing how NJEA HELPS MAKE PUBLIC SCHOOL GREAT!
Come here NJEA, make your office here if things are sooooooooooooooooooo GREAT!
THIS PLACE IS ABSOLUTELY HORRIBLE.
THE NEW JERSEY TAXPAYERS ARE GETTING SO SCREWED AND THE TEACHERS WHO HAVE TO WORK IN THESE CONDITIONS ARE BEING SACRIFICED.

### May 15, 2012, I sent an e-mail to the president & vice president of the PEA & a representative of the NJEA. Below is a narrative.
The behavior in this building would never ever be tolerated any place in public a setting.
A custodian is cleaning the hallway all day because it is filled with food, bottles, wrappers, garbage not to mention ketchup, mustard and mayonnaise and its aluminum packet from the cafeteria.
FREE LUNCH, yet it is thrown all over the place and they do not have to pick it up.
Taxpayers are being killed paying for all of this while a public school is encouraging this behavior by allowing it to go on unabated.
This is not setting an example? We are not teaching and reinforcing right and wrong!

A student is screaming I mean absolute screaming right now at the top of her lungs FUCK YOU, FUCK ALL OF YOU, I DON'T CARE, FUCK, FUCK, FUCK!
As an administrator was walking by and did nothing.
Now other students will follow and do the same.
A major lawsuit is in order. What the heck are we waiting for?
NJEA, WHY ARE YOU ABANDONING US?
END

### May 15, 2012, I sent another e-mail to the president & vice president of the PEA & a representative of the NJEA to give them on the spot report of what I am seeing. Now everything is actually being documented. With every email I send, now there's a paper trail. Narrative to follow.

Two big fights! One was in the cafeteria with girls. Hair all over the place! No one is suspended or arrested. What happened to ZERO TOLERANCE TO VIOLENCE?
As for bullying, why can't students be arrested for bullying teachers and staff?
Bottom line, there is NO LAW AND ORDER HERE. Cops are standing here shaking their heads.
JFK is nothing more than a money pit to the taxpayers.
Only certain students are suspended for not wearing uniforms when most of the students do NOT?
During testing, the people of SRA where doing what they can to get a student to pass and graduate. This fine upstanding young gentleman became obscenely obnoxious and gave Ms. Huwiggins* a bad time and was more than disrespectful and filled with foul language.
This is the mindset here, students know they don't have to do anything, and they will graduate.
We just push them out and doctor up everything. The idea of working for something is not instilled here.
The message here is, it is a right to have everything given to you
It is 2:34, the bell rang minutes ago, the hallways are filled with kids and not one administrator is around. Students are actually wrestling and rolling around on the floor.
END

### May 16, 2012, I sent another email to the president & vice president of the PEA & a representative of the NJEA, adding to the paper trail. Below is a narrative

Something is going on. One of the (2) building principals along with (2) of the heads of security are in the hallways. My guess is we are getting visitors? I haven't seen the principal since last week. It was easy to spot him because he has a brand-new suit on. It looks as if some of the security guards are actually rounding up students and bringing them into the security office. Our poor security guards take such abuse. The foul language and the verbal threats are atrocious, and nothing is done about it.

There's a kid right now yelling at the top of his lungs, "SUCK MY DICK!" and he keeps yelling it over and over. NOTHING IS BEING DONE ABOUT IT. Everybody acts as if this is normal.
I do not understand how this can be allowed let alone tolerated; ESPECIALLY being that this school and District is a State Takeover, Run and Operated School District.

The bell just rang to go to 6th period. It is absolutely worse than any street corner and you do not see the now (3) heads of security people, or the principal. I guess he doesn't want to get his new suit dirty by students throwing something at him. AND this is exactly the time when their presence is most necessary.

It's about 30 minutes later and the rest of the day is so out of freaking control.
One more thing Mr. (Omitted NJEA reps name), I'm not the only one who feels that the NJEA has abandon us. Everybody here feels, NJEA has abandoned us and only cares about suburban schools.

An entire year has been wasted and out of those who do graduate how many SHOULD NOT?
WE ARE DUMBING DOWN AND RUINING A NATION.
THIS IS ALL UNACCEPTABLE.
END

### May 18, 2012, I sent another email to the president & vice president of the PEA & a representative of the NJEA, adding to the paper trail. Below is a narrative.

I explained during 6th period and late 7th I had 3 videos showing the schools out of control conditions.
Shows 2 administrators Stevenson* and Little* who both did nothing to get students to go to class.
You'll see Mr. Dickinson* in the wing by the entrance to the auditorium when and where a boy was yelling by the stairwell cursing how he is going to fuck up some girl or girls.
I said there is so much commotion going on you can't focus on anything.

You hear one girl as she is walking in the hallway talking on the phone about a situation and nobody was suspended.

I finished up with Taxpayers are constantly being screwed with the money allotted to each student for a free public education. The administration I believe does this on purpose and now taxpayers have to pay for "BUY BACK PROGRAMS," "TWILIGHT PROGRAMS," and NOW COMING UP "SUMMER SCHOOL." Taxpayers are paying and paying, and the governor is telling them it's the teachers' fault. This is a state run & operated school district.     THIS IS NEGLECT, NEGLECT, NEGLECT!
SOMEONE HAS TO BE HELD ACCOUNTABLE.
END

**May 21, 2012, I sent an email to the president & vice president of the PEA & a representative of the NJEA, adding to the paper trail. Below is a narrative**

It is the same stuff. Have more video. Nothing changes I am just keeping up with my paper trail that the administration keeps hushed up. In fact, kids are now coming from the old art wing along with Mr. Dickinson*. The kids were really acting up and obviously not in class. Mr. Dickinson* yells to get to class, let's go, but kept on walking and students remain in the hallways acting up. Eventually, it just got worse and worse. Mr. Jim* and a security guard arrive. The security guard blew his whistle and the kids laughed. THE END, nothing else was done about it. I asked again, how can teachers be held responsible, if one of the principals of the building does absolutely nothing?
END

**May 22, 2012, I sent an email to the president & vice president of the PEA & a representative of the NJEA, adding to the paper trail.    Below is a narrative.**

I let them know the administration is showing a video in the auditorium that has NOT been released to the public (boot leg version) "THE AVENGERS" that's dubbed in Greek! I guess laws don't apply to JFK. The auditorium is just like the rest of the building out of control. Students, 100s of them, are in there because of testing. So much for making sure students get a good education, not to mention losing time to prepare for the up and coming Final Exams.

Oh silly me, it doesn't matter here. Everyone graduates and gets passed to the next level.
END

**May 22, 2012, this is the second email I sent to PEA & NJEA about the videotaping with more details and continuing with my own paper trail.    Below is a narrative.**

I wrote telling them I have terrible video but good audio of the auditorium. Then, as I was walking out of the auditorium, I was talking with one of the counselors. He too is so disgusted with everything going on here and even made the remark, "this is restructuring?"

Meanwhile the same kids are in the hallway, (can't see them or not to well) but you can hear them. You will hear the counselor saying to a young lady, every day all day long you're in the hallway. I told him about one of my female students who has 76 cuts and is a senior. I told her if I was the principal, I would not allow you to graduate. That's the point. Everybody can and will graduate.

You will also hear two other girls cursing up a storm and yelling at who or whomever.

Bottom line, the audio tells it all.

Why is this allowed to carry on every day, all day long without any recourse or anybody to stop this?
THIS IS ILLEGAL!  THERE ARE MAJOR LAWSUITS A WAITING!
END

**May 22, 2012, I sent an e-mail to the president & vice president of the PEA & a representative of the NJEA, adding to the paper trail.    Below is a narrative.**

Have a video. You can hear the horn sound to BEGIN 6th period. The students will not move. Mr. Stevenson* was in the hallway and only for a short time. However, you will notice the kids ignored him.

He tells them to move, saying ladies, ladies, where do you belong, go to class on and on. All they did was move a few feet and resume with their conversation and foul mouths. You'll see a student storm out of the security office and a woman I assume a security guard followed and apprehended him.

I went to the 2$^{nd}$ floor and it was out of control. Students were walking in and out of class as class is and has been in session. Came back down and the same section of the old art wing you see the very same kids just acting up and no administrators.

There is absolutely no supervision here. The hallways are filled, and I mean filled, with students screaming. How can any teacher be held responsible for students who do NOT and are allowed not to attend class?
Yet students will pass and graduate. Am I the only one that sees this as being wrong?
Why isn't anything being done about this?
The NJ taxpayers have to see that their tax dollars are being flushed down the toilet.
As I continue typing, I am recording the hallways are still filled and you can hear all of the noise.
When are we going to get help? How long does it take to stop this?
An entire period shot again! An entire year shot, wasted and nobody did anything to help?
There must be another food fight or something going on in the cafeteria right now.
END

**May 22, approximately 9:00am -** I received a reply from the president of the PEA about the Bootleg Video. He said he sent an email to one of the assistant superintendents saying, pretty much (copying and pasting) what I had written to him.

He received a reply from the assistant superintendent thanking him and said she will reach out to Mr. Dickinson*.
As with ALL email, I still have the originals in my files.

**May 22 -** later that day, Ms. Sweetness* was telling me she is so disgusted and angry the way this place is always soooo out of freaking control and then started talking about the Bootleg Video. She was so upset she went to one of the heads of security saying the movie isn't released yet and it is illegal to show it. The jackass replied, "It's only illegal if you are caught purchasing the video." She blew up and was even more upset with that remark. I told her I sent 2 email to the president of the PEA about this and if nothing was wrong, then why did the administration all of a sudden stopped showing it? We just shook our heads, kept talking how disgusting this place is and especially with all of the added administrators in this building, why do they allow this place to be so out of control every day, all day long.

**May 23 -** I was told that a male student shot another student (girl) in the arm with a BB gun on a school bus. During the investigation, the student who shot the girl made accusations against the investigating Police Officer Lt. Mike Recca. The student who shot the young lady complained, trying to make LT. Recca look as if he was doing something wrong because he spoke HARSH to him. It also appears because of this incident, Lt. Mike Recca was banned from working security at JFK. Can you imagine he was banned for doing his job, protecting students, and in retaliation for NOT protecting the false image that is constantly portrayed by the District Administration and the school administrators here at JFK? In fact, he is NOT the ONLY police officer who was banned in retaliation from JFK for doing their job.
The boy with the BB gun was never arrested because the action stayed within the school & school district. Thankfully, Lt. Recca was exonerated because once again, the administration did NOT want to go through the Police Department because there would have to be an ACTUAL paper trail/police report. That would also mean that the student with the BB gun would have been arrested.

Bottom line, the district, and JFK wanted it squashed and hushed up.

> *__This started to make me think of more questions.__*
> - What happened to or with the girl that was shot?
> - Did the young lady's parents know, get involved and pressed charges?
> - Did the bus driver get involved and or pressed charges?
> - Did the bus company press charges?
> - Lastly, I wanted to know if that boy the shooter was allowed to still use the bus.
> - That, I received an answer for! *"YES!"*

**May 23 -** Police found a gun outside the school. Not on school grounds but close to the school itself.

## May 23, 2012, I sent an email to the president & vice president of the PEA & a representative of the NJEA, adding to the paper trail.   Below is a narrative

**It is 11:11,** almost the end of 4th period. I just came back from the Phys. Ed Department. There were exactly 24 students (only 1 wearing a uniform) in the hallway all bunched up gathered around, banging on lockers, jumping, wrestling cursing and yelling.
If the administration can't enforce the simplest of rules, then how do we expect them to have control of the building?
It should ALL be on the school surveillance VIDEO.
Why can't the PEA get copies of the school surveillance videos?

Two years ago, the entire district had a staff meeting at William Paterson College. The Superintendent told us how things were going to change. It will be about education. If any student refuses to follow rules they will NOT be denied an education, but they will be removed from the school population so as not to **infect** the rest of the students. He also said, **all rules** will be enforced and on and on and on.

I said the PEA should get a copy of that video.
Then I commented about this is supposed to be "RESTRUCTURING"? With the school being so out of control is this the reason why, all of us teachers had to go through a hiring process in order to keep our jobs such as; fill out an application, get references, submit resumes and have an interview?
I suggested that the PEA have all JFK staff fill out and submit an evaluation for the school.
Including comments explaining what is going on.
Then have the PEA, send a copy to the superintendent, NJEA, the commissioner of education and Governor. Do this for ALL Paterson Public Schools. We start creating our own paper trail.  **END**

## May 25, 2012 - I sent an email to the president & vice president of the PEA & a representative of the NJEA, adding to the paper trail.          Below is a narrative.

Did you know that JFK's Prom is June 6th?
Did you know the first day of FINAL EXAMS at JFK is June 7th?
Hope everyone has a Great Memorial Day Weekend.
This is why we are celebrating to remember our veterans and especially those who gave their lives for our FREEDOM and a right to a freeeee public education, while JFK is out of freakin control!
END

**May 29 -** testing for freshman and sophomores to see if they need special HSPA classes. I have to laugh, all day after the testing was over students were in the hallways all day long, not in uniform and wearing flip flops. I expect it to be worse tomorrow, because it is another day of testing. Testing, testing, testing, that's all students have been doing for months. If students were made to be in class, we wouldn't have or need for all this testing. It doesn't matter, students here don't have to go to class, just attend their testing, in which they show up 30 to 60 minutes late and are still allowed to be tested. Meanwhile these students are not in class preparing or going over their work for next week's final exam. Isn't that important too?

**May 30, 2012 - I sent an email to the president & vice president of the PEA & a representative of the NJEA, adding to the paper trail.** **Below is a narrative.**

Subject: Why has this gone on an entire school year?
Testing is over, homeroom is in session, yet the hallways are PACKED. Not one administrator to be seen. During testing I had 14 students. They were really well-behaved. However, 7 were wearing uniforms. The hallway as I am typing this doesn't look as if anyone has their uniforms on.
Also, speaking with a teacher this morning, he said last week he called security to come and remove all the students in the hallway between rooms 117 & 118. He said the area was FILLED with students cutting class, hanging out and pitching quarters. Security arrived and said, what do you want us to do? If we pick them up, we are told only to let them go? It is worse than any street corner here. Is this what veterans fought and died for? Is this what taxpayers pay taxes for?

As of right now, the front hallway has increased by 200 hundred more students just hanging out, yelling and screaming. How has attendance supposedly improved, if students are not in homeroom?
I said again that we should get a copy of the superintendent speech at William Paterson College making all the promises about how things will be in Paterson Public Schools and catching him in all of these lies!
END

A little later I sent them all another email, an addendum stating,
It's 11:12 and supposed to be 4th period and the hallways are still out of freakin' control and no administrators seen. Several young ladies should not be allowed in the building the way they are dressed. They look as if they are getting ready to either go to bed or just woke up.
Why are the hallways cleared during testing but just days prior to final exam, why are students allowed to be in hallways instead of being in classes preparing for their exams?
Why can't there be a class action or civil lawsuit?
All teachers and police who work at JFK and especially those who were made to leave because the administration did not want them to be involved in some of the situation could be subpoenaed.
END

**May 30, 2012 - I received an email from a case worker about one of my students.**
This email had my name and all of the names of teachers failing this senior/student for poor attendance.
Subject: Progress Report
Good Afternoon,
I am the Case Manager for the classified student listed below. In order to complete their IEP I am in need of a current Progress Report from you. Please email me a brief summary of the students' status in your class. If you have any questions, please feel free to contact me at ext. 50167.
Student: (Name omitted)
Thank you,
Ms. (Name omitted)
CST Case Manager / JFK Education Complex
END

**NOTE OF INTEREST:** - I want to make it perfectly clear it is May 30, 2012, and this is the *first* time all year this person who is supposed to be his case worker has contacted me. WHY, because he is failing, and he is a SENIOR!

**Here is my reply to the case worker.**
RE: Progress Report (Progress Reports = Warning Notices, same thing, different words)
Good Afternoon (Name omitted),
Mr. (Students name omitted) WILL FAIL. One needs to come to class in order to pass.
**TOTAL ABSENTS (79)**     **CUTS (76)**     **LATES (29)**
Why he hasn't been suspended for his POOR ATTENDANCE AND CUTTING is unacceptable!
ATTACHED are his record/s.

Thank you and most respectfully,

Lee E McNulty (Metal Shop 114)     ex. 50114
                                    END

## May 30, 2012- I sent an email to the president & vice president of the PEA & a representative of the NJEA adding to the paper trail.     Below is a narrative.
Subject: AN IDEA
Why don't we have all teachers turn in their attendance for every class at the end of the year? Let's see if the absents, cuts and lateness match with what the school/s and Superintendent's office have and send in to the state?
We all know it will not correlate with what the teachers have.
*Example-*
My 4th period class changes every marking period.
Here is the information I have for 1st, 2nd & 3rd marking periods.
I had a total of **50** students.
**Total absences (371)**     **Cuts (103)**     **Lates (84)**
Fourth Marking Period I have 1 student, who has never showed up.
                                    END

## May 31, 2012 - I sent an email to the president & vice president of the PEA & a representative of the NJEA, adding to the paper trail.     Below is a narrative.
Subject: ADDENDUM
At 1:27, I'm speaking with Dave* and he's was really upset. As he was talking, he was talking loud (meaning in the video) because he wanted everybody to hear. He also said, he and Mr. Jim* a TAP have been suspending students only to be rescinded by the building principal.
Dave* and all of our security guards are so disgusted.
Today is worse than ever. If having all of these students in the hallways NOT dangerous, then what is?
Mr. Stevenson* is by the elevator with a BIG coffee playing with the kids. Not making them go to class.

I also forgot, in my last email on the 2nd floor a female teacher was asking for a security guard because there were students that did not belong in her class and would not leave. Furthermore, she was Spanish and these students especially this one boy who is in the hallway all day, every day, all year was making fun of her and her Spanish. If this young man graduates, I want to know how because he is never, ever, do you understand *never,* in class.
As I am getting ready to send this, kids are throwing plastic bottles at each other.
I feel so helpless. This is so wrong, and it goes on and on and on.
Also have 6th period video & documentation. You'll hear the wood shop teacher saying how bad his 4th period students are. I know because I had them last marking period. He said they told him that they aren't going to do anything and don't care if they fail. I replied you better fail them. He said he is. We'll see!

Then 9th period, I went to the gym to drop off and pick up some equipment I fixed and to work on. Kids were still all over the place hanging out and playing. No security/No administration.
However, on my way back to my classroom, I see an administrator Mr. Little* in the middle of the school, standing there with hands crossed as everything all around was going berserk.

END

**Jun 1, around 10:00** -no administrators or the heads of security? Went to the 2nd floor absolutely - disgusting, it was wall to wall students and still no administrators. I couldn't take it and wanted to get out of here, so I went back down to my room. I do not want to be exposed to this nonsense anymore. I am freaking tired and the noise is exhausting. Meanwhile, New Jersey taxpayers will now pay BIG BUCKS for CREDIT RECOVERY because the administration did NOT allow students to attend class.

I had enough and started again just prior to the horn sound for 6th period. The video shows it all. Bottom line - all day it just kept on getting worse. I guess students don't have to go to class to review for final exams because the administration will always give them credit recovery. And the New Jersey taxpayers will have to pay MORE now so teachers and administrators can be paid overtime because of credit recovery. New Jersey Taxpayers just pays and pays. As I walked from the 1st floor to the 2nd floor and back down to the first you will NOT see one administrator or the heads of security!

I started again right after the horn sound to begin 8th period and the hallways are a mess, complete chaos and disrespect. You'll even see several times the three heads of security walking around. The reason is because *Congressman Pascrell and former President Clinton* are coming to JFK's auditorium to speak. Even with these high-profile people coming, the school is STILL out of control. I guess it doesn't matter because the Congressman and Mr. Clinton will be here hours *AFTER* school is OUT. I went to the 2nd floor and even went to the opposite side of the building where there should be nobody in the building and who do I see, the (3) Heads of Security and so are the students. Have video.

**June 15, 2012 - I sent another email to the president & vice president of the PEA & a representative of the NJEA, adding to the paper trail. Below is a narrative.**
*I omitted the rest of the email because it was the same as the last few email sent.

WE ARE RUINING A NATION

How much did it cost for this so-called restructuring?<br>
As of June 15, 2012, here are my numbers / statistics, compared with the year 2010 - 2011

2010- 2011 TOTAL ABSENCES, CUTS, TARDIES & STUDENTS

| | | | |
|---|---|---|---|
| 1ST Period | Absents 44 | Lates 30 | Cuts 23 @ 4 Total students |
| 2nd Period | Absents 176 | Lates 86 | Cuts 57 @ 38 Total students |
| 4th Period | Absents 154 | Lates 32 | Cuts 8 @ 29 Total students |
| 5th Period | Absents 668 | Lates 97 | Cuts 203 @ 20 Total students |
| 6th Period | Absents 410 | Lates 95 | Cuts 134 @ 19 Total students |
| 9th Period | Absents 440 | Lates 131 | Cuts 164 @ 17 Total students |
| **Grand total:** | **Absents 1892** | **Lates 471** | **Cuts 589 @ 127 Total students** |

### 2011- 2012 TOTAL ABSENCES, CUTS, TARDIES & STUDENTS
### RESTRUCTURING YEAR

| | | | |
|---|---|---|---|
| 1ST Period | Absents 545 | Lates 134 | Cuts 288 @ 12 Total students |
| 2nd Period | Absents 378 | Lates 89 | Cuts 153 @ 15 Total students |
| 4th Period | Absents 400 | Lates 84 | Cuts 127 @ 51 Total students |
| 5th Period | Absents 452 | Lates 65 | Cuts 95 @ 24 Total students |
| 7th Period | Absents 122 | Lates 24 | Cuts 40 @ 11 Total students |
| 9th Period | Absents 32 | Lates 10 | Cuts 9 @ 3 Total students |
| **Grand total:** | **Absents 1929** | **Lates 406** | **Cuts 712 @ 116 Total students** |

I am not telling you these stories and information as a teacher who actually witnesses what goes on here at JFK, but as a *New Jersey taxpayer!*

In 2011- 2012 the very last week of school there was "CREDIT RECOVER" conducted by Dr. Myers*.
When I submit my grades, I print them out.
My attendance does NOT jive with the district computer printout. Naturally mine are greater.
Even still if you look at the attendance or should I say absences the numbers are 20, 30, 40, 50 as much as 80 + days absent and nothing was done about it and students still *PASSED AND GRADUATED!*
END

**Jun 20** - a student was finally kicked out of school (name omitted), and only because he and a female student where caught in stairwell while she was giving/performing Oral Sex on him. This student and his posse were continuously in the hallways all day, every day, all year for years. He never went to class, was always in trouble, fighting, mostly causing and starting it and the list just goes on. This IDIOT would constantly threaten teachers and get away with it. If a teacher wrote him up or complained, it was ALWAYS ignored. He was one of many students who constantly walked in and out of classrooms he did not belong in along with his jackass friends/followers which were growing constantly. HOWEVER, because of this sexual incident he was finally removed from school. Where did he go? Or what happened after that? Once again it was all hushed up! If it weren't for some students and teachers telling me, I would have never known! How many other staff members are not aware of this? If she was a minor shouldn't there been a police report? Shouldn't he have been arrested? Bottom line, if these two kids were NOT allowed to be in the hallways this would have never happened. This is only what I know/found out! Can you imagine how much that goes on here that I / *we don't know* and is and has been hushed up? Worse than that, neither does the parents and the guardians who send their children here.

**Jun?** - just prior to graduation a building principal was being screamed and cursed at by a student. She did nothing and allowed it to go on as it continued in the center of the building in front of every student, security, teachers, and Paterson police officers. As usual that student was not disciplined and was still allowed to attend their graduation. Obviously, students are rewarded for poor, inappropriate, unacceptable and dysfunctional behavior here. Meanwhile this showed all of those other students that they too can act this way to the principal of the building and will get away with it. It was absolutely disgusting!

**June 21** - have a video documentation of the last day of school when the Act Academy principal is speaking about the school year.

I am absolutely beat, exhausted, burnt out and dread going back in September!
I really can't be subjected to this out of control and state of lawlessness here at JFK anymore!

## 2012 – 2013 SCHOOL YEAR
## 2ND YEAR OF RESTRUCTURING

**September 4, 2012** - first day back to school, just teachers. Now the entire perimeter is enclosed by a 10-foot fence. What a waste of money. When we have to evacuate the building, where are the students going to go? TWO PLUS THOUSAND students will now be standing next to the building and the parking lot which will make it dangerous for the police and fire departments to get through. Absolutely ridiculous! Doesn't anybody ever think things through? Meanwhile students/seniors do not have textbooks!

We were told for the 2012 – 2013 school year there WILL be less school suspensions. Already students will know that they will NOT be punished or discipline. It will be another freaking joke here. All to say JFK has improved. By NOT filling out reports, NOT documenting what *truly* goes on here all in the manipulation of numbers and statistics is LYING and illegal.

EXAMPLE: ISS = In School Suspension. NO MORE. It is still ISS but they now call it, In School Support. Already the administration is playing political games with names/semantics with words.

NOW 2012 – 2013 we are back to having a cut office. However, each academy (4) will have their own, instead of having one cut and tardy office like we use to. That means more teachers will be taking care of cuts then what we had originally prior to this restructuring. First of all, there should be no cutting at all especially when there are now 17 assigned administrators for discipline compared to when we only had 7 prior to RESTRUCTURING.

We were also told that attendance will be closely monitored. Administration said you know how students leave for a few months or so and come back and pick up where they left off! There will be accountability for their attendance. Once again *supposedly,* because that's not what the principal said on 12/16/11!

**Sept 5, 2012,** speaking with Ms. White* a guidance counselor, she said this place is unbelievable and CANNOT believe the students who graduated. She said she had so many students who were not supposed to graduate and this was back in March. There was no way, no how, they could have graduated and yet they DID GRADUATE! She said she couldn't believe it and is so disgusted. Then she said what can I do, I'll just come in and whatever happens, happens. There is nothing more I can do.

**During our meeting** the administration said teachers will be held accountable. If students do NOT progress (pass), it will reflect on our evaluations. We were also told the state exam reflects 50% towards our evaluation and the other 50% reflects on the teacher? They are making it so teachers are the escape goats for students who do NOT do their work, do not come to class, who have poor attendance, whose parents do not care and to make the superintendent look good by passing BLAME onto teachers. Does this mean teachers will now *HAVE* to pass students to protect their careers? Teachers brought up that many to most of our students are between a 4th and 5th grade level. The principal replied, "and even lower in some cases." Then why are these students in high school? You CANNOT expect High School teachers to be held responsible for teaching *13 years* of school in 4 years and then be held accountable if they fail?

**Sept 6, 8:07 am - here we go, the very first day of school for students**, I am watching police, security and administrators running out the front door because there was a BIG FIGHT ALREADY. As I watched from my classroom, NO ONE was brought into the security office. It was squashed and hushed up already. The school day and year hasn't begun yet. We still had 8 more minutes before the bell rang to begin the NEW SCHOOL YEAR. *WELCOME TO JOHN F. KENNEDY EDUCATIONAL COMPLEX!*

Mary* a security guard had some problems today with students running around the entire building. She tried to call for back up but like last year her walkie-talkie didn't work. Again, just like last year and on the very first day of school, chaos and the state of being out of control prevails. I don't understand it, with the supposedly new surveillance camera system in the building, why doesn't anyone see this and STOP IT? Plus, why don't the walkie-talkies work it is only the first day of school?

Sept 7 - 1st period and all during homeroom, already students are gathering, hanging out in hallways, stairwells and bathrooms. They are walking into school late, any time, but not on time, not wearing uniforms, wearing hats, carrying drinks, eating food, throwing wrappers, spitting on the floor and just taking their sweet time as if they are taking a stroll in the park. No one makes them get to class or writes them up for being late. Oh yeah, NO PAPER TRAIL, silly me. The administration has to show everything has improved and is better now. However, IF we don't stop this right away, this year will be lost too!

**Sep. 7, 2012 - today is the first time I checked my work email.**
There was an email from my principal Mr. Baker* dated August 29, 2012.
Below, is the last paragraph of his email, explaining why he chose to resign and leave the district.

"Unfortunately, throughout the course of the year many decisions were made that affected our ability **to provide the best educational environment for our students.** We as a team were able to prevail and surmount all obstacles before us. However, decisions continued to be made (without consultation) that jeopardized not only our success, **but our students' ability to succeed and maintain their trajectory.** Such decisions lead me to question Paterson's dedication to excellence. If such decisions were made that support personal agendas and "adult issues" over the best interests of the students of Paterson, I could no longer (in good conscious) sit by the wayside and witness our students' being wronged and our successes and sacrifices being dismissed. After much thought and despair, I came to the conclusion that I must resign as the Director of the School of Architecture and Construction Trades. I will undoubtedly miss each and every one of you and can't thank you enough for your belief in me. Each of you shares a special place in my heart.

As always, I thank you for all your hard work and dedication and I will always make myself readily available for any of your needs." **END**

Sept 18 - I was looking over the new John F. Kennedy Educational Complex Handbook to see all the administrators. There were 23. That is NOT including those who are in administration. but they are called students teacher coordinators. They do not teach any classes. They are NOT like guidance Counselors or those who work in scheduling, these people are administrators, and have administrative duties.

With all these NEW people how many millions of dollars more are the taxpayers paying now for the so-called change here in PATERSON, NJ? This State Takeover Run and Operated and UNCONTROLLED School District is nothing more than a bottomless, MONEY PIT.

Sept 18 - already the administration is covering up incidents using the old rule of thumb, if it isn't written down, then it never happened. That is exactly what has been going on here and looks like it will be continuing again this year but to a higher degree. This administration must cover up and hush it all up to make it appear as if everything is going smooth here!

**Below is a copy of a discipline report.** This student was only in my class maybe a total of 2 minutes before I removed him. All they did was assigned him ISS. As I predicted he never showed up. The next day the head of Guidance told me she is having him transferred back to YES ACADEMY, whatever the hell that is and supposedly where he came from. I told her that he will stay in ISS until then during my class. She replied I can't do that. I made it clear he is NOT coming back into my class and he can then sit with you or the building principal.

Then on Friday, **September 21,** I saw this student whom I never met, got to learn his name by hearing it in the hallways, defiantly wearing his hat, obviously NOT in ISS, not with the head of guidance or the building principal and just roaming FREE. Just like I said, here at JFK it is all about cover up and no paperwork to make this place appear as if it is better and running without incident.

**DISCIPLINE REFERRAL**

September 18, 2012,
Lee E McNulty (Room 114)

On Tuesday, September 18, 2012, a student, whose name I did not get entered my class about 5 minutes into the period. As soon as I was done giving instructions to my students, I attempted to explain what I needed for this student to do.

Before I could even finish explaining this young filthy mouth student wanted to go to the bathroom. I said no. He kept acting up, insisting, ignoring what I said and kept trying to talk over me. I stopped him right then and made it clear, to knock it off and made it extra clear no one is leaving my room.
He continues, I walked away, and he walked out of class.
About 4 or 5 minutes later, he came back in with Mr. Stevenson*. At that time, I was giving a lesson to my students. When I was done, Mr. Stevenson* had left and this young man was now on his cell phone. I told him to put it away. He ignored me. I asked him 3 more times.

This young man snaps at me and says who the fuck am I talking too. I said again, put the phone away. His reply, "SUCK MY DICK.!"

That's when I took him out of my room and escorted him to security.
All the while this filthy mouth little man was trying to intimidate me and start a further confrontation.
SIMPLE:
I will NOT accept him in class.
I expect the proper disciplinary actions taken. Not the usual; give him another chance.

He had another chance when Mr. Stevenson* brought him back into my classroom from walking out.

Thank you and most respectfully,

Lee E McNulty
973-321-0500 ex. 50114

END

**Sept 20 -** I was absent; however, there were several incidents. Enough for the building principal to make announcement over the PA system today about people acting up, being disrespectful and about parents who come in and act up. They will be arrested and prosecuted to the fullest extent of the law. I have the announcement on video.

**Later** I also have students from my 4$^{th}$ period class knowing & allowing me to videotape them talking about what had happened. How it is starting again between BLACKS and the DOMINICANS. It seems a boy was jumped, stabbed, slashed, and beaten with a bat. They said it was really bad yesterday when students were leaving to go home. Nothing happened in school; however, it was really bad outside the school building and going all the way down several blocks. *AS USUAL NOTHING IN NEWS!*

**Sept 21 - FIGHTS all day long in and outside of the building.** Hallways are a disaster already. The horn blew for students to be in class and the hallways are filled with screaming, swearing, cursing running and fooling around students. By not suspending anyone, the administration has lost control of the building already. Students know this so they do whatever they want making the school more out of control and dangerous. Meanwhile the administration wants everyone to think JFK has changed, improved and is safe. Look what I have documented already! The REAL reason for not suspending is to manipulate the numbers and statistics so the administration can say look how much suspensions are down this year and JFK is running MUCH better. Once again, the administration is controlling, manipulating and falsifying documentation and reports. By NOT writing up the required documents and reports, there is nothing to be filed and processed, alleviating any type of paper trail. Meanwhile our brave service men and women are all over the world fighting, dying and building schools. When right here in Paterson, NJ, JFK and the entire school system is *still* under STATE CONTROL! Maybe our military should be here instead?

**Sept 21 -** 4 to 5 students were arrested today. I am NOT sure if they are involved with yesterday's incidents and full day of VIOLENCE! However, I was told weapons were confiscated. And it is all hushed up? Don't parents have the right to know what is going on in JFK and if their child or children are safe?

**Oct 4 -** my God there were fights all day long and everywhere. Today, there are NOT as many kids in the hallways. That's because students are now walking out of the building and hanging out outside. Or they are gathering and hanging out more in the stairwells. What makes it worse is parents are coming into the building and have to walk through all of this. Do you know how intimidating that looks when they unexpectedly see gangs of students just hanging out in the stairwells, instead of being in class? I would PULL my children out of here and SUE the district and the State of New Jersey!

**Oct 5 - it is 8:41** and hundreds of kids are just now coming into the building. They are ALL LATE and nothing is and has been done about it. Then we wonder why they cannot hold a job after they graduate, if you really want to call it graduating. Let's just say after they leave school with a diploma. The importance of being on time is NOT taught or enforced here. As I am still typing, I am still watching, witnessing students pouring into the building as if this is normal. Then again here at JFK anything abnormal in the real world is normal here and allowed to flourish. The majority of the students are NOT wearing their uniforms and wearing hats. The students do this out of defiance. Anything students are told NOT to do, they do and will do it right in front of you hoping to start a confrontation and make a big scene, which insights other students to do the same. They come to school late and NOT by a little. They are eating cake, cookies sandwiches, drinking coffee or soda, making a mess, throwing the garbage, wrappers, bottle caps or spilling everything all over the floor. They just don't care or have any respect. What you don't see is them carrying anything that they DO need for school or their classes. It is just a place to meet up with friends, hangout, walk around, play, fight and cause havoc.

**Oct 5 - it is so out of freaking control again** on all three (3) floors, all hallways and wings, all day and there is NOT one administrator present. No change same as last year and it's only the 5th week of school.

**Oct 16 -** NO CHANGE, it is the same out of control crap again today. As usual loooong after the horn sounds for students to be in classes they just gather and congregate in the hallways and stairwells again. NO administrators, heads of security are to be seen! Just ONE lone security guard, Arnie*. This poor guy works his ass off every day and for what? Whatever he does, he has to do over and over again dealing with the same students over and over again, because the administration allows students to run wild. Once Arnie* does his job, the administration tell him to release them. It's like fishing, "Catch and Release."

**OCT 18 - 8:30am**, it has been first period for a looooooong time. Large groups of students are still coming in as if it is NOW time to enter school. In reality it has nothing to do with time. Time is whenever they want to come to school and doesn't mean a thing. They are walking slow, eating, drinking, talking, deliberately cursing as loud as can be looking for attention and being disruptive in hopes of starting a confrontation with anyone who tells them to STOP! As usual there is NOT one administrator present. NOTHING is done about student's attendance and obviously tardiness and cutting.

Furthermore, the administration came up with something new in order to manipulate, hide, adjust, and falsify records by lowering the number of student's absences, cutting and tardiness. Teachers are now told NOT to write and submit cuts on a student if they do NOT show up for their 1st or 2nd period classes. The administrations' reasoning is, because students did not go to homeroom which is after 1st and 2nd periods. Even if teacher knows a student was in school the rest of the day, they still cannot write cuts.

Meanwhile because students are not showing up for 1st and 2nd periods they are failing, and the administration blames the teachers. The administration is actually causing these problems to grow by continuing allowing and ignoring students to be late, cut and NOT show up for classes?

**It is 8:48am** and students are still pouring into the building. HOW can students pass their class or classes and graduate if they do NOT go to class? Meanwhile it is ALL on the school's surveillance cameras.

**October 18, 2012 - below is a narrative to an email I sent to the president of the PEA, giving him an actual timeline of events while keeping up with and adding to the paper trail.**
**UNFREAKINBELIEVABLE, FIGHTS ALL DAY. SO FAR EVERYONE INVOLVED GIRLS.**
It is so bad here. The hallways are a disaster. What do we expect, if there is no discipline? This is not a place of learning and education. How can it be when students are in the hallways looooooong after the horn sounded to be in class? How in the world can they pass and later graduate? As I am writing this another fight is going on and a student is swinging at a security woman. Where are the administrators?
END

**Below is a narrative to another email I sent on the same day to the president of the PEA, keeping up with and adding to the paper trail.**
I was going to see Ms. Sweetness*, when I saw and heard a parent saying how bad this school is. She was cursing and mad. As soon as we were next to each other she stopped. I hesitate and then called to her. We had a big discussion. She is so disgusted. She said when she went to JFK and it was never like this. I told her and made it clear this is only what I know, but there have been 4 fights here today. She said she heard a security guard telling someone that there were actually 6 BIG fights today in the building. I said "what did I just tell you, what I ONLY KNOW!"
She said her daughter likes coming here. I said and in front of her daughter the only reason why she likes this place is because she can come here in PLAY. Moms exact words were, "that's right, I know that!" She said she was going to contact the newspapers. I told her to tell everyone she knows and get parents involved because this place is not only bad it is absolutely DANGEROUS!
END

**Below is a narrative to another email I sent on Oct. 18 to the president of the PEA, giving him an actual timeline of events while keeping up with and adding to the paper trail.**
**1 p.m. ANOTHER FIGHT JUST BROKE OUT.**
Dave* the security guard is escorting a kid and this kid is constantly screaming I'm going to get your boy. The hallways are a disaster, not one administrator present, it is so dangerous here.
The kids are like sharks in a feeding frenzy. They are waiting and looking to start more fights and cause more chaos. There is no way classes can be conducted. Everyone is in the hallways as if it is a riot.
It is now 1:07, the number of students in the hallways is ridiculous. The noise is absolutely defining.
What in the hell is going on here? Why is this allowed to go?
Nobody is stopping any of this or making students go to class. IT IS OUT OF FREAKING CONTROL!
With all the administrators we in this building, not one is present and getting things under control.
HELP! WE ARE SINKING!
SOMEONE IS GOING TO GET KILLED HERE
END

**Oct. 19, 2012 - below is a narrative to another email I sent to the president of the PEA, giving him an actual timeline of events while keeping up with and adding to the paper trail.**
*I GUESS WE HAVE TO GO THROUGH ANOTHER YEAR LIKE OR WORSE THAN LAST YEAR. WHY?*
**I have video of** students (with their permissions) talking about how bad it was yesterday and especially with so many students in the building who had weapons (machetes) in their book bags. Also, how bad thing were at the end of the school day. It is so dangerous for these kids. Then when they heard a gunshot, students ran to get away and tried to get back into the building, but the administration and security would not allow them in! This is just a real short version. The students were telling me how a car or cars pulled up with tinted windows, open up their trunks and started pulling out weapons. The police were spraying mace at everyone. There was a big police present, and nothing was on TV, radio and or in the newspapers.
THIS IS NOT RIGHT TO PARENTS, THE COMMUNITY AND TAXPAYERS.
THIS IS A CRIME IN ITSELF.
Students (and you will hear it on video) were saying it is unfair because so many students have to bring weapons to school just to protect themselves. This is what I have been saying all along. Unless something has already happened then the district will allow security to use metal detectors.
This school and district is NEVER PROACTION.
END

Oct 19 - students told me that many kids were locked up yesterday and again today for fighting. Some had weapons. Just like the kids in the video were saying, "SOMEONE IS GOING TO GET KILLED!"

Oct 20 - a substitute and I we were talking about how dangerous it is here. She said she saw a boy with a knife. I asked if she summoned security. She said, "NO!" She was afraid of the student retaliating, but was actually *MORE* afraid of the District retaliating and NOT calling her back to be a substitute.

Oct 23 - the school print shop teacher was so MAD because he's been constantly printing up tardy to school slips. He says it is ridiculous. At this stage of the game no one should be late, and the school shouldn't be writing that many tardy slips.

This proves what I've been saying. Every day I witness students enter the building 9:30 and later. Many times, the building principal is standing right there joking around with the two heads of security ignoring the students as they are just strolling on into the building.

Remember the superintendent, the school principal and all of the school administrators do not want teachers to write cuts for 1st & 2nd period classes. Me, I still and will write cuts. I will not change, and my class rules are the same. THREE cuts and you fail the marking period. However, I do allow students to make up those cuts by coming in early in the morning for detention. Depending on what time they start school, they are to report to me either at 7:00 or 7:30. I allow them to make the time up by working on their assignments, notes and or projects. Furthermore, I make sure I create a paper trail. So in May and especially June when the administration suddenly shows an interest in students with poor attendance and excessive cutting because teachers are failing them which ultimately brings the graduation numbers, rate and statistics lower, I have a record. However, even though these students did NOT show up especially for their 1st and 2nd period classes miraculously they still passed and GRADUATED!
Remember, according to the politicians and the superintendent it is the teachers fault for failing students. So, why don't they blame teachers for students not coming to school on time too?

**Big fight** first thing this morning by the ACT Academy Office. Then at 11:48 police took a student out in handcuffs. That is odd, I wonder if the principal knows about this. If a police officer did this without permission, by the end of the day, that officer will be BANNED from the building. That's why I have to document as much as I can and write the book. However, my biggest concern is will everything I say STILL be ignored? Will everything here at JFK as well as the entire school district of Paterson, continue and remain the same? OR finally, will *all* of the superintendents, their administration, commissioners of education and governors be held responsible because of everything that has been going on here ever since the State of New Jersey took over, and has been in control, running and operating the Paterson Public School District?

**As usual students** are in the hallways loooong after the horn sounded for students to be in class. I didn't see the heads of security or one administrator. So many teachers are now more concerned/afraid of failing students because it will be marked against them in their evaluations. Which can and will affect them in rehiring, being fired, losing an increment, and tenure? This is another political BS scare tactic, so teachers just pass their students. I want to know, who in the hell evaluates the building principals, all of the academy principals and every single administrator at JFK? There is NO WAY, this nonstop, out of control behavior, chaos and riot like violent, lawlessness atmosphere, where students do not have to come to school or class on time and can constantly hangout in the hallways, stairwells, bathrooms, walk in and out of classrooms they do NOT belong in, disrupt classes, disrupt teachers, where foul language and inappropriate behavior is normal, accepted and is policy for any educational setting/high school in the world? Boy that is some sentence, but it is the TRUTH! Have Video

**Oct 24 -** I was just updated by Lt. Mike Recca, a Paterson police officer, about the last school year's June 20, 2012 entry. It wasn't one student; it was a major GANG BANG down in the basement stairwell by the auto shop! It WAS on the school surveillance cameras, but not everything. However, it did view all the guys lined up. Furthermore, being it was on the school surveillance cameras, it proves what I have been saying, "NOTHING" is done until after something has happened. Also being that this incident was on video then so is everything else that I have been writing about proving that the building principal and administrators ignore it all and allow it all to continually go on unless and *only* if something happens. I bet the administration worked their asses off trying to keep it hushed up. Obviously, it worked. I am just learning about it four months later. I wonder if the parents SUED the administration for allowing this to happen.

**7:41am -** a bunch of kids were dragged into security office by security and the building principal. Already, there has been nothing but FIGHTING going on all day. However, my guess for the building principal to be present was to make sure everything gets squashed and hushed up.

**FOOD FOR THOUGHT - SECOND YEAR OF ACADEMIES AND WHAT A JOKE!**
What's the point of the academies? Nothing has changed! The only change is the district program called Genesis which teachers must use to enter student attendance which shows absolutely no record of cutting. An academy is supposed to have its own classes, teachers and courses. So why are there so many Math, English, etc. classes all shared within all four academies? The superintendent is making everything sound as if it is better. It is NOT. If the NJ taxpayers should actually see what goes on here and how their tax dollars are spent/wasted HEADS WILL ROLL. That is my argument, am I not a NJ taxpayer?

Last year, so many students failed all 4 marking periods. However, with the buyback/credit recovery program, in 3 to 4 four weeks *supposedly* showing up for buyback, students were allowed to graduate? I would like to have every student who participated with buy back/credit recovery and graduated last year take the same test for the GED and let's see what happens?

The way things work around here, it would be best to shut this place down and let students get a GED. They may have a better chance of getting an education.

**October 25, 2012 - below is a narrative to another e-mail I sent to the president of the PEA, giving him an actual timeline of events while keeping up with and adding to the paper trail.**
It is 7$^{th}$ period and the bell rang to be in class looooooooooooooooooooong ago. The hallways are filled with students. I can hear my academy principal Mr. Arthurs* yelling at students to get to class. They're talking back to him. He is asking some girls, "Where do you belong?" He yells [for them] to get upstairs and get there. The kids are all talking back and cursing. He is upset. I have never ever heard him lose his temper and or raise his voice. Some students move, but just to someplace else and NOT TO CLASS.

7$^{th}$ period starts at 12:59. It is now 1:23. The hallways look as if it's the last weekend before Christmas at the Mall. THE NOISE IS SOOOOOOOOOOOOOOOOOOO BAD.
THE SCREAMING IS UNBELIEVABLE! Where is the building principal?
He supposed to be in charge of the building/facility. Why is he not getting control of the building? It is out of freaking control here. The hallway in the center of the building first floor is filled with students. Taxpayers are getting screwed as well as we are ruining a nation.
END

**Nov 9 - I have been out 2 days and this is the first I have been back since the Hurricane SANDY!** I didn't want to come in because I knew this place would be out of control. WELL, I WAS RIGHT. Kids were in the hallways and all over the place, all day long. Around 10 a couple of TAPs were doing hall sweeps. Right after that, the building was back to normal, meaning not normal, out of control and chaos. I have yet to see the principal. The only administrator I have seen in the hallways today was my Academy

Principal Mr. Arthurs* He is the ONLY administrator who is actually TRYING to get students out of the hallways and back into classes. It is 20 minutes or maybe longer when there was the hall sweep. However, the hallways are as if there weren't a sweep and students are still not in class. Now students are just flat out walking out of the building. So much for the new security cameras and the 10-foot-high fence going around the building all at taxpayers' expense to help with JFK's security! It's the same students all day long in the hallways and I know in my heart no matter what, they will ALL still pass and graduate.

**Nov 14 - it is 8:30 and students are all over the place.** There's no point because there is no change. The only difference/change is the date on the calendar.

**November 14, 2012 - below is a narrative to another e-mail I sent to the president of the PEA, giving him an actual timeline of events while keeping up with and adding to the paper trail.**
Have video that starts a few seconds after the horn sound for students to be in class. You will see students still roaming the 1st floor. You will hear one of the guidance counselors telling me how she had a fit yesterday and went storming to principal office complaining how bad it is in the hallway. She asked him "what planet is this where 16-year-old students run things." And here it's the next day, the hallways are a disaster and still there is NO administration. You will also see a big waste of money is some of these part time security guards. The kids are all over the place, but they do nothing. What's the point and especially if the students do not listen or respect them? Finally, you will see 2 administrators a male & female. They did nothing other than the female administrator told a student to take off his hood. He refused and the two administrators just went on their merry way. Many kids who are in the hallway walking around are seniors. They know it doesn't matter and they will graduate because the Superintendent does NOT want a low graduation rate. Meanwhile the administration is recording it all!
Why doesn't the PEA acquire a copy of the school video on a daily basis?
END

**Nov 14 -** 2nd period a big fight involving several girls, hair extensions all over the place and not one administrator. Students came from all over filling the hallways like sharks on a feeding frenzy. It's absolute lawlessness here and it has been this way all day.

**Have video #2, starts before the horn to begin 5th period and for a long time after.** This freaking place is so out of control. It baffles my mind how this nonstop, day in and day out chaos, out of control atmosphere can just go on and on and no one other than teachers are held accountable? I really cannot blame students. The administration allows them to carry on this way. There is absolutely NO SUPERVISON HERE and because there are no consequences students act and carrying on the way they do. Another FIGHT just broke out with a little girl and the boy who shoved her down to the floor. Its 12:05 and I stopped but the hallways are still filled with roaming students going berserk.

**Kids in the hallway all 7th period.** They are walking in and out of my class. I tell them to leave, they tell me to go FUCK MYSELF. They refuse to leave and start messing with my books, tools, students anything and everything they want just to disrupt my class. I had it and went out into the hallway yelling "why are there students in the hallways? "Who runs this school?" A kid yells, "we run this fucking school!" I yelled, "That boy is absolutely right!" There was not one administrator to be seen. After about 3 or 4 minutes the head of Guidance comes over and tells me to be quiet. I said who the hell are you to tell me to be quiet when this place is out of control; students are in the hallway making noise, acting up, walking in and out of my classroom telling me FUCK YOU. I had it and then told her, "get out of here and do your job, obviously you're clueless or an excellent actress in playing DUMB!"

**November 15, 2012 - below is a narrative to another e-mail I sent to the president of the PEA, giving him an actual timeline of events while keeping up with and adding to the paper trail.**
It's all on video, just prior to the beginning of 6th period and looooooooooooooooooong after the beginning of 6th period. You will hear the horn to begin class. Not one administrator present. There is NO WAY, this should be allowed let alone be LEGAL. What makes it all more disgusting JFK and the entire district is STILL under STATE CONTROL. Is this what every NJ citizen can expect by having the state of New Jersey running this school and district? UNFREAKIN believable, the hallways are absolutely out of freaking control and shear chaos. Students just do and saying whatever they want and NOT going to class.

Sometime afterwards, the building Principal came around, but the kids didn't care and obviously either did he. Why didn't he have them swept up? The period started long ago and every one of these students is cutting and he just walks by as if it is another day at the park.

Students were banging on my door. I was trying to leave my classroom and the students would not allow me to open the door. They would deliberately shove the door close in my face. It is way-out of control and all of these students were defiant and looking to start a confrontation. I had enough and forced my way out. Then once I forced my way out the students who were deliberately trying to keep me from opening my door were yelling at me, fuck you, fuck you, fuck you over and over and so much other vial crap. All because I did not let them bully me so now, they will try to lure me into a confrontation knowing damn well the building principal and all of the other administrators in this building will not back me up and blame me or any teacher for causing the problem instead of disciplining students. And so, the lawlessness, out of control chaos prevails and continues to go on, all day, every day, all year and again for another year. I have had about enough of this BULL XXXX!

WHY IS THERE NOT A LAWSUIT! PARENTS SHOULD, COULD AND WOULD WIN BIG TIME IF THEY KNOW WHAT IS REALLY GOING ON.

How can teachers be held responsible, if the administration allows the building to behave in this grossly inappropriate non-educational manner? It is absolutely disgusting here.

END

**November 16, 2012 - below is a narrative to another e-mail I sent to the president of the PEA, giving him an actual timeline of events while keeping up with and adding to the paper trail.**

As homeroom announcements were going on and during the Pledge Allegiance to the Flag, hundreds of students are now entering and still roaming the building. No one stops during the Pledge of Allegiance. No one is disciplined for being late to school. School starts at 7:30 and 8:05 for others. No one should be entering the building at this time. They are late and supposed to be accompanied with a parent.

**Speaking with Mary\* the security guard I found out yesterday, November 15, there was a fire in the boys' bathroom by the cafeteria AND we did NOT evacuate the building.** They caught the boy and gave him 10 days' suspension and supposedly will have to undergo psychological evaluation. Why wasn't he arrested? Obviously to be HUSHED UP! PLUS, there was another fire somewhere in or around JFK yesterday. I have been getting conflicting information. One teacher said that the grounds were set a fire. Another said students were trying to set a bus on fire. I don't know the truth. Bottom Line, the fire department did come. Just prior to the fire department arriving I heard Dave\* the security guard yell it's a 43. I have no idea what a 43 is. However, he and other security people along with a few police officers were running, I assume to wherever the 43 was. I have a funny feeling the smoke and fire detectors are OFF in the bathrooms by the cafeterias. I do NOT understand why the administration allows students to smoke in there. You CANNOT walk in there any time of the day, on any day, without walking out smelling like an ash tray.

**Fights all period long in cafeteria during 7th period.** This place is so bad and out of control. As far as I can tell NOTHING was done about any of the chaos all period. To think we have Paterson police officers in the building and cafeteria, and they are NOT allowed to do anything. If these students acted like this any place else, they would be arrested and jailed. Have video.

END

**November 19, 2012 - below is a narrative to an email I sent to the president & vice president of the PEA, giving an actual timeline of events while keeping up with and adding to the paper trail.**

**Update Video 1,** is during homeroom. You will see students all over the place and NOT in homeroom Bottom line, the video speaks for itself.

**Video 2,** 3rd period students wanted to talk with me on camera. They did NOT want their faces, but they talked about how dangerous this school is and many things that has been going on here. It is absolutely disturbing. You have to see and hear the video.

**Video 3**, 4th period and it is out of freaking control. Same crap! However, there was a VP (don't know his name) asking why I had a propane tank. Yet he did and said nothing to the students.
You even see and hear a disgusted police officers say he would NOT send his children here.
END

### November 20, 2012 - below is a narrative to another email I sent to the president & vice president of the PEA, keeping up with and adding to the paper trail.

One of my seniors gave me a video (see attached) that shows students fighting outside of JFK after school. You will see 2 students with machetes. One is very visible and will see it glisten from the sun. The other student has it in his book bag and you can clearly see the outline of it as he is holding it by the handle (Names omitted). All of my students say the number of weapons that are being brought into school is ridiculous. I have them telling me on video with permission. You received that email yesterday, 11/19/12. Students want to know why they aren't using metal detectors at JFK. They also told me students are purchasing uniforms so intruders can come into the building because IDs are never checked! Many are street thugs and gang members.
Now you have this video showing weapons as students leave JFK.
With all the info I have sent you just this year can we write up a major grievance for JFK being unsafe?
END


**Nov 20 - 3rd period, they tried again to elect a class president**. Key word is AGAIN. You still see students with no uniforms, no ID, talking, when confronted by teachers or administrators they continued being disruptive, disrespecting, ignoring, cursing them in defiance and would not leave when told to do so. I was there and saw it with my own eyes! It was *absolutely disgusting*. Students know there are no consequences for poor behavior and defiance of authority, so they continue and boy did they push it. Later the building principal enters the auditorium, and he did nothing either. The following administrators were there: the building principal, Ms. Corfu*, Mr. Wilt*, Mr. Naptha* and a VP from Stem.

Have video just as horn sounded to begin 6th period. Poor quality and bad angle! However, LOOOOOOOOOOOOOOOOOOOONG after the sound to start class and on both floors, hallways are an absolute disaster. However, I saw 3 administrators upon occasion. There was Mr. Wilt* & Ms. Corfu* on the 2nd floor. On the 1st floor a Spanish lady. Basically, they did absolutely nothing other than talk. That is why the school is so out of freaking control and again right after the building principal said about changes were going to happen. ALL B/S! On my way through the 2nd floor a boy was right in front of Ms. Corfu*, inches away from her deliberately, defiantly, disgustingly and obnoxiously, acting as if he was HUMPING/FUCKING her. Ms. Corfu* looked me right in the eye and she did absolutely nothing. I just shook my head in absolute disgust. Finally, the boy left and ran down the hall. Not a thing was done about it, as if this is normal and accepted behavior. To think that Ms. Corfu* is a PRINCIPAL and she allowed this student to degrade and humiliate her in front of everyone who was in the hallway watching. What would her husband say, no do, if he saw that? You have to see and hear this to believe it.


### November 21, 2012 - below is a narrative to an email I sent to the president & vice president of the PEA and the NJEA, keeping up with and adding to the paper trail.

Received another VIDEO (See attached) from a student. It was a FIGHT, 2 girls, yesterday, Tuesday, November 20, 2012 during 9th period. Notice it is right by Office #1 and the building principal's office. Where was the building principal, the heads of security and administrators?

Also, there were many BIG FIGHTS/BRAWLS last Friday by the cafeterias. No one was suspended. They all received ISS, creating no paper trail and teaching students they are allowed to fight here.
*GREAT PLACE TO SEND YOUR CHILDREN!*
END

**Nov 26 - have video of homeroom announcements and pledge of allegiance to the flag.** It shows how unprofessional, unpatriotic and low class of a school it is here.

**November 28, 2012 - below is a narrative to another email I sent to the president & vice president of the PEA, keeping up with and adding to the paper trail.**
I was absent, but everyone was telling me the fire alarms went off. It was snowing very badly yesterday. It was a FALSE ALARM, pulled by the trailers. There was a major snowball fight. Several people were injured and had to go to the nurse's office. AND nothing was done about it. So, what good are the cameras in and around the building for? These videos are on file for 30 days before erased! Be sure to add this to your date & times of fire alarms.

**November 28, 2012,** I was talking to a security guard. He was so upset. He said because they don't want to suspend students and just send them to ISS, now ISS is out of control. It is held in the auditorium and students just fight, destroy property, and don't listen because the students know there are no consequences. It is so bad here. Those were his exact words. He said everything I have been saying.
END

**NOTE OF INTEREST: -** To date, with all the emails I sent to the PEA and the NJEA, especially those telling them about students talking on video about weapons being brought into the building and how dangerous JFK is, I have never received a reply from them other than the time about the "bootleg video."

**November 30, 2012 - below is a narrative to an email I sent to the president and vice president of the PEA, the NJEA Uniserv assistant director and two NJEA region 27 Field Reps.**
**During 5th period** the Affirmative Action Officer came to visit me. She was concerned about the remarks Mr. Dickinson* made at the teachers meeting when he was calling students animals. She wanted video of it or if I knew of anyone who had video. I told her no. She asked if I knew of anyone who had video and audio of the way things are here in the building. I said I do.
She asked if I would ask that person to release them. I said NO. No one trusts anyone from the district. She said she knows and that's a problem. Then said the Superintendent knows and wants the info, video, documentation anything and has a paper that guarantees any retaliation. I said that means nothing, what's a piece of paper going to do? There is NO WAY, I trust anyone from the district. I told her to send someone here anonymously as a janitor to see and capture what really goes on. She asked if I would try to convince that person or persons to give her video/s. I said NO! She asked if I would get copies and send them to her. I said NO, I would not betray the trust of that person or persons.
I FIND THIS QUITE COINCIDENTAL?
END

**Nov 30 -**today is the last of 15 emails since October 24, between the president of the PEA, the NJEA Uniserv Assistant Director and myself. two NJEA region 27 Uniserv Field Reps also received copies. I was attempting to arrange a meeting to acquire help to put a stop to what has been and is still going on a JFK. Below is a narrative of all the e-mail correspondences. It starts -

**1. October 24, 2012,** I received an email from the Uniserv Assistant Director which was also cc'd to the President of the NJEA and two Uniserv field reps.

Subject: your email to NJEA

Mr. McNulty,
The NJEA President has asked me to contact you regarding your recent emails to her. As Uniserv Assistant Director, I work closely with the Passaic County Regional office that serves Paterson. I would be happy to meet with you and the NJEA field representatives to discuss the concerns you raised. I am in the process of getting dates that we could meet and will be in touch.

**2. October 24, 2012** - I replied, Thank you and looking forward to meeting with you.

**3. October 24, 2012** - The Uniserv Assistant Director replied, I am meeting with the field reps on Monday and will nail it down. It may have to wait until after the convention to get all of our calendars in sync, but I will do my best and keep you posted. Thanks

**4. October 25, 2012** - I replied, Thank you. I understand. Looking forward to meeting with you.

**5. November 15, 2012** - I sent an email to the Uniserv Assistant Director asking if we will be meeting soon and stating if you can believe it, JFK is getting WORSE!

**6. November 14, 2012** - The Uniserv Assistant Director wrote, Hello Lee, I am sorry things were delayed. As you know the storm knocked out power to much of the northern part of the state and meetings were cancelled. All NJEA offices in the north were just restored this week. Obviously, that took some of my time. I will be sending you new dates to meet soon. Thanks.

**7. November 16, 2012** - I replied, I look forward to hearing from you.
When we meet, I suggest you bring a laptop and several flash drives.

**8. November 28, 2012** -The Uniserv Assistant Director wrote, Hi Lee, I hope you had a good holiday. I am told that the PEA has arranged to visit JFK and meet with you and other reps on Dec 4. I am glad to hear this. I also think it is best to wait until after you have had the mtg. Good luck and let me know if you still want to meet after that.

**9. November 29, 2012** - I replied, Sir, I want this meeting with you (NJEA) NOT JUST THE PEA. They know it all. I have sent them everything and spoke with them for YEARS. We are wasting time. I wrote the President of the NEA as well as the President and Vice President of the NJEA because it has taken tooooo long.

My letters were sent out in the beginning of September. It will be December this Saturday.
Too much time has been wasted. I want a meeting with the NJEA and want these situations corrected. If it were your children attending this school or if you were working here, would you want to WAIT and waste more time?

Either we all meet together OR DO NOT WASTE MY TIME.
You have no idea how upset I am at this moment. I feel that you are taking this lightly. There needs to be a lawsuit filed against JFK and the district for allowing student not to go to class all day, every day, all year and still graduate them. As well as a dangerous environment we are working in.
If not, I want a DIRECT meeting with the PRESIDENT of the NJEA.
I'm tired of playing games. No more jerking me around.
This is about RUINING A NATION! I am sending a copy to the Presidents of the NEA & NJEA.

This is not just ridiculous; it is a waste of precious time. I await your response.

**10. November 29, 2012** - the president of the PEA wrote, I'm sorry that you do not wish to meet with us on December 4 during your lunch period. This was our first opportunity to get the parties together. I will now wait until the Uniserv Assistant Director arranges a meeting for you.

**11. November 29, 2012** - The Uniserv Assistant Director wrote, I am suggesting Lee go to the meeting. I would also be happy to meet after that. I think we are all on the same side, no?

**12. November 30, 2012** - I replied to the president of the PEA, it is NOT that I do not want to meet with you or anyone else. I want you and all involved parties to be present along with the Assistant Director. I don't want to go over and over and over meeting after meeting discussing the same stuff. I wanted a meeting to get things DONE! MORE TALKING is a waste of time. What is there to say that you don't already know?
PLEASE, respectfully explain the reason for this meeting. Give me an outline.
I am so frustrated and disgusted. It is long overdue and time for action.
I sent my letter to the President of the NEA & NJEA as well to VP of the NJEA.
90 days have gone by. A 1/2 of the school year, and I am right back where I started. NO WHERE!
Unfortunately, it seems obvious that the NJEA is not concerned or not interested and blowing it off.
This is unacceptable. None of you would like it if your child or children had to go to a school or schools like this. Then we graduate students, not because they are ready, but to increase the numbers to make the school, the district & superintendent look good.
What the hell is wrong with all of you? WE ARE RUINING A NATION!
PLEASE, explain to me what would another meeting do?
WHEN ARE WE GOING TO TAKE ACTION? What is the plan of attack?
For years I have been sending documentation and information to you and the NJEA rep. NO CHANGE!
I will call you approximately 10:00 am, Friday November 30, 2012. I AM SO DISGUSTED.

**13. November 30, 2012** - I replied to the Assistant Director, I did NOT say I was not going to be here. I explained my concerns and outrage and these situations being taken lightly. Too much time has been wasted all ready. There is NO EXCUSE when there is wrong being done and most likely breaking of educational laws continuously. I do NOT want to waste my time to go over and over and over the same stuff. I am not going to go all over this again with you. You received a copy of my reply to Pete which was cc to all. NO MORE TIME WASTED. 90 days, 1/2 a school year is gone and wasted.
I look forward to you being present also on the 4th of December. I am so disgusted.

**14. November 30, 2012** - The Assistant Director replied, Lee, I can assure you I am not taking your concerns lightly. I have direct experience with these types of issues. I am sympathetic to your sense of urgency, but my experience also tells me that these are complex and deep-seated problems that cannot be solved quickly or easily. I am happy to meet with you. I cannot be there on December 4 which is early next week. I will get dates for all of us to talk. This is about process and organizing, and unfortunately there are no quick and easy answers.

**15. November 30, 2012** - I replied, I am sure you can sense my frustration. This has NOT just started. This has been going on for YEARS! Two plus decades! I have sent PEA/NJEA information for years! Sense of urgency is an understatement. How many years does it take?
Meanwhile, students who should still be in grammar school are getting high school diplomas.
You state, "this is about process and organizing, and unfortunately there are no quick and easy answers."
You have to be kidding me? The Vietnam War was over quicker. Absolutely disgusting.

END
There was finally a meeting and NOTHING was done about ANYTHING.
However, it is not the same here at JFK. It is worse! The PEA & NJEA received the very same information you are reading in this book. It is obvious the unions do not care.

**And the NJEA has the nerve to have a TV commercials saying,**
***"MAKING PUBLIC SCHOOLS GREAT FOR EVERY CHILD!"***

**December 7, 2012 - below is a narrative to another email I sent to the president and vice president of the PEA, the NJEA Uniserv assistant director and two NJEA region 27 Field Reps.**
Speaking with guidance counselors, they were told to CHANGE students' schedules. What is happening students who are failing classes because of extreme cutting and poor attendance, and even if they say they do NOT like a teacher, guidance is to ACCOMMODATE students and change their schedules. Furthermore, now all of their past attendance, cuts and lateness and do not count. They have a clean slate.

I was also informed by a guidance counselor -
**1.** Started on December 4, 2012, for the next 2 weeks, students will be removed from their $2^{nd}$, $3^{rd}$, $4^{th}$ & $5^{th}$ period classes in order to prepare for the *state exam* in March. Then they will be removed again once we come back from Christmas break for 2 more weeks. Then another 2 weeks prior to the exam dates. A total of 6 weeks, missing 4 periods, a total of 30 days out from each of their scheduled classes / courses.
- *Why bother having school when it is nothing more than preparing for a test?*

**2.** A student on December 5, 2012, (Students name omitted) was suspended for 10 days for defecating in the stairwell. The cameras must work because he was caught via the school surveillance cameras.
- *Meanwhile students are in the hallways all day long, every day and the cameras don't see that?*

**3.** Lastly, if students weren't just pushed through grammar school with a $3^{rd}$ or $4^{th}$ grade level of education, then while they are at JFK High School were made to go to class instead of roaming the hallways all day, all year long, they wouldn't have to be missing 4 classes a day for 6 weeks to prepare for the *state exam* that their regular classes should have already prepared them for!
- *Taxpayers are getting screwed big time and not by teachers!*
END

The following is a **NORTHJERSEY.COM: NEWS** newspaper article about an announcement the principal made the day we were leaving for Thanksgiving Holiday.
**"Paterson principal is under scrutiny for alleged Thanksgiving announcement"**
By Nick Clunn and Leslie Brody / Staff writers, December 7, 2012 / The Record
http://www.northjersey.com/news/paterson-principal-is-under-scrutiny-for-alleged-thanksgiving-announcement-1.361987

PATERSON – School officials said Thursday that they were investigating a complaint that a high school principal made an inappropriate announcement before Thanksgiving break.

Superintendent Donnie Evans said the district's lawyers were looking into a report that Amod Field, principal of operations at the John F. Kennedy Educational Complex, allegedly made inappropriate comments over the school's public-address system. Evans said privacy rules barred him from discussing details of a personnel matter, but he expected to have the results of the investigation next week.

A purported recording of the announcement has been emailed among teachers and was sent to The Record and Herald News.

In the recording, a man can be heard saying: "We must [be] very, very, very, very understanding to our Native Americans, who lost and sacrificed because of the scalping that took place on Thanksgiving. They were invited to a dinner, and then their lives were taken from them."

When first contacted by a reporter on Thursday, Field said, "There's been altered tapes sent out," but that he hadn't heard them. After the recording was emailed to him, he said he hadn't had time to listen to it, but he did remember telling students in an announcement to "remember the need to be sensitive about what took place" at an early Thanksgiving celebration and that "lives were lost" at the event.

He said in the second interview he did not recall using the word "scalping" in the school announcement, but he cited several websites — including a blog post titled "The Truth About Scalping" on the Tumblr site Rarely in History — that he said offered evidence that Native Americans were scalped at the second Thanksgiving.

"There's different variations in history," Field said. "My thing is about being informative to young people. ... I stand for love and caring of people of all kinds."

The Rev. John Norwood, tribal council member of the Nanticoke Lenni-Lenape Nation, based in Bridgeton, said that while Field might have mangled the history of the first Thanksgiving, he succeeded in raising the mixed feelings that some Native Americans have about the holiday.

While many Native American families gather for a meal on Thanksgiving, others protest the holiday, citing the massacre of American Indians that occurred after that moment of goodwill.

"For some American Indians, Thanksgiving is a time for gratitude that we are surviving, that we are still here, but not a feeling that everything was OK," said Norwood, who also leads a non-denominational Christian church in Ewing.

But Daniel K. Richter, director of the McNeil Center for Early American Studies at the University of Pennsylvania, said there was no murder of Native Americans at the first Thanksgiving, in 1621.

"There are several well-documented occasions on which colonists invited native people to share a meal and then murdered them," he said in an email, "but I am not aware of any connection to what might be called a Thanksgiving feast."

Grace Giglio, the Paterson school district's representative to the New Jersey Principals and Supervisors Association, described Field as a "nice guy" and said the district has yet formally to notify the association about the nature of the complaint filed against him.

**Dec 12** - receive a video. It starts at 8:31. There was a malfunction and it was restarted 5 or 10 minute later. Its first period and it's an absolute mess nothing changes here. It's mostly the same kids. JFK is just a place to hang out and play. You will hear security telling students to go to class, but the students are defiant and disrespectful to him. You'll see some students are running away from somebody. You'll eventually see an administrator Mr. Wilt* arrive and only because security went to get him. Mr. Wilt* did NOTHING. You will see students walking into a classroom that they don't belong in. In fact, you'll hear a young lady in the hallway even saying that. A few seconds later they came out. Little later, you'll see another administrator Mr. Stevenson*. All he did was tell students to go. Not get to class? Not escorting them to security for cutting and being in the hallway. JUST GO!

**Dec 12** - finally met with everyone from the NJEA, but disappointed. To sum it up, they stressed it is a loooooooooooooooooooong and slooooooooow process to get anything done. They both said it may take years! It has been 20 plus years already are you freaking kidding me? They said they wanted to go after the principal. I said what if the principal and all of the administrators are just following orders? I know that's NOT an excuse, but my colleagues and I are doing it too? I believe the way things are here will keep going on and on and teachers will be the escape goats. The NJEA is absolutely useless. Where is the experience? Go back to the email dated, November 20, 2012, when Al states, "I have direct experience with these types of issues." It is just frustrating. I am convinced they too DO NOT CARE!

**Dec 13** - have video, during the latter part of 1st period and on into homeroom. Students are talking so disrespectfully to Principal Ms. Corfu*. Every day, I see students sexually disrespecting her. WHY does she allow this? How can she go home feeling good about herself when she is constantly being walked over, talked to in the most disrespectfully, sexually degrading way and with the foulest of language spoken to her by children?

**Have video starting** just prior to 7th period and long into the period. The only administrator present was Mr. Arthurs*. His office is on the 2nd floor. He came down to the 1st floor in attempt to get students out of the hallways, stairwells and into class. You will see he was trying very hard to get students moving. Unfortunately, the students just ignored him. You will NOT see any of the other administrators present.

**NOTE OF INTEREST: -** Principal Mr. Arthurs* is the ONLY administrator who actually cares and tries very hard throughout the day to make a difference in changing the school climate and atmosphere. Unfortunately, he too is getting frustrated. Think about it, if students are so disrespectful to Principals Ms. Corfu* and Mr. Arthurs* how do you think students act and treat teachers? The video shows it all.

**Dec 14** - this is the FIRST YEAR of NO SCHOOL NEWS PAPER. WHY, because the journalism teacher is not able to produce the newspaper as she and her students use to. The reasons for this is because she has students assigned to her class/course that do not want to be there, not interested, do not want to work or create a newspaper and this is the saddest reason of all, she said so many students are not able to read or write. And because of their handicap the students are basically incapable. Where have you heard of a school without a school newspaper? THIS IS PROGRESS? NO, this is "RESTRUCTURING!"

**The school/board print shop person** told me they have printed 6000 tardy slips. (That's 8 reams of paper. 10 reams make a case). The reason I was told this is because the person whose job it is to be in the cafeteria until 10:15 every day writing tardy slips for students that come to school late asked him for 750 more tardy slips today. ARE YOU FREAKING KIDDING ME, and there is no record of it and or recourse for students who are habitually LATE.
A copy of this notation was sent via email to the president of the PEA, the NJEA Uniserv Assistant Director and two NJEA Region 27 Uniserv Field Reps, just to keep up with my paper trail.

**Dec 19 - 6th period**. UNBELEIVABLE, with all of the added administrators we have in this building NOT ONE makes themselves visible? What's to say that hasn't been said before? What an absolute disgrace this place is. If you reread my entry for December 14, 2012, do you really wonder why those poor students could not read or write? *How can no one be held accountable?* Have video!

**January 3, 2013** - 2nd day back from Christmas break. IT IS ABSOLUTELY OUT OF FREAKING CONTROL HERE. The kids are all over and every place other than in their classrooms all day long. To add insult to all of this the building principal made an announcement about students signing up for credit recovery. Now taxpayers will have to pay more for "CREDIT RECOVERY," because the building principal and all of the administrators allow students NOT to attend their classes. What other programs they will come up with in order to beef up student graduation numbers?

I have to laugh, every month we have CODE BLUE DRILLS. This is to shut/lock down the building. Everyone *has* to be in class. This is the only time students are in class. We should have CODE BLUE ALL THE TIME, THIS WAY STUDENTS WOULD BE IN CLASS.

**January 4, 2013 - below is a narrative to an email I sent to the president and vice president of the PEA, keeping up with and adding to the paper trail.**
**8:19am** - no student should be out of class. However, gangs of students are in the center hallway screaming, yelling cursing and carrying on and not one administrator present. I HADE ENOUGH and went out there and told them all to get to class. They cursed me out and continue to carry on.
A week or so prior to Christmas vacation Mr. Dickinson* tells me to identify the students who are acting up. I replied that he has them on video. What's the point of the taxpayers paying for the surveillance cameras *if* they are not being used? What makes it more sickening, Mr. Dickinson* made an announcement yesterday about CREDIT RECOVERY.

Once a month we have a CODE BLUE DRILL. Maybe we should have a code blue drill every day. JFK is NOT a safe place to work. There is NO discipline and students are NOT held accountability for any of their actions. As of this week, I will have to pay 1 to 2 thousand dollars more a year from my salary in taxes, yet students do not have to be in class. As a NJ taxpayer, I am getting screwed.

Can I send a copy of this email again to you, Mr. Dickinson*, all of the administrators in the building as well as all of the superintendents?
It's 8:41, students are still entering the building with bags of food, eating, drinking and not going to class.
CREDIT RECOVERY, ARE YOU KIDDING ME?
END

**January 7, 2013 - below is a narrative to an email I sent to the president and vice president of the PEA, keeping up with and adding to the paper trail.**
Interesting it is 10:07, for 90 minutes or more, there has been NO STUDENTS in the hallway.
NO NOISE.    ABSOLUTELY PERFECT!
REASON: some sort of assessment test being administered.
QUESTION: why isn't the school day like this every day?
END

**Below is a narrative to another email I sent on Jan. 7 to the president and vice president of the PEA, keeping up with and adding to the paper trail.**
CONTAMINATED WATER!
January 3 and 4, I noticed all water fountains and sinks in the building were covered with plastic and taped closed. There were signs on them saying DO NOT USE, CONTAMINATED.
REASON: LEAD in the water.
If the water is contaminated, then how does the cafeteria cook?
How do students get a drink of water other than purchasing bottled water from the vending machines?
END

**January 7, 2013** - I received a reply from the president of the PEA pertaining to the contaminated water along with an attached message / letter he sent to the Superintendent mistakenly dated 2012.

January 7, 2012

Via Facsimile and US Mail

Dr. Donnie W. Evans
State District Superintendent of Schools
Paterson Public Schools
90 Delaware Avenue
Paterson, New Jersey 07503

re: Water in the Schools

Dear Dr. Evans,

Just prior to the Christmas/Recess, the Association received notification from the Passaic Valley Water Commission reminding us once again that the water in Paterson is contaminated with lead. This is, unfortunately, no news to the Association, since the water contamination has been problematic for a very long time. It is, however, an extremely serious health and safety issue for our schools.

However, the Association has been notified by several schools that the response to this matter seems to be to block off all water fountains, covering them with bags without providing alternate water sources for staff and students. As you are aware, especially in the winter months, the heat in the buildings is extremely dry and creates an even higher need for alternative refreshment options in the schools (in the past, bottled water and water coolers were provided in some locations).

Preventing people in the schools from accessing water is an unacceptable solution. We urge you to reverse the inane solution that has been imposed and provide clean water for the people (both students and staff) who work in our schools and buildings.

Your prompt response in this matter is awaited.
Sincerely,

Peter A. Tirri
President
cc: ▓▓▓ NJEA UniServ Representative
 ▓▓▓ NJEA UniServ Representative
P.E.A. Joint Worksite Safety & Health Committee Members
▓▓▓, Deputy Superintendent of Schools
▓▓▓ Labor Relations Officer
▓▓▓ Director of Facilities

END

**NOTE OF INTEREST:** - Other than the above email, I have never heard anymore about the contaminated water/lead, situation in our school/s.

Needless to say, in March of 2016, a major crisis hit the Newark Public Schools in Newark, NJ where the water fountains in many of their schools were covered in plastic and taped off so students and faculty could not drink from them because of high levels of lead. Once I heard about the water contaminated with lead in the Newark school systems, I contacted several TV stations and a local newspaper. I sent them (via email) a copy of the email above informing them about the Paterson Public School system.

Unfortunately, as of April 1, 2016, nothing was reported. Furthermore, Newark and Paterson school districts are still and have been operated and under state control for over 25 years each.

**January 7, 2013 - below is a narrative to an email I sent to the president & vice president of the PEA keeping up with and adding to the paper trail.**
It's 2:10 and the hallways are a total disaster. Since testing was over, all you see is students in the hallways, playing, wrestling, screaming and cursing at the top of their lungs saying the most vial and disgusting things. In the last 20 minutes, Ms. Conscientious* had come out of her office several times yelling at students to go, to get to class and knock it off with the foul language. Only to be yelled and cursed at by students. She is in charge of the testing and is trying to get her work done. The hallways are a disaster and not one administrator is present. There is no way the administration in this building cannot know what is going on here. *IF* the information is true, the surveillance videos are also tied in with central office. Then all of the superintendents should know what is going on.
END

**January 8, 2013 - Below is a narrative to a pair of email I sent today to the president and vice president of the PEA, keeping up with and adding to the paper trail.**
2nd day of testing! Testing is over and we are back to normal, meaning not normal! Have video - shows and tells it all. Ms. *Conscientious* and Ms. Huwiggins* are in the hallway trying to get students to leave. They're just ignored. You will hear a security guard telling me how bad it is and there are NO administrators. Shortly afterwards a female VP walks by and did tell a student to remove his hat. The student refused and had a lot of wise remarks for her. I thought academies were to make things better?
**PART II**
**It is out of freaking control!** Not one administrator until LATE in the video when Mr. Arthurs* was trying to move students and was ignored. You will hear him tell students come on, let's get an education. Bottom line, not a thing is done about all of the students constantly in the hallways.
Send me a flash drive; I'll down load them to you. Very damaging!
END

**Jan 9 - have video 18 plus minutes long prior to 1st period.** However, I do NOT know if these students belong to ZERO PERIOD. Bottom line, no one belongs in hallway. It is absolutely disgusting the language and the way these students carry on and are allowed to continue to carry on. EXAMPLE - 4:56 into the video you will hear then see a security guard making an attempt to have a student remove his hood. It wasn't until the security guard started to walk over then the boy removed his hood, but not without his defiant attitude, disrespectful and vulgar back talk. You will NOT see any administrators. At approximately 8:40 – 8:55 minutes you will see a guidance counselor walking toward her office, stop and look at all the kids in front of her office screaming and cursing. She is so disgusted and just walks away. Every day, all day long, the guidance counselors and SRA teachers have difficulty doing their work in their offices even with the doors closed because of all of these students are being allowed by the administrators to constantly hang around making noise, swearing, screaming, yelling, wrestling and horsing around. The horn sounds to start first period but students don't care. The video shows it all. The video was shot from my room and my desk. That's how loud it is. If my little camera can pick it all up from here, can you imagine how loud it is out in the hallway?

**Jan 11** - I don't know what's going on. I only have rumors. Can't get info out of anyone! However, every student this morning was checked with handheld metal detectors. Rumor has it someone was stabbed. As always, everything is hushed up. Interesting and coincidentally, last night JFK staff received a phone call about a meeting next Wednesday, to hear Superintendent Donnie Evans talk about school/s security.

**January 14, 2013 -** I received an email from my principal about the state exam. Below is a narrative.
I need your help. Please encourage your 11th grade students to attend the HSPA prep programs. If they cannot attend after school, they should attend on Saturdays or vice versa. *We have to get the scores up.* These classes will help them in this regard.
Saturday Program 8:30 – 12:30
Weekday Afterschool Program: Tuesdays and Thursdays 3:30 – 5:30
Mentors, talk with the students you mentor. Attending these classes should be mandatory.
END

**Another fight** (that I know about) today involving one of my students and another boy.
Rule of thumb, fighting equals mandatory 10 days suspension. They both received three days of **In-School Suspension**. This is part of covering up and falsification of records.

**Jan 15 -** 7th period you can hear the panic over the walkie-talkies that there's a fight going on in room 235. What do they expect if there are no consequences for fighting, inappropriate, bad or poor behavior?

I sent an email to the president of the PEA asking if I can send a letter to my principal, vice principal, a tap, the building principal and all of the superintendents.
Later that day, I went directly to Mr. Arthurs* about my letter. Mr. Arthurs* was very supportive and understanding. He asked me if I would go with him to speak with Mr. Dickinson*. I said absolutely. However, I never received a reply from the president of the PEA.

**Jan 16 -** I still have not heard from the president of the PEA so I decided to send my letter with some additions to the original this morning to my principal and two VPs.

January 15, 2013

Dear Mr. Arthurs*, Mr. Naptha* and Mr. Lawrence*,

It is absolutely unbelievable down here. The noise is so loud you can't even hear my machines being on my classroom. Right now, there are students, 100s of them, all over the place. They are falling and rolling into my classroom fighting, cursing and carrying on.
When I say something to them, I am cursed at. UNACCEPTABLE!

No place else in the world is this allowed and definitely not acceptable in an educational complex. However, it goes on all day every day. I have had enough. There is NO CONTROL IN THIS BUILDING.

With all of the added administrator's in this building this type of behavior should not be going on. EVERY student should be in class BEFORE the bell sounds to start class.

The simplest of rules, no hat, wearing of uniforms, no phones, iPods, etc., are NOT enforced as was promised on the first day of school during our meeting in the auditorium.

One student in particular, a senior, the same student as above December 8, 2011 named FOOL* (and there are HUNDREDS more just like him is in the hallway all day, every day and NOT wearing a uniform, wearing hats, cursing, play fighting, continually cutting class and it goes on and on day after day every day all year) was never ever in class at all last year. HOW CAN HE BE A SENIOR????
This is NOT restructuring, this is NEGLECT.

We teachers cannot be held responsible and liable for students acting this way and for NOT going to class. I see administrators once and awhile and it's 15, 20 PLUS minutes after the bell rang to be in class. All they say is take your hat off and keep walking. Are you kidding me, they should have escorted them to security and given detention and or suspension? They are supposed to be swept up 2 minutes after the bell rings to be in class. This is going on 20 minutes INTO the class.

Having students in the hallway and not in class is a safety/security violation. How can you have security of the building when students are in the hallways, stairwells, walking in and out of the building, any place and every place other than being in class?

If a teacher says something to these students we are met with a barrage of threats, cursing, etc. This is BULLYING. What happened to the seriousness of BULLYING? Or did that also go by the way of ZERO TOLERANCE TO VIOLENCE?

Obviously, the student/s ignore all of us including administrators. WHY? Because administration has taught them that students can do whatever they want, and NOTHING WILL BE DONE ABOUT IT.

Then you have the nerve to have HSPA Boot Camp, HSPA Saturday Program, Credit Recovery and all these other programs especially just prior to the end of year to increase the graduation numbers and at the taxpayers' expense all because students are NOT made to go to class?

Meanwhile, students walk into the building by the 100s during homeroom.

Every student should be in school already. Not meandering eating and drinking as they are taking their sweet time going who knows where, and obviously NOT to homeroom.

Even during 3rd period, students are still entering the building. This is education? There is NOTHING in the realm of discipline or responsibility for being late, cutting and or having poor attendance.

It is January 15, 2013 and I have students with well over 40 days of absence, 20 plus cuts and 20 plus lateness and NOT one thing is done about it.

Students walk in and out of the building all day unabated. This is NEGLECT. We will NOT have an educational complex until we have order and discipline instead of a free for all and chaos.

If a parent does not send their child to school or makes sure they attend school, they are held liable, can be arrested and DYFS is brought in for NEGLECT. WELL, who is responsible for not having students attend their classes?

It's the same students every day, all day, all year for the last 2 years who are in the hallways, stairwells and any place else other than their respective classes and it's allowed??????

Then the district wants to increase the school day? Why? So, students can be in the hallway longer.

**_Simple Math -_** Using 10 minutes as a means, when it is usually 20 PLUS minutes.
If students were to be in class on time for nine periods, you have just increased the school day by 90 minutes without increasing the school day.

Can you imagine how much you have increased the school day at 20 PLUS minutes??????
I don't get it. Mr. Dickinson* tells me to identify these students when all of this is supposedly recorded on the so-called state of the art surveillance system?

I don't know about anyone else; however, with what goes on inside here every day and I did NOT write everything down bothers me. As a conscientious teacher and employee, I do NOT feel good about what is going on here.

I will NOT take the blame or responsibility for any student who fails when administration fails to enforce rules and discipline.

Ask yourselves, would YOU send your children here? I already know the answer.
Then why is this acceptable for the people/citizens of Paterson, NJ? It is 12:38, as I am finishing this up; there are about 9 students, 4 girls and 5 guys SCREAMING, CURSING at the top of their lungs, playing music loud and dancing. Are you kidding me!

THERE IS NO ONE HERE TO MAKE THEM GO TO CLASS! WHY?
This is NOT a place to play, hang out, or act as if it is a STREET CORNER.
OUR MAIN PRIORITY IS SUPPOSED TO BE EDUCATION.

This morning, January 16, 2013, a bunch of students were outside my door screaming yelling, boxing, cursing up a storm. One of the STEM guidance counselors came out and told these students to go and go to class. In defiance, these girls actually started bullying and threatening her.
They were cursing her and telling her to go FUCK herself, looking her up and down, in an act of intimidation. All this guidance counselor wanted is for them to go to class, and get out of the hallway, so she can work. WHY should she have to be placed into this position? Why is everything reactive and not proactive? Why was this allowed in the first place? WHY where these students in the hallway? Where are the administrators? Once again, with all the added administrators and the two heads of security why is this allowed to go on and on every day?
As for these young ladies they were BULLYING, YES BULLYING IN DEFIANCE TO THIS GUIDANCE COUNSELOR.

These young ladies MUST be held responsible for their actions and for the ACT OF BULLYING!
THIS IS A SCHOOL, not the streets.

Most respectfully,

Lee E. McNulty (TEACHER)

Surprise, surprise, I never received reply, a response or anything about the above email from anyone.
The email and I were ignored.
\*\*\*\*\*\*\*\*\*\*\*\*\*\*\*\*\*\*\*\*

**Jan 16** - as soon as the horn sound to end 5th period a BIG FIGHT breaks out with girls in the hallway. The hallways were so bad, and dangerous. Then another girl started cursing Fuck you, Fuck this, as loud as she could at a female security guard in attempts of starting a fight with her. And NOTHING was done about it. It is so freaking out of control. The ONLY administrator you see in the hallways is Mr. Arthurs*. He truly TRIES to get students out of the hallways, stairwells and back into class. Unfortunately, the students ignore and are very disrespectful to him. Can you imagine only (1) administrator trying to get control of this huge school all by himself when there are about 20 other administrators all hibernating. It is SICKENING! Where is the building principal? He continually allows this to go on every day. It was at least 20 plus minutes before the riot like situation to somewhat subside. It's the same students all day long. There needs to be an investigation on how so many students, who do not go to class, pass and are promoted. The fighting that is continuously allowed to go on inside here all day, every day, all year is unfreakinbelievable and insane! So much for *"ZERO TOLERANCE TO VIOLENCE!"*

**January 16, 2013** - I sent a copy of my January 15, letter to the presidents of the NEA and NJEA via USPS with a cover page; "What is taking so long to get help here at John F. Kennedy High School." I did this so I could continue creating a paper trail about JFK High School.

**Jan 17** - approximately 8:10, Mr. Dickinson* and Mr. Wilt* were going to the elevator on the 1st floor. Just prior to stepping in Mr. Dickinson* yells, "Good Morning." I replied, "Good Morning." He asked if there are any problems, is everything ok today? I knew he was being a wise ass and sarcastic so I smiled and said, "Everything is fine, no problems YET!" I realized Mr. Arthurs* gave him my letter. He wanted me to let him know who is using the foul language. He confirmed they do have everything on the security cameras but there is no sound. Next, he said that he will stand with me during the changing of classes. I replied, that has nothing to do with students being in the hallways all day. Then he asks do my students like me? I replied that has nothing to do with it. He asks again, do my students like me? I knew what he was getting at and said some of them. He said that's why. The students don't go to class because they don't like the class. I said that is unacceptable. I told him if I don't like you and you're my boss that's too bad. Students are to be in class not in the hallways. Typical, he tried to turn it around and blame the teachers for students not being in class. Even IF it is the teachers fault then why does he and all of the administrators with EXCEPTION of Mr. Arthurs* continually hide and deliberately allow students NOT to go to class all day, every day and for the entire year? The conversation died and he left.

**NOTE OF INTEREST:** - At no time did Mr. Dickinson* ever stand with me during the changes of any classes on any day for the rest of the year as he said he would.

**Jan 16** - I received an email from the president of the PEA saying he will be meeting with NJEA on the 24th.

**January 17, 2013, below is my reply email (narrative version) to the president of the PEA, keeping up with and adding to the paper trail.**
I gave my letter to Mr. Arthurs* and he is also quite upset with everything that is going on here. Mr. Arthurs* is the ONLY administrator who is trying and especially now after my letter. ALL DAY, he was really trying to get students moving out of the hallways and to class. I spoke with him yesterday because I was afraid, he would get sick or worse because it was getting to him too. The students were absolutely DISGRACEFUL. Even with him, they show no respect or fear of consequences. What does that tell you? Mr. Arthurs* said that himself.
END

**Jan 18** - received VIDEO from two students today on fighting in and on school grounds. I have two more videos from one of my female students involving a fight with girls on 1/17, approximately 2:30 right by the school's front doors. The other is on Monday, 1/14, involving one of my students and another kid fighting in the gymnasium. A total of 4 videos from students.

January 18, 2013 - below is a narrative to an email I sent with an attached video from my female student to the president and vice president of the PEA, the NJEA Uniserv assistant director and two NJEA regions 27 Uniserv Field Reps, keeping up with and adding to the paper trail.
See attached fight video. How much do you want to bet there is no V&V report? For the last 2 weeks there has been nothing but fights all day every day.
The administration wants to give the impression everything is going smoothly and safe, so no student/s is to be suspended creating a paper trail. So why would students care if nothing is going to happen to them? Example: A big fight is in a classroom the other day, the students received 3 days ISS.
END

(V&V = Vandalism & Violence report)

**Jan 25 – 29** - have video of students acting up outside my classroom.

**Feb 1** - I sent an email to Mr. Dickinson* and sent copies to Mr. Arthurs*, Mr. Naptha*, Mr. Lawrence* the president of the PEA and myself, to continue creating a paper trail. This time Mr. Dickinson* did reply back. However, typically he says the video footage he has shows something differently. Gee that's a surprise! However, he did come to see me along with his two bodyguards/heads of security and was more concerned WHY I copied the PEA. I told him I wanted my email documented. I can see on the look on his face he did NOT like that. He didn't say anything after that and left.
Once again, NOTHING changes, and everything remains the same OUT OF FREAKING CONTROL!

**Feb 20** - received video, starting in janitor's office and long after the horn for students to be in class. NO administrators! You'll see students punching one another in the nuts. Meanwhile every student will graduate and or pass to their next level?

**Video #2** - starts before the horn to begin 7$^{th}$ period with some sort of riot like atmosphere. Horn sounds 2:15 minutes into the video and students are in the hallways looooong after. Approximately 5minutes into the video, students are throwing toilet paper. 9 minutes into the video shows toilet paper all over and teachers asking if it's toilet paper. Approximately 11 minutes into video, a building principal told a bunch of kids to move, get to class and one of them was THE FOOL* who was absolutely disrespectful to her. He continued making fun of and cursing at her. You might be able to see and make it out in the video. There is nothing but foul language and cursing throughout the video. The principal did absolutely NOTHING. It just continued and she allowed it to continue. Other than this principal you do not see another administrator. If students know they can act and talk that way to a principal what the hell kind of example, message, and standards is the administration setting by allowing this type of behavior. I do NOT feel sorry for her. I say GOOD! After all these administrators created this dangerous out of control atmosphere to go and continually grow here! Video is almost 15 minutes long.

**February 21** - I sent an email to Mr. Dickinson*, Mr. Arthurs*, Mr. Naptha*, Mr. Lawrence*, the president and vice of the PEA, the president of the NJEA, the NJEA Uniserv assistant director and two NJEA regions 27 Uniserv Field Reps and to myself.
I am continuing with the paper trail that the administration is desperately trying to keep hushed up.

Gentlemen,

Attached, is my updated list of total students, absents, cuts and lateness per class (5 periods) up to the end of the second marking period. Not INCLUDING from then to present day.

NOT GOOD!
Thank you and most respectfully,
Lee E. McNulty

HERE IS THE ATTACHED UPDATED LIST

## 2012 -2013 SCHOOL YEAR METAL SHOP

| 2nd Period | As of the first day of school | | 17 Total students |
|---|---|---|---|
| 1st Marking period total | Absents (149) | Cuts (101) | Lates (30) |
| 2nd Marking period total | Absents (110) | Cuts (72) | Lates (21) |
| *Total 2 marking periods | **(259)** | **(173)** | **(51) & still counting.** |

| 4th Period | As of the first day of school | | 6 Total students |
|---|---|---|---|
| 1st Marking period total | Absents (27) | Cuts (7) | Lates (1) |
| 2nd Marking period total | Absents (9) | Cuts (1) | Lates () |
| *Total 2 marking periods | **(36)** | **(8)** | **(1) & still counting.** |

| 5th Period | As of the first day of school | | 21 Total students |
|---|---|---|---|
| 1st Marking period total | Absents (67) | Cuts (40) | Lates (10) |
| 2nd Marking period total | Absents (91) | Cuts (36) | Lates (20) |
| *Total 2 marking periods | **(158)** | **(76)** | **(30) & still counting.** |

| 8th Period | As of the first day of school | | 18 Total students |
|---|---|---|---|
| 1st Marking period total | Absents (88) | Cuts (63) | Lates (41) |
| 2nd Marking period total | Absents (70) | Cuts (31) | Lates (23) |
| *Total 2 marking periods | **(158)** | **(94)** | **(64) & still counting.** |

| 9th Period | As of the first day of school | | 18 Total students |
|---|---|---|---|
| 1st Marking period total | Absents (226) | Cuts (167) | Lates (32) |
| 2nd Marking period total | Absents (141) | Cuts (93) | Lates (38) |
| *Total 2 marking periods | **(367)** | **(260)** | **(70) & still counting.** |

**Grand total students (80)**    **Absents (978)**    **Cuts (611)**    **Lates (216) & still counting.**

END

**Feb 22** - below is a narrative email I sent to the president of the PEA.

**10:54am** - center hallway FILLED with students MOST not even in uniform. Mr. Dickinson* and Mr. Stevenson* are both present as students are just moseying as cattle grazing. Not one word was said to students to get to class. Get a copy of the school video. This is PROOF that the administration does NOTHING with safety, education and the following of rules and discipline here at JFK.

END

**Feb 22** - a couple of the Special-Ed counselors were telling me how overwhelmed they are in paperwork filing parents request for social security because their child is classified as ADHD & AHD? They receive money because their child is hyper. Most of them are not hyper, they are used to running free with no discipline at home and can do what they want here in school and so the district classifies them, and taxpayers have to pay MORE. You wonder why there's no money for social security!

**Feb 22** - I saw Mr. Piel*, a TAP, talking to one of my students. I purposely walked over and said this student has NOT been in my class since September. The student (name omitted) replied, I am trying to get my guidance to change it. I replied try nothing, it is NOT up to you, it is up to your guidance counselor and for five months you have been cutting class. You're to be in class. You do NOT make decisions on what classes you're going to have. The conversation was typical it just went on and on and it went nowhere. I wasted my time. All Mr. Piel* said to the kid, you have to keep going to class or you will keep getting cuts. I laughed, and said five months of cutting, how does a student make up five months of cutting? I was so disgusted, I just walked away. I could see Mr. Piel* didn't care and wasn't going to do anything and the students will keep on cutting knowing that nothing will be done about it!

Do you believe this? All these cuts and has yet to be disciplined? While the conversation was going on the hallways were filled with students just walking around. Why do we need administrators? WHAT DO THEY DO? For (5) months the administration has allowed this kid to cut my class!

**Feb 25 -** there is something going on allegedly with a teacher and some students sexually. Police arrested the teacher, and the newspaper reporters were outside. So, with all of this going on the administration is putting on the ye ole dog and pony show by being present, keeping students moving, picking them up and assigning them Saturday detention for NO UNIFORMS. However, in defiance you will still see small groups of students still just roaming. We should have reporters here all the time. Maybe this place would be a school instead of an indoor street corner. Something has to be done!

**February 26, 2013 - below is a narrative to another email I sent to Mr. Dickinson*, Mr. Arthurs*, Mr. Naptha*, Mr. Lawrence*, the president of the PEA and to myself. I continue creating and increasing the paper trail that the administration is desperately trying to keep hushed up.**
Once again, I am contacting you as you requested for me to do when I see something wrong. As for identifying them, once again, you have it all on video. It is 12:52, all period students outside screaming, yelling, wrestling playing hitting one and other, cursing worse than any sailor at the top of their lungs and no one stops them. Why is this allowed to continue over and over every day?
Why does guidance, Ms. Conscientious* and I have to put up with this inappropriate behavior.
IT IS WORSE THAN A STREET CORNER.
END

**Feb 28 -** I have 8 sections of lighting that are not working in my classroom/shop. I told the head janitor that I need bulbs replaced. He said there are NO BULBS in the district! Unfreakinbelievable!

Also, the district print shop teacher told me he now has to make and deliver 250 late slips every day. On 12/14/12, he had already printed 6000 slips and they asked for another 750 more for that day. WHAT A WASTE OF TIME AND MONEY! In fact, several of the print shop teacher's students come to school late every day and they get their late slips. We both asked them what happens. The students say, they give us detention, but we don't go. I asked what happens next. They said, "NOTHING!"
Why should they show up when they know nothing is going to be done about it?

**Mar 5, 6 & 7, week of HSPA state testing.** What a joke, time and being on time means NOTHING here. After testing students have maybe four, 15 - 20 minute classes. Most students don't even show up. Instead, the building is chaos and out of freaking control. The kids are all over the place, walking the hallways, playing, acting up or breaking something long after the horn sounds to be in class as other students are pouring out of the building through every door. The noise and cursing in the hallway is absolutely ridiculous and deafening. Even with the door shut the noise is unfreakinbelievable! So much for the state-of-the-art surveillance cameras! Meanwhile the Paterson police officers just stand there shaking their heads watching it all and cannot do anything because the administration will not allow them. However, if this was any place else, the police would be arresting students and would need a tractor trailer to take them to booking. So many students have over 60 days of absence and have not been dropped from roll. Another joke is we have 40 to 50 students on TWILIGHT PROGRAM. The teacher working that program told me maybe a dozen will pass. The others still act up and expect to pass. In reality our students get so many added advantages to pass the state exam/HSPA compared to schools in other districts. They have summer school prep for HSPA, weekend school for HSPA, HSPA Boot Camp twice a year, their regularly assigned classes are specifically designed and geared for taking the test. This is absurd and would NOT be necessary if students were made to be in class all day, every day and NOT hanging out in the building. THIS IS NEGLECT AND IN-HOUSE TRUANCY! Even after all of that so many students still do NOT pass the HSPA/state exam. Then in May and especially in June watch all the BS and alternative programs the administration will come up with to manipulate in changing student's grades and status to have students and especially seniors pass and graduate. It is NOT about giving students a quality well rounded education and preparing them for the REAL WORLD. It is about the "TEST," making the superintendent and the administration LOOK GOOD! It is all BS, lies and a big waste of taxpayers' money in the name of education.

**March 8, 2013 - below is a narrative email I sent to my principal, Mr. Arthurs*, VP Mr. Naptha*, TAP Mr. Lawrence* & myself, in keeping up with and adding to the paper trail.**
- I would like to know why, Mr. (Students name is omitted, I have been calling him, FOOL*), is allowed to come to school every day without wearing his uniform?
- I would like to know why he is allowed to be in the hallways every day, all day long.
- I would like to know why last week when the building principal told him and other students to move and get to class, he can curse at her, make fun of her and get away with it?
- I would like to know why he was allowed to enter school late today without having to get a pass.
- It is now 1:06 and he is in the hallway cursing up a storm and nobody finds this unacceptable?
- I find it degrading, inappropriate & unacceptable, yet it continues every day all day long, WHY?
- I would like to know why, is this allowed?
- Bottom Line, if (FOOL*) and other students are allowed to act this way every day, without any disciplinary action, then other students will follow adding to this GROWING problem.
- I would like to know, is this what has become of our Public School System?
- Is this what restructuring means?
- I am writing this because I am concerned not only as a teacher but a taxpayer!

END

As expected I never received a reply back. Like all of the other emails this went IGNORED!

**Mar 12 - during 2nd period,** a student was escorted out of the building in handcuffs, by two police officers. REASON is for putting his hands on a security guard. I was lucky enough to get that info. It's getting harder and harder to get any info anymore. The administration works so hard trying to keep everything hushed up. The administration should work half as hard in running this school properly and safely.

**Mar 13 - literally 100s** of students coming into school late. It is 8:41 and they are still coming in as if the bell just rang for school to begin. They get detention, but they don't show up.

**7th period -** students are in the hallways carrying on as if they are on the streets with all of the screaming and yelling. I finally had enough and yelled as loud as I could "nobody belongs in the hallway," and told them to get out of the hallway. The students were defiant and carried on as if I wasn't even there. I was fed up and said I will record them and WILL give it to the principal. As you will see they still didn't care. Their behavior and attitude show that there are NO consequences for being late and or cutting class. I went upstairs, told and downloaded the video to my principal Mr. Arthurs*. He said he will show it to building Principal. Mr. Arthurs* is the ONLY administrator that actually TRIES to make a difference. The video shows it all and not one administrator present!

**Next is an email my colleagues and I received about senior failures.**
From: Mr. Arthurs*
Sent: Wednesday, March 13, 2013 5:02 PM
To: All Names are omitted
Cc: Naptha*, Lentes*
Subject: Senior failures
Colleagues:
One of our school's goals is to increase the graduation rate. It therefore means that our seniors have to pass your classes. There are 65 seniors who are in danger of failing for the year, which means that it is likely that they will not graduate. This is not acceptable. Believe it or not, this is a serious problem which will affect every one of us.

Please meet with your seniors and ensure that they complete all obligations so they can graduate.
Thank you for your hard work, support and commitment to the success of our students.
Mr. Arthurs*

END

---

*NOTATION TO THE ABOVE EMAIL*
- Sentences 2, 4 & 5; says it all.
- Now the pressure is on to pass seniors no matter what!
- This is only March; watch what happens, come May and June to pass students/seniors?
- Then why did the administration allow students to be in the hallways, stairwells, bathrooms and every place else other than being in class all day long, every day, and all year long?
- I will guarantee the students who are failing are those who have *poor* attendance & cutting!

---

**March 15, 2013 - below is a narrative to an email I sent to Mr. Dickinson*, Mr. Arthurs*, Mr. Naptha*, Mr. Lawrence*, Mr. Jim*, the President of the PEA and to myself adding to the paper trail.**
As per our conversations about wanting me to inform you if I see anything wrong or have concerns, I am to let you know so you can fix them. As you said, "if you don't see it, you can't fit it."

I thank you for this opportunity and unfortunately I do have some. **March 15, 2013 at 8:23**, a female administrator went up to a group of students in the center hallway and told them to go to class. They never left, but she did. Five minutes later she tells them again. Once again, she is ignored and leaves.

A guidance counselor asks students to move away from her office. She was met with a ration of BS and had to call security. The students finally moved only because the two heads of security moved them.

When a teacher or any staff members, especially an administrator tells a student/s to move, go to class, students should move or be swept up and given appropriate consequences. Now other students are acting up because they see that this behavior is allowed and now it's growing.
With the surveillance cameras and the added administration in the building why are students in the hallways? Even as I am writing this at 8:38a.m. hundreds of students are still entering the building. Why is this allowed and continues to go on every day? Please do not tell me they are assigned Saturday detention, because students tell me that they don't go and NOTHING is done about it.
Can students just come to school whenever they want? Think about it. If 100s of students come to school late every day and receive Saturday detention, if they showed up, you would have to open the entire building to hold all of the students, plus pay 20 or more teachers to be here, every Saturday.

Furthermore, most students don't wear their uniforms. You told us 2 minutes after the bell rings to begin class any student without a proper pass or is not wearing their uniform will be swept up. Just 2 weeks ago, for the umpteenth time, you made an announcement telling students that they MUST be in uniform. NO EXCEPTIONS. WELL? If the simplest of rules cannot be enforced and there are no consequences for not following school and district policy, what's the point?

It is now 8:47 and students are still pouring in. We are supposed to be preparing students not just academically, but for their future, for our future and the future of our country. Wonder why our students cannot hold down a job because they have no idea why and how important it is to be ON TIME!

Teachers received an email about seniors being in danger of failing and it may cause problems for us. If students are allowed in the hallways every day, all day, all year please explain how can they pass? This is NOT the teachers fault.
Just like the conversation I had with you a few months back, are we at the time of the year when the administration is going to go crazy trying to figure out how to get more students to pass and graduate? Are we going to just give out diplomas, put on a dog and pony show, lie and say see, everything is better?
SEE BELOW STUDENTS WITH THE WORSE ATTENDANCE
As of March 14, 2013 the numbers have increased dramatically.
NJ TAXPAYERS ARE GETTING SCREWED!

I don't understand how everyone can put their head in the sand and believe this is normal. The only administrator trying to make a difference is Mr. Arthurs*.

It is 9 am, homeroom, the announcements are being made and students are still in the hallways and still entering the building. You have it on video.
Do all of the superintendent/s, the Commissioner of Education and Governor Christie ever get to see these videos as proof on how things run and have supposedly improved here?
As a teacher and a NJ TAXPAYER I am writing my observations and my deepest concerns.

Mr. Dickinson*, I wrote and sent this and other messages because I care A GREAT DEAL! My goal and love of what I do is not about having a job and collecting a paycheck. I want every student to be better than me. I want every parent to know that I will do my job pertaining to education, reinforce appropriate behavior and give their child the best education within my ability and this school setting allows.

Unfortunately, that's not going to happen and makes it very difficult for me as well as with all of my colleagues. Not until we have control of our building, rules are enforced and there are appropriate consequences for students and their inappropriate actions and behavior.

It is now, 11:25 and the center hall is filled with 100s of students who are out of control.

Wonder why students are failing? Class is 41 minutes long. Not whenever they get there. It is now 1:10 and the hallways are still filled with students and not one administrator present? That's 11 minutes after the bell rang to be in class, losing precious lesson and class time. 11 minutes more behind and on top of how many other minutes all day, every day, all year?

It is March 15 and NOW the administration is concerned about SENIORS GRADUATING?
What happened between September and February, two report cards and three supplementary notices?

I have 30 seniors total, equaling 37.5% of my student population.

## STUDENTS WITH THE WORSE ATTENDANCE

**Name Omitted**

| | | | |
|---|---|---|---|
| 1st Marking Period Grade (F) | Absents (18) | Cuts (6) | Lates (9) |
| 2nd Marking Period Grade (F) | Absents (37) | Cuts (12) | Lates (2) |
| Grand Total as of 3/1/13 | Absents (76) | Cuts (29) | Lates (11) |

**Name Omitted**        9/14 First day assigned to class.

| | | | |
|---|---|---|---|
| 1st Marking Period Grade (F) | Absents (39) | Cuts (39) | Lates () |
| 2nd Marking Period Grade (F) | Absents (41) | Cuts (18) | Lates () |
| Dropped from roll 2/26 | | | |
| Grand Total as of 2/26/13 | Absents (97) | Cuts (18) | Lates () |

**A Senior        Name Omitted**

| | | | |
|---|---|---|---|
| 1st Marking Period Grade (F) | Absents (8) | Cuts (5) | Lates () |
| 2nd Marking Period Grade (F) | Absents (18) | Cuts (12) | Lates (3) |
| Grand Total as of 3/1/13 | Absents (34) | Cuts (22) | Lates (4) |

**Name Omitted**

| | | | |
|---|---|---|---|
| 1st Marking Period Grade (F) | Absents (20) | Cuts (20) | Lates (7) |
| Dropped from roll 2/23 | | | |
| Grand Total as of 2/23/13 | Absents (36) | Cuts (24) | Lates (6) |

**A Senior        Name Omitted**

| | | | |
|---|---|---|---|
| 1st Marking Period Grade (F) | Absents (25) | Cuts (27) | Lates (4) |
| 2nd Marking Period Grade (F) | Absents (14) | Cuts (3) | Lates (3) |
| Grand Total as of 3/1/13 | Absents (42) | Cuts (3) | Lates (3) |

**A Senior        Name Omitted**

| | | | |
|---|---|---|---|
| 1st Marking Period Grade (F) | Absents (5) | Cuts (2) | Lates () |
| 2nd Marking Period Grade (F) | Absents (17) | Cuts (11) | Lates (1) |
| Grand Total as of 3/1/13 | Absents (26) | Cuts (16) | Lates (1) |

**Name Omitted**        2/25 First day assigned to class.

- Has never shown up for class?

**Name Omitted**        9/25 First day assigned to class.

| | | | |
|---|---|---|---|
| 1st Marking Period Grade (F) | Absents (21) | Cuts (21) | Lates (5) |
| Dropped from roll 12/4 | | | |
| Grand Total as of 12/4/12 | Absents (31) | Cuts (24) | Lates (5) |

**Name Omitted**        10/09 First day assigned to class.

| | | | |
|---|---|---|---|
| 1st Marking Period Grade (F) | Absents (7) | Cuts (1) | Lates (1 |
| 2nd Marking Period Grade (F) | Absents (12) | Cuts (8) | Lates () |
| Grand Total as of 2/28 13 | Absents (26) | Cuts (14) | Lates (1) |

**Name Omitted**

| | | | |
|---|---|---|---|
| 1st Marking Period Grade (F) | Absents (6) | Cuts (9) | Lates (8) |
| 2nd Marking Period Grade (F) | Absents (7) | Cuts (11) | Lates (16) |
| Grand Total as of 2/28/13 | Absents (24) | Cuts (23) | Lates (25) |

**Name Omitted**

| | | | |
|---|---|---|---|
| 1st Marking Period Grade (F) | Absents (35) | Cuts (35) | Lates () |
| Dropped from roll 1/15 | | | |
| Grand Total as of 1/15/13 | Absents (66) | Cuts (39) | Lates () |

**A Senior     Name Omitted     1/04 First day assigned to class.**

| | | | |
|---|---|---|---|
| 2nd Marking Period Grade (F) | Absents (12) | Cuts (14) | Lates (2) |
| Grand Total as of 2/28/13 | Absents (34) | Cuts (36) | Lates (2) |

**Name Omitted**

| | | | |
|---|---|---|---|
| 1st Marking Period Grade (F) | Absents (31) | Cuts (17) | Lates () |
| Dropped from roll 12/4 | | | |
| Grand Total as of 12/4/12 | Absents (40) | Cuts (17) | Lates () |

**A Senior     Name Omitted**

| | | | |
|---|---|---|---|
| 1st Marking Period Grade (F) | Absents (4) | Cuts (7) | Lates (12) |
| 2nd Marking Period Grade (F) | Absents (12) | Cuts (11) | Lates (6) |
| Grand Total as of 2/28/13 | Absents (27) | Cuts (29) | Lates (19) |

**Name Omitted     This is the student from entry Feb 22, 2012, talking with Mr. Piel***

| | | | |
|---|---|---|---|
| 1st Marking Period Grade (F) | Absents (28) | Cuts (22) | Lates () |
| 2nd Marking Period Grade (F) | Absents (41) | Cuts (34) | Lates () |
| Grand Total as of 2/28/13 | Absents (87) | Cuts (74) | Lates () |

**Name Omitted     9/10 First day assigned to class.**

| | | | |
|---|---|---|---|
| 1st Marking Period Grade (F) | Absents (3) | Cuts (4) | Lates (6) |
| 2nd Marking Period Grade (F) | Absents (18) | Cuts (11) | Lates (1) |
| Grand Total as of 2/28/13 | Absents (30) | Cuts (26) | Lates (9) |

**Name Omitted**

| | | | |
|---|---|---|---|
| 1st Marking Period Grade (F) | Absents (39) | Cuts (39) | Lates () |
| Dropped from roll 11/28 | | | |
| Grand Total as of 11/28/12 | Absents (44) | Cuts (44) | Lates () |

END

Once again, I never received a reply. It all went ignored!

**March 17** - Mr. Dickinson* met me outside my room during 1st period. He was upset. The first thing he said, you send me an email with all that information on it, you cc other people, you also cc the president of the PEA, you made it look like I am not doing anything about this. I replied, you're not. If you are then how can I have sent so much information in one day? He said he suspends students. I told him if you did then why are the same people in the hallway, coming to school late every day and that this school is out of control. I said you know I am against suspension. It is a vacation. If students don't want to come to school, follow rules, behave, etc., etc. then they should be made to come to school and have to spend even more time in here. Give them early morning, after school and Saturday detentions. They have to WORK, do assignments not just sit and sleep during detention. He said I assign detention. I said yeah, maybe they are assigned detention, but they don't show up and you administrators let it go. Then he asks me to give him the names of the students who said that. I said what does that have to do with anything? Obviously, he was upset, but so am I. So should the parents and guardians of Paterson and all of the NJ taxpayers. Then I realized his only real concern and the main reason for being upset is because I am creating a major paper trail with major documentation that cannot be disputed!

AGAIN, on March 20 an announcement was made about uniforms. Almost 2 years of RESTRUCTURING have gone by and he still cannot enforce the rule of students wearing uniforms.

**Mar 20 -** Mr. Piel* came to my room to speak with me about the March 15 email. He was upset and made a comment about being in the same union as me because he is a TAP. I was under the impression he was a VP. Nevertheless, I should have at least and as a courtesy sent him a copy of the email or kept his name out of it. However, he came in trying to prove that's the way things are here, they have been this way for years, they are not going to change, and he is not going to try to change them.

I said that is unacceptable. I told him I am going to try to make a difference and a change. He tried to tell me that cutting, and attendance has improved. I told him he was out of his mind. I showed him my documentation. He insisted that cutting is way down. Again, I said, you are out of your freaking mind. NO WAY, you guys are doctoring the numbers and statistics. He invited me to come up and see and speak with the teachers in the cut office. I told him I don't care what they have to say. I showed him that my numbers are off the chart compared to any year previous and only at the end of the 2nd marking period.

Mr. Piel* kept coming up with excuses such as he's only been here since November, the district will not allow us to do this, can't do that, we are not from Paterson, parents complain, and we get in trouble. I blew up and said get in trouble for what, telling the truth! Are you kidding me? Angrily, I said I challenge anyone to my documentation. Then he changed his tune by saying that the DISTRICT WON'T ALLOW US! **He also said, "It is the district's policy not to have students get to class on time." I snapped at him and said, "I want a copy of that policy."**

I asked him, "How do you sleep at night? He then tried to use for an excuse that my classroom is in right in the middle of the school hallway. His asinine logic was if my room wasn't here, I wouldn't see anything. I snapped at him and said are you nuts. Are you telling me if it isn't seen, if it isn't written or talked about (See No Evil, Hear No Evil & Speak No Evil), then it never happened? I said it again, is there something wrong with all of you? And if I didn't see all of this, I cannot be reporting all of this, and then none of this is happening? That would be OK with you too? ARE YOU FREAKING KIDDING ME? Unfortunately, I didn't think fast enough and should have said, would you send your children here? I kept telling him what is going on inside here is wrong and so are you. All of a sudden, he looked at his phone or walkie-talkie and just turned around and left.

Bottom line, Mr. Piel* was upset because I mentioned his name in the email about a student who has been cutting since September. I sent Mr. Piel* via email all of my documentation that I sent to Mr. Dickinson*and all of the other administrators in the last two emails pertaining to attendance, cutting and tardiness. I never received a reply.

**NOTE OF INTEREST: -** Typical administration, Mr. Piel* is more concerned about what I wrote and sent in an email to Mr. Dickinson*. They don't care about the student documentation I supplied.

**I sent an email to Mr. Piel* requesting a copy of the school's suspension list for the year.**
I never received a reply or a copy of the suspension list. However, I did go up to his office and asked for a copy of the absentee list. He tells me it is confidential and that I have to see the building principal for it. I said, "CONFIDENTIAL, since when!" They were never confidential. They were always placed in our mailbox every day. I still have almost everyone since I have been working here. This makes me believe this is part of the administration's plan on hiding the paper trail with student attendance.

**Mar 20 & 21** - students are all over the place, out of control and all day long. During 9th period another big brawl breaks out. From what I could make out, it was all girls fighting. Bottom line, if students weren't allowed to hang out in the hallway, there would not be any problems. As usual NOTHING was or will be done about it. The administrators just hushed it all up.

Same thing on March 21, with Dominicans fighting black students. There was nothing but large chaotic brawls and gangs starting fights in the hallways and stairwells all day. Some fights started in the hallways and were brought right into classrooms. Security just gets done breaking up a fight and a few minutes later, another starts. It is the same thing starting all over again and the hallways for the remainder of the day are just jam packed filled with students threatening one another, instigating more fights and trouble and actually fighting. It just continues to go on and on here all day every day and you do NOT see one administrator, or the building principal. The chaos just doesn't stop. It is so freaking dangerous here and to think we have six uniformed police officer in the building at all times. This is not a school. REMEMBER, THIS IS A SCHOOL THAT IS STILL UNDER STATE TAKEOVER AND CONTROL. I would love to see every New Jersey Politician have to send their children and grandchildren to school here. After all aren't they running things here in Paterson, NJ?

**Mar 21 -** to continue with my documentation and creating a paper trail I sent an email to the president of the PEA detailing my conversation and a copy of the email I sent to Mr. Piel* on March 20th. I also included the same attachments asking him to PLEASE look over my figures.

**March 25, 2013 - below is an email of a V&V report I sent to the president of the PEA and two NJEA representatives keeping up with and adding to the paper trail.**

Subject: VIOLENCE & VANDALISM REPORT
Good Morning Pete,
On Friday, March 22, 2013 I had an incident TWICE with a student.
Attached, explains it all and will be submitted today along with a Violence and Vandalism Form.
Thank you and most respectfully,
HERE IS THE ATTACHED

VIOLENCE & VANDALISM REPORT
On Friday, March 22, 2013, approximately 12:15pm, as I have been for the last few weeks, I take a walk during my lunch period, around the perimeter of JFK.
Ever since I have been released from the hospital approximately 5 weeks ago and taking blood thinning medications, it is important that I take walks. I stay within the perimeter of the building. I figured since the district had spent 10's of thousands of dollars for the security fence that wraps around the entire perimeter of the building and a state-of-the-art surveillance system it would be SAFE to go for a walk.

As I was approaching the lower section of the parking lot (the pit), I noticed 3 boys trying to break into the building. I kept walking and the tall one all dressed in dark clothes says to me, "what you looking at mother fucker." Being I have a catheter, I am basically handicapped right now and there's 3 of them, I figured the best thing I could do to protect myself was to pull out my camera, to make them think I am videotaping them and have proof who they were.

It worked, their first reaction was to run and hide. Two of the kids, were more concerned about getting away, not getting caught for being out of the building and cutting. They never really said or did anything. However, the tall one with the dark clothes (NO UNIFORM TO IDENTIFY WHAT ACADEMY HE WAS IN) kept it up with the threats, telling me the next time he sees me he is going to beat my ass along with a continuation of foul language and hand gestures. However, he still kept walking away.

I went about my business and continued with my walk then went back inside the building. It should all be on the school surveillance system.

At the beginning of 8th period, guidance counselor (name omitted) came to speak with me about one of my students. To keep our conversation private from the other students, we went outside my door to talk. All of a sudden, the same big kid in the dark clothes walked right up to (name omitted) and me. Once again and obviously he is cutting class again. My first reaction was he is hunting for me? So, I just said hi.

Again, he begins with the obscenities, foul mouth and threatening remarks to me. He started by calling me mother fucker, who is you, who do you think you is and now what are you going to do, now? I replied "Who do you think you're talking to? You don't like something, tell a cop." This kid continued calling me mother fucker, that he was going to fuck me up, who do I think I am, etc. etc. etc. I had enough of him cursing and threatening me and I yelled, "Are you threatening me?" The kid continued. I yelled again, "I'll ask you again, are you threatening me?!"
With all the people in the center hall not one person came over. However, this kid realized I wasn't going to take it anymore. He walked away and brazenly went directly to an administrator, Ms. Weiland*. I was shocked and disgusted. It is so typical, a teacher has a problem, and nobody came to see or help. However, if the students can't get his or her way they go running to an administrator as if I DID SOMETHING WRONG!
What makes me laugh as well as even more disgusted -
- This student who obviously was cutting class when we were both outside of the building earlier.
- He and the other two kids shouldn't even have been outside of the building in the first place.
- No uniform to identify which academy he is part of.
- Threatens me while I was outside the building
- All three students finally succeeded to make their way back into the building without getting caught. Every day that week those 3 kids as well as others are outside. So much for the security system.
- 8th period he is now cutting class again.
- Curses and threatening me again brazenly and defiantly and in front of a guidance counselor.
- Then goes running to an administrator because his threats and **bullying** tactics didn't work on me as it does with so many of the other teachers.
- As I have been saying all year if these students and so many others were not allowed to roam the building, enter and exit the building whenever they want, this incident would have never happened.

Does the BULLYING ACT only refer to students on students?
Are we at the point where teachers must stay in a group, do not leave our rooms or unless we go directly to our cars stay inside, too. I don't want to end up like Mr. Robles.
Whatever happened to the District's Policy on "ZERO TOLERANCE to VIOLENCE?"

With that being said, it is imperative that a police report be filed and copies given to me and the PEA.
For the record, my name is Mr. McNulty, not "MOTHER FUCKER!"
Copies of this will be added to the Violence and Vandalism Form, sent to Pete Tirri of the PEA and to the NJEA.

                                          Thank you and most respectfully,
                                              Mr. Lee E. McNulty (Teacher)

**END**

**NOTE OF INTEREST TO THE V&V REPORT & EMAIL:**

I sent a copy of the above information and police report to the President of the PEA and two NJEA representatives. I did this for my added protection because if anything should happen to me, the district will not only blame me, they would find me at fault for NOT filing a report.
Even though I placed a copy of the V&V report in every administrator's mail box not one came to see if I was alright or to ask me what happened.

I never heard back from the President of the PEA or anyone from the NJEA.

Here is the Police Report.

| PATERSON POLICE DEPARTMENT | NARRATIVE | FILE CONTROL # 13-27155 |

On March 25, 2013 this officer was assigned to work at John F Kennedy High School. At approximately 1030 hours this officer was approached by a teacher Mr. McNulty, who related that he wanted to file report for threats against a student.

Mr. McNulty related on Friday March 22, 2013 at approximately 1:15 pm, he went outside for a walk during his lunch period around John F Kennedy perimeter. As Mr. McNulty approached the lower section of the parking lot he noticed three boys trying to get into the building. Mr. McNulty continued walking while [REDACTED] stated to him "what you looking at motherfucker". Mr. McNulty became alarm and pulled out his cellphone since he is handicapped right now and there's three boy, so he act like he was videotaping them and the boys took off running in an unknown direction.

[REDACTED] stated that he is going to assault the complainant specifically stating "I going to beat your ass the next time I see you" while he walk away. The complainant continued his walk and went back inside J.F.K. Building. Mr. McNulty related during 8th period he was in the hallway when [REDACTED] approached him and again states threatening him stating "motherfucker I going to fuck you up" while throwing up hand gestures.

This officer advised Mr. McNulty to the courts to file complaint for threats if he wishes to pursue this incident. Also school officials was notified about this incident. Mr. McNulty stated the school surveillance system probably capture this incident.

END

**Mar 26 - my student gave me a video** showing students sneaking out of school 3rd period. You'll see them going through the gate to change clothes and looking for their weapons. My student watched the whole thing but could only videotape so much. The school cameras should have it all recorded.

**March 27 - I sent the following information from the Paterson Public Schools website via email to the president of the PEA and a NJEA representative.**

MEANWHILE JFK IS OUT OF FREAKING CONTROL

On District web site: http://www.paterson.k12.nj.us/11_superintendent/superintendent.php

### Office of the Superintendent

A Message from the Superintendent on School Safety

First I want to express my heartfelt condolences to the parents and family members of the young children and staff members who lost their lives during the tragic event in Newton, Connecticut on December 14th.

It is never easy for any of us to hear about the loss of life – especially of those so young – and our thoughts and prayers go out to all who are grieving.

Certainly, a tragedy like this causes all of us who are responsible for school safely to pause and reflect on our own safety practices and question if we are doing all we can to ensure that our school buildings are safe.

Let me start by reassuring parents that we consider *your* children to be *our* children, and I firmly believe that our schools are among the safest places here in the City of Paterson.

Over the years, we have institutionalized many best practices including ensuring we have highly trained security personnel, conducting annual training of our staff which includes regular practice of drills including lock down drills and active shooter drills (recently reviewed by Homeland Security), and collaborating with City and County law enforcement officials to share and evaluate our district's safety procedures and practices.

Although I am proud of what we have done to make our schools safe for our students and staff, there is always room for us to continue to improve on our practices and procedures. To that end, we are currently examining our policies to ensure they are consistently implemented throughout the district, and we are evaluating each and every facility for areas that may be deemed vulnerable to someone who has the intent to do harm.

> **I have said many times that learning cannot take place in an environment where students and staff do not feel safe – and for this reason "Safe, Caring and Orderly Schools" has been and will remain one of our district's top priorities.**
>
> Parents, students, and staff should know that I am firmly committed to this priority and I have advised my staff that we all need to ensure we are addressing any potential issues and pursuing any required "fixes" immediately. In fact, I have asked our Deputy Superintendent, Ms. Eileen Shafer, to lead an initiative to update our Safety & Security Plan. You will hear more about this plan in the second half of January, and we will ask our Board, and our community members to review the plan and provide any feedback or concerns that you may have. Once this Safety & Security Plan is finalized, it will ultimately go to our Board of Education for a final review.
> Thank you.

END
ONCE AGAIN NO RESPONSE, NO REPLY, IGNORED!

Do they work in and in charge of the same school I work in?

**Apr 16** - guidance counselors were telling me that their supervisor told them that they are going to graduate everyone. As long as they passed HSPA, they will graduate! It does not matter about school or classes. One guidance counselor pointed out a student who just returned to school for being out a month after being locked up for possession saying, even he will graduate. I said just a month? I bet he's been out of school MORE than a month in total. She just made a face of disgust.

**May 18** - Ms. Conscientious* made an announcement to seniors. She explained if they DO NOT bring in their appeal forms SIGNED BY THEIR PARENTS, you CANNOT GRADUATE!
They have failed the HSPA and whatever else for testing. Now the school & District wants to appeal their scores. These kids DO NOT CARE. They DO NOT want to do anything. Their attitude is YOU DO IT FOR ME. They don't even want to bring in a paper to graduate. This attitude and behavior is taught and reinforced here, because teachers and everybody else did and still does everything for them. This is NOT fair to all of the students that DO their work, have GOOD attendance, participate and follow the rules.

**April 19, 2013 - below is another email I sent to the president and vice president of the PEA, the President of the NJEA, the NJEA Uniserv assistant director and two NJEA regions 27 Uniserv Field Reps keeping up with and adding to the paper trail.**

Subject:        DOCUMENTATION

Good Morning All,

A little information to show how well things are going here and especially with the restructuring.

The second attachment you can compare to the past years.

Yet nothing is done about it.

I don't understand how this cannot only continue but allowed to get progressively worse?

Am I the only one who cares?

Most respectfully,

Lee

ATTACHEMENT #1

METAL SHOP
3rd MARKING PERIOD REPORT & GRADES

**2nd PERIOD**
- **Grades:**        **(11) Students total**
- A = 2
- B = 4
- C = 1
- D = 0
- F = 4

| As of 4/17/13 | (17) total students have been assigned to this class. | | |
|---|---|---|---|
| 1st Marking period total | Absents (149) | Cuts (101) | Lates (30) |
| 2nd Marking period total | Absents (110) | Cuts (72) | Lates (21) |
| 3rd Marking period total | Absents (117) | Cuts (45) | Lates (19) |
| **Total 3 marking periods:** | **Absents (376)** | **Cuts (218)** | **Lates (70)** |

**4th PERIOD**
- **Grades:**        **(3) Students total**
- A = 3

| As of 4/17/13 | (6) total students have been assigned to this class. | | |
|---|---|---|---|
| 1st Marking period total | Absents (27) | Cuts (7) | Lates (1) |
| 2nd Marking period total | Absents (9) | Cuts (1) | Lates () |
| 3rd Marking period total | Absents (25) | Cuts (9) | Lates (3) |
| **Total 3 marking periods:** | **Absents (61)** | **Cuts (17)** | **Lates (4)** |

**5th PERIOD**
- Grades:         (10) Students total     New students every marking period.
- A = 3

| | | | |
|---|---|---|---|
| As of 4/17/13 | (31) total students have been assigned to this class. | | |
| 1st Marking period total | Absents (67) | Cuts (40) | Lates (10) |
| 2nd Marking period total | Absents (91) | Cuts (36) | Lates (20) |
| 3rd Marking period total | Absents (32) | Cuts (9) | Lates (10) |
| **Total 3 marking periods:** | **Absents (190)** | **Cuts (85)** | **Lates (40)** |

**8th PERIOD**     (12) Students total
- Grades:
- A = 2
- B = 5
- C = 0
- D = 1
- F = 4

| | | | |
|---|---|---|---|
| As of 4/17/13 | (19) total students have been assigned to this class. | | |
| 1st Marking period total | Absents (88) | Cuts (63) | Lates (41) |
| 2nd Marking period total | Absents (70) | Cuts (31) | Lates (23) |
| 3rd Marking period total | Absents (118) | Cuts (43) | Lates (31) |
| **Total 3 marking periods:** | **Absents (276)** | **Cuts (137)** | **Lates (95)** |

**9th PERIOD**     (11) Students total
- Grades:
- A = 3
- B = 0
- C = 1
- D = 0
- F = 7

| | | | |
|---|---|---|---|
| As of 4/17/13 | (19) total students have been assigned to this class. | | |
| 1st Marking period total | Absents (226) | Cuts (167) | Lates (32) |
| 2nd Marking period total | Absents (141) | Cuts (93) | Lates (38) |
| 3rd Marking period total | Absents (158) | Cuts (118) | Lates (33) |
| **Total 3 marking periods:** | **Absents (525)** | **Cuts (378)** | **Lates (103)** |

**Total students for 3rd marking period = (47)**
- Total   A's = 20
- Total   B's = 9
- Total   C's = 2
- Total   D's = 1
- Total   F's = 15
- As of 4/17/13 a grand total of **(92)** students.
- Grand total for only **three** marking periods all **5** periods.
- **Absents (1428)**     **Cuts (835)**     **Lates (312)**

**STILL HAVE ONE MARKING PERIOD LEFT**

## ** ATTACHMENT #2 **

### 2009 - 2010 TOTAL ABSENCES, CUTS, TARDIES & STUDENTS

| | | | | |
|---|---|---|---|---|
| 1st Period | Absents 301 | Lates 147 | Cuts 253 | @ 13 Total students |
| 2nd Period | Absents 141 | Lates 47 | Cuts 41 | @ 36 Total students |
| 4th Period | Absents 230 | Lates 53 | Cuts 55 | @ 38 Total students |
| 5th Period | Absents 390 | Lates 168 | Cuts 186 | @ 21 Total students |
| 6th Period | Absents 327 | Lates 189 | Cuts 98 | @ 17 Total students |
| 9th Period | Absents 215 | Lates 114 | Cuts 145 | @ 16 Total students |
| **Total** | **Absents 1604** | **Lates 718** | **Cuts 778** | **@ 141 Total students** |

### 2010 - 2011 TOTAL ABSENCES, CUTS, TARDIES & STUDENTS

| | | | | |
|---|---|---|---|---|
| 1st Period | Absents 44 | Lates 30 | Cuts 23 | @ 4 Total students |
| 2nd Period | Absents 176 | Lates 86 | Cuts 57 | @ 38 Total students |
| 4th Period | Absents 154 | Lates 32 | Cuts 8 | @ 29 Total students |
| 5th Period | Absents 668 | Lates 97 | Cuts 203 | @ 20 Total students |
| 6th Period | Absents 410 | Lates 95 | Cuts 134 | @ 19 Total students |
| 9th Period | Absents 440 | Lates 131 | Cuts 164 | @ 17 Total students |
| **Total** | **Absents 1892** | **Lates 471** | **Cuts 589** | **@ 127 Total students** |

### 2011 - 2012 TOTAL ABSENCES, CUTS, TARDIES & STUDENTS
### RESTRUCTURING YEAR

| | | | | |
|---|---|---|---|---|
| 1st Period | Absents 545 | Lates 134 | Cuts 288 | @ 12 Total students |
| 2nd Period | Absents 378 | Lates 89 | Cuts 153 | @ 15 Total students |
| 4th Period | Absents 400 | Lates 84 | Cuts 127 | @ 51 Total students |
| 5th Period | Absents 452 | Lates 65 | Cuts 95 | @ 24 Total students |
| 7th Period | Absents 122 | Lates 24 | Cuts 40 | @ 11 Total students |
| 9th Period | Absents 32 | Lates 10 | Cuts 9 | @ 3 Total students |
| **Total** | **Absents 1929** | **Lates 406** | **Cuts 712** | **@ 116 Total students** |

Homeroom is taking attendance, but students do not attend class? An entire week wasted!

- Restructuring year compared to 2010 – 2011 School year
- **Absents** = 37 More    **Lates** = 65 Less    **Cuts** = 123 More    **11 Less students**

Student's absenteeism *is* increasing every year.
END E-MAIL

---

**NOTATION TO THE ABOVE INFORMATION:**
- The administration says our attendance has improved.
- I sent the same information to all administrators.
- Not one administrator has gotten back to me or shown concern.
- However, below are my final numbers.

## 2012 – 2013 TOTAL ABSENCES, CUTS, TARDIES & STUDENTS
## 2nd YEAR OF RESTRUCTURING

I stopped taking attendance Wednesday, June 26, 2013.
Last 7 or so days of school no students showed up for any classes or even make ups.

| | | | |
|---|---|---|---|
| 2nd Period | Absents 577 | Lates 99 | Cuts 255 @ 17 students |
| 4th Period | Absents 98 | Lates 8 | Cuts 33 @ 6 students |
| 5th Period | Absents 370 | Lates 67 | Cuts 207 @ 42 students |
| 8th Period | Absents 364 | Lates 107 | Cuts 175 @ 19 students |
| 9th Period | Absents 745 | Lates 124 | Cuts 546 @ 19 students = 103 students |
| **Grand Total** | **Absents (2154)** | **Lates (405)** | **Cuts (1216) & only 5 periods this year** |

### Note of Interest:
- I had 5 periods this year. I usually have 6 and look at the increases.
- 4th Marking Period I ended up with only 44 students' total.
- 2012-2013 has 13 students less than 2011- 2012. Student absences & cutting is HIGHER!
- 2012-2013 has 24 students less than 2010 - 2011. Student absences & cutting is HIGHER!
- 2012-2013 has 38 students less than 2009 - 2010. Student absences & cutting is HIGHER!

**Apr 22 - 9th period, 2:45pm**, the noise and commotion is absolutely deafening. All of this is on school video. Class started at **2:29**. However, the hallways are jam packed and filled with students yelling, screaming, playing, running, cursing and not one administrator present. Meanwhile teachers are receiving email and notices about FAILING students. Remember the March 13, 2013 email stating, "This is not acceptable. Believe it or not, this is a serious problem that will affect everyone." Meanwhile the hallways, stairwells, bathrooms the entire building is filled with students/SENIORS who are NOT in class. How can teachers be held accountable? It is failing ADMINISTRATION NOT TEACHERS!

### Here is a perfect example of manipulating the graduation and passing numbers.

**Last week, I sent a student (name omitted) to the office with a disciplinary form.** Friday, my principal removed him from my class. I said he didn't need to do that. He insisted and said he is done and would be best to have him out of my class so I can work with the other students. I thought, *today*.

**April 22, 2013, I learned** the administration removed him because he has failed three PLUS marking periods, poor attendance, a great many cuts and lateness. They placed him in a class he already has earlier in the day, now having two classes of the same woodshop. Now he starts fresh with a few weeks left of classes before final exams. With a stroke of a pen, his failing grades, absences, cuts and lateness disappear because the administration wants the numbers/statistics to increase by any means possible for graduation.

Anybody can get a diploma here and you DON'T have to go to class.
- **Below are his totals from my class prior to removal.**
- **Grand Total as of 4/19/13**   Absents (30)   Cuts (20)   Lates (26)
- **Update - June 27, 2013, he did pass and graduate.**

**Apr 23 - 12:20,** I watched three girls place an object between the door and jam so the door doesn't close, then leave the building. They do this so they can get back in but so can unwanted intruders. My biggest concern is God Forbid if something should happen to those girls because they left the school? Doesn't anyone monitor the security cameras? I do NOT blame the girls. The administration is allowing this.

**Apr 24 -** this place is out of freaking control. Bottom line, it doesn't matter, the administrators are all scrambling now to do whatever it takes to have as many students pass and graduate. Meanwhile nothing has changed. Hallways are filled with students looooooooooooooooooong after the horn to BEGIN class. There is *NO* accountability for attendance, cuts &lateness's.

**Apr 26 - it is absolutely ridiculous here.** NOTHING changes. Students are still in the hallway. Shocking, there ARE a few administrators telling students to move and the students are ignoring them or maybe they may move 2 feet. The students don't care; they stay defiant knowing damn well that there is no recourse or disciplinary action going to be taken. PROOF, LOOK AT MY ATTENDANCE! It is the same kids and seniors to boot. What the administrators are doing NOW is removing seniors who failed all three marking periods, placing them in another class with 6 weeks left of school so they can start fresh. Making their 3 marking period grades, attendance, cutting and lateness not count, will all be ignored just so they will pass and to increase the graduation rate. Then the superintendent will get his bonus!
NEW JERSEY TAXPAYERS ARE GETTING SO SCREWED!

**It is UNFREAKINBELIEVABLE, nothing but problems and fighting ALL DAY.** It was so bad during 8th period, one of my girls (name omitted) came up to me and said the other day she went to the ladies' room and some girls gave her a bad time, got in her face saying she's not allowed to use this bathroom, started threatening and bullying her. I was upset because she didn't tell me until today. I immediately went to find a security guard, a TAP, an administrator– anyone - but they were all too busy with all of the commotion that was going on inside and around here. Even the Mr. Dickinson* was involved. The administrators are working like crazy trying to figure out how to keep all of this from becoming a major paper trail and what do they need to do to keep it all hushed up. There were no visitors in the building, so it is NOT a dog and pony show. It is a mess here and the administrators are afraid if any of this is going to get out. Little do they know IT IS, but a little later thanks to me!

There is so much going on all over the place with fighting, students walking in and out of classes they don't belong in, carrying on, teachers are calling security to come and remove students from class, from the hallways every place, it is just absolute chaos/bedlam, and the noise is deafening. Then to boot, there was a situation including some *parents*, who came into the building who themselves were so out of control, started a great deal of commotion and actually started fighting with everyone.

UNFREAKINBELIEVABLE! Nothing surprises me here anymore. As I have been saying all along and especially these last 2 restructuring years, it is OUT OF CONTROLL HERE. There is NOTHING about RESTRUCTURING or EDUCATION here. It is about BS and LIES! Bottom line, I couldn't get anyone to help my student. She is so afraid that these girls are going to attack her. I told her if you see them or thinks something is going to happen, do NOT disrespect a teacher, you excuse yourself and come directly to me. I'll take care of everything. I also told her to make sure she tells her mother what is going on. Later that day she was told to see a TAP on Monday and if she sees them again, to report them then. I said, NO, they should have it on video. Bottom line, nothing was done about it.

**Then to end the day,** one of the Child Study Team Counselors was telling me how the principal and other administrators want him and all of the counselors to change and make any necessary arrangements so seniors can graduate. I said, "Isn't that against the law?" He said, **"YES, it is against the law!"** He said the administration wants all of the counselors to say, (LIE) all of these students are exempt from mandated class, such as Health, Gym and etc. He refuses and realizes that the administration will place a great deal of pressure upon him & them. He even said it is just about pushing these kids through to make the numbers higher for graduation and to make the superintendent look good.

**May 1, 2013 - below is a narrative to another email I sent to the president and vice president of the PEA, the president of the NJEA, the NJEA Uniserv assistant director and two NJEA regions 27 Uniserv Field Reps. keeping up with and adding to the paper trail.**

It's update time.
I enclosed my documentation for April 26.
**April 30, 2013,** no change, the hallways were absolutely insane all day and more so after 4th period. Students were running as fast as they can, throughout the building, slap boxing, wrestling, throwing kids down on the floor and acting as if they are mugging them, cursing and swearing instead of being in class.

If it wasn't for taking students out of classes to prepare for all of these state tests there is no education going on! NO administrators around. My students were commenting how bad the hallways are. I don't understand how this can continue day after day, all year and nothing changes?

Students/seniors who are failing classes all 3 marking periods are removed from class, placed into another class so they will pass and graduate.

The administration is doing anything and everything to increase the number of students graduating. Many of these students' seniors have an enormous number of cuts and more than 30 days absent. One in particular has NOT been in school for the last 3 months and will be graduating?
Is this what is meant by RESTRUCTURING?
In the local media, NJEA sends their support to Camden? Why doesn't Paterson get any support?

The superintendent and his administration MUST be held liable. THIS IS NEGLECT!
Parents have their children taken away by DYFS for less.
Every day 100s of students and they are the same students who are late to school. Obviously, if it is the same students, there are NO CONSEQUENCES!

Would anyone from the NEA, NJEA and the PEA send their children here? I know the answer. Then why is this allowed to continue and nobody does anything, especially when there is so much proof available?

Can't we obtain copies of the school surveillance videos? Doesn't the superintendents look at them? Even with the cameras outside the building it would show students coming and going all day long.

WE ARE RUINING A NATION! Speaking of which, take a walk around the school during the Pledge of Allegiance to the Flag. It is absolutely DISGUSTING. AND THIS IS A PUBLIC SCHOOL?
Is this what our service men and women have died for and are still dying for?

I write, collect and send information for years to those who I thought would help.
Especially this year, I wrote to the presidents of the NEA & NJEA and nothing. Not a god damn thing

I don't know how anybody can sleep at night knowing this is going on.
I KNOW I CAN'T.
AND THIS IS A STATE RUN AND OPERATED SCHOOL DISTRICT!
SHAME ON US ALL!
END
*NO ONE EVER RESPONDED BACK!*

**May 1 - at the end of 5th period,** surprisingly, Mr. Wilt* was out in the hallways telling students to come on let's go, walk and talk, let's get to class. The students just ignored him. Before a minute was up, he gave up and just walked away. So much for an administrator having authority or actually caring!

**May 3 -** another guidance counselor was telling me that she was upset and has a problem. She has a student (name omitted) who is 20 years old, was locked up for selling drugs, has been absent/out of school for 90 plus days, was brought back to JFK and told he WILL GRADUATE!

**May 3 - below is an email I sent (narrative version) to the president of the PEA and two NJEA regions 27 Uniserv Field Reps keeping up with and adding to the paper trail.**
I wrote explaining I have been marking some students down for cutting only to find out they were not cutting. They had (ISS) In School Suspension. Naturally, I changed their cuts to WB which means ISS on Genesis. However, whoever is in charge of ISS is marking / changing students to present, NOT ISS. It seems that the administration is controlling and falsifying these records too.
END

**May 9 -** Ms. Conscientious* made announcement again as she has every day for the last two weeks, for all seniors who DID NOT bring in a signed EPP (which is an appeal from the state) in order to graduate they must bring it in by tomorrow, Friday, May 10, 2013. They just don't care.

**May 10 - 10:04, FIRE! Had to evacuate building!** The fire was in a locker in boys' locker room. Fire department and extra police came into the building. We came back in approximately 10:36.

**May 14 -** a parent Mrs. Moore* came into see me along with her son's guidance counselor. She was concerned that her son Lenny Moore* is failing my class and that some sort of deal was made where my class wasn't an issue for graduation. I said, I didn't understand. This is ACT academy, meaning Architect, Construction and Trades Academy. My class metal shop, just as woodshop, graphic arts, auto shop are the supposedly CORE classes of the academy. They left to speak with my principal.

**On May 15 -** speaking with the guidance counselor again, we were discussing Lenny Moore* and yesterday's situation. She said Lenny* will go to Credit Recovery for INTRO to Microsoft Word in lieu of my class. He also has credit recovery for 1 or 2 other classes in order to graduate. I said that makes no sense, CREDIT RECOVERY is for failing a particular class NOT starting from scratch to just get credits. Plus, how does someone get credit for the entire year for a class they didn't have at all? Then if (the operative word is "IF") CREDIT RECOVERY starts tomorrow May 15, 2013, how does he receive credit for an entire year for a couple of hours worth of work and if he even bothers to show up? ARE YOU FREAKING KIDDING ME? All week the administration has been making announcements saying, NO student can go to the PROM if they are failing any classes. It is the middle of MAY and this is the first time I have seen or spoke with his mother. Where has she been since September? Her son has been failing all year and now after eight plus months, three report cards, four warning notices later, she is concerned? Plus, she seems to be more concerned about Lenny* NOT attending the PROM!
Once again, how can a student go to the prom when a school stipulation is no student can attend if they are failing? As always, it is all lies, BS, smoke & mirrors. The students all know this and that is why they don't care. They know some way, somehow, they WILL GRADUATE and don't have to do a thing.

**On March 22,** I had a meeting with Lenny* and his guidance counselor. We decided on a way he could pass my class. The next morning, he never shows up for makeup. He also decides to cut class, adding to his already high absentee rate. Just with his absenteeism, how can he be allowed to graduate?
As of May 14, 2013, he has the following;    **Absents (42)    Cuts (18)    Lates (1)**

There is no reason for anyone to drop out of school here, anyone can get a diploma.
*JUST AS LONG AS THEY JUST HANG OUT INSIDE HERE.*

**May 15 - it is 9:42** students are still walking in and not being brought to the office for being late. In fact, one student who just walked in came over and asked me what period is this. I told him but I couldn't help it, I busted out laughing out of disgust! It just doesn't matter here.
**BIG FIGHT** again at the end of 7th period. The hallways were packed with 100s maybe more than 1/2 the school population. My 8th period students could not get to class on time because of all the commotions. So, I refused to mark them late.

**May 16 -** one of the guidance counselors was telling me she was so damn disgusted. She was at a meeting last week at Central Office and was told by a superintendent (name omitted), that any senior who has passed the HSPA, no matter what, they are graduating. "WE ARE GETTING THEM OUT OF HERE!" I relayed this information via email to the president of the PEA & a NJEA field rep.

**May 21 -** Ms. Sweetness* is so disgusted. She told me she wrote a letter to the Governor as a spokesperson for the teachers here and nothing was done about anything. I told her that I have written so many letters, 25 just to Governor Whitman alone. I have written so many letters to Governor Christie. NOTHING is ever done about anything. I said I never use my name. I use a pseudo-name. She believes the Governor doesn't care. She also said she went to Mr. Wilt* and told her how upset and disgusted she is about everything here. He replies, "***His hands are tied. It is all about numbers.***" I replied, NO KIDDING. It is all lies, smoke and mirrors here. But at least he was HONEST!

**Four of us teachers have a 5th period class that rotates and changes every marking period.** During this 4th marking period I have a student (name omitted) who has cut every day with exception of 3 absences and 2 lates. As of today, he has a total of 19 cuts. I have sent in all the necessary paperwork along with the student under school security escort to Mr. Piels* office who is supposedly *now* the *new* cut officer in charge and yet this student defiantly is standing outside my room just staring and glaring at me. Not one administrator challenges him to see where he belongs. This is just one kid. There are literally 100s all day, every day and all year.
At the end of the marking period, this student had; **Absences (39)**     **Cuts (32)**     **Lates (2).**
Remember, this is only a one marking period class.

**May 21 -** there is Biology testing go on. So the building principal allows the school to be MORE out of control. There were 100s of students in the hallways playing, wrestling, screaming, cursing, banging, kicking classroom doors, nothing but chaos all over the place and you never see the building principal anytime in the hallway moving, directing, or anything when it comes to the taking charge and control of the building. Plus it was a tad warm, so students are pulling off their shirts, wearing slippers and flip flops as if they are at the beach. So much for the morning announcements when the girls say at the end, "In the words of our principal Mr. Dickinson*, EDUCATION IS THE KEY TO LIFE." Then I always yell out, "YEAH, BUT YOU DON'T HAVE TO GO TO CLASS."

The administrators are *NOW* signing seniors up for credit recover? The school year is OVER? My question is how can students who have failed all year long, be allowed to take CREDIT RECOVERY and be able to pass *any* class in less than three weeks? Because it doesn't matter! The administration will make sure these seniors pass and graduate. All the administration cares about is to increase the graduation numbers. It is not about education. It is the administration not teachers who are sending students (NOT ALL OF THEM) but a great many of them out in the world unprepared.

**May 31, 2013 - below is another email I sent to the president of the PEA, the president of the NJEA, the NJEA Uniserv assistant director and two NJEA regions 27 Uniserv Field Reps.**
**Subject:      SCHOOL IS QUIET AND UNDER CONTROL TODAY**

Good Afternoon All,

What a difference today.      School is in somewhat under control.
Not perfect, BUT MUCH, MUCH, MUCH, BETTER that I have seen all year.
Even at this moment when it is usually just chaos there is hardly anyone or even student/s in the hallway.

Do you think it may be because the Passaic County Commissioner of Education and some other dignitaries' have been in the building since early this morning and are still here now?

And WAIT I just noticed something else.
I just saw the 2 heads of security (the 2 retired Paterson police officers) walking the hallway telling students to get going, move, get to class. This is a first for me and I am right in the major combat area.

Nothing like the Ye Old Smoke & Mirrors routine.

WHY CAN'T IT BE LIKE THIS ALL THE TIME?      CAN ANYBODY EXPLAIN THIS TO ME?
This is proof, that what has been going on the administration knows it is WRONG!
 Or why the Dog & Pony Show today?    Get the school video/s!
ABSOLUTELY FRUSTRATING!

Most respectfully,

Lee
                                              END

**June 4 - I was so upset today. I didn't want to forget what to write so I videotaped myself on my way home.** Maybe three weeks left of school and the administration is now starting students with CREDIT RECOVERY. And these three weeks are supposed to make up for an entire year? It's even shorter than a summer school program. Most students still won't even show up. It's NOT about education. It is about perception, numbers, and statistics. First of all, why did the administration allow students to continually be in the hallways and every place else, all day, every day, all year long instead of being in class? The CREDIT RECOVERY IS NOTHING more than a scam so the administration and can give seniors phony credit in order to graduate. Many of my students told me, students who have credit recovery just show up at the end of the day, sign in and then told to go home. Talk about setting an example of GOOD WORK ETHICS. I want to know, who monitors this credit recovery? New Jersey taxpayers are getting screwed and by the very state that is running and operating this school district!

**Jun 5 & 6 - WHY, is the school so out of control?** Students should be in class preparing for Final Exams which starts next Monday. EDUCATION is not a priority here. It is just about passing the state exam and other BS testing. I sent an email yesterday to the PEA & NJEA about not one administrator is making a presence. How do you expect students to take school and testing serious when the school administrators don't take discipline, responsibility and accountability serious? There is no way anyone should have to send their children here. TAXPAYERS ARE GETTING SCREWED BIG TIME. As I have said over and over and to the PEA, NJEA and the NEA, I must be the only one who cares.

**Jun 10 - first day of *FINAL EXAM'S*.** Students just come and go as they please. The first final exam period is over. We have been in homeroom for quite some time. It is **10:35** and students are now just pouring into the building. Even during the pledge of allegiance to the flag, the hallways were filled with students and no one stops to honor colors. Most of them go about their business, eating, drinking, talking and playing. What do I expect? I have been here long enough to know the administration doesn't care!

*NOTE OF INTEREST - I HAVE THOUGHT OF THIS SO MANY TIMES.*

It's a shame, I come to school and many times I have to sit and wait before I am able to park my car because parents are dropping off their children. Then they wait to make sure they go inside safely. **Unfortunately,** these poor conscientious parents have no idea once their child or children are in the school building the administration allows them to walk in and out of the building all day as well as being any place else throughout the entire school day instead of being in class.

**Jun 17 - the entire final exam week was an absolute waste and a freaking disaster. I have never seen it this bad before!** For example, the beginning of 6th period two kids come running in my room. I asked them to leave. They said no. Obviously they were hiding from other kids or possibly security. I made it real clear to get out and quit playing around. They start cursing at me, fuck you, go fuck yourself mother fucker, shut the fuck up, you can't tell us what to fucking do mother fucker, fuck this and that and on and on. Then one big kid yells as he is walking out of my class, "Suck my dick!" Several teachers and staff members all yelled, "HEY" (meaning watch your mouth) but he ignored them and just kept it up. Nobody did a thing. He was allowed to continue.

A few minutes later, two other kids come by and started to come in. One was hanging on the door. I figured before something happens, I'll just close my door and stay inside. I said to the student, excuse me. He replies, "You're excused." Here we go, I knew right then and there I am going to have a problem. I go to close my door, he blocks me. I said excuse me again and he continues with his nonsense and defiance deliberately holding the door keeping me from closing it. I go to pull the stop out from underneath the door, he swings around. I moved him. The first thing out of his mouth is don't touch me. I said, "MOVE!" He defiantly keeps it up. I turn to the rent a security guard who is just standing there doing NOTHING, and said would you please remove this "PUNK!" Security took his time to move them. I closed the door, but the kids kept it up. They were banging, kicking, punching the door and this went on for quite a while as the rent a security guard just stood there.

I went about my business trying to ignore it all. After about 10 minutes I had it. To keep from having a confrontation with the kids and instead of going outside to get a security guard I called the security office. A female security guard answered, and I explained everything to her. I walked by my door and she was already there talking to the security guard. I knew she was asking him questions and when I opened the door, he started to say something to the effect "he" and then stopped. I assume "he" was ME! Then said which had nothing to do with anything, they will be back. Basically, admitted he knows what was going on, did NOTHING and allowed these kids to act up. I HATE THIS PLACE.

**Jun 18** - I am still aggravated from yesterday. The more I thought about it just shows how out of control, the lack of respect from students and what makes it worse the out-of-control behavior the administration allows to continually go on every day all day. Even as I was getting ready to come in this morning, I was getting this sick, anxious feeling inside. It is worse than any movie you have ever seen where things are so out of control and wrong is right and right is wrong, and you feel so uneasy and disgusted. I just don't want to be here anymore. Even with 8 days left and ½ day schedule, the building is worse, and students still don't have go to class. So much for students having to be in school for 181 days! It is 7:47am and I want to go home and get away from this "F'ed up out of control PLACE. I hate this place.

**Videotaped myself on my way home.** I was so disgusted and talking about how administrators are approaching all the guidance counselors in order to come up with ways for seniors to pass and graduate. It is all BS with false paperwork to say seniors took and passed CREDIT RECOVERY. But *not* one administrator will sign off on it. They want guidance to sign off and be held responsible.

**Jun 19 -** I am so disgusted; the administration is implementing all these programs in order to graduate more students. If students were in class instead of being everyplace else all day, every day, all year, taxpayers wouldn't have to pay for these programs, including overtime for everyone to stay after the workday to implement these programs. I believe the district wants this to be their paper trail to say see what we did in order to have students pass, increased the graduation rate and lowered the dropout rate but not being truthful on HOW they achieved it! Bottom line it is costing the NJ Taxpayer *BIG BUCKS*!

You truly cannot blame some of these kids. When you get the unfortunate pleasure to meet the parent/s then you understand why. The old saying, "The apple doesn't fall far from the tree" is sooooooooooooooooooooo true! Please make sure you understand this is *NOT* with *all* students and *all* parents. This is with many of the main extreme students who cannot be controlled, are the most disrespectful, defiant, arrogant, destructive and foul specimens you can imagine.

**Jun 20 - NO STUDENTS** are attending any classes. In fact, from June 17 – 27, the remaining two weeks of school, students *did not* show up for class, most not even to school and their attendance *did not* count. As if it ever really counted at all this year. *IF* they should show up for school, they're every place else but in class, walking and running, playing, eating, drinking and anything else they want to do and it's allowed. Even my students who still haven't taken their final exam won't even show up. Once again, you cannot blame the students, especially the seniors who all know that they don't have to and they *will* graduate.

If students are *required to attend* 181 plus days of school and *have* to make up days for inclement weather (Super Storm Sandy) and such, why was this allowed?
Unfortunately, because students were not going to class or school one teacher was in hot water. One of his students was caught being at home by her mother. The mother wanted to know why she was not in school. The young lady tells her the teacher said she can go home. The teacher never said that.
To cover their tracks and protect themselves the school administration tried to hang the teacher. Are you going to tell me with all of the added administration in this building and the surveillance cameras, that administration did not notice, did not realize, did not see there were *NO* students in classrooms or hardly in the building until a parent complained? Even after that incident nothing changed, still no students.

Here is a copy of the "FINAL EXAM SCHEDULE."<br>
Please note final exams started June 10, 2013, and ended June 14, 2013, with make ups starting on June 17 & 18, 2013. End of the year for students was June 27, 2013.

## High School

|  | MAY |  |  |  |
|---|---|---|---|---|
|  |  | 1st | 2nd | 3rd SGO Principal Training |
| 6th | 7th SGO Principal Training | 8th | 9th | 10th |
| 13th | 14th Early Dismissal for PD | 15th | 16th | 17th |
| 20th STAR Reading & Math OFF | 21st STAR Reading & Math 28th STAR Reading & Math | 22nd STAR Reading & Math 29th STAR Reading & Math | 23rd 30th | 24th Early dismissal PEA 31st |
| **JUNE** | | | | |
| 3rd LA & Math Unit Test | 4th LA & Math Unit Test | 5th LA & Math Unit Test | 6th LA & Math Unit Test Early Dismissal for PD | 7th LA & Math Unit Test |
| 10th EXAMS | 11th EXAMS | 12th EXAMS | 13th EXAMS | 14th EXAMS |
| 17th MAKE-UP EXAMS | 18th MAKE-UP EXAMS | 19th | 20th | 21st |
| 24th | 25th | 26th | 27th Graduation | 28th Last Day for Staff |

Last Day for Staff – <u>June 28, 2013</u> – 9:00 a.m. – 12 Noon

**All Subjects including Language Arts and Math will have an exam**       Revised 4/23/13

**June 21** - I just had an epiphany; the superintendent wants to increase the school day. As I always say what for so students can be in the hallway longer. Well, if they want to increase the day then why don't students have to show up during the last 2 weeks of school? There's two weeks less or MORE right there! I was just told the name of a student who is not only *passing* he is *graduating*. It seems the only class he failed because the teacher was not going to pass him for being out 6 months while in jail, plus all of his other days absent, cuts, comes back and still does nothing in class was woodshop. However, all his other teachers *passed* him. How much do you want to bet the administration was involved big time in order to have him pass and graduate! ABSOLUTELT DISGUSTING!

**Jun 27** - I was talking with Lenny Moore's* guidance counselor again. See May 14th & 15th as a reference. She was so upset and kept apologizing. She said yesterday she was so upset, went home crying and was upset all night. Then had reservation about telling me what was going on being afraid I would get mad and do something stupid. I told her I was glad that she told me and that I WILL confront my principal and VP about this. Especially when my principal said to me that this student was NOT going to graduate! He reassured me that he was not going to sign off on Lenny* because he is NOT going to put his licenses on the line for falsifying records. In fact, just last week I spoke with my principal again and he reassured me that this student is NOT graduating. I repeated it, "He is NOT GRADUATING!" My principal replied, "That's correct."
Well, as of today, June 27, 2013, Lenny Moore* is not only *GRADUATING* he has supposedly passed CREDIT RECOVERY in those few days. In fact, his guidance counselor only found out he was graduating yesterday. She told me she has been running around in order to set him up for SUMMER SCHOOL! All that time wasted and in the meantime the administrators all knew he was going to graduate

and waited to the last minute to tell her. The administration purposely did this so there would be less time for me and others to find out and complain about what is going on and it would be too late to do anything about it. This is a prime example how they just pass everybody and anybody just to increase the numbers and fudge the percentages.

Lenny* has supposedly completed "Art Appreciation" in order to have received credit for his CREDIT RECOVERY. It has come to my attention that "Art Appreciation" IS NOT part of fine arts. It was supposedly changed and approved by central office to make up this BS story in order for him to graduate.

**Jun 27 -** talking with one of the social workers. He is so disgusted. He said one of his students was out over 50 days this year. She had F's in 3 subjects for 3 marking periods. She now has straight D's in those subjects and is *GRADUATING!*
*WILL SOMEBODY PLEASE EXPLAIN TO ME HOW THIS IS NOT ILLEGAL?*

**Jun 27 -** when I walked into the SRA office there were several people from guidance, a few secretaries, other counselors and several SRA officers who take care of the testing. They were all upset and disgusted just as I am about the lies and graduation rate this year. One of the secretaries said, only 40 students are NOT graduating. This goes along with what I have said pertaining to my student Lenny Moore*.
As I figured what was done with him in order to graduate was done with so many other students. The only students who will NOT graduate are those who did not pass the HSPA.
See April 16 entry when guidance counselors were told by their administrator if students passed HSPA, they will graduate! "WE ARE RUINNING A NATION!"

**Jun 27 - approximately 10:17 am,** I spoke to my principal about my student Lenny Moore*. I said it has come to my attention he is graduating. All of a sudden, he puts his head down and starts looking in the graduation booklet. I said Lenny* will not be in the booklet because this decision was just made the other day and these were already printed. Then said even if Lenny* did credit recovery for my class in 5 days and at 5 hours each time, which I know he did NOT, how can 25 hours represent and satisfy my entire class for a year? As I was talking, he kept his head down and acted as if he was writing notes. Then all of a sudden, he jumped up saying, I will check into it, made a dash for the door saying, "and I will get back to you." He acted as if he knew nothing about it. I know he did, because he sent an email to the guidance counselor about Lenny* and she replied, "It seems he will graduate." He replied, "GREAT!" So, I don't understand why he would say he'll check into it. He knows everything about seniors especially who is and is NOT graduating. Then I found out Mr. Naptha* a VP signed off on Lenny's* failing and credit recovery situation. Interesting! If you remember my principal told me he was not going to sign off on Lenny* because he is NOT going to put his licenses on the line for falsifying records.

I am so upset but my colleagues keep saying don't let it bother you, there's nothing you can do about it. I said that's the problem, everybody says and feels that way. I am going to try to make a difference. IT IS WRONG and ILLEGAL!

**At 12:20,** I was talking with my principal again and he said that some seniors will have to attend summer school. He told me the names of a couple of them. I asked him who is paying for their summer school. He replied you and I. Meaning the New Jersey taxpayers, AGAIN! Once again, these students were constantly in the hallway all day for (4) years and now they will get to go to summer school for a few weeks and get a diploma. So many teachers like me are upset and disgusted about all of this.
Then he said, I have NOT asked anyone to change a student's grade. I replied you didn't have to; the district did it with BULL CRAP maneuvering and lies with CREDIT RECOVERY.
Angrily, I asked him,

- Why do you need teachers? Teacher's records and grades don't mean anything.
- Student attendance doesn't mean anything. You change student's grades with a BS credit recovery program that they don't attend.
- The superintendent and all of you administrators LIE and change everything, to make as if everything here has improved and going well.
- This is wrong and it is ILLEGAL!
- And next year the administration wants to have a more stringent system for evaluating teachers? ARE YOU FREAKING KIDDING ME?
- The superintendent and all of you administrators just want teachers to place blame on.
- It would be better to get rid of all the teachers and have students when they turn 18 pay for a diploma. This way it will save taxpayers a big expense with all of these BS programs.

I was so upset and disgusted when I was speaking with my principal and forget that everything I just said was already written on my blackboard as a reminder. He had to see it. Talk about perfect timing.

**Jun 27** - just prior to going home I was speaking with the teacher again, who said earlier today there's nothing you can do about it. Don't get sick over it. He said he knows and was telling me about one of the boys who is always cursing at teachers and security, always in the hallways etc., had come into his room yesterday and asked if he could use one of the computers for CREDIT RECOVERY. He told the student yes, but you're in school and have to take your hat and earphones off. The kid ignored him. The teacher said it again. The kid replied, that's ok, I'm going to go. My teacher said as long as I sign in and log on to a computer for at least 10 minutes, I'll get credit. THAT'S "CREDIT RECOVERY!"
That was the reason why this teacher was telling me not to get sick over this. He kept saying there is nothing you can do about any of this. I replied, it's wrong and at least I will try, instead of putting my head in the sand. New Jersey taxpayers are paying BIG BUCKS for student's education and they don't have to go to class, they can hang out, play in school, all day, every day, all year and on top of that they have to pay for CREDIT RECOVERY, TWILIGHT PROGRAM AND SUMMER SCHOOL?
This is all unacceptable especially when this is a State Takeover, Run and Operated School District.
GOVERNOR CHISTIE WHERE'S THE SAVINGS NOW TO THE TAXPAYERS?

We were allowed to leave at 1:10 today. I was so upset I thought about stopping at the Drs. Office for a blood pressure check. I cannot and do not want to be a part of or subjected to, any of this anymore.

**Jun 28** - woke up at 4:15am, could not sleep. I was still so disgusted, aggravated and had that lousy anxious feeling, even though it was the last day. I do not want to go there anymore. First thing this morning a friend of mine asked me, if I was in a better mood today. I said NO! I just blew up and was so mad. Then he tells me about a student (name omitted) and yep he is a SENIOR. He had over 100 days absent. He would leave school every day around 11:30/12:00. He never spent a full day in school all year and he GRADUATED! I can't make these things up. "WE ARE RUINING A NATION!"
Wonder why our students want everything given to them? What do you expect? They were taught and it was reinforced in school that you don't have to do, work for or earn anything, they will give it to you.
IS THIS WHAT I SERVED IN THE MILITARY AND WENT TO COLLEGE FOR?

The guidance counselor told me it was obvious my principal Mr. Arthurs* was just speaking with me before he came to see her. She said the first thing out of his mouth was, "Is everything in order with Mr. McNulty and Lenny Moore*. She said, as far as she was concerned and that VP Mr. Naptha* signed off on everything. She said Mr. Arthurs* was good with that. She said he was so concerned about me (Lee), obtaining information and all of the necessary documentation. She said in reality he was looking to cover his own ass. The bottom line the district approved it. It was done.

What bothers me the most is Mr. Arthurs*, a man who I really looked up to and respected so much, LIED right to my face. I always thought of him as being a straight up guy.

I even said to the guidance counselor it is obvious that Mr. Arthurs* knew that I would be looking for all of the documentation and proof on Lenny* receiving and completing CREDIT RECOVERY, because for the last few days I have been asking VP Mr. Naptha* for the paperwork and I wanted to see it all. Realizing this he kept stalling me. Probably was told by Mr. Arthurs*, (just guessing) but probably right, NOT to give me anything, knowing I WILL make a BIG fuss about it. Later that day, I asked Mr. Naptha* again and as expected, he said he forgot and he'll send it to me later. I said, "How, we will be going home shortly?" Then like a little kid he changed the subject by talking about what a good man I am and thanked me for showing him how to solder copper pipes. Games these people play. If they were trying to cover their rear ends by not letting me get a hold of the documentation on this student do, they actually think I would fall for a stalling and changing the topic tactic? I have HAD IT. All the way home I could not relax. I was so antsy, mad and disgusted. How do these people sleep at night? So many of the graduating class should have never even been in high school let alone graduated.

I can't do this anymore. It is 8:29 pm and I'm finishing up my entries in my *diary* as of June 28, 2013. I cannot go back there and go through all of this again. It is tooooo dangerous there.

**Jun 29** - could not sleep. Tossed and turned all night. Finally woke up at 3:30am, was so anxious and hyper. I have been hyper for the last 3 days now. I deliberately stayed in bed until 6am. I was tired and my entire body felt hard as a rock. I guess because being so upset I was so tense. I keep thinking about everything over and over. How students didn't go to class day after day, all year and not only passed but graduated. I can't relax. I feel anxious and can't concentrate on anything. Last night I couldn't even concentrate on TV. I feel so sick inside. I can't do or be subjected to *this* anymore. What makes it even more upsetting is this is a state controlled, run &operated school district. What do I do? Who do I turn to for help? I wrote so many letters to the PEA, NJEA and the NEA.NOBODY CARES!

**July 22, 2013 - below is a narrative email I sent to the president and a NJEA rep.**
Attached are three items.
1. Is an article from a local newspaper saying that the governor at that time signed into law that DYFS is to be contacted when there are a long-term and unexcused absences?

We have proof, videos, documentation and email just as it was all happening. What is more disgusting, these last two school years were restructuring. What a waste at the expense of NJ taxpayers.

2. End of the year and final exam schedule.
Please note Final exams started June 10, 2013, and ended June 14, 2013, with make ups on June 17 & 18, 2013. End of the year for students was June 27, 2013.
From June 17 through June 27, where were students?
I had three or maybe four students who showed up almost every day.

The kids that did show up I asked them what happens when students don't go to class and turn in their texts. They replied, what texts. Two of the kids were seniors and said we haven't had textbooks in years.

Until about noon, the building was absolutely worse than I have described to you all year long.
The remaining two weeks there were no students going to classes. If students are to have 181 days of school and are to make up days for inclement weather and such, why was this allowed?

Then it hit me. Most students do not show up for final let alone a makeup exam because they don't have to. They know they will pass and graduate. That's when I realized about the end of year schedule. These last two weeks are used for administrators to find out which seniors are not passing and what can they do to get them to pass and graduate.

One of the biggest scams is CREDIT RECOVERY. I have an email going back and forth asking if a certain Credit Recovery Course may be used to give a Lenny* credit for my class. It clearly states that they have done this in the past but should not be used next year. I asked for the documentation on a particular student showing the dates, and times along with the signatures on all who signed off on his satisfactory completion of Credit Recovery. As expected, I never received them. There should be some type of documentation in his records, with the guidance department chairperson and his counselor. Especially when I spoke with an administrator one week prior to graduation about this student and was told he has NOT met your requirements and will fail and will not graduate.
Then miraculously this student not only passed, he graduated?

3. Lastly is my documentation on my classes Attendance, Cuts &Lateness. (Start 2006 - 2013 End) The 2012 - 2013 is the absolute worse. This is the first and only year I had only 5 classes. I have always had 6 classes. This is added proof students are NOT going to class without any disciplinary actions taken.

This district is deliberately passing and graduating students who have not met the necessary classroom requirements, to make the superintendent/s look good at the expense of the taxpayers and the country.

THIS IS NOT JUST NEGLECT IT IS A CRIME!

Please let me know if the information I have provided will help and if there is anything else you need?

**SCHOOL YEAR 2013 - 2014**

When September came, I was not ready to go back. I was still burnt out. So, I decided to take a leave of absence. I was not going to subject myself to the insanity of working in a school that is out of control, allows violence without impunity, where students do *not* have to go to class, and only teachers are *HELD* responsible and is still a part of a State Takeover, Run and Operated School District.

After a while I realized I did *NOT* want to go back to John F. Kennedy High School and decided to retire.

On May 1, 2014, I sent in my letter of intent to retire.
May 1, 2014

Ms. Jaime Cangialosi-Murphy
Director of Human Resources
Paterson Public Schools
90 Delaware Avenue
Paterson, New Jersey 07503

Dear Ms. Cangialosi-Murphy,

It is a sad day in my life where I must write and submit this letter; however, due to the failure of the administration to instill a sense of order and discipline in the student body at John F. Kennedy High School, I feel it is time for me to leave.
Over the past few years, I have reported a situation where cutting is rampant, poor attendance and unacceptable behavior is acceptable, continual fights occur, students are allowed to hang out in the hallways, stairwells, walk in and out of classrooms they don't belong in, walk in and out of the building at

will all day, every day, all year. All of these matters have been recorded on the school's surveillance cameras and can be easily verified as they occurred. Yet, many of the students who participate in these actions are promoted to their next grade, or because they are seniors, are permitted to graduate.

As a result, please be advised that as of the end of the month of June 2014, (2013 - 2014 School Year), I will retire. It is unfortunate. Up until the 2011 - 2012, the first so-called restructuring year I never had any intentions of ever retiring. However, when students are allowed to cut class being pushed through the system and my colleagues and I are made to be held accountable for failing, it is time to go.
I can no longer be part of an educational facility where any and all sense of right or wrong does not exist. My sense of morality and health is more important than having to be continually exposed to an atmosphere that is dangerous, where I do not feel safe in and I am forced to keep a close eye and make believe that out of control behavior is supposed to be the norm.

It is so sad to see that our Public Educational system has so dramatically been permitted to change and has come to this.

I will miss my children / students dearly and pray for their forgiveness, because I was not allowed to give them a better education; an education which they not only deserved but is their right.

Thank you.

Most respectfully,

Lee E. McNulty

cc : Dr. Donnie W. Evans, State District Superintendent of Schools
: ███████ Principal, JFK-ACT
END

Don't misunderstand me; I was quite nervous about submitting my retirement letter. I always feared retaliation. Even though I was telling the truth, I feared it even more and was anticipating a response. Surprisingly, I never received a reply from the superintendent, my principal or anyone from the district in reference to my reasons for retiring. After a few days, I realized why they didn't respond? They would have to acknowledge what I had written. It was more IMPORTANT for them to keep it HUSHED UP!

Remember, what I have written is *ONLY* what I know and or was made aware of. There are probably tens of thousands more stories that went and were never documented. Furthermore, I ONLY wrote about JFK High School. There are over 30 schools in the State controlled and operated School District of Paterson, NJ. Many of them have the same problems. Hopefully, once this book is out teachers will come forward and tell New Jersey parents and taxpayers, everything that has been going on in their schools.
With everything I have written and documented, how many state and federal, OSHA&PEOSH laws have been and still remain broken?

Is this what our American service men & women have fought for & died for? They are all over the world building schools and helping to educate people in other countries. Meanwhile, John F. Kennedy High School is not only *disgusting*, but a *disaster*; a war zone within itself!

Throughout my career, I had some really terrific students. I had more GOOD students than bad. I was really blessed and enjoyed their company and friendship. Some attended college and graduated, became successful and obtained excellent careers.

*Examples* -Obtained pilots licenses, Air Traffic Controllers, Bankers, Engineers, Nurses, Case Workers for DYFS (Division of Youth and Family Services); a career in the US Army, Police Officers, Fireman, Welders, and yes even Teachers. Unfortunately, and sadly, some did not and went directly to jail.

*NOBODY* should have to endure or be exposed to what I have written about while attending High School. JFK High School should have been a SAFE haven as well as a good educational facility. The superintendents, the administration and the State of New Jersey had FAILED students and teachers.

How do all of you bastards sleep at night knowing you deliberately helped to "RUIN A NATION?"

---

**The Paterson Public Schools**
33 Church Street
Paterson, New Jersey 07505
(201) 881-6213/4
Fax. (201) 523-9561

Laval S. Wilson, Ph.D.
State District Superintendent of Schools

**Public Forum to Review
Paterson School District Priorities
During the Next Two Years**

Place: Eastside High School Auditorium

Date: Thursday, February 23, 1995

Time: 6:30 p.m. - 9:30 p.m.

Paterson became State-Operated on August 7, 1991. The District will probably be State-Operated for another two to three years.

The State District Superintendent of the Paterson Public School System, Paterson Advisory Board, Paterson Education Association, Paterson Administrators Association, Paterson Principals Association, and the Paterson Education Fund will sponsor a public forum on February 23, 1995. The purpose of the forum is to obtain suggestions about possible priorities of the District during the remaining time Paterson will be State-Operated.

We are encouraging comments and suggestions from the parents of the City's students, citizens of Paterson, District staff, and representatives of community organizations.

Although a number of reforms have been implemented successfully in the District, there is still a great deal of work to be done to improve our schools and our educational programs. We would like to hear from you at the forum about additional reforms and improvements which you believe would help to improve the school system.

*Our schools can use the help of all who desire to make a difference.*

---

The State was only supposed to be here for three years.
Its 2015, things are worse and the State is still here!
A total of 9 Governors and countless Commissioners of Education since the State of New Jersey took over the Public School District of Paterson, NJ.
During my leave of absence, I was so upset and determined to still do something about the conditions at John F. Kennedy High School. There is no way a school and worse yet an entire district should be allowed to get away with what goes on and unchallenged.

On January 23, 2014, I met with a senator and explained in detail as outlined in this book. I also submitted a large packet containing copies of my documentation. I could see the senator was shocked and asked if I spoke with the superintendent. I said "NO, because I was afraid of losing my job and pension." I also said why, would I go to the enemy with all of these major violations, grievances and complaints which are all against him, being he is the one in charge of the school and district. It would be career suicide. The only thing the superintendent and his administration care about is perception."

Then I was asked if I have ever contacted the Governor. I said YES and have been for years. However, because I fear retaliation, losing my job, career and pension, I sent letters under a pseudo name. I also said so did many of my colleagues. You would think with all of those letters someone would have investigated by now.

The senator asked me if I took the day off to come here. I explained I am on a leave of absence because I can no longer work under and be subjected to those conditions anymore and plan on retiring in July. I also explained and made it very clear that I am writing a book and the information and documentation that I was going over is in my book.

The senator promised to read everything and will have me come back in a month.

In February 2014, I was called back. After a few minutes the senator asked me is everything they read was the truth. I assured the senator it's the gospel and that I have documentation to back up everything I say and what I gave you was nothing compared to what I have.

Then the senator tried to explain the feelings felt after reading all of the information. We both agreed it was disturbing. I replied. "Try having to work under those conditions day after day, all day, for years and worse, being a child having to attend a school under those conditions and thinking that this is normal."

The senator was concerned why security and the police were allowing all of this to go on. I explained, it is not their fault. The administration will not allow them to do their jobs. It is the administration allowing the school to be out of control. Students have 60, 70, 80 PLUS days of absences and the same amount in cuts. I explained everything as I had written in this book. The senator asked if I knew the head of security. I said yes. The senator said that then he would have to know why things are the way I described. I said absolutely, however, he too is following orders.

Then just before I left, I handed the senator another large packet of information and documentation.

In April many of my colleagues were telling me JFK is so out of control and how nothing ever changes. So I decided to contact Choice Media in Hoboken, New Jersey and agreed once I officially retire, I will make an appointment for an interview.

Then in June and July of 2014 many of my colleagues would either come to my house or called me on the phone telling me nothing has changed at JFK and how disgusted, fed up, and burnt out they all were. July 2014, I officially retired. However, I was not going to quit. I started to write this book, contacted Choice Media again and made an appointment to meet with them in August, 2014.

In August, I met Mr. Bob Bowdon of the education news group, **"Choice Media,"** who not only interviewed me but video recorded it. A month or so later, I was interviewed by a reporter Ms. Hannan Adely, from the newspaper The Record. On November 25, 2014, the newspaper article was published;

"Ex-teacher says chaos was the norm; officials dispute view of Paterson school." Along with the article and to my surprise an embedded video of the interview by Mr. Bob Bowdon was included.
Here is the link to the article and video interview.
http://www.northjersey.com/news/ex-teacher-says-chaos-was-norm-officials-dispute-view-of-paterson-school-1.1141171

On the morning of November 25, 2014, around 8:30 am, I was contacted by a fellow teacher at JFK. She was screaming and yelling on how happy and proud she was of me. I could hear all of the other teachers in the background, yelling thank you, Lee. I was stunned and asked what the heck are you talking about? She said, "We've seen it!" I still didn't understand. She yells "the newspaper article with your video!" I said "are you kidding me. I had no idea it was going to be out. I was under the impression it wouldn't be out until after the 1st of the NEW YEAR."
Everybody at JFK was soooo happy. All day the phone was ringing.
I was contacted by so many of my colleagues (teachers, secretaries, guidance counselors, case workers, everybody) who are still working at JFK as well as others throughout the district, including firemen and police officers. They were thanking me, telling me I'm HERO and how happy they all are and how pleased and excited that finally someone has come forward and told the truth. They were saying now the people know what is really going on inside here. They were also so grateful and finally felt good about themselves knowing that someone was not just standing up for them but more importantly for the children the students.

In the mist of all these conversations some teachers were telling me that there is now "SOMETHING NEW" they called it "THE WORD IS OUT!"

It means students especially SENIORS, from other school districts who are failing come March, April and in even May REGISTER for school in Paterson. They not only pass they too graduate. Their records from the other school and districts doesn't matter or count. I said just like when any of our students / seniors are failing. It is strictly about the numbers, statistics', the perception and obvious the bonuses!
I said, I guess this is all part of the *CHANGE!*

Unfortunately, and disgustingly the administration cannot undo the damage they have already done by pushing through the system by passing and graduating so many of our children, who were not properly educated and prepared for the future. This is not wrong this is a crime. However, according to the Herald News Superintendent Donnie Evans said, "it's a very different school today compared to two years ago because of leadership changes and a relentless focus on improving student achievement." All of a sudden, everything has changed and is better since I have left.

It is obvious that the superintendent and his administration never thought anyone would come forward and make a splash like the November 25th, newspaper article and interview/video. They figured they already survived a teacher coming forward before relatively quietly with the Paterson Times article on Mrs. Simonetta in the Sunday, September 13, 2013, news article, "Teacher, morally disgusted, resigns from Paterson school" by Jayed Rahman.

## ARTICLES

Here's the link to Mrs. Simonetta's article.
http://patersontimes.com/2013/09/13/teacher-morally-disgusted-resigns-from-paterson-school/

Next is my reply to the superintendent's comments' on the November 25, 2014, newspaper article and link. http://www.northjersey.com/opinion/opinion-letters-to-the-editor/the-record-letters-friday-dec-19-1.1169741?page=2

**"Turmoil inside"**          **The Record: Letters, Friday, Dec. 19**

Paterson schools
Regarding "Ex-teacher says chaos was the norm" (Page L-1, Nov. 26):
I'm the teacher involved.
Why would a superintendent continually allow John F. Kennedy High School in Paterson to be out of control all those years and now all of a sudden, after I left, it has changed? Are Paterson police and school security now allowed to do their jobs?

How does JFK go from 400,000 cuts in one year to zero the next?

In 2013, I had five classes and a total of 103 students. In all, student absents totaled 2,154, and students were late a total of 405 times. There was also a total of 1,216 cuts.

That same year, six seniors failed my class having an average of 315 absences and 201 cuts, but miraculously they all graduated.

The day the article came out, I received phone calls from JFK staff saying how happy they were that someone told the public what really goes on inside the school. With all of the articles prior and since about the school, doesn't anybody care?
For more than 23 years, the Paterson School District has operated with a state-appointed superintendent of schools.
There is no other school district in the state that receives so much negative press.

Lee E. McNulty

On January 23, 2105, at NJ School Choice Summit 2015 at St. Peters University in Jersey City, NJ, Superintendent Evans and I were to be on a panel for Urban Education Policy.

However, one week before on January 17, 2015, Mr. Bob Bowdon calls me that afternoon, saying that the superintendent made a demand, if I was to be a part of the panel; he was not going to attend.

Not to ruin anything I agreed to attend but only as part of the audience. On that day, I said to the superintend (Paraphrasing) you say things are so much better at JFK, however, according to all of the teachers and students I have spoken with and still speak with they all say NOTHING has changed it is the same. The change came only after the article and interview video came out in November.

The superintendent responded confidently declaring these violence problems are a thing of the past. However, on the very same day a young man was arrested for attacking and assaulting his teacher which happened days before. This young man was ONLY arrested because the video was leaked to the press.

Obviously, the district already knew about this incident and was already trying to cover and hush it up. Otherwise, why wasn't that young man arrested days earlier?

What makes it even more disturbing NOT one student came to help the teacher or tried to stop the attack. In fact, in all of my years working there, I have never seen students' being more behaved all the while the student was attacking, manhandling and body slamming his teacher and acted as if this was normal. Think about it, there are 6 uniformed Paterson police officers in the building at all times, a dozen or so security guards, so if a student can attack and assault a teacher without fear of being arrested what does that tell you on how safe John F. Kennedy High School really is?

Here's something to think about. The video recording of the teacher being attacked and assaulted started before it happened. This makes me think it was deliberate and planned out ahead of time. Which makes me wonder how much was actually edited compared to what we viewed on TV and social media?

Furthermore, according to a few of my friends, who are still working at JFK they said; this is NOT the first time this teacher was assaulted. They said there was an incident earlier this school year and once the previous year. Which makes me wonder what else remains covered and hushed up?

** Below is the article and link showing how much John F. Kennedy High School has not changed. **

**"Paterson freshman charged with assault after classroom attack on teacher"**
By Joe Malinconico / January 23, 2015/ Paterson Press
http://www.northjersey.com/towns/paterson/paterson-freshman-charged-with-assault-after-classroom-attack-on-teacher-1.1239201

A ninth grader at John F. Kennedy High School in Paterson was arrested Friday and charged with assaulting a teacher in a classroom.

The attack, captured on video, shows the teen slamming the 62-year-old educator to the floor in front of other students in an effort to get his cell phone back.

City school officials confirmed that criminal charges have been filed against the student, who has been suspended from school.

Someone in the classroom recorded the assault, which officials say took place at about 1 pm on Tuesday, and the **video has been posted on YouTube**.

The 23-second video shows the 16-year-old with his arms wrapped around the teacher, knocking him into an empty desk. The student then wrestles the teacher across the front of the classroom before slamming him to the floor. The teen then reaches down and wrests something from the teacher before breaking away when someone in the classroom yelled: "Security."
The district filed a complaint against the student earlier this week, a spokeswoman said, and Paterson police said they arrested him at his home on Friday
"We took a statement from the teacher today," said Capt. Heriberto Rodriguez. "After that, we went out and found the juvenile and arrested him." The teenager was charged with third-degree aggravated assault, the captain said.

David Cozart, principal of operations at JFK, said the incident happened during a physics class.

He said the teacher apparently confiscated the phone — which belonged to the assailant — from another student. The principal said students are allowed to use cell phones in class for academic purposes, but staff may take the devices and return them at the end of the day if students use them for other reasons.

District officials have not revealed the name of the teacher or student. Peter Tirri, president of the Paterson Education Association, the teacher's union, said the teacher has worked in the district since 2003.

"Let me say that this is a very upsetting incident and certainly one that we take seriously as the safety of our students and staff is our top priority," said Terry Corallo, district spokeswoman.

She said the student while on suspension will receive home instruction and a disciplinary hearing will determine "an appropriate, educational placement" for the rest of the school year.
"I'm disappointed I didn't see any other kids in the classroom help [the teacher] out," Tirri said about the events depicted in the short video. "Maybe they were afraid. I don't know."
"What strikes me is that the teacher never even defended himself," said Lee McNulty, a retired JFK teacher who has been vocal recently with criticism about violence and disorder in the high school. "That just shows how much teachers are afraid of losing their job."

"It's troubling that in our society today students think that inside a school they can put their hands on each other and teachers as well," said Jonathan Hodges, a veteran school board member. "I went online trying to find this video and I found numerous videos of teachers being attacked by their students."

In press interviews last year, McNulty called JFK a chaotic place where fights were common.
But city education officials said they have improved conditions at JFK in the past few years.

"This district has worked extremely hard to provide a safe and caring environment for our students and our staff, and we have succeeded in this area," Corallo said in a written statement. "The superintendent feels very confident in Mr. Cozart's leadership and knows that Mr. Cozart will continue to work aggressively to ensure that the JFK building is a safe place for teachers to teach and for students to learn."

This attack was shown literally all over the world with all the news media and YouTube.

Here is the link to the video.     https://www.youtube.com/watch?v=iJ0FvPGr5BA

** Next is another letter and its link I submitted. **

**"Problems at Kennedy are not thing of past"**
January 26, 2015 / Paterson Press
http://www.northjersey.com/news/paterson-press-letter-problems-at-kennedy-are-not-thing-of-past-1.1258795

Dear Editor,
I cannot believe it. Superintendent Donnie Evans keeps telling everybody that John F. Kennedy High School has changed and it is not the school of the past. Meanwhile he never apologized to the students, their parents or to everyone who worked there, for allowing it to be that way in the first place under his control.

Just this past Friday, January 23, 2015, Superintendent Evans sat in a panel at the NJ School Choice Summit at St. Peters University in Jersey City, responding to the Choice Media video of me, confidently declaring these violence problems a thing of the past.

I am so disturbed, upset and receive no satisfaction to see on the very same day Superintendent Evans was trying to convince us that the unruly, violent image of Paterson schools was a thing of the past, almost as he spoke, a 16-year-old Kennedy student was being arrested for allegedly assaulting a 62-year old teacher and throwing him to the floor.

I believe if it wasn't reported, nothing would have been said about it.

Unfortunately, it makes me wonder and more so concerned on what else has been going on inside JFK that we don't know about.

It is time that the parents, community, the city of Paterson as well as the entire State of New Jersey should know the truth and finally begin to hold Paterson Public Schools which is a State Run and Operated School District accountable for the environment they continue to allow.

I would like to know if Donnie Evans or anyone in his administration would send their children or grandchildren to this school. If not, they should be forced to.

Most respectfully,
Lee E. McNulty
McNulty is a former teacher at Kennedy

Only to be followed up with days later with TWO more horrendous acts of violence at John F. Kennedy High School's cafeteria that were caught on camera and submitted to Chasing NJ, a part of Channel 9 News of New Jersey and local Newspapers.

Next article and link are about a security guard being bitten in an attack by a student at JFK High School.

Police report: "Paterson Kennedy student bit school security officer in the stomach"
By Joe Malinconico / January 28, 2015/ Paterson Press
http://archive.northjersey.com/news/police-report-paterson-kennedy-student-bit-school-security-officer-in-the-stomach-1.1259953

PATERSON – Five days prior to the **Jan. 20 classroom attack on a teacher by a Kennedy high school freshman**, a different student at the school bit a security officer in the stomach while the youth allegedly was being restrained from wrecking the nurse's office, according to a police report.

The guard suffered "a bite mark/visible bruising," according to the report. But authorities say no charges were filed against the student, whom the report described as "emotionally disturbed."

Meanwhile, the president of the teachers' union says the organization will file a complaint over a determination last week by the district's medical contractor that the 62-year-old victim of the classroom attack – an assault captured in a video on YouTube - is well enough to report back to work. The original video posting on YouTube exceeded 900,000 views.

"That's absurd," said the union president, Peter Tirri. "The guy took a body slam onto a hard floor and they're telling him he doesn't need to stay out."

District officials have not revealed whether or when they plan to require the teacher who was attacked to return to work. "There are options that are made available, but as this is a personnel matter, I cannot discuss," said Paterson Public Schools spokeswoman Terry Corallo.

Tirri said he met with the teacher, whose name has not been made public, on Wednesday.

"He's still in a lot of pain," the union president said. "His head, his shoulder, his back, his wrist."

Based on the medical evaluation by the district's health care vendor, the teacher may have to use sick days and eventually file a worker's compensation claim against the district when those run out, Tirri said.

"It's a way for the district to save money on his salary until the worker's comp case goes to court, which could take two years," Tirri said.

Tirri said the district's doctor told the teacher to take pain pills and return to work.

The 16-year-old student in the classroom attack was arrested last week and charged with aggravated assault, police said. The district said he has been suspended from school.

Despite the two incidents, district officials say Kennedy provides a safe environment for its students. Last Friday, Paterson schools' superintendent Donnie Evans attended an education conference in Jersey City during which organizers played a portion of a video in which a retired Kennedy teacher, Lee McNulty, asserts that the high school is a dangerous place.

"That represents the Paterson of the past," Evans said at the conference. "It is not Paterson anymore."
But Tirri said recent incidents at Kennedy indicated that the district needed to review its policies regarding security at city schools. Tirri said he was not familiar with the details of the Jan. 16 incident in which the student allegedly bit the security. Paterson Press asked Corallo about the incident on Monday and she has not yet responded.
The police report says security personnel had to restrain the 18-year-old student "on the floor" because the student was "destroying the nurse's office."

The report says the security officer, an employee of the district, was taken to the medical provider that the district uses for staff injuries – the same place that determined the attacked teacher was ready to resume work.
Paterson Press contacted the student named in the police report on his cell phone. When asked about the incident, the student replied, "What does this have to do with school?" Then he hung up.

There is no job / position in the world where anyone can keep their job / position than the superintendent of the Paterson Public School where he does nothing wrong, is never held accountable, where he receives bonuses for improving student attendance even though most students have over 30 days of absences and more in cutting, students do not have textbooks, he and his administration can place all blame on teachers and where you can't even go two weeks without some sort of negative press is written about the school district.

What's worse than that is you do *NOT* hear not one politician coming forward asking for an investigation. Or is it because their children do *not* have to attend schools in Paterson, NJ which is under State Control? There was more excitement, coverage, and interest with the teacher being body slammed by a 9th grade student to the point if you go to YouTube there is over900 thousand views in a matter of days and was viewed all over the world.

What bothers me is where are the parents, the community don't they care, want answers, demand a better education and a safer environment for their children?

Am I sadly and disgustingly right, NO ONE CARES?

No other School District in the entire State of New Jersey receives as much negative press, spends God knows how much money on damage control, is still a state controlled, run and operated school district that has had 2 generations of students pushed through its system and NOTHING HAS CHANGED!

- **One generation of students = 1st grade to senior in High School.**

With the all of the negative newspaper articles above and in the resource section about the State Takeover Run and Operated School District of Paterson, NJ you can write another book.

March 4, 2015, I wrote another lengthy letter and sent a copy to each of the following: Governor Christie, Commissioner of Education Hespe and the Attorney General of the State of New Jersey, John Jay Hoffman.

On April 27, 2015, I also sent a copy to the **_SENATE EDUCATION COMMITTEE,_**
Diane Allen, James Beach, Michael J. Doherty, Shirley K. Turner, and M. Teresa Ruiz

**It is August 24, 2015 and I still await their response.**

On May 25, 2015, I sent a very lengthy detailed letter to President Barrack Obama, asking for help. I even said I would gladly pay my own way to meet and talk with him so we could get something done to correct these problems. I also said, "The best way to have a secure, prosperous and strong nation is by having ALL of our citizens educated and gainfully employed."
Happily, I receive a reply dated July 23, 2015.
The president wrote about what is needed, he proposed plans, etc. Then the happiness went away.
His last sentence said it all, "*That is what I'll keep fighting for as long as I hold this office.*"
That sentence only proves what I have said earlier about politics and politicians on how truly unconcerned they all are about the Public Educational System.

**We are all responsible for what we DON'T DO as much as what we do!**

*I did everything I can think of to get the public's attention.*
*After seeing and reading all of this, now you know why I titled my book*

**"RUINING A NATION**
**and**
**Nobody Cares"**

## *MY FINAL THOUGHTS*

Over the past 27 years I have seen the high school I worked at deteriorate. I have witnessed first-hand out-of-control students, teachers becoming fearful and frustrated and administrators failing to supervise.

This book is filled with eyewitness testimonials, videos, newspaper articles and photos. It is my diary, depicting real events that occurred at JFK HS in Paterson, NJ from March 1994 to December 2015.

I hope when you have finished reading this book you will have gained insight into the every day "goings-on" in one real life public high school, that has lost its identity after becoming a State Run District.

Visit your children's school frequently and if you can unannounced. Hold the school district accountable for teaching sound educational practices. It is a parent's right to visit their children's school on days other than just an open house. If need be make an appointment with their teacher/s or guidance counselor and be suspicious if they refuse to allow you to see the entire facility as it operates.
Do not accept that your son or daughter is graduating high school and cannot read adequately or do simple math. Question, question, question the administration and DEMAND better for your child...if you don't...then I ask you...WHO WILL?

*LASTLY, DO NOT ALLOW YOUR SCHOOL DISTRICT TO BECOME STATE CONTROLLED.*

## RESOURCES

***Below are some of the negative newspaper articles during Donnie Evans tenure as Superintendent.***
- From January 2014 – September 29, 2016, there are 263.
- 104 of the 263 are between, January 2016 – September 29, 2016.
- If you would like a list of *every* negative newspaper article about the Paterson Public School system, that I have resourced starting from 2010, e-mail me; chaoswasthenorm@gmail.com and I will send a complete chronological list and in the same format as in the resource section below.

**"Attacks outside Eastside: Problems on the Rise with Fewer Cops at High School"**
By Joe Malinconico / October 25, 2011/ Paterson Press
http://tapinto.net/articles/attacks-outside-eastside-problems-on-the-rise-wi

**"City School Principal Says Her Six-Figure Job Requires No Work"**
By Joe Malinconico / February 1, 2013 / Paterson Press
http://tapinto.net/towns/paterson/articles/city-school-principal-says-her-six-figure-job-req

**"Paterson schools superintendent Donnie Evans collects $15,759 bonus"**
By Joe Malinconico / August 12, 2013 / Paterson Press
http://www.northjersey.com/news/education/paterson-schools-superintendent-donnie-evans-collects-15-759-bonus-1.597678

**"Administrative salaries at Paterson school prompt inquiry by unions"**
By Joe Malinconico / September 13, 2013 / Paterson Press
http://www.northjersey.com/story-archives/administrative-salaries-at-paterson-school-prompt-inquiry-by-unions-1.635487

**"Paterson, New Jersey district: Administrators make six figures while schools fail"**
By Steve Gunn / October 3, 2013
http://eagnews.org/paterson-new-jersey-district-administrators-living-in-comfort-while-schools-fail-and-kids-drop-out/

**"Mother of Paterson high school student severely beaten in cafeteria sues school, city"**
By John Petrick / January 27, 2014 / Staff Writer, The Record
http://www.northjersey.com/news/mother-of-paterson-high-school-student-severely-beaten-in-cafeteria-sues-school-city-1.668039

**"Paterson school's chief gets $10,750 bonus"**
By Joe Malinconico /September 11, 2014 / Paterson Press
http://www.northjersey.com/news/paterson-schools-chief-gets-10-750-bonus-1.1086304

**"Paterson Letters: Disappointed that NJ appointed Superintendent of the Paterson Schools"**
October 17, 2014 / Paterson Press
http://www.northjersey.com/news/paterson-letters-disappointed-that-nj-appointed-superintendent-of-the-paterson-schools-1.1112083

**"Evans fails our children"**
"Letter to the Paterson Press: November 18, 2014
http://www.northjersey.com/news/letter-to-the-paterson-press-evans-fails-our-children-1.1136300

**"Only NINETEEN of 600 students in New Jersey school district scored high enough on SATs to get into college"**
- Just over 3 per cent of students from Paterson deemed 'college-ready'
- Pupils have to score at least 1,500 out of 2,400 to reach the benchmark
- A decrease from the 26 (4.2 percent) who reached those levels last year
- Education officials have alleged the administration of 'hiding something' after they gave optimistic projections of test results

By Willis Robinson / December 2, 2014
http://www.dailymail.co.uk/news/article-2857013/Only-NINETEEN-600-students-New-Jersey-school-district-scored-SATs-college.html

**"Student punches School 21 security guard in the face"**
By Jayed Rahman / January 6, 2015 / Paterson Times
http://patersontimes.com/2015/01/06/student-punches-school-21-security-guard-in-the-face/

**"Seventh grader threatens to beat, shoot substitute teacher"**
By Jayed Rahman / January 8, 2015 / Paterson Times
http://patersontimes.com/2015/01/07/seventh-grader-threatens-to-beat-shoot-substitute-teacher/

**"Security at Paterson's JFK High School under scrutiny"**
By Joe Malinconico and Abbott Koloff / Paterson Press and The Record/ January 28, 2014
http://www.northjersey.com/news/security-at-paterson-s-jfk-high-school-under-scrutiny-1.1260066

**"Paterson's Kennedy High to reopen after repairs done on heating system"**
By Joe Malinconico / February 19, 2015 / Paterson Press
http://www.northjersey.com/news/paterson-s-kennedy-high-to-reopen-after-repairs-done-on-heating-system-1.1274639

- This is nothing new. This problem has been going on forever. About 10 years ago, an entirely new and updated heating system was installed and never worked. It was supposed to be state of the art, where each room can be individually controlled.

**"Paterson schools cited for violating state's Special Education requirements"**
By Joe Malinconico, February 23, 2015 / Paterson Press
http://www.northjersey.com/towns/paterson/paterson-schools-cited-for-violating-state-s-special-education-requirements-1.1276624

**"Paterson 7th grader arrested with 23 bags of heroin in classroom, police say"**
By Joe Malinconico, March 13, 2015 / Paterson Press
http://www.northjersey.com/news/education/paterson-principal-resigns-amid-stir-over-bogus-tests-scores-in-previous-job-1.582823#sthash.bx5yvWB6.dpuf

**"Paterson Press letter: NJ should take action against schools superintendent"**
By Joe Malinconico, March 23, 2015 / Paterson Press
http://www.northjersey.com/news/paterson-press-letter-nj-should-take-action-against-schools-superintendent-1.1294200

**"Paterson Press letter: Parent says she's fed up with school superintendent"**
By Joe Malinconico, April 10, 2015 / Paterson Press
http://www.northjersey.com/news/paterson-press-letter-parent-says-she-s-fed-up-with-school-superintendent-1.1306826

**"Critics Say Paterson's Special Ed Program Heading Toward Disaster with Layoffs"**
Brenda Flanagan, Correspondent NJTVONLINE / June 2, 2015   Has Video
http://www.njtvonline.org/news/video/critics-say-patersons-special-ed-program-heading-toward-disaster-with-layoffs/

**"Paterson Press letter: Former Paterson HS teacher questions timing of final exams"**
June 17, 2015 / Paterson Press
http://www.northjersey.com/news/paterson-press-letter-former-paterson-hs-teacher-questions-timing-of-final-exams-1.1357378

**"Paterson Press letter: End state control of Paterson schools"**
June 17, 2015 / Paterson Press
http://www.northjersey.com/news/paterson-press-letter-end-state-control-of-paterson-schools-1.1357398

**"Auditor report warns of possible $186M deficit for Paterson school district"**
By Joe Malinconico, June 19, 2015 / Paterson Press
http://www.northjersey.com/news/auditor-report-warns-of-possible-186m-deficit-for-paterson-school-district-1.1359719

**"Resumes show Paterson's special education supervisors lacked credentials for the job"**
By Joe Malinconico, August 3, 2015 / Paterson Press
http://www.northjersey.com/news/resumes-show-paterson-s-special-education-supervisors-lacked-credentials-for-the-job-1.1385638

**"Paterson Press letter: Stop the foolishness at Paterson Public Schools"**
August 13, 2015 / Paterson Press
http://www.northjersey.com/news/paterson-press-letter-stop-the-foolishness-at-paterson-public-schools-1.1392148

**"Busing problems arise on Paterson's first day of school**
By Joe Malinconico, September 3, 2015 / Paterson Press
http://www.northjersey.com/news/busing-problems-arise-on-paterson-s-first-day-of-school-1.1403489

**"Parent: School bus dropped off 8-year-old with autism when nobody was home in Paterson"**
By Joe Malinconico, September 18, 2015 / Paterson Press
http://www.northjersey.com/news/parent-school-bus-dropped-off-8-year-old-with-autism-when-nobody-was-home-in-paterson-1.1413343

**"Paterson Press letter: Legislator gives superintendent an 'F'"**
September 23, 2015 / Paterson Press
http://www.northjersey.com/news/paterson-press-letter-legislator-gives-superintendent-an-f-1.1416155

**"Complaint says staff shortages undermining Paterson special education program"**
By Joe Malinconico, October 2, 2015 / Paterson Press
http://www.northjersey.com/news/complaint-says-staff-shortages-undermining-paterson-special-education-program-1.1424188

**"Paterson's School 21 struggling with vacancies"**
By Joe Malinconico, October 22, 2015 / Paterson Press
http://www.northjersey.com/news/paterson-s-school-21-struggling-with-vacancies-1.1438798

**"Paterson school official says state will speed up review on local control"**
By Joe Malinconico, October 22, 2015 / Paterson Press
http://www.northjersey.com/news/paterson-school-official-says-state-will-speed-up-review-on-local-control-1.1438793

**"District: Updated numbers show Paterson schools did not have a surge in enrollment this year"**
By Joe Malinconico, November 3, 2015 / Paterson Press
http://www.northjersey.com/news/district-updated-numbers-show-paterson-schools-did-not-have-a-surge-in-enrollment-this-year-1.1447414

**"Freeholder among 14 administrators in Paterson school district to receive promotions"**
By Joe Malinconico, November 17, 2015 / Paterson Press
http://www.northjersey.com/news/freeholder-among-14-administrators-in-paterson-school-district-to-receive-promotions-1.1457258

**"Paterson School District Least Ready to Reclaim Local Control"**
By Michael Hill, December 15, 2015 / NJTVNEWS     (With a Video)
http://www.njtvonline.org/news/video/paterson-school-district-least-ready-to-reclaim-local-control/

**"Paterson school official mentions possibility of employee furloughs to state legislators"**
By Joe Malinconico, December 15, 2015 / Paterson Press
http://www.northjersey.com/news/paterson-school-official-mentions-possibility-of-employee-furloughs-to-state-legislators-1.1474045

**"Paterson's lack of teachers in first marking period forces afterschool instructions for school 21 and 10 students"**
By Jayed Rahman, December 28, 2015 / Paterson Times
http://patersontimes.com/2015/12/28/patersons-lack-of-teachers-in-first-marking-period-forces-after-school-instructions-for-school-21-and-10-students/

**"Audit signals possibility of another fiscal crisis for Paterson school district"**
By Joe Malinconico, January 15, 2016 / Paterson Press
http://www.northjersey.com/news/audit-signals-possibility-of-another-fiscal-crisis-for-paterson-school-district-1.1493107

**"Education advocates call Paterson's PARCC scores 'alarming'**
By Joe Malinconico, January 16, 2016 / Paterson Press
http://www.northjersey.com/news/education-advocates-call-paterson-s-parcc-scores-alarming-1.1494265

**"N.J. gives Paterson schools chief $8,720 bonus"**
By Joe Malinconico, August 12, 2016
http://www.northjersey.com/news/n-j-gives-paterson-schools-chief-8-720-bonus-1.1644977

**"Paterson teachers' union votes 'no confidence' on schools superintendent"**
By Joe Malinconico, September 16, 2016
http://www.northjersey.com/news/paterson-teachers-union-votes-no-confidence-on-schools-superintendent-1.1668886

Made in United States
North Haven, CT
01 November 2025